The
WILEY
advantage

W9-DCD-782

Dear Valued Customer,

We realize you're a busy professional with deadlines to hit. Whether your goal is to learn a new technology or solve a critical problem, we want to be there to lend you a hand. Our primary objective is to provide you with the insight and knowledge you need to stay atop the highly competitive and ever-changing technology industry.

Wiley Publishing, Inc., offers books on a wide variety of technical categories, including security, data warehousing, software development tools, and networking — everything you need to reach your peak. Regardless of your level of expertise, the Wiley family of books has you covered.

- For Dummies® – The *fun* and *easy* way® to learn
- The Weekend Crash Course® – The *fastest* way to learn a new tool or technology
- Visual – For those who prefer to learn a new topic *visually*
- The Bible – The *100% comprehensive* tutorial and reference
- The Wiley Professional list – *Practical* and *reliable* resources for IT professionals

The book you now hold is part of our new *60 Minutes a Day* series which delivers what we think is the closest experience to an actual hands-on seminar that is possible with a book. Our author is a veteran of hundreds of hours of classroom teaching, and he uses that background to guide you past the hurdles and pitfalls to confidence and mastery of Java in manageable units that can be read and put to use in just an hour. If you have a broadband connection to the Web, you can see Richard introduce each topic — but this book will still be your best learning resource if you download only the audio files or use it strictly as a printed resource. From fundamentals to network and database programming, you'll find this self-paced training to be your best learning aid.

Our commitment to you does not end at the last page of this book. We'd want to open a dialog with you to see what other solutions we can provide. Please be sure to visit us at www.wiley.com/compbooks to review our complete title list and explore the other resources we offer. If you have a comment, suggestion, or any other inquiry, please locate the "contact us" link at www.wiley.com.

Finally, we encourage you to review the following page for a list of Wiley titles on related topics. Thank you for your support and we look forward to hearing from you and serving your needs again in the future.

Sincerely,

Richard K. Swadley

Richard K. Swadley
Vice President & Executive Group Publisher
Wiley Technology Publishing

15 HOUR WEEKEND CRASH COURSE

V Visual™

Bible

DUMMIES FOR

Wiley Publishing, Inc.

more information on related titles

Wiley Going to the Next Level
— Available from Wiley Publishing

60 Minutes a Day Books...
- Self-paced instructional text packed with real-world tips and examples from real-world training instructors
- Skill-building exercises, lab sessions, and assessments
- Author-hosted streaming video presentations for each chapter will pinpoint key concepts and reinforce lessons

 0-471-43023-4

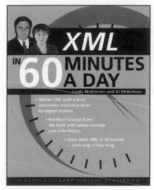 0-471-42548-6

 0-471-42314-9

 0-471-42254-1

WILEY
Wiley Publishing, Inc.

Available at your favorite bookseller or visit www.wiley.com/compbooks

Java™ in 60 Minutes a Day

Java™ in 60 Minutes a Day

Richard F. Raposa

WILEY

Wiley Publishing, Inc.

Executive Publisher: Robert Ipsen
Vice President and Publisher: Joe Wikert
Senior Editor: Ben Ryan
Editorial Manager: Kathryn A. Malm
Developmental Editor: Jerry Olsen
Production Editor: Vincent Kunkemueller
Media Development Specialist: Angie Denny
Text Design & Composition: Wiley Composition Services

Published by Wiley Publishing, Inc., Indianapolis, Indiana

Published simultaneously in Canada

For general information on our other products and services please contact our Customer Care Department within the United States at (800) 762-2974, outside the United States at (317) 572-3993 or fax (317) 572-4002.

Wiley also publishes its books in a variety of electronic formats. Some content that appears in print may not be available in electronic books.

Library of Congress Cataloging-in-Publication Data: See Publisher

ISBN: 0-471-42314-9

Printed in the United States of America

10 9 8 7 6 5 4 3 2 1

A Note from the Consulting Editor

Instructor-led training is proven to be an effective and popular tool for training engineers and developers. To convey technical ideas and concepts, the classroom experience is shown to be superior when compared to other delivery methods. As a technical trainer for more than 20 years, I have seen the effectiveness of instructor-led training firsthand. *60 Minutes a Day* combines the best of the instructor-led training and book experience. Technical training is typically divided into short and discrete modules, where each module encapsulates a specific topic; each module is then followed by "questions and answers" and a review. *60 Minutes a Day* titles follow the same model: each chapter is short, discrete, and can be completed in 60 minutes a day. For these books, I have enlisted premier technical trainers as authors. They provide the voice of the trainer and demonstrate classroom experience in each book of the series. You even get an opportunity to meet the actual trainer: As part of this innovative approach, each chapter of a *60 Minutes a Day* book is presented online by the author. Readers are encouraged to view the online presentation before reading the relevant chapter. Therefore, *60 Minutes a Day* delivers the complete classroom experience—even the trainer.

As an imprint of Wiley Publishing, Inc., Gearhead Press continues to bring you, the reader, the level of quality that Wiley has delivered consistently for nearly 200 years.

Thank you.

Donis Marshall
Founder, Gearhead Press
Consulting Editor, Wiley Technology Publishing Group

To my wife, Susan, for her motivation and support, and to our children, Megan, Ryan, Katelyn, and Emma, for letting me use the computer for hours at a time.

Contents

Acknowledgments   xix

About the Author   xxi

Introduction   xxiii

Chapter 1   **Getting Started with Java**   1
             Why Java?   1
             The Java Virtual Machine   2
             The Editions of Java   4
                 J2SE   4
                 J2ME   5
                 J2EE   5
             Downloading the Java 2 SDK   6
             Installing the SDK   7
             Running the SDK Tools   8
                 Running the javac Compiler   9
                 Running the JVM   10
             A Simple Java Program   10
                 Step 1: Write the Source Code   11
                 Step 2: Compile the Program   13
                 Step 3: Run the Program   14
             Summary   17

Chapter 2   **Java Fundamentals**   21
             Java Keywords   21
             Identifiers   22
             Java's Eight Primitive Data Types   23
             Variables   24
                 Assigning Variables   25
             Integral Types   27

Floating-Point Types   29
Boolean Data Type   30
Char Data Type   31
Strings   33
References versus Primitive Data   35
Constants   37
Java Operators   37
   Increment and Decrement Operators   39
   Assignment Operators   40
   Shift Operators   40
   Comparison Operators   42
   Boolean Operators   43
   Ternary Operator   43
Java Comments   44
Summary   46

Chapter 3   **Control Structures**   **51**
Flow of Control   51
Boolean Logic   52
   The and Operator   52
   The or Operator   53
   The exclusive or Operator   54
   The not Operator   54
Boolean Operators   55
The if Statement   57
The if/else Statement   59
The switch Statement   61
The while Loop   64
The do/while Loop   67
The for Loop   70
The break Keyword   74
The continue Keyword   76
Nested Loops   78
Summary   80

Chapter 4   **Classes and Objects**   **85**
Overview of Classes and Objects   85
Procedural Programming   86
Object-Oriented Programming   87
Object-Oriented Analysis and Design   88
Writing a Java Class   89
   Adding Fields to a Class   89
   Adding Methods to a Class   90
Instantiating an Object   92
Garbage Collection   94
Accessing Fields and Methods   97
Using the Dot Operator   97
   Step 1: Write the Employee Class   97
   Step 2: Compile the Employee Class   98

	Step 3: Write the EmployeeDemo Class	98
	Step 4: Compile the EmployeeDemo class	99
	Step 5: Run the EmployeeDemo program	99
	The this Reference	100
	Summary	103
Chapter 5	**Methods**	**107**
	Method Call Stack	107
	Invoking Methods	108
	Method Signature	111
	Arguments and Parameters	113
	Call-by-Value	116
	Overloading Methods	121
	Constructors	125
	Default Constructor	128
	Using Constructors	129
	A Class with Multiple Constructors	130
	Using this in a Constructor	131
	Summary	136
Chapter 6	**Understanding Inheritance**	**139**
	An Overview of Inheritance	139
	The *is a* Relationship	144
	Implementing Inheritance	145
	Instantiating Child Objects	146
	Single versus Multiple Inheritance	149
	The java.lang.Object Class	150
	The Methods of the Object Class	151
	Method Overriding	154
	The super Keyword	157
	The final Keyword	160
	final Methods	161
	The Instantiation Process	162
	Invoking a Parent Class Constructor	165
	Summary	170
Chapter 7	**Advanced Java Language Concepts**	**175**
	An Overview of Packages	175
	Adding a Class to a Package	176
	The Namespace Created by Packages	178
	The import Keyword	180
	The Directory Structure of Packages	183
	Step 1: Write and Save the Source Code for Vehicle	185
	Step 2: Compile the Source Code Using the -d Flag	185
	Step 3: Write the CarDealer Class	186
	Step 4: Set the CLASSPATH	187
	Step 5: Compile and Run the CarDealer Program	188
	The Access Specifiers	190
	Encapsulation	194

	Benefits of Encapsulation	197
	Understanding Static Members	198
	Accessing Static Fields and Methods	199
	Static Initializers	203
	Instance Initializers	205
	Summary	209
Chapter 8	**Polymorphism and Abstraction**	**213**
	An Overview of Polymorphism	213
	Using Parent Class References to Child Objects	214
	Casting References	218
	The instanceof Keyword	221
	Polymorphic Parameters	225
	Heterogeneous Collections	229
	Virtual Methods	230
	Taking Advantage of Virtual Methods	233
	An Overview of Abstraction	238
	Abstract Classes	239
	Abstract Methods	241
	Summary	247
Chapter 9	**Collections**	**253**
	Arrays	253
	Accessing Arrays	255
	The length Attribute	255
	Arrays of References	256
	Array Initializers	259
	Copying Arrays	261
	Multidimensional Arrays	263
	Example of a Heterogeneous Collection	265
	Overview of the Java Collections Framework	272
	The Vector Class	273
	Adding Elements to a Vector	275
	Accessing and Removing Elements in a Vector	277
	The Hashtable Class	281
	Adding Elements to a Hashtable	283
	Accessing Elements in a Hashtable	285
	Summary	290
Chapter 10	**Interfaces**	**295**
	An Overview of Interfaces	295
	Declaring Interfaces	296
	User-Defined Interfaces	298
	Write the Interface Source Code	299
	Compile the Interface	299
	Implementing an Interface	300
	Write a Class That Implements Paintable	300
	Save and Compile the Rectangle Class	301
	Add the paint() Method	302
	Write a Class That Uses Paintable	302

	Using Interfaces	303
	Exposing Methods via an Interface	304
	Forcing Behavior on a Class	310
	Declaring Fields in Interfaces	316
	Extending Interfaces	317
	Extending Multiple Interfaces	319
	Interfaces and Polymorphism	321
	Summary	326
Chapter 11	**Exception Handling**	**329**
	Overview of Exception Handling	329
	Flow of Control of Exceptions	330
	Throwable Classes	333
	Methods of the Throwable Class	333
	Catching Exceptions	334
	Writing try/catch Blocks	335
	Multiple catch Blocks	337
	Handle or Declare Rule	341
	Declaring Exceptions	343
	The throws Keyword	345
	Throwing Exceptions	348
	The finally Keyword	351
	Overridden Methods and Exceptions	354
	User-Defined Exceptions	357
	Summary	361
Chapter 12	**An Introduction to GUI Programming**	**367**
	AWT versus Swing	367
	Creating Windows	369
	java.awt.Frame Class	369
	javax.swing.JFrame Class	372
	Containers and Components	375
	Adding Components to a Container	375
	Layout Managers	378
	FlowLayout Manager	379
	BorderLayout Manager	383
	Panels	385
	GridLayout Manager	388
	BoxLayout Manager	390
	Nesting Panels	392
	Using No Layout Manager	396
	Summary	401
Chapter 13	**GUI Components and Event Handling**	**405**
	The Delegation Model	405
	The Event Listener Interfaces	407
	Creating an Event Listener	409
	Registering a Listener with an Event Source	410
	The Event Adapter Classes	412

Buttons   417
   AWT Buttons   417
   Swing Buttons   418
Check Boxes   421
   AWT Check Boxes   421
   Swing Check Boxes   423
Radio Buttons   425
   AWT Radio Buttons   425
   Swing Radio Buttons   427
Labels   429
Text Components   430
   AWT Text Components   430
   Swing Text Components   434
Lists   437
   AWT Lists   437
   Swing Lists   439
Combo Boxes   440
   AWT Choice   440
   Swing Combo Boxes   442
Progress Bars   445
Menus   445
Summary   452

Chapter 14 Applets   **457**
An Overview of Applets   457
The java.applet.Applet Class   459
Swing Applets   462
Life Cycle of an Applet   465
   Step 1: Write the Applet Class   467
   Step 2: Write the HTML Page   468
   Step 3: View the HTML Page   468
   Step 4: View the Java Console   469
The <applet> Tag   473
Document and Code Base   478
The appletviewer Tool   479
Sandbox Security   481
The Applet Context   485
Displaying Images   488
Playing Audio   490
JAR Files and Applets   494
Summary   500

Chapter 15 Threads   **503**
Overview of Threads   503
Life Cycle of a Thread   506
Creating a Thread   507
Implementing Runnable   508

Extending the Thread Class   511
Methods of the Thread Class   516
Timer and TimerTask Classes   519
Scheduling Tasks   522
Multithreading Issues   526
synchronized Keyword   530
Deadlock Issues   532
Ordering Locks   534
wait() and notify() Methods   536
Summary   546

Chapter 16   Input and Output   551
An Overview of the java.io Package   551
    The Output Streams   552
    The Input Stream Classes   553
    The Writer Class   553
    The Reader Class   554
Low-Level and High-Level Streams   557
    Low-Level Streams   557
    High-Level Streams   559
Chaining Streams Together   561
Low-Level Readers and Writers   564
High-Level Readers and Writers   564
File I/O   565
The RandomAccessFile Class   566
Using Pipes   570
An Overview of Serialization   574
Serializing an Object   577
Deserializing an Object   578
The Logging APIs   579
    An Example of Logging   581
Summary   587

Chapter 17   Network Programming   591
An Overview of Network Programming   591
    Transmission Control Protocol   592
    User Datagram Protocol   592
Using Sockets   594
The ServerSocket Class   596
Socket Class   599
Communicating between Sockets   600
Java Secure Socket Extension (JSSE)   602
Secure Server Socket   603
Secure Client Socket   607
Communicating over a Secure Socket   610
Overview of Datagram Packets   612
    DatagramSocket Class   612
    DatagramPacket Class   613

Receiving a Datagram Packet   614
Sending a Datagram Packet   615
Working with URLs   617
URL Connections   619
Summary   625

Chapter 18   Database Programming   629
An Overview of JDBC   629
JDBC Drivers   632
Connecting to a Database   633
    Using the DriverManager Class   634
    Using the DataSource Class   636
An SQL Primer   637
    Creating Data   638
    Reading Data   639
    Updating Data   640
    Deleting Data   641
Creating Statements   641
Simple Statements   642
Working with Result Sets   647
Navigating a Result Set   647
Viewing a Result Set   648
Updating a Result Set   651
Prepared Statements   652
    Step 1: Preparing the Statement   652
    Step 2: Setting the Parameters   654
    Step 3: Executing a Prepared Statement   654
Callable Statements   656
Summary   663

Chapter 19   JavaBeans   669
Overview of JavaBeans   669
Simple Properties   672
Packaging a Bean   675
    Step 1: Write the Bean Class   676
    Step 2: Write the Manifest File   676
    Step 3: Create the JAR File   677
    Step 4: Download the Bean Builder   678
    Step 5: Run the Bean Builder   678
    Step 6: Load the Movie Bean into the Bean Builder 681
    Step 7: Using the Movie Bean in the Builder Tool 681
Bound Properties   684
    Step 8: Binding Properties in the Bean Builder   687
Constrained Properties   690
Vetoing an Event   693

Overview of Events   694
    Step 9: Hooking up Buttons to the Movie Bean   695
    Step 10: Viewing Beans in Preview Mode   696
Generating User-Defined Events   698
BeanInfo Class   703
Summary   708

Appendix   About the 60 Minutes Web Site   713

Index   717

Acknowledgments

I would like to thank the editors for their hard work on this book: J.W. (Jerry) Olsen, Nancy Sixsmith, and Susan Hobbs, and everyone at Wiley Publishing who helped in this project, especially Ben Ryan. Thanks also to Donis Marshall for the opportunity to write a book for the *60 Minutes a Day* series as well as to Jerry for managing the editors on behalf of Gearhead.

And then there is everyone out there who played a role, whether small or large, in my writing of this book: Susan Raposa, javalicense.com, my Mom (who can read it now), and most importantly, Megan, Ryan, Katelyn, and Emma.

And finally, to all of those who kept asking me when my book would be published: Leo and Linda Schaefbauer; Steve, Beth, Geoffrey, Nathan, and Aurora Venteicher; Michael and Tammy Schaefbauer; David Schaefbauer; Betty Haefner; Mark, Margaret, Marie, Melissa, and Jay VanDerWerff; Michele, Gabe, and Seth Raposa; Allen, Denise, Joseph, Rechele, Kathalena, Kurstin, Joshua, and Kristina Raposa; Dave, Maryann, Daniel, Duke, Davey, Dylan, and Darby Knoll; and Barb and Steve Sachs.

About the Author

Richard F. Raposa is a Java instructor for JLicense, Inc., a Java courseware and training firm based in Rapid City, SD. One of the first Sun Certified Java Instructors, Rich has taught courses on Java, J2EE, XML, Web Services, C++, Visual C++/MFC, Win32 Internals, UML, and other object-oriented technologies at companies around the country. He has developed courses on almost every aspect of Java and the J2EE technologies.

Introduction

An Overview of *Java in 60 Minutes a Day*

I will never forget taking my first Java class at Sun Microsystems in Dallas, Texas, in May, 1998. I had heard the many promises about Java and how it would revolutionize software development, but I was skeptical and arrogant as I sat in the back of the class anxious to make life hard on the instructor.

At the time, I was programming and teaching C++, mostly Visual C++ and the Microsoft Foundation Classes. For some reason, after I learned C++, I figured that would be the last programming language I would ever need to learn. My boss, on the other hand, had different ideas, because I was slated to become a Sun Certified Java Instructor.

Contrary to my expectations, I was blown away by Java! It was logical, predictable, powerful, and simple (compared to C++). Sun had taken the best of the existing object-oriented programming languages and removed many of the idiosyncrasies and problem areas. And the best part: Java is platform independent! You write a program once, and it can be executed on different operating systems and devices without your even having to recompile your code.

I have been travelling the country teaching Java now for the last 5 years, and I still get excited about standing up in front of a classroom of students who are seeing Java for the first time. One of my goals was to capture that enthusiasm on the pages of this book. I want you to appreciate why Java has become one of the most popular and widely used programming languages in software development today.

How This Book Is Organized

The goal of this book is for you to be able to study each chapter in one hour, like a student sitting through a one-hour lecture. After you finish a chapter, there are labs that solidify what you learned by having you write code. You will also find review questions and answers at the end of each chapter to help you review the key points of the chapter. Also throughout the book are Classroom Q&A sections where I answer questions that I have frequently been asked by students in the classroom.

The book contains 19 chapters. The first eight chapters discuss the fundamentals of the Java language, and should be read in order. The order of the last 11 chapters isn't quite as important, although you will find that many of the labs build on the ones from previous chapters. The following sections describe what you will learn in this book's chapters.

Chapter 1: Getting Started with Java

It just wouldn't be a programming class if I didn't start with the "Hello, World" application. In Chapter 1, you will learn what all the hype is about with Java. I will discuss the life cycle of a Java program, then you will see how to write, compile, and execute a Java program using the Java 2 Platform, Standard Edition (J2SE) Standard Developer Kit (SDK).

Here's a tip: If you have a slow Internet connection, you might want to start downloading the J2SE SDK before you start reading the chapter.

Chapter 2: Java Fundamentals

This chapter covers the fundamentals of Java, such as keywords, the built-in data types, strings, variables, references, and arithmetic operators. The information in this chapter establishes the foundation for the remainder of the book, so take your time and make sure you understand everything.

If you are a C or C++ programmer, don't skip over this chapter thinking you already know what's in it. Java looks similar to C++, but it behaves quite differently.

Chapter 3: Control Structures

In this chapter, you will learn the various control structures in Java and the details of how to use them, including if/else, switch, do/while, and if statements. I will also cover Boolean operators and the truth tables.

There are some fun labs in this chapter, including one where you write a program to simulate the Powerball lottery.

Chapter 4: Classes and Objects

In my opinion, this is the most important chapter in the book, whether or not you are new to object-oriented programming (OOP). Java is purely object-oriented, so to be a Java programmer is to understand classes and objects. In this chapter, you will learn how to think like an object-oriented programmer, as opposed to thinking procedurally. The basics of OOP are discussed: that objects consist of attributes and behaviors, and that classes describe objects. I will also briefly discuss the Unified Modeling Language (UML) and give you a taste of Object Oriented Analysis and Design (OOAD). The important topic of Java references is also covered in detail.

Spend extra time on this chapter if you need to, because all of the topics require your complete understanding before you can write Java programs.

Chapter 5: Methods

The behaviors of an object becomes methods in a class. By Chapter 5, you will be familiar with writing classes, so it's time to discuss all of the details about writing and invoking Java methods. Topics covered in this chapter include the method call stack, method signatures, parameters, arguments, method overloading, constructors, and the always-important discussion of call-by-value in Java.

The labs in this chapter give you the opportunity to really get a feel for objects and OOP. You will write classes, instantiate objects, and invoke methods on those objects.

Chapter 6: Understanding Inheritance

Object-oriented programming has four major aspects: inheritance, encapsulation, polymorphism, and abstraction. This chapter focuses on the most important of the four: inheritance. A new child class can be written that extends an existing class, inheriting the attributes and behaviors of its parent. This chapter discusses when and how to use inheritance, including the "is a" relationship, the extends keyword, the Object class, method overriding, and a repeat discussion on constructors and how they are affected by inheritance.

If I were to rank chapters in order of their importance, I would put this one second behind Chapter 4, "Classes and Objects." An understanding of inheritance is essential to understanding the remaining chapters of the book.

Chapter 7: Advanced Java Language Concepts

In this chapter, I tie up some loose ends and discuss the details of some of the more advanced topics of Java. Topics covered in this chapter include packages, the access specifiers, encapsulation, static fields and methods, and the javadoc tool.

Some of these topics, such as packages and the javadoc tool, are of special interest because they are concepts unique to Java. I think javadoc is one of the most impressive features of the Java language, as you may also agree after you see how it works.

Chapter 8: Polymorphism and Abstraction

Polymorphism is the capability of an object to take on different forms. Abstraction refers to the use of abstract classes, classes that cannot be instantiated. In this chapter, I discuss the details of these two object-oriented concepts, including polymorphic parameters, heterogeneous collections, the instanceof keyword, virtual methods, and abstract methods.

This is likely the most difficult chapter in the book. The concept of polymorphism is crucial but difficult to explain, so I make an asserted effort to simplify my discussions. Read this chapter carefully, and refer back to it whenever you need to.

Chapter 9: Collections

After eight days of building a foundation for programming in Java, you will now be ready to start using some of the many Java APIs that compose the Java 2 Platform, Standard Edition (J2SE). Chapter 9 covers the classes in the Java Collections API. If you have ever had to write code to create a linked list, hash table, tree, or other data structure, you will be happy to find that the J2SE contains classes for all the commonly used data structures.

This is a useful chapter for anyone, no matter what types of problems you will be solving in your Java programming future.

Chapter 10: Interfaces

The Java language contains the concept of interfaces, which allow you to create data types based on a set of behaviors. A class implements an interface, thereby causing the class to take on the data type of the interface. The class must also implement the methods of the interface, which is how interfaces can be used to force behavior on classes.

This chapter covers the details of writing and implementing interfaces. Knowledge of interfaces is an absolute must in Java, so study this chapter closely.

Chapter 11: Exception Handling

Exception handling is a built-in feature of Java, and you need to know how to catch an exception before continuing further in the book. This chapter discusses the two types of exceptions: runtime and checked. You will learn the details of a try/catch block and how it affects the flow of control of a method. Other topics include the Handle or Declare Rule, the finally keyword, and writing user-defined exceptions.

Chapter 12: Introduction to GUI Programming

Now, we get to the fun part of Java: GUI (graphical user interface) programming. I am still impressed with the ability to be able to write a GUI program that runs on different operating systems. In this chapter, you will learn how to lay out GUI components in a container using the various layout managers. You have two options in Java for creating a GUI: AWT or Swing. This chapter compares these two APIs and shows you how to use them both.

The labs in this chapter are the start of a project that has you create an Instant Messaging application. The program will gradually evolve throughout the rest of the book.

Chapter 13: GUI Components and Event Handling

There is a lot of information in creating GUIs and handling the events of the components, so I separated the topics into two days. In this chapter, you will learn how to handle the events from the GUIs you created in the previous chapter. Different components generate different types of events, and my goal in this chapter is to show you how to determine for yourself what types of events a component generates. Event handling is accomplished using the Delegation Model, which I discuss in detail.

By the end of this chapter, you will be able to write fully functional Java GUI applications.

Chapter 14: Applets

An applet is a Java program that runs in a Web browser. Applets are actually GUI containers, so you will be writing applets in no time, knowing what you learned in the previous two chapters. This chapter discusses the details of writing applets and embedding them in an HTML page.

Don't worry if you are new to HTML. I will show you enough so that you can create simple Web pages containing your applets.

Chapter 15: Threads

Java has built-in support for threads. In this chapter, I will discuss the details of multithreaded Java applications, including how to write and start a thread, the life cycle of a thread, and a discussion of synchronization. You will learn three techniques for writing and starting a thread: implementing the Runnable interface, extending the Thread class, and using the Timer class. The wait() and notify() methods of the Object class are also discussed in detail.

You can do some fun things with threads, as you will discover by doing the labs in this chapter.

Chapter 16: Input and Output

The java.io package contains some great classes for performing just about any type of input and output you will need to perform in a Java program. This chapter discusses how to find and use the classes you need from the java.io package. Topics covered include a comparison of streams vs. readers and writers, chaining streams together, high-level and low-level streams, and serialization, another one of those subtle but powerful features of the Java language.

J2SE 1.4 introduced new classes for performing error and message logging, the details of which are covered also.

Chapter 17: Network Programming

By this point in the book, you will begin to realize how Java simplifies common programming tasks, allowing you to focus on the problem at hand, and this chapter is yet another example. I will discuss the various classes in the java.net package that allow you to perform network programming. Topics discussed include creating socket connections using TCP/IP, creating secure socket connections using the Java Secure Sockets Extension, sending datagram packets using the User Datagram Protocol (UDP), and how to connect to and read from a URL.

In the labs in this chapter, you will finish up the Instant Message application, which will allow you to send instant messages between multiple computers on a network or over the Internet.

Chapter 18: Database Programming

In this chapter, I will show you how to write a Java program that connects to a Java database. Included in this chapter is a discussion on SQL (the Structured Query Language), the common technique for accessing data in a database. You will learn about JDBC, the various types of drivers, connecting to a data source, using prepared statements, using callable statements, and working with result sets.

It's hard to get far in the programming world without needing to access a database, so this is an important chapter and a great reference for using the JDBC API.

Chapter 19: JavaBeans

A JavaBean is a software component written in Java. A software component is a reusable piece of software designed to be "plugged in" to an application, allowing for easier code reuse and faster application development. Topics discussed in this chapter include an overview of JavaBeans, the Bean Builder, properties, events, and hooking beans together in a builder tool.

JavaBeans are used in many of the Java technologies, including an important role in JavaServer Pages, a popular Java technology for simplifying Web page development.

Who Should Read This Book

This book is targeted towards programmers who want to learn Java. I make very few assumptions about what you already know, but general programming knowledge is helpful. This is an introductory book, and I assume you have no prior knowledge of Java.

To be specific, if you are familiar with COBOL, Visual Basic, C, C++, C#, Fortran, Ada, or any other programming language, and if you want to learn Java, this book is for you.

Tools You Will Need

To run the sample code in this book as well as complete the lab assignments, you will need:

J2SE SDK. The compiler, JVM, libraries, and other tools to create and execute Java programs are found in the Java 2 Platform, Standard Edition (J2SE) Standard Developer Kit (SDK). This SDK is freely downloadable from the Sun Microsystems Web site at http://java.sun.com/j2se. In Chapter 1, I will show you how to download and install the SDK.

A text editor or IDE. You will need a text editor to write and edit the source code for your Java programs. You can use a text editor that you already have, like Microsoft Notepad, or you can download one of the dozens of text editors on the Internet, in both free and shareware versions. Alternatively, you can use an IDE that you may already have, such as IBM's Visual Age, Symantec's Visual Café, or Borland's JBuilder, to name only a few.

What's on the Web Site

Sample code in this book, the book's labs, and more are provided on the book's Web site at the following URL: www.Wiley.com/compbooks/60minutesaday

Summary

Reading this book is the next best thing to sitting in on one of my classes. After 5 years of teaching Java to hundreds of students, I have learned what's important to new Java programmers and what's not. The book is written in the first person, as if I am lecturing in front of a class, and it contains notes and tips that I'm sure you will find useful.

I hope you enjoy the book. So now that the introductions are over, let's get started!

CHAPTER 1

Getting Started with Java

When learning a new programming language, students are often anxious to get started, so let's not waste any time. In this chapter, you will learn why Java has become one of the most popular programming languages being used today, even though it is a relatively new language. You will download and install the necessary software for developing Java programs, and we will go through the steps of writing, compiling, and running a Java program using the Java Standard Developer's Kit (SDK) provided by Sun Microsystems.

Why Java?

You might ask, "Why Java?" That's a good question, especially if you are new to the language and have not heard all the buzz about it yet. How does a programming language that has only been around since 1995 and is quite similar in syntax and design to C++ become so widely adopted? Why not just stick to languages that have been used for decades: C, C++, COBOL, Fortran, and so on?

Relative to the other programming languages used today, Java is in its infancy. (Sun Microsystems released the first version of Java in 1995.) Yet Java has become one of the most popular languages used in programming today. Java is an object-oriented programming language with syntax and keywords almost identical to C++, another object-oriented language that has been used extensively for over 20 years.

So why learn a new programming language that is similar to an established programming language? First of all, Java is easier to learn than other object-oriented languages. When developing Java, its creators took all of the good features of the existing object-oriented programming languages such as C++, Ada, and Smalltalk, and removed most of their flaws and peculiarities. There are a lot of aspects of the Java language that are consistent and make sense, thereby making it easier to learn.

When I first learned C++ in college, we spent weeks learning just to manipulate and display strings. It was hard to remember which function to use when, and none of it ever made any sense to me. When I first started to learn Java, I was immediately impressed with the ease with which strings are handled. It was one of the first simplicities of Java that got me excited about the language.

 I want to emphasize that I did not say Java is *easy* to learn. I said Java is *easier* to learn than other object-oriented programming languages, specifically C++. You still have some work ahead of you, but I think you will find that Java is straightforward, powerful, well designed, and an enjoyable language with which to program.

The Java Virtual Machine

The elegance and power of how Java is designed is only part of the reason why Java has become so prevalent in today's software development. Platform independence is what Sun boasts the loudest about regarding Java—and with good reason!

A Java program can be written once and then run on many different devices. Sun uses the slogan "write once, run anywhere." I used the term *boast* because the validity of the claim to true platform independence has been argued by some; however, in an ideal situation, most Java programs can be moved from one device to another without any modifications to the code.

For example, suppose that you want to develop a program that is to run on a PC with Microsoft Windows and a hand-held PC running the Palm OS. These two platforms have little in common. If you were to write this program using a language other than Java, you would likely write the program twice— once for Windows, and again for the Palm version. The programs would probably look quite different, and possibly would be written in different languages.

With Java, you are not concerned with the target platform. The exact same program can run on Windows and the Palm OS, without changing the code at all. This "write once, run anywhere" capability is an exciting feature of Java that makes it appealing for anyone developing software.

Classroom Q & A

Q: So, how is platform independence possible?

A: Well, I have been leading you up to that question. How do you think it is possible?

Q: I am assuming you recompile the program, using a compiler designed for the specific platform you are targeting.

A: Yes and no. You do use a compiler for a specific platform, but there is no recompiling. In fact, compiled Java code, which is referred to as *bytecode*, is well defined and looks the same no matter what type of device you are targeting. This is because in Java, the platform you target is a Java Virtual Machine, or JVM for short. You do not write Java programs for Windows, Unix, a Palm PC, or any other device. You write Java programs to run on a JVM.

Q: So if I want my Java program to run on Windows, I need a JVM for Windows?

A: Exactly. And if you want your Java program to run on your watch, you need a JVM for your watch. If you want a Java program to run on your cell phone, you need a JVM for your cell phone, and so on.

Q: And the JVMs are written in Java?

A: No. Interestingly enough, most JVMs are written in C or C++. When you run a Java program, you are really running a JVM, and the JVM is interpreting your Java code.

Q: This must make Java programs considerably slower.

A: That is a definite concern. Five years ago, I would have had to concede that a Java program was noticeably slower than a C or C++ program. But modern JVMs are much more efficient and include a feature known as a Just-In-Time (JIT) compiler. A JIT compiler actually takes your Java bytecode and translates it into native code. This translated code will run just as fast as any C++ program. There is more overhead at the beginning of the Java program when the code is being translated, but the end result of a JIT compiler is well worth it.

Q: Can you look at this translated Java code and just use it directly?

A: No. Most JIT compilers do all of their work in RAM, so this translation takes place each time you run the Java program. The point of Java is not to focus on trying to create native code, since native code is inherently non-platform-independent. The point of Java is to write code that will run on a JVM. That way, your Java program can run on any device that has a JVM. Think about this: You can write a Java program, and three years from now that program can run on an electronic device that doesn't even exist today, as long as the device has a JVM for it.

The Editions of Java

When Java was introduced, it primarily consisted of two components: the programming language specification, and the Java runtime environment specification that described the features of a JVM. As the Java language evolved over the years, Sun Microsystems gradually added new specifications and technologies that made Java more than just a programming language.

For example, servlets and JavaServer Pages were introduced to provide a mechanism for using Java to create dynamic Web pages. JavaBeans provide a Java software component architecture. Enterprise JavaBeans provide a mechanism for developing distributed applications. Each of these technologies has its own specification.

Soon after the release of Java 2, however, (which coincided with the release of version 1.2 of the Java Development Kit), to create common runtime environments for Java developers to target, Sun grouped their major Java programming technologies into three editions:

- J2ME: Java 2 Platform, Micro Edition
- J2SE: Java 2 Platform, Standard Edition
- J2EE: Java 2 Platform, Enterprise Edition

J2SE

J2SE is what I like to call the core Java language. This book focuses on the key elements of this Standard Edition. J2SE provides an environment for developing many different types of Java applications and includes support for GUI programming, threads, input/output, networking, XML, CORBA, applets, JavaBeans, remote method invocation, security, and database access.

If you are interested in eventually taking the exam to become a Sun Certified Java Programmer, you need to become familiar with the J2SE.

J2ME

J2ME is not a slimmed-down version of J2SE. Instead, it establishes a procedure for defining what a particular JVM designed for an electronic device will provide. The J2ME technology has two components:

Configurations.   Define the type of JVM that is being targeted.

Profiles.   Describe specification details about the device that is being targeted. Each device has a profile listing the standard Java APIs available for that device.

Configurations are composed of Java APIs and virtual machines designed to run on two different types of devices. The first type of device is those with 128–512K of memory. This configuration is called the Connected Limited Device Configuration (CLDC), and the corresponding JVM is referred to as the K Virtual Machine, or KVM.

The second configuration is for devices with more than 512K of memory. This configuration is called the Connected Device Configuration and uses the standard JVM, with all the same capabilities of a regular desktop computer.

Profiles are defined by the Java Community Process (JCP), which allows for input from any industry interested in a profile for a particular type of electronic device. For example, a profile would be created for wireless phones, with the profile defining the configuration to use for wireless phones and the Java APIs that will be available. Any company that had an interest in wireless phones could join the Java Community Process to help determine which configuration to choose and what the Java API would look like for developing Java applications for wireless phones.

J2EE

J2EE is a collection of Java technologies that create a platform for distributed applications. Along with the J2SE (some of the J2EE technologies are actually a part of the Java 2, Standard Edition), J2EE allows for the most complex of multitier software applications to be portable across multiple platforms.

J2EE consists of the following technologies:

Enterprise JavaBeans (EJB).   An EJB is a component architecture for the development and deployment of object-oriented distributed business applications. Applications written using the EJB architecture are scalable, transactional, and multiuser secure.

Java Servlets.   A servlet is a Java application that runs in a Web server.

JavaServer Pages (JSP).   A JavaServer Page is similar to a servlet and allows for the creation of dynamic Web pages.

Java Database Connectivity (JDBC).   JDBC allows Java applications to access a database.

Extensible Markup Language (XML).   XML provides a mechanism for describing data using tags in a platform-independent manner.

Java Naming and Directory Interface (JNDI).   JNDI allows Java applications to access naming services and directory services.

Java Transaction API (JTA).   JTA allows Java applications to access a transaction service.

Java Transaction Service (JTS).   JTS defines the implementation of a transaction manager that supports the JTA.

Java Messaging Service (JMS).   JMS allows for Java applications to access a message service.

Java IDL.   The Java IDL allows Java applications to use CORBA implementations.

JavaMail.   JavaMail allows Java applications to access an email service.

RMI-IIOP.   RMI-IIOP is for using Remote Method Invocation over the Internet InterOrb Protocol.

Connectors.   Connectors allow Java applications to access enterprise information systems.

Java Web Services.   Java Web Services allow Java applications to take advantage of the emerging Web services technologies.

Similar to J2SE programs run in a JVM, J2EE applications run in a J2EE-compliant application server. The application server implements the J2EE specification, allowing developers to create applications that use any or all of the J2EE technologies, but that still are platform independent. Some of the more popular applications servers are IBM's WebSphere, BEA Systems' WebLogic, and Macromedia's JRun.

Downloading the Java 2 SDK

As mentioned earlier, this book focuses on the J2SE, the Java 2 Platform, Standard Edition. By the way, there is no Java 1. Before Java 2, the versions of Java were referred to by the version of the Java Development Kit (JDK). The first release of Java was JDK 1.0, which was released in 1995. The next release was JDK 1.1 with enough changes and additions to JDK 1.0 to make the two versions not backward compatible. With the release of JDK 1.2, Sun started referring to the language as Java 2, and the developer's kit is now called the Standard Developer's Kit (SDK).

The SDK contains many tools for developing and running Java applications, most importantly a compiler and JVM. The current version of the Java 2 SDK is 1.4, but Sun updates Java 2 frequently; don't be surprised if you find versions 1.5 or beyond on Sun's Web site. No matter what the version is, the SDK is free for developers to download and install.

The SDK can be found at http://java.sun.com/j2se. To download the SDK, click the link for J2SE Downloads, and you will taken to the SDK download page. This page has two columns for each platform: one for the JRE and one for the SDK. JRE stands for Java Runtime Environment, which is what you would download if you wanted to just run Java applications. The JRE is essentially the JVM for your platform.

If you are actually going to write Java programs, which is what we are going to do throughout this book, you will need the SDK. The SDK contains the JRE plus all the necessary development tools.

Click the SDK that's right for you. For example, if you are going to be using Windows to write your Java programs, click the Windows SDK. Notice that there are versions available for Linux and Solaris as well. You need to agree to Sun's license agreement before downloading.

 The SDK is a large download that will take more than an hour for those with a dial-up connection.

Installing the SDK

After you have downloaded the installation file, execute it to install the SDK. The downloaded file will be unpacked and Install Wizard will begin. You will be prompted to accept Sun's license agreement; then you will be asked to select the folder where the SDK is to be installed.

It is best to install the SDK in the default folder that the Install Wizard displays. For example, for SDK 1.4, the default folder is c:\j2sdk1.4.0. If you do change the install folder, however, be sure not to pick a directory with spaces in the directory name such as Program Files. Spaces in directory names tend to cause problems with the compiler and JVM.

Figure 1.1 shows the step in the Install Wizard where you can choose which components of the SDK to install. If you have plenty of hard drive space, you might as well install all the components; however, if you want to save some hard drive space, you can choose to not install the Native Interface Header Files, Demos, and the Java Sources. These components will not be needed for what we are going to be doing.

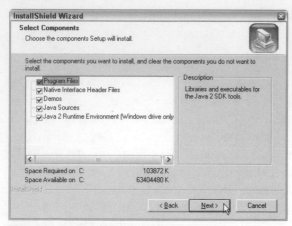

Figure 1.1 Choosing the SDK components to install.

The installation is complete when you see the InstallShield Wizard Complete page. Click the Finish button to complete the installation.

Running the SDK Tools

After you have successfully installed the SDK, you need to set your PATH environment variable so the compiler and JVM can be executed easily from a command prompt. The folder to add to your path is the bin folder where you installed the SDK, such as c:\j2sdk1.4.0\bin. Setting the PATH environment variable is different on each operating system. For Windows 2000/NT/XP users, the PATH can be set by clicking the System icon of the Control Panel. (In Windows XP, the System icon is located in the Performance and Maintenance section of the Control Panel.) Select the Advanced tab, and then click the Environment Variables button to display the Environment Variables dialog box. Click on Path in the System Variables list, then click the Edit button to display the dialog box shown in Figure 1.2. Add the \bin folder where you installed the SDK to your PATH.

Figure 1.2 Setting the PATH in Windows 2000/NT/XP.

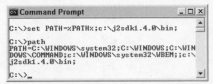

Figure 1.3   Using the SET command to set the PATH environment.

For other versions of Windows, the PATH environment variable is edited in the c:\autoexec.bat file. You then need to restart your system. In all versions of Windows, you can also set the PATH manually at the command prompt (also called the DOS prompt) by using the SET command, as shown in Figure 1.3.

 If you use the SET command as shown in Figure 1.3, the PATH will only be set for that particular DOS window, and the changes will be lost when you close that DOS window.

Running the javac Compiler

The javac tool is the Java compiler you will use to compile the Java code you write into bytecode. To run javac, type javac at the command prompt and press Enter. Figure 1.4 shows the output that you should see. If an error message occurs along the lines of a file not being found, your PATH might not have been set correctly.

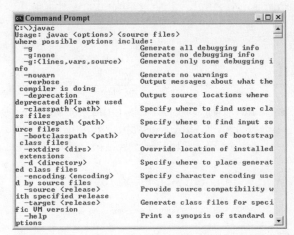

Figure 1.4   The javac tool compiles Java source code into bytecode.

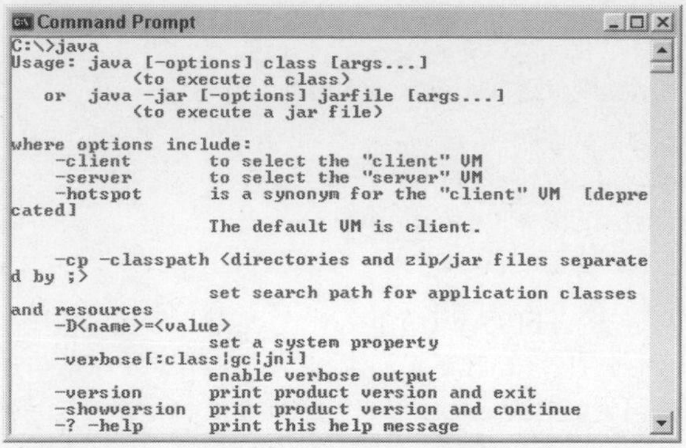

Figure 1.5   Use the java tool to interpret your Java bytecode.

Normally, when you run javac, you enter the name or names of Java source code files that you want to compile. Because you just ran javac without entering any source code files, the help topics for javac were displayed, as shown in Figure 1.4.

Running the JVM

After javac is running successfully, you should be able to type java and then press Enter to run the JVM that comes with the SDK. Figure 1.5 shows the output that you should see.

Normally, when you run java, you enter the name of the bytecode file that contains the Java program you want to execute. If you saw an output similar to Figure 1.5, you are ready to compile and run Java programs using the SDK. So let's get started!

A Simple Java Program

It is common practice when learning a new programming language to start out with a *Hello, World* program that simply displays the message, "Hello, World." So, we will now write a simple Java program that displays a greeting at the command prompt.

Here are the steps we will follow in writing our first Java program:

1. Write the source code.
2. Compile the source code.
3. Run the program.

Step 1: Write the Source Code

The first step is writing the code for our Java program. We will write the Java programs in this book using a simple text editor such as Windows Notepad. (You Unix folks can use emacs or vi.) The Java code is initially text, and the javac tool will compile our text files into bytecode.

Figure 1.6 shows you the Hello, World program typed into Notepad. Open your text editor and then type in the program just as you see it in Figure 1.6. Keep in mind that Java is case sensitive, meaning, for example, that *String* and *string* are not the same in Java.

Let's save this file first and then discuss what the program does. Java is a highly structured and organized language. One of the rules that must be followed is that the name of a source code file must match the name of the public class defined in that file, and the file extension must be .java.

Create a new directory off your root directory (off your c:\ drive in Windows) named javafiles. Save the HelloWorld.java file in that javafiles directory. This way you can access it quickly from the command prompt. The name of the public class in Figure 1.6 is HelloWorld, so this file must be saved as HelloWorld.java.

Some programs such as Notepad use a default extension like .txt for text files. Because this won't work in Java, make sure that you save the source file correctly. One way to ensure a correct filename is to enclose the filename in quotation marks.

 Do not save your Java source files in a directory with spaces in the name of the directory. This may cause problems, depending on the version of Windows you are using; therefore, do not save your files in the My Documents folder.

```
Untitled - Notepad
File  Edit  Format  View  Help
public class HelloWorld
{
        public static void main(String [] args)
        {
                System.out.println("Hello, World");
        }
}
```

Figure 1.6   The source code of the Hello, World program.

The program in Figure 1.6 contains a single class (see the *An Introduction to Classes and Objects* sidebar) named HelloWorld. Within HelloWorld is one method: main(). The main() method is declared as public, static, and void, which are Java keywords that are discussed later in the book. The main() method is unique because it is the method invoked by the JVM when this program is executed.

The main() method must look like:

```
public static void main(String [] args)
```

♦ An Introduction to Classes and Objects

You should understand two important object-oriented terms: object and class. A *class* is a description of an object, and an *object* is an instance of a class.

In Java, you *write* classes. Because Java is purely object oriented, all of the statements in your Java programs appear inside a Java class. Notice that the Hello, World program in Figure 1.6 is a public class. We will discuss *public* in detail later, but for now I will just say that almost every class you write in Java will be declared public.

The purpose of a class is to describe an object. An object is just what the word means in English: a thing, an item, a noun. For example, a car, a house, an employee of a company, a window that opens on the computer screen, or a TCP/IP socket connection between two computers.

An object consists of two major components: attributes and behaviors. The *attributes* of an object are what the object consists of, and the *behaviors* of the object are what the object does.

You do not write an object in object-oriented programming (OOP); you *instantiate* one. You get to describe what an object will look like when it gets instantiated by defining the attributes and behaviors of the object in a class. My favorite analogy when explaining classes and objects is to compare blueprints to a class. A blueprint of a house tells you what the house will look like when it is built, but it is clearly not a house—just a description of one. When a contractor follows the blueprints and actually builds an instance of a house, that house is an object.

How many houses can you build from a set of blueprints? As many as you want. How many instances of a class (that is, objects) can you create? As many as you want.

A class contains the attributes and behaviors of the object it is describing. In the HelloWorld class in Figure 1.10, there are no attributes and only one behavior, main(). By the way, the behaviors are often referred to as methods, and HelloWorld contains a single method: main().

What is interesting (and often confusing) about the HelloWorld example is that it is not object oriented in any way. But just because our HelloWorld program does not use any OOP concepts, we still need to write a class because the Java language requires all methods to appear within a class.

The only term you can change in this signature of main() is the name of the parameter args, which can be any valid identifier name. The array of strings (String []) will contain the command-line arguments, if any, when the program is executed from the command prompt.

Within main() is a single statement:

```
System.out.println("Hello, World");
```

This statement is what causes "Hello, World" to appear at the command prompt—or in this case, the standard output. System.out represents the standard output of the device where this program is running, and the println() (short for print line) method displays the given string along with a line feed.

Notice the semicolon at the end of the System.out.println() statement. The Java compiler ignores all whitespace and indenting, so it is necessary to use a semicolon to denote the end of all statements in Java.

Step 2: Compile the Program

The javac tool compiles Java classes into bytecode. Figure 1.7 shows how to compile the HelloWorld.java class from Figure 1.6. Notice the use of the cd command to change directories to the one where the HelloWorld.java file is located.

If the compiler is successful, no message will be displayed and the command prompt will come back. Notice in Figure 1.7 the use of the dir command to display the contents of the current directory. You should see a new file: HelloWorld.class. This is the bytecode file generated from the compiler.

All bytecode appears in .class files. The extension is appropriate because within that .class file is the bytecode describing a single class. In this case, HelloWorld.class contains the bytecode of the HelloWorld class, which is a class containing one method, main().

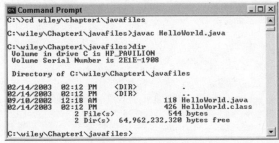

Figure 1.7 Use the javac tool to compile HelloWorld.java.

If there are compiler errors, they will be displayed on the command prompt with a description of what the compiler did not understand. For example, Figure 1.8 shows the compiler error that occurs if the word String in Figure 1.6 was not capitalized.

Be sure to read your compiler errors closely. Many of my students simply glance at a compiler error and quickly jump back to their code to look for the error. However, if you read the error carefully, you will notice that the compiler tells you the name of the file and the line number where the error occurred. In the case of Figure 1.8, line 3 of HelloWorld.java has a problem.

Upon closer examination of the compiler error, it appears that the compiler "cannot resolve symbol," which happens to be my most common compiler error. The compiler does not know what "string" means. That was my fault, of course, because I changed String to string. The compiler doesn't know what I meant; all it knows is that it cannot figure what a string is.

Step 3: Run the Program

After you have successfully compiled HelloWorld.java and created the Hello-World.class file, you can now run the program using the java tool. The java tool requires the name of the bytecode file that you want to execute. (The class being executed must contain the main() method within it, or an error will occur.)

Figure 1.9 shows the proper use of the java tool to run the HelloWorld program. Keep in mind that Java is case sensitive, even though Windows and DOS are not. You need to type in the name of the class using proper case, such as HelloWorld, as shown in Figure 1.9.

Notice also in Figure 1.9 that you do not use the .class extension when running Java programs with the java tool. The JVM only interprets bytecode in .class files, so the .class extension is not needed. An error occurs if you include the extension.

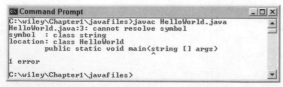

Figure 1.8   The compiler does not know what a string is, as stated by the compiler error.

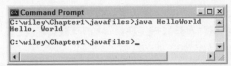

Figure 1.9 Running the Hello, World program.

Lab 1.1: Your First Java Program

In this lab, you will write a Java program that uses the System. out.prinlnt() method to display an email signature (name, title, email address, and so forth).

Perform the following steps:

1. Create a new subdirectory in your javafiles directory, called Lab1_1.

2. Using your text editor, start with a public class called Signature. Add the main() method within the Signature class.

3. Within main(), use the System.out.println() method to print your name at the command prompt.

4. Similarly, print your title on a line, then your email address, Web site URL, or phone numbers. (Display any information you want in your signature. Just remember to use a semicolon after each println() statement.)

5. Save your Signature source code in the Lab1_1 folder in a file called Signature.java.

6. Compile Signature.java using the javac tool.

7. Run the Signature program using the java tool.

You should see an output similar to that in Figure 1.10.

Figure 1.10 Sample output for Lab 1.1.

Lab 1.2: Using Command-Line Arguments

When you run a Java program from the command prompt, you can input arguments that get passed to the main() method as strings. For example, suppose that you entered the following command to run your Signature program from Lab 1.1:

```
java Signature hello 27 "Rich Raposa"
```

This command has three command-line arguments beyond the java Signature command: hello, 27, and Rich Raposa. (Arguments are separated by spaces unless placed in double quotes.) These three arguments are passed into main() and placed in the args parameter. The args parameter is an array of strings that can hold as many command-line arguments as you enter.

To access these arguments within main(), you use args with a subscript in square brackets. For example, args[0] is the first argument, args[1] is the second, and so on. In the current example, args[0] will be the string "hello," args[1] will be "27," and args[2] will be "Rich Raposa."

In this lab, you will display the title and author of a book, where the title and author are entered as command-line arguments such as:

```
Title: Green Eggs and Ham
Author: Dr. Seuss
```

Now, follow these steps:

1. Create a new subdirectory of javafiles, called Lab1_2.

2. Open your text editor, and write a public class called Book.

3. Add main() within your Book class.

4. The title will be args[0] and the author will be args[1]. You need to concatenate "Title: " with args[0], which is done by using the + operator. For example:

```
System.out.println("Title: " + args[0]);
```

5. Similarly, use the concatenation operator to display "Author: " and args[1].

6. Save your Book class in the Lab1_2 directory in a file called Book.java.

7. Compile the Book class.

8. Run the Book program, using two command-line arguments:

```
java Book "Green Eggs and Ham" "Dr. Seuss"
```

 If you run the Book program and forget to enter two command-line arguments, you will see an "exception in thread main" java.lang.Array IndexOutOfBounds-Exception. This would happen, for example, if you tried to access args[1], and there was no string at that position in the args array.

Summary

- Java is an object-oriented programming language that is interpreted by a Java Virtual Machine (JVM), allowing it to be platform independent.

- There are three editions of Java: J2SE, the Java 2 Platform, Standard Edition, which is covered in this book; J2ME, the Java 2 Platform, Micro Edition, which is for electronic devices with limited resources; and J2EE, the Java 2 Platform, Enterprise Edition, which is a collection of Java technologies that includes servlets, JavaServer Pages, and Enterprise JavaBeans.

- Writing Java code involves writing classes. A class is saved in a .java file, and only one public class can appear in a .java file. The name of the .java file must be the name of the public class declared in the file.

- Compiled Java code is referred to as bytecode. Bytecode appears in a .class file.

- To compile a Java program, you use the javac tool that comes with the Standard Developer Kit (SDK), which is freely downloadable from Sun's Web site.

- To run a Java program, you use the java tool that comes with the SDK. The java tool is a JVM.

- The JVM invokes the main() method. The signature of main() is public static void main(String [] args).

Review Questions

1. Name the three editions of the Java 2 platform.

2. Compiled Java code is referred to as _____.

3. A class is a description of a(n) _____.

4. An object is an instance of a(n) _____.

5. The main() method has to be declared as _____.

6. True or False: A Java program written for Windows needs to be recompiled to run it on Linux or Unix.

7. What are the two major components of an object?

8. What does the JIT acronym stand for? What does it mean?

Answers to Review Questions

1. The three editions of the Java 2 platform are J2ME, J2SE, and J2EE.

2. Compiled Java code is bytecode.

3. The answer is object. Classes describe objects.

4. The answer is class. You write a class to define an object, and an instance of the class is an object.

5. public static void main(String [] args). The only term you can change is "args"; otherwise, main() must look like this.

6. No, you do not need to recompile Java code for different platforms because Java only runs on one platform—a Java Virtual Machine implementation.

7. Attributes and behaviors, also referred to as fields and methods.

8. JIT stands for Just-In-Time and refers to a JVM that compiles portions of the bytecode of a Java program into native code when the program is executed.

Java Fundamentals

This chapter builds your foundation for using the Java programming language. It discusses the details of the fundamentals of Java. The keywords are discussed as well as how to declare identifiers and variables. The chapter also discusses literals, constants, strings, references, and the Java arithmetic operators.

Java Keywords

The keywords of a programming language are the words that define the language, have special meaning to the compiler, and cannot be used as identifiers. Table 2.1 displays all the Java keywords.

Table 2.1 Java Keywords

abstract	default	if	private	this
boolean	do	implements	protected	throw
break	double	import	public	throws

(continued)

Table 2.1   *(continued)*

byte	else	instanceof	return	transient
case	extends	int	short	try
catch	final	interface	static	void
char	finally	long	strictfp	volatile
class	float	native	super	while
const	for	new	switch	
continue	goto	package	synchronized	assert

The keywords const and goto cannot be used in Java. They were added to the list of keywords so they would generate compiler errors for developers who were converting C and C++ code over to Java. The keyword *assert* is a new Java keyword added to the J2SE in version 1.4.

There are three more reserved words in Java: true, false, and null. Technically, they are literal values and not keywords. However, they cannot be used as identifiers, and they have a specific meaning to the Java compiler.

Take a look back at the HelloWorld example in Chapter 1. The keywords used are public, class, static, and void. The other words in the HelloWorld class are identifiers, which are discussed next. Notice that main is not a keyword, even though main is a special name used to denote the method in which a Java program starts.

Identifiers

Identifiers are those words in your Java code that you choose. For example, in Lab 1.1, you wrote a class named Signature. Signature is not a Java keyword, nor does it have any special meaning in Java. You had to name the class something, and Signature was chosen to make the code more readable because the program displayed an email signature.

In Java, you will need to identify many elements in your code, including class names, methods, fields, variables, and package names. The names you choose are called identifiers and must adhere to the following rules:

- An identifier cannot be a keyword or true, false, or null.
- An identifier can consist of letters, digits 0–9, the underscore, or the dollar sign.
- An identifier must start with a letter, an underscore, or a dollar sign.

For example, x, X, x1, x2, HelloWorld, Signature, System, String, age, $color, and _height are valid identifiers. Don't forget that Java is case sensitive. That means Public is a valid identifier because it is different from the keyword public.

 The following are not valid identifiers: 1x because it starts with a digit, public because it is a keyword, a@b or x+y because @ and + are not valid characters for use in identifiers.

Java's Eight Primitive Data Types

Java has eight data types that are built into the language. These eight data types, often referred to as the primitive types, are the building blocks from which classes are written. Table 2.2 shows the eight data types, the number of bits they consume in storage, and the range of values that can be stored in each type.

Notice that the size of the data types (except for boolean) is strictly defined. For example, an int is a signed, 32-bit data type. The reason Java can define the exact size of its primitive data types, independently of the platform that the program runs on, is because Java programs run on a JVM. The underlying platform does not affect the size or range of values of Java's primitive data types.

We will discuss each of the data types in Table 2.2 in detail. But before we do, I want to discuss declaring variables in Java. For more information on data types, be sure to read the sidebar *Understanding Classes and Data Types*.

Table 2.2   Eight Primitive Data Types

DATA TYPE	SIZE	MIN VALUE	MAX VALUE
byte	8 bits	−128	127
short	16 bits	−32768	32767
int	32 bits	−2147483648	2147483647
long	64 bits	−9223372036854775808	9223372036854775807
float	32 bits	±1.40239846E-45	±3.40282347E+8
double	64 bits	±4.94065645841246544E-324	±1.79769313486231570E+308
char	16 bits	\u0000	\uFFFF
boolean	n/a	true or false	

♦ Understanding Classes and Data Types

Programming involves working with data. Data is stored in the computer's memory, and the program creates and manipulates this data. In Java, the type of data you are working with needs to be specifically declared. For example, if you want to store something simple such as an integer value, you need to specify exactly how much storage space that integer needs. If you want to store complex data such as all the information that an employer needs to know about employees, this data also needs to be specifically defined.

In the case of storing an integer value, you can use one of the eight built-in data types. In the case of an employee, you would write a class describing the type of data that makes up an employee. By writing a class to describe an employee, you are creating a new data type, one that was not built into the Java language.

This employee class would most likely consist of a combination of the built-in data types and other classes. (These other classes are either ones you wrote or those in the J2SE.) For example, there is a String class in the J2SE to represent strings. The employee class could use the String class to store the employee's first and last name. There is a Data class in the J2SE for representing a calendar date. The Date class could be used to store the hire date of an employee.

By combining built-in data types and classes (either J2SE classes or user-defined classes), you create new data types. Your new data types can now be used just like any of the existing data types.

I want to emphasize this point again: When you write a class in Java, you are creating a new data type. This concept of creating data types and developing programs based on the program's data is the basis of object-oriented programming. We will discuss the details of writing classes in Chapter 4, "Classes and Objects."

Variables

Variables are used to store data. In Java, a variable needs to be declared. Declaring a variable involves two steps: giving the variable a name and stating what type of data is to be stored in the variable.

For example, the following statements are variable declarations:

```
short x;
int age;
float salary;
```

Because x is a short, x consumes 16 bits of memory and can contain any integer value between –32768 and 32767 (refer to Table 2.2). Similarly, age is an int and consumes 32 bits of memory, whereas salary is a float and also consumes 32 bits of memory.

 The variables age and salary consume the same amount of memory: 32 bits. However, they are quite different in the way they can be used. The variable age can store only integer numbers, those without a decimal value. Because salary is a float, it stores numbers with decimals, using the IEEE 754 standard for floating-point values. This allows salary to store much larger values than age, with some loss of accuracy in large values.

Assigning Variables

The term variable is used because the data stored in a variable can vary. In other words, you can change the value of a variable. In Java, you use the assignment operator = to assign a variable to a particular value.

For example, the following statements declare an integer x and assign it the value 12.

```
int x;
x = 12;
```

Note that a variable can assign a value at the time it is declared. The previous two statements could have been replaced with the following single statement:

```
int x = 12;
```

Java is strict about letting you assign variables only to values that match the variable's data type. If x is an int, you cannot assign it to other data types unless you use the cast operator.

For example, the following statements declare x as an int and then attempt to assign x to a floating-point value.

```
int x;
double d = 3.5;
x = d;        //This does not compile!
x = (int) d; //This does compile since I used the cast operator.
```

The cast operator consists of placing the data type that the value is being cast to in parentheses. In this example, f was being cast to an int, so int was placed in parentheses right before f.

 Casting tells the compiler that you are aware of the invalid assignment, but you want to do it anyway. In the example above, x was assigned to d by casting, and x will be the value 3. Casting a floating-point number to an integer data type causes the decimal part of the number to be truncated.

Classroom Q & A

Q: Why would you ever need to assign a double to an int? It seems like the cast operator would not be used very often.

A: I am not going to say that you will use the cast operator every day, but it is an important operator in any programming language that requires strict data typing. If you hand me a floating-point number, and I want to store it as an integer value, I will need to use the cast operator.

Q: What if I give you an integer value and you want to store it as something smaller? In other words, suppose that I give you a short and you want to store it as a byte. Why would you need to cast then?

A: I still need the cast operator because you are giving me 16 bits of data (a short) and I want to store it in eight bits of data (a byte). Any time you try to store something "bigger" into something "smaller," the cast operator is required or the code will not compile.

Q: Why? In C or C++, that would generate only a compiler warning, not an error.

A: You are getting your first taste of the strictness of Java when it comes to data types. Besides, there is a possibility of data being lost, so generating an error draws attention to this, just as when I take 3.5 and cast it to an int, and the decimal part is lost and I get 3. If the short that you give me is between −128 and 127, casting it to a byte does not result in the loss of any data. However, if you give me a short whose value is, say, 250, casting that to a byte causes the loss of the upper 8 bits of the short, making the value meaningless. The result of casting 250 to a byte is essentially a programming error on my part.

Q: So you need the cast operator only when working with numeric values?

A: No. In fact, the cast operator is probably used more often when working with object references, as we will see in Chapter 8, "Polymorphism and Abstraction." By the way, the Java compiler rarely gives warnings. There is typically only one way to do something in Java, and anything that doesn't follow the rules generates a compiler error. That is part of the reason why Java is easier to learn and understand than C++.

Integral Types

Of the eight primitive data types, four of them are integer types that differ only by their size: byte, short, int, and long. All four of them are signed, meaning that they store both positive and negative numbers.

The following IntegerDemo program demonstrates using the integral types. Study the program and try to determine what the output is.

```java
public class IntegerDemo
{
    public static void main(String [] args)
    {
        int x = 250;
        System.out.println("x is " + x);
        short a, b, c;
        c = 21;
        b = 9;
        a = (short) (b + c);      //why cast to a byte?
        System.out.println("a is " + a);
        long y = 12345678987654321L;      //notice the "L"
        System.out.println("y is " + y);
        y = x;
        byte s;
        s = (byte) c;
        System.out.println("y is now " + y + " and s is " + s);
    }
}
```

Let's take a look at the IntegerDemo program in detail. Assigning x to the value 250 and displaying it is fairly straightforward. Notice that you can declare more than one variable at a time, with a, b, and c all being declared shorts in one statement. An interesting note about Java is that it performs integer arithmetic at the int level, so b+c returns an int. This means that the sum must be cast to a short before assigning it the value to a because a is a short.

The variable y is declared as a long and assigned to an integer literal that is larger than 32 bits. The literal is appended with an L to denote it as a long. This line of code would not compile if the L were omitted.

 When you hard-code a numeric value in your code, that value is referred to as a literal. For example, in the IntegerDemo program shown in Figure 2.1, the numbers 250, 21, 9, and 12345678987654321 are integer literals. (They are integer literals because they do not contain a decimal point.) In Java, integer literals are treated as int values, which is fine in most situations.

However, when an integer literal is too large to fit into a 32-bit int, the literal cannot be treated as an int. In these situations, you need to append the literal with an L to denote that the literal is to be stored as a long, not an int.

Take special note of the statement y = x, where y is a long and x is an int. These two variables are different data types, but no cast operator is used. This is because an int is assured of fitting into a long without any loss of data. When y is assigned to x, the value of x is simply promoted to a long and stored in y.

However, assigning the byte s to the short c requires the cast operator. The short c is 16 bits and s is only 8, so there is a possible loss of data. Without the cast operator, the assignment will not compile.

The output of IntegerDemo is shown in Figure 2.1.

Figure 2.1 Output of the IntegerDemo program.

Floating-Point Types

Two of the eight primitive data types are used for storing floating-point numbers: float and double. The only difference between them is their size, with a float being 32 bits and a double being twice that size (which explains where the term *double* comes from). Floating-point values are stored using the IEEE 754 standard format.

In the previous section, I discussed how integer literals are treated as ints, except when an L is appended to the number, thereby making it a long. Similarly, floating-point literals are treated as a double value by default. A floating-point literal is any literal that contains a decimal point.

If you want a floating-point literal to be treated as a float, you need to append an F to the literal. The following FloatDemo program demonstrates using the float and double data types. Study the code and see if you can guess the output. Figure 2.2 shows the actual output of the FloatDemo program.

```java
public class FloatDemo
{
    public static void main(String [] args)
    {
        double pi = 3.14159;
        float f = 2.7F;
        System.out.println("pi = " + pi);
        System.out.println("f = " + f);
        int n = 15, d = 4;
        f = n/d;
        System.out.println("15/4 = " + f);
        int radius = 10;
        double area = pi * radius * radius;
        System.out.println("area = " + area);
    }
}
```

 In the FloatDemo program, 3.14159 and 2.7F are floating-point literals. The first one is treated as a double, whereas 2.7 is treated as a float because it has an F appended. Assigning f to 2.7 without the F generates a compiler error because 2.7 would be a double, and you cannot assign a double to a float (unless you use the cast operator).

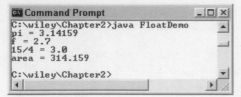

Figure 2.2   Output of the FloatDemo program.

You may be surprised by the result of 15/4 in the FloatDemo program. Because both 15 and 4 are int values, their quotient is also an int, in this case 3. (The remainder is truncated.) The value of f is assigned to the int 3, so f becomes 3.0.

In the expression pi * radius * radius, a double is being multiplied by two ints. Before the multiplication occurs, the int values are promoted to doubles, and the result is therefore a double.

Boolean Data Type

Java has a built-in data type, boolean, to represent Boolean values. A variable of type boolean can be either true or false. Note that true and false are special literals in Java.

The following BooleanDemo program demonstrates using the boolean data type. Study the BooleanDemo program and try to determine what the output will be.

```
public class BooleanDemo
{
    public static void main(String [] args)
    {
        boolean t = true;
        System.out.println("t is " + t);
        int x = 10;
        boolean y = (x > 15);
        System.out.println("y is " + y);
        // y = x;      // Does not compile!
    }
}
```

In the BooleanDemo program, t is declared as a boolean variable and is assigned the value true. When t is printed out as a string, true is displayed. The boolean y is assigned to an expression that evaluates to false because x is less than 15. The string false is displayed when y is printed out (see Figure 2.3).

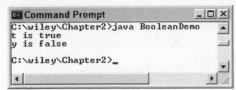

Figure 2.3   Output of the BooleanDemo program.

 In Java, a boolean data type is not an integer value. A boolean can be only true or false, two special Java literals. In other languages, Boolean values are integer types, with 0 being false and a nonzero entry being considered true. Notice in the BooleanDemo program that the boolean y cannot be assigned to the int x, even if casting is attempted.

Char Data Type

The char data type represents characters in Java. The size of a char is 16 bits, which allows characters to be represented as integers using the Unicode character mapping. A char can be treated as an integer value, allowing you to perform arithmetic and make comparisons using greater than or less than. Just keep in mind that char is an unsigned data type.

Single quotes are used to denote a character literal. For example, the literal 'A' in your code would be treated as a char. (If a literal appears in double quotes, like "A", it is not a char, it is a String.) Some characters that are not printable are denoted using the escape sequence \. Table 2.3 provides a list of some of the more commonly used escape sequence characters.

Table 2.3   Escape Sequence Characters

ESCAPE SEQUENCE	DEFINITION
\t	tab
\b	backspace
\n	newline
\r	carriage return
\'	single quote
\"	double quote
\\	backslash

If you need to denote a character by its Unicode value, you use the escape sequence \u followed by its Unicode value in hexadecimal format, as in '\uF9A4', or octal format, as in '\071'. (The octal format is for the Latin-1 encoding.)

The following CharDemo program demonstrates the use of the char data type and character literals. Study it carefully and try to determine the output, which is shown in Figure 2.4. You will likely be surprised.

```java
public class CharDemo
{
    public static void main(String [] args)
    {
        char a = 'A';
        char b = (char) (a + 1);
        System.out.println(a + b);
        System.out.println("a + b is " + a + b);
        int x = 75;
        char y = (char) x;
        char half = '\u00AB';
        System.out.println("y is " + y + " and half is " + half);
    }
}
```

 In the CharDemo program, a and b are declared as char variables. When b is assigned to (a + 1), the cast operator is required because the result of adding 1 to a is an int. We saw this in the IntegerDemo program, when the sum of two shorts was an int. Java promotes the smaller integer types to int values before performing any arithmetic.

Adding (a + b) results in the sum of two ints, which is 65 + 66, or 131. The second println() statement is not adding 'A' and 'B', but concatenating the two characters. The result of concatenation is a string, in this case "AB".

Notice in the CharDemo program that the int x is cast to a char. The value 75 corresponds with a 'K', which is the value of y. The variable half demonstrates using the '\u' escape sequence, and the character '\u00AB' is the 1/2 character.

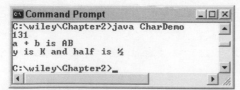

Figure 2.4 Output of the CharDemo program.

Strings

A *string* is a sequence of characters. Keep in mind that strings are not primitive data types in Java, and therefore need to be represented by a class. Java has a class named String to represent string objects. I have always liked the String class from the moment I first learned Java because it makes working with strings much simpler than in other languages.

A String object is created automatically for the string literals in your Java code. For example, suppose that you had the following println() statement:

```
System.out.println("Hello, World");
```

The string literal "Hello, World" is converted to a String object, which is then passed into the println() method. Consider the following statements:

```
int x = 10;
System.out.println("x = " + x);
```

The string literal "x = " is converted to a String object. The + operator then becomes string concatenation, so the variable x needs to be converted to a String and then concatenated to "x = " to create a third String, "x = 10". It is this third String object that gets passed to println().

 In Java, every primitive data type being concatenated to a String will be automatically converted to a new String object. This simplifies the process of working with built-in types and displaying or outputting them. In fact, any object in Java (not just the built-in types) is convertible to a String because every object in Java will have a toString() method. The toString() method is discussed in detail in Chapter 6, "Understanding Inheritance."

The following StringDemo program demonstrates string literals and String objects. Study the program and try to determine what the output will be.

```
public class StringDemo
{
    public static void main(String [] args)
    {
        String first = "Rich", last = "Raposa";
        String name = first + " " + last;
        System.out.println("Name = " + name);
        double pi = 3.14159;
        String s = "Hello, " + first;
        System.out.println(s + pi + 7);
        System.out.println(pi + 7 + s);
    }
}
```

I want to make a few comments about the StringDemo program. I count five string literals in the program: "Rich", "Raposa", " ", "Name = ", and "Hello, ". Each of these literals is converted to a String object. So when name is assigned to first + " " + last, that is the concatenation of three String objects. Similarly, "Name = " + name is the concatenation of two String objects.

I specifically added the last two println() statements of the StringDemo program to demonstrate the importance of order of operations. When s + pi +7 is calculated, the s + pi occurs first, which is string concatenation, not addition. This new string is then concatenated to a 7 to create the string "Hello, Rich3.141597".

In the last println() statement, the order was changed, and pi + 7 is evaluated first. The 7 is an integer literal, and therefore is treated as int. So, pi + 7 is a double plus an int, and the 7 is promoted to a double and the addition is calculated, resulting in the double 10.14159. This double is concatenated to s, creating the string "10.14159Hello, Rich".

The output of the StringDemo program is shown in Figure 2.5.

A String object in Java is immutable, meaning that the string of characters being represented by a String object cannot be changed. For example, the StringDemo program declared a String called name and assigned it to the literal "Rich". The "Rich" string cannot be altered. If, for example, you want name to be "RICH", you would have to assign name to a new String object "RICH". You cannot change the individual characters of name.

It may seem like a waste of resources to have to create a new String object each time a String is used, but having immutable strings actually allows the JVM to efficiently handle strings. However, there are times when you may want to alter a string's characters without having to create new String objects each time. The sidebar on the StringBuffer class discusses how this can be done.

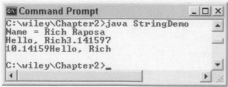

Figure 2.5 Output of the StringDemo program.

♦ The StringBuffer Class

Java has another class for representing strings, the StringBuffer class. A String object cannot be altered because String objects are immutable. If you are working with strings that need to be altered, the StringBuffer is a flexible alternative.

Strings represented as StringBuffer objects are basically an array of characters, allowing you to change, insert, or delete individual characters of the StringBuffer. You can also append characters, change the length of the buffer, view characters at a specific location in the string, and reverse the order of characters.

This is all accomplished by using the many helpful methods of the StringBuffer class. (In Chapter 5, "Methods," you will learn the details of invoking a method on an object.)

References versus Primitive Data

I showed you in the earlier section titled *Variables* how to declare a variable, and then we saw some sample programs that used variables of the primitive data types. However, there is one other type of variable in Java, called a reference, which is used when the data involved is not a primitive data type. You saw this initially in the StringDemo program, but I purposely avoided discussing references at the time because the point of the StringDemo program was to demonstrate String objects.

Now, I want to focus on the details of references versus primitive types because understanding references is an essential component of understanding Java. For example, suppose that you need to allocate memory for a String to represent someone's name. Your code might look like the following:

```
String name;
name = "Rich";
```

In this example, name is a variable of type String. String is not one of the eight primitive data types. It is a commonly used class that is a part of the J2SE. When you declare a variable of a class type, that variable is referred to as a *reference*. The term reference is used because a reference *refers* to an object.

A reference is different from a primitive data type in that a reference does not contain the actual data of the object that it refers to. Instead, a reference points to the location in memory where the object is located.

In other words, the name variable above does not contain the string "Rich". Instead, "Rich" is somewhere else in memory, and name points to that location. This is quite different from the values x and pi, which are primitive data types. The value 250 is in the 32 bits consumed by x, and the value 3.14159 is in the 64 bits consumed by pi.

I need to emphasize the importance of the difference between a variable that is a reference and a variable that is a primitive data type. (Those of you that are familiar with C++ should definitely pay attention here because what I am about to say is not true for C++.) A variable in Java is either one of the eight primitive data types or it is a reference to an object. Those are your only two options.

If the variable is a primitive data type, the value of that variable is stored in the same memory location as the variable.

If the variable is a reference, the value of that variable is a memory address. This memory address is the location of the object that the reference refers to. The object contains the actual data.

Classroom Q & A

Q: Wait a minute. Isn't a reference just another name for a pointer?

A: No. Sun has made specific efforts to not use the term *pointer* in Java. A pointer is a term used to describe a variable that points to a certain memory address. A reference is a variable that refers to a particular object.

Q: That doesn't sound different at all. You just said a reference contains a memory address.

A: You're right. It is a subtle difference, but an important one to understand when learning Java. Both pointers and references are 32- or 64-bit integer values that contain a memory address. However, pointers can be treated as integers in other languages, allowing for tasks such as pointer arithmetic. Also, in other languages, a pointer can point to a primitive data type. In Java, a reference can either refer to an object or null. Also, there is no such thing as pointer arithmetic in Java. Unlike pointers, you cannot see the actual value of a reference. So, although a reference is a memory address, nowhere in your code can you take advantage of that fact.

Q: Why not just cast the reference to an int and view it that way?

A: Nice try, but the compiler won't let you cast a reference to any numeric value. Not allowing programmers direct access to memory is one of the security features of Java, and it also leads to more stability in your programs. With pointers, it is easy to run off the end of an array or alter memory that you had no business accessing. These are issues that cannot occur in a Java program.

Q: So how do you use a reference to access the data in an object?
A: That is a question I will answer in great detail in Chapter 4, "Classes and Objects."

Constants

The final keyword is used in Java to declare a variable as a constant. A final in Java cannot be changed after it is assigned a value. Consider the following statements, some of which compile and some of which don't.

```
final double pi = 3.14159;
pi = -5.0; //Does not compile!
final int x     //A blank final
x = 12;    //ok
x = 100    //Does not compile!
```

The variable pi is declared final and initialized to 3.14159, so attempting to change it to –5.0 is not valid.

The variable x is declared final, but is not initialized. This can be done in Java, and x is referred to as a blank final. Assigning it to 12 at a later time is valid, but it cannot be changed after it is assigned. Trying to change it to 100 is invalid and causes a compiler error.

Java Operators

Table 2.4 shows the various operators in Java. The operators are listed in the precedence that they are evaluated, with the pre- and postincrement/decrement operators having the highest precedence.

Table 2.4 Java Operators and Precedence

OPERATOR	SYNTAX
Pre- and postincrement/decrement	++, --
Unary operators	+, -, ~, !, (cast)
Multiplication/division/modulus	*, /, %
Addition/subtraction/concatenation	+, -, +
Shift Operators	<<, >>, >>>
Comparison	<, <=, >, >=, instanceof

(continued)

Table 2.4 *(continued)*

OPERATOR	SYNTAX
Equality	==, !=
Bitwise AND, OR, XOR	&, |, ^
Conditional AND, OR	&&, ||
Ternary operator	? :
Assignment operator	=
Assignment with operation	*=, /=, %=, +=, -=, <<=, >>=, >>>=, &=, ^=, |=

The following ArithmeticDemo demonstrates some of the operators and their order of operations. For example, notice that an int m is declared and assigned to 15%4, read "15 modulus 4". The modulus operator % returns the remainder when the two integers are divided.

Study all the statements in the ArithmeticDemo program carefully and try to determine what the output is. The actual output is shown in Figure 2.6.

```java
public class ArithmeticDemo
{
    public static void main(String [] args)
    {
        System.out.println(5 + 4 * 6 / 3 - 2);
        System.out.println((5 + 4) * 6 / (3 - 2));
        int x = 5, y, z;
        y = x++;
        System.out.println("x = " + x + " y = " + y);
        x = 5;
        z = ++x;
        System.out.println("x = " + x + " z = " + z);
        int m = 15%4;
        System.out.println("m = " + m);
        m = 29;
        System.out.println("m << 2 = " + (m >> 2));
        double d = 5.0;
        d *= 4.0;
        System.out.println("d = " + d);
        System.out.println("Ternary: " + (x==5 ? "yes" : "no"));
    }
}
```

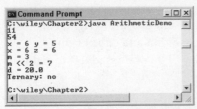

Figure 2.6   Output of the ArithmeticDemo program.

Increment and Decrement Operators

The increment operator ++ adds one to a number, and the decrement operator
-- subtracts one from a variable. The two operators are applied as either a
prefix or a suffix to any variable that represents a number.

Using these operators as a prefix is referred to as preincrement and pre-
decrement, and this causes the increment or decrement to occur immediately,
using the new value in the statement.

Using these operators as a suffix to a variable is referred to postincrement
and postdecrement, and this causes the increment or decrement to occur after
the variable is used in the statement. The variable is then incremented or
decremented after the statement.

For example, in the ArithmeticDemo program, x is assigned the value 5 and
then the following statement occurs:

```
y = x++;
```

This is a postincrement, so x gets incremented to 6 after it is used in the statement. Therefore, y is 5 after this statement and x is 6.

The variable x is then assigned to 5 again, then you see the following
statement:

```
z = ++x;
```

This is a preincrement, so x becomes 6 before it is used in the statement.
Therefore, z will be 6, as you can see in the output of the ArithmeticDemo
program in Figure 2.6.

When two operators of the same precedence appear in a statement, the Java language specifies that they be evaluated from left to right. For example, in the following statement, the addition and subtraction operators have the same precedence and will be evaluated left to right:

```
int x = 5 + 4 - 3;
```

The 5 + 4 will be evaluated, and then the 3 will be subtracted from 9 to get 6.

Assignment Operators

Java provides a collection of shortcut assignment operators that are based on a similar feature of C++. A variable can be used in a statement and assigned to the result, all in one statement.

For example, the following statement uses the multiplication with assignment operator:

```
d *= 4.0;
```

In the preceding statement, d is multiplied by 4.0, and the result is stored in d. The statement is equivalent to the following:

```
d = d * 4.0;
```

Table 2.4 contains a list of all the operators with assignment. This is another one of those features of Java that you do not use every day, but I want you to at least be familiar with it because you may run into it when reading other developers' Java code.

Shift Operators

There are three shift operators in Java: one left-shift operator (<<) and two right-shift operators (>> and >>>). Shift operators act on integer values by shifting their binary values (how they are stored in memory) to the right or left.

Shifting an integer to the left causes a 0 to be placed in the least-significant digit, shifting all the other 1s and 0s one place to the right, and having the most significant digit "pushed" off the end and lost. For example, the following is 45 represented in binary format:

```
0 0 1 0 1 1 0 1
```

If this value were shifted once to the left, you would get the following:

```
0 1 0 1 1 0 1 0
```

The number is 90, which just happens to be twice 45. Because it is a binary shift to the left, this is equivalent to multiplying by two.

Similarly, the right-shift operators shift the binary digits to the right. The only difference between the two right-shift operators is that one is signed (>>) and the other is unsigned (>>>). The signed right-shift brings in the sign bit on the right, whereas the unsigned right-shift always brings in a 0 on the right, no matter what the sign bit is.

For example, the following is 45 represented in binary format:

```
0 0 1 0 1 1 0 1
```

The most significant bit is a 0, so shifting to the right using >> or >>> produces the same result:

```
0 0 0 1 0 1 1 0
```

If the sign bit is a 1, as in the following binary representation of –4, the shift operators do make a difference:

```
1 1 1 1 1 1 0 0
```

Shifting this value to the right using >> produces the following, which is the value –2:

```
1 1 1 1 1 1 1 0
```

Shifting to the right using >> is equivalent to dividing the number by 2. Shifting –4 to the right using >>> results in the following, which has no meaningful mathematical result:

```
0 1 1 1 1 1 1 0
```

The following ShiftDemo program demonstrates the use of the shift operators. Study the program and try to determine its output, which is shown in Figure 2.7.

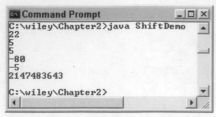

Figure 2.7 Output of the ShiftDemo program.

```
public class ShiftDemo
{
    public static void main(String [] args)
    {
        byte b = 11;
        System.out.println(b << 1); //Shift to the left
        System.out.println(b >> 1); //Signed shift to the right
        System.out.println(b >>> 1); //Unsigned shift to the right
        byte c = -10;
        System.out.println(c << 3); //Shift to the left three
        System.out.println(c >> 1); //Sign shift to the right
        System.out.println(c >>> 1);
    }
}
```

Comparison Operators

Table 2.5 shows the comparison operators in Java, as well as the data types that each can be used with. Notice that the "equal to" and "not equal to" operators can be used on both primitive data types and references, but it does not make sense to compare references to see if one reference is less than another. (C++ programmers will be interested here to know that Java does not allow for operator overloading.)

Table 2.5 Comparison Operators

OPERATOR	SYNTAX	VALID DATA TYPES
Less than	<	byte, short, int, long, float, double, char
Less than or equal to	<=	byte, short, int, long, float, double, char
Greater than	>	byte, short, int, long, float, double, char
Greater than or equal to	>=	byte, short, int, long, float, double, char

Table 2.5   *(continued)*

OPERATOR	SYNTAX	VALID DATA TYPES
Equal to	==	byte, short, int, long, float, double, char, boolean, references
Not equal to	!=	byte, short, int, long, float, double, char, boolean, references
Instance of	instanceof	references

We will see the comparison operators used extensively in Chapter 3, "Control Structures." The instanceof operator is discussed in Chapter 8, "Polymorphism and Abstraction."

Boolean Operators

The Boolean operators are used for combining two or more Boolean expressions into a single Boolean expression. The conditional operators *and* (&&) and *or* (||) can be used to combine two Boolean expressions, whereas the bitwise operators *and* (&), *or* (|), and *exclusive or* (^) can be used on both Boolean expressions and integers.

The Boolean operators are discussed in detail in Chapter 3, "Control Structures."

Ternary Operator

Another carryover from C++ is the ternary operator. It is called the *ternary operator* because it has three operands, and it is basically a shortcut mechanism for writing an if/else control structure. The syntax is the following:

```
(boolean expression) ? x : y
```

The first part is a Boolean expression followed by a question mark. If the Boolean expression is true, the x statement is executed. If the Boolean expression is false, the y statement is executed.

The ternary operator was demonstrated in the ArithmeticDemo program.

```
(x == 5) ? "yes" : "no";
```

If x is 5, then "yes" is displayed, otherwise "no" is displayed. As you will see in Chapter 3, "Control Structures," this can be accomplished in a much less elegant manner by using the following if/else statement:

```
if(x == 5)
     System.out.println("Ternary: yes");
else
     System.out.println("Ternary: no");
```

Java Comments

I have been using comments sporadically in some of the previous examples, but I have not discussed them yet in detail. There are three techniques for adding comments to your Java code, each of which has their own particular usage. The three techniques are the following:

- **//** Use the two forward slashes to comment out text that appears after the forward slashes but on the same line.

- **/* and */** Use the /* to turn on comments, and all text will be commented until a */ is reached. This is useful for commenting out multiple lines of code.

- **/** and */** A special type of comment used specifically with the javadoc tool for generating HTML files that contain your comments. This feature of Java is widely used, and it is expected that these HTML pages accompany any Java code that is distributed among developers.

The following Television class demonstrates all three types of comments. The javadoc-style comments will be discussed in detail in Chapter 9, "Collections."

```
/* Filename: Television.java
   Author: Rich Raposa
   Date: 9/20/02
*/
public class Television
{
     private int channel; //current channel
     private int prev;   //previous channel
     /** This method changes the channel
     *    of this television.
     *    @param newChannel The channel to be changed to
     */
     public void setChannel(int newChannel)
     {
          prev = channel; //Keep track of the previous channel.
          channel = newChannel; //Change to the new channel.
     }
}
```

Lab 2.1: Temperature Converter

In this lab, you will write a Java program that converts Celsius to Fahrenheit.

1. Write a public class called TempConverter, and declare the main() method within the class.

2. The value for Fahrenheit will be input from the command line. Because all command-line arguments are String objects, the first thing you need to do within main() is convert the String to a double. Use the following statement, which converts the first command-line argument into a double:

   ```
   double F = Double.parseDouble(args[0]);
   ```

3. The formula for converting Fahrenheit to Celsius is C = (5 / 9) x (F - 32) where F is Fahrenheit and C is Celsius. Compute this value using the double passed in from the command line, and display the result.

4. Save, compile, and run your TempConverter program. Be sure to enter a command-line argument for the Fahrenheit temperature. For example:

   ```
   java TempConverter 85
   ```

You should see the output in Celsius of the Fahrenheit temperature entered on the command line.

Lab 2.2: Mortgage Calculator

In this lab, you will write a program that computes the monthly payment of a mortgage, given the amount of the loan (principal), the interest rate, and the number of years required to pay back the loan.

1. Write a class called Mortgage, and add the main() method to it.

2. The first command-line argument will be the principal of the loan, which will be a double. Parse this argument into a double using the Double.parseDouble() method.

3. Similarly, the second command-line argument will be the interest rate. Parse this argument into a double.

4. The third command-line argument is the number of years for the loan. This value needs to be parsed into an int, which can be done using the Integer.parseInt() method.

5. You now have all the data you need to compute the monthly payment. Use the following formulas for computing the mortgage, and display the result using the println() method.

```
N = years x 12       //Number of payments
R = interest_rate / (12 x 100)    //Monthly interest rate
Monthly payment = principal x (R / (1 - (1 + R)^-N))
```

6. To compute the power of $(1 + R)$ to the $-N$, use the following Java function, which computes a to the power b:

```
Math.pow(a, b)
```

The return value is a double.

7. Save, compile, and run the Mortgage program. Be sure to enter the three command-line arguments. For example, the following statement computes the monthly payment for a $200,000 mortgage at 6.5 percent for 30 years:

```
java Mortgage 200000 6.5 30
```

The output should display the monthly payment of the mortgage information input on the command line.

Summary

- The keywords goto and const are reserved words, meaning they have no implementation in Java. The terms true, false, and null are special literal values and technically are not Java keywords.

- A valid identifier cannot be a keyword; must start with a character, underscore, or dollar sign; and can contain the digits 0–9 as long as the identifier does not start with a digit.

- Java has eight primitive data types: byte, short, int, long, float, double, char, and boolean. Their size does not depend on the underlying operating system or platform. The numeric values are all signed, meaning that they hold both positive and negative values. The char data type is 16 bits and is unsigned. The size of a boolean is not specified, and it can only contain the values true or false.

- An integer literal is treated as an int by the JVM. The literal can be appended with an L to denote that the literal is a long. A floating-point literal is treated as a double by the JVM. An F can be appended to the literal to denote it as a float.

- String literals are treated as java.lang.String objects. A String object is immutable, meaning that once it is instantiated, its contents cannot be changed.

- A variable in Java is either one of the eight primitive data types or a reference.

- The final keyword in Java is used to declare a constant.

- There are three ways to declare comments in Java: two forward slashes // comment out the remainder of the current line of text; the format /* ... */ is used to comment out multiple lines of text; the /** ... */ format is a special type of comment used by the javadoc tool.

Review Questions

1. Which two Java keywords have no implementation and cannot be used in Java?

2. A boolean in Java can only be assigned to which two special literals?

3. True or False: main is a Java keyword.

4. True or False: An identifier must begin with a letter, underscore, or dollar sign.

5. Name the eight primitive data types in Java and give their size in bits.

6. True or False: You can use the unsigned keyword to make an int store all positive values.

7. If you need to create a new data type beyond the eight built-in types, you need to write a(n) _____.

8. True or False: The size of an int depends on the underlying platform that the Java program is running on.

9. What Java keyword is used to declare a constant?

10. A string literal in Java is automatically instantiated into what data type?

11. True or False: String objects in Java are immutable.

12. In Java, a variable is either one of the eight primitive data types or a(n) _____.

13. True or False: A reference in Java contains the memory address of an object, but there is no way for you to view or access that memory address.

14. If x is an int equal to 25, what will x be after the statement x /= 4?

15. If b is a byte equal to −24, what is the result of b >>= 2?

16. Assuming that x is 10, what will y be after the statement y = (x > 0) ? 1 : 2; ?

17. Name the three techniques in Java used to add comments to source code.

Answers to Review Questions

1. goto and const.

2. true or false.

3. False. *main* is the name of the method that the JVM invokes on a standalone Java application, but *main* is not a keyword.

4. True.

5. byte (8 bits), short (16 bits), int (32 bits), long (64 bits), float (32 bits), double (64 bits), char (16 bits), boolean (size is not defined).

6. False. Unsigned is not a Java keyword.

7. class. We will do this throughout the remainder of the book.

8. False. The "underlying platform" is always a JVM, and an int is 32 bits on all JVMs.

9. final. Variables declared as final cannot be changed.

10. A String object.

11. True. A String object cannot be changed.

12. reference.

13. True. A reference holds a memory address, but you cannot use this fact in your Java programs.

14. 6. This is integer division, so the result is an int. Any remainder is truncated.

15. −6. The right-shift operator is equivalent to integer division by 2, so shifting twice is equivalent to integer division by 4. −24/4 equals −6.

16. 1. 10 is greater than zero, so the value of y is the expression immediately following the question mark.

17. // is used for single-line comments, /* ... */ is used for commenting multiple lines, and /** ... */ is used for javadoc comments.

CHAPTER

3

Control Structures

In this chapter, I will discuss the control structures of the Java language, covering decision making and repetition. Topics in this chapter include a discussion on Boolean logic, truth tables, the if/else statement, the switch statement, the for loop, and while and do/while loops. If you are new to programming, spend some time in this chapter. Control structures are fundamental to any programming language, not just Java. If you are already familiar with structures like if statements and while loops, pay close attention to the details of how these are implemented in Java.

Flow of Control

In the programs I have shown you so far and in the programs you have written in the labs, there has been a public class with a main() method declared in it. These programs have begun executing at the first statement in main(), then each subsequent statement has executed in order until the end of main() is reached, at which point the programs terminated.

Frequently in programming you need to change the flow of control—that is, the order in which statements are executed. There are three basic techniques for changing the flow of control of a program:

Invoke a method.   This involves the flow of control leaving the current method and moving to the method being invoked. For example, when you invoke the println() method, flow of control leaves main(), jumps to println(), and returns to main() when the println() method is finished. We will cover methods in detail in Chapter 5, "Methods."

Decision making.   This is when a certain criterion determines which path the flow of control takes. Java has two mechanisms for making decisions: the if/else statement and the switch statement. (The ternary operator can also be used for decision making, but it is basically a shortcut version of an if/else statement.)

Repetition.   Repetition occurs when a task needs to be repeated a certain number of times, and is often referred to as a loop. Java has three looping mechanisms: the for loop, the while loop, and the do/while loop.

The decision-making and repetition statements are known as *control structures*, because you use them to control the flow of a program. All of the control structures involve some type of Boolean decision, so you will need a good understanding of Boolean logic and truth tables, which I will discuss next.

Boolean Logic

Boolean logic refers to the logic of combining two or more Boolean expressions into a single Boolean expression. I will discuss four types of logic when working with combined Boolean statements:

and.   The combined expression is true only if both parts are true.

or.   The combined expression is true if either part is true.

exclusive or.   The combined expression is true only if one part is true and the other part is false.

not.   Negates a Boolean expression.

I will now discuss the logic and truth tables for these Boolean operators.

The and Operator

Suppose I make the following statement:

```
It is raining out today and x is equal to 4.
```

This expression is a combination of two Boolean statements. The statement "It is raining out today" is either true or false. The statement "x is equal to 4" is either true or false. The *and* combines these two Boolean expressions into a single, larger expression that is either true or false.

We use what is called a truth table when determining whether a combination of Boolean expressions is true or false. In the case of the *and* operator, the only time the larger expression is true is when both smaller expressions are true, as shown in Table 3.1.

Therefore, the earlier comment about the rain and variable x is only true when it is actually raining out *and* x is indeed the value 4. If x is 4, but it is not raining out, the entire expression becomes false. Similarly, if it is raining but x is not 4, the expression is false. Finally, if it is not raining and x is not 4, the entire expression is again false.

 Just like the old saying that two wrongs don't make a right, two false statements do not make a true statement. An expression of the form *false and false* is false.

The or Operator

Suppose that I make the following comment:

```
Today is Monday or I will buy lunch for everyone today.
```

With the *or* operator, if either of the two expressions is true, the entire expression is true. Therefore, in my statement about Monday and lunch, if it is indeed Monday, I do not need to take anyone to lunch and the statement is still true. Similarly, if I buy lunch for everyone and it is not Monday, the statement is true. If it is not Monday, and I do not buy lunch for anyone (which is the likely outcome), the statement is false.

Table 3.2 shows the truth table for the or operator. Notice in Table 3.2 that the only time an or expression is false is when both of the statements in the expression are false.

Table 3.1   The Truth Table for the *and* Operator

AND	TRUE	FALSE
TRUE	TRUE	FALSE
FALSE	FALSE	FALSE

Table 3.2   The Truth Table for the *or* Operator

OR	TRUE	FALSE
TRUE	TRUE	TRUE
FALSE	TRUE	FALSE

The exclusive or Operator

The *exclusive or* operator is used when you want a combined Boolean expression to be true only when exactly one of the two statements is true. Table 3.3 shows the truth table for the exclusive or operator.

For example, a Boolean expression of the form true exclusive or false is true, while true exclusive or true is false.

The not Operator

The final Boolean operator I want to discuss is the *not* operator, which negates a single Boolean expression. If I say something that was not true, it must be false. Similarly, if I say something that is not false, it must be true. The not operator performs this logic in your code.

 There is no truth table for the not operator because it is only performed on a single expression.

Consider the following statement:

```
Not (it is raining out today).
```

This example may not sound grammatically correct, but it is programmatically correct. The not operator is placed at the beginning of a Boolean expression. The statement above is true when it is not raining out today. If it is raining out today, the statement is false.

Table 3.3   The Truth Table for the *exclusive or* Operator

EXCLUSIVE OR	TRUE	FALSE
TRUE	FALSE	TRUE
FALSE	TRUE	FALSE

Boolean Operators

Now that you have seen the logic behind the operators, let's look at the corresponding programming syntax. Table 3.4 shows the Boolean operators available in Java.

The & and && operators only differ in that the && will *short-circuit* when the first Boolean expression is false. To demonstrate, consider the following Boolean expression:

```
(a > 0) && (a < 1)
```

If a is not greater than 0, the first part of the expression is false. Because the operation is *and*, we can now say that the entire expression will be false, no matter what the result of the second expression is. In the case of using the two ampersands &&, the expression will short-circuit and the (a < 1) will not be checked.

There are many situations where short-circuiting is the desired result. For example, consider the following expression:

```
(x != 0) && (y/x < 1)
```

If x is 0, then you do not want the second expression to be evaluated because it involves integer division by zero, which causes a runtime exception and will make your program crash. If x is not 0, the first part is true, and the second part must be evaluated to determine the result of the entire Boolean expression. Because we are assured that x is not zero, the division y/x is no problem.

 In some situations, you might not want the short-circuit behavior. In the following example, the second part of the expression contains an operation that changes the value of the variable x:

```
(x != 0) && (x++ > 10)
```

I consider the preceding statement to be poor programming practice, but it illustrates my point. If x is 0, then the x++ increment will not occur. If you want the x++ to be evaluated in all situations, you would use the single ampersand (&):

```
(x != 0) & (x++ > 10)
```

No matter if x is 0 or not, the expression (x++ > 10) will be tested. In other words, the single ampersand guarantees that both Boolean expressions will be checked. The same is true for the *or* operator (|).

Table 3.4   The Boolean Operators

OPERATOR	SYNTAX
short-circuit and	&&
and	&
short-circuit or	||
or	|
exclusive or	^
not	!

The or operator also has two versions. The || operator will short-circuit if the first Boolean expression is true. (If the first part of the expression is true, it does not matter what the second part evaluates to. The entire expression will be true.)

For example, the following statement will short-circuit:

```
int x = 10;
(x > 0) || (x-- != 10)
```

The previous expression is true because the first part is true. What is x after the code above? Because it short-circuits, x will still be 10. The second part of the Boolean expression is not evaluated.

As with the single ampersand, &, you can use the single | to ensure that an *or* expression never short-circuits:

```
int x = 10;
(x > 0) | (x-- != 10)
```

What is x after the code above? This time, no short-circuiting occurs and x will be decremented to 9. The expression still evaluates to true because *true or false* is true.

The not operator, !, may be placed at the beginning of any Boolean expression or variable. Consider the following statements:

```
short a = 10, b = 5;
boolean test = !(a > b);
```

Because a is greater than b, the expression in parentheses is true. The not operator is then applied to true, which results in false (not true equals false); therefore, the value of test is false.

You can combine the Boolean operators to create a more complex Boolean expression. For example, try to determine the result of the following code:

```
int x = 5, y = 6, z = -3;
boolean b = ((x + 3 > y) ^ (z >= y)) && !(x == 5 | ++x == y);
```

Pay close attention to the parentheses. If you replace the comparisons with true and false, you get the following logically equivalent statement:

```
(true ^ false) && !(true | true)
```

Evaluating the ^ and | expressions gives you:

```
true && !(true)
```

This is the same as true and false, which is false; therefore, the variable b in the code above will be the value false.

Now that you have seen the Boolean operators, I am ready to talk about the various control structures in Java, all of which involve some type of Boolean expression.

The if Statement

An *if* statement consists of a Boolean expression followed by one or more statements. If statements have the following syntax:

```
if(Boolean_expression)
{
     //Statements will execute if the Boolean expression is true
}
```

If the Boolean expression in parentheses is true, the statements within the curly brackets are executed. If the Boolean expression is false, the statements in curly brackets are skipped over. In the case of false, the flow of control will jump to the statement that is immediately beyond the curly brackets.

The IfDemo program that follows demonstrates using if statements. Study the program and try to determine what the output will be. A sample output is shown in Figure 3.1.

```
public class IfDemo
{
     public static void main(String [] args)
     {
          int x = Integer.parseInt(args[0]);
```

```
double half = 0.0;
if(x != 0)
{
     half = x / 2.0;
     System.out.println(x + "/2 = " + half);
}
if(x == 0)
{
     System.out.println("The value of x is 0");
}
int y = x * 5;
char grade = 'F';

if(y >= 85)
{
     grade = 'A';
}
if(y >= 70 && y < 85)
     grade = 'C';

System.out.println("y = " + y + " and grade = " + grade);
     }
 }
```

In the IfDemo program, I wanted to divide an int in half. If I had used the statement x/2, the 2 would be treated as an int because 2 is an integer literal. This would have given me an int as a result, meaning that any remainder would have been lost. For example, 19/2 would result in 9, not 9.5.

By using the statement "x/2.0," I forced the x to be promoted to a double before the division was calculated, thereby not losing any remainder. For example, 19/2.0 results in 9.5, which is what I wanted in this particular situation.

Figure 3.1   Sample outputs of the IfDemo program.

The curly brackets of an if statement are not required if you only have one statement that follows the if. For example, in the preceding IfDemo program, the following if statement does not need the curly brackets since there is only one statement that follows: grade = C.

```
if(y >= 70 && y < 85)
     grade = 'C';
```

In the if statement comparing (y >= 85), the curly brackets appear, but are not necessary.

 Try to use curly brackets all the time, even if they are not required. They make code easier to read and modify.

The if/else Statement

An if statement can be followed by an optional *else* statement, which executes when the Boolean expression is false. The syntax for an if/else looks similar to:

```
if(Boolean_expression)
{
     //Executes when the Boolean expression is true
}
else
{
     //Executes when the Boolean expression is false
}
```

With an if/else statement, you are guaranteed that either the if block or the else block will execute, depending on the value of the Boolean expression.

 An else can only follow a corresponding if. It does not make sense (nor is it valid) to have a standalone else statement.

The else block can also contain another if statement, creating a series of if/else statements in which only one if block of code will execute. The syntax looks similar to:

```
if(Boolean_expression)
{
}
else if(Boolean_expression)
```

```
{
}
else if(Boolean_expression)
{
}
//And so on, until
else
{
}
```

When using an if/else statement as in the format above, the final else block is optional. The following StudentGrade program demonstrates using an if/else control structure by assigning a letter grade to an exam score between 0 and 100. Study the program and try to determine what the output will be for the various possible exam scores. Figure 3.2 shows some sample outputs of the program.

```
public class StudentGrade
{
    public static void main(String [] args)
    {
        int score = Integer.parseInt(args[0]);
        char grade;
        if(score >= 90)
        {
            grade = 'A';
            System.out.println("Way to go!");
        }
        else if(score >= 80)
        {
            grade = 'B';
            System.out.println("Good job");
        }
        else if(score >= 70 && score < 80)
        {
            grade = 'C';
        }
        else if(score >= 60)
        {
            grade = 'D';
        }
        else
        {
            grade = 'F';
            System.out.println("Try again");
        }
        System.out.println("Your grade is a " + grade);
    }
}
```

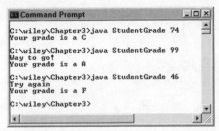

Figure 3.2 Sample outputs of the StudentGrade program.

In the StudentGrade program, exactly one of the if/else blocks must execute. Notice that if the value of score is, say, 92, all the if statements are true; however, because they are checked in order, the (x >= 90) block will be checked first, which is true. The grade will be assigned as 'A', the message "Way to go!" will be displayed, and the flow of control will jump out of the if/else structure. The next line of code to execute will be the println() statement displaying "Your grade is a A," and none of the subsequent Boolean expressions will be checked.

 Notice the truth logic in the if/else control structure of the StudentGrade program. You might ask why I checked for the score greater than or equal to 70 *and* less than 80.

Well, to be honest, I did not need to check for the score to be less than 80. I added that to make you think about the logic and bring attention to the fact that I already knew score was less than 80 by the time I got there. If x is not less than 80, it must be greater than or equal to 80, and one of the two previous Boolean expressions would have evaluated to true.

That being said, having the less than 80 in the expression might make the code more readable, even though it is not needed.

The switch Statement

A *switch* statement allows a variable to be tested for equality against a list of values. Each value is called a *case*, and the variable being switched on is checked for each case.

The syntax for a switch statement looks similar to the following:

```
switch(variable)
{
    case value :
        //Statements
```

```
        break;          //optional
    case value :
        //Statements
        break;          //optional
    //You can have any number of case statements.
    default :           //Optional
        //Statements
}
```

The following rules apply to a switch statement:

- The variable used in a switch statement can only be an integer value 32 bits or smaller. That means the only data types that can be switched on are byte, short, int, and char.

- You can have any number of case statements within a switch. Each case is followed by the value to be compared to and a colon.

- The value for a case must be the same data type as the variable in the switch, and it must be a constant or a literal.

- When the variable being switched on is equal to a case, the statements following that case will execute until a break is reached.

- When a break is reached, the switch terminates, and the flow of control jumps to the next line following the switch statement.

- Not every case needs to contain a break. If no break appears, the flow of control will "fall through" to subsequent cases until a break is reached.

- A switch statement can have an optional *default case*, which must appear at the end of the switch. The default case can be used for performing a task when none of the cases is true. No break is needed in the default case.

I always find it is easier to understand a switch by going through an example. The following CongratulateStudent program contains a switch statement that prints out a message to a student, depending on the student's letter grade. The first statement within main() retrieves the first character from the first command-line argument, which is supposed to be the student's letter grade.

Study the switch statement and try to determine what the output will be for the various possible values of grade. Figure 3.3 shows some sample outputs of the program.

```
public class CongratulateStudent
{
    public static void main(String [] args)
    {
```

```
char grade = args[0].charAt(0);
switch(grade)
{
    case 'A' :
        System.out.println("Excellent!");
        break;
    case 'B' :
    case 'C' :
        System.out.println("Well done");
        break;
    case 'D' :
        System.out.println("You passed");
    case 'F' :
        System.out.println("Better try again");
        break;
    default :
        System.out.println("Invalid grade");
}
System.out.println("Your grade is a " + grade);
}
}
```

Notice that when the grade is an A, the first case statement is true. The string "Excellent!" is displayed, a break is reached, and the flow of control jumps down to the statement following the switch.

When the grade is a B, the first case is false, the second case is true, and all subsequent statements following case B will execute until a break is reached. Even though the case of a C is false when the grade is a B, the flow of control falls through, since there is no break between case B and case C.

A similar falling through occurs when the grade is a D, when "You passed" is displayed and so is "Better try again."

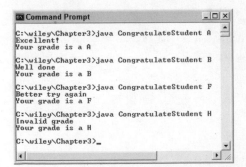

Figure 3.3 Sample outputs of the CongratulateStudent program.

Classroom Q & A

Q: What are the benefits of using a switch statement?

A: Switch statements are a carry-over from C and C++, and there are many situations where a switch statement is more elegant and easier to write than a series of if/else statements.

Q: It seems like the StudentGrade program would have been easier to write using a switch. Why not use a switch every time?

A: You have to be careful here. A switch statement only tests for equality. The StudentGrade program was checking to see if a variable fell within a range of values, which required less than and greater than comparisons. You can't do those types of comparisons with a switch, only equality.

Q: Can you list more than one value after a single case?

A: No. If you want a case to have multiple values, you need to use the case keyword each time followed by a single value, similar to case B and C in the CongratulateStudent program.

Q: So you are limited by a switch statement.

A: It's not so much that you are limited, but that a switch is only useful in certain situations. That being said, you never need to use a switch statement. Every switch statement can be written using an equivalent if/else statement. In my experience, though, programmers use switch statements all the time.

The while Loop

A *while* loop is a control structure that allows you to repeat a task a certain number of times. The syntax for a while loop is:

```
while(Boolean_expression)
{
    //Statements
}
```

When a while loop is first reached, the Boolean expression is checked. If the Boolean expression is true, the statements in the body of the loop execute. The flow of control then goes back up to the Boolean expression, which is checked again. If it is still true, the statements in the loop execute again. This process repeats until the Boolean expression is false.

Study the following while loop. How many times will it execute? How will the output look?

```
int x = 1;
while(x <= 10)
{
     System.out.println(x);
     x++;
}
```

Notice that x starts at 1 and is incremented by 1 each time through the loop; therefore, the println(x) statement executes 10 times, and the output is:

```
1
2
3
4
5
6
7
8
9
10
```

Note that when the loop is done executing, the value of x will be 11. In this example, the variable x is referred to as the *loop counter* because x changes each time through the loop, and it is the value of x that determines when the loop will terminate.

It is possible to write a while loop that never executes. If the Boolean expression is initially false, the statements in the loop are not executed. For example:

```
int i = -10;
while(i > 0)
{
     System.out.println("You will not see this.");
}
```

Similarly, it is possible to write an infinite while loop that never terminates. For example:

```
int i = 1;
while(i > 0)
{
     System.out.println(i++);
}
```

It is not difficult to inadvertently write an infinite while loop. Your program will simply run indefinitely. To stop an infinite loop, you need to stop the JVM. This is done by pressing Ctrl+C at the command prompt window in which you are running your Java program.

The following WhileDemo program has three while loops. Study the program carefully and try to determine what each while loop is doing.

 The first loop in the WhileDemo program uses the print() method, which is similar to println(), except that it does not move the cursor down to the next line.

```java
public class WhileDemo
{
    public static void main(String [] args)
    {
        //Loop #1
        int i = 10;
        while(i > 0)
        {
            System.out.print(i + " ");
            i--;
        }
        System.out.println();

        //Loop #2
        int x = Integer.parseInt(args[0]);
        long sum = 0;
        i = 0;
        while(i <= x)
        {
            sum += x;
            i++;
        }
        System.out.println("sum = " + sum);
        //Loop #3
        long f = 1;
        while(x >= 1)
            f *= x--;
        System.out.println("f = " + f + " and x = " + x);
    }
}
```

In the first while loop in the WhileDemo program, the variable i is the loop counter. It starts at 10 and is decremented by 1 each time through the loop.

Figure 3.4 Output of the WhileDemo program.

Because the loop terminates when x becomes 0, it executes 10 times. The output of the first loop is the numbers 10 down to 1, all on the same line.

The variable i is the loop counter in the second while loop, also. It is incremented by 1 each time, and the loop executes until i equals x, so the actual number of executions is x + 1 (since i starts at 0). The value of i is added to sum, so mathematically sum is the result of adding 0 + 1 + 2 + 3 + 4 + ... + x.

I made the third while loop intentionally confusing. The loop counter is x, which is the value input from the command line. The value of x is decremented by 1 each time, and the loop executes while x is greater than or equal to 1. The loop will therefore execute x number of times. Each time through the loop, the value of x is multiplied by f before it is decremented. The result of f is x * (x-1) * (x-2) * ... * 1, which is the factorial of x.

 Notice I did not use any curly brackets in loop #3 of the WhileDemo program. As with an if statement, when you have only one statement in the body of a loop, the curly brackets are not needed.

Figure 3.4 shows the output of running the WhileDemo program when x is equal to 5.

The do/while Loop

A *do/while* loop is similar to a while loop, except that a do/while loop is guaranteed to execute at least one time. The syntax of a do/while loop is:

```
do
{
     //Statements
}while(Boolean_expression);
```

Notice that the Boolean expression appears at the end of the loop, so the statements in the loop execute once before the Boolean is tested. If the Boolean expression is true, the flow of control jumps back up to do, and the statements in the loop execute again. This process repeats until the Boolean expression is false.

The semicolon at the end of the do/while statement that immediately follows the Boolean expression is easy to forget.

How many times does the following do/while loop execute?

```
int y = 10;
do
{
    System.out.println(y);
     y += 10;
}while(y <= 100);
```

The loop counter is y, which starts at 10 and is incremented by 10 each time through the loop. Because it repeats until y equals 100, that is 10 times through the loop. The output will be the multiples of 10:

```
10
20
30
40
50
60
70
80
90
100
```

Classroom Q & A

Q: Why did you use a do/while loop to display the multiples of 10? It seems like you could have just used a while loop.

A: You're right. In fact, I think a while loop in that example would have made the code more readable.

Q: So, are there situations where a do/while is required?

A: No. In fact, a while loop is the only repetition control structure you would ever need in Java. If you can write something with a do/while loop, a while loop can be written to do the same thing. The upcoming section *The for Loop* shows you how to write a for loop, and the same is also true with them. If you can perform a task with a for loop, a while loop can be written that does the same thing.

Q: Why not just use while loops exclusively, then?

A: I suppose you could; however, in many situations, a do/while loop or a for loop can make code more readable or make a repetition problem easier to solve. The upcoming RandomLoop program is a good example of a do/while loop solving a problem more efficiently than a while loop. Study this program and try to determine what the do/while loop is doing.

 The RandomLoop program uses the Math.random() function to generate random numbers. The return value of Math.random() is a random double between 0 and 1 (but never equal to 0 or 1). Multiplying this result by 10 gives you a random number r in the range $0 < r < 10$. Adding 1 changes this range to $1 < r < 11$. Casting this value to an int gives you a random integer between 1 and 10 (including 1 and 10).

```
public class RandomLoop
{
    public static void main(String [] args)
    {
        int a, b;
        a = (int) (Math.random() * 10 + 1);
        System.out.println("a = " + a);
        do
        {
            b = (int) (Math.random() * 10 + 1);
            System.out.println("Trying b = " + b);
        }while(a == b);

        System.out.println("a = " + a + " and b = " + b);
    }
}
```

The RandomLoop program starts by declaring two ints, a and b. The variable a is assigned to a random number between 1 and 10, and this number is displayed. Inside the do/while loop, b is also assigned to a random number between 1 and 10, and this value is displayed. If a is equal to b, the loop repeats. This means that the loop repeats until b is not equal to a.

Therefore, when a and b are displayed after the do/while loop, it is assured that they are two random but different numbers between 1 and 10. Figure 3.5 shows some sample outputs of the RandomLoop program.

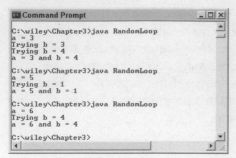

Figure 3.5   Sample outputs of the RandomLoop program.

The for Loop

A *for* loop is a repetition control structure that allows you to efficiently write a loop that needs to execute a specific number of times. The syntax of a for loop is:

```
for(initialization; Boolean_expression; update)
{
    //Statements
}
```

Here is the flow of control in a for loop:

1. The initialization step is executed first, and only once. This step allows you to declare and initialize any loop control variables. You are not required to put a statement here, as long as a semicolon appears.

2. Next, the Boolean expression is evaluated. If it is true, the body of the loop is executed. If it is false, the body of the loop does not execute and flow of control jumps to the next statement past the for loop.

3. After the body of the for loop executes, the flow of control jumps back up to the update statement. This statement allows you to update any loop control variables. This statement can be left blank, as long as a semicolon appears after the Boolean expression.

4. The Boolean expression is now evaluated again. If it is true, the loop executes and the process repeats itself (body of loop, then update step, then Boolean expression). After the Boolean expression is false, the for loop terminates.

Let's go through an example to demonstrate the preceding steps. Consider the following for loop:

```
for(int j = 1; j <= 1024; j = j * 2)
{
     System.out.println(j);
}
```

The first step that occurs is j being initialized to 1; j then is tested to see if it is less than or equal to 1024, which is true, so the body of the for loop executes and 1 is displayed. The flow of control then jumps up to the update statement j = j * 2, and j becomes 2. Because 2 is less than or equal to 1024, the loop repeats again and 2 is displayed.

This process repeats, and j becomes 4, 8, 16, and so on until it equals 2048, at which point the loop terminates. The output will look similar to:

```
1
2
4
8
16
32
64
128
256
512
1024
```

 This could have been done using a while loop similar to the following:

```
int j = 1;
while(j <= 1024)
{
     System.out.println(j);
     j = j * 2;
}
```

The end result is the same, so I do not want to imply that one technique is better than the other. For loops are widely used, though, and are an important fundamental piece of Java.

 As with while loops and do/while loops, it is possible to write a for loop that never executes, which happens when the Boolean expression is initially false. Similarly, you can write an infinite for loop that never terminates, which happens when the Boolean expression never becomes false.

♦ Comparing the Looping Control Structures

I want to make a general observation about while loops, do/while loops, and for loops. The number of times that a loop repeats does not need to be predetermined. For example, how many times does the do/while loop repeat in the RandomLoop program? Statistically, assuming that the random number generator is truly random, the loop should only have to repeat itself three or four times at the most.

However, it is possible for the loop to have to repeat 10 times or more until a second random number is finally generated that is different from the first random number. So, to answer my own question, the loop will repeat an indeterminate number of times. You have to run the program to see how many times through it takes to generate a second, unique random number.

What if you knew exactly how many times you needed to repeat something? For example, suppose that I have 20 students in a calculus class and I need to compute the exam score for each student. I will need to repeat a task 20 times. I can use a while loop or a do/while loop, but my preferred choice in this situation would be a for loop.

You can write a for loop that executes an indeterminate number of times, and you can write a while or do/while loop that executes a predetermined number of times. In general, however, when you know ahead of time exactly how many times you need to repeat a task, a for loop is the control structure of choice. Otherwise, if you need to repeat a task in indeterminate number of times, a while loop or do/while loop is your best bet.

The following ForDemo program contains three for loops. Study the program and try to determine what the output of the program will be. By the way, I added one statement in the program that does not compile. See if you can guess which line of code it is.

```java
public class ForDemo
{
    public static void main(String [] args)
    {
        //Loop #1
        int x = Integer.parseInt(args[0]);
        long f = 1;
        for(int i = 1; i <= x; i++)
        {
            f = f * i;
        }
        System.out.println("f = " + f);
        System.out.println("i = " + i);
        //Loop #2
        for(int k = 1; k <= 100; k++)
        {
            if(k % 7 == 0)
            {
                System.out.println(k);
```

```
            }
        }
        //Loop #3
        for(int a = 1, b = 100; a < b; a = a + 2, b = b - 4)
        {
            System.out.println("a = " + a + " and b = " + b);
        }
    }
}
```

One nice feature of for loops is that you can often tell how many times they will repeat just by looking at the for declaration. For example, the first loop in the ForDemo program repeats x number of times, where x is a value input from the command-line arguments. The second for loop repeats 100 times. It is not clear how many times the third for loop executes, but I will discuss that in detail in a moment.

The first for loop multiplies 1 * 2 * 3 * ... * x, which is the factorial of x. When the variable i is equal to x + 1, the for loop terminates. For example, when x is 7 the output is:

```
f = 5040
```

The statement I added that does not compile is:

```
System.out.println("i = " + i);
```

The variable i was declared in the initialization step, and i goes out of scope once the for loop terminates.

 If you want i to have scope outside of the for loop, you need to declare it outside of the for loop.

For example, you could change the beginning of the loop to:

```
int i;
for(i = 1; i <= x; i++)
```

Now, the variable i can be used after the for loop, and it will be the value x + 1.

The second for loop in the ForDemo program executes 100 times and prints all of the numbers between 1 and 100 that are divisible by 7. This for loop generates the following output:

```
7
14
21
28
```

```
35
42
49
56
63
70
77
84
91
98
```

The third for loop demonstrates using the comma operator to perform multiple statements in the update step. The for loop is declared as:

```
for(int a = 1, b = 100; a < b; a = a + 2, b = b - 4)
```

Two variables, a and b, are declared and initialized in the initialization step. In the update step, I wanted to add 2 to a and subtract 4 from b. You can have more than one statement in the update step by separating the statements with a comma. This loop executes 17 times, which is how many times it takes for a to become larger than b, and generates the following output:

```
a = 1 and b = 100
a = 3 and b = 96
a = 5 and b = 92
a = 7 and b = 88
a = 9 and b = 84
a = 11 and b = 80
a = 13 and b = 76
a = 15 and b = 72
a = 17 and b = 68
a = 19 and b = 64
a = 21 and b = 60
a = 23 and b = 56
a = 25 and b = 52
a = 27 and b = 48
a = 29 and b = 44
a = 31 and b = 40
a = 33 and b = 36
```

The break Keyword

The *break* keyword can be used in any of the loop control structures to cause the loop to terminate immediately. When a break occurs, no matter what the value is of the loop counter or the Boolean expression, the flow of control will jump to the next statement past the loop.

The following BreakDemo program contains a while loop with a break in it. Study the program and see if you can determine how many times the while loop executes.

```java
public class BreakDemo
{
    public static void main(String [] args)
    {
        int k = 1;
        while(k <= 10)
        {
            System.out.println(k);
            if(k == 6)
            {
                break;
            }
            k++;
        }
        System.out.println("The final value of k is " + k);
    }
}
```

It looks as though the while loop will execute 10 times, since k starts at 1 and the Boolean expression has k less than or equal to 10; however, when k is 6, the break occurs, the loop terminates, and flow of control jumps down to the println() that displays the final of value of k. This final value is 6, as you can see by the output in Figure 3.6.

A common use of the break keyword is in while loops that execute indefinitely, or at least until a problem arises. For example, consider the following while loop:

```java
while(true)
{
    try
    {
        //Perform certain tasks.
    }catch(IOException e)
    {
        break;
    }
}
```

At first glance, this while loop looks like an infinite loop. Theoretically, it could run forever if no IOException occurs; however, if an IOException does occur while performing the certain tasks, the catch block will execute and the break will cause the loop to terminate. (Try/catch blocks are discussed in detail in Chapter 11, "Exception Handling.")

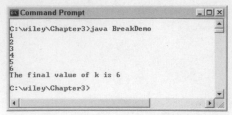

Figure 3.6 Output of the BreakDemo program.

The continue Keyword

The *continue* keyword can be used in any of the loop control structures. It causes the loop to immediately jump to the next iteration of the loop.

- In a for loop, the continue keyword causes flow of control to immediately jump to the update statement.

- In a while loop or do/while loop, flow of control immediately jumps to the Boolean expression.

The following ContinueDemo program demonstrates how the continue keyword works. Study the program carefully and try to determine what the output is.

```java
public class ContinueDemo
{
    public static void main(String [] args)
    {
        System.out.println("The for loop");
        for(int i = 10; i > 0; i--)
        {
            if(i % 2 == 0)
            {
                continue;
            }
            System.out.println(i);
        }
        System.out.println("The while loop");
        int j = 20;
        do
        {
            if(j % 3 != 0)
            {
```

```
                continue;
            }
            System.out.println(j);
        }while(j-- > 0);
    }
}
```

The for loop in the ContinueDemo program has a continue statement that executes each time the loop counter is divisible by 2. For example, the first time through the loop, the value of i is 10. Because 10 percent of 2 is 0, the continue occurs and flow of control jumps to the update statement, i--. Therefore, the 10 is not displayed because the println() statement is skipped. Notice in the output in Figure 3.7 that only the odd values less than 10 are displayed.

The while loop in the ContinueDemo program has a continue that occurs each time the loop counter j is not divisible by 3. The first time through the loop, j is 20 and the continue occurs. Flow of control jumps to the Boolean expression, which decrements j. This process repeats, with the println() statement getting skipped over each time the value of j is not divisible by 3. The output of this while loop is the numbers less than 20 that are divisible by 3, as you can see in Figure 3.7.

 Excessive use of the break and continue statements is not going to impress any of your programming colleagues. The main reason these keywords appear in the Java language is that they are used in C and C++. They do serve a purpose, especially the break keyword (as discussed earlier); however, in many situations you can avoid using a break or continue simply by redesigning your code.

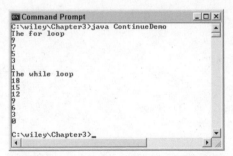

Figure 3.7 Output of the ContinueDemo program.

Nested Loops

A *nested* loop is a loop that appears within the body of another loop. For example, within the body of a for loop, you can have another for loop. The following Alphabet program demonstrates nested loops by displaying the letters of the alphabet in rows and columns. Study the program, and try to determine the output, which is shown in Figure 3.8.

```
public class Alphabet
{
    public static void main(String [] args)
    {
        char current = 'a';
        for(int row = 1; row <= 3; row++)
        {
            for(int column = 1; column <= 10; column++)
            {
                System.out.print(current + " ");
                current++;
            }
            System.out.println();
        }
    }
}
```

The outer for loop executes three times, and the inner for loop executes 10 times. That means the print() statement that displays the current variable is going to execute 3 × 10 = 30 times. Ten characters are printed in a row, and there are three rows.

Figure 3.8   The output of the Alphabet program.

Lab 3.1: Cell Phone Bill

This lab shows you how to write a Java program that computes a customer's monthly cell phone bill given the number of minutes used.

You have written several Java programs in the labs in the previous two chapters, so I am going to give you more freedom in writing the solutions for this chapter. For example, I will not tell you what to name your classes or step you through saving, compiling, and running the programs. Instead, I will describe a problem to be solved, providing you with all the details needed to solve the problem.

 Keep in mind that there is no correct answer in programming, as long as you write a program that solves the problem at hand.

- The program should take in two integer command-line arguments—one for the number of peak minutes used, and one for the number of weekend and night minutes used.

- Each customer pays $29.95 a month, which includes 400 peak minutes and 750 weekend and night minutes.

- The price for going over the allotted time is $.40/minute for both peak and weekend/night calls.

Lab 3.2: Using if/else

Write the CongratulateStudent program discussed in the section *The switch Statement* using if/else statements instead of a switch statement.

Lab 3.3: Summation Problem

Write a program that inputs an integer, n, from the command line and displays the string "1 + 2 + 3 + 4 + ... + n = sum." For example, if the command-line argument is 7, the output should be:

```
1 + 2 + 3 + 4 + 5 + 6 + 7 = 28
```

Make sure the number entered on the command line is positive.

Lab 3.4: Using do/while

Write the RandomLoop program from the section *The do/while Loop* using a while loop instead of a do/while loop.

Lab 3.5: The Powerball Lottery

Powerball is a lottery played in many of the United States. The lottery numbers are chosen randomly from two containers of numbered balls. Five white balls are chosen from a container of 49 balls, and one red ball is chosen from a container of 42 balls.

Write a program that simulates the selection of the Powerball lottery numbers. Use the Math.random() function to simulate the random selection of a numbered ball. Keep in mind that you cannot just randomly generate six numbers. The five white numbers must be unique and between 1 and 49. (After a ball is removed from the container, it can't be selected again.) The one red number must be between 1 and 42. Note that the red number can possibly be the same number as one of the selected white balls.

Summary

- The && and || operators are the short-circuit *and* and *or* operators, respectively.

- The if and if/else statements are used for decision making.

- A switch statement consists of one or more case statements. The value in a switch statement can be of type byte, short, int, or char. The value of a case must be either a literal or a constant expression.

- A while loop is used for repeating tasks. The statements in the body of a while loop execute until the Boolean expression of the while loop is false. It is possible to write an infinite while loop and also a while loop that never executes.

- A do/while loop is similar to a while loop, except that a do/while loop is guaranteed to execute at least once.

- A for loop is useful when you know how many times a task is to be repeated.

- The break keyword terminates the execution of a loop. The continue keyword causes the loop to jump to the next iteration of the loop.

Review Questions

1. Name the two control structures in Java used for making decisions.

2. Name the three control structures in Java used for repetition.

3. True or False: 2 + 2 = 4 "and" 5 − 3 = 1.

4. True or False: 2 + 2 = 4 "or" 5 − 3 = 1.

5. Which of the following data types can be used in a switch statement? Select all that apply.

   a. byte

   b. int

   c. float

   d. String

   e. char

   f. boolean

6. True or False: The value of each case in a switch statement must be either a final variable or a literal.

7. What is the output of the following code?

```
int k = 20;
while(k > 0)
     System.out.println(k);
```

8. What is the output of the following code?

```
int point = 15;
switch(point)
{
     case 0 :
         System.out.println("point is 0");
         break;
     case 15 :
         System.out.println("point is 15");
     case 30 :
         System.out.println("point is 15 or 30");
         break;
     case 40 :
         System.out.println("point is 40");
     default :
         System.out.println("Invalid point");
}
```

9. In the switch statement in the previous question, what would the output be if point was the value 40?

10. What is the output of the following code?

```
double rate = 1.5;
double price = 0.0;
if(rate >= 0.0 && rate < 1.0)
{
     price = 20 * rate;
}
else if(rate >= 1.0 && rate < 2.0)
{
     price = 15 * rate;
}
else if(rate >= 2.0)
{
     price = 10 * rate;
}
System.out.println(price);
```

11. What would the output be in the code in the previous question if the value of rate was −0.75?

12. How many times does the following loop repeat? What is the output?

```
byte b = 1;
do
{
     b++;
}while(!(b < 10));
System.out.println(b);
```

13. What is the output of the following code?

```
int y = 100, x = 5;
while(y > 0)
{
     y--;
     if(y%x != 0)
     {
          continue;
     }
     System.out.println(y);
}
```

Answers to Review Questions

1. if/else and switch.

2. while, do/while, and for loops.

3. False, because one of the two expressions is false.

4. True, because one of the two expressions is true.

5. Only 32-bit integer types can be used in a switch statement, so a, b, and e are the correct answers.

6. True.

7. That is an infinite loop because the value of k does not change. The output will be the number 20 printed over and over until the program is terminated.

8. Because the case of 15 does not contain a break, the output is "point is 15" followed by "point is 15 or 30."

9. Again, because the case of 40 does not contain a break, the output is "point is 40" and "Invalid point."

10. Because rate is 1.5, the price is 15 * 15, which is 22.5. The output is 22.5.

11. If rate is –0.75, none of the if expressions will evaluate to true, and price will remain 0. The output is 0.

12. The loop will execute only one time. The value of b will be 2.

13. The loop outputs the multiples of 5, starting at 95 and ending at 0. The output is:

```
95
90
85
80
75
70
65
60
55
50
45
40
35
30
25
20
15
10
5
0
```

Classes and Objects

In the last two chapters, I discussed the fundamentals of the Java programming language: keywords, primitive data types, references, strings, arithmetic operators, and control structures. We are now ready to discuss the most important aspect of learning and understanding Java: object-oriented programming (OOP). In this chapter, I will discuss classes and objects, how object-oriented programs differ from procedural programs, how to write a class in Java, and how to instantiate and use objects.

Overview of Classes and Objects

Java is strictly an objected-oriented programming language. All the Java code that you write will appear in either a class or an interface. (Interfaces are discussed in Chapter 10, "Interfaces.") When you write a program using an object-oriented programming language, you design your program around the objects in the problem being solved. For each object, a class is written to describe the object's attributes and behaviors.

By definition, a *class* is a description of an object. Similarly, an *object* is defined to be an instance of a class. An object consists of attributes and behaviors. An attribute is a feature of the object, something the object "has." A behavior is something the object "does."

Each attribute of an object is denoted as a field in the class. Each behavior of an object becomes a method in the class.

Procedural Programming

In the early days of programming, programs were designed using flowcharts and a sort of top-down design. With this type of design, a large problem is solved by breaking it down into smaller tasks. For each of the smaller tasks, a procedure is written. One main procedure was written to start the process and subsequently flow through to the solution, invoking the desired procedures along the way.

This type of programming is referred to as *procedural programming*. There are many procedural programming languages widely used today, most notably COBOL and C.

Procedural programming involves writing a procedure that performs a specific task. Any data that the procedure needs to use is passed in to the procedure via its *parameters*. The procedure can view and alter the data passed in and optionally return a value back to whoever called the procedure.

To demonstrate procedural programming, let's look at an example. Suppose that you want to write a program to weekly pay the employees of a company (a realistic problem to solve). Paying employees involves computing their pay based on hours worked or a portion of an annual salary. In addition, you have to compute Social Security and Medicare taxes, as well as any federal income taxes to be withheld.

Each of these computations has to be repeated for each employee in the company. Because these tasks are repeated, you can write a procedure for each one. For example, you might write a procedure called computePay() that inputs an employee's payment data and returns his or her pay. You may also have procedures called computeMedicareTax(),computeSSTax(), and so forth.

 In the example of writing the program to pay the employees of a company, many procedures will be written, and each of these procedures needs to have the employee's data passed in to it. For example, if you want to invoke the computePay() procedure, you will need to pass in the employee's payment information such as hours worked or hourly pay.

This is a common occurrence in procedural programming, in which data is passed around between procedures. The procedures modify the data passed in and/or return data back to whoever called the procedure. As you will soon see, object-oriented programming uses a different approach.

As your employee program evolves, you will certainly find yourself adding and changing procedures so that everything works successfully. For example, as you start writing the computePay() procedure, you might realize that there are two different types of employees (at least in terms of how they get paid): hourly employees and salaried employees. In this situation, you might decide to write two computePay() procedures, one for hourly employees and a different one for salaried employees.

Writing a procedure to solve a specific task is a fundamental programming concept used in both procedural languages and in object-oriented programming. As you design and write Java programs, procedures will be an essential element for solving the problem at hand.

 In Java, procedures are referred to as methods. Methods in Java appear within a class. Procedures in a procedural language typically appear at a global level so that they can be invoked from anywhere.

Object-Oriented Programming

Object-oriented programming (OOP) originated from research done by Xerox's Palo Alto Research Center (PARC) in the 1970s. OOP takes an entirely different approach to developing computer applications. Instead of designing a program around the tasks that are to be solved, a program is designed around the objects in the problem domain.

 You can think of procedural programming as writing a procedure for the *verbs* in the problem domain, such as paying an employee or computing taxes. You can think of object-oriented programming as writing a class for each of the *nouns* in the problem domain. Granted, this may be oversimplifying OOP, but I want you to conceptually understand this important difference between OOP and procedural programming.

Let's take another look at the example in which a program is to be written to pay employees of a company on a weekly basis. Instead of approaching this problem from the point of view of all the little tasks that need to be performed, such as computing an employee's pay and taxes, you begin by determining the objects in the problem domain.

An object is any person, thing, or entity that appears in the problem domain. In our example, we want to pay employees, so the employees are objects. The employees work for a company, so the company is another object. After further analysis, you might decide that the payroll department is an object. After you start writing the program, other objects will be discovered that were not apparent in the initial design.

After you have determined the objects in the problem, you write a class to describe the attributes and behaviors of each object. For example, we will need an Employee class that contains the attributes and behaviors of an employee.

The attributes of an Employee object will be what the employee "has," such as a name, address, employee number, Social Security number, and so on. Each of these attributes will be represented by a field in the Employee class.

The behaviors of an Employee object are what the employee object "does" (or, more specifically, what we want the object to do). Employees do many things, but for our purposes, we want to be able to compute their pay and mail them a paycheck once a week. These desired behaviors become *methods* in the Employee class.

For each employee in the company, we would instantiate an Employee object. If we have 50 employees, we need 50 Employee objects. In memory, this would create 50 names, addresses, salaries, and so on. Each employee would be distinguished by a reference, so we would need 50 references as well. Later in this chapter, you will see how to instantiate an object and assign a reference to it.

 With object-oriented programming, data is still passed around between method calls as in procedural programs. However, there is an important distinction to be made when comparing procedural programming with object-oriented programming. The data that is passed around in an object-oriented program is typically varying data, such as the number of hours an employee has worked in a week. It is not the entire Employee object that gets passed around.

If a procedure in a procedural program needs data to perform a task, the necessary data is passed in to the procedure. With object-oriented programming, the object performs the task for you, and the method can access the necessary data without having to pass it in to the method.

For example, if you want to compute an employee's pay, you do not pass the corresponding Employee object to a computePay() method. Instead, you invoke the computePay() method on the desired Employee object. Because it is a part of the Employee object, the computePay() method has access to all the fields in the Employee object, including the Employee object's hourly pay, salary, and any other required data.

Object-Oriented Analysis and Design

Programs written with an object-oriented language revolve around the objects in the problem domain, not the individual tasks that need to be performed in solving the problem. How you decide what the objects are and what the objects look like is an important but unique process.

Two architects asked to design a house will certainly come up with two unique but satisfactory solutions. Two developers asked to solve a problem using an OOP language will certainly come up with two unique (and hopefully satisfactory) solutions. One solution may be more elegant than the other. One solution might be easier to maintain or change than the other.

Entire books are written on how a problem can be solved using OOP. Object-oriented analysis and design (OOAD) refers to this process of designing programs that will be solved using an OOP language.

We do not have time to delve into the various OOAD approaches and give them the justice they deserve. My goal for you at this point in your OOP learning is to have you understand the big picture about OOP so that you can start developing and understanding Java programs.

At its core, OOP is based on writing classes for the objects in the problem domain: that is, the objects in the problem being solved. An object is any noun that appears in your problem or that can be used to help solve the problem.

A class is written for each object in the problem domain. These classes are then instantiated in your program, thereby creating the objects in memory for use by your program.

Writing a Java Class

A class in Java is declared using the *class* keyword. A source code file in Java can contain exactly one public class, and the name of the file must match the name of the public class with a .java extension.

 You can declare more than one class in a .java file, but at most one of the classes can be declared *public*. The name of the source code file must still match the name of the public class. If there are no public classes in the source code file, the name of the file is arbitrary.

The fields and methods of a class appear within the curly brackets of the class declaration. The following code shows a simple class with no fields or methods declared yet.

```
public class Employee
{
}
```

Adding Fields to a Class

The attributes of an object become fields in the corresponding class. A field within a class consists of the following:

- Access specifier, which can be public, private, or protected; or the access specifier can be omitted, giving the field the *default* access.
- Data type.
- Name, which is any valid identifier that is followed by a semicolon.

Access specifiers are discussed in detail in Chapter 7, "Advanced Java Language Concepts." Until then, we will use public access for fields and methods. Specifying *public* allows access to the field or method from any other object.

The following Employee class has five fields: name, address, number, SSN, and salary. When an Employee object is instantiated in memory, memory will be allocated for each of these five fields.

```
public class Employee
{
    public String name;        //First and last name
    public String address;       //Mailing address
    public int number;        //Employee number
    public int SSN;            //Social Security number
    public double salary;        //Employee's salary
}
```

 Keep in mind that a class describes what an object looks like. The Employee class is being used to describe employees of a company in the context of paying them weekly. The fields that appear in the Employee class represent information about an employee that is needed to compute his or her pay.

For example, an employee has a name and address, so the Employee class has a name field and an address field. An important piece of information in our example is the salary field used to represent the employee's salary.

Employees have other attributes that may not be relevant in our situation. Suppose, for example that every employee has a manager or supervisor. The Employee class does not contain a field for this information. However, in computing someone's pay, his or her supervisor is probably not relevant. This Employee class might look quite different if it were going to be used for other purposes besides paying employees.

Adding Methods to a Class

Behaviors of an object become methods in the corresponding class. A method within a class typically consists of the following:

- Access specifier
- Return value

- Name, which can be any valid identifier
- List of parameters, which appears within parentheses
- Definition of the method

In Java, the *definition* (often referred to as the *body*) of a method must appear within the curly brackets that follow the method declaration. The details of writing and invoking a method are discussed in Chapter 5, "Methods." The following class demonstrates methods by adding two methods to the Employee class.

```
public class Employee
{
    public String name;
    public String address;
    public int number;
    public int SSN;
    public double salary;
    public void mailCheck()
    {
        System.out.println("Mailing check to " + name
                                + "\n" + address);
    }
    public double computePay()
    {
        return salary/52;
    }
}
```

Keep in mind that this Employee class demonstrates how to add a method to a class, so the method implementations are kept simple. For example, the mailCheck() method simply prints out the name and address of the employee receiving the check. The computePay() method simply divides the employee's salary by 52, which assumes that the salary is an annual amount. The details of computing taxes and so forth are omitted for brevity.

Methods have access to the fields of the class. Notice in the Employee class that the mailCheck() method prints out the name and address of the employee being paid using the name and address fields of the class. Similarly, the computePay() method accesses the salary field.

What I want you to notice about this Employee class is the following:

- The name of the class is Employee.
- The class has five public fields.
- The class has two public methods.

The Employee class needs to appear in a file named Employee.java, and the compiled bytecode will appear in a file named Employee.class.

Instantiating an Object

In Java, the new keyword is used to instantiate an object. The new operator creates the object in memory and returns a reference to the newly created object. This object will remain in memory as long as your program retains a reference to the object.

The following statements declare an Employee reference and use the new keyword to assign the reference to a new Employee object.

```
Employee e;
e = new Employee();
```

The reference e is pointing to the Employee object in memory. The new operator allocates memory for the object and then "zeroes" the memory so that none of the object's fields will contain garbage. Instead, all fields will have an initial value of zero. Table 4.1 shows what the initial value of a field will be, depending on its data type.

When I first teach students about instantiating objects, I like to declare a reference first and then use the new keyword in a second statement to assign the reference to a new object. This emphasizes the important fact that two entities are being created in memory: the reference and the object. In the preceding statements, e is declared as a reference to an Employee, meaning that e can refer to any Employee object. In the second statement, e is then assigned to a new Employee object.

Table 4.1 Initial Value of an Object's Fields

FIELD DATA TYPE	INITIAL VALUE
byte	0
short	0
int	0
long	0
float	0.0
double	0.0
char	the null character
boolean	false
reference of any type	null

◆ Understanding References

A reference is (typically) a 32-bit integer value that contains the memory address of the object it refers to. I use the term "typically" because the size of a reference is not strictly defined in the Java Language Specification. In the future, references will likely be 64-bit integers or larger. Similarly, they can be smaller than 32 bits when used with operating systems for small electronic devices.

Because references are essentially integers, you may wonder why they need to be declared as a particular data type. This is because data types are strictly enforced in Java. A reference must be of a particular class data type.

For example, in the following statements, two Employee references and one String reference are allocated in memory.

```
Employee e1, e2;
String s;
```

Each of these three references consumes the same amount of memory and is essentially an integer data type. However, the references e1 and e2 can refer only to Employee objects. The reference s can refer only to a String object. To illustrate this point, the following statements attempt to break this rule and are not valid:

```
s = new Employee();      //Does not compile
e1 = "Rich";             //Does not compile
```

You might think that using the cast operator could create a work-around to this situation:

```
e1 = new Employee();     //Valid
s = e1;            //Does not compile
s = (Employee) e1;     //Still doesn't compile
```

However, the compiler knows that String objects and Employee objects are not compatible and will generate compiler errors in the statements above. (Other languages such as C++ have similar data type concerns, but they are often not as strictly enforced as they are in Java.)

The references e1 and e2 are the same data type and can be assigned to each other. For example:

```
e1 = new Employee();
e2 = e1;            //Valid
```

The e1 reference is assigned to a new Employee object, and the e2 reference is assigned to e1. This is valid because e1 and e2 are both Employee references and therefore are the same data type. This new Employee object now has two references pointing to it. (Note that there is only one Employee object in memory because we only used the new keyword once. Assigning e1 to e2 does not create a new object.)

We could have declared the reference e and instantiated the Employee object in a single statement:

```
Employee e = new Employee();
```

This statement creates two separate elements in memory: the reference e and the Employee object. The reference e is *not* an object. The object itself does not have a variable name, and the only way you can access and use the object is to use a reference to the object.

Garbage Collection

In the previous section, I showed you how the new keyword is used to instantiate objects. However, I have not discussed how to delete an object after you are finished with it so the memory that the object is consuming can be freed.

In other OOP languages such as C++, memory has to be explicitly freed by the programmer. In fact, C++ has a delete keyword that needs to be used to free the memory of an object. If you forget to delete an object in C++ and you lose any references to it, the memory can never be freed and you have created what is referred to as a *memory leak*, which can wreak havoc on your programs, especially programs that use large amounts of memory or run for long periods.

In Java, there is no keyword or operator that you can use to remove an object from memory. Java was designed to avoid the problems of memory leaks that arise in other languages. A JVM has a low-level thread known as the garbage collector that is constantly running in the background, looking for objects in your Java program that are no longer being used and freeing their memory.

The concept of automatic garbage collection makes programmers both excited and nervous. Garbage collection is appealing because programmers do not have to spend hours upon hours worrying about and/or trying to fix memory leaks. Programmers get nervous, however, because they lose the control of being able to free memory at any point in a program because memory will be freed in a Java program only when the garbage collector concludes that the memory is no longer being used.

Classroom Q & A

Q: How does the garbage collector know when to remove an object from memory?

A: Good question. It is important to understand the answer because there are times when you want the garbage collector to free up memory. An object is marked for garbage collection when it is no longer *reachable* in your program.

Q: Does reachable mean when there are no more references to the object?

A: No, but that is a common misunderstanding of garbage collection. You might think that the garbage collector keeps count of how many references there are to an object and then frees the object when the reference count is zero. However, it is easy to come up with a situation in which two objects need to be garbage collected, but each object has a reference to the other. If reference counting was being used, these two objects would never be freed.

Q: Then how do you make an object unreachable?

A: You need to make sure that the references that are still within the scope of your Java application are no longer referring to the object you want to be garbage collected. You can assign these references to null, assign them to point to some other object, or make the references go out of scope.

Q: Suppose that I have a very large object that I have just made unreachable and I want it to be garbage collected right now. Can I force the garbage collector to free the memory instantly?

A: Unfortunately, no. In Java, you cannot explicitly free memory. However, there is method you can invoke, System.gc(), which causes the garbage collector to "expend effort towards recycling unused objects," as quoted from the method's documentation. The gc() method is very much JMV dependent, so its behavior is hard to predict. However, it is your only mechanism for communicating with the garbage collector.

The following GCDemo program instantiates three Employee objects. Study the program carefully and try to determine at which point in the program that each Employee will be eligible for garbage collection.

```
public class GCDemo
{
    public static void main(String [] args)
    {
        Employee e1, e2, e3;
        e1 = new Employee();      //Employee #1
        e2 = new Employee();      //Employee #2
        e3 = new Employee();      //Employee #3
        e2 = e1;
        e3 = null;
        e1 = null;
    }
}
```

The GCDemo program creates three references and assigns each to a new Employee object. The new keyword is used three times, so there are three objects in the program. The result of assigning e2 to e1 is that employee #2 no longer has a reference to it and can be garbage collected at any point after the statement e2 = e1. Note that now employee #1 has two references pointing to it.

Assigning e3 to null causes employee #3 to be immediately eligible for garbage collection because the object can no longer be reached. In fact, if we decide that the object should be retrieved for some reason, it is too late. There is no way to relocate the object after all references to it have been lost.

Assigning e1 to null does not cause employee #1 to be garbage collected because e2 still refers to the object. The reference e2 goes out of scope at the end of main(), so the employee #1 object can be garbage collected immediately after main() is done executing.

◆ Methods Are Associated with an Object

A common mistake that I often see students make is to try to invoke a method without using a reference, because this is how methods are invoked in procedural languages. Consider the following statements, the second of which does not compile:

```
Employee e1 = new Employee(), e2 = new Employee();      //Valid
mailCheck();              //Error. Mail check to whom?
```

To demonstrate my point, I instantiated two Employee objects and then attempted to invoke mailCheck() without a reference. First of all, this can never be done in Java. A method can be invoked only by using a reference unless the method is static, in which case a class name is used with the dot operator.

Second, because there are two Employee objects, there are two mailCheck() methods. Which one do I want to invoke? I need to specify this using the appropriate reference and the dot operator.

Just as each Employee object has its own name, address, salary, and so on, each Employee object has its own mailCheck() and computePay() methods. To invoke mailCheck(), I need to specify whose mailCheck() method I want to invoke using the dot operator. For example, the following invokes the mailCheck() method of the Employee object that e1 refers to:

```
e1.mailCheck();
```

The statement invokes the mailCheck() method of the Employee object that e2 refers to:

```
e2.mailCheck();
```

Accessing Fields and Methods

When you instantiate an object using the new keyword, memory is allocated for each of the fields and methods in the class. You need a reference to the object to access these fields and methods using the *dot* operator.

For example, the following statements declare an Employee object and change the name field of the object:

```
Employee e = new Employee();
e.name = "Robert Smith";
```

The operation e.name is the way to access the name field of the Employee object that e refers to. Similarly, the following statement uses the dot operator to invoke the mailCheck() method of this particular Employee object:

```
e.mailCheck();
```

Using the Dot Operator

Let's go through an example that demonstrates writing a class, creating instances of that class, and using the dot operator to access the fields and methods of the objects.

We have been discussing the Employee class throughout this chapter, so we will begin by writing and compiling the Employee class. We will then write a second class that uses the Employee class. Follow along with the subsequent steps, which will help you to understand the process of using multiple classes in a program.

Step 1: Write the Employee Class

Open Notepad (or the text editor of your choice) and type in the following Employee class.

```
public class Employee
{
    public String name;
    public String address;
    public int number;
    public int SSN;
    public double salary;
    public void mailCheck()
    {
        System.out.println("Mailing check to "
            + name + "\n" + address);
```

```
        }
        public double computePay()
        {
            return salary/52;
        }
    }
```

I want you to save the file in a new empty folder on your hard drive named c:\payroll (assuming that you are using your c: drive). Be sure to name the file Employee.java.

Step 2: Compile the Employee Class

Open a command prompt window, change directories to the c:\payroll folder, and compile Employee.java, as shown in Figure 4.1.

You should now see the bytecode file Employee.class in the c:\payroll folder.

Step 3: Write the EmployeeDemo Class

You will now write a second class that instantiates and uses Employee objects. Using your text editor, type in the following EmployeeDemo class.

```
public class EmployeeDemo
{
    public static void main(String [] args)
    {
        Employee e1, e2;
        e1 = new Employee();
        e2 = new Employee();
        e1.name = "Robert Smith";
        e1.address = "123 Main St., Anytown, USA";
        e1.number = 101;
        e1.SSN = 111223333;
        e1.salary = 10000.00;
        System.out.println(e1.computePay());
        e1.mailCheck();
        e2.name = "Jane Smith";
        e2.address = "321 Main St., Anytown, USA";
        e2.number = 202;
        e2.SSN = 333221111;
        e2.salary = 100000.00;
        System.out.println(e2.name + " " + e2.SSN);
        System.out.println(e2.computePay());
        e2.mailCheck();
    }
}
```

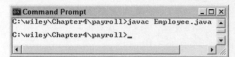

Figure 4.1   Use javac to compile the Employee class.

Be sure to save the EmployeeDemo class as c:\payroll\EmployeeDemo .java. (It needs to be in the same folder as the Employee class.)

Step 4: Compile the EmployeeDemo class

Assuming that Employee.java and EmployeeDemo.java are in the same folder, go back to your command prompt and compile the EmployeeDemo class. Look at the contents of the c:\payroll folder. You should now have four files in there: the source code and bytecode for Employee and the source code and bytecode for EmployeeDemo.

 In Chapter 7, "Advanced Java Language Concepts," the CLASSPATH environment variable will be discussed. Until then, if you are writing a Java program that consists of more than one class, the bytecode for each class must appear in the same folder on your hard drive. Otherwise, your dependent classes will not compile. For example, EmployeeDemo will compile only if the compiler can find the Employee.class file because the EmployeeDemo class uses (and therefore is dependent on) the Employee class.

Step 5: Run the EmployeeDemo program

After both classes are written and compiled, you can run the EmployeeDemo program. Figure 4.2 shows the output.

Figure 4.2   Output of the EmployeeDemo program.

In the EmployeeDemo program, two Employee objects are instantiated and referenced using two Employee references: e1 and e2. Each of the fields is initialized in both objects using the dot operator. For example:

```
e1.name = "Robert Smith";
e2.name = "Jane Smith";
```

There are two Employee objects in memory, which means that there are two fields called name, two fields called salary, two methods called computePay(), and so on. How do you tell them apart? They are distinguished by which reference you use. The Employee reference e1 points to the Employee object whose name is Robert Smith. The Employee reference e2 points to the Employee object whose name is Jane Smith.

If you want to compute the pay of Robert Smith, you invoke computePay() using e1:

```
e1.computePay();
```

If you want to mail a check to Jane Smith, you invoke mailCheck() using e2:

```
e2.mailCheck();
```

The references do more than keep the object from being garbage collected. They represent your only access to the fields and methods of the object—using a reference along with the dot operator.

The *this* Reference

Every object has a reference to itself represented by the *this* keyword. The *this* reference is used in the methods of a class whenever a method accesses the fields or other methods of the class.

For example, notice in the Employee class that the computePay() method accesses the salary field, as follows:

```
public double computePay()
{
     return salary/52;
}
```

The only way to access a field or method of an object is to have a reference to the object. But in the computePay() method, we did not use a reference to access salary. We simply used the salary variable, and everything worked fine.

The reason everything worked is that the compiler realizes that compute-Pay() is accessing the salary field, so the compiler adds the reference for us. Which reference does the compiler add? Well, computePay() needs a reference to whatever object that computePay() was invoked on, which in every case is the *this* reference.

The computePay() method actually looks like the following:

```
public double computePay()
{
    return this.salary/52;
}
```

Notice that the *this* reference and the dot operator were prefixed to salary. The compiler adds the *this* reference for you if you do not explicitly add it yourself. You can add the *this* reference if you like, or you can simply let the compiler do it for you.

For example, in the Employee class, the mailCheck() method accesses the name and address fields. In each case, the *this* reference is used, whether you add it to your code or the compiler adds it. The actual mailCheck() method looks like the following:

```
public void mailCheck()
{
    System.out.println("Mailing check to " +
              this.name + "\n" + this.address);
}
```

Notice that name and address are prefixed with *this*.

Classroom Q & A

Q: The *this* reference seems a little confusing. Is it necessary?

A: The *this* reference is one of those fundamental concepts of OOP that tends to be confusing the first time you see it. To explain the need for the *this* reference, I always try to emphasize the fact that a field or method cannot be accessed without a reference. The *this* reference is the only way a method in a class can access the other fields or methods of the class.

Q: Why does the compiler add *this.* automatically?

A: It is strictly for convenience. It would be fairly tedious (although certainly feasible) to add *this.* every time it was required in a class. In a large class, there could easily be hundreds of accesses to the fields or methods of the class, each requiring the *this* reference. For now, keep in mind that the *this* reference is implicitly being used when a method in your class accesses a field of the class.

 You can also use the *this* reference as an argument to a method, in which an object passes a reference of itself to another object.

Lab 4.1: The Video Rental Store

In this lab, you will design a solution to a problem that is to be solved using an object-oriented programming language. You will use the concepts of OOAD to determine the classes needed and what they look like. (Keep in mind that there is no single correct solution to any programming problem, as long as the program solves the problem at hand.)

Suppose that a program is to be written in Java to solve the following problem: A video rental store wants a program to keep track of its movies. It rents VHS and DVD movies, with each movie given a unique inventory number. Each customer must have a phone number, which is used as his or her membership number. The program needs to keep track of every customer and every movie, including information such as whether a movie is rented or available, who has it rented, and when it is due back. Employees of the store receive a commission on sales of non-movie items such as candy and popcorn, so this information needs to be maintained as well.

1. Determine the objects in the problem domain.

2. For each object, determine its attributes and behaviors.

Lab 4.2: Writing Classes

In this lab, you will write a class for each of the classes you described in Lab 4.1.

1. Write a Java class for each of the classes you came up with in Lab 4.1. When writing your classes, keep the following in mind:

   - Each class you write should be public; therefore, each class needs to appear in a separate source code file.

   - We have not discussed the details of writing methods. (Methods are discussed in the next chapter.) Focus on which methods each class should have, but don't worry about how they should be implemented. Within each method, use the System.out.println() method to display the name of the method.

   - Be sure to save all your classes in the same directory on your hard drive.

2. Writing a program to tie the classes together to make everything functional is not feasible without implementing all the methods. For now, just write and compile each class to match your design from Lab 4.1.

3. Write a program named VideoStore that creates an instance of each of your classes, initializes their fields, and invokes the methods to practice accessing the fields and methods of objects.

4. Compile and run your VideoStore program.

You should see the output of all the methods you invoked within your classes.

Summary

- Procedural programming involves designing a program around the tasks that the program needs to accomplish. Object-oriented programming involves designing a program around the objects in the problem domain.

- Object-oriented analysis and design is the process of determining the objects in a problem domain, determining any relationships between these objects, and also determining the attributes and behaviors of each object.

- A class is a description of an object, and an object is an instance of a class.

- The class keyword is used to declare a class in Java. A class consists of fields and methods.

- The new keyword instantiates an object. The new operator returns a reference to the newly created object. The object remains in memory until it can no longer be reached by any reference, at which point the object becomes eligible for garbage collection.

- The garbage collector is a low-priority thread of a JVM that is constantly looking for unreachable objects and freeing them from memory.

- The dot operator is used to access the fields and methods of an object using a reference to the object.

- Every object has a reference to itself referred to as the this reference.

Review Questions

1. A class is a description of a(n) _____ .
2. An object is an instance of a(n) _____ .
3. When designing a class to describe an object, how are the attributes of the object represented in the class?
4. When designing a class to describe an object, how are the behaviors of the object represented in the class? Use the following BaseballGame and Team classes to answer the ensuing questions.

```
public class Team
{
    public String name;
    public String city;
    public int numberOfWins, numberOfLosses;
}


public class BaseballGame
{
    public Team home, visitor;
    public int homeScore, visitorScore;

    public void homeTeamScored(int numberOfRuns)
    {
        homeScore += numberOfRuns;
    }
    public void visitorTeamScored(int numberOfRuns)
    {
        visitorScore += numberOfRuns;
    }
    public void gameOver()
    {
        if(homeScore > visitorScore)
        {
            home.numberOfWins++;
            visitor.numberOfLosses++;
        }
        else
        {
            visitor.numberOfWins++;
            home.numberOfLosses++;
        }
```

```
        }

        public void setHomeTeam(Team t)
        {
            home = t;
        }
        public void setVisitingTeam(Team visitor)
        {
            visitor = visitor;
        }
    }
```

5. How many fields are in the Team class? Name them.

6. How many fields are in the BaseballGame class? Name them.

7. How many methods are in the Team class? Name them.

8. How many methods are in the BaseballGame class? Name them.

9. After the following statement, what is the value of each field of the game object?

    ```
    BaseballGame game = new BaseballGame();
    ```

10. After the following statement, what is the value of each field of the giants object?

    ```
    Team giants = new Team();
    ```

Consider the following statements when answering questions 11 and 12:

```
Team angels;
BaseballGame worldSeries;
```

11. How many objects are there in memory after the previous two statements are done executing?

12. Which consumes more memory: angels or worldSeries?

13. How many Team objects are there in memory after the following two statements?

    ```
    Team a = new Team();
    Team b = a;
    ```

14. In the previous question, how many Team references are there in memory after the two statements execute?

15. After some testing, it has been determined that the setVisitingTeam() method of the BaseballGame class does not work successfully. After it is invoked, the visitor field does not change. What is the problem, and how can it be fixed?

Answers to Review Questions

1. Object.

2. Class.

3. Attributes are represented as fields in the class.

4. Behaviors are represented as methods in the class.

5. Four: name, city, numberOfWins, numberOfLosses.

6. Four: home, visitor, homeScore, visitorScore.

7. Zero. The Team class has only fields.

8. Five: homeTeamScored, visitorTeamScored, gameOver, setHomeTeam, and setVisitingTeam.

9. Home and visitor are references, so they will both be null. homeScore and visitorScore are of type int, so they will both be zero.

10. Name and city are references and will both be null, whereas numberOfWins and numberOfLosses will be zero because they are ints.

11. There are no objects in memory because the new keyword was not used.

12. Angels and worldSeries are references, and even though they are of different data types, they consume the same amount of memory.

13. The new keyword was used once, so there is one Team object in memory. Both a and b refer to this one object.

14. There are two Team references, a and b.

15. The parameter visitor is the same name as the field visitor. Setting the following assigns the visitor parameter equal to itself and does not change the field visitor:

    ```
    visitor = visitor;
    ```

    To distinguish the parameter from the field, the field needs to explicitly use the *this* reference. To fix the problem, change the body of the method to the following:

    ```
    this.visitor = visitor;
    ```

CHAPTER

5

Methods

The behaviors of an object are represented as methods in a class. In this chapter, we will discuss the details of methods in Java, including the signature of a method, invoking a method, and how data is passed back and forth between method calls.

Method Call Stack

I want to begin with a discussion on how methods change the flow of control of a program. A method is *invoked* (also referred to as *called*), which causes flow of control to jump to the method that is being invoked.

Flow of control then executes the statements within the method. Of course, the method being executed might invoke another method, causing flow of control to jump to this other method. All method calls are maintained in a structure known as the *call stack*. The current method that is executing is at the top of the call stack. When this method completes executing, it is removed from the top of the call stack, and the flow of control returns to the previous method on the stack. When a new method is invoked, this new method gets placed at the top of the call stack.

The first method that is invoked in your Java program is main(), which is invoked by the JVM. Therefore, main() is at the bottom of your method call stack.

Suppose that main() invokes a method called turnOn(), and the turnOn() method invokes a setVolume() method, which in turn invokes the println() method. Because println() is at the top of the call stack, the flow of control is currently within println(). The setVolume() method is waiting for println() to finish, the turnOn() method is waiting for setVolume() to finish, and so on down the call stack.

 A Java program can have more than one call stack if it is a multithreaded application, but all the programs so far in this book have a single call stack. We will discuss multithreaded applications in Chapter 15, "Threads."

Invoking Methods

A method is invoked, causing it to be placed at the top of the call stack until it is finished executing. When a method is done executing, three things can occur:

- The method returns a value, in which case a primitive data type or reference is passed back to the caller of the method.

- The method does not return a value, in which case the return value is declared as void.

- The method throws an exception, which is thrown back to the caller of the method. Exceptions are discussed in Chapter 11, "Exception Handling."

In all three of these cases, the flow of control jumps back to the caller of the method. To demonstrate the flow of control of methods, let's look at an example. The following Date class is a simple class that could be used to represent a calendar date. How many fields does the Date class have? How many methods?

```
public class Date
{
    public int day, month, year;
    public int getDay()
    {
        System.out.println("Inside getDay method");
        return day;
    }
    public void printDate()
    {
        System.out.println("Inside printDate method");
```

```
                    System.out.println(month + "/" + day + "/" + year);
        }
    }
```

The Date class has three fields, all of type int: day, month, and year. The Date class also has two methods: getDay() and printDate(). The getDay() method declares that it returns an int, and notice within getDay() it returns the day field, which is an int. The printDate() method is declared void and does not return a value. Both methods have an empty parameter list, which is denoted by the empty parentheses.

In the following DateProgram, a Date object is instantiated and the two methods in the Date class are invoked. Study the DateProgram carefully and try to determine its output.

```
public class DateProgram
{
    public static void main(String [] args)
    {
        System.out.println("Within main...");
        Date today = new Date();
        today.day = 25;
        today.month = 12;
        today.year = 2003;
        System.out.println("The day is " + today.getDay());
        System.out.println("Printing the date...");
        today.printDate();
        System.out.println("What is displayed next?");
        today.getDay();
    }
}
```

The first line of output of the DateProgram is as follows because it is the first statement in main():

```
Within main...
```

A Date object is then instantiated, and its fields are initialized to represent December 25, 2003.

Another System.out.println() statement occurs, and the string "The day is " is concatenated with today.getDay(). The getDay() method is invoked on the today object, causing flow of control to jump to the getDay() method.

 Notice that the string "The day is " is not displayed yet. The call to System.out.println() has not occurred yet because order of operations requires that the method call to getDay() occur before the call to println(). After getDay() returns a value, the string concatenation is evaluated, and then println() will be invoked.

Flow of control is now within getDay(), and the following string is displayed:

`Inside getDay method`

Then the return statement is reached, which in this example returns the number 25. The return also causes flow of control to jump back to the calling method, which was main(). The 25 is concatenated with "The day is ", then the System.out.println() method is invoked, which outputs the following:

`The day is 25`

The next statement to execute is the println() in main(), which outputs the following:

`Printing the date...`

Then, today.printDate() executes, which invokes the printDate() method on the today object. The flow of control jumps to within printDate(), and the first statement in printDate() displays the following:

`Inside printDate method`

The next statement in printDate() prints out the fields of the object in the following format:

`12/25/2003`

That is the end of printDate(), and it does not return a value, so the flow of control simply returns to main(), and the following is displayed:

`What is displayed next?`

The statement in question here is today.getDay(). I wanted to demonstrate that you can invoke a method that returns a value and not do anything with the return value. We just invoked getDay() again on the today object, so flow of control goes back to the getDay() method. The following statement is displayed again:

`Inside getDay method`

Then the number 25 is returned to main(). The flow of control jumps to main(), but we did not do anything with the return value 25. The main() method simply keeps executing, and because we are at the end of main(), our program ends. Figure 5.1 shows the entire output of the DateProgram.

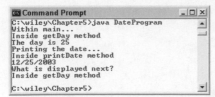

Figure 5.1   Output of the DateProgram.

 Methods in Java can appear only within a class because Java is a strictly object-oriented programming language. In many languages, methods appear at a global level and can be invoked at any time. In Java, methods (not declared as static) can only be invoked on instances of the class. For example, the getDay() method can be invoked only on instances of the Date class.

If you do want to write a global-type method that can be invoked by anyone at any time without requiring an instance of a class, you write a static method. In Chapter 7, "Advanced Java Language Concepts," static methods are discussed. A static method is essentially equivalent to the concept of a global method.

Method Signature

You can determine everything you need to know about invoking a method by looking at the method's *signature*. The signature includes information such as the method name, the parameter list, and the data type of any return value. For example, the signature of main() is as follows:

```
public static void main(String [] args)
```

Notice that the signature of a method does not include any of the statements in the body of the method. The signature is the declaration part of the method.

The following list discusses each of the components in a method signature, shown in the order they appear when declaring a method.

Access specifier.   The possible values of the access specifier are public, private, protected, or default access, which is obtained by leaving off the access specifier. Public access allows anyone to invoke the method from anywhere. Private access means that no one else can invoke the method, thereby hiding it within the class. The protected and default access apply to inheritance and packages, respectively, and are discussed in detail in Chapter 7, "Advanced Java Language Concepts."

Optional specifier.   The next part of a method signature is a list of any optional specifiers. The possible values for these specifiers are static, final, abstract, native, and synchronized. A native method is used for writing a Java method that maps to a method written in a different programming language, a topic not discussed in this book. The other specifiers are discussed in detail later. A method might not use any of these specifiers, or a method might use more than one of them.

 The order of the access specifiers and optional specifiers is arbitrary. For example, you can declare main() as:

```
static public void main(String [] args)
```

However, you will almost always see the access specifier appear first in a method signature because it is the preferred style among Java programmers.

Return value.   A method signature must contain a return value type. If the method does not return a value, void is used. Otherwise, the data type of the return value is specified. Possible values for the return value are one of the eight primitive data types or a reference. Note that this allows you to return anything you want from a method because every variable in Java is either one of the eight primitive data types or a reference to an object.

Method name.   The name of the method must appear directly after the return value. The method name can be any valid Java identifier. The Java naming convention calls for naming a method in mixed case, so the first letter will be lowercase and other terms in the method name will be capitalized. Examples of mixed case include main, toString, getDay, and setPreferredSize. A common exception to mixed case is a term that is an acronym. For example, the name accessURL would be preferred to accessUrl.

 Using mixed case for naming methods is not required. It is strictly a naming convention only. However, keep in mind that Java's naming convention is widely used and accepted. You should have a specific reason for not following this convention.

Parameter list.   Immediately following the method name must appear a set of parentheses that contain the parameter list of the method. When a method is invoked, data can be passed in by the caller of the method. This passed-in data is copied into the parameters. A parameter consists of a data type and an identifier. For example, the following method signature declares two parameters, an int and a float:

```
public float divide(int x, float f)
```

Parameters and arguments are discussed in detail later in this chapter.

List of thrown exceptions. Methods can throw an exception back to the caller of the method. An exception is thrown when a problem arises that the method is unable (or does not want) to handle itself. If a method throws a checked exception, the exception must be declared in the signature using the throws keyword. A method can declare multiple exceptions after the throws keyword, in which case they are separated by commas. For example, the following method signature declares that the method throws two possible exceptions:

```
public void readFromFile() throws IOException, SecurityException
```

If a method does not need to declare any exceptions using the throws keyword, this part of the signature is simply left off. Exceptions are discussed in detail in Chapter 11, "Exception Handling."

Here are some examples of method signatures:

```
public int getDay()
private void setName(String f, String g)
int calibrate(double radius, int multiplier, boolean metric)
public void addListener(Listener a) throws TooManyListenersException
public Employee findEmployee(int number) throws SQLException
```

From these signatures, you can determine everything you need to know about invoking each of these methods. For example, if you want to invoke getDay(), you do not pass in any data and you get back an int. With setName(), you must pass in two Strings, and nothing is returned.

To invoke the calibrate() method, you must pass in a double, an int, and a boolean, in that order, and an int will be returned. The addListener() method takes in a Listener object, returns nothing, and possibly throws a TooManyListeners exception. The findEmployee() method takes in an int, returns a reference to an Employee object, and possibly throws an SQLException.

Now that you have seen the information that can be obtained by analyzing the signature of a method, let's look at how data is passed from one method to another.

Arguments and Parameters

The signature of a method contains a list of *parameters*, which are used to declare what type of data needs to be passed in to the method. The term *argument* refers to the data that is passed in to a parameter. When a method is invoked, an argument must be passed in to each parameter in the method's parameter list.

The following Radio class has several fields and methods. Study the class and determine how many fields and methods it has. What is the parameter list for each method in the Radio class?

```java
public class Radio
{
    public int volume;          //0 -10
    public float tuning;          //Current station tuned in
    public char band;          //'A' for AM or 'F' for FM

    public void turnOn(int v, float t, char b)
    {
        System.out.println("Turning on the radio");
        setVolume(v);
        setBand(b);
        tuning = t;
    }

    public void setVolume(int volume)
    {
        //Make sure the input is valid (between 0 and 10).
        System.out.println("Setting the volume to " + volume);
        if(volume >= 0 && volume <= 10)
        {
            this.volume = volume;
        }
        else
        {
            this.volume = 0;
        }

        //Let's see what happens here.
        volume = -5;
    }

    public void setBand(char b)
    {
        System.out.println("Setting the band to " + b);
        //Make sure the input is valid ('A' or 'F').
        if(b == 'A' || b == 'F')
        {
            band = b;
        }
        else
        {
            band = 'F';
        }
```

```
    }

    public void turnUp()
    {
        System.out.println("Turning the volume up");
        if(volume < 10)
        {
            volume += 1;      //Increase volume by 1
        }
    }

    public void turnDown()
    {
        System.out.println("Turning the volume down");
        if(volume > 0)
        {
            volume -= 1;      //Decrease volume by 1
        }
    }

    public float getTuning()
    {
        System.out.println("Inside getTuning");
        return tuning;
    }

    public void changeBand()
    {
        System.out.println("Switching bands");
        if(band == 'A')
        {
            band = 'F';
        }
        else
        {
            band = 'A';
        }
    }
}
```

Notice that the Radio class has three fields: volume, tuning, and band. The Radio class also has seven methods. The turnOn() method has three parameters: an int, a float, and a char. To invoke turnOn(), you must pass in an int, float, and char (in that order) as arguments.

The setVolume() has one parameter: an int. To invoke setVolume(), you must pass in an int argument. The setBand() method also has one parameter: a char. Similarly, to invoke setBand() you must pass in a char argument.

The other four methods have no parameters. No arguments can be passed in to these methods.

Call-by-Value

When an argument is passed in to a parameter, the argument's data is copied into the parameter. The process of copying data between method calls is referred to in programming as *call-by-value*.

 In Java, you do not specify that an argument is to be passed using call-by-value. It happens automatically, and is, in fact, your only option. Other programming languages use call-by-reference and/or call-by-pointer, in which an argument is not copied into a parameter. You cannot do call-by-reference or call-by-pointer in Java. No matter what type of argument you pass in to a method, the corresponding parameter will get a copy of that data, which is exactly how call-by-value works.

For example, to invoke the setVolume() method of the Radio class, you must pass in an int argument:

```
int x = 7;
someRadio.setVolume(x);
```

In the previous statements, the integer x is passed in to setVolume(). The contents of x are copied into the int parameter of setVolume(), which is the variable volume. There are now two 7s in memory. The value of volume is 7, and the value of x is still 7.

The following ListenToRadio program demonstrates passing arguments to parameters. Try to determine the flow of control of the program and also what the output will be.

```
public class ListenToRadio
{
    public static void main(String [] args)
    {
        System.out.println("Creating a radio...");
        Radio radio = new Radio();
        System.out.println("...and turning it on...");
        float initialStation = Float.parseFloat(args[0]);
        int initialVolume = 5;
        radio.turnOn(initialVolume, initialStation, 'F');
        System.out.println("The tuning is " + radio.getTuning());
        int x = 7;
        radio.setVolume(x);
        System.out.println("x = " + x);
        radio.turnUp();
        radio.turnUp();
        radio.changeBand();
```

```
System.out.println("The volume is now " + radio.volume
        + ", the band is " + radio.band
        + ", and the tuning is " + radio.tuning);
    }
}
```

Let's follow the flow of control of the ListenToRadio program. The JVM invokes main() when you run the program, so main() is at the bottom of the call stack. The first line of code within main() is a call to the println() method, which displays the following:

```
Creating a radio...
```

The next statement in main() instantiates a new Radio object, followed by another call to println():

```
...and turning it on...
```

 I want to emphasize that before a Radio object is instantiated, none of the methods in the Radio class can be invoked. Until there is a Radio object in memory, there is no setVolume() method or turnOnRadio() method (and so on) to invoke. You cannot turn on a radio until a radio exists, and no radio exists until you instantiate one using the new keyword.

The first command-line argument of the ListenToRadio program is the initial station to be tuned in. The command-line argument is parsed into a float and stored in the initialStation variable. An int is declared (initialVolume) and is set equal to 5.

The turnOn() method is then invoked, causing it to be pushed onto the top of the call stack. To invoke turnOn(), you must pass in an int, float, and char, in that order. The int passed in is initialVolume, which is 5. The value 5 is copied into the corresponding parameter of turnOn(), which is v. Similarly, the contents of initialStation are copied in to the parameter t. Finally, the character F is copied in to the parameter b.

The flow of control is now within turnOn(), and the first statement within turnOn() is a call to println(), displaying the following:

```
Turning on the radio
```

The setVolume() method is then invoked, pushing setVolume() onto the top of the call stack. You must pass an int into setVolume(), and v is passed as an argument. The contents of v are copied in to the parameter volume, which in this case is 5. There are now three variables in memory equal to 5: initialVolume in main(), v in turnOn(), and volume in setVolume().

Within setVolume(), the println() method is invoked and pushed onto the call stack. We now have the situation illustrated by the call stack discussed in the earlier section *Method Call Stack*. The following is displayed:

```
Setting the volume to 5
```

The parameter volume is assigned to the field volume, so now the 5 is in memory in four different places. The parameter volume is assigned to –5, a statement I added to emphasize that this is call-by-value. What does changing volume to –5 do to the argument v that was passed in to volume? It does nothing to v because volume is a copy of v and not the actual variable v.

 Within the setVolume() method, the parameter name is volume, which also happens to be the name of one of the fields of the Radio class. This might seem like a naming conflict, but it is okay and is done regularly in Java. To distinguish between the local variable volume and the field volume, you must use the *this* reference whenever referring to the field. Therefore, using just volume refers to the parameter and using this.volume refers to the field.

At one point in the ListenToRadio program, the initial volume of 5 was in four different variables in memory: initialVolume, v, volume, and this.volume. Keep in mind that the variables volume, v, and initialVolume are local variables (sometimes aptly referred to as temporary variables). They are allocated in memory on the call stack, and when the method is done executing, these variables go away.

For example, when setVolume() is done, the parameter volume goes out of scope. When turnOn() is done, the parameter v goes out of scope. When main() is done, initialVolume goes out of scope. But the field volume in the Radio object stays in memory until the object is garbage collected, which can be long after these temporary variables have gone away.

After setVolume() finishes, control returns to the turnOn() method, which invokes setBand(). The setBand() method has a char parameter, and the b in turnOn() is passed as an argument in to the b parameter of setBand(). There are now two variables in memory named b, both of value F, but their scopes are different. The b in turnOn() is not accessible from within setBand(). Nor is the b in setBand() accessible to the turnOn() method. This is why the value F was passed into setBand() because the F was needed within the scope of setBand().

The setBand() method prints out the following:

```
Setting the band to F
```

The field band is assigned to F, and the setBand() method returns. We are back in the turnOn() method, which sets the field tuning equal to the parameter t. The turnOn() method is now complete, so flow of control jumps back down to main().

The next line of code in main() is a println() statement, but before println() is invoked, the getTuning() method of radio is called. Notice that no arguments are passed in because getTuning() has no parameters. Control jumps to getTuning(), which prints out the following:

```
Inside getTuning
```

The getTuning() method declares that it returns a float, so it must do so somewhere in the method. Notice that it returns the tuning field, which is a float containing the current radio station. The value of tuning is returned-by-value, meaning that a copy of tuning is sent back to main(), similarly to how arguments are copied into parameters.

The copy of tuning is sent back as a float and then concatenated to "The tuning is ", displaying something like the following:

```
The tuning is 100.3
```

Control is back within main(), and the volume is set to 7. Recall that the setVolume() sets the volume parameter to –5 to demonstrate that the argument has not changed. The output of displaying the contents of x looks like the following:

```
x = 7
```

The volume is then turned up by invoking turnUp() twice. The band is changed by invoking changeBand(), and the final output looks similar to the following:

```
The volume is now 9, the band is A, and the tuning is 100.3
```

Figure 5.2 shows a sample output of the ListenToRadio program.

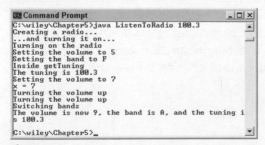

Figure 5.2   Sample output of the ListenToRadio program when the command-line argument is 100.3.

Classroom Q & A

Q: What if I want the method to be able to change the contents of the argument?

A: This cannot be done in Java. It's as simple as that. When using call-by-value, changing the parameter in the method does not change the argument. Look closely at the setVolume() method of the Radio class discussed earlier. The last line of code in that method sets the parameter to −5. This does not change the argument to −5. We simply can't change the argument, even if we want to.

Q: I suppose I can live with parameters not being able to change arguments, but what if I have a large amount of data that needs to be passed in to a method. I'm talking very large. Typically, I would want to pass in a pointer so as to not waste the time and memory of copying large data. Can I avoid passing large objects in Java?

A: Not only can you avoid passing large objects, you can't do it even if you want to. I need to reiterate a very important aspect of Java: A variable in Java is either one of the eight primitive data types or it is a reference. If the argument is a primitive data type, it is at most 64 bits in size (a double or a long). If the data I want to pass to a method is a very large object, it is not the object that is passed. It is a reference to the object, which is no larger than 64 bits, and in most cases is 32 bits. It is the reference that is copied, not the large amount of data.

Q: So the largest amount of data that is copied with call-by-value in Java is only 64 bits?

A: Correct! And copying 64 bits in today's computing world is rarely a concern in terms of performance or overhead.

Q: What if I really want the method to change the argument passed in?

A: Well, you just can't do it. But notice what you can do with the parameter if it is a reference to an object. The method can use this reference to do anything it wants to the object (depending on the access specifiers of the object's fields and methods). The method can change the data of the object being pointed to and invoke methods on the object. The only restriction arising from call-by-value is that the method cannot change where the reference is pointing to.

♦ A Class with No main() Method?

A common point of confusion that new OOP students of mine have arises when they write a class that does not have main() method in it. A Java class without main() is not a program.

For example, you cannot execute the Radio class. The Radio class is a description (albeit a simple one) of an AM/FM radio. If you try to run Radio by entering the following command, you will get an error message from the JVM, stating that no main() method was found:

```
java Radio
```

The Radio class is meant to be used by other classes that need a radio.

In a large Java application with dozens or even hundreds of classes, you might define main() methods all over the place. However, it is likely that only one class has main() in it. If the Java application is using other Java technologies such as Servlets or Enterprise JavaBeans, no class will have a main() method in it.

On a similar note, just because Radio has a bunch of nice methods in it, it does not mean that the methods are automatically invoked. If you want a method to execute, you need to explicitly invoke it. Similarly, if you do not want a method to execute, don't invoke it.

For example, the ListenToRadio program creates a Radio object, but at no point is the turnDown() method invoked. We could have invoked turnDown() if we wanted to because it is available to us, but we do not have to and it is not invoked automatically at any point in time.

Overloading Methods

Java allows a method to be overloaded. *Method overloading* occurs when a class has two or more methods with the same name but different parameter lists. Having more than one method with the same name might seem unnecessary, but method overloading is used quite frequently in Java (and other programming languages).

 Method overloading is used most commonly with constructors, which are discussed in the next section.

For example, the println() method that we used throughout the book so far is an overloaded method of the java.io.PrintStream class, as you can see by the documentation of PrintStream shown in Figure 5.3.

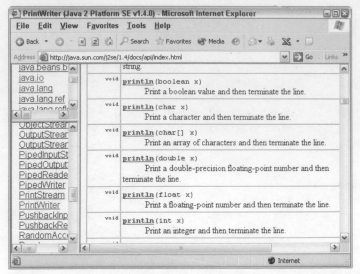

Figure 5.3   The println() method is overloaded 10 times in the PrintStream class.

The PrintStream class has 10 println() methods. How does the compiler know which one you want to invoke? If you look carefully, you will also notice that the parameter list is different for each version of println(). For example, calling println() and passing in an int invokes that overloaded version whose signature is as follows:

```
public void println(int x)
```

Invoking println() and passing in a String invokes the following version:

```
public void println(String x)
```

If method overloading were not an option, the println() methods would each have to use a unique name such as printlnInt(), printlnString(), println-Double(), and so on. In this case, method overloading simplifies both the writing of the PrintStream class and the usage of the class. Developers do not need to remember 10 different names for printing a line of text to the system output; they can simply remember that the method to use is println(), and it is overloaded for every data type.

Let's look at an example using method overloading. The following Calculator class contains five multiply() methods. Study the method signatures carefully and determine whether this is valid method overloading.

```
public class Calculator
{
    public int multiply(int x, int y)
    {
```

```
        System.out.println("Multiply int * int");
        return x * y;
    }
    public double multiply(double x, double y)
    {
        System.out.println("Multiply double * double");
        return x * y;
    }
    public double multiply(int x, double y)
    {
        System.out.println("Multiply int * double");
        return x * y;
    }
    public int multiply(int x)
    {
        System.out.println("Multiply int * itself");
        return x * x;
    }
    public int multiply(int x, int y, int z)
    {
        System.out.println("Multiply three ints");
        return x * y * z;
    }
}
```

♦ Method Overloading

You can overload a method as long as the parameter lists are distinct enough for the compiler to be able to distinguish which method you want to invoke. Certainly if the number of parameters is different, the overloading is valid, as shown in the following two method signatures:

```
public float computePay(double d, int x);     //Two parameters
public float computePay(double d);            //One parameter
```

If you simply change the name of the parameter, it is not valid. For example, the following two methods could not appear in the same class because this is not valid overloading:

```
public void setDay(int x, int y, long z);
public boolean setDay(int a, int b, long c)        //No!
```

The preceding two methods have the same name and the same number of parameters, and the parameters appear in the same order. The compiler would not be able to distinguish between the two methods and would generate a compiler error. Note that changing the return value does not affect whether the overloading is valid or not.

However, changing the order of parameters is just like changing the parameter list. For example, the following two methods demonstrate valid method overloading:

```
public void setDay(int x, int y, long z    ;
public boolean setDay(long a, int b, int c);
```

Of the five multiply() methods in the Calculator class, the parameter lists are different for each one. Therefore, this is an example of valid method overloading.

The following OverloadDemo program instantiates a Calculator object and invokes the various multiply() methods. Study the OverloadDemo program carefully and try to determine the output. The actual output is shown in Figure 5.4.

```java
public class OverloadDemo
{
    public static void main(String [] args)
    {
        System.out.println("Instantiating a Calculator...");
        Calculator calc = new Calculator();
        System.out.println("Initializing some variables...");
        int a = 5;
        int b = 8;
        double d1 = 2.5;
        double d2 = -1.0;
        float f = 4.0F;
        int intAnswer = 0;
        double doubleAnswer = 0.0;
        intAnswer = calc.multiply(a, b);
        System.out.println(a + " * " + b + " = " + intAnswer);
        doubleAnswer = calc.multiply(d1, d2);
        System.out.println(d1 + " * " + d2 + " = " + doubleAnswer);
        intAnswer = calc.multiply(b);
        System.out.println(b + " * " + b + " = " + intAnswer);
        intAnswer = calc.multiply(a, b, a);
        System.out.println(a + " * " + b + " * " + a + " = "
                         + intAnswer);
        doubleAnswer = calc.multiply(b, f);
        System.out.println(b + " * " + f + " = " + doubleAnswer);
        doubleAnswer = calc.multiply(d2, f);
        System.out.println(d2 + " * " + f + " = " + doubleAnswer);
    }
}
```

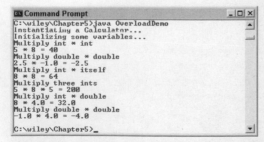

Figure 5.4   Output of the OverloadDemo program.

In the first call to multiply() in the OverloadDemo program, a and b are passed in. Because a and b are both ints, the following version of multiply() in the Calculator class is invoked:

```
public int multiply(int x, int y)
```

When the two doubles d1 and d2 are passed in to multiply(), the corresponding overloaded version in Calculator is invoked:

```
public double multiply(double x, double y)
```

In the following statement, only a single int is passed in, so the version of multiply that takes in a single int is invoked:

```
intAnswer = calc.multiply(b);
```

Similarly, invoking multiply() with three int arguments causes the corresponding multiply() with three int parameters to be invoked.

I want to make an observation about the following statement in the OverloadDemo program:

```
doubleAnswer = calc.multiply(b, f);
```

The arguments are of type int and float, in that order. There is no multiply() method in the Calculator class that has a parameter list with an int and a float. However, because a float can be promoted to a double, notice that the multiply() method that gets invoked is the following:

```
public double multiply(int x, double y);
```

 This situation in which the float is passed in to a double arises all the time when invoking methods (not just when a method is overloaded). When an argument does not exactly match a parameter, but the argument can be promoted to match a parameter, then the promotion will occur automatically.

Constructors

A *constructor* is a special method in a class that is invoked when the object gets instantiated. The purpose of a constructor is to allow the fields of the object to be initialized when the object is instantiated.

Remember that when an object is instantiated using the new keyword, the memory is allocated and zeroed out. Therefore, the initial values of the fields of an object are zero values (see Table 4.1). Without a constructor, you have to go in and initialize all the fields so that the object has meaningful data. A constructor provides an opportunity to construct the object so that its fields have meaningful data while the object is being instantiated.

What makes a constructor different from a method is that a constructor satisfies the following two properties:

- The name of the constructor must match the name of the class.

- A constructor does not declare a return value, not even void.

For example, if we want to add a constructor to the Radio class discussed earlier, the name of the constructor has to be Radio and no return value is declared. Listing 5.1 shows the Radio class with two constructors added.

```
public class Radio
{
    public int volume;          //0-10
    public float tuning;          //Current station tuned in
    public char band;          //'A' for AM or 'F' for FM
    public Radio()
    {
        System.out.println("Inside no-argument constructor");
        tuning = 80.0F;
        band = 'F';
        volume = 5;
    }
    public Radio(float t)
    {
        System.out.println("Inside float constructor");
        tuning = t;
        band = 'A';
        volume = 8;
    }
    //The remainder of the class definition...
}
```

Listing 5.1   This Radio class has two constructors.

 When adding multiple constructors to a class, the rules of method overloading apply. Each constructor must have a unique parameter list that makes it distinguishable from the other constructors.

Have you noticed throughout the book so far that parentheses appear when using the new keyword to instantiate an object? For example, a new Radio object is instantiated as follows:

```
Radio r = new Radio();
```

I have not explained those empty parentheses, but I am ready to now. Any time you see parentheses, it looks as if a method is being invoked. This is exactly what is happening when you use the new keyword, except that a method is not invoked. One of the constructors in the class is invoked.

In fact, the only time you can invoke a constructor is when the object is being instantiated. Constructors are similar to methods, but keep in mind that they are not methods. They behave quite differently, as you will see in Chapter 6, "Understanding Inheritance."

Classroom Q & A

Q: Wait a minute. We haven't added a constructor to any of the classes we have seen up until now. Do you have to add a constructor to every class?

A: You are right. We must not have to add a constructor because our classes seem to be fine without one, so the answer to your question is no. If you do not add a constructor to your class, the compiler writes one for you. This "free" constructor is known as the *default constructor*.

Q: How does the compiler know what I want my default constructor to do?

A: The compiler doesn't know. The default constructor that you get for free has an empty parameter list and doesn't do anything.

Q: Then why bother? It seems like a waste of code to have a constructor that doesn't do anything.

A: Because every class must have a constructor. When you instantiate a class, the new operator must invoke a constructor. The fact that the compiler adds a default constructor to your class is purely for convenience. In almost all development situations you find yourself in, you will add at least one constructor yourself to all of your classes. Before we write our own constructors, though, let's take a quick look at this default constructor.

Default Constructor

If you write a class and do not add a constructor, the compiler generates a default constructor in your class. This default constructor is public, has no parameters, and does not do anything.

For example, if the Radio class does not declare a constructor, the compiler adds the following:

```
public Radio()
{}
```

Notice that this follows the rules of a constructor: The constructor name matches the class name, and there is no return value. Also notice that the constructor contains no statements.

♦ A Class with No Default Constructor

If you do not add a constructor to a class, the compiler generates a default constructor for the class. This default constructor does not contain any parameters. If you add one or more constructors to your class, no matter what their parameter lists are, the compiler does not add a default constructor to your class.

The following class does not have a default constructor:

```
public class Television
{
    public int channel;
    public Television(int c)
    {
        channel = c;
    }
}
```

Because there is only one constructor in this Television class, the only way to instantiate a new Television object is to pass in an int:

```
Television t1 = new Television(4);
```

The point I want to make with this example is that the following statement does not compile:

```
Television t2 = new Television();
```

This statement is attempting to invoke a no-argument constructor, but the Television class does not contain a no-argument constructor, thereby causing a compiler error. It is not uncommon to write a class without a no-argument constructor, as demonstrated by many classes in the Java API.

If you do add a constructor to your class, the compiler does not add the default constructor to your class. Consider the Radio class shown in Listing 5.2.

```
public class Radio
{
    public int volume;
    public float tuning;
    public char band;
    public Radio(int v, char b)
    {
        volume = v;
        band = b;
    }
}
```

Listing 5.2 This Radio class declares a constructor and therefore does not have a default no-argument constructor.

The Radio class shown in Listing 5.2 declares a constructor that has two parameters: an int and a char. Because we added a constructor to this Radio class, the compiler does not add another one for us.

Using Constructors

A constructor must be invoked when an object is instantiated using the new keyword. A class can (and often does) have multiple constructors. You determine which constructor is invoked with the arguments used with the new operator.

If a class has one constructor, there is only one way to instantiate an object of that class type. For example, the Radio class shown in Listing 5.2 has only one constructor. The signature of this constructor is the following:

```
public Radio(int v, char b)
```

Therefore, the only way to instantiate a Radio using the class shown in Listing 5.2 is to pass in an int and a char:

```
int volume = 7;
char band = 'A';
Radio radio = new Radio(volume, band);
```

The following statement does not compile with the Radio class shown in Listing 5.2:

```
Radio radio = new Radio();  //invalid!
```

The previous statement attempts to invoke a no-argument constructor, but the Radio class shown in Listing 5.2 does not declare a no-argument constructor.

A Class with Multiple Constructors

If a class has multiple constructors, the new operator can be used for each constructor in the class. For example, the Radio class shown in Listing 5.1 has two constructors. Their signatures are as follows:

```
public Radio()
public Radio(float t)
```

This gives us two ways to instantiate a new Radio. To invoke the no-argument constructor, use the new operator with no arguments:

```
Radio x = new Radio();
```

To invoke the constructor that has a float parameter, pass in a float with the new operator:

```
float station = 100.3F;
Radio y = new Radio(station);
```

Study the following ConstructorDemo program and try to determine the output. (Note that the ConstructorDemo program is using the Radio class defined in Listing 5.2.) The program output is shown in Figure 5.5.

```
public class ConstructorDemo
{
    public static void main(String [] args)
    {
        System.out.println("Instantiating the first Radio");
        Radio x = new Radio();
        System.out.println("Instantiating the second Radio");
        float station = 100.3F;
        Radio y = new Radio(station);
        System.out.println(x.volume + " " + x.tuning
+ " " + x.band);
        System.out.println(y.volume + " " + y.tuning
+ " " + y.band);
    }
}
```

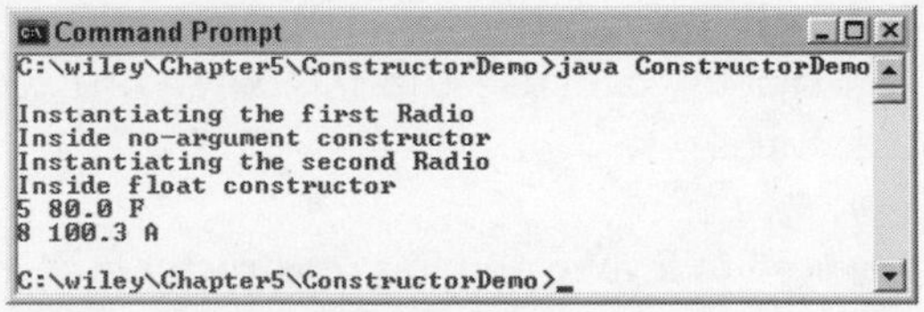

Figure 5.5   Output of the ConstructorDemo program.

Using *this* in a Constructor

The following Television class has three constructors in it. Notice that the three constructors have different parameter lists, but the body of each one essentially does the same thing.

```
public class Television
{
    public int channel;
    public int volume;
    public Television()
    {
        System.out.println("Inside no-arg constructor");
        channel = 4;
        volume = 10;
    }
    public Television(int c)
    {
        System.out.println("Inside one-arg constructor");
        channel = c;
        volume = 10;
    }
    public Television(int c, int v)
    {
        System.out.println("Inside two-arg constructor");
        channel = c;
        volume = v;
    }
}
```

The problem with the Television class is that code is repeated three times. If you needed to change code in one of the previous constructors for some reason, you would need to change the code in three places, which is an undesirable situation in any programming language.

To avoid repeating code, you can have all the constructors invoke one constructor that does all the work. A constructor can use the *this* keyword to invoke another constructor within the same class.

 If a constructor uses the *this* keyword to invoke another constructor in the class, the *this* statement must appear as the first line of code in the constructor. (Otherwise, a compiler error will occur.)

The following Television class demonstrates using the *this* keyword to make one constructor invoke another constructor. Notice that the *this* statement is the first line of code in the constructor.

```
public class Television
{
    public int channel;
    public int volume;
    public Television()
    {
        this(4, 10);
        System.out.println("Inside no-arg constructor");
    }
    public Television(int c)
    {
        this(c, 10);
        System.out.println("Inside one-arg constructor");
    }
    public Television(int c, int v)
    {
        System.out.println("Inside two-arg constructor");
        channel = c;
        volume = v;
    }
}
```

 The *this* keyword used within a constructor is not the same as the *this* reference that every object has to itself. The *this* keyword has two different uses in Java.

The following ThisDemo program instantiates three Television objects by using each of the three constructors in the Television class. Study the program carefully and try to determine the output. The output is not obvious, so follow the flow of control carefully. The actual output is shown in Figure 5.6.

```
public class ThisDemo
{
    public static void main(String [] args)
```

```
{
        System.out.println("Instantiating first television");
        Television t1 = new Television();
        System.out.println(t1.volume + " " + t1.channel);
        int channel = 206;
        System.out.println("Instantiating second television");
        Television t2 = new Television(channel);
        System.out.println(t2.volume + " " + t2.channel);
        int volume = 7;
        System.out.println("Instantiating third television");
        Television t3 = new Television(channel, volume);
        System.out.println(t3.volume + " " + t3.channel);
    }
}
```

The first statement within main() outputs the following:

```
Instantiating first television
```

Then, a Television object is instantiated using no arguments. Flow of control jumps to the no-argument constructor of the Television class. The first statement in the following constructor causes flow of control to jump to the two-argument constructor in the Television class:

```
this(4,10);
```

The two-argument constructor executes, then control jumps back to the one-argument constructor, which executes. Therefore, the output is as follows:

```
Inside two-arg constructor
Inside no-arg constructor
```

Notice that the default constructor creates a Television object with an initial volume of 10 and channel 4. The second Television object in ThisDemo uses the one-argument constructor, which uses the *this* keyword to invoke the two-argument constructor, creating the following output:

```
Inside two-arg constructor
Inside one-arg constructor
```

The third Television object invokes the two-argument constructor directly, creating the following output:

```
Inside two-arg constructor
```

The entire output is shown in Figure 5.6.

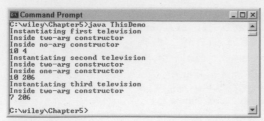

Figure 5.6 Output of the ThisDemo program.

Lab 5.1: Simulating an Elevator

In this lab, you will write an Elevator class containing various methods. Then, you will write a program that creates Elevator objects and invokes the various methods. The purpose of the lab is to help you understand how to write methods and how methods manipulate the data of an object.

1. Using your text editor, write a class named Elevator. Add fields for the following attributes: an int for the current floor, an int for the floor that the elevator is heading to, a boolean to denote whether the elevator is going up or down once it reaches its destination, and a boolean to denote whether the elevator doors are open or closed.

2. Add a method named goToFloor() that changes the floor that the elevator is heading to. Use the System.out.println() method to display a message that you are changing the value.

3. Add methods named openDoors() and closeDoors() that change the appropriate boolean field accordingly. Again, display a message within each method so that you can see when the methods are invoked.

4. Add methods named goingUp() and goingDown() that change the appropriate boolean field accordingly.

5. Save and compile your Elevator class.

6. Write a class named ElevatorProgram that contains main().

7. Within main(), instantiate two Elevator objects. Invoke the various methods of the Elevator class on these two objects, ensuring that all your Elevator methods work successfully.

Lab 5.2: Using Constructors

The purpose of this lab is to become familiar with working with constructors. You will add two constructors to your Elevator class.

1. Begin by opening your Elevator class from Lab 5.1 in your text editor.

2. Add a constructor that has a single parameter of type int to represent the current floor of the elevator. Within the constructor, assign the parameter to the appropriate field in your class. Also, display a message using System.out.println() that shows which constructor you are currently in.

3. Add a no-argument constructor that uses the *this* keyword to invoke your constructor in the previous step, passing in a 1 for the initial floor. Display a message that states you are currently in the no-argument constructor.

4. Modify your ElevatorProgram in Lab 5.1. Instantiate one of the Elevator objects using the no-argument constructor, and instantiate the other Elevator object using the one-argument constructor.

5. Run the ElevatorProgram and ensure that the constructors are working successfully.

Lab 5.3: Redesigning the Powerball Lottery

In this lab, you will make your Powerball program object oriented by writing a class called Powerball.

1. Write a class named Powerball that contains six fields to represent the five white balls and one red ball.

2. Add a method named play() that simulates the playing of Powerball. (See Lab 3.5 for details of the lottery.) This method should assign a value to each of the six fields.

3. Add a method named displayResults() that prints out the values of the five white balls and one red ball.

4. Save and compile your Powerball class.

5. Write a class named PlayLottery that contains main(). Within main(), instantiate a Powerball object and invoke the methods of the Powerball class to ensure that they are working successfully.

Summary

- Methods must appear within a class in Java. A method's signature denotes the name of the method, its access specifier, its return value, any arguments that need to pass into the method, and any checked exceptions that the method may throw.

- Arguments are passed to methods in Java using call-by-value, meaning that a copy of the argument is passed to the method.

- A method can be overloaded, allowing a class to have more than one method with the same name as long as the parameter lists are different.

- Every class has at least one constructor, a unique type of method that is invoked when the class is instantiated. The name of a constructor must match the name of the class, and no return value is declared.

- If a class does not declare a constructor, the compiler adds the default constructor to the class. The default constructor has no parameters and does not do anything.

- A constructor can invoke another constructor in the same class using the this() syntax, which must be the first statement in the constructor.

Review Questions

1. A method uses what keyword to return a value within the body of the method?

2. A method uses what keyword to denote that it does not return a value?

3. True or False: A method can have private access.

4. True or False: All methods must be declared static.

5. True or False: The parentheses are optional in a method signature.

Use the following method signature to answer the next five questions:

```
protected double findInRange(int x, int y, boolean b)
                throws NotFoundException
```

6. What is the name of the method?

7. What is the data type of the return value?

8. How many parameters does it have?

9. What is the access specifier?

10. True or False: The method will throw a NotFoundException every time the method is invoked.

11. What keyword is used within a constructor to invoke another constructor in the same class?

12. True or False: If you write a class and do not put a constructor in it, the compiler generates a constructor for you.

13. True or False: Every class must have a no-argument constructor.

14. When arguments are copied into parameters, this is referred to as

_____.

15. True or False: If a Java method changes a parameter, it changes the corresponding argument as well.

Answers to Review Questions

1. return.

2. void.

3. True, although private methods can be invoked only by other methods in the class.

4. False. In fact, most methods you write will not be static.

5. False. A method signature must contain parentheses immediately following the method name. If there are no parameters, the parentheses will be empty.

6. findInRange.

7. double.

8. Three: two ints and a boolean.

9. protected.

10. Hopefully false, even though the method could be written so that it did throw an exception every time. However, the throws keyword in a method signature means that the method *might* throw an exception, not that it *will* throw an exception.

11. The *this* keyword.

12. True. The generated constructor is referred to as the default constructor.

13. False. It is your decision whether you want your class to have a no-argument constructor.

14. Call-by-value.

15. False. With call-by-value, methods cannot change arguments, no matter what.

Understanding Inheritance

Inheritance is one of the most important benefits of object-oriented programming. It allows a new class to be written that extends an existing class. This chapter discusses the details of understanding and implementing inheritance, including the *is a* relationship, the extends keyword, the Object class, method overriding, the super keyword, and how inheritance affects constructors.

An Overview of Inheritance

In object-oriented programming (OOP), a new class can be built upon an existing class with the new class extending the existing class and inheriting its attributes and behaviors. Extending a class is called *inheritance*.

The existing class is referred to as the *parent class*, and the new class is referred to as the *child class*.

 Other common OOP terms for the parent class are *base* class and *super* class. The child class is often referred to as the *derived* class or *subclass*. These different terms for the parent and child class are used interchangeably but have the same meaning.

Inheritance is arguably the single most important aspect of OOP. The ability to create a new class as an extension of an existing class has many benefits, including the important concepts of polymorphsism and abstraction, discussed in Chapter 8, "Polymorphism and Abstraction."

Inheritance is best explained with an example. Recall the example where a program is needed to pay employees of a company every week. One obvious object in this problem domain is the employee, and it was decided that an Employee class is to be written.

Consider the following Employee class, which includes attributes for the employee's name, address, SSN, number, and salary. The methods are compute-Pay() and mailCheck().

```
public class Employee
{
    public String name;
    public String address;
    public int SSN;
    public int number;
    public float salary;

    public void mailCheck()
    {
        System.out.println("Mailing a check to " + name + " " + address);
    }
    public float computePay()
    {
        return (float) salary/52.0;
    }
}
```

The design of the Employee class might seem fine initially. An employee has a name, address, and number, and we want the employee objects to compute their pay and mail a check.

Keep in mind that we are using the Employee class in the context of paying employees. Is it true that every employee has a salary? What about employees who are paid by the hour, or contractors who are paid by the day, or those in other situations where an employee is not paid by an annual salary? Perhaps the Employee class needs further analysis.

The first mistake in the Employee class is adding a field of type salary. Does every employee have a salary? If the answer is no, the Employee class should not have a field of type salary.

What do we do instead? We need to realize that although employees are objects in our problem domain, there are actually two different types of employee objects: salaried employees and hourly employees. Therefore, we should write two classes: Salary and Hourly.

♦ When to Use Inheritance

The Employee class has a field named salary, which implies that an employee *has a* salary; however, hourly employees have an hourly rate, which is quite different from a salary.

A tempting fix for this situation is to add a Boolean field to the Employee class named isSalary that is true for salary employees and false for hourly employees. The salary field could be used to represent an annual salary when isSalary is true or an hourly rate when isSalary is false.

The isSalary field could also be used within the computePay() method to determine which arithmetic to use because computing pay for salaried employees is different than for hourly employees. For example,

```
public float computePay()
{
    if(isSalary)
    {
        //Perform arithmetic for salaried employee
    }
    else
    {
        //Perform arithmetic for hourly employee
    }
}
```

Adding a field such as isSalary and trying to use one class to represent two different types of objects is not a good OOP design. You could make it work, but you are not taking advantage of the benefits of inheritance.

If you use a field to determine the type of an object, your end result is a class that looks object-oriented but is really procedural. For example, an Employee object will need to check this added Boolean field just to know what type of object it is, causing the design of the program to not be focused on objects.

A bigger problem arises when something needs to be changed. What happens to the isSalary field when a new type of employee needs to be added? Suppose that the company starts hiring contractors who are paid by the day. The Boolean no longer works because it can't be used to distinguish between three types. You could change the field to an int, name it employeeType, and use an enumeration like 0 for salary, 1 for hourly, and 2 for contractor.

Again, you could make this work, but you have to make serious modifications to the Employee class. The computePay() method will have to entirely rewritten:

```
public float computePay()
{
    switch(employeeType)
    {
        case 0:
```

continued

◆ When to Use Inheritance *(continued)*

```
            //Perform arithmetic for salaried employee
            break;
            case 1:
            //Perform arithmetic for hourly employee
            break;
            case 2:
            //Perform arithmetic for contractor employee
            break;
            //and so on if necessary
        }
    }
```

And the computePay() method will keep getting longer and longer as different types of employees arise. Any time you find yourself writing classes that do not know what type they are, you probably should rethink your design. With inheritance, all of these issues are avoided.

The common features of employees appear in a parent class. Each different type of employee is represented by a child class. When a new type of employee such as a contractor comes along, a new child class is written that extends the parent class. *None of the existing code needs to be touched.*

This benefit is difficult to achieve with procedural programming and also with poorly designed OOP applications. To avoid these situations, constantly test your OOP design against these simple rules: An object "has" an attribute, and an object "does" a behavior.

In our employee example, if it is not true that an employee "has" a salary, an Employee class should not have a salary field, and we should redesign our program.

The Salary class should have a field to represent the employee's annual salary because a Salaried employee has a salary. The Hourly class should have fields to represent the employee's hourly pay and number of hours worked because these are attributes of an Hourly employee.

The following classes demonstrate what the Salary and Hourly classes might look like. Look closely at the attributes and behaviors of these two classes. As with the Employee class, there is something flawed with this design also.

```
public class Salary
{
    public String name;
    public String address;
    public int SSN;
    public int number;
    public float salary;
    public void mailCheck()
    {
```

```
        System.out.println("Mailing a check to " + name
            + " " + address);
    }

    public float computePay()
    {
        return (float) salary/52.0;
    }
}
public class Hourly
{
    public String name;
    public String address;
    public int SSN;
    public int number;
    public float hourlyRate;
    public float hoursWorked
    public void mailCheck()
    {
        System.out.println("Mailing a check to " + name
            + " " + address);
    }
    public float computePay()
    {
        return (float) hoursWorked * hourlyRate;
    }
}
```

The Salary and Hourly classes demonstrate the need for inheritance. Although Salary and Hourly employees are different types, they are not entirely different. In fact, the two types of employees have a lot in common, as seen by the repetition of fields and methods in these two classes. Using inheritance will improve this design considerably, so keep in mind that writing two separate classes for the two different types of employees is not yet a satisfactory solution.

As you can see, the Salary and Hourly classes are repeating code. Salary and hourly employees are still employees, and there is a lot of information in common between the two. Inheritance can be used in this situation not only to avoid repeating code, but also to create a program design that allows for better maintenance and code changes later.

When two or more classes are different but share similar features, take the common elements of the classes and put them in a parent class. The classes can extend this parent class, thereby inheriting all the features of the parent, yet the different features can remain in each child class.

A better design for the Salary and Hourly classes is to take their common elements and put them in a parent class, leaving the unique elements in the child classes. For example, the mailCheck() method could appear in the Employee parent class, and the computePay() method could appear in each of the child classes. The assumption is that the process of mailing a check is the same for all employees, but computing their pay is directly affected by how they are paid.

Employees do not share a common computePay() method. By placing computePay() in each child class, the method will be written twice. This is not repeating code, though, because computePay() in Salary is quite different than computePay() in Hourly.

The *is a* Relationship

The *is a* relationship is a simple but powerful rule for testing if your inheritance is a good design. Whenever you use inheritance, you should be able to say that a child *is a* parent. If this statement is true, your inheritance is likely a good design.

For example, it is true that a salaried employee is an employee. Similarly, an hourly employee is an employee; therefore, it is reasonable that the Salary and Hourly classes extend the Employee class.

Let's look at an example where inheritance is not a good idea. Suppose that you have a Date class that represents a calendar date, and you want to use that class to keep track of the date when an employee was hired.

Because inheritance has so many benefits, you decide to have the Employee class extend the Date class. When you instantiate an Employee object, you will also get a Date object for storing the employee's hire date; however, is it true that an employee *is a* date? The *is a* relationship clearly fails here. Although the result might work for us, an Employee class inheriting from a Date class is not a good design and should not be used.

 The solution to the improper use of inheritance with the Employee and Date classes is to realize that an employee *has a* hire date, not that an employee *is a* hire date. If an object *has* an attribute, the attribute should be a field in the class. The Employee class should add a field of type Date to represent the hire date of an employee, as opposed to extending the Date class.

Implementing Inheritance

Now that we have seen why inheritance is useful in OOP, let's look at how it is implemented in Java. A class uses the *extends* keyword to inherit from another class. The extends keyword appears after the class name when declaring the class and is followed by the name of the class being extended.

For example, the following statement is used to declare that the Salary class is a child of the Employee class:

```
public class Salary extends Employee
```

Similarly, the Hourly class can extend Employee with the statement:

```
public class Hourly extends Employee
```

The following Employee class will be used as the parent of Salary and Hourly. Note that you do not add any special code to denote that Employee is a parent class.

```
public class Employee
{
    public String name;
    public String address;
    public int SSN;
    public int number;
    public void mailCheck()
    {
        System.out.println("Mailing a check to " + name
+ " " + address);
    }
}
```

The following Salary class uses the extends keyword to denote Salary is a child class of Employee.

```
public class Salary extends Employee
{
    public float salary;      //Annual salary
    public float computePay()
    {
        System.out.println("Computing salary pay for " + name);
        return salary/52;
    }
}
```

Similarly, the following Hourly class extends the Employee class using the extends keyword.

```java
public class Hourly extends Employee
{
    public float hourlyRate;      //Pay rate
    public float hoursWorked;     //Weekly hours worked
    public float computePay()
    {
        System.out.println("Computing hourly pay for " + name);
        float pay = 0.0F;
        if(hoursWorked <= 40)
        {
            pay = hourlyRate * hoursWorked;
        }
        else    //Need to compute overtime
        {
            pay = (hourlyRate * 40) +
                    (hourlyRate * (hoursWorked - 40) * 1.5F);
        }
        return pay;
    }
}
```

A child class has access to the fields and methods in the parent class, depending on the access specifier, which is discussed in Chapter 7, "Advanced Java Language Concepts." The computePay() method of the Salary class displays the name of the employee being paid, but there is no name field in the salary class. The name field is in Employee, the parent of Salary. In this example, because name is public, Salary has acces to it and can use it at any point in the Salary class.

Notice that the Hourly class prints out the employee's name within its computePay() method, using the name field inherited from the Employee class.

Instantiating Child Objects

Now that we have defined the Employee, Salary, and Hourly classes, let's look at a program that instantiates and uses these classes. The following Inherit-Demo program creates an Employee, Salary, and Hourly object. Study the program carefully and try to determine its output.

```java
public class InheritDemo
{
    public static void main(String [] args)
    {
        System.out.println("Instantiating an Employee");
```

```
Employee e = new Employee();
e.name = "Robert Smith";
e.address = "111 Java Street";
e.SSN = 999001111;
e.number = 1;
System.out.println("Instantiating a Salary");
Salary s = new Salary();
s.name = "Jane Smith";
s.address = "222 Oak Drive";
s.SSN = 111009999;
s.number = 2;
s.salary = 100000.00F;
System.out.println("Instantiating an Hourly");
Hourly h = new Hourly();
h.name = "George Washington";
h.address = "333 Espresso Lane";
h.SSN = 111990000;
h.number = 3;
h.hourlyRate = 10.00F;
h.hoursWorked = 50;
System.out.println("Paying employees");
//e.computePay();       //Does not compile!
System.out.println(s.number + " " + s.computePay());
System.out.println(h.number + " " + h.computePay());
System.out.println("Mailing checks");
e.mailCheck();
s.mailCheck();
h.mailCheck();
   }
}
```

The InheritDemo program starts by instantiating each of the three employee types and initializing their fields. Up until the "Paying employees" statement, the only output is:

```
Instantiating an Employee
Instantiating a Salary
Instantiating an Hourly
```

The computePay() method is then invoked on the Salary and Hourly objects. Notice within main() the salary object can access the number field inherited from its parent using:

```
s.number
```

The same is true for the Hourly object, which accesses the number field using the statement:

```
h.number;
```

Invoking the computePay() methods on the Salary and Hourly objects generates the following output:

```
Paying employees
Computing salary pay for Jane Smith
2 1923.0769
Computing hourly pay for George Washington
3 550.0
```

 Notice that the Employee object referenced by e in the InheritDemo program cannot invoke the computePay() method because the object does not have a computePay() method. In fact, there is no place to put information about how or what Robert Smith is paid. It is safe to say that no employee at the company will want to be of type Employee.

This does not mean that the Employee class is not useful. In fact, the opposite is true. Even though we will not be needing objects of type Employee, the Employee class plays a fundamental and essential role in the design of our program.

The mailCheck() method is available to all three objects in the InheritDemo program. Invoking them causes the following output:

```
Mailing checks
Mailing a check to Robert Smith 111 Java Street
Mailing a check to Jane Smith 222 Oak Drive
Mailing a check to George Washington 333 Espresso Lane
```

The entire output of the InheritDemo program is shown in Figure 6.1.

 The bytecode for Employee, Salary, Hourly, and InheritDemo all need to be in the same folder on your hard drive. Putting the bytecode in the same folder is necessary for the compiler and the JVM to find these files, at least until you become familiar with CLASSPATH, discussed in Chapter 7, "Advanced Java Language Concepts."

```
Command Prompt                                    _ □ ×
C:\wiley\Chapter6>java InheritDemo
Instantiating an Employee
Instantiating a Salary
Instantiating an Hourly
Paying employees
Computing salary pay for Jane Smith
2 1923.0769
Computing hourly pay for George Washington
3 550.0
Mailing checks
Mailing a check to Robert Smith 111 Java Street
Mailing a check to Jane Smith 222 Oak Drive
Mailing a check to George Washington 333 Espresso Lane

C:\wiley\Chapter6>
```

Figure 6.1   Output of the InheritDemo program.

Single versus Multiple Inheritance

Some OOP languages (such as C++) allow a child class to have more than one parent; however, this is not allowed in Java. A Java class can only have one parent. For example, the Salary class cannot extend both the Employee class and a Manager class. Multiple inheritance is not allowed in Java.

 One of the goals of the Java language was to create an OOP language that was simple to use and understand. Multiple inheritance is one of those capabilities that only tends to add confusion to a language.

In terms of design issues, there are no situations where multiple inheritance is the only option. (Some may argue that it is needed at times, but I have yet to be convinced of this by anyone who has attempted to sway me with a specific example.) Therefore, there is no need to waste time going into the details of why multiple inheritance is not a requirement of OOP. We can simply appreciate the fact that when learning Java we do not need to bother ourselves with figuring out the many details and issues of multiple inheritance.

 Be aware of what I said about multiple inheritance. I said a Java class can only have one parent. However, this does not mean a class cannot have a grandparent, great grandparent, and so on up the hierarchy tree. Keep reading!

A Java class can have a parent class, and that parent class can have a parent, and so on. This hierarchy can continue as long as you want.

For example, the Salary class discussed earlier extends the Employee class. The Salary class can also be a parent class. Any child classes of Salary inherit the fields and methods of Salary and Employee.

Suppose that you determine that a class is needed to represent part-time salaried employees, who have an annual salary but must keep track of the hours they work. Then a new class named PartTimeSalary can be written that extends the Salary class.

This results in the PartTimeSalary class being a child of Salary, and Salary being a child of Employee. A PartTimeSalary object inherits everything from Salary and Employee.

The following class shows the definition of PartTimeSalary. The extends keyword is used to extend Salary, but you do not specify any inheritance with Employee. The compiler and JVM know that Salary extends Employee.

```
public class PartTimeSalary extends Salary
{
    public int hoursWorked;
    public int getHoursWorked()
```

```
        {
            System.out.println("Getting hours for " + this.name
                                    + " earning " + salary);
            return hoursWorked;
        }
    }
```

The PartTimeSalary class has one field and one method; however, a PartTimeSalary object will have six fields: name, address, SSN, number, salary, and hoursWorked.

Similarly, the PartTimeSalary class has one method, getHoursWorked(), but a PartTimeSalary object has three methods: getHoursWorked(), computePay(), and mailCheck().

Notice that the getHoursWorked() method in the PartTimeSalary class accesses the name field inherited from Employee, the salary field inherited from Salary, and the hoursWorked field in its own class.

The this reference is used for accessing this.name in the getHoursWorked() method of the PartTimeSalary class to emphasize that the name field is a member of this object, even though name is not a field in this class. The same is true for accessing salary. Keep in mind that the compiler prefixes *this.* to salary and hoursWorked for us, as it would have done with name had we not explicitly used the this reference ourselves.

The *is a* relationship should also be maintained. A child is a parent, a child is a grandparent, and so on. In our example, a part-time salaried employee is a salaried employee, and a part-time salaried employee is an employee.

The java.lang.Object Class

The Java language API includes a special class named Object that is the root class of the entire Java hierarchy. The Object class, found in the java.lang package, is the parent of every Java class, either directly (meaning the class is an immediate child of Object) or indirectly (meaning Object is an ancestor further up the inheritance tree).

For example, consider the following Employee class that does not declare a parent class.

```
public class Employee
{
    //Class definition
}
```

Because this Employee does not explicitly extend another class, it implicitly extends Object. In fact, we could have added the extends keyword as follows:

```
public class Employee extends Object
{
    //Class definition
}
```

 If you write a class and do not explicitly extend another class, the compiler adds "extends Object" to your class declaration. If you write a class that extends another class besides Object, the class still is a child of Object, since eventually one of its ancestors must have extended Object.

Suppose that a Salary class is written that extends Employee:

```
public class Salary extends Employee
{
    //Class definition
}
```

The Salary class extends Employee, and because a Java class can only have one parent class, Salary does not extend Object directly. Because Employee extends Object, however, the Salary class is an indirect child of the Object class. Note that the compiler does not add "extends Object" to a child class that already extends another class.

The Methods of the Object Class

Object is a parent of every class, so the methods in the Object class are inherited by every Java object. Therefore, the methods in the Object class can be invoked on any Java object, no matter what class type the object is.

The following list contains the signatures of the methods in the Object class and a description of what each method does:

public final Class getClass().   Every class used in a Java program is loaded by the JVM. When the JVM loads a class, the information about the class is stored in a Class object. Use this method to obtain a reference to the Class object of the object you invoke the method on.

public int hashcode().   This method returns a hashcode value for the object, which is useful when working with hash tables and other data structures that use hashing.

public boolean equals(Object x).   Use this method to check if two objects are equal to each other. This method is often overridden (method over- riding is discussed in the next section) and allows a class to determine what it means for two objects of that type to be equal. Note if two objects are equal as determined by this method, then the hashcode() method of the two objects should generate the same hash code.

protected Object clone() throws CloneNotSupportedException.   The clone method is used to create a copy of an object. The exception occurs when the object being cloned does not support cloning. The details of cloning objects are not discussed in this book.

public String toString().   This method returns a string representation of the object. Representing an object as a String can be helpful for debug- ging or testing purposes. The Java documentation recommends that you add the toString() method to all of your classes, a widely used practice in Java programming.

protected void finalize() throws Throwable.   This method is invoked on an object right before the object is to be garbage collected. The finalize() method allows for an object to free up any resources or perform any nec- essary cleanup before the object is removed from memory.

public final void wait() throws InterruptedException.   The wait() method has two other overloaded versions in the Object class. Invoking wait() on an object causes the current thread to stop executing until some other thread invokes notify() on the same object. The wait() and notify() methods are used for thread synchronization.

public final void notify().   There is also a notifyAll() method in the Object class. These methods are used to restart any threads that were blocked by invoking one of the wait() methods on the object.

The final methods in the Object class, such as wait() and notify(), cannot be changed by the child classes of Object; however, the nonfinal methods are intended to be included in classes that want or need to change the default behavior of the corresponding method in the Object class.

For example, the default behavior of the toString() method in Object is to print out the name of the class, followed by the @ symbol, followed by the hashcode value. If you do not want this behavior, add toString() to your class and generate any string you like.

The following ToStringDemo program invokes the toString() method of the following Radio class. Notice the Radio class does not contain a toString() method but inherits the default toString() method in Object.

Study the ToStringDemo program carefully and try to determine the output. (Note that I added something that we have not discussed yet, printing out just a reference.)

```
public class Radio
{
    public int volume;
    public double channel;
    public char band;
    public Radio(int v, double c, char b)
    {
        volume = v;
        channel = c;
        band = b;
    }
}

public class ToStringDemo
{
    public static void main(String [] args)
    {
        Radio radio = new Radio(7, 100.3, 'F');
        System.out.println("toString returns " + radio.toString());

        System.out.println("Just printing the reference: " + radio);
    }
}
```

Figure 6.2 shows the output of the ToStringDemo.

The toString() method invoked on the radio object created the following String:

```
Radio@1ea2dfe
```

The output of printing out the reference generated the same String:

```
Just printing the reference: Radio@1ea2dfe
```

The toString() method was invoked implicitly by the JVM when the reference was concatenated with a String.

 When the radio reference is concatenated to the string "Just printing the reference: ", the reference needs to be converted to a String before the concatenation can occur. Notice that the toString() method is invoked automatically. Because every object in Java is a child of Object, every object has a toString() method, and the JVM will invoke toString() implicitly anytime the object needs to be converted to a String.

```
Command Prompt                                    _ □ ×
C:\wiley\Chapter6>java ToStringDemo
toString returns Radio@1ea2dfe
Just printing the reference: Radio@1ea2dfe

C:\wiley\Chapter6>_
```

Figure 6.2 The output of the ToStringDemo program.

The default toString() method, although sometimes useful, is not very exciting. Instead of using the default version, the Radio class can include its own toString() method, allowing the Radio class to create its own string representation of a Radio object. Adding toString() to the Radio class replaces the toString() method in Object. This is an example of method overriding, which we will now discuss.

Method Overriding

A child class can override a method that it inherits from a parent, thereby allowing the child class to add or change the behavior of the method in the parent. This is referred to as *method overriding* and is a feature of OOP.

Here is a list of rules that must be followed when a child class overrides a method in a parent class:

- The return type, method name, and parameter list must be identical.

- The access specifier must be at least that of the parent. For example, if the parent method is public, the child must be public. If the parent method is protected, the child must be protected or public (public allows more access than protected).

- The overriding exception cannot throw more exceptions than the parent. (The reason for this is discussed in Chapter 11, "Exception Handling.")

 If a method in the child class has the same name as a method in the parent class, but the child class method changes the parameter list, then this is method overloading, not method overriding. Try not to confuse the two concepts, since their usages are quite different.

The Radio class discussed earlier inherited all the methods of Object but did not override any of them. The following Radio in class overrides the toString() method, thereby replacing the toString() behavior of toString() in Object.

```
public class Radio
{
    public int volume;
    public double channel;
    public char band;
    public Radio(int v, double c, char b)
    {
        volume = v;
        channel = c;
        band = b;
    }
```

```
public String toString()
{
    System.out.println("Inside Radio toString");
    String rep = "Radio volume = " + volume + ", channel = "
                    + channel + " and band = " + band;
    return rep;
}
}
```

♦ The equals() Method

The Object class has an equals() method for determining whether two objects are equal. The idea is that every class you write will override the equals() method, allowing users of your class to determine when instances are equal.

What does it mean for two Employee objects to be equal? You get to decide. For example, maybe two employees are equal if they work in the same department, or have the same manager, or get paid the same amount. More likely, suppose that two employees are the same if they have the same number. Whatever logic you decide on, you perform that logic by overriding equals() in the Employee class.

The following Employee class overrides equals() and determines that two objects are equal if they have the same number.

```
public class Employee
{
    public String name;
    public String address;
    public int SSN;
    public int number;
    public void mailCheck()
    {
        System.out.println("Mailing a check to " + name
+ " " + address);
    }
    public boolean equals(Object x)
    {
        if(x == null)
            return false;
        Employee other = (Employee) x;
        if(this.number == other.number)
        {
            return true;
        }
        else
        {
            return false;
```

continued

◆ The equals() Method *(continued)*

```
        }
    }
    public int hashcode()
    {
        return this.number;
    }
}
```

Testing for a null reference is a good idea because it is a possibility. The reference passed in is then cast to an Employee type, which is necessary because we want to treat this object as an Employee. (Casting down the hierarchy such as this is risky, and typically we should use instanceof to ensure that x is of type Employee. I have not discussed this yet, though, so I have omitted it for now. The details of casting down the hierarchy tree are discussed in Chapter 8, "Polymorphism and Abstraction.")

Notice that the hashcode() method is also added to the Employee class. The general rule of hash codes that should be followed is that if two objects are equal, they should generate the same hash code; therefore, classes that override the equals() method typically need to override the hashcode() method as well.

The following statements instantiate two Employee objects and test for equality.

```
Employee e1  = new Employee();
Employee e2 = new Employee();
e1.number = 101;
e2.number = 102;
if(e1.equals(e2))
    System.out.println("This will not print.");
e2.number = 101;
if(e2.equals(e1))
    System.out.println("This will print.");
if(e1 == e2)
   System.out.println("This will not print either.");
```

In the previous statements, two Employee objects are instantiated, so two equals() methods are available to us: e1's and e2's. It does not matter if you invoke e1.equals(e2) or e2.equals(e1), the result will be the same.

The equals() method compares two objects to see if they are equal. The == comparison operator checks to see if two references point to the same object, which is an entirely different comparison. If e1 and e2 point to different objects, the == operator will be false, no matter if e1 equals e2 or not.

 note   The toString() method in the Object class is declared as public in Object; therefore, toString() must be declared public in Radio. If a weaker access privilege is attempted for toString() in Radio, then the Radio class will not compile.

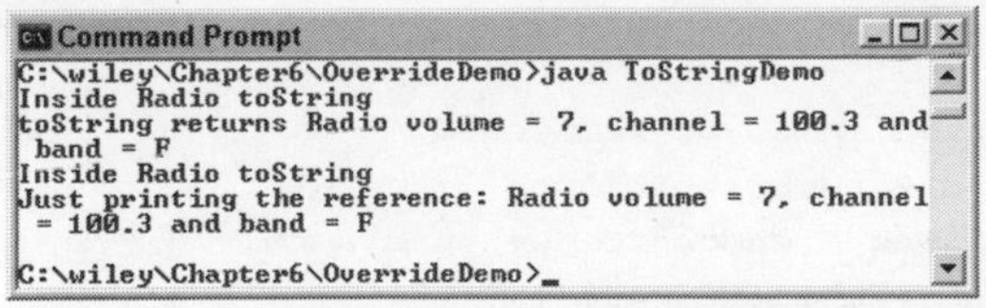

```
Command Prompt                                    _ □ ×
C:\wiley\Chapter6\OverrideDemo>java ToStringDemo
Inside Radio toString
toString returns Radio volume = 7, channel = 100.3 and
 band = F
Inside Radio toString
Just printing the reference: Radio volume = 7, channel
 = 100.3 and band = F

C:\wiley\Chapter6\OverrideDemo>_
```

Figure 6.3   The overridden toString() method in the Radio class is invoked.

Now when toString() is invoked on a Radio object, the toString() method in the Radio class will be invoked, not the toString() method in the Object class. The toString() method in the Object class is essentially hidden for Radio objects, which is the result we wanted.

Let's run the ToStringDemo program again, this time using our new Radio class. Try to determine how the output will change. Figure 6.3 shows the output.

 The toString() method in the Radio class of Figure 6.3 demonstrates a child class that wanted to completely change the behavior of an inherited method, in this case, toString() from Object. There are times when a child class might want to add to the behavior of an inherited method and not completely replace the parent method. A child class can use the super keyword to invoke the overridden method in the parent. The details of using super are discussed next.

The super Keyword

Every object has a reference to itself called the *this* reference, and there are situations where a class needs to explicitly use the this reference when referring to its fields or methods. Similarly, a class can use the super keyword to explicitly refer to a field or method that is inherited from a parent. You can think of super as a child object's reference to its parent object.

To demonstrate using super, the following Employee class explicitly uses the super keyword to invoke the toString() method inherited from Object. (Notice that the Employee class also explicitly uses the this reference to access its fields name and address, although it is not necessary in this particular instance.)

```
public class Employee
{
    public String name;
    public String address;
    public int SSN;
    public int number;
```

```
        public void mailCheck()
        {
                System.out.println("Inside Employee mailCheck: "
                                        + super.toString());
                System.out.println("Mailing a check to " + this.name + " "
                                        + this.address);
        }
}
```

**In the Employee class, the super keyword is not needed to invoke
toString(). Not only is super not needed, but the call to toString()
could have used the this reference instead:**

```
this.toString()
```

**The toString() method can be invoked using this because Employee
inherits toString(). It can be invoked using super because toString()
is in the parent class.**

The super keyword can also be used in the child class when the child wants
to invoke an overridden method in the parent. This allows the child class to
override a method when the child needs to add to the parent method, not completely change the behavior.

The following Salary class extends Employee and overrides the mailCheck()
method. Within mailCheck(), the Salary class uses super to invoke mailCheck()
in Employee.

```
public class Salary extends Employee
{
    public float salary;       //Annual salary
    public float computePay()
    {
        System.out.println("Computing salary pay for " + super.name);
        return salary/52;
    }
    public void mailCheck()
    {
        System.out.println("Inside Salary mailCheck");
        super.mailCheck();
        System.out.println("Mailed check to " + this.name
                        + " with salary " + this.salary);
    }
}
```

The following SuperDemo program instantiates a Salary object and invokes
the mailCheck() method. Study the program carefully and try to determine the
output, which is shown in Figure 6.4.

```
Command Prompt                                    _ □ ×
C:\wiley\Chapter6\super>java SuperDemo
Instantiating an Employee
Instantiating a Salary
*** Invoking mailCheck on e ***
Inside Employee mailCheck: Employee@17182c1
Mailing a check to Robert Smith 111 Java Street

*** Invoking mailCheck on s ***
Inside Salary mailCheck
Inside Employee mailCheck: Salary@13f5d07
Mailing a check to Jane Smith 222 Oak Drive
Mailed check to Jane Smith with salary 100000.0

C:\wiley\Chapter6\super>_
```

Figure 6.4 The output of the SuperDemo program.

```
public class SuperDemo
{
    public static void main(String [] args)
    {
        System.out.println("Instantiating an Employee");
        Employee e = new Employee();
        e.name = "Robert Smith";
        e.address = "111 Java Street";
        e.SSN = 999001111;
        e.number = 1;
        System.out.println("Instantiating a Salary");
        Salary s = new Salary();
        s.name = "Jane Smith";
        s.address = "222 Oak Drive";
        s.SSN = 111009999;
        s.number = 2;
        s.salary = 100000.00F;
        System.out.println("*** Invoking mailCheck on e ***");
        e.mailCheck();
        System.out.println();
        System.out.println("*** Invoking mailCheck on s ***");
        s.mailCheck();
    }
}
```

note The super keyword is required when a child method wants to invoke an overridden method in the parent. For example, if the super keyword was omitted in the mailCheck() method of the Salary class in Figure 6.4, the compiler would add *this.*:

```
this.mailCheck()
```

The previous statement creates an infinite recursion because this.mailCheck() invokes mailCheck() in the Salary class. Your program would keep calling mailCheck() in Salary until it eventually crashed when it ran out of memory.

Classroom Q & A

Q: I noticed in the Salary class you used this.name in the mailCheck() method and super.name in the computePay() method. How do you know which one to use?

A: It doesn't matter, as I demonstrated in the Salary class when I used both this and super. The name field is inherited from the Employee class. I can use super to access fields or methods in the parent.

Q: Then why can you use this.name also?

A: Because a Salary object has a field called name, and an object can use this to access its own fields.

Q: So super and this refer to the same thing?

A: No! When a child object is referring to an inherited field or method, then this or super can be used. However, when a child is accessing a field or method from its own class, then only the this reference can be used, as with this.salary in the mailCheck() method of the Salary class. Using super.salary in that case would not compile because the parent class does not have a salary field.

Q: Then why is the super reference needed?

A: The super reference must be used when a child class wants to invoke an overridden parent class method.

 The super keyword has another use that is not related to overridden methods. This other use of the super keyword is discussed later in this chapter in the section *Invoking a Parent Class Constructor*.

The final Keyword

We have seen the final keyword used for creating constant variables. A final variable cannot be changed after it has been assigned a value.

Now that we have seen inheritance and method overriding, I can show you the other two uses of the final keyword.

Final class.   A class can be declared final. A final class cannot be subclassed.

Final method.   A method can be declared final. A final method cannot be overridden.

Several of the classes in the Java API are declared final. For example, the String class is final, so you cannot write a class that extends String.

The final keyword appears before the class keyword when declaring a final class. For example:

```
public final class Hourly extends Employee
{
      //Class definition...
}
```

A compiler error is generated if you try to write a class that subclasses Hourly. The following class declaration will not compile:

```
public class PartTime extends Hourly                //error!
{
      //Class definition...
}
```

 You won't write final classes every day, but there are certain situations where you might write a class that you do not want anyone to subclass. For example, the designers of Java decided that no one should extend the String class because it is such a fundamental class in the Java language.

If a class was allowed to extend String, this child class could override the methods of String, changing the behaviors with undesired results. By making String final, you can be assured that the implementation of String objects is consistent and reliable.

final Methods

When a child class overrides a method in the parent class, the overridden method is essentially hidden. The only way the parent method can be invoked is if the child method explicitly invokes it. If you write a method with important behavior that you do not want a child class to override, you can declare the method final. A final method cannot be overridden by a child class.

 The getClass(), wait(), and notify() methods of the Object class are declared final. Their implementations are essential for the proper behavior of an object, and these methods cannot be overridden by any class.

When declaring a method final, the final keyword can appear anywhere before the return value. (Typically it appears after the access specifier.) The following Employee class demonstrates declaring a final method.

```
public class Employee
{
    public String name;
    public String address;
    public int SSN;
    public int number;
    public final void mailCheck()
    {
        System.out.println("Inside Employee mailCheck: "
                        + super.toString());
        System.out.println("Mailing a check to " + this.name + " "
                        + this.address);
    }
}
```

 The Employee class declares its mailCheck() method as final. By doing this, the Salary class will no longer compile because it attempts to override mailCheck().

The Instantiation Process

A child object is an extension of its parent. When a child class is instantiated, the parent class object needs to be constructed first. More specifically, a constructor in a parent class must execute before any constructor in the child class executes.

In addition, if the child class has a grandparent, the grandparent object needs to be constructed first. This process continues up the tree.

When an object is instantiated, the following sequence of events occurs:

1. The new operator invokes a constructor in the child class.

2. The child class may use the this keyword to invoke another constructor in the child class. Eventually, a constructor in the child class will be invoked that does not have this() as its first line of code.

3. Before any statements in the child constructor execute, a parent class constructor must be invoked. This is done using the super keyword. If a constructor does not explicitly make a call using super, the compiler will call super() with empty parentheses, thereby invoking the no-argument parent class constructor.

4. If the parent class is also a child of another class, the parent class constructor must invoke a constructor in its parent before executing any statements. Again, this is done using the super keyword.

5. This process continues until we reach the top of the hierarchy tree, which must be the Object class.

6. The constructor in the Object class executes, then the flow of control returns to the constructor in the class just below Object in the inheritance hierarchy tree.

7. The constructors execute their way down the hierarchy tree. The last constructor to execute is actually the one that was invoked first in Step 1.

Let's look at an example. Suppose we have the following BigScreenTV class that extends the following Television class, and Television extends Object.

```
public class Television
{
    public int channel, volume;
    public Television()
    {
        this(4,5);
        System.out.println("Inside Television()");
    }
    public Television(int c, int v)
    {
        System.out.println("Inside Television(int, int)");
        channel = c;
        volume = v;
    }
}
public class BigScreenTV extends Television
{
    public String aspectRatio;
    public short size;
    public BigScreenTV()
    {
        super();
        aspectRatio = "unknown";
        size = 40;
        System.out.println("Inside BigScreenTV()");
    }
}
```

Notice that the BigScreenTV constructor explicitly invokes the no-argument constructor in Television using the statement:

```
super();
```

A call to super() or this() must be the first line of code in every constructor. If a constructor does not contain either, the compiler adds super() with empty parentheses as the first line of code in the constructor. In the BigScreenTV class, if the call to super() did not appear, the compiler would have added it for us.

In the Television class, the constructor with two int parameters does not call super() or this(), so the compiler adds super() as the first line of code, thereby invoking the no-argument constructor in the Object class.

The following ConstructorDemo program instantiates a BigScreenTV object. Follow the flow of control carefully and try to determine the output, which is shown in Figure 6.5.

```
public class ConstructorDemo
{
    public static void main(String [] args)
    {
        System.out.println("Constructing a big screen TV");
        BigScreenTV tv = new BigScreenTV();
        System.out.println("Done constructing TV");
    }
}
```

Within main() of ConstructorDemo, we instantiate a BigScreenTV object:

```
BigScreenTV tv = new BigScreenTV();
```

This statement invokes the no-argument constructor in the BigScreenTV class. The constructor in BigScreenTV invokes the no-argument constructor in Television. The no-argument Television constructor invokes the other Television constructor, which does not have a this() or super() statement. Therefore, the compiler added super(), causing the no-argument constructor in Object to be invoked.

When the Object constructor is finished, control returns to the Television constructor with two arguments, which executes and outputs:

```
Inside Television(int, int)
```

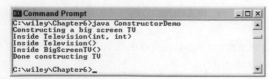

Figure 6.5 The output of the ConstructorDemo program.

Control then returns to the no-argument Television constructor, which executes and outputs:

```
Inside Television()
```

Control then returns to the BigScreenTV constructor, which executes last and outputs:

```
Inside BigScreenTV()
```

After all three constructors are done, the object is instantiated and the new operator returns a reference to the new BigScreenTV object. The entire output of the ConstructorDemo program is shown in Figure 6.5.

Invoking a Parent Class Constructor

The super keyword is used to invoke a parent class constructor. The compiler adds super() with empty parentheses if a constructor does not explicitly use the super keyword, causing the parent's no-argument constructor to be invoked.

What happens, however, if the parent class does not have a no-argument constructor? Calling super() with empty parentheses does not compile, and the child class constructors need to explicitly invoke a parent constructor, passing in the appropriate arguments to the parent class constructors.

For example, suppose we modify the Television class as follows so that it no longer has a no-argument constructor.

```
public class Television
{
    public int channel, volume;
    public Television(int c)
    {
        this(c,5);
        System.out.println("Inside Television(int)");
    }
    public Television(int c, int v)
    {
        System.out.println("Inside Television(int, int)");
        channel = c;
        volume = v;
    }
}
```

Figure 6.6 shows what happens when the BigScreenTV class is compiled using this new Television class.

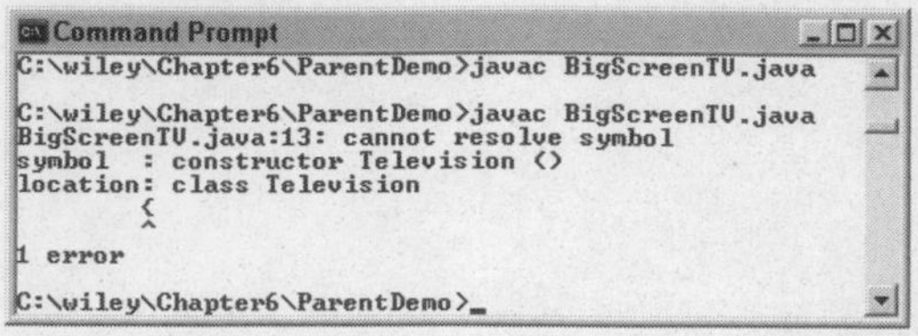

Figure 6.6   The call to super() no longer works, since Television does not have a no-argument constructor.

The BigScreenTV constructors must explicitly invoke one of the constructors in the parent class. The following class shows a whole new BigScreenTV class that uses the super() keyword and passes in arguments to a specific Television constructor.

```
public class BigScreenTV extends Television
{
    public String aspectRatio;
    public short size;
    public BigScreenTV(int channel)
    {
        this("unknown", (short) 40, channel);
        System.out.println("Inside BigScreenTV(int)");
    }
    public BigScreenTV(String r, short s, int channel)
    {
        super(channel);
        System.out.println("Inside BigScreenTV(String, short, int)");
        aspectRatio = r;
        size = s;
    }
    public BigScreenTV(String r, short s, int channel, int volume)
    {
        super(channel, volume);
        System.out.println("Inside BigScreenTV(String, short, int,
int)");
        aspectRatio = r;
        size = s;
    }
```

The following ParentDemo program invokes two BigScreenTV objects using the new Television and BigScreenTV classes. Try to determine what the output will be. Compare your answer with the actual output shown in Figure 6.7.

```
public class ParentDemo
{
    public static void main(String [] args)
    {
```

```
        System.out.println("*** big screen #1 ***");
        int channel = 4;
        new BigScreenTV(channel);
        short size = 53;
        channel = 3;
        String ratio = "16:9";
        System.out.println("\n*** big screen #2 ***");
        new BigScreenTV(ratio, size, channel);
        ratio = "5:4";
        size = 42;
        channel = 4;
        int volume = 7;
        System.out.println("\n*** big screen #3 ***");
        new BigScreenTV(ratio, size, channel, volume);
    }
}
```

♦ The Default Constructor

In Chapter 5, "Methods," I discussed how the compiler generates a default constructor for any class that does not explicitly declare a constructor. I mentioned that the default constructor does not contain any statements, but that is only partially true. Because the default constructor is a constructor that does not invoke this() or super(), the compiler adds a call to super() for you.

For example, suppose the BigScreenTV class looked similar to:

```
public class BigScreenTV extends Television
{
    public String aspectRatio;
    public short size;
}
```

The compiler would then generate and add the following constructor to this BigScreenTV class:

```
public BigScreenTV()
{
    super();
}
```

This BigScreenTV class will not compile for the Television class that did not include a no-argument constructor. The BigScreenTV default constructor does not work in this situation.

By writing a class without a no-argument constructor, you are forcing all child classes to explicitly add a constructor that contains a call to super(). For the most part, this is not a major concern; however, this is another instance of why you should have a specific reason to write a class that does not contain a no-argument constructor.

```
Command Prompt                                    _|□|×|
C:\wiley\Chapter6\ParentDemo>java ParentDemo
*** big screen #1 ***
Inside Television(int, int)
Inside Television(int)
Inside BigScreenTU(String, short, int)
Inside BigScreenTU(int)

*** big screen #2 ***
Inside Television(int, int)
Inside Television(int)
Inside BigScreenTU(String, short, int)

*** big screen #3 ***
Inside Television(int, int)
Inside BigScreenTU(String, short, int, int)

C:\wiley\Chapter6\ParentDemo>_
```

Figure 6.7   The output of the ParentDemo program.

Lab 6.1: Implementing Inheritance

The purpose of this lab is to become familiar with implementing inheritance in Java. You will write a class named Polygon that is subclassed by a Triangle class.

1. Write a class called Polygon that has two fields: an int for the number of sides and a double for the area. Add a method called get-NumberOfSides() that prints out and returns the number of sides.

2. Override the toString() method in Polygon to return a nice string representation of your Polygon class.

3. Add a constructor to Polygon that takes in an int to represent the number of sides and prints out the message "Inside Polygon constructor."

4. Save and compile the Polygon class.

5. Write a class called Triangle that extends Polygon. Add two int fields: one for the base and one for the height. (Triangles have a base and a height.)

6. Add a constructor to Triangle that takes in two int's for the base and height. The constructor needs to use super() to invoke the constructor in Polygon, passing in 3 for the number of sides. Print out the message "Inside Triangle constructor."

7. Add a toString() method to Triangle that prints out the triangle's base and height.

8. Add a getArea() method to Triangle that computes and returns the area. The formula for the area of a triangle is:

```
area = 1/2 (base * height)
```

9. Save and compile the Triangle class.

10. Write a program that instantiates at least one Polygon object and one Triangle object. Invoke the various methods to ensure that everything is working.

When you instantiate a Triangle object, the output should display "Inside Polygon constructor" before displaying "Inside Triangle constructor."

Lab 6.2: Overriding Methods

This lab is a continuation of Lab 6.1 and demonstrates overriding methods.

1. Write a class called RightTriangle that extends your Triangle class from Lab 6.1.

2. Add a field of type double called hypotenuse to represent the longest side of a right triangle.

3. Add a constructor that takes in two int's to represent the base and height. Pass these two values up to the Triangle constructor and then use these two values in the constructor to compute the hypotenuse field. The formula is:

   ```
   hypotenuse = sqrt(base*base + height*height)
   ```

4. Use the Math.sqrt() function to compute the square root. Math.sqrt() takes in a double and returns a double. Also, print out a message stating "Inside RightTriangle constructor."

5. Add the toString() method to RightTriangle. Use super to invoke toString() in the parent and concatenate the result with the hypotenuse.

6. Save and compile the RightTriangle class.

7. Write a program that instantiates a RightTriangle object and invokes the toString(), getArea(), and getNumberOfSides() methods. Run your program, and verify that everything is working correctly.

When you instantiate a RightTriangle object, the output of the constructors should be in the following order: "Inside Polygon constructor," "Inside Triangle constructor," and "Inside RightTriangle constructor."

Summary

- Inheritance is the most important feature of object-oriented programming. It allows a new class to be written that extends an existing class. This new class inherits all of the attributes and behaviors of its parent.

- The *is a* relationship is a simple but important step used to determine if inheritance is a good design. You should be able to say "A child object *is a* parent object."

- The extends keyword is used to implement inheritance. A class in Java can only extend one class.

- If a class does not explicitly extend another class, then its parent class is java.lang.Object. The Object class is at the top of the entire Java hierarchy, and it contains useful methods that can be invoked on any object, such as toString(), equals(), and hashcode().

- Method overriding is when a child class contains the same method as its parent class.

- The super keyword is used by a child class to explicitly access a field in the parent class or explicitly invoke a method in the parent class.

- A final class cannot be extended. A final method cannot be overridden.

- A child class can invoke a constructor in its parent using the super() syntax, which must be the first statement in a constructor. If a constructor does not explicitly invoke super() or this(), then the compiler adds a call to super() (with no arguments) to the constructor.

Review Questions

1. In OOP, a class can extend another class. This concept is referred to as _____.

2. Suppose a class is declared as

   ```
   public class Rectangle extends Triangle
   ```

   What might be wrong with this design?

3. True or False: A child inherits all the fields of its parent class.

4. True or False: The first line of code in every constructor is either a call to this() or a call to super() (possibly with arguments in both cases).

5. True or False: The compiler adds a call to this() if a constructor does not add it explicitly.

6. If a class does not declare that it extends another class, the parent of this class is _____.

7. True or False: A class in Java can extend more than one class.

   Use the following class definitions to answer the next four questions.

   ```java
   public class Vehicle
   {
        public int numOfWheels;
        public Vehicle(int x)
        {
             numOfWheels = x;
        }
        public void drive()
        {
             System.out.println("Driving a vehicle");
        }
   }
   public class Car extends Vehicle
   {
        public int numOfDoors;
        public Car(int d, int w)
        {
             numOfDoors = d;
             super(w);
        }
        public void drive()
        {
             System.out.println("Driving a car");
        }
   }
   ```

8. The Car class does not compile. Why? How can it be corrected?

9. (Assume from here on that the problem with the Car class has been corrected.) What is the output of the following statements?

```
Car audi = new Car();
Car.drive();
```

10. What is the output of the following statements?

```
Car porsche = new Car(2, 4);
porsche.drive();
```

11. What is the output of the following statements?

```
Vehicle v = new Vehicle(18);
v.drive();
v.numOfDoors = 2;
```

Answers to Review Questions

1. Inheritance.

2. A rectangle is not a triangle, so the *is a* relationship is not satisfied.

3. True. Child classes inherit all fields from their parent class, no matter what the access specifier of a parent field is.

4. Except for the constructor in the Object class, this statement is true.

5. False. The only call the compiler adds is super() if this() or super() does not appear explicitly.

6. java.lang.Object.

7. False. Multiple inheritance is not allowed in Java, so a Java class can only have one parent.

8. The statement super(w) must be the first line of code in the Car constructor. Move it to before the numOfDoors = d statement, and the class will work fine.

9. Neither of those two statements compiles. The statement new Car() implies that the Car class has a no-argument constructor, but it does not. The statement Car.drive() tries to invoke drive() using the name of the class, which does not make any sense.

10. The output is "Driving a car."

11. The output is "Driving a vehicle" for the first two statements. The third statement does not compile. A Vehicle object does not have a field of type numOfDoors.

CHAPTER

7

Advanced Java Language Concepts

This chapter is a potpourri of Java topics that are essential to your understanding of how Java works. Topics discussed in this chapter include packages, the access specifiers, encapsulation, the static keyword, and Java documentation.

An Overview of Packages

Every class belongs to a package. Packages have two basic purposes:

- Packages provide a mechanism for organizing classes.
- Packages provide a namespace for the classes within the package.

When developing a Java program, you put classes that go together in the same package. For example, in the J2SE, the classes that are used to perform input and output are in the java.io and java.nio packages. The fundamental classes of the Java language are in the java.lang package. The classes used for networking and sockets are in the java.net package. The classes used for creating GUI applications are in the java.awt, javax.swing, and other packages. I can go on and on because there are about 136 packages in the J2SE, depending on the version of J2SE.

Classroom Q & A

Q: You said every class is in a package. What package are all the classes we have written so far in?

A: Good question. You use the package keyword to declare a class in a package, and I haven't shown you how to do this yet. If you do not explicitly declare a class in a package, the class belongs to the *default package*. The default package contains every Java class ever written that does not use the package keyword, and that includes every class we have written so far.

Q: Is there something wrong with having a class in the default package?

A: It's not the end of the world, but I will say this: If you write a Java class for a real-world application (as opposed to code you are just playing around with or learning with), you will declare the class in a package. Packages are a fundamental but essential part of the Java language.

Q: Why are packages necessary? What if I have a small program that is only a dozen classes?

A: Packages are more than just a mechanism for organizing your classes. A more important aspect of packages is the namespace they create. For example, suppose that your small program contains a class named Vehicle. What if I wrote a Vehicle class as well? How would you be able to tell them apart? What if someone wanted to use my Vehicle class and your Vehicle class in their program?

Q: I have seen this problem before. Why don't you change the names of the classes, such as Vehicle1 and Vehicle2?

A: No thanks. I would have to rewrite and recompile a bunch of code, and with packages I don't have to worry about it. If the two Vehicle classes are in different packages (which they will be, see the sidebar on package names), my Java program can distinguish the two Vehicle classes. I will discuss the namespace feature of packages in detail after I show you how to create a package and put classes in it.

Adding a Class to a Package

A class is added to a package using the package keyword. The package statement must be the first statement in your source code file (except for comments). For example, suppose we wanted to create a package named payroll for the Employee, Salary, and Hourly classes used in our program to pay employees.

```
package payroll;
public class Employee
{
    public String name;
    public String address;
    public int SSN;
    public int number;
    public Employee(String name, String address, int SSN, int number)
    {
        System.out.println("Constructing an Employee");
        this.name = name;
        this.address = address;
        this.SSN = SSN;
        this.number = number;
    }
    public void mailCheck()
    {
        System.out.println("Mailing a check to " + this.name
                                + " " + this.address);
    }
}
```

The payroll package is not something that needs to be instantiated or physically created. The compiler sees the package declaration and treats Employee as being in the payroll package, even if Employee is the first class written in payroll.

 The package declaration must appear first in the class file. Notice the following statement, which is the first statement in the Employee source code. The class will not compile if an attempt is made to put any statement besides comments before the package declaration.

```
package payroll;
```

If we want Salary and Hourly in the payroll package also, we simply add the package statement to their class definition as well. For example, the Salary class would look similar to:

```
package payroll;
public class Salary extends Employee
{
    //Salary definition...
}
```

and the Hourly class would look similar to:

```
package payroll;
public class Hourly extends Employee
{
```

```
    //Hourly definition...
}
```

The Employee, Salary, and Hourly classes are all now in the same package, which is named payroll. These classes do not need to be in the same package; this was a design decision. Part of designing a Java application is deciding what packages to create and in which package each class will belong.

 The Java naming convention recommends package names be all lowercase, unless an acronym is part of the name. Typically, your package name will be multiple terms, and each term is separated by the dot operator. Examples include java.lang, java.awt.event, org.omg.CORBA, and org.omg.stub .java.rmi.

The Namespace Created by Packages

Packages create a namespace for all classes. If a class is in a package, *the name of the package becomes a part of the name of the class*. The package name is prefixed to the name of your class, separated by the dot operator.

For example, the Employee class is declared in the payroll package. The Employee class is now referred to:

```
payroll.Employee
```

The Employee class can no longer be referred to as simply Employee. The package name payroll must be used by any other class outside of the payroll package that wants to use the Employee class. Similarly, the Salary and Hourly classes become:

```
payroll.Salary
payroll.Hourly
```

 Classes in the same package do not need to use the package name when referring to each other. This is one of the benefits of putting classes that go together in the same package. For example, the Salary class extends Employee and can use the name Employee instead of payroll.Employee because Salary is also in the payroll package.

Packages create a namespace that is useful in avoiding naming conflicts. Two classes named Employee that both appear in the default package cannot be distinguished from each other; however, if one of the Employee classes is in the payroll package and the other is in a package named people, the two classes no longer have a naming conflict. The Employee class in payroll is referred to as payroll.Employee, while the other class is referred to using people.Employee:

```
payroll.Employee e1 = new payroll.Employee();
people.Employee e2 = new people.Employee();
```

In the previous statements, e1 refers to a payroll.Employee object, while e2 refers to a people.Employee object.

♦ Naming Packages

Packages create a namespace, with the name of the package becoming the prefix for the name of the class. The purpose of a namespace is to avoid naming conflicts where two classes have the same name.

Suppose that you write a Vehicle class, and I write a Vehicle class. How can we tell them apart? That's easy if they are in two different packages. For example, I can put my Vehicle class is in a package named rich:

```
package rich;
public class Vehicle
{
      //My vehicle class
}
```

Your Vehicle class can be in a different package:

```
package student;
public class Vehicle
{
      //Your vehicle class
}
```

The name of my Vehicle class is now rich.Vehicle, and the name of your Vehicle class is now student.Vehicle. The following statements instantiate one of each type:

```
rich.Vehicle mine = new rich.Vehicle();
student.Vehicle yours = new student.Vehicle();
```

Of course, this works fine if you and I use different package names; but what if we both choose rich for the package name? We are then right back where we started with the naming conflict because both of our classes would be named rich.Vehicle.

Thankfully, this is not a problem in the world of Java development because companies use a universally agreed-upon naming convention of including the company's Web site URL as part of the package name. Because Web site URLs are unique, the only possible naming conflicts that can occur are within a company.

continued

♦ Naming Packages *(continued)*

For example, Wiley Publishing's Web site URL is www.wiley.com. If you write a Vehicle class as an employee of Wiley, your package name would be similar to:

```
package com.wiley.rich;
public class Vehicle
{
    //Your Vehicle class
}
```

I work for a company whose Web site is www.javalicense.com. The package name for my Vehicle class would include com.javalicense:

```
package com.javalicense.rich;
public class Vehicle
{
    //My vehicle class
}
```

Even though we both picked rich as part of our package name, the two Vehicle classes no longer have a naming conflict. One of the classes is named com.javalicense.rich.Vehicle, and the other is named com.wiley.rich.Vehicle.

Many of the packages in the J2SE begin with java, to denote their role in the standard Java language. Most of the packages in the J2EE APIs begin with javax in the their name, such as javax.servlet and javax.ejb. The "x" is for extension, denoting that the package is an extension of the Java language.

The import Keyword

If a class wants to use another class in the same package, the package name does not need to be used. Classes in the same package "find each other" without any special syntax.

For example, suppose a class named Boss is added to the payroll package that already contains Employee. The Boss can then refer to the Employee class without using the payroll prefix, as demonstrated by the following Boss class.

```
package payroll;
public class Boss
{
    public void payEmployee(Employee e)
    {
        e.mailCheck();
    }
}
```

The payEmployee() method of the Boss class has a parameter of type Employee. The parameter is actually of type payroll.Employee, but because Boss is in the payroll package, the payroll prefix of Employee is not needed.

What happens if Boss is not in the payroll package? The Boss class must then use one of the following techniques for referring to a class in a different package.

- The fully qualified name of the class can be used. For example,

```
payroll.Employee
```

- The package can be imported using the import keyword and the wild card (*). For example,

```
import payroll.*;
```

- The class itself can be imported using the import keyword. For example,

```
import payroll.Employee;
```

 A class file can contain any number of import statements. The import statements must appear after the package statement and before the class declaration.

Suppose that the Boss class is in a package named management. The following Boss class uses the fully qualified name when referring to the Employee class in the payroll package.

```
package management;
public class Boss
{
    public void payEmployee(payroll.Employee e)
    {
        e.mailCheck();
    }
}
```

Because Boss uses the full name payroll.Employee, the payroll package does not need to be imported. If the Boss class imports the payroll package, however, it can refer to Employee without using the payroll prefix, as demonstrated by the following Boss class.

```
package management;
import payroll.*;
public class Boss
{
    public void payEmployee(Employee e)
    {
        e.mailCheck();
    }
```

```
        public void payEmployee(Salary s)
        {
            s.computePay();
        }
        public void payEmployee(Hourly h)
        {
            h.computePay();
        }
    }
```

This Boss class has three overloaded versions of payEmployee(), one for each type of employee, and therefore needs to refer to three classes in the payroll package: Employee, Salary, and Hourly. The statement:

```
import payroll.*;
```

tells the compiler to look in the payroll package when attempting to locate the classes used by Boss; therefore, this Boss class does not need to use the payroll prefix when referring to classes from the payroll package.

 You never need to use import statements, because you can always refer to a class by its fully qualified name (the name of the class prefixed with its package name). The import keyword is strictly a convenience. In fact, when compiling your classes, the compiler removes all import statements and replaces all class names with their fully qualified name. That said, you will use import statements all the time. Using the fully qualified name for every class is tedious and can actually make your code more difficult to read.

The third option when using a class from another package is to import the class itself. The following Boss class individually imports each class that it is using from another package.

```
package management;
import payroll.Employee;
import payroll.Hourly;
import payroll.Salary;
public class Boss
{
    public void payEmployee(Employee e)
    {
        e.mailCheck();
    }
    public void payEmployee(Salary s)
    {
        s.computePay();
    }
```

```
    public void payEmployee(Hourly h)
    {
        h.computePay();
    }
}
```

Importing each class individually is obviously more typing, but this option is actually preferred over using the import statement with the wild card. There are some rare instances where importing the wild card either does not work or causes a naming conflict. These situations will not arise in anything we do in this book, however, so I will use the wild card import statement regularly.

 There is no size or performance benefit gained from importing classes individually versus importing an entire package. The compiled bytecode will look the exact same because the compiler removes your import statements and replaces all class names with their fully qualified name.

We have been using classes such as String, System, Math, and Object throughout the examples so far in this book. Why did we not have to use the import keyword? Because each of these classes is in the java.lang package. The java.lang package is implicitly imported in every source code file.

In fact, you can import java.lang if you like, as the following class does, but it is never necessary to do so:

```
package electronics;
import java.lang.*;
public class Radio extends Object
{
    public String make, model;
}
```

The Radio class imports java.lang.* explicitly. The Radio class uses both Object and String from java.lang, but the code will compile just fine without the import statement.

The Directory Structure of Packages

Two major results occur when a class is placed in a package:

- The name of the package becomes a part of the name of the class, as we just discussed in the previous section.
- The name of the package must match the directory structure where the corresponding bytecode resides.

In other words, the name of the package affects where you store your byte-code. Suppose, for example, a class named Vehicle is in the com.wiley.trans package, which contains classes representing modes of transportation. The fully qualified name of this class is:

```
com.wiley.trans.Vehicle
```

The corresponding bytecode for the Vehicle class is in a file named Vehicle .class. Because Vehicle is in the com.wiley.trans package, Vehicle.class needs to be in a directory named trans, which is a subdirectory of wiley, which is a sub-directory of com.

The com directory can appear anywhere on your hard drive. For example, if com is in a folder called c:\my_bytecode, the path for Vehicle.class would be:

```
c:\my_bytecode\com\wiley\trans\Vehicle.class
```

The folder c:\my_bytecode is arbitrary, but the \com\wiley\trans directory structure must exist and contain the file Vehicle.class.

 Java is case sensitive. Because the package name com.wiley.trans is all lowercase, the directory names need to be all lowercase, even though directory names in Windows and DOS are not case sensitive.

The necessary file structure can be created in two ways:

- You can manually create the directories and save your *.java files in the same folder as your *.class files. The *.java files can then be compiled in the usual manner, with the *.class being generated in the same directory as the *.java file.

- You can use the -d flag of the javac compiler, specifying an output directory where you want your bytecode to go. If the required package directory structure does not exist, the -d flag will create the directories and put the *.class file in the appropriate folder.

Both options have their advantages. The first option is convenient in terms of managing your source code on your hard drive, plus the files are in the required format for using the javadoc tool (discussed later in this chapter). The second option is convenient if you want to separate your bytecode from your source code, a common need in Java when deploying applications (because the bytecode is all that is needed).

Whichever method you choose, the process of creating the directories can be confusing and frustrating, especially when classes no longer can find each other; therefore, I want to go through an example so that you can see how the process works first hand. Open your text editor, and follow along with me through the following steps.

Step 1: Write and Save the Source Code for Vehicle

Begin by writing the following Vehicle class, declaring it in a package named com.wiley.trans. Type in the class, but do not save it yet.

```
package com.wiley.trans;
public class Vehicle
{
     public String make, model;
     public int year;
     public double purchasePrice;
     public Vehicle(String make, String model, int year)
     {
          System.out.println("Constructing Vehicle");
          this.make = make;
          this.model = model;
          this.year = year;
     }
     public double sellVehicle(double sellPrice)
     {
          System.out.println("Selling " + this.toString());
          return purchasePrice - sellPrice;
     }
     public String toString()
     {
          return year + " " + make + " " + model;
     }
}
```

Save the Vehicle.java file in a directory you create named c:\src (src is short for source code).

Step 2: Compile the Source Code Using the -d Flag

Before you compile Vehicle.java, create a folder on your hard drive named c:\my_bytecode.

 The -d flag allows you to specify an output directory for the bytecode; however, for the -d flag to work successfully, the output directory must already exist.

Open a DOS window and use the cd command to change directories into the c:\src directory you created in the previous step. To compile Vehicle.java, use the -d flag of javac, specifying the output directory as c:\my_bytecode. The command to enter follows.:

```
javac -d c:\my_bytecode Vehicle.java
```

Notice that the bytecode file Vehicle.class is not in the c:\src folder. To find the bytecode, look in your c:\my_bytecode folder. You should see a com directory, and in com a wiley directory, and in wiley a trans directory.

By the way, we are not done with this example. Vehicle.class is where it needs to be, but how does the compiler or JVM find it, especially because we put it in an arbitrary folder named c:\my_bytecode? The compiler and JVM need to know about c:\my_bytecode, and they find it by checking the CLASS-PATH environment variable, discussed next.

Suppose that we write a class called CarDealer that uses our Vehicle class in the com.wiley.trans package. No matter what package we put CarDealer in, the compiler is going to have to find Vehicle.class before CarDealer compiles.

The compiler knows that Vehicle is in the com.wiley.trans package, because we are going to import that package. The compiler therefore knows to look for a directory structure \com\wiley\trans; however, and this is an important point in Java that tends to cause much frustration, the compiler does not know to look in the c:\my_bytecode folder. That directory was arbitrarily named, and in fact, \com\wiley\trans could easily be somewhere else on our hard drive or out on a network file system somewhere.

The Java compiler and JVM look for bytecode located in directories found in the CLASSPATH environment variable. With the CLASSPATH environment variable, the bytecode can be in arbitrary directories. In our Vehicle example, because we put the bytecode in the c:\my_bytecode directory, we need to add this directory to our CLASSPATH.

 Why have we not had to use CLASSPATH until now? Because in all of the examples and labs up until now, all of the bytecode needed has been in the same folder, and if no CLASSPATH environment variable is found, the compiler and JVM look in the current directory.

The best way to see how CLASSPATH works is hands on, so let's finish our example with the Vehicle class that we started earlier. Continue with the following steps.

Step 3: Write the CarDealer Class

The following CarDealer class is a program that uses the Vehicle class. CarDealer is in a different package, so the import statement is used to import the Vehicle class. Type in the CarDealer class, and save it in the c:\src directory with Vehicle.java.

```
package com.wiley.programs;
import com.wiley.trans.Vehicle;
public class CarDealer
```

```
{
     public static void main(String [] args)
     {
          Vehicle porsche = new Vehicle("Porsche", "911", 2003);
          porsche.purchasePrice = 45000.00;
          System.out.println(porsche);
     }
}
```

Step 4: Set the CLASSPATH

Try to compile the CarDealer class using the -d flag:

```
javac -d c:\my_bytecode CarDealer.java
```

You should get a compiler error stating that the com.wiley.trans package cannot be found and also that the Vehicle symbol cannot be resolved, similar to the compiler errors in Figure 7.1.

The compiler cannot find the com.wiley.trans package because the compiler does not know to look in c:\my_bytecode. The CLASSPATH environment variable needs to be set.

 CLASSPATH contains all the directories and JAR files where the necessary bytecode can be found. A collection of bytecode files can be compressed into a single file known as a Java Archive (JAR). If the bytecode you need is in a JAR file, the JAR file needs to appear in the CLASSPATH environment variable.

The easiest way to set the CLASSPATH variable is to use the set command, as shown in Figure 7.2. Keep in mind that setting CLASSPATH in this manner only sets it for that particular command prompt window.

 The DOS command echo is used to see the current definition of an environment variable, as demonstrated in Figure 7.2.

```
Command Prompt                                    _ □ ×
C:\src>javac -d c:\my_bytecode CarDealer.java
CarDealer.java:3: package com.wiley.trans does not exi
st
import com.wiley.trans.Vehicle;
                      ^
CarDealer.java:9: cannot resolve symbol
symbol  : class Vehicle
location: class com.wiley.programs.CarDealer
                      Vehicle porsche = new Vehicle("Porsche
", "911", 2003);
```

Figure 7.1 CarDealer will not compile until the CLASSPATH is set.

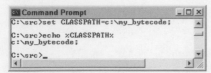

Figure 7.2 The DOS command set is used to define an environment variable.

Step 5: Compile and Run the CarDealer Program

After your CLASSPATH is set, try to compile the CarDealer class again. Be sure to use the -d flag, as follows:

```
javac -d c:\my_bytecode CarDealer.java
```

♦ Setting the CLASSPATH Environment Variable

There are several ways to set environment variables, depending on your operating system. If you are using a version of Windows that is Windows NT/2000/XP, then CLASSPATH can be set in the Control Panel.

Open your Control Panel, and open the System icon. (Windows XP users need to click Performance and Maintenance first.) You will see either the Environment or Environment Variables tab. XP users need to click the Advanced tab and then click the Environment Variables button. In either case, you should see the Environment Variables dialog window.

Click the New button for User Variables, or Edit if you already have a CLASSPATH environment variable defined, and define your CLASSPATH. The window will look similar to Figure 7.3.

Figure 7.3 Setting the CLASSPATH using the Environment Variables dialog window.

Click the OK button when you are finished. The settings will not take place in command prompts that are currently open, but will take effect in all subsequent command prompts.

Be aware that setting the CLASSPATH in the Control Panel sets it for all command prompt windows that you open. We might not want to set our CLASSPATH in the Control Panel to only include c:\my_bytecode because we only want this directory in our CLASSPATH for our Vehicle example. Notice that I included a . in the CLASSPATH. The dot (.) represents the current directory.

There are many situations where you want folders and JAR files in your CLASSPATH all the time. In these cases, set the CLASSPATH in the Control Panel so you do not have to set it every time you open a command prompt.

It should work fine this time. (If not, make sure that your CLASSPATH is set correctly.) Notice the -d flag created the directory \programs in the \com\ wiley directory, then output the CarDealer.class file there.

Now that both the Vehicle and CarDealer classes are compiled, try running the CarDealer program by entering the command:

```
java CarDealer
```

You should get the following error message:

```
Exception in thread "main" java.lang.NoClassDefFoundError: CarDealer
```

The JVM cannot find the CarDealer class. The reason is not a CLASSPATH problem because we set the CLASSPATH environment variable to include c:\my_bytecode, which is the correct directory. The reason the CarDealer class cannot be found is that we are using the wrong name.

The CarDealer class is in the com.wiley.programs package, so the name of the class is com.wiley.programs.CarDealer. Try entering the command:

```
java com.wiley.programs.CarDealer
```

Figure 7.4 shows the output of running the CarDealer program. Notice that you can run the CarDealer from any directory of the command prompt because the JVM is not looking in the current directory but the CLASSPATH.

Do not include any part of the package directory structure in your CLASSPATH. For example, the compiler and JVM will not be able to find Vehicle or CarDealer if your CLASSPATH is set to:

```
set CLASSPATH=c:\my_bytecode\com\wiley;
```

There are no situations where CLASSPATH should contain package directories. It should only contain the directories where the package directories can be found. If you are having a problem with classes not being found, it is likely a CLASSPATH problem. Be sure to check your CLASSPATH carefully for any mistakes or typos.

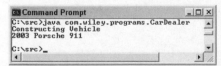

Figure 7.4 Run the CarDealer program by using its fully qualified name.

I want to point out that this directory structure for packages absolutely must be used. There is no shortcut or simple technique to bypass it. The bytecode for a class in a package must appear in a directory structure that matches the package name.

The Access Specifiers

Every member of a class (that is, the fields, methods, and constructors) has an *access specifier* that determines who has access to the member. Access specifiers allow the design of your programs to take into account who should be accessing the various attributes and behaviors of an object.

For example, you might want to add a method to your class that performs repetitive tasks and that is only invoked by the other methods in the class. You can declare this method private, thereby hiding the method from anyone outside the class.

Similarly, you might have a method that needs to be available to any other objects. Then you should declare this method as public, which allows universal access to members.

Java provides four levels of access for members of a class:

Public access.   Granted using the public keyword, public access is often referred to as universal access because public members are accessible to any other object.

Private access.   Granted using the private keyword, private is the most restrictive of the four access specifiers. A private member cannot be accessed outside of the class.

Protected access.   Granted using the protected keyword, a protected member is accessible to any other class in the same package and also child classes, no matter which package the child class is in.

Default access.   Also referred to as package access, you grant default access by not using any of the other three access specifiers. (There is no keyword used to grant the default access.) A member with default access is accessible to any other classes in the same package.

 Notice that protected and default are similar because they grant access to other classes in the same package. Protected is actually less restricted than the default because protected also grants access to child classes that may be outside of the package.

Let's look at an example that demonstrates how the access specifier of a member controls access to the members of an object. The InventoryItem class defined in the following code is in the products package. Review the class and determine its fields, methods, and constructors, and their corresponding access.

```java
package products;
public class InventoryItem
{
    private long partNumber;
    public String description;
    public InventoryItem(long n, String d)
    {
        partNumber = n;
        description = d;
    }
    protected InventoryItem()
    {
        partNumber = 0;
        description = "N/A";
    }
    long getPartNumber()
    {
        return partNumber;
    }
}
```

The DVDPlayer class in the following extends InventoryItem, but is in a different package. DVDPlayer can therefore only access the public and protected members of InventoryItem, and does not have access to the private or default members.

```java
package electronics;
import products.InventoryItem;
public class DVDPlayer extends InventoryItem
{
    public String make, model;
    private double retailPrice;
    public DVDPlayer(String make, String model, long partNumber)
    {
        super(partNumber, "DVD player");
        this.make = make;
        this.model = model;
    }
    public DVDPlayer(String make, String model)
    {
        super();
```

```
            this.make = make;
            this.model = model;
            //partNumber = 11223344L;        //Does not compile
        }
        private void setRetailPrice(double p)
        {
            //System.out.println(getPartNumber());    //Does not compile
            retailPrice = p;
        }
    }
```

In the DVDPlayer class, the commented-out statement that follows does not compile because partNumber is private in the parent. A DVDPlayer object gets a field named partNumber of type long in memory, but the DVDPlayer class does not have access to partNumber because it is private. The only place part-Number can be accessed is within the InventoryItem class.

```
partNumber = 11223344L;
```

Similarly, the attempt to invoke getPartNumber() fails in the statement:

```
System.out.println(getPartNumber());
```

The getPartNumber() method has default access and is only accessible from classes in the products package. The DVDPlayer class is in the electronics package and therefore cannot invoke getPartNumber().

The InventoryItem class has a protected constructor. Only classes in the products package or that subclass InventoryItem can access this constructor. The child class DVDPlayer invokes the protected constructor in InventoryItem with the statement:

```
super();
```

This is allowed because DVDPlayer is a child of InventoryItem. In the following AccessDemo program, an attempt is made to use the protected Inventory Item constructor with the statement:

```
InventoryItem x = new InventoryItem();
```

This statement in AccessDemo does not compile because the AccessDemo class is not a subclass of InventoryItem, nor is it in the products package.

The AccessDemo program attempts to instantiate and use objects of type InventoryItem and DVDPlayer. The AccessDemo class is in a different package than both classes and does not extend either class; therefore, AccessDemo only has access to the public members of both classes.

The AccessDemo class does not compile, and generates seven compiler errors, all access violations. Study the AccessDemo program carefully and see if you can spot all seven errors. Figure 7.5 shows the output when an attempt is made to compile AccessDemo.

```java
package programs;
import electronics.*;
import products.*;
public class AccessDemo
{
    public static void main(String [] args)
    {
        InventoryItem x = new InventoryItem();
        InventoryItem y = new InventoryItem(5005678L, "cell phone");
        y.partNumber = -1;
        System.out.println(y.getPartNumber());
        DVDPlayer z = new DVDPlayer("Acme", "2000DV", 11223344L);
        z.setRetailPrice(199.99);
        z.retailPrice = 199.99;
        DVDPlayer w = new DVDPlayer("Acme", "1000DV");
        System.out.println(w.getPartNumber());
        System.out.println(w.partNumber);
    }
}
```

AccessDemo is compiled in Figure 7.5 using the -d flag, which is needed since AccessDemo is in a package (named programs). The dot (.) following -d represents the current directory. This means that a program's directory will be created as a subdirectory of whatever directory the AccessDemo.java file is in.

Attempting to access the partNumber field or invoke the getPartNumber() method accounts for four of the compiler errors in AccessDemo. Neither the field nor the method is public, so they cannot be accessed from within Access-Demo.

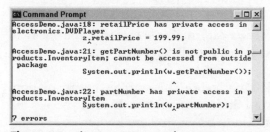

Figure 7.5 The AccessDemo class generates seven compiler errors.

Two of the compiler errors stem from the retailPrice field and the setRetailPrice() method of DVDPlayer, both of which are private. Neither of the following two statements compiles:

```
z.setRetailPrice(199.99);
z.retailPrice = 199.99;
```

A DVDPlayer object has a field named retailPrice and a method setRetailPrice(), but making them private hides them in the class, not allowing access to them by any other class.

There seems to be a design flaw with DVDPlayer; the DVDPlayer class does not change retailPrice from its initial value of zero, and no one else can change or view the retailPrice field. Making a field private and hiding it in the class is a common OOP practice known as encapsulation (discussed in the next section), and has many positive side effects. Encapsulation, however, typically involves adding public methods that allow the field to be viewed or changed, something our DVDPlayer class does not contain.

 A class can also have an access specifier. The only two access specifiers that can be used for a class are public and the default. Every class we have seen up until now has been declared. A public class can be used by any other class. A class with the default access can only be used by other classes in the same package.

Encapsulation

Encapsulation is the technique of making the fields in a class private and providing access to the fields via public methods. If a field is declared private, it cannot be accessed by anyone outside the class, thereby hiding the fields within the class. For this reason, encapsulation is also referred to as data hiding.

 Encapsulation is one of the four fundamental OOP concepts. The other three are inheritance, polymorphism, and abstraction.

The SalesPerson class in the following code demonstrates encapsulation. Each of its fields is marked private, and there are public methods to access the fields. The get methods that allow a field to be viewed are known as accessor methods. The set methods that allow a field to be changed are known as mutator methods.

Naming the accessor and mutator methods with the get and set convention is not only widely used, but is highly recommended by the Java naming convention. Other Java technologies such as JavaBeans and Enterprise JavaBeans rely on the set and get notation for accessor and mutator methods.

```java
public class SalesPerson
{
    private String name;
    private int id;
    private double commissionRate;
    private double sales;
    public SalesPerson(String name, int id, double commissionRate)
    {
        setName(name);
        this.id = id;
        setCommissionRate(commissionRate);
    }
    public void setName(String n)
    {
        name = n;
    }
    public String getName()
    {
        return name;
    }
    public void setCommissionRate(double newRate)
    {
        if(newRate >= 0.0 && newRate <= 0.20)
        {
            commissionRate = newRate;
        }
        else
        {
            System.out.println("Rate must be between 0 and 20%");
        }
    }
    public double getCommissionRate()
    {
        return commissionRate;
    }
    public int getId()
    {
        return id;
    }
    public void addToSales(double s)
    {
        sales += s;
```

```
    }
    public double computeCommission()
    {
        double commission = 0.0;
        if(sales > 0.0)
        {
            commission = sales * commissionRate;
        }
        sales = 0.0;      //Start over
        return commission;
    }
}
```

Here are a few points I want to make about the SalesPerson class:

- All of the fields are private, which is commonly done even if the accessor and mutator methods of a field do not do anything special. For example, setName() and getName() simply change and return the name field, respectively.

- The id field only has a corresponding accessor method, but no mutator method. In other words, you can get the contents of the id field, but it cannot be changed. This makes id a read-only field. A field can also be made write-only by including only a set method.

- The only way to change commissionRate is to invoke setCommission-Rate(), and this method only changes the field when the value passed in is between 0 and 20 percent.

- The constructor invoked the set methods for the name and commission-Rate fields, even though the constructor can access these fields directly. The advantage of a constructor using the accessor methods is that the logic for assigning a value to a field is centralized in one location and does not need to be repeated. For example, if the constructor did not invoke setCommissionRate(), the constructor would have needed to check the rate passed in to ensure that it was in the proper range of 0 to 20 percent. But setCommissionRate() already contains this logic.

- The sales field has neither a set nor a get method; however, the field is still an important part of the class because it keeps track of the amount of sales for the salesperson.

Benefits of Encapsulation

There are many benefits of encapsulation, including:

- The fields of a class can be made read-only or write-only, as was done with the id field in the SalesPerson class. There is no way to change the id field of a SalesPerson object after the object has been instantiated.

- A class can have total control over what is stored in its fields. The Sales-Person class demonstrates this with the commissionRate field, which can only be a value between 0.0 and 0.20.

- The users of a class do not know how the class stores its data. A class can change the data type of a field, and users of the class do not need to change any of their code.

Let me demonstrate that last benefit of encapsulation with the SalesPerson class. Notice that the commissionRate field is a double. Because it only can be a value between 0.0 and 0.20, there is no reason we couldn't have used a float; however, changing the data type of a field can have serious repercussions on any other class that relies on the commissionRate field.

 Because we used encapsulation, we can change the commissionRate field to a float, and no existing code elsewhere will be affected or need to be changed (or even recompiled, for that matter). The users of the SalesPerson class did not know that the commissionRate was stored as a double because the field is hidden in the class.

The only thing the users of SalesPerson know is that setCommissionRate() takes in a double and getCommissionRate() returns a double. As long as we leave the signatures of these two methods alone, existing code that invokes these methods does not need to be modified.

The following code shows a modified SalesPerson class with the commission-Rate changed from a double to a float. Notice that we did not change the signatures of any of the methods. The only changes made were within the setCommissionRate() method with the statement:

```
commissionRate = (float) newRate;
```

The cast operator was added to cast the incoming double to a float because the commissionRate field is now a float.

```
public class SalesPerson
{
            private float commissionRate;       //Changed to a float
public void setCommissionRate(double newRate)
    {
```

```
            if(newRate >= 0.0 && newRate <= 0.20)
            {
                commissionRate = (float) newRate;
            }
            else
            {
                System.out.println("Rate must be between 0 and 20%");
            }
        }
        //Remainder of the SalesPerson class stays the same
    }
```

Understanding Static Members

I have repeatedly mentioned that Java is strictly an object-oriented programming language and that all code must appear within a class; however, there are situations where it would be nice if a field or method did not have to be associated with instances of a class. Sometimes a global-type field or method is needed or would perhaps result in a better design.

The static keyword allows a field or method to not be associated with any particular instance of a class. Instead, the field or method can be thought of as global, and any other class can access the field or invoke the method without requiring an instance of the class.

 The important point to remember about static is that static members are associated with the class, not particular instances of the class. In fact, a static field or method can be accessed without any instances of the class existing.

A static member of a class is often referred to as a *class member* because static members are associated with the class and not with individual instances of the class. Fields and methods that are not static are often referred to as *instance members* because nonstatic fields and methods only exist within instances of the class.

We have used static many times because it is a required attribute of the main() method, as seen in the following ConstructorDemo program.

```
public class ConstructorDemo
{
    public static void main(String [] args)
    {
        System.out.println("Constructing a big screen TV");
        BigScreenTV tv = new BigScreenTV();
        System.out.println("Done constructing TV");
    }
}
```

To run this program, you enter the following command:

```
java ConstructorDemo
```

The ConstructorDemo class has no fields and one method. At no point in time did we instantiate a ConstructorDemo object. So how can the JVM invoke a method in a class if no instances of the class exist? Remember, a class is only a definition. Fields and methods do not exist until the class is instantiated.

Well, actually, that last sentence is only partly true. To be more accurate, the *nonstatic* fields and methods of a class do not exist until the class is instantiated. However, static members are associated with the class. Static fields and methods are allocated in memory and can be used once the class is loaded by the JVM. (Class loading takes place throughout a program's execution as classes are needed by the JVM.)

Because main() is static in ConstructorDemo, main() can be invoked without requiring a new ConstructorDemo object to be instantiated. The question now becomes: If we don't need an instance of a class to invoke a static method or access a static field, what is the syntax for accessing a static member? The answer is to use the name of the class, which is discussed next.

Accessing Static Fields and Methods

Static fields and methods are not accessed using a reference because references refer to instances of the class, and we do not need instances of the class to access static members. Instead, the name of the class is used to access a static member.

For example, if you wanted to invoke main() in the ConstructorDemo class, you would use the syntax:

```
ConstructorDemo.main(null);     //Or replace null with an array of String's
```

Of course, main() is not a method we typically invoke because the JVM does that for us. Notice that if the JVM wants to invoke main(), the JVM needs the name of the class. But we give the JVM the name of the class when we run the program:

```
java ConstructorDemo
```

And now you know why the java command requires the name of the class that contains main().

We have used static fields and methods in the examples and labs. You can tell when a field or method is static whenever you see it being accessed with a class name. For example, throughout the book we have used:

```
System.out
```

Because System is a class, we can assume (correctly) that out is a static field in the System class. The out field represents the standard output, and you do not need to instantiate a System object to access this field.

Let's look at an example that demonstrates writing and accessing static fields and methods. The following Employee class contains a static field, a counter, and a static method, getCounter().

```
public class Employee
{
    private String name;
    private String address;
    private int SSN;
    private int number;
    public static int counter;
    public Employee(String name, String address, int SSN)
    {
        System.out.println("Constructing an Employee");
        this.name = name;
        this.address = address;
        this.SSN = SSN;
        this.number = ++counter;
    }
    public void mailCheck()
    {
        System.out.println("Mailing a check to " + name
            + ", number " + number);
    }
    public static int getCounter()
    {
        System.out.println("Inside getCounter");
        return counter;
    }
}
```

 Notice that the Employee constructor accesses counter without using the class name prefix, assigning it to the number field. The methods in a class can access the static fields in the same class without using the class name; therefore, in the Employee class, we can simply use counter instead of Employee.counter.

The following StaticDemo program accesses the counter field and get-Counter() method of Employee. Because these members are static, you use the Employee class name when referring to them. For example, to access the counter field, use:

```
Employee.counter
```

To invoke the getCounter() method, use the syntax:

```
Employee.getCounter()
```

Study the StaticDemo and try to determine its output, which is shown in Figure 7.6.

```
public class StaticDemo
{
    public static void main(String [] args)
    {
        Employee.counter = 100;
        System.out.println("Counter = " + Employee.getCounter());
        Employee e = new Employee("John Wayne",
                "101 Hollywood Blvd.", 123456789);
        System.out.println("Counter now = " + Employee.getCounter());

        System.out.println("Using e: " + e.getCounter());
    }
}
```

The first statement within main() of the StaticDemo class is:

```
Employee.counter = 100;
```

Notice that there are no Employee objects in memory yet. We can only access counter because it is static and the counter field was created in memory when the Employee class was loaded (which would be right away when the program begins executing). The counter field is 100, which is printed out with the statement:

```
System.out.println("Counter = " + Employee.getCounter());
```

Again, we used the class name to invoke getCounter(), which exists in memory even though no Employee objects have been instantiated yet.

Figure 7.6 Output of the StaticDemo program.

Notice you can access a static field using a reference to an instance of that particular class. For example, you can access the counter and getCounter() fields using any Employee reference, as demonstrated by the method call:

```
e.getCounter()
```

in the StaticDemo program. Although it is valid, I would discourage using a reference instead of the preferred syntax of using the class name. Using a class name makes it clear that the field or method is static.

◆ Static Methods Cannot Access Instance Members

What happens if an instance field or method is accessed from within a static method? For example, the getCounter() method in the following Employee class attempts to set the name field to "Rich."

```
public class Employee
{
    private String name;
    private String address;
    private int SSN;
    private int number;
    public static int counter;
    public Employee(String name, String address, int SSN)
    {
        System.out.println("Constructing an Employee");
        this.name = name;
        this.address = address;
        this.SSN = SSN;
        this.number = ++counter;
    }
    public static int getCounter()
    {
        System.out.println("Inside getCounter");
        name = "Rich";       //does not compile!
        return counter;
    }
}
```

I want to make a couple of important observations about the getCounter() method's setting name to "Rich." The getCounter() method is static, so the method does not belong to any particular instance of Employee. In fact, we can invoke getCounter() with zero Employee objects in memory. If there are no Employee objects in memory, there are no name fields in memory; therefore, in this case, it does not make sense to set name equal to "Rich" because there are no name fields anywhere.

Similarly, what happens if there are 100 Employee objects in memory? There are 100 name fields in memory. Which name am I setting equal to "Rich?" All of them? That would be an interesting company to work for. Again, it does not make sense to set name equal to "Rich" because it is not clear which name is being changed.

For these reasons, static methods cannot access nonstatic fields or methods. It does not make any sense, as we can see with trying to change the name field to "Rich." Also, accessing a nonstatic member requires the this reference. Static methods do not have a this reference.

Therefore, static methods cannot access nonstatic fields. The statement:

```
name = "Rich";
```

does not compile in the static getCounter() method. The compiler generates the following error:

```
Employee.java:26: non-static variable name cannot be
referenced from a static context
                name = "Rich";
                ^
1 error
```

This compiler error would have occurred whether or not the this reference was explicitly used to access name.

Static Initializers

The static keyword has another use outside of declaring a field or method static. A Java class can contain a static initializer, which is a group of statements that execute when the class is being loaded by the class loader of the JVM.

Classes are loaded once by the class loader, and the purpose of a static initializer is to allow the class to perform any necessary setup tasks that would only need to occur once.

A static initializer is declared by using the static keyword followed by a set of curly brackets to enclose the statements of the initializer:

```
static {
    //Statements appear here.
}
```

The following Radio class contains a static initializer.

```
public class Radio
{
    private int station;
    public Radio(int x)
    {
        System.out.println("Constructing a Radio");
```

```
            station = x;
        }
        static {
            System.out.println("Inside static initializer");

        }
    }
```

The following StaticInitDemo program instantiates a Radio object. Study the program and try to determine the output. Pay particular attention to when the static initializer executes. The output is shown in Figure 7.7.

```
public class StaticInitDemo
{
    public static void main(String [] args)
    {
        System.out.println("Inside main");
        Radio r1 = new Radio(1380);
        Radio r2 = new Radio(850);
    }
}
```

 The only purpose I have seen for static initializers occurs when a Java program is using the Java Native Interface (JNI) to invoke a native function (typically written in C or C++). For the Java program to be able to invoke a native function, the function needs to appear in a function library, which needs to be loaded exactly once.

We will not be discussing JNI, nor will we ever have a reason to use static initializers in this book. I just wanted you to be aware that static initializers exist, in case you run into one someday or find a need to use one in a class.

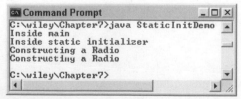

Figure 7.7 The output of the StaticInitDemo program.

Instance Initializers

An instance initializer is similar to a static initializer, except that an instance initializer executes each time an object of the class is instantiated. The difference between an instance initializer and a constructor is that an instance initializer executes before the constructor is invoked.

An instance initializer is simply a block of code within curly braces that appears in a class. For example, the CDPlayer class in the following contains an instance initializer. Notice that no keyword is used and no name is given to the instance initializer.

```java
public class Electronics
{
    public Electronics()
    {
        System.out.println("Constructing an Electronics");
    }
}
public class CDPlayer extends Electronics
{
    private int songNumber;

    public CDPlayer(int x)
    {
        super();
        System.out.println("Constructing a CDPlayer");
        songNumber = x;
    }
    {
        System.out.println("Inside instance initializer");
    }
}
```

The instance initializer in the CDPlayer is the following block of code:

```java
{
    System.out.println("Inside instance initializer");
}
```

The statements in an instance initializer execute after any parent class constructors are invoked, but before the child class constructor executes. When an object is instantiated and the class contains an instance initializer, the following events occur in the order shown:

1. The appropriate constructor in the child class is invoked.

2. A call to super() is made, and the flow of control jumps to the appropriate parent class constructor.

3. When the parent class constructor completes, the flow of control jumps back to the child class constructor.

4. Before any statements that follow super() within this child constructor execute, the instance initializer executes.

5. Finally, the statements in the child class constructor following the call to super() execute.

The following InstanceInitDemo program demonstrates this series of events by instantiating two CDPlayer objects. Study the program carefully and try to determine the output, which is shown in Figure 7.8.

```
public class InstanceInitDemo
{
    public static void main(String [] args)
    {
        System.out.println("Inside main");
        CDPlayer c1 = new CDPlayer(1);
        CDPlayer c2 = new CDPlayer(7);
    }
}
```

As with static initializers, I wanted to discuss instance initializers just in case you run into one someday or a situation comes up where you need to use one. You will not see or use them everyday, since in almost all situations a constructor or other method in the class can accomplish the same result without needing an instance initializer.

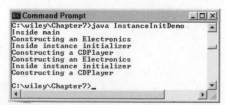

Figure 7.8   The output of the InstanceInitDemo program.

Lab 7.1: Working with Packages

The purpose of this lab is to become familiar with writing, compiling, and running Java classes that appear in packages.

1. After completing Lab 6.2, you had written four classes: Polygon, Triangle, RightTriangle, and a class with main() in it that you executed to test the other three classes. Copy and paste the four source code files (the *.java files) for these four classes into a directory named c:\src (or similar folder).

2. Add the Polygon, Triangle, and RightTriangle classes to the geometry .shapes package, and compile these classes using the -d flag. The output directory can be any folder you choose, or you can use the c:\my_bytecode folder from the example in this chapter.

3. Add the fourth class (the program you wrote) in a package named geometry.programs. Compile this class using the -d flag.

4. Set your classpath to include the directory where the compiler output the bytecode.

5. Run the program again.

The output of running your program will be the same. However, you now need to include the package name when running the program from the DOS prompt, and you should be able to run the program from any directory at the DOS prompt.

Lab 7.2: Using Encapsulation

In this lab you will write a class that takes advantage of the benefits of encapsulation.

1. Declare a class named Television. Add two fields: channel and volume. Declare both fields as private.

2. Add accessor and mutator methods for both fields. The valid values for volume are 0 to 10, so disregard any attempts to set the volume to a value outside that range. Similarly, the channel field should only be set to a value between 2 and 999.

3. Add a constructor to Television that takes in two ints, one for channel and one for volume. Be sure to invoke the mutator methods instead of having the constructor assign the parameters to the fields.

4. Save and compile the Television class.

5. Write a class named WatchTelevision that contains main(). The first command-line argument will be the volume, and the second one will be the channel. Use the Integer.parseInt() method to parse these values into ints.

6. Instantiate a Television using the two command-line arguments; then print out the channel and volume using the accessor methods of Television.

7. Try to change the volume or channel to an invalid value.

8. Save, compile, and run the WatchTelevision class.

Run the program several times with different values for the volume and channel. You should not be able to set the volume outside of the range 0 to 10 nor set the channel outside the range 2 to 999.

Lab 7.3: Using static Methods

The purpose of this lab is to become familiar with writing and using static methods.

1. Begin by declaring a class named FormatTest. This class is going to be used to verify that data fits a certain format.

2. Add a static field of type int named maxStringLength. Also add a static field of type double named minSize.

3. Add a static method named testStringLength() that has a String parameter and returns a boolean. This method should return true if the string passed in is less than or equal to the maxStringLength field; otherwise, the method should return false.

4. Add a static method named testDouble() that has a double parameter and returns a boolean. It should return true if the double parameter is greater than or equal to the minSize field; otherwise, it should return false.

5. Save and compile the FormatTest class.

6. Write a class named TestProgram that contains main(). The first command-line argument (args[0]) is going to be the String to be tested, and the second command-line argument (args[1]) is going to be the double to be tested. Use the Double.parseDouble() method to parse the second command-line argument into a double.

7. Within main(), assign the maxStringLength field of FormatTest to 12 and the minSize field to 100.00.

8. Invoke the testStringLength() and testDouble() methods, passing in the corresponding command-line argument. Display the result.

9. Save, compile, and run the TestProgram class several times, making sure that everything is working correctly.

If you enter a String for args[0] that is longer than 12 characters, the result of testStringLength() should be false. If args[1] is a double that is smaller than 100.00, the result of testDouble() should be false.

Summary

- Every class belongs to a package. The package keyword is used to declare a class within a package, and the package declaration must be the first statement in a .java source file. If a class is not declared within a package, then the class appears in the default package.

- A package creates a namespace. The package name becomes a part of the class name.

- The import keyword is used to import a package into a source file. Importing a package allows you to use a class from that package without prefixing the package name to the class name. The java.lang package is implicitly imported into each source file.

- The .class file for a class must appear in a directory structure that matches the package name that the class is declared in. You can use the -d flag of the javac tool to have the compiler generate these folders for you automatically.

- The compiler and JVM use the CLASSPATH environment variable to determine where to look for bytecode.

- There are four levels of access in Java that can be applied to the fields and methods of a class: public, protected, private, and default.

- Hiding the fields in a class by making them private is referred to as encapsulation.

- A static field or method is not associated with each instance of the class. Instead, there is only a single instance of the field or method, and it is shared among all instances of the class and also the other classes in your program.

- A static initializer is executed when a class is loaded. An instance initializer is executed right when a class is instantiated and is invoked right before the constructor is invoked.

Review Questions

1. What are the two basic purposes of packages?

2. If you do not declare a class in a package, the class is in the _____ package.

Use the following A and B class definitions to answer the ensuing five questions:

```java
//filename A.java
package a;
public class A
{
    private int x;
    public int y;
    protected int z;
    double d;

    public A()
    {
    }
}
//filename B.java
package b;
import a.A;
public class B extends A
{
    private byte s;
    public byte t;
    public B()
    {
    }
}
```

3. Which variables are accessible within the constructor of the B class?

4. Suppose that a class, C, is declared in a package named c. Which variables in A and B will C have access to?

5. In what directory does A.class need to appear? In what directory does B.class need to appear?

6. What are the fully qualified names of the A and B classes?

7. Suppose that A.class is in a directory named c:\code\review\a\. What directory should appear in the CLASSPATH environment variable so that the A class can be found in the classpath?

8. What package never needs to be explicitly imported?

9. Hiding the fields of a class by making them private is referred to as _____.

10. True or False: If a class has a static field, the field cannot be accessed until at least one instance of the class is created in memory.

Answers to Review Questions

1. Packages allow you to organize your classes that share a common theme or are closely associated with each other. Packages also create a namespace for the classes within the package.

2. The default package.

3. The fields of B, along with the public and protected fields of A, so the answer is y, z, s, and t.

4. C will only have access to the public fields of A and B, so C will only have access to the fields y and t.

5. The directory names must match the package names. A.class must be in a folder named \a, and B.class must be in a folder named \b.

6. The fully qualified names include the package name, so the answer is a.A and b.B.

7. The folder that represents the package name should not appear in the CLASSPATH environment variable, so the answer is c:code\review.

8. java.lang is implicitly imported into each source file.

9. encapsulation.

10. False because no instance of a class is needed.

CHAPTER

8

Polymorphism and Abstraction

Two important effects that stem from inheritance in object-oriented programming (OOP) are polymorphism—where an object can take on many forms—and abstraction—allowing for the creation of abstract classes. This chapter discusses both of these OOP concepts in detail and how they are implemented in Java.

An Overview of Polymorphism

When we discussed inheritance, I explained how the *is a* relationship is used to determine if your inheritance is a good design. The *is a* relationship is also helpful when learning polymorphism. Polymorphism is the term used to describe how an object can take on many forms. An object takes on many forms because an object can be treated as a child type, a parent type, a grandparent type, and so on up the hierarchy tree.

 The term *polymorphism* is a combination of *poly*, meaning many or multiple, and *morph*, meaning shapes or forms. Polymorphism in OOP refers to the ability of an object to have many forms, which is a direct result of inheritance.

213

Suppose, for example, that a Salary class extends an Employee class. We discussed in Chapter 6, "Understanding Inheritance," how this was a good design because a salaried employee is an employee. From the point of view of polymorphism, a Salary object is an Employee object. This means a Salary object can be treated as an Employee object.

A child object being treated as a parent class type has the following benefits:

- Using a parent class reference to a child object.

- Using polymorphic parameters and return values.

- Creating heterogeneous collections of objects, where not all objects in the collection are of the same type.

We will now discuss each of these benefits of polymorphism in detail.

Using Parent Class References to Child Objects

A child object can be referenced using a parent class reference. This is the most fundamental use of polymorphism because using a parent class reference to refer to a child object is what allows you to take advantage of the benefits of polymorphism.

To demonstrate polymorphism in action, I will use the following Employee and Salary classes, which represent classes used to pay employees of a company. (I am going to use this employee example throughout this chapter.)

Notice in Listing 8.1 that the Employee class has three fields: name, address, and number; one constructor; a mailCheck() method; the toString() method; and various accessor methods. There are no fields in the Employee class used to represent the employee's pay because we decided in Chapter 6 that this data should appear in the child classes.

```
public class Employee
{
    private String name;
    private String address;
    private int number;

    public Employee(String name, String address, int number)
    {
        System.out.println("Constructing an Employee");
        this.name = name;
        this.address = address;
        this.number = number;
```

Listing 8.1   The Employee class extends Object implicitly.

```
        }

    public void mailCheck()
    {
        System.out.println("Mailing a check to " + this.name
+ " " + this.address);
    }

    public String toString()
    {
        return name + " " + address + " " + number;
    }

    public String getName()
    {
        return name;
    }

    public String getAddress()
    {
        return address;
    }

    public void setAddress(String newAddress)
    {
        address = newAddress;
    }

    public int getNumber()
    {
        return number;
    }
}
```

Listing 8.1   *(continued)*

The Salary class, shown in Listing 8.2, has one field named salary to represent the annual pay of an employee. The Salary class also has one constructor, a computePay() method, and various accessor and mutator methods. The idea behind this design is that not every Employee has a salary, so adding a salary field in the Employee class would cause issues later; therefore, the child classes of Employee will contain the fields and methods needed to compute the employee's pay. Later in this chapter, we will define the Hourly class that also extends Employee, and it will have fields for an hourly wage and number of hours worked, as well as a computePay() method.

```
public class Salary extends Employee
{
    private double salary;      //Annual salary

    public Salary(String name, String address, int number,
                double salary)
    {
        super(name, address, number);
        setSalary(salary);
    }

    public double getSalary()
    {
        return salary;
    }

    public void setSalary(double newSalary)
    {
        if(newSalary >= 0.0)
        {
            salary = newSalary;
        }
    }

    public double computePay()
    {
        System.out.println("Computing salary pay for " + getName());
        return salary/52;
    }
}
```

Listing 8.2 The Salary class extends the Employee class.

Now, let's look at a couple of statements that might be familiar to you. Suppose that we instantiated an Employee object as follows:

```
Employee e = new Employee("George W. Bush", "Houston, TX", 43);
```

The previous statement creates two entities in memory: the Employee reference e, and the Employee object to which the e gets assigned. The reference is of type Employee, and so is the object it refers to.

Similarly, the following statement is valid:

```
Salary s = new Salary("George Washington", "Valley Forge, DE", 1, 5000.00);
```

In this statement, s is a Salary reference, and it is assigned to a new Salary object. Both the reference and the object are of type Salary.

Now, take a look at a new type of statement that at first glance might not seem valid:

```
Employee p = new Salary("Rich Raposa", "Rapid City, SD", 47, 250000.00);
```

The left side of the equation creates a reference p of type Employee. The right side of the equation is a new Salary object. Can you assign an Employee reference to point to a Salary object? Are they compatible data types?

The answer to both questions is yes. The *is a* relationship carries over to polymorphism. The right side of the equation is a Salary object. A Salary object is an Employee object. Can p refer to an Employee object? Certainly. In fact, p can refer to an Employee object, and because a Salary object is an Employee object, p can refer to a Salary object as well.

 An Employee reference can refer to any Employee object. Because a Salary object is an Employee object, an Employee reference can be used to refer to a Salary object. This is an example of a parent class reference referring to a child class object.

Classroom Q & A

Q: Why use an Employee reference to refer to a Salary object? Why not just use a Salary reference?

A: There are situations where using a parent class reference can make your code easier to write and easier to maintain. You can think of an Employee reference as a more generic reference than a Salary reference. Suppose that we have Hourly and Salary classes that both extend Employee. I can then reference each employee's object as either a Salary or Hourly, using a Salary or an Hourly reference. Or I can treat each employee's object as an Employee, and use an Employee reference to refer to any employee, no matter what data type the employee actually is.

Q: OK, but what do you gain from doing this?

A: By treating Hourly and Salary objects as type Employee, I can store them in the same data structure (an example of a heterogeneous collection). I can also write a method that has an Employee parameter, which allows both Salary and Hourly objects to be passed in to that method (an example of polymorphic parameters).

Q: If you treat a Salary object as an Employee, don't you lose the Salary part of the object?

A: No. The object does not change, just the data type of the reference to it. This is an important point to understand. If I instantiate a Salary object, I get a Salary object, no matter what data type its reference is.

Q: So why not always use a parent class reference if it doesn't change anything?

A: Well, be careful. I said the *object* does not change, but *how it is viewed* does change. If I use an Employee reference to a Salary object, the object does not lose any data, but I lose the ability to access those fields and methods from the Salary class using the parent class reference.

Q: You can never access them? Then you have lost something.

A: No, you can still access them, but you have to cast the Employee reference to a Salary reference. Let's discuss the casting process first. I will then show you examples where using a parent class reference to a child object is advantageous.

Casting References

We saw in Chapter 2, "Java Fundamentals," that the cast operator can be used to cast primitive data types. For example, suppose that you have a double that you want to store in a float. Even if the double fits easily in the float, the compiler still requires you to use the cast operator:

```
double pi = 3.14159;
float a = pi;              //Does not compile!
float b = (float) pi;      //Works fine
```

You might think the compiler should be smart enough to realize that 3.14159 fits into a float, so no casting is necessary; however, it is important to realize that the compiler only knows data types. When you assign a 64-bit double to a 32-bit float, the compiler only sees a larger piece of data being stored in a smaller piece. Because data could be lost, the cast operator tells the compiler you know what you are doing, and any loss of data is acceptable.

 By the way, casting a float to a double is acceptable because they are compatible data types. You cannot cast a String to a float, a boolean to an int, an Employee to a char, and so on, because these data types are not compatible.

I want to relate the casting of references to the casting of primitive data types. Using the Employee and Salary classes in Listings 8.1 and 8.2, suppose we instantiate two Salary objects as follows:

```
Salary s = new Salary("George Washington",
            "Valley Forge, DE", 1, 5000.00);
Employee e = new Salary("Rich Raposa", "Rapid City, SD", 47, 250000.00);
```

I want to emphasize that these two statements create *two* Salary objects; each object consumes the same amount of memory and has the same methods and fields allocated in memory. The only difference between these two objects is the particular data stored in their respective fields.

Because s is a Salary reference, we can use s to invoke the accessible fields and methods of both the Salary and Employee class. For example, the following statements are valid:

```
s.setSalary(100000.00);    //A Salary method
s.computePay();            //A Salary method
s.mailCheck();             //An Employee method
```

 When going up the inheritance hierarchy, no casting is needed. For example, a Salary reference can be used to invoke an Employee method without casting because Employee is a parent of Salary. Going down the hierarchy, however, requires an appropriate cast, as we will see next.

Because e is an Employee reference, we can use e to only invoke the accessible methods of the Employee class. For example, we can use e to invoke mailCheck(), but we cannot use e to invoke setSalary() or computePay():

```
e.setSalary(500000.00);    //Does not compile!
e.computePay();            //Does not compile!
e.mailCheck();             //An Employee method, so this compiles
```

The Salary object referenced by e has a setSalary() and a mailCheck() method; however, the compiler thinks e refers to an Employee, and attempting to invoke setSalary() or mailCheck() generates a compiler error. We need to use the cast operator on e, casting e to a Salary reference, before the Salary methods can be invoked using e. The following statements demonstrate two techniques for casting e to a Salary reference:

```
((Salary) e).computePay();
Salary f = (Salary) e;
f.computePay();
```

In the first statement, e is cast to a Salary reference, but the resulting Salary reference is not preserved. Notice that an extra set of parentheses is required because of the order of operations. We want the cast to occur before the method call. In the second statement, e is cast to a newly declared Salary reference f, and f is subsequently used to invoke computePay(). This technique is more convenient if you need to invoke more than one method after casting.

The CastDemo program shown in Listing 8.3 demonstrates polymorphism and casting references down the hierarchy tree. Study the program and try to determine the output, which is shown in Figure 8.1.

```java
public class CastDemo
{
    public static void main(String [] args)
    {
        Salary s = new Salary("George Washington", "Valley Forge, DE",
 1, 5000.00);
        System.out.println(s.getName() + " " + s.computePay());

        Employee e = new Salary("Rich Raposa", "Rapid City, SD",
47, 250000.00);
        System.out.println(e.getName());

        //e.computePay();       //Does not compile!
        Salary f = (Salary) e;
        System.out.println(f.getName() + " " + f.computePay());

        s.mailCheck();
        e.mailCheck();
        f.mailCheck();
    }
}
```

Listing 8.3   The CastDemo program casts an Employee reference to a Salary reference.

The Salary object in CastDemo for George Washington is referenced by a Salary reference, so we can invoke methods like getName() and computePay() with s. The Salary object for Rich Raposa is referenced by an Employee reference, so we can only invoke the Employee class methods like getName() using e; however, when e is cast to a Salary reference:

```java
Salary f = (Salary) e;
```

we can now use f to invoke any method in Salary or Employee.

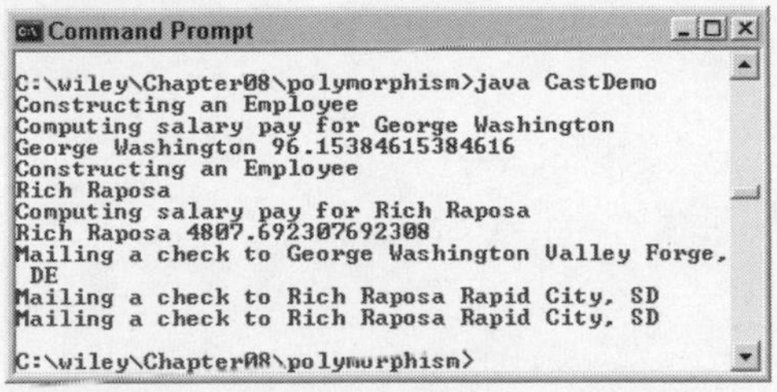

Figure 8.1 The output of the CastDemo program.

note **In the CastDemo program, there are two references to the Rich Raposa object: e and f. We can use either reference to access the object. With e, only the Employee methods can be invoked. With f, we can invoke methods from either Salary or Employee. Invoking mailCheck() with both references, as in:**

```
e.mailCheck();
f.mailCheck();
```

simply invokes the method twice on the same object, since e and f point to the same Salary object. Notice in Figure 8.1 that the output from invoking mailCheck() with e or f is identical.

The instanceof Keyword

In the CastDemo program in Listing 8.3, an Employee reference was cast to a Salary reference. The cast was successful because the object being cast was actually a Salary object. If we had attempted to cast the object to something that it wasn't, however, an exception would have occurred.

Let me demonstrate this with a specific example. The Salary class extends Employee. Suppose that in Listing 8.4, the class named Hourly also extended Employee.

```
public class Hourly extends Employee
{
    private double hourlyRate, hoursWorked;

    public Hourly(String name, String address, int number,
                double hourlyRate)
    {
```

Listing 8.4 The Hourly class extends the Employee class. *(continued)*

```
            super(name, address, number);
            setHourlyRate(hourlyRate);
    }

    public double getHourlyRate()
    {
        return hourlyRate;
    }

    public void setHourlyRate(double newRate)
    {
        if(newRate >= 0.0 && newRate <= 200.00)
        {
            hourlyRate = newRate;
        }
    }

    public double getHoursWorked()
    {
        return hoursWorked;
    }

    public void setHoursWorked(double h)
    {
        if(h >= 0 && h <= 80)
        {
            hoursWorked = h;
        }
    }

    public double computePay()
    {
        System.out.println("Computing hourly pay for " + getName());
        if(hoursWorked <= 40)
        {
            return hourlyRate * hoursWorked;
        }
        else
        {
            return hourlyRate * 40.0
+ hourlyRate * 1.5 * (hoursWorked - 40);
        }
    }
}
```

Listing 8.4   *(continued)*

The following valid statements instantiate an Hourly object, referring to it with an Employee reference. The reference is cast to Hourly to invoke the methods of the Hourly class.

```
Employee h = new Hourly("Abe Lincoln", "Springfield, IL", 16, 8.00);
((Hourly) h).setHoursWorked(40);
((Hourly) h).computePay();
h.mailCheck();
```

However, suppose I tried to cast the Hourly object to a Salary object:

```
Salary s = (Salary) h;        //This compiles OK!
s.computePay();               //Which computePay() gets invoked?
```

Keep in mind that the compiler thinks h is an Employee, and casting an Employee to a Salary is a compatible cast. This statement compiles, but there is a problem looming. At run time, when h is cast to an Hourly object, a Class-CastException will occur and the program will terminate. Java is very strict about data types, and casting an Hourly object to type Salary is not valid because the two types are not compatible.

 By the way, invoking computePay() with s also compiles. Notice, too, in the comment, that I asked "Which computePay() method gets invoked?" More specifically, is it the computePay() in Hourly or the one in Salary? The answer is neither because the cast one line above causes an exception, and any ensuing statements will not execute.

What if you are not sure of the actual data type of h? Because h is of type Employee, h can refer to an Employee object, a Salary object, or an Hourly object. The instanceof keyword can be used to determine the data type of a reference. The syntax for using instanceof looks like:

```
reference instanceof ClassName
```

The instanceof operator returns true if the reference is of the given class type, and false otherwise. For example, before casting h to a Salary object, we should have made the following check:

```
if(h instanceof Salary)
{
    Salary s = (Salary) h;
    s.computePay();
    //And so on
}
```

The cast above occurs only when h actually refers to a Salary object, so we are guaranteed to avoid a ClassCastException when using the instanceof operator in this manner.

ClassCastException is the type of exception that occurs from poorly written code. You should always use the instanceof operator to check the data type of a reference before casting the reference, thereby averting any chance of a ClassCastException.

The following InstanceOfDemo program in Listing 8.5 demonstrates the instanceof operator. Study the program carefully and try to determine the output, which is shown in Figure 8.2.

```java
public class InstanceOfDemo
{
    public static void main(String [] args)
    {
        Employee h = new Hourly("Abe Lincoln", "Springfield, IL",
16, 8.00);
        System.out.println(h.getName() + " " + h.getNumber());

        if(h instanceof Salary)
        {
            System.out.println("Casting to a Salary reference");
            Salary x = (Salary) h;
            System.out.println("Pay = " + x.computePay());
            x.mailCheck();
        }
        else if(h instanceof Hourly)
        {
            System.out.println("Casting to an Hourly reference");
            Hourly x = (Hourly) h;
            x.setHoursWorked(80);
            System.out.println("Pay = " + x.computePay());
            x.mailCheck();
        }

        System.out.println("\nDeliberately cast to the wrong type");
        Salary s = (Salary) h;
        s.computePay();
        s.mailCheck();
        System.out.println("End of main");
    }
}
```

Listing 8.5 The InstanceOfDemo program uses instanceof to verify the data type of a reference before casting.

```
Command Prompt                                    _ □ ×

C:\wiley\Chapter08\polymorphism>java InstanceOfDemo
Constructing an Employee
Abe Lincoln 16
Casting to an Hourly reference
Computing hourly pay for Abe Lincoln
Pay = 800.0
Mailing a check to Abe Lincoln Springfield, IL

Deliberately cast to the wrong type
Exception in thread "main" java.lang.ClassCastExcept
ion
        at InstanceOfDemo.main(InstanceOfDemo.java:2
5)

C:\wiley\Chapter08\polymorphism>_
```

Figure 8.2 The output of the InstanceOfDemo program.

note

Notice in the output of the InstanceOfDemo program in Figure 8.2 that the statement "End of main" is not displayed. A ClassCastException occurs at the statement:

```
Salary s = (Salary) h;
```

This exception causes main() to stop executing, and your program terminates. Therefore, the last three statements in main() do not execute. The flow of control when an exception occurs is discussed in detail in Chapter 11, "Exception Handling."

Polymorphic Parameters

Now that we have discussed parent class references and the instanceof keyword, I want to show you a benefit of polymorphism known as polymorphic parameters. When a method has a parameter that is a reference, any object that is compatible with that reference can be passed in, allowing a method to accept parameters of different data types.

For example, suppose that a method has an Employee parameter:

```
public void payEmployee(Employee e)
```

An Employee object needs to be passed in to the payEmployee() method. If Salary and Hourly extend Employee, a Salary or Hourly object could also be passed in to payEmployee() because through polymorphism a Salary or Hourly object is also an Employee object.

note

Having an Employee parameter makes payEmployee() a more generic method in that its parameter is loosely defined. Presently, it can accept Employee, Hourly, and Salary objects. If a new class came along that extended Employee, say a class named Contractor, Contractor objects could also be passed in to payEmployee().

The Boss class in Listing 8.6 contains a payEmployee() method with an Employee parameter. The method casts the parameter to its appropriate data type and invokes computePay().

```
public class Boss
{
    public void payEmployee(Employee e)
    {
        double pay = 0.0;

        if(e instanceof Salary)
        {
            pay = ((Salary) e).computePay();
        }
        else if(e instanceof Hourly)
        {
            pay = ((Hourly) e).computePay();
        }

        System.out.println("Pay = " + pay);
        e.mailCheck();
    }
}
```

Listing 8.6 The Boss class demonstrates polymorphic parameters.

The payEmployee() method in the Boss class cannot simply invoke com-putePay() on the parameter e because the parameter is an Employee type, and the Employee class does not contain a computePay() method. To invoke com-putePay(), the reference e must be cast to its appropriate data type, which is determined by using the instanceof keyword. Notice that the mailCheck() method can be invoked without casting because mailCheck() is in the Employee class and e is an Employee reference.

The payEmployee() method can be invoked passing in any Employee object. If a new Contractor class is written that extends Employee, Contractor objects can be passed into the existing payEmployee() method without changing the method's signature.

Unfortunately, we would have to modify the body of payEmployee() and add an instanceof check for Contractor, which is not good design. In the upcoming *Taking Advantage of Virtual Methods* section, I will show you a payEmployee() method that can pay all Employee objects without requiring modification when new child classes of Employee come along.

The PayDemo program in Listing 8.7 instantiates one Hourly object, two Salary objects, and one Employee object, and passes them to the payEmployee() method. Study the program and try to determine its output.

```
public class PayDemo
{
    public static void main(String [] args)
    {
        Boss boss = new Boss();

        Hourly h = new Hourly("Abe Lincoln", "Springfield, IL",
16, 8.00);
        Salary s = new Salary("George Washington", "Valley Forge, DE",
1, 5000.00);
        Employee x = new Salary("Rich Raposa", "Rapid City, SD",
47, 250000.00);
        Employee y = new Employee("George W.", "Houston, TX", 43);

        System.out.println("** Paying Abe Lincoln **");
        boss.payEmployee(h);
        System.out.println("\n** Paying George Washington **");
        boss.payEmployee(s);
        System.out.println("\n** Paying Rich Raposa **");
        boss.payEmployee(x);
        System.out.println("\n** Paying George W. **");
        boss.payEmployee(y);
    }
}
```

Listing 8.7 The PayDemo program passes Employee objects to the payEmployee() method of a Boss.

In the PayDemo program, an Hourly reference h and a Salary reference s are passed in to the payEmployee() method. This is valid because the parameter is of type Employee and Salary and Hourly objects are Employee objects:

```
boss.payEmployee(h);
boss.payEmployee(s);
```

The reference x is of type Employee but refers to a Salary object. When this object is paid:

```
boss.payEmployee(x);
```

the instanceof statement in payEmployee() is true when compared to Salary, even though the reference is of type Employee, because x actually refers to a Salary object.

The last Employee object in PayDemo is neither a Salary nor Hourly employee, but simply an Employee object. It can certainly be passed in to payEmployee():

```
boss.payEmployee(y);
```

Notice, though, that the pay is 0.0 for this object, as shown in the output in Figure 8.3. In a real-world use, we likely would not allow any objects that were only of type Employee (and not one of the child class types) because there is no way to determine that employee's pay. I will make this observation again in the upcoming sections on abstraction.

 Because java.lang.Object is a parent of all classes, every object in Java can take on the form of type Object. There are many instances in the Java API where Object is used as either a parameter or return value of a method. For example, the following method signature is found in the java.util.Vector class:

```
public Object elementAt(int index)
```

Because this method declares a return value of type Object, it can return any type of object it wants; all objects in Java are of type Object. Similarly, if a method has an Object parameter, any type of object can be passed in to that parameter. For example, the java.util.Hashtable class contains the method:

```
public boolean contains(Object value)
```

Any reference of any data type can be passed in to this method. In fact, the only variables that cannot be passed in to the contains() method are the eight primitive data types. (See the following sidebar titled *The Wrapper Classes*.)

```
Command Prompt                                    _ □ ×
C:\wiley\Chapter08\polymorphism>java PayDemo
Constructing an Employee
Constructing an Employee
Constructing an Employee
Constructing an Employee
** Paying Abe Lincoln **
Computing hourly pay for Abe Lincoln
Pay = 0.0
Mailing a check to Abe Lincoln Springfield, IL

** Paying George Washington **
Computing salary pay for George Washington
Pay = 96.15384615384616
Mailing a check to George Washington Valley Forge, DE

** Paying Rich Raposa **
Computing salary pay for Rich Raposa
Pay = 4807.692307692308
Mailing a check to Rich Raposa Rapid City, SD

** Paying George W. **
Pay = 0.0
Mailing a check to George W. Houston, TX

C:\wiley\Chapter08\polymorphism>
```

Figure 8.3 The output of the PayDemo program.

♦ The Wrapper Classes

There are situations in Java programming where you want a primitive data type to take on the form of java.lang.Object. The developers of Java realized this and created what is referred to as the wrapper classes. There are eight wrapper classes, one for each of the eight primitive data types. We use the term *wrapper* because their main purpose is to wrap a primitive data type into a Java object.

For example, the java.lang.Integer class is used to wrap an int. The Integer class has two constructors:

```
public Integer(int value)
public Integer(String value) throws NumberFormatException
```

(Note that the String parameter is parsed into an int.) Whichever constructor you use, the int value is stored as a field in the class and is retrieved using the method:

```
public int intValue()
```

Why create an object to store a simple 32-bit int? Because the wrapper class Integer is just that—a class. It therefore extends Object, and can be used in any situation where an Object is required.

Wrapper classes are commonly used with the Java Collections Framework, a set of classes that represent commonly used data structures such as sets, trees, and hash tables. (Collections are discussed in detail in Chapter 9, "Collections.") These data structures only store objects of type Object, which is great when working with Java objects, but unfortunate when you want to use the data structures for storing primitive data types.

The solution is to wrap each primitive type in its corresponding wrapper class. The wrapper classes are found in the java.lang package, and include:

Byte

Short

Integer

Long

Float

Double

Character

Boolean

Each wrapper class has constructors similar to the two in Integer, and each class has methods for retrieving the primitive type from the wrapper object. View the J2SE documentation to view the constructors and methods of each class.

Heterogeneous Collections

A common use of polymorphism is to create a collection of data that is not all the same type, but has a common parent. A collection of different objects is referred to as a *heterogeneous collection*.

For example, suppose that we wanted to use an array to keep track of the employees of a company. When creating an array, all the data in the array must be of the same type. Because there are two types of employees, we could create an array for Salary objects and a second array for Hourly objects.

Because Salary and Hourly objects are Employee objects, however, we can create a single array for Employee objects that can contain both Salary and Hourly objects. This is an example of a heterogeneous collection because the elements in the array will not all be the same. They will all be Employee objects, but some will be Salary objects and some will be Hourly objects. While Salary and Hourly have a common parent, they are different objects.

 Chapter 9 discusses arrays and other data structures used for containing large amounts of data. In that chapter, I will show you how to create an array of Employee objects and fill it with different Object types.

The data structures in the Java Collections Framework, such as Vector and Hashtable, store java.lang.Object types. These collections can be quite heterogeneous because you can store Employee objects alongside Radio objects alongside Vehicle objects alongside anything because every object is of type Object.

Virtual Methods

In this section, I will show you how the behavior of overridden methods in Java allows you to take advantage of polymorphism when designing your classes. In Chapter 6, "Understanding Inheritance," we discussed method overriding, where a child class can override a method in its parent. An overridden method is essentially hidden in the parent class, and is not invoked unless the child class uses the super keyword within the overriding method.

For example, suppose that we modify the Salary class in Listing 8.8, and override the mailCheck() method from the Employee class.

```
public class Salary extends Employee
{
    private double salary;      //Annual salary

    public Salary(String name, String address, int number, double
salary)
        {
```

Listing 8.8   This Salary class overrides the mailCheck() method of Employee.

```
            super(name, address, number);
            setSalary(salary);
      }

      public void mailCheck()
      {
            System.out.println("Within mailCheck of Salary class");
            System.out.println("Mailing check to " + getName()
+ " with salary " + salary);
      }
      //The remainder of the class definition...
}
```

Listing 8.8 *(continued)*

The mailCheck() method in the Employee class displays a message containing the employee's name and address. The mailCheck() in Salary displays a message stating that execution is in Salary as well as the employee's name and salary. Try to determine the output of the following statements:

```
Salary s = new Salary("Thomas Jefferson", "Monticello, VA", 3, 2400.00);
s.mailCheck();
```

Because s refers to a Salary object, mailCheck() from the Salary class is invoked and the output is:

```
Within mailCheck of Salary class
Mailing check to Thomas Jefferson with salary 2600.0
```

Now, let me put a spin on this example. Suppose that I instantiate a Salary object and use an Employee reference to it, as I did in the VirtualDemo program in Listing 8.9. I want you to study this program carefully and try to determine its output. In particular, I want you to pay close attention to the statement:

```
e.mailCheck();
```

where e is an Employee reference referring to a Salary object.

```
public class VirtualDemo
{
      public static void main(String [] args)
      {
            Salary s = new Salary("Thomas Jefferson", "Monticello, VA",
                                3, 2600.00);
```

Listing 8.9 The VirtualDemo program demonstrates virtual methods in Java. *(continued)*

```
            Employee e = new Salary("John Adams", "Boston, MA",
                                 2, 2400.00);

            System.out.println("** Call mailCheck using
                                          Salary reference **");
            s.mailCheck();
            System.out.println("\n** Call mailCheck using
                                          Employee reference **");
            e.mailCheck();
        }
    }
```

Listing 8.9   *(continued)*

The output of the VirtualDemo program is shown in Figure 8.4. The program instantiates two Salary objects—one using a Salary reference s, and the other using an Employee reference e.

We saw earlier that invoking mailCheck() with s causes mailCheck() to execute in the Salary class. In the following statement, the compiler sees mailCheck() in the Salary class at compile time, and the JVM invokes mailCheck() in the Salary class at run time:

```
s.mailCheck();
```

Invoking mailCheck() on e is quite different because e is an Employee reference. When the compiler sees the following statement, the compiler sees the mailCheck() method in the Employee class:

```
e.mailCheck();
```

Does this mean that mailCheck() in the Employee class is invoked at run time? No! Look closely at the output in Figure 8.4. At compile time, the compiler used mailCheck() in Employee to validate this statement. At run time, however, the JVM invokes mailCheck() in the Salary class.

 This behavior is referred to as *virtual method invocation*, and the methods are referred to as *virtual methods*. All methods in Java behave in this manner, whereby an overridden method is invoked at run time, no matter what data type the reference is that was used in the source code at compile time.

With virtual methods, the JVM must look down the inheritance hierarchy and determine if a method is overridden. If the method is overridden, the child method executes at run time, not the one in the parent that was invoked at compile time.

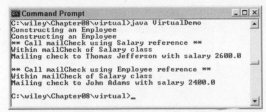

Figure 8.4   The output of the VirtualDemo program.

For example, when the statement executes in the VirtualDemo program, the JVM searches down the inheritance hierarchy and discovers that Salary overrides mailCheck() in Employee. The JVM then invokes mailCheck() on Salary, resulting in a virtual method invocation.

```
e.mailCheck();
```

In C++, virtual methods are not the default behavior of methods. In fact, you must use the C++ keyword virtual to "turn on" the behavior of virtual method invocation. The opposite is true in Java. All methods in Java are virtual by default (virtual is not a keyword in Java), and the only way to avoid this behavior of virtual methods is to declare a method final.

Final methods cannot be overridden, so the JVM does not need to worry about looking down the inheritance hierarchy and trying to determine if a child has overridden the method. For this reasons, final methods have a performance benefit because the overhead of virtual method invocation is avoided.

That being said, you should only declare a method as final if it is truly part of the design of your class.

Taking Advantage of Virtual Methods

Let's look at an example where virtual methods are used to simplify and improve the design of a Java application. In the Boss class discussed earlier, the payEmployee() method has an Employee parameter, allowing any type of Employee object to be passed in to the method. Within payEmployee(), we needed to know what type of Employee was passed in so we could cast the Employee parameter and invoke the appropriate computePay() method.

I like the Boss example because it demonstrates the instanceof keyword, an important operator in Java that is necessary at times; however, anytime I can avoid casting down the hierarchy tree, I will. It saves me from having to use instanceof, and it improves the maintenance of my code when I do have to worry about what type an object is.

Classroom Q & A

Q: In the Boss class, why did you cast the Employee parameter to either a Salary or Hourly reference?

A: I wanted to invoke computePay() on the parameter, but there are two computePay() methods: one in Salary, and one in Hourly. I had to cast the parameter to its appropriate type so I could explicitly invoke the proper computePay() method.

Q: But you just said all methods in Java are virtual by default. Why didn't the JVM at runtime figure out which computePay() method to invoke?

A: You cannot invoke computePay() with an Employee reference because there is no computePay() method in the Employee class. Plus, virtual methods only apply to overridden methods. The computePay() methods in Salary and Hourly are not overriding anything.

Q: Why don't we just put computePay() in the Employee class so that we can take advantage of virtual methods?

A: Good idea. In fact, we will do that next and see what happens. This points out a flaw in the design of our employee program. We started this example with the idea that our program would pay employees on a weekly basis. We quickly discovered that we had different types of employees, depending on how they were paid. Subclassing Employee is a good design because it allows us to write multiple computePay() methods, instead of a single, decision-filled computePay() method that has to determine which formula to use based on how the employee is paid. In the process of subclassing Employee, however, we removed computePay() from our Employee class entirely.

Q: That's because all the information to compute an employee's pay is in one of the child classes. Why put computePay() in the Employee class when the data it needs is down in a child class?

A: It's a design issue. I think we should put computePay() back in the Employee class because, from the outset, we wanted to be able to compute an employee's pay. Therefore, one of the behaviors of the Employee class should be computePay().

Q: What is the computePay() method in Employee going to do?

A: For now, we will add a computePay() method to Employee that returns 0.0, as seen in Listing 8.10, just so we can override it in Salary and Hourly and take advantage of virtual methods.

```
public class Employee
{
    private String name;
    private String address;
    private int number;

    public double computePay()
    {
        System.out.println("Inside Employee computePay");
        return 0.0;
    }

    public void mailCheck()
    {
        System.out.println("Mailing a check to " + this.name
+ " " + this.address);
    }
    //Remainder of class definition...
}
```

Listing 8.10 The Employee class with a computePay() method added.

With computePay() in the Employee class and also in the Salary and Hourly classes, the following statements now compile:

```
Employee e = new Salary("George Washington", "Valley Forge, DE",
                        1, 5000.00);
e.computePay();
```

More important than compiling, the previous statements behave in the manner that we want. The compiler sees computePay() in the Employee class, which simply returns 0.0. At run time, however, the JVM invokes computePay() in the Salary class because e references a Salary object.

The SmartBoss class in Listing 8.11 is a modification of the Boss class. The payEmployee() method in the SmartBoss takes advantage of virtual methods, and does not need to worry about casting or using the instanceof operator.

```
public class SmartBoss
{
    public void payEmployee(Employee e)
    {
        double pay = e.computePay();
        System.out.println("Just paid " + e.getName() + " $" + pay);
        e.mailCheck();
    }
}
```

Listing 8.11   The SmartBoss class takes advantage of virtual methods.

The payEmployee() method in the SmartBoss class simply invokes computePay() on the Employee reference passed in, and at no time does the SmartBoss know or care what type of Employee object was actually passed in. At run time, virtual method invocation occurs, and the appropriate computePay() method is invoked in one of the child classes of Employee.

 Notice that the SmartBoss also invokes mailCheck(), which appears in the Employee class. The Salary class overrides mailCheck(), so when the argument passed in is of type Salary, mailCheck() in Salary is invoked. The Hourly class does not override mailCheck(), so the mailCheck() method in Employee is invoked when an Hourly object is passed in to payEmployee().

The PayDemo2 program in Listing 8.12 instantiates and pays several employees. Study the program carefully, determine when virtual methods apply, and try to determine the output, which is shown in Figure 8.5.

```
public class PayDemo2
{
    public static void main(String [] args)
    {
        SmartBoss boss = new SmartBoss();

        Salary s = new Salary("Thomas Jefferson", "Monticello, VA",
3, 2600.00);
        Hourly h = new Hourly("John Adams", "Boston, MA", 2, 2.50);
        h.setHoursWorked(40);
        Employee e = new Employee("George W.", "Houston, TX", 43);

        System.out.println("** Paying Salary object **");
```

Listing 8.12   The PayDemo2 program pays employees using the SmartBoss.

```
            boss.payEmployee(s);

            System.out.println("\n** Paying Hourly object **");
            boss.payEmployee(h);

            System.out.println("\n** Paying Employee object **");
            boss.payEmployee(e);
        }
    }
```

Listing 8.12 *(continued)*

Within the PayDemo2 program, a Salary, Hourly, and Employee object are instantiated and passed in to the payEmployee() method of SmartBoss. (We can pass each type in to payEmployee() because it has an Employee parameter.) The payEmployee() method invokes computePay() which, by the nature of virtual methods, invokes computePay() in the appropriate child class. The same occurs when invoking mailCheck(), and the output is shown in Figure 8.5.

 warning **You should have a good reason to override a parent class method. Due to the behavior of virtual method invocation, which is the default behavior of all Java methods, overriding a method hides the parent class version of the method. In most cases, that is the desired result; however, if you just want to add to the tasks being performed in the parent method, be sure to invoke the parent method using the super keyword in the child method.**

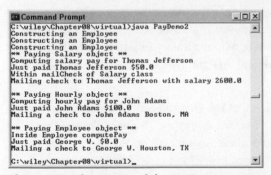

Figure 8.5 The output of the PayDemo2 program.

An Overview of Abstraction

Abstraction refers to the ability to make a class abstract in OOP. An abstract class is one that cannot be instantiated. All other functionality of the class still exists, and its fields, methods, and constructors are all accessed in the same manner. You just cannot create an instance of the class.

An abstract class might initially seem like an odd design. Why write a class and not allow anyone to create instances of it? In most situations, the design of the class is such that no one would want an instance of the class.

The Employee class is a perfect example of a class that really does not need to be instantiated from a design perspective. The PayDemo2 program created an Employee object, but notice that the employee did not have any information about how much it is paid, and its computePay() method simply returns 0.0. It is safe to say that no employee of our company would want to be strictly an Employee object (and not one of the child class types).

We can make it so that no one can instantiate an Employee object, by declaring the Employee class abstract. This has no effect on how the fields, methods, and constructors behave. The only result of making Employee abstract is that we can no longer create an instance of Employee. For example, the following new statement would not compile:

```
Employee e;          //This statement is OK.
e = new Employee("George W.", "Houston, TX", 43); //Compiler error!
```

You can still create Employee references, such as the reference e in the previous statements; however, you cannot use the new operator on Employee if the Employee class is declared abstract.

 If Employee is abstract, this does not affect the child classes Salary and Hourly. Assuming that Salary and Hourly are not abstract, you can create any number of instances of them. When a Salary object is instantiated, its Employee part is constructed, and an Employee constructor is invoked, just as before.

Similarly, the methods and fields of the Employee class behave the same and are accessed in the same manner as before. The only change that occurs by making the Employee class abstract is that we can no longer instantiate a new Employee object. Everything else about Employee remains the same.

If a class is abstract and cannot be instantiated, the class does not have much use unless it is subclassed. This is typically how abstract classes come about during the design phase. A parent class contains the common functionality of a collection of child classes, but the parent class itself is too abstract to be used on its own.

I like to use an example about mammals when discussing abstraction. If I asked you to draw me a picture of a mammal, you would likely draw a dog, horse, person, or something similar. If I asked you to draw a picture of something that was just a mammal, you can see how the concept of a mammal is abstract. Many animals are mammals, but no animal is *just* a mammal. It seems logical, therefore, that no one would need to instantiate an object of type Mammal (assuming that we wrote a Mammal class). Similarly, all of our employees in our company are of type Employee, but no one is *just* an Employee. It seems logical that no one would need to instantiate an object of type Employee, and it should be declared abstract.

Let's now look at how to declare a class abstract in Java.

Abstract Classes

Use the abstract keyword to declare a class abstract. The keyword appears in the class declaration somewhere before the class keyword. For example, the Employee class in Listing 8.13 is declared as abstract.

```java
public abstract class Employee
{
    private String name;
    private String address;
    private int number;

    public Employee(String name, String address, int number)
    {
        System.out.println("Constructing an Employee");
        this.name = name;
        this.address = address;
        this.number = number;
    }

    public double computePay()
    {
        System.out.println("Inside Employee computePay");
        return 0.0;
    }

    public void mailCheck()
    {
        System.out.println("Mailing a check to "
                            + this.name + " " + this.address);
    }

    public String toString()
```

Listing 8.13   The Employee class is declared abstract by using the abstract keyword.

```
        {
            return name + " " + address + " " + number;
        }

        public String getName()
        {
            return name;
        }

        public String getAddress()
        {
            return address;
        }

        public void setAddress(String newAddress)
        {
            address = newAddress;
        }

        public int getNumber()
        {
            return number;
        }
    }
```

Listing 8.13   *(continued)*

Notice that nothing else has changed in this Employee class. The class is now abstract, but it still has three fields, seven methods, and one constructor. We cannot instantiate a new Employee, but if we instantiate a new Salary object, the Salary object will inherit the three fields and seven methods from Employee. Similarly, an Hourly object will inherit the fields and methods as well.

The AbstractDemo program in Listing 8.14 contains one compiler error. See if you can find it, and try to determine the output of the program, assuming that the statement with the compiler error is omitted.

```
public class AbstractDemo
{
    public static void main(String [] args)
    {
        Employee s = new Salary("Thomas Jefferson", "Monticello, VA",
3, 2600.00);
        Employee h = new Hourly("John Adams", "Boston, MA", 2, 2.50);
```

Listing 8.14   The AbstractDemo program declares an Employee reference but cannot instantiate an Employee object.

```
        Employee e = new Employee("George W.", "Houston, TX", 43);

        System.out.println(s.getName() + "'s pay is $"
+ s.computePay());

        ((Hourly) h).setHoursWorked(50);
        System.out.println(h.getName() + "'s pay is $"
+ h.computePay());
    }
}
```

Listing 8.14   *(continued)*

The only problem with the AbstractDemo program is the statement:

```
Employee e = new Employee("George W.", "Houston, TX", 43);
```

This statement does not compile, and generates the following compiler error:

```
C:\wiley\Chapter8\abstract\AbstractDemo.java:7: Employee is abstract;
cannot be instantiated
              Employee e = new Employee("George W.", "Houston, TX", 43);
                           ^
1 error
```

If this statement is commented out, the program will compile and execute fine, and the output is shown in Figure 8.6.

Abstract Methods

The abstract Employee class still has one peculiarity that I want to fix, and that is the computePay() method that does not do anything except return 0.0. Don't get me wrong—I want the computePay() method in the Employee class. Having it there allowed us to take advantage of virtual method invocation in the SmartBoss class.

Figure 8.6   The output of the AbstractDemo program.

If you think about it, we really don't care what computePay() does in the Employee class because it will not ever be invoked. Our assumption is that child classes of Employee will override computePay(), so the implementation of computePay() is insignificant.

This is where abstract methods become useful. If you want a class to contain a particular method but you want the actual implementation of that method to be determined by child classes, you can declare the method in the parent class as abstract. Abstract methods consist of a method signature, but no method body.

Listing 8.15 shows the computePay() method declared abstract. Notice the method has no definition, and its signature is followed by a semicolon, not curly braces.

```
public abstract class Employee
{
    private String name;
    private String address;
    private int number;

    public abstract double computePay();

    //Remainder of class definition
}
```

Listing 8.15   The computePay() method is declared abstract and has no implementation in the Employee class.

Declaring a method as abstract has two results:

- The class must also be declared abstract. If a class contains an abstract method, the class must be abstract as well.

- Any child class must either override the abstract method or declare itself abstract.

From a design point of view, putting an abstract method in a parent class forces that particular behavior onto any child classes. A child class that inherits an abstract method must override it. If they do not, they must be abstract, and any of their children must override it. Eventually, a descendant class has to implement the abstract method; otherwise, you would have a hierarchy of abstract classes that cannot be instantiated.

Why make a method abstract then? Because forcing a behavior on other classes has its benefits. For example, suppose if computePay() is abstract in the Employee class, we can be guaranteed that any nonabstract child class of Employee will contain a computePay() method.

The Salary and Hourly classes already contain computePay(), so we can declare computePay() abstract in Employee without modifying Salary or Hourly. If we write a new class named Contractor that extends Employee, the Contractor must override computePay() or be declared abstract. If we want to instantiate Contractor objects, our only option is to override computePay(), as demonstrated by the following Contractor class in Listing 8.16.

```java
public class Contractor extends Employee
{
    private double dailyRate;
    private int daysWorked;

    public Contractor(String name, String address, int number,
double dailyRate)
    {
        super(name, address, number);
        setDailyRate(dailyRate);
    }

    public double computePay()
    {
        System.out.println("Computing contractor pay for "
+ getName());
        return dailyRate * daysWorked;
    }

    public void setDailyRate(double newRate)
    {
        if(newRate >= 0.0 && newRate <= 2000.00)
        {
            dailyRate = newRate;
        }
    }

    public double getDailyRate()
    {
        return dailyRate;
    }

    public void setDaysWorked(int daysWorked)
    {
        if(daysWorked >= 0)
        {
            this.daysWorked = daysWorked;
        }
    }
}
```

Listing 8.16 The Contractor extends Employee and overrides the abstract computePay() method.

♦ The Benefits of Using Abstract Classes and Methods

Declaring the Employee class as abstract has several important benefits in terms of the overall design of our program to pay employees. First, no Employee objects can be instantiated. This makes sense in our application because no employee of the company probably wants to be just an Employee object anyway. The Employee class does not contain any information about how that employee is paid.

In addition, if we used a heterogeneous collection of Employee references to manage the company's employees, every object in the data structure needs to be of type Employee. This is fine for Salary and Hourly employees because these two classes extend Employee. Suppose, however, that a new Contractor class is needed. If the Contractor objects want to appear in the company's data structure, they need to be of type Employee. This forces the Contractor class to extend the Employee class.

This leads to another benefit of abstraction, in which a method can be declared abstract. If Contractor extends Employee, Contractor must override the abstract computePay() method, thereby forcing the Contractor class to contain a computePay() method. That fits in perfectly with our design because we want the Contractor class to have a computePay() method anyway. Forcing behavior on a class is a typical and widely used OOP design. (Interfaces, discussed in Chapter 10, "Interfaces," are used extensively for this purpose.)

By using inheritance, abstraction, and polymorphism, the design of our employee program is now taking advantage of the fundamental benefits of OOP. If a new type of employee is needed, the class written to represent these new employees has to extend Employee if it wants to appear in the data structure. Because this new class must extend Employee, it must contain a computePay() method, which is what we wanted to accomplish in the first place with this program.

Most importantly, none of the existing classes are affected when a new type of employee comes along. When the Contractor class is added, the Employee class does not change; it is merely extended. The Salary and Hourly classes are not affected at all. The SmartBoss class that pays employees doesn't have to worry about new types of employees either because virtual methods are used, so the SmartBoss has no problem paying Contractor objects.

The PayEmployees class in Listing 8.17 uses the SmartBoss class to pay some Employee objects. What I want you to notice about this example is that the SmartBoss class discussed earlier does not need any modifications, even though the Employee class has since been made abstract and we added an entirely new class named Contractor.

Study the PayEmployees program, which compiles and executes successfully, and try to determine its output, which is shown in Figure 8.7.

```
public class PayEmployees
{
    public static void main(String [] args)
    {
        Salary s = new Salary("Thomas Jefferson", "Monticello, VA",
3, 2600.00);

        Hourly h = new Hourly("John Adams", "Boston, MA", 2, 2.50);
        h.setHoursWorked(40);

        Contractor c = new Contractor("M. Mouse", "Anaheim, CA",
44, 1000.00);
        c.setDaysWorked(5);

        SmartBoss boss = new SmartBoss();

        boss.payEmployee(s);
        boss.payEmployee(h);
        boss.payEmployee(c);
    }
}
```

Listing 8.17 The PayEmployees program instantiates and pays several types of employees.

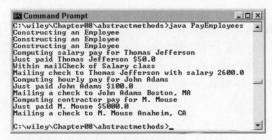

Figure 8.7 The output of the PayEmployees program.

Lab 8.1: Using Polymorphism

The purpose of this lab is to become familiar with using polymorphism in Java. You will use polymorphic parameters to write a class that can "draw" any shape, and use virtual method invocation so that the appropriate shape is drawn without requiring any casting of references.

1. Write a class called Shape that only contains a method named draw(), with no parameters and a void return value. The draw method should print out "Drawing a Shape".

2. Save and compile the Shape class.

3. Write a class named Rectangle that extends Shape. Add two int fields for the width and height of the rectangle, and add a constructor with two int parameters that are used to initialize these fields. Use encapsulation to ensure that the value of width and height are between 1 and 15.

4. In your Rectangle class, override the draw() method in Shape. Using nested for loops and asterisks (*), print out the rectangle using its proper width and height. For example, if width is 7 and height is 3, the draw() method should display:

    ```
    *******
    *     *
    *******
    ```

5. Save and compile the Rectangle class.

6. Write a class named RightTriangle that extends Shape. Add two int fields for the base and height of the triangle, and add a constructor with two int parameters that are used to initialize these fields. Use encapsulation to ensure that the value of base and height are between 1 and 20.

7. In your RightTriangle class, override the draw() method in Shape. Using nested for loops and asterisks, print out the triangle similarly to the way you printed out the Rectangle. For example, if the base is 8 and the height is 4, the output should look similar to:

    ```
    *
    ***
    *****
    *******
    ```

8. Save and compile the RightTriangle class.

9. Write a class named Artist that contains a method named drawShape(). The method has one parameter of type Shape and returns void. The drawShape() method should invoke the draw() method on whatever Shape object is passed in.

10. Save and compile the Artist class.

11. Write a class named ArtistDemo that contains main(). Within main(), instantiate a Shape, a Rectangle, and a RightTriangle object.

12. Within main(), also instantiate an Artist object. Using your Artist object, invoke drawShape() three times, once for each of the three shapes instantiated in the previous step.

13. Save, compile, and run the Artist class.

Lab 8.2: Abstract Classes

The purpose of this lab is to become familiar with writing abstract classes and methods. This lab is a continuation of the work you did in Lab 8.1.

1. Within your Shape class from the previous lab, remove the body of the draw() method, and declare the method abstract.

2. Save and compile your Shape class.

3. Write a class named Ladder that extends Shape. Add a field of type int to represent the number of rungs in the ladder, and add a constructor that initializes this field. Use encapsulation to ensure the number of rungs is between 1 and 10.

4. Your Ladder class needs to override draw(). Using asterisks, draw a ladder with the appropriate number of rungs. For example, a five-rung ladder should look similar to:

```
*************************
    *    *    *    *    *
    *    *    *    *    *
*************************
```

5. Save and compile the Ladder class.

6. Modify your ArtistDemo program so that it also instantiates and draws a Ladder object.

Summary

- Polymorphism is the ability of an object to take on many forms. The most common use of polymorphism in OOP occurs when a parent class reference is used to refer to a child class object.

- There are two key benefits to polymorphism: polymorphic parameters and heterogeneous collections.

- The instanceof keyword is used to determine if an object is an instance of a particular class.

- Methods in Java are virtual methods, meaning that an overridden method invoked at run time is dynamically invoked in the appropriate child class.

- Abstraction is the ability to write an abstract class. An abstract class is a class that cannot be instantiated. The abstract keyword is used to declare a class as abstract.

- The abstract keyword is also used to declare a method as abstract. An abstract method does not have any method body, and a class that contains an abstract method must be declared abstract as well. An abstract method must be overridden in any child classes, or the child class must also be abstract.

Review Questions

1. Where does the term polymorphism originate?
2. What is the only effect that the abstract keyword has on a class?
3. What are the two main effects of declaring a method abstract?

Use the following three class definitions to answer the remaining questions.

```java
//filename: Mammal.java
public abstract class Mammal
{
    public void breathe()
    {
        System.out.println("Mammal is breathing");
    }

    public abstract void nurse();
}


//filename: Cat.java
public class Cat extends Mammal
{
    public void breathe()
    {
        System.out.println("Cat is breathing");
    }

    public void nurse(int t)
    {
        System.out.println("Cat is nursing");
    }
}


//filename: Whale.java
public class Whale extends Mammal
{
    public void breathe()
    {
        System.out.println("Whale is breathing");
        super.breathe();
    }

    public void nurse()
    {
        System.out.println("Whale is nursing");
    }
}
```

4. The Whale class compiles fine, but the Cat class does not. Why not? What can be done to fix the problem?

5. Is the following statement valid?

```
Mammal m = new Whale();
```

6. What is the output of the following statements?

```
Whale w = new Whale();
w.breathe();
w.nurse();
Mammal m = w;
m.breathe();
m.nurse();
```

7. Using the statements in the previous question, is the expression *m instanceof Whale* true or false?

8. Similarly, is the expression *w instanceof Mammal* true or false?

9. What about the expression *m instanceof Cat*?

Answers to Review Questions

1. Poly means many, and morph means form. Polymorphism refers to the ability of an object to take on many forms.

2. A class declared abstract cannot be instantiated.

3. The class must also be declared abstract, and any child classes either must override the abstract method or declare themselves abstract as well.

4. The Cat class does not override the abstract nurse() method in Mammal. The Cat class contains a nurse() method, but it has a different parameter list than nurse() in Mammal. This is an example of method overloading, not method overriding. The Cat class can either be declared abstract or define a nurse() method that is public, void, and has no parameters, similar to the one in Mammal.

5. Yes. A Mammal reference can refer to a Whale object because a Whale *is a* Mammal.

6. Invoking breathe() and nurse() on a Whale object has the same result, whether the reference used is of type Whale (like w) or of type Mammal (like m). The output is:

```
Whale is breathing
Mammal is breathing
Whale is nursing
Whale is breathing
Mammal is breathing
Whale is nursing
```

7. True. m is a reference of type Mammal, but it is an instance of a Whale.

8. True. w refers to a Whale object. A Whale object *is a* Mammal object, so w is an instance of Mammal.

9. False. m refers to a Whale, and a Whale object is not a Cat object.

CHAPTER

9

Collections

A *collection* is an object that represents a group of objects. In this chapter, we will discuss the various types of collections in Java. I will begin with a discussion on arrays, including how to declare, instantiate, and access arrays. Then, I will discuss the *Java Collections Framework*, which is the term used to denote the various classes and interfaces in the J2SE that represent collections. Collections discussed in this chapter include vectors, hash tables, maps, and sets.

Arrays

An *array* is a collection of elements stored in a contiguous block of memory. Each element in an array must be the same data type, and they are distinguished by an index. The first element in the array is at index 0.

Creating an array involves two steps, as follows:

1. Declaring a reference for the array.

2. Instantiating the array using the new keyword and specifying the size of the array.

In Java, data is either a primitive data type or an object. Because arrays are not one of the eight primitive data types, they must be objects. Therefore, an array requires a reference to access it and the new keyword to instantiate it.

Use square brackets to declare an array reference. For example, the following statement declares a reference to an array of ints:

```
int [] sums;
```

 In Java, you can also declare an array with the square brackets following the variable name, instead of preceding it. For example, sums can be declared as follows:

```
int sums [];
```

This is for compatibility with C and C++. My preference is to place the square brackets before the variable name, because it makes the reference declaration clearer.

The sums reference can refer to any array of ints, no matter how many elements are in the array. Because sums is a reference, it can also be assigned to null.

The size of the array is determined when the array is instantiated. An int is placed in square brackets to specify the size. For example, the following statement assigns sums to a new array of 20 ints:

```
sums = new int[20];
```

Because an array must be in contiguous memory, its size cannot be changed after the memory is initially allocated. If the array of size 20 is deemed too small, a new larger array is instantiated and the old array is garbage collected. For example, the following statement assigns sums to a larger array of 30 ints:

```
sums = new int[30];
```

The array of 20 ints is garbage collected, assuming that it is no longer being referenced in your program. Assigning sums to an array of 20 ints and then to an array of 30 ints demonstrates how sums can refer to any size array of ints.

An array reference can be declared and the array object can be instantiated in the same statement. The following statement declares temps a reference to an array of doubles, and temps is assigned to a new array of 31 doubles in the same statement:

```
double [] temps = new double[31];
```

As with sums, temps can refer to any size array of doubles. Right now, it refers to an array of 31 doubles.

 Because an array object is instantiated using the new keyword, the memory is zeroed after it is allocated. Therefore, the initial values of the elements in the array will be their zero value (these values were found in Table 4.5). For example, the 31 doubles in the temps array are initially 0.0, and the 30 ints in the sums array are initially 0.

Accessing Arrays

The elements in an array are accessed by using a reference to the array and an index, an int value denoting which element in the array you want to access. The first element in the array is index 0, the second element is index 1, and so on.

For example, the following statements declare an array of 20 ints and place 1 in the first element, 2 in the second element, and 191 in the last element:

```
int [] sums = new int[20];
sums[0] = 1;
sums[1] = 2;
sums[19] = 191;
```

It takes 20 statements to assign the 20 ints in sums to a value, so for loops go hand in hand with arrays, as you might imagine. The following for loop assigns the values in sums to the sum of the first $n + 1$ numbers, where n is the index:

```
sums[0] = 1;
for(int i = 1; i < 20; i++)
{
     sums[i] = sums[i-1] + i;
}
```

The first element in sums is assigned to 1; the for loop initializes the remaining 19 elements.

The length Attribute

Suppose that the size of the sums array is 20 ints:

```
int [] sums = int[20];
```

The index of the last element in sums is 19. Using the index 20 is not valid, although the compiler will let you. Be careful because the following statement compiles:

```
sums[20] = 211;
```

However, at run time this statement causes an ArrayIndexOutOfBoundsException to occur. Java arrays are different from arrays in other languages in that Java arrays are objects. One benefit of this is that every array in Java has a *length attribute* that contains the size of the array.

By using the length attribute, you can greatly reduce the likelihood of inadvertently accessing elements beyond the end of an array. The following for loop prints out the elements in the sums array, using the length attribute as the upper limit of the loop control variable:

```
for(int i = 0; i < sums.length; i++)
{
    System.out.println("sums[" + i + "] = " + sums[i]);
}
```

 Notice that the Boolean expression in the for loop uses "less than" sums.length, as opposed to "less than or equal to" sums.length. Because sums is of size 20, the value of sums.length is 20. If we use less than or equal to, we would access sums[20] in the loop and cause an exception to occur. This is a common programming error.

Arrays of References

There are nine types of arrays in Java: There is an array type for each of the eight primitive data types, and there is an array type for arrays of references. The sums and temps array are examples of arrays of primitive data types. The other type of array is an array of references. You can declare an array of any reference type.

For example, the following statement declares a reference to an array of Employee references:

```
Employee [] myCompany;
```

The variable myCompany can refer to any array of Employee references. The following statement assigns myCompany to a new array of 500 Employee references:

```
myCompany = new Employee[500];
```

This array is 500 references of type Employee, each initialized to null.

 If you want 500 Employee objects, you need 500 new statements. The following statement uses new only once, and the object that is instantiated is the array. No Employee objects are instantiated.

```
new Employee[500]
```

The elements in myCompany are accessed just like any other array element: by using an index. The following statement assigns the 228th element to a new Employee object:

```
myCompany[227] = new Employee("George Washington", "Mount Vernon", 1);
```

To invoke a method on this Employee object, you use both the index and the dot operator. Assuming that the Employee class has a mailCheck() method, the following statement invokes it on the 228th element in the myCompany array:

```
myCompany[227].mailCheck();
```

To demonstrate using an array of references, we will create an array for a collection of Employee objects, using the following Employee class:

```
public class Employee
{
    public String name;
    public String address;
    public int number;

    public Employee(String name, String address, int number)
    {
        System.out.println("Constructing an Employee");
        this.name = name;
        this.address = address;
        this.number = number;
    }

    public void mailCheck()
    {
        System.out.println("Mailing a check to " + this.name
                            + " " + this.address);
    }
}
```

The following ArrayDemo program instantiates and uses several arrays. Study the program and try to determine its output:

```java
public class ArrayDemo
{
    public static void main(String [] args)
    {
        int [] sums;
        sums = new int[20];

        sums[0] = 1;
        for(int i = 1; i < 20; i++)
        {
            sums[i] = sums[i-1] + i;
        }

        for(int i = 0; i < sums.length; i++)
        {
            System.out.println("sums[" + i + "] = " + sums[i]);
        }

        System.out.println(sums.toString());

        double [] temps = new double[31];
        temps[0] = 85.0;
        temps[1] = 79.5;
        temps[2] = 76.0;

        Employee [] myCompany;
        myCompany = new Employee[500];
        myCompany[227] = new Employee("George Washington",
                                        "Mount Vernon", 1);
        myCompany[227].mailCheck();
        System.out.println("The length of myCompany is "
                                + myCompany.length);

        System.out.println(temps[31]);
    }
}
```

I want to make a few observations about the ArrayDemo program:

- Because arrays are objects, their class types extend java.lang.Object. This means that you can invoke any of the Object methods on arrays. In ArrayDemo, the toString() method is invoked on the sums array.

- The statement "Constructing an Employee" prints out only once, meaning that only one Employee object is created in memory.

- The final statement in main() accesses temps[31], which compiles but causes an ArrayIndexOutOfBoundsException, as shown in the output in Figure 9.1.

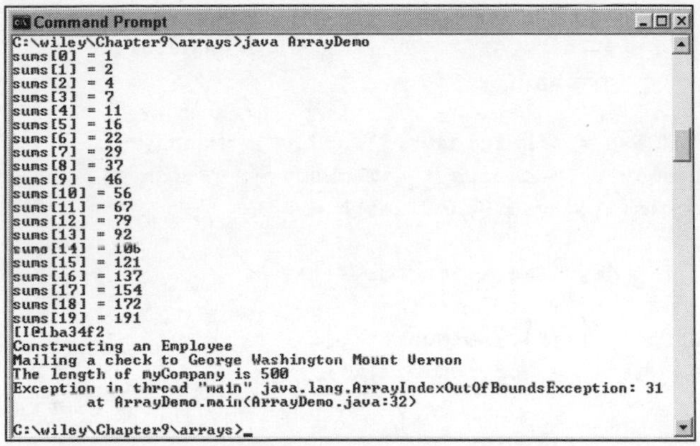

```
Command Prompt                                              _ □ ×
C:\wiley\Chapter9\arrays>java ArrayDemo
sums[0] = 1
sums[1] = 2
sums[2] = 4
sums[3] = 7
sums[4] = 11
sums[5] = 16
sums[6] = 22
sums[7] = 29
sums[8] = 37
sums[9] = 46
sums[10] = 56
sums[11] = 67
sums[12] = 79
sums[13] = 92
sums[14] = 106
sums[15] = 121
sums[16] = 137
sums[17] = 154
sums[18] = 172
sums[19] = 191
[I@1ba34f2
Constructing an Employee
Mailing a check to George Washington Mount Vernon
The length of myCompany is 500
Exception in thread "main" java.lang.ArrayIndexOutOfBoundsException: 31
        at ArrayDemo.main(ArrayDemo.java:32)

C:\wiley\Chapter9\arrays>_
```

Figure 9.1   Output of the ArrayDemo program.

Array Initializers

In Java, you can declare an array reference, instantiate an array, and fill the array with elements all in a single statement. This process, which is referred to as an *array initializer*, is useful when creating small arrays that contain predetermined data.

An array initializer creates an array without using the new keyword. The elements in the array are listed within curly braces, separated by commas. For example, the following array initializer creates an array of five ints:

```
int [] odds = {1, 3, 5, 7, 9};
```

The first element in the odds array is 1, the second element is 3, and so on. Note that a semicolon is required after the right curly brace.

The following ArrayInitDemo program demonstrates array initializers. Study the program and try to determine its output, which is shown in Figure 9.2.

```
public class ArrayInitDemo
{
    public static void main(String [] args)
    {
        int [] odds = {1, 3, 5, 7, 9};
        System.out.println("odds.length = " + odds.length);
        for(int i = 0; i < odds.length; i++)
```

```
        {
              System.out.println("odds[" + i + "] = " + odds[i]);
        }

        String [] daysOfWeek = {"Saturday", "Sunday", "Monday",
                   "Tuesday", "Wednesday", "Thursday", "Friday"};
        System.out.println("\ndaysOfWeek.length = " +
daysOfWeek.length);
        for(int i = 0; i < daysOfWeek.length; i++)
        {
              System.out.println("daysOfWeek[" + i + "] = "
                                  + daysOfWeek[i]);
        }

        Employee [] employees = {
                   new Employee("M. Mouse","Main St. USA", 1),
                   new Employee("D. Duck", "Lake Buena Vista", 2),
                   new Employee("W. Pooh", "100 Acre St.", 3)
                   };

        System.out.println("\nemployees.length = " +
employees.length);
        for(int i = 0; i < employees.length; i++)
        {
              employees[i].mailCheck();
        }
    }
}
```

note

An array initializer can be used only when a new array reference is being declared. For example, the following statement is a valid use of array initializers:

```
String [] weekend = {"Saturday", "Sunday"};
```

However, declaring the reference in one statement and assigning it to an array initializer in another statement is not valid:

```
String [] weekend;
weekend = {"Saturday", "Sunday"};            //Does not compile!
```

An array initializer can be used only when assigning it to a newly declared array reference, all in a single statement.

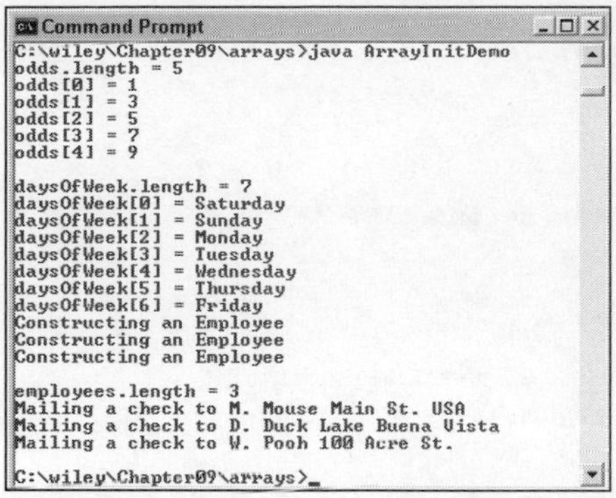

Figure 9.2   Output of the ArrayInitDemo program.

Copying Arrays

Because arrays are fixed in size, it is not unusual when working with arrays to have to create a larger or smaller array and then copy the contents of an existing array into a new one. You can write a *for* loop that copies the contents of one array to another. An alternative to a *for* loop is the static method array-copy() in the System class.

The arraycopy() method has the following signature:

```
public static void arraycopy(Object source, int sourcePos,
                             Object destination, int destinationPos,
                             int length)
```

The arraycopy() method is a good example of using Object as a polymorphic parameter. Because arrays are objects, they are of type Object. Therefore, any array reference can be passed in to the source and destination parameters.

sourcePos indicates where in the source array to copy from, and destinationPos indicates the location in the destination array to copy to. The length parameter represents the number of elements to copy.

The ArrayCopyDemo program demonstrates the use of the arraycopy() method by copying 10 ints from one array to another. Study the program and try to determine its output, which is shown in Figure 9.3.

```
public class ArrayCopyDemo
{
    public static void main(String [] args)
    {
        int [] odds = {1, 3, 5, 7, 9, 11, 13, 15, 17, 19};
        System.out.println("** odds the first time **");
        for(int i = 0; i < odds.length; i++)
```

```
        {
               System.out.println("odds[" + i + "] = "
                                               + odds[i]);
        }

        System.out.println("** odds the second time **");
        int [] temp = odds;
        odds = new int[20];

        System.arraycopy(temp, 0, odds, 4, temp.length);
        for(int i = 0; i < odds.length; i++)
        {
               System.out.println("odds[" + i + "] = "
                                               + odds[i]);
        }
    }
}
```

In the ArrayCopyDemo program, the odds reference is assigned to the temp reference:

```
int [] temp = odds;
```

At the time of this assignment, odds is referring to an array of 10 ints. Therefore, temp is also referring to the array of 10 ints. Then, odds is assigned to a new array of 20 ints, all of which are initially 0. The first 10 elements in temp (which is all of the elements in temp) are copied into the new array of 20 ints, starting at the element at index 4. Notice in the output in Figure 9.3 that the other elements in odds are 0 because they have not been assigned a value yet.

Figure 9.3   Output of the ArrayCopyDemo program.

Multidimensional Arrays

The arrays discussed up until now have been one-dimensional (often referred to as single arrays). In Java, you can create an array of any dimension. For example, a two-dimensional array (or double array) can be used to store data that is viewed as rows and columns. A three-dimensional array can be used to store data that is viewed as rows, columns, and a height dimension. You can create higher-dimensional arrays as well, although they become hard to visualize.

As with single arrays, multidimensional arrays are objects and require a reference. The reference is declared using multiple square brackets between the data type and the variable name. For example, the following statement declares a reference to a double array of ints:

```
int [] []  sums;
```

When instantiating a double array, two ints are used to specify the number of rows and columns. The following statement assigns sums to a new 10 x 12 array of ints:

```
sums = new int[10][12];
```

This array consists of 120 ints because in memory there will be 10 arrays of 12 ints. The sums reference points to an array of size 10, which contains 10 int array references. Each of the 10 int array references points to an array of 12 ints, resulting in 120 ints.

 A three-dimensional reference looks similar to the following:

```
String [] [] [] dims;
```

Instantiating the array involves three values, one for each dimension, as follows:

```
dims = new String[5][5][4];
```

The dims array consists of 5 * 5 * 4 = 100 String objects.

Each element in a two-dimensional array requires two indexes to access it. In the sums array, the first value is between 0 and 9, and the second value is between 0 and 11. The following statement assigns the value 5 to the element in the third column of the fourth row:

```
sums[3][2] = 5;
```

Working with double arrays often involves nested loops because rows and columns are involved. The DoubleArray program contains nested for loops that fill the sums array with values. (The values are the sum of the row index plus the column index.) Study the program carefully and try to determine its output, which is shown in Figure 9.4.

```java
public class DoubleArray
{
    public static void main(String [] args)
    {
        System.out.println("Instantiating a double array");
        int [] [] sums = new int[10][12];

        System.out.println("Filling the array with data");
        for(int row = 0; row < 10; row++)
        {
            for(int col = 0; col < 12; col++)
            {
                sums[row][col] = row + col;
            }
        }

        System.out.println("Displaying the array");
        for(int row = 0; row < sums.length; row++)
        {
            for(int col = 0; col < sums[row].length; col++)
            {
                System.out.print(sums[row][col] + "\t");
            }
            System.out.println();
        }

    }
}
```

Notice in the DoubleArray program that the first set of nested for loops used 10 and 12 as the upper limits of their respective loop control variables. This works fine, but with arrays you should take advantage of the length attribute.

Notice that the second set of nested for loops uses sums.length for the row loop control variable. The value of sums.length is 10 because sums refers to an array of 10 references. For the column loop control variable, the for loop uses sums[row].length, which is 12 for each value of row.

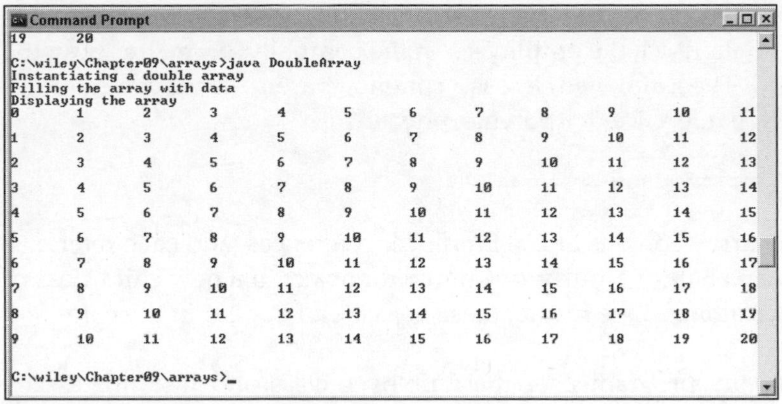

Figure 9.4   Output of the DoubleArray program.

Example of a Heterogeneous Collection

I promised in Chapter 8, "Polymorphism and Abstraction," that I would show you how to create a heterogeneous collection of Employee objects. The abstract Employee class has three child classes: Salary, Hourly, and Contractor. Suppose that we have a company that never has more than 200 employees. We could create three different arrays to keep track of the employees:

```
Salary [] salaries = new Salary[200];
Hourly [] hourlies = new Hourly[200];
Contractor [] contractors = new Contractor[200];
```

Using three different arrays has its disadvantages. First of all, using 200 references of each type is a waste of memory. But how do we distribute the employee types? What if one year we have 100 salaried, 100 hourly, and no contract employees, but a year later we have 150 salaried, 25 hourly, and 25 contract employees? I suppose we could start out with smaller arrays, but if any one of three arrays was too small, a larger array would have to be instantiated and the data from the smaller array copied into the larger array.

The second disadvantage has to do with changes to our program in the future. What if a new type of Employee is added? Then, a new array is needed, and the question about how big it should be arises again.

We can avoid these types of situations by creating a single heterogeneous collection that contains all the employees of the company, no matter how the employee is paid. The Employee class is a common parent, so we can create an array of Employee references by polymorphism:

```
Employee [] company = new Employee[200];
```

The company array consists of 200 Employee references, and each reference can refer to either a Salary, Hourly, or Contractor object. If a new child class of Employee comes along in the future, these objects can appear in the company array as well.

The MyCompany program uses the Employee class and instantiates 200 employees of random pay types, storing them in a single heterogeneous collection:

```java
public class MyCompany
{
    public static void main(String [] args)
    {
        Employee [] company = new Employee[200];

        System.out.println("Randomly fill the array with employees");
        for(int i = 0; i < company.length; i++)
        {
            int random = (int) (Math.random() * 3);
            if(random == 0)
            {
                company[i] = new Salary("Salary " + i,
                            "New York, NY", i, 50000.00);
            }
            else if(random == 1)
            {
                company[i] = new Hourly("Hourly " + i,
                            "Chicago, IL", i, 10.00);
                ((Hourly) company[i]).setHoursWorked(40);
            }
            else
            {
                company[i] = new Contractor("Contractor " + i,
                            "Denver, CO", i, 200.00);
```

```
                    ((Contractor) company[i]).setDaysWorked(5);
                }
            }

            SmartBoss boss = new SmartBoss();

            System.out.println("Paying each employee");
            for(int i = 0; i < company.length; i++)
            {
                boss.payEmployee(company[i]);
            }
        }
    }
```

The payEmployee() method in SmartBoss has an Employee parameter, so all the elements in the company array can be passed in. Within payEmployee(), the computePay() and mailCheck() methods are invoked on the Employee passed in; and by virtual method invocation, the appropriate computePay() method is invoked on each of the 200 Employee objects.

Because the MyCompany program generates random types of employees, the output will look different each time the program is executed. Figure 9.5 shows an example of its output.

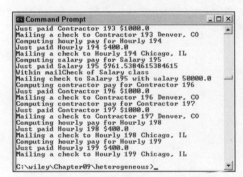

Figure 9.5 Sample output of the MyCompany program.

♦ Java Documentation

A unique and extremely useful feature of the Java language is the javadoc tool, which takes comments from Java source code and generates HTML pages. This encourages developers to add comments to their code because the HTML pages can be used by fellow developers and anyone else who wants to know about a class, without looking at the actual source code.

The documentation for the J2SE APIs was generated using the javadoc tool. This documentation is found on Sun's Web site at http://java.sun.com/j2se/ at the same URL from which the SDK is downloaded (refer to Figure 1.1). You can download the documentation or view it online. Note that the documentation does not come with the J2SE SDK that you downloaded earlier.

Running the javadoc tool creates an HTML page for each class, which contains details about the class. Information on a class's page includes its inheritance hierarchy; a summary of the fields, constructors, and methods in the class; and detailed descriptions of each field, constructor, and method.

Figure 9.6 shows a portion of the javadoc page for the java.lang.String class.

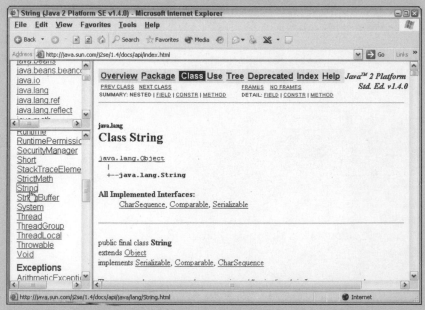

Figure 9.6   Documentation page for the String class.

Notice that the J2SE documentation is split into three frames. In the upper-left frame is a list of all the packages in the J2SE. Click on a package name, and all the interfaces and classes in that package appear in the lower-left frame. Clicking on a class name in the lower-left frame causes that class's documentation page to appear in the large frame in the center.

Find the documentation online and either download it or bookmark the Web page so that you can access it quickly. Throughout the remainder of the book, I will ask you to view the J2SE documentation for further information about specific classes and interfaces. The javadoc looks for special comments in your source code that appear in the following format:

```
/**
*/
```

Comments that contain general information about the class appear directly before the class declaration. Comments about a field, method, or constructor appear directly before the member's declaration in the class. In addition, you can use one of the following javadoc tags for specific types of comment information:

@author.   Represents the name of the author or authors of the source code.

@depracated.   Denotes a member of the class as deprecated, meaning that the API should no longer be used.

{@docRoot}.   Represents the relative path to root directory where the current page will be output. This is useful when providing a link to an outside URL.

@exception.   Used by a method to list thrown exceptions.

{@link package.class#member label}.   Creates a link to specified class member.

{@linkplain package.class#member label}.   Same as {@link}, except that the plain text font is used instead of the code font.

@param.   Used to describe the parameters of a method.

@return.   Used to describe the return value of a method.

@see.   Creates a "See also" heading for providing links or comments about other information the reader can check.

@since.   Denotes a version number indicating when the member existed or was changed.

@serial, @serialField, and @serialData.   Used for serialization purposes.

@throws.   Same as the @exception tag.

{@value}.   Used for displaying the value of a constant static field.

@version.   Denotes the software version of the class.

The Television class, shown in the following listing, contains javadoc comments and demonstrates using the javadoc tags:

```
package electronics;

/** The Television class is used to represent a standard TV
 *     that contains a channel and volume setting. This
 *     particular javadoc comment will appear at the beginning
 *     of the documentation page.
 *
```

continued

◆ Java Documentation *(continued)*

```
*      @author Rich Raposa
*      @version 1.2
*/


public class Television
{
    /**
    *      The channel field represents the current channel
    *      being watched.
    */
    public int channel;

    /**
    *      This field is private and by default will not
    *      appear on the documentation page.
    */
    private int volume;

    /**
    *      Constructs a Television object with a channel of
    *      4 and a volume 5.
    */
    public Television()
    {
        this(4,5);
        System.out.println("Inside Television()");
    }

    /**
    *      Constructs a Television object with a channel c
    *      and volume v.
    *      @param c The initial channel.
    *      @param v The initial volume.
    */
    public Television(int c, int v)
```

```
    {
        System.out.println("Inside Television(int, int)");
        channel = c;
        setVolume(v);
    }


    /**
    *     Accessor method for the volume field.
    *     @return the current volume.
    */
    public int getVolume()
    {
        return volume;
    }


    /**
    *     Changes the volume as long as the parameter is
    *     a value between 0 and 10.
    *     @param v The new volume of the television. This value
    *     should be between 0 and 10.
    */
    public void setVolume(int v)
    {
        if(v >= 0 && v <= 10)
        {
            volume = v;
        }
    }
}
```

You can run javadoc on one or more classes or on one or more packages. There are many options for javadoc. To view them, open a command prompt, type in javadoc, and press Enter.

The following javadoc command is used to generate the HTML pages for the electronics package, with the author and version tags included:

```
javadoc -author -version -d . electronics
```

Many pages are generated from this command. The Television documentation page is shown in Figure 9.7. Notice that the private field volume does not appear because we did not specify private as one of the javadoc options.

continued

♦ **Java Documentation** *(continued)*

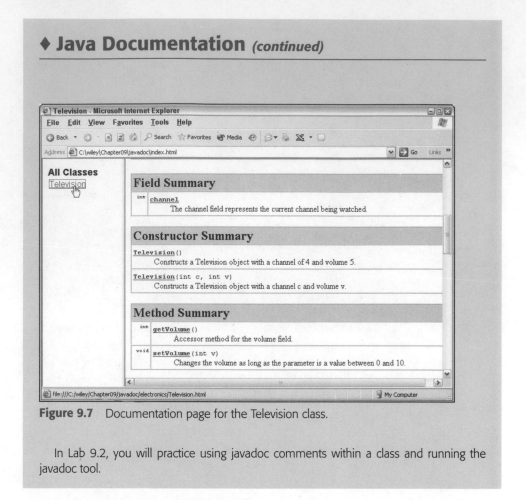

Figure 9.7   Documentation page for the Television class.

In Lab 9.2, you will practice using javadoc comments within a class and running the javadoc tool.

 For the javadoc tool to work successfully, your source code must be saved in a directory structure that matches the package name of the classes (the same rule that applies for bytecode). For example, a class named Television in an electronics package must be saved in a file named .\electronics\Television.java.

Overview of the Java Collections Framework

The J2SE contains a collection of classes and interfaces referred to as a collections framework. The goal of the *collections framework* is to provide a common architecture for working with collections, reducing the amount of code that developers need to write by providing the basic data structures. Data structures fit into three basic categories:

Lists.   Also known as a *sequence*, a *list* is a collection of ordered elements, and each element is accessed by an index. Lists allow for multiple entries and multiple null elements. An array is an example of a list, and other examples include the Vector, ArrayList, and LinkedList classes (all in the java.util package).

Sets.   A *set* is similar to a list except that a set does not allow multiple elements to appear in the set. More specifically, if x1 and x2 are in the set, x1.equals(x2) must result in false. In addition, sets can contain at most one null element. Examples of sets include the HashSet, TreeSet, and LinkedHashSet classes (all in the java.util package).

Maps.   Elements in a *map* consist of (key, value) pairs, in which each value in the collection has a key associated with it. Each key can map to at most one element, and duplicate keys are not allowed. Examples of maps include Hashtable, HashMap, IdentityHashMap, TreeMap, and WeakHashMap classes (all in the java.util package).

 Notice that the same type of data structure can be used to implement different types of collections. For example, sets are implemented as a hash table using the HashSet class and as a balanced tree using the TreeSet class. Lists are implemented as a resizable array with the ArrayList class and a linked list with the LinkedList class. Maps are implemented as both hash tables (Hashtable and HashMap) and trees (TreeMap).

Different collections result in different levels of performance, depending on how the data structure is being used. For example, an element in a list can be quickly accessed by using its index, but lists take longer when searching for an element. Trees have more overhead when accessing elements, but can be extremely efficient when searching for an element. Adding elements to a tree or list takes longer than adding elements to a hash table.

The purpose of the collections framework is to create a collection of classes that have similar methods, so using the classes is simple and makes code more manageable. My goal in the remainder of this chapter is for you to become familiar with the way these classes work. After you have worked with the more popular classes such as Vector and Hashtable, you will find that the other classes in the collections framework are similar.

The Vector Class

The java.util.Vector class is a list implementation that represents a growable array of elements. In fact, you can think of a Vector as an array that (after it reaches its capacity) simply grows larger the next time an element is added to it.

The elements in a Vector are accessed by using an index, just like array elements. The elements also must be of type java.lang.Object, which means that the only elements that cannot appear in a Vector are the eight primitive data types.

 If you want to add a primitive data type to a Vector, use its corresponding wrapper class found in the java.lang package. For example, if you want to add an int to a Vector, wrap the int in an Integer object and add the Integer object to the Vector.

A Vector has two attributes: a capacity and a capacity increment. The capacity represents the size of the Vector in memory. After the capacity is reached, the Vector must grow before a new element can be added. The capacity increment denotes how much the Vector should grow by when the Vector needs to increase in size. If the capacity increment is 0, the array simply doubles in capacity each time it needs to grow.

For example, if a Vector has a capacity of 50 and a capacity increment of 10, the Vector does not need to grow in memory until after 50 elements are added. When the 51st element is added, the Vector will grow to size 60 because its capacity increment is 10.

The Vector class has four constructors:

public Vector().   Creates an empty Vector with an initial capacity of 10 and a capacity increment of 0.

public Vector(int initialCapacity).   Creates an empty Vector with the given initial capacity and a capacity increment of 0.

public Vector(int initialCapacity, int capacityIncrement).   Creates an empty Vector with the given initial capacity and capacity increment.

public Vector(Collection c).   Creates a Vector that initially contains the elements in the given Collection. Collection is an interface that all of the data structures in the collections framework have in common. This constructor allows you to create a new Vector from the elements stored in a hash table or tree, for example, because the hash table or tree will be of type Collection through polymorphism.

The following statement instantiates an empty Vector with an initial capacity of 50 and a capacity increment of 10:

```
Vector employees = new Vector(50, 10);
```

The employees Vector is initially empty, so its size is 0. Elements are added to the Vector by using the various methods in the Vector class, which we will discuss next.

Size and capacity are two entirely different attributes of a Vector. The size of a Vector is the number of elements in the Vector. The capacity of a Vector is the amount of room available for adding elements before the Vector needs to grow. For example, the employees Vector is empty, so its size is 0. However, it has room for 50 objects, so its capacity is 50.

Adding Elements to a Vector

The following methods from the Vector class are used to add elements to a Vector. Keep in mind that Vectors are similar to arrays, and each element is associated with an index in the array. Also notice that there are some redundancies in the functionality of some of these methods, which was done to make the Vector class similar to the other classes in the collections framework. (The Vector class has been around since JDK 1.0, whereas the collections framework is new as of Java 2.)

public void add(int index, Object element). Inserts the Object at the specified index within the Vector.

public boolean add(Object element). Appends the Object to the end of the Vector. The method returns true if the element is added successfully.

public void addElement(Object element). Appends the Object to the end of the Vector and is identical to the add(Object) method.

public void insertElementAt(Object element, int index). Inserts the Object at the specified index, causing elements after the index to be shifted down one index spot in the Vector. This method is identical to the add(int, Object) method.

public boolean addAll(Collection c). Adds the elements in the given Collection to the end of the Vector and returns true if the Vector changed.

public boolean addAll(int index, Collection c). Adds the elements in the given Collection to the Vector at the specified index and returns true if the Vector changed.

The VectorDemo program, shown in the following listing, creates a Vector of capacity 50 and capacity increment 10. Then, a for loop randomly inserts 51 Employee objects. Study the program carefully and try to determine not only the output of the program, but what the Vector will look like at the end of the for loop.

```
import java.util.Vector;

public class VectorDemo
{
```

```
    public static void main(String [] args)
    {
        Vector employees = new Vector(50, 10);

        System.out.println("Add some Employee objects
                    to the vector...");
        int numSalary = 0;
        for(int i = 1; i <= 51; i++)
        {
            Employee e = null;
            int random = (int) (Math.random() * 3);
            if(random == 0)
            {
                e = new Salary("Salary " + i,
                    "Palo Alto, CA", i, 100000.00);
                employees.add(0, e);
                numSalary++;
            }
            else if(random == 1)
            {
                e = new Hourly("Hourly " + i,
                    "Cupertino, CA", i, 100.00);
                employees.insertElementAt(e, numSalary);
            }
            else
            {
                e = new Contractor("Contractor " + i,
                    "Milpitas, CA", i, 1000.00);
                employees.add(e);
            }
        }

        System.out.println("The size of the vector is "
                        + employees.size());
        System.out.println("The capacity of the vector is "
                        + employees.capacity());
    }
}
```

 The Vector class contains a size() method that returns the current number of elements in the Vector and a capacity() method that returns the current capacity of the Vector().

In the VectorDemo program, if the employee added to the Vector is of type Salary, the object is added to the first element in the Vector:

```
employees.add(0, e);
```

This is not an efficient add because all subsequent elements in the employees Vector must shift down one to make room for the new employee. The Hourly objects are added to the Vector using the following statement:

```
employees.insertElementAt(e, numSalary);
```

The same result could have been achieved by using the following statement:

```
employees.add(numSalary, e);
```

The numSalary value is the number of Salary objects already added to the Vector, so the Hourly objects are inserted somewhere in the middle of the employees Vector.

The Contractor objects are added to the Vector by using the following statement:

```
employees.add(e);
```

This appends the Contractor object to the end of the employees Vector. The result is a Vector of 51 Employee objects with the Salary objects appearing at the beginning, the Hourly objects in the middle, and the Contractor objects at the end. This means that the size of employees is 51, because 51 objects were added. Because its capacity was initially 50, employees needed to grow once by its capacity increment of 10, so the capacity of employees is 60, as shown by the output of the VectorDemo program shown in Figure 9.8.

Accessing and Removing Elements in a Vector

Elements can be removed from a Vector, which causes the remaining elements to move up one (subtracting one from their index) in the Vector to fill in the space made by the removed element. The Vector class contains the following methods for removing elements:

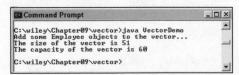

Figure 9.8 Output of the VectorDemo program.

public void clear().   Removes all the elements from the Vector, causing the Vector to become empty. The same result can be achieved by using the public void removeAllElements() method.

public Object remove(int index).   Removes the Object at the specified index and returns a reference to the Object. The same result can be achieved by using the public void removeElementAt(int index) method.

public boolean remove(Object element).   Removes the first occurrence of the specified Object, as determined by the equals() method. The return value is true if the Vector actually contained and removed the element Object. The same result can be achieved by using the public boolean removeElement(Object element) method.

public boolean removeAll(Collection c).   Removes the elements in the Vector that appear in the given Collection. The method returns true if the Vector is changed.

public boolean retainAll(Collection c).   Removes the elements in the Vector that do not appear in the given Collection. The method returns true if the Vector is changed.

public void setElementAt(Object element, int index).   Adds the given Object to the Vector at the specified index, removing any previous element at that index.

The Vector class also contains various methods for accessing the elements in the Vector, as well as obtaining general information about the Vector. Some of these methods include the following:

public Object get(int index).   Returns a reference to the element in the Vector at the specified index. The public Object elementAt(int index) method can also be used for this purpose.

public Object firstElement().   Returns the element at index 0.

public Object lastElement().   Returns the last element in the Vector.

public int indexOf(Object element).   Returns the index in the Vector of the first occurrence of the given element as determined by the equals() method. The return value is −1 if the element is not found.

public Object [] toArray().   Returns an Object array containing all the elements in the Vector.

The VectorDemo2 program, shown in the following listing, demonstrates using some of these methods for accessing and removing elements from a Vector. Note that the Employee class was modified to include an equals() method that returns true if two Employee objects have the same number. Study the program and try to determine its output, which is shown in Figure 9.9.

```java
import java.util.Vector;

public class VectorDemo2
{
    public static void main(String [] args)
    {
        Vector employees = new Vector(10);  //initial capacity of 10

        System.out.println("Add some Employee
                        objects to the vector...");

        int numSalary = 0;
        for(int i = 1; i <= 10; i++)
        {
            Employee e = null;
            int random = (int) (Math.random() * 3);
            if(random == 0)
            {
                e = new Salary("Salary " + i,
                    "Palo Alto, CA", i, 100000.00);
                employees.add(0, e);
                numSalary++;
            }
            else if(random == 1)
            {
                e = new Hourly("Hourly " + i,
                    "Cupertino, CA", i, 100.00);
                employees.insertElementAt(e, numSalary);
            }
            else
            {
                e = new Contractor("Contractor " + i,
                    "Milpitas, CA", i, 1000.00);
                employees.add(e);
            }
        }

        System.out.println("The size of the vector is "
                            + employees.size());
        System.out.println("The capacity of the vector is "
                            + employees.capacity());

        Salary s = new Salary("","",4, 0.0);
        if(employees.remove(s))
        {
            System.out.println("Just removed employee number 4");
        }

        employees.remove(7);
        System.out.println("Just removed employee number 7");
```

```
int size = employees.size();
System.out.println("The size is now " + size);
System.out.println("The capacity is now "
                        + employees.capacity());


for(int i = 0; i < size; i++)
{
    Employee current = (Employee) employees.elementAt(i);
    if(current instanceof Hourly)
    {
        ((Hourly) current).setHoursWorked(40);
    }
    else if(current instanceof Contractor)
    {
        ((Contractor) current).setDaysWorked(5);
    }

    current.computePay();
    current.mailCheck();
    }
  }
}
```

The VectorDemo2 program adds 10 Employee objects to the employees Vector. The following statement removes employee number 4:

```
employees.remove(s)
```

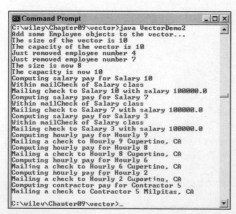

Figure 9.9 Output of the VectorDemo2 program.

The remove() method searches the Vector for the first Employee that is equal to s. Because two Employee objects are equal if they have the same number, the employee who is number 4 is removed. The index of the removed employee is different each time the program is executed because of the random order in which the Vector is filled.

The following statement removes the object at index 7 from the employees Vector:

```
employees.remove(7);
```

The size of the vector is now 8, and the for loop uses the elementAt() method to traverse through the Vector and pay each Employee object. Figure 9.9 shows the output.

 The Vector class is useful in situations in which you need a resizeable array. However, in terms of performance, Vectors can be quite inefficient if elements are continually being added and removed. Each time an element is added in the middle, all the elements beyond the inserted element need to be moved up one (index increases by one). Similarly, deleting an element causes all elements beyond the deleted element to be moved back one (their index decreases by one). When using a Vector, try to limit the number of arbitrary insertions and deletions.

The Hashtable Class

A *hash table* is a data structure that maps keys to values. A hash table can be viewed as a collection of buckets, with each bucket able to hold any number of entries. Adding an object to a hash table involves deciding which bucket to place the object in, a process referred to as hashing.

Every object in the hash table generates a hash code as determined by its hashcode() method. Every object has a hashcode() method that it inherits from java.lang.Object. A class that is to be used with hash tables should override the hashcode() method and return a unique value for different objects. The general rule is that if two objects are not equal as determined by their equals() method, the two objects should return different hash codes.

For example, the Employee class in the following listing uses the employee's number as its hash code. Notice that the equals() method in Employee defines two Employee objects as equal if they have the same number, which means that different Employee objects have a different hash code.

```java
public abstract class Employee
{
    private String name;
    private String address;
    private int number;

    public Employee(String name, String address, int number)
    {
        this.name = name;
        this.address = address;
        this.number = number;
    }

    public int hashcode()
    {
        return number;
    }

    public boolean equals(Object x)
    {
        if(x == null || !(x instanceof Employee))
        {
            return false;
        }
        else
        {
            return this.number == ((Employee) x).number;
        }
    }
}
```

The java.util.Hashtable class implements a hash table. A Hashtable object has two attributes that determine how the hash table grows in memory: an initial capacity and a load factor. The initial capacity of a Hashtable is similar to the initial capacity of a Vector. It is the initial available memory for the hash table.

Vectors grow by a fixed amount when they become completely filled. Hash tables would be terribly inefficient if they behaved in this manner. Instead, a hash table grows when the buckets start to get too many elements in them. How many is too many? This is determined by the load factor, a value between 0 and 1 that is used in the following formula:

*number of entries > capacity * load factor*

When the number of entries in the hash table is greater than the load factor times the capacity, the hash table automatically resizes and rehashes itself. Suppose, for example, that you have a hash table whose capacity is 100 and whose load factor is 0.75. The point it resizes occurs after 100 * 0.75 = 75 elements are added to the hash table. After 75 elements, the hash table grows in size, which means that there are more buckets. Each entry has to be rehashed because it will likely now appear in a different bucket. This entire process happens automatically in the Hashtable class.

 A load factor of 0.75 tends to be a good balance between the amount of memory consumed by the hash table and the amount of time it takes to add, remove, and access elements. If a hash table is too large, memory is wasted. If a hash table is too small, a performance loss occurs, especially if the table has to be rehashed.

The Hashtable class has four constructors:

public Hashtable(). Creates an empty Hashtable with an initial capacity of 11 and a load factor of 0.75.

public Hashtable(int initialCapacity). Creates an empty Hashtable with the given initial capacity and a load factor of 0.75.

public Hashtable(int initialCapacity, float loadFactor). Creates an empty Hashtable with the given initial capacity and load factor.

public Hashtable(Map t). Creates a Hashtable from the given Map, with an initial capacity large enough to hold the contents of the Map and a load factor of 0.75.

The following statement creates a hash table with an initial capacity of 10 and a load factor of 0.75:

```
Hashtable myCompany = new Hashtable(10);
```

The myCompany hash table will support 7.5 (actually 7) insertions before needing to be rehashed.

Adding Elements to a Hashtable

A mapping is added to a hash table by "putting" the mapping into the hash table using the put() method in the Hashtable class:

```
public Object put(Object key, Object value);
```

The key parameter is the hash code of the value parameter. Neither of these two parameters can be null. Notice that the key is an Object, so using a primitive data type requires using the corresponding wrapper class.

The HashtableDemo program, shown in the following listing, creates a Hashtable and puts some Employee objects in it by using the previous Employee class listing.

```java
import java.util.Hashtable;

public class HashtableDemo
{
    public static void main(String [] args)
    {
        Hashtable myCompany = new Hashtable(10);

        System.out.println("Add some Employee
                    objects to the hash table...");

        Salary e1 = new Salary("Salary1", "Palo Alto, CA",
                        1, 100000.00);
        Hourly e2 = new Hourly("Hourly2", "Cupertino, CA",
                        2, 100.00);
        Contractor e3 = new Contractor("Contractor3", "Milpitas, CA",
                        3, 1000.00);

        myCompany.put(new Integer(e1.hashcode()), e1);
        myCompany.put(new Integer(e2.hashcode()), e2);
        myCompany.put(new Integer(e3.hashcode()), e3);

        System.out.println("The size of the hash table is "
                        + myCompany.size());
    }
}
```

 The Hashtable class has a size() method that returns the number of mappings in the hash table.

In the HashtableDemo, three Employee objects are put into the myCompany Hashtable. The following statement adds the Salary object e1, whose hashcode() returns an int equal to 1 (because that is the employee number of e1):

```java
myCompany.put(new Integer(e1.hashcode()), e1);
```

The int is wrapped in an Integer object and used as the key.

Notice that the other two Employee objects are put into the Hashtable using their respective hash codes:

```java
myCompany.put(new Integer(e2.hashcode()), e2);
myCompany.put(new Integer(e3.hashcode()), e3);
```

The result is a myCompany hash table of size three, which you can see in the output shown in Figure 9.10.

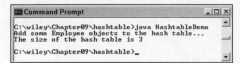

Figure 9.10 Output of the HashtableDemo program.

Accessing Elements in a Hashtable

To view an element in a hash table, you "get" it using the get() method of the Hashtable class:

```
public Object get(Object key)
```

The key parameter is the key of the Object you are looking for. The get() method returns a reference to the Object that matches the given key, or null if the key is not found.

Here are some other useful methods in the Hashtable class for determining information about the hash table and the elements within it:

public boolean isEmpty(). Returns true if there are no mappings in the Hashtable.

public void clear(). Removes all mappings from the Hashtable.

public boolean containsValue(Object value). Returns true if the Hashtable contains at least key mapping to the specified value.

public boolean containsKey(Object key). Returns true if the Hashtable contains a mapping for the specified key.

public Object remove(Object key). Removes the object mapped to by the specified key (and the key as well) and returns a reference to the value.

The HashtableDemo2 program, shown in the following listing, demonstrates getting values using keys and also removes an element from the Hashtable. Study the program and try to determine its output, which is shown in Figure 9.11.

```
import java.util.Hashtable;

public class HashtableDemo2
{
    public static void main(String [] args)
    {
        Hashtable myCompany = new Hashtable(10);

        System.out.println("Add some Employee
                objects to the hash table...");
```

```
Salary e1 = new Salary("Salary1", "Palo Alto, CA",
                        1, 100000.00);
Hourly e2 = new Hourly("Hourly2", "Cupertino, CA", 2, 100.00);
Contractor e3 = new Contractor("Contractor3", "Milpitas, CA",
                        3, 1000.00);

myCompany.put(new Integer(e1.hashcode()), e1);
myCompany.put(new Integer(e2.hashcode()), e2);
myCompany.put(new Integer(e3.hashcode()), e3);

System.out.println("The size of the hash table is "
                        + myCompany.size());

int size = myCompany.size();
for(int i = 1; i <= size; i++)
{
    Employee current =
                (Employee) myCompany.get(new Integer(i));
    if(current instanceof Hourly)
    {
        ((Hourly) current).setHoursWorked(40);
    }
    else if(current instanceof Contractor)
    {
        ((Contractor) current).setDaysWorked(5);
    }

    current.computePay();
    current.mailCheck();
}

myCompany.remove(new Integer(2));
System.out.println("The size is now " + myCompany.size());
    }
}
```

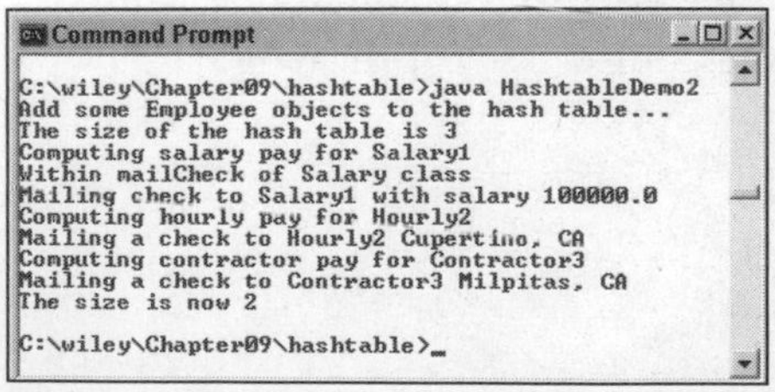

Figure 9.11 Output of the HashtableDemo2 program.

The other classes in the Java collections framework are similar to the Vector and Hashtable class in terms of construction and adding, deleting, and accessing elements. If you are interested in the other list, set and map classes, browse the Java documentation in the java.util package, which is where the collections framework classes are found.

Classroom Q & A

Q: Why have all these different classes in the collections framework? Why not just use a class like Vector all the time?

A: The Vector class is a list data structure, like an array or a linked list. The Hashtable class is a map data structure and is entirely different internally from a Vector, even though the two classes are similar to use. Your question really should be: Why not just use a list all the time?

Q: Sounds good. Why not just use a list all the time?

A: Good question! Well, with a list, all the elements are accessed by using an index, which means you can iterate (traverse) a list quickly. However, insertions and deletions all take linear time, which can really add up if you are performing lots of these types of operations or working with a large list.

Q: Why not use a map all the time then?

A: A map is very efficient when adding and removing elements, but iterating a map is time-consuming. So there is the trade-off between lists and maps.

Q: So which is better to use?

A: You can answer that question only on a case-by-case basis because it depends entirely on your situation. If you are looking for a good data structure to use, my advice is to browse the java.util package in the Java documentation and read up on some of the different types of classes provided in the collections framework.

Lab 9.1: Using Arrays

In this lab, you will modify your Powerball class from Lab 5.3 so that it keeps track of each colored ball in a single array.

1. In your text editor, open your Powerball class from Lab 5.3.

2. Remove the five fields that represent the five white balls. Add a single field that is a reference to an array of type int.

3. Within the Powerball constructor, assign the field in the previous step to a new int array of size five.

4. Modify the remainder of the Powerball class so that it uses the array of ints to store the values of the five white balls. Use a for loop and the length attribute of arrays when displaying the results in the displayResults() method.

Lab 9.2: Using javadoc

In this lab, you will run the javadoc tool to create documentation for your Powerball class.

1. First off, delete the bytecode file Powerball.class from your hard drive. (I do not want the Powerball.java and Powerball.class files in the same directory.)

2. Add your Powerball class to a package named lottery.

3. Compile the class using the -d flag, which will create a \lottery directory.

4. Move Powerball.java from its current directory to the \lottery directory.

5. Add javadoc comments throughout your Powerball class, for all fields, methods, and constructors. Use the @param tag for any method parameters, and the @return tag for any return values. Add an @author and @version tag as well, and any other javadoc tags that you want to experiment with.

6. Run javadoc on the lottery package using the command line:

```
javadoc -author -version -private lottery
```

7. If you get an error stating that a package or class is not found, either run the command from the directory that contains \lottery or add the directory that contains \lottery to your CLASSPATH.

8. Open the index.html file that was created, and check out your comments!

Lab 9.3: Using the Vector Class

This lab demonstrates using the Vector class. You will write a class called GuessingGame that randomly tries to "guess" a number you pick between 1 and 100. Each guess is saved in a Vector.

1. Write a new class named GuessingGame. Add a field of type int named target and a field of type Vector named guesses.

2. Add a constructor that takes in an int, which is stored in the target field. Within the constructor, initialize guesses to a new Vector with an initial capacity of 100 and a capacity increment of 25.

3. Add a public void method named startGuessing(). This method should contain a while loop that randomly generates an int between 1 and 100. If the random number matches the target, then break out of the for loop. If it doesn't, add the random number to the guesses Vector and keep repeating the loop.

4. Add a public void method named printGuesses() that uses a for loop to print out all of the elements in the guesses Vector. After the for loop, print out the size of the Vector.

5. Add main() to the GuessingGame class. Within main(), parse the first command-line argument to an int to represent the target. Use the method Integer.parseInt().

6. Within main(), instantiate a new GuessingGame object, passing in the int from the command line. Invoke startGuessing(), and then printGuesses().

7. Save and compile the GuessingGame class.

8. Run the GuessingGame program, making sure that you pass in an int on the command line. The startGuessing() method will randomly generate ints between 1 and 100 until your number is guessed. You should see the output of the Vector after your number is guessed.

Lab 9.4: Using the LinkedList Class

The purpose of this lab is to become familiar with using a collection class for the first time. The class you will use is java.util.LinkedList, which represents a linked list. A *linked list* is a list implementation in which each element contains a reference to both the next and previous elements in the list.

1. Find the java.util.LinkedList class in the Java documentation. Look over its constructors and methods.

2. Write a class named StringSorter. Add a field of type LinkedList and initialize this field in the StringSorter constructor.

3. Add a method named addString() that has a String parameter. This method should add the given String to the LinkedList, maintaining the list in alphabetical order. You will need to search the list and determine where in the list the String should appear.

4. Write a method named printList() that displays all the String objects in the LinkedList.

5. Save and compile the StringSorter class.

6. Write a program named AddString that contains main(). Within main(), instantiate a StringSorter object.

7. Add about a dozen Strings using the addString() method.

8. Print out the list using the printList() method.

9. Save, compile, and run the StringSorter program. Verify that it is working properly.

Summary

- An array is a collection of elements stored in a contiguous block of memory. Arrays are fixed in length and cannot grow or shrink once they are declared. Every array has a length attribute that contains the size of the array.

- Arrays can be initialized using the new keyword or by using an array initializer.

- Java allows for multidimensional arrays of any dimension.

- The javadoc tool generates HTML pages that contain information about your classes, including any javadoc comments that may appear in your source code.

- The java.util.Vector class is a useful class for creating a heterogeneous collection of type Object that grows and shrinks dynamically.

- The java.util.Hashtable class represents a hash table of elements of type Object.

- The Java collections framework consists of the classes in the java.util package that represent the various data structures.

Review Questions

1. True or False: An array object can be made smaller, but not larger.

2. How many String objects are instantiated in memory after the following statement:

   ```
   String [] values = new String[10];
   ```

3. In the previous question, what is the value of values.length?

4. Suppose that we declare the following array. What is the value of types[1]?

   ```
   char [] types = {'a', 'b', 'c', 'd'};
   ```

5. In the previous example, what is the value of types.length?

6. If a Vector is instantiated with an initial capacity of 20 and a capacity increment of 0, how many elements can be added to the Vector?

7. If a Vector is instantiated with an initial capacity of 20 and a capacity increment of 0, how many elements can be added to the Vector before it needs to be resized? What will the capacity of the Vector be after the first resizing?

8. Where does the add(Object) method from the Vector class add the given Object in the Vector?

9. Suppose that a Hashtable has a capacity of 50 and a load factor of 0.8. At what point does the hash table need to grow and be rehashed?

Answers to Review Questions

1. False. Arrays are not resizable.

2. Zero. You get a reference to an array (values) and an array of 10 String references, but no String objects.

3. 10

4. 'b'

5. 4

6. A Vector is only limited in size by memory constraints. You can add as many elements as you have room for. The initial capacity and increment are not relevant in this question.

7. When the 21st element is added, the Vector will need to be resized. Vectors with a capacity increment of 0 double in size, so the capacity of the Vector after the 21st element is added will be 40.

8. The add(Object) method adds the given element at the end of the Vector.

9. 50 * 0.80 = 40, so adding the 41st element causes the Hashtable to be resized and rehashed.

CHAPTER

10

Interfaces

Interfaces are a fundamental feature of the Java language and need to be understood before we can delve much further into the Java language. This chapter discusses what an interface is and how it is used, including writing and implementing an interface, declaring constants in interfaces, extending interfaces, and the effect of interfaces on polymorphism.

An Overview of Interfaces

An *interface* is a collection of abstract methods. A class implements an interface, thereby inheriting the abstract methods of the interface. Unless the class that implements the interface is abstract, all the methods of the interface need to be defined in the class. An interface is similar to a class in the following ways:

- An interface can contain any number of methods.

- An interface is written in a file with a .java extension, with the name of the interface matching the name of the file.

- The bytecode of an interface appears in a .class file.

- Interfaces appear in packages, and their corresponding bytecode file must be in a directory structure that matches the package name.

However, an interface is different from a class in several ways, including:

- You cannot instantiate an interface.

- An interface does not contain any constructors.

- All of the methods in an interface are abstract.

- An interface cannot contain instance fields. The only fields that can appear in an interface must be declared both static and final.

- An interface is not extended by a class; it is implemented by a class.

- An interface can extend multiple interfaces.

 An interface is not a class. Writing an interface is similar to writing a class, but they are two different concepts. A class describes the attributes and behaviors of an object. An interface contains behaviors that a class implements.

Interfaces have many uses and benefits. For example, an interface can be used to expose certain behaviors of a class, without exposing all of the behaviors of a class. Interfaces can be used to force behavior on other objects, ensuring that certain methods are implemented by an object. Interfaces can be used for polymorphism reasons, since an object can take on the form of an interface type.

We will discuss all of these uses and benefits of interfaces throughout this chapter. I want to start by discussing the details of writing interfaces and writing classes that implement interfaces.

Declaring Interfaces

The interface keyword is used to declare an interface. The source code file for an interface has the format shown here:

```
//A package declaration
package package_name;
//Any number of import statements
import java.lang.*;
public interface NameOfInterface
{
    //Any number of final, static fields
    //Any number of abstract method declarations
}
```

Interfaces have the following properties:

- An interface is implicitly abstract. You do not need to use the abstract keyword when declaring an interface (although it is acceptable to use it).

- Each method in an interface is also implicitly abstract, so the abstract keyword is not needed. You can explicitly declare a method in an interface as abstract, but typically the abstract keyword is left off.

- Methods in an interface are implicitly public. It is common practice to use the public keyword when writing an interface, but if you do not explicitly declare a method in an interface as public, it will be public anyway.

The Java API contains hundreds of interfaces. For example, the following Runnable interface is defined in the java.lang package.

```
package java.lang;
public interface Runnable
{
    public void run();
}
```

The Runnable interface contains one method named run(). The Runnable interface is abstract, as is the run() method, even though the abstract keyword was not explicitly used in either place.

 The Runnable interface is used when writing multithreaded applications. The design of threads in Java requires a class to implement Runnable to be a thread, thereby forcing the class to have a run() method. When the thread is started, the run() method is invoked. You will see the Runnable interface again when we discuss threads in Chapter 15, "Threads."

The MouseListener interface is another example of an interface in the Java API. It is defined in the java.awt.event package and contains five methods:

```
package java.awt.event;
public interface MouseListener extends java.util.EventListener
{
    public void mouseClicked(MouseEvent m);
    public void mouseEntered(MouseEvent m);
    public void mouseExited(MouseEvent m);
    public void mousePressed(MouseEvent m);
    public void mouseReleased(MouseEvent m);
}
```

Any class implementing MouseListener needs to implement all five of these methods. Notice that the MouseListener interface has a parent interface named EventListener. Any class that implements MouseListener must also implement the methods of EventListener; however, EventListener does not contain any methods:

```
package java.util;
public interface EventListener
{}
```

The EventListener interface is an example of a *tagging interface*, which is discussed in a sidebar later in this chapter.

 The EventListener interface is the parent class of all listener interfaces (such as MouseListener). The listener interfaces are used extensively in handling GUI events, discussed in Chapter 13, "GUI Components and Event Handling." Listener interfaces are also an essential element of JavaBeans, discussed in Chapter 19, "JavaBeans."

User-Defined Interfaces

You can also write your own interfaces. The following PhoneHandler interface is a user-defined interface that contains three methods:

```
package customer.service;
public interface PhoneHandler
{
    public void answer();
    public boolean forward(int extension);
    public void takeMessage(String message, String recipient);
}
```

The PhoneHandler interface must be saved in a file named PhoneHandler .java, and the bytecode file PhoneHandler.class needs to appear in a \customer\ service directory.

Let's work through an example where you write your own interface and then a class that implements it. Open your text editor and follow along through the following steps.

Write the Interface Source Code

Start by writing the .java file for an interface named Paintable. The interface will represent any object that can be painted onscreen. It will contain a single method named paint().

Type in the Paintable interface shown in Figure 10.1.

Compile the Interface

Save the source code file in a new directory named c:\interfaces\display. Create this directory, and save the file there as Paintable.java. Interfaces are compiled the same way as classes, using the javac compiler. Because you already created the \display directory, and Paintable.java is saved in that directory, you do not need to use the -d flag. You can compile it using the command line shown in Figure 10.2.

You should see a new file named Paintable.class in the \display folder. The display.Paintable interface is now ready to be implemented by a class, which we will do next.

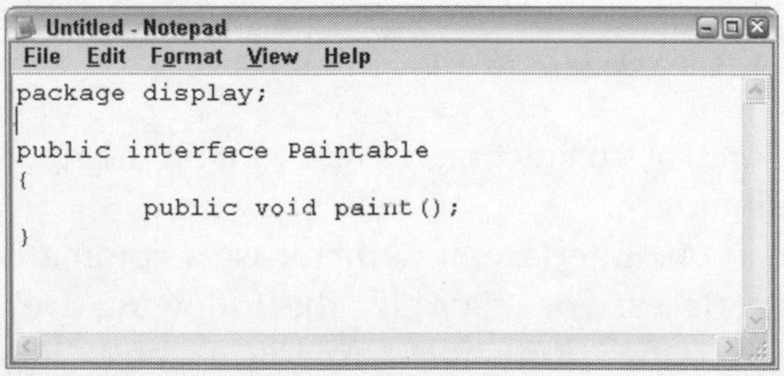

Figure 10.1 The Paintable interface is in the display package.

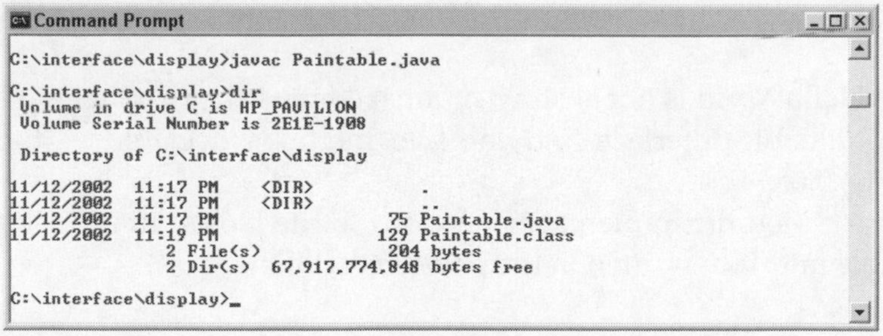

Figure 10.2 Compile the interface using the javac compiler.

Implementing an Interface

When a class implements an interface, you can think of the class as signing a contract, agreeing to perform the specific behaviors of the interface. If a class does not perform all the behaviors of the interface, the class must declare itself as abstract.

More specifically, when a class implements an interface, the class has two options:

- Implement all of the methods in the interface
- Be declared as abstract

A class uses the implements keyword to implement an interface. The implements keyword appears in the class declaration following the extends portion of the declaration. The format for implements looks similar to:

```
public class ClassName extends ParentClassName implements InterfaceName
```

For example, the following HelloWorld class declares that it implements the Runnable interface:

```
public class HelloWorld implements Runnable
```

The HelloWorld class is not declared as abstract, so it must contain the run() method declared in the Runnable interface.

A class can implement more than one interface, in which case a comma is used to separate the multiple interfaces. For example, the following HelloWorld class implements both the Runnable interface and the java.awt.event.MouseListener interface:

```
public class HelloWorld implements Runnable,
java.awt.event.MouseListener
```

Again, because HelloWorld is not abstract, it must contain the run() method declared in the Runnable interface and the five methods declared in the MouseListener interface.

Now that we have seen the implements keyword, write a class that implements our Paintable interface written in the previous section.

Write a Class That Implements Paintable

In this step, we will write a class named Rectangle that implements the Paintable interface. Open your text editor, and type in the class shown in Figure 10.3.

```
Untitled - Notepad
File  Edit  Format  View  Help
import display.Paintable;

public class Rectangle implements Paintable
{
        public int width, height;

        public Rectangle(int w, int h)
        {
                width = w;
                height = h;
        }
}
```

Figure 10.3   The Rectangle class implements the Paintable class.

Notice that the Rectangle class declares that it implements Paintable, but it does not contain the paint() method. I did this intentionally to show you the compile error that is generated. Continue on to the next step, and see what happens.

Save and Compile the Rectangle Class

Save the Rectangle class in your c:\interface directory. Compile Rectangle.java using javac. You should get a compiler error similar to the one in Figure 10.4 because Rectangle is neither declared abstract, nor implements the paint() method in Paintable.

 If you want a quick fix for your Rectangle class, simply declare it as abstract:

```
public abstract Rectangle implements Paintable
```

It will compile now, but you will not be able to create any Rectangle objects because it is an abstract class.

```
Command Prompt
11/12/2002  11:19 PM             129 Paintable.class
                 2 File(s)           204 bytes
                 2 Dir(s)  67,917,414,400 bytes free

C:\interface\display>cd..

C:\interface>javac Rectangle.java
Rectangle.java:3: Rectangle should be declared abstract; it does not define pain
t() in Rectangle
public class Rectangle implements Paintable
       ^
1 error

C:\interface>
```

Figure 10.4   The Rectangle class does not properly implement Paintable.

Add the paint() Method

Let's add the paint() method to the Rectangle class so that it compiles properly. Add the paint() method shown in Figure 10.5, and compile your Rectangle class again. It should compile successfully this time.

You have now written both an interface and a class that implements the interface. Next, you will write a class that paints Paintable objects, and we will use the Rectangle class as an example.

Write a Class That Uses Paintable

Write the MyPainter class in Figure 10.6, which contains a paintAnything() method. The paintAnything() method can paint any object of type Paintable. Within main(), a MyPainter object paints a Rectangle object passed in to the paintAnything() method. Type in the MyPainter program and save it in your c:\interface directory.

Run the MyPainter program, and you should see output similar to that in Figure 10.7.

```
Rectangle - Notepad
File   Edit   Format   View   Help

import display.Painting;

public class Rectangle implements Paintable
{
        public int width, height;

        public Rectangle(int w, int h)
        {
                width = w;
                height = h;
        }

        public void paint()
        {
                for(int row = 1; row <= height; row++)
                {
                        for(int col = 1; col <= width; col++)
                        {
                                System.out.print("*");
                        }
                        System.out.println();
                }
        }
}
```

Figure 10.5   The Rectangle class properly implementing Paintable.

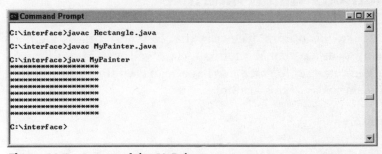

Figure 10.6   The MyPainter class uses the Paintable interface as a method parameter.

```
C:\interface>javac Rectangle.java

C:\interface>javac MyPainter.java

C:\interface>java MyPainter
***********************
***********************
***********************
***********************
***********************
***********************
***********************
***********************

C:\interface>
```

Figure 10.7   Output of the MyPainter program.

Using Interfaces

Interfaces have two equally important but different usages:

- An interface can be used to expose the methods of a class, allowing users of the class to interface with objects of the class via the methods in the interface.

- An interface can be used to force certain behaviors on a class.

These two usages create a wealth of design opportunities for Java applications. Being able to expose methods of a class using an interface is used extensively in distributed computing, which includes technologies such as RMI (Remote Method Invocation), CORBA, and Web Services.

Forcing certain behaviors on a class allows you to create more generic and flexible classes that can communicate with completely different objects that share a common interface. The MouseListener interface is an example of forcing behavior on an object. When a mouse is clicked, a MouseEvent object is instantiated and passed to a listener, invoking the mouseClicked() method. How can the source of the MouseEvent know that a listener has even bothered to write the mouseClicked() method? Because the listener was forced to implement the MouseListener interface, or it would not have been allowed to listen for mouse clicks. Because the listener was forced to implement MouseListener, the mouseClicked() method must have been written, so the source of the event is guaranteed to be able to invoke mouseClicked() successfully on the listener.

Let's look at examples of both of these interface uses. We will start with a class that uses an interface to expose certain methods in the class.

Exposing Methods via an Interface

The following code shows an Employee class that contains various methods for accessing an employee's personal information, as well as methods for paying an employee. The details of the methods have been kept simple so as to not to detract from the emphasis of this example.

```java
public class Employee
{
    private String name, address;
    private double weeklyPay;
    public Employee(String name, String address)
    {
        this.name = name;
        this.address = address;
    }
    public String getName()
    {
        return name;
    }
    public void setName(String n)
    {
        name = n;
    }
    public String getAddress()
    {
        return address;
    }
    public void setAddress(String a)
    {
        address = a;
    }
```

```
        public double getWeeklyPay()
        {
            return weeklyPay;
        }
        public void computePay(int hoursWorked)
        {
            weeklyPay = hoursWorked * 6.50;
            System.out.println("Weekly pay for " + name
                                    + " is $" + weeklyPay);
        }
        public void mailCheck()
        {
            System.out.println("Mailing check to " + name
                                    + " at " + address);
        }
    }
```

Imagine that we have two departments in our company—a Payroll Department for handling the weekly payroll duties, and a Human Resources Department for managing general information about employees. The Payroll Department does not need to access or change the personal information about an employee. The Human Resources Department needs access to an employee's information, but should not be accessing any paycheck details.

The methods pertinent to the Payroll Department can be exposed in one interface, and the methods pertinent to the Human Resources Department can be exposed in another interface.

For example, the following interface named Payable exposes three methods from the Employee class.

```
public interface Payable
{
    public void computePay(int hoursWorked);
    public void mailCheck();
    public double getWeeklyPay();
}
```

The following interface named EmployeeInfo exposes four methods from the Employee class.

```
public interface EmployeeInfo
{
    public String getName();
    public void setName(String n);
    public String getAddress();
    public void setAddress(String a);
}
```

Now that we have written the interfaces, we need a class to implement them. But in our example, the Employee class already implements these methods, so all we need to do is make a quick change to Employee, having it declare that it implements both Payable and EmployeeInfo, as shown here:

```
public class Employee implements Payable, EmployeeInfo
{
    //The class definition remains the same.
}
```

 By implementing Payable and EmployeeInfo, through polymorphism an Employee object becomes a Payable object and an EmployeeInfo object. If someone in payroll needs an Employee object, we can pass the Employee object to a Payable reference. If someone in human resources needs an Employee object, we can pass the Employee object to an EmployeeInfo reference. With a Payable reference, only the Payable methods can be invoked. With an EmployeeInfo reference, only the methods in EmployeeInfo can be invoked.

In Chapter 8, "Polymorphism and Abstraction," we saw a SmartBoss class that has a payEmployee() method with an Employee parameter. This allows SmartBoss to pay any Employee object. The SmartBoss can use the Employee reference and invoke any of the methods in the Employee class.

The following Payroll class represents the Payroll Department of the company. The parameter of payEmployee() in Payroll is a Payable reference, meaning that we can pass in any object that is of type Payable. Because the Employee class implements Payable, Employee objects are of type Payable, so we can pass Employee objects in to the Payable reference of the payEmployee() method.

```
public class Payroll
{
    public void payEmployee(Payable p)
    {
        p.computePay(40);
        p.mailCheck();
    }
    public void printPaycheck(Payable p)
    {
        System.out.println("Printing check for $" + p.getWeeklyPay());
    }
}
```

In the Payroll class, the payEmployee() method uses the Payable parameter to invoke computePay() and mailCheck(). The Payroll class cannot invoke any of the methods in Employee that do not appear in Payable. For example, within payEmployee(), the statement:

```
p.setName("Bill Gates");        //Will not compile
```

is not valid. Only the three methods in Payable can invoked using p because p is a Payable reference. This was the whole purpose of this example, to create a situation in which specific methods of the Employee class are exposed through an interface. The way the Payroll class is designed, Payroll objects cannot access or change an employee's name or address. Payroll objects can only invoke the three methods in Payable that pertain to an employee's weekly paycheck.

The following PayableDemo program instantiates a Payroll object and pays an Employee. Study the program and try to determine its output, which is shown in Figure 10.8.

```
public class PayableDemo
{
    public static void main(String [] args)
    {
        Employee e = new Employee("George Washington", "Mt. Vernon");
        Payroll payroll = new Payroll();
        payroll.payEmployee(e);
        payroll.printPaycheck(e);
    }
}
```

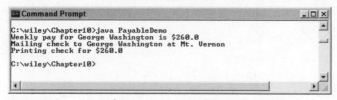

Figure 10.8   The output of the PayableDemo program.

The Payroll class is a more generic and adaptable class than the SmartBoss class. The SmartBoss can only pay Employee objects, which limits it to child classes of Employee. The Payroll class can pay any Payable object, which is any object whose class implements Payable. This includes all Employee objects because Employee implements Payable.

Imagine that the Payroll Department needs to send checks to members of the Board of Directors, who are represented by a Director class. If the Director class does not extend Employee, the SmartBoss will not be able to pay Director objects. However, if the Director class implements Payable:

```
public class Director implements Payable
```

Director objects can be passed in to the payEmployee() method of Payroll without any modifications to the Payroll class. The payEmployee() method does not know the actual data type of the Payable argument passed in. It only knows that the argument is Payable, and therefore has a computePay() and mailCheck() method.

The Payable interface demonstrates how an interface is used to expose methods of a class. The Payroll class is handed Payable objects, not Employee objects. Similarly, suppose that we have a class named HumanResources to represent the Human Resources Department. If we want the human resources department to only be able to invoke the methods of Employee that are exposed in the EmployeeInfo interface, we can design the methods of the HumanResources class so that they use EmployeeInfo references.

The following HumanResources class contains methods for changing an employee's name and address. Notice that a HumanResources object cannot invoke methods like computePay() or mailCheck() in Employee. It can only invoke those methods in the EmployeeInfo interface.

```
public class HumanResources
{
    public String getInfo(EmployeeInfo e)
    {
        return e.getName() + " " + e.getAddress();
    }
    public void changeName(EmployeeInfo e, String name)
```

```
    {
        System.out.println("Changing name for " + e.getName());
        e.setName(name);
        System.out.println("New name is " + e.getName());
    }
    public void updateAddress(EmployeeInfo e, String address)
    {
        System.out.println("Changing address for " + e.getName());
        e.setAddress(address);
        System.out.println("New address is " + e.getAddress());
    }
}
```

The following HRDemo program instantiates a HumanResources object and demonstrates changing an employee's name and address. Study the program and try to determine its output, which is shown in Figure 10.9.

```
public class HRDemo
{
    public static void main(String [] args)
    {
        Employee e = new Employee("George Washington", "Mt. Vernon");
        HumanResources hr = new HumanResources();
        System.out.println(hr.getInfo(e) + "\n");
        hr.changeName(e, "Bill Gates");
        hr.updateAddress(e, "Redmond, WA");
        System.out.println("\n" + hr.getInfo(e));
    }
}
```

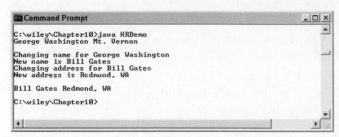

Figure 10.9   The output of the HRDemo program.

Forcing Behavior on a Class

An interface can be used as a parameter to a method, as we saw earlier in this chapter in both the Payroll class and the HumanResources class. For example, the payEmployee() method in Payroll has a Payable parameter. In that example, the purpose of using the Payable interface was to expose certain methods of the Employee class to the Payroll object, while hiding the other methods in Employee.

You can also use interface parameters to force classes to implement a particular interface. By forcing a class to implement a particular interface, you are forcing the class to contain certain methods.

 This type of design is used throughout Java programming, and we will see several important examples of interface parameters in the remainder of this book, including GUI event handling, threads, and JavaBeans.

For example, imagine that we have written a program that updates an audience of a football game every time the score changes. The audience in this example could be someone waiting for updates on a cell phone or PDA, or someone at home watching the scores change on a Web site, or a restaurant that flashes the scores on an electronic scoreboard for its customers. In these examples, each audience is an example of a listener. They are waiting and listening for a particular event to occur. We need to keep track of all these different types of listeners. This heterogeneous collection of listeners will not be too difficult to create because we saw in Chapter 9, "Collections," that the collections framework classes hold objects of type Object, which is any object.

However, we need a mechanism for notifying listeners when the score of the football game changes. How do we do this? Well, we are going to invoke a method on each listener. Which method will we invoke? And more importantly, how do we know that the listener has implemented the method we want to invoke?

By using an interface parameter, we will force anyone who wants an update of the football score to implement an interface named FootballListener. The FootballListener interface is defined as follows:

```
public interface FootballListener
{
    public void homeTeamScored(int points);
    public void visitingTeamScored(int points);
    public void endOfQuarter(int quarter);
    public void setHomeTeam(String name);
    public void setVisitingTeam(String name);
}
```

The following FootballGame class represents a live football game, and as events happen during the game, the listeners of the game receive updated information. Notice that the FootballGame class uses a Vector to keep track of all listeners. More importantly, notice how listeners get into the Vector.

```
import java.util.Vector;
public class FootballGame
{
     private String homeTeam, visitingTeam;
     private int homeScore, visitingScore;
     private Vector audience;
     public FootballGame(String homeTeam, String visitingTeam)
     {
          this.homeTeam = homeTeam;
          this.visitingTeam = visitingTeam;
          audience = new Vector(10);
     }
     public void addFootballListener(FootballListener f)
     {
          //Add the listener to the Vector.
          audience.add(f);
          //Tell them who is playing.
          f.setHomeTeam(homeTeam);
          f.setVisitingTeam(visitingTeam);
     }
     public void homeTeamScored(int points)
     {
          //Notify the audience that the home team scored.
          int size = audience.size();
          for(int i = 0; i < size; i++)
          {
               FootballListener current =
                         (FootballListener) audience.elementAt(i);
               current.homeTeamScored(points);
          }
     }
     public void visitingTeamScored(int points)
     {
          //Notify the audience that the visiting team scored.
          int size = audience.size();
          for(int i = 0; i < size; i++)
          {
               FootballListener current =
                         (FootballListener) audience.elementAt(i);
               current.visitingTeamScored(points);
          }
     }
     public void quarterEnded(int quarter)
     {
```

```
            //Notify the audience which quarter just ended.
            int size = audience.size();
            for(int i = 0; i < size; i++)
            {
                FootballListener current =
                            (FootballListener) audience.elementAt(i);
                current.endOfQuarter(quarter);
            }
    }
}
```

Classroom Q & A

Q: How do listeners get into the audience Vector of the FootballGame class?

A: Look at the addFootballListener() method and you will see a call to add() invoked on the Vector. This adds the parameter f to the audience Vector.

Q: Sure, but how exactly does the FootballGame class force its audience to implement the FootballListener interface?

A: Two specific design techniques are used. The audience Vector is a private field, so no one outside the class can access the audience Vector directly. The only changes to audience occur in the addFootballListener() method. Also, the parameter is a FootballListener, so the only way to invoke addFootballListener() is to pass in a FootballListener object.

Q: But FootballListener is an interface. I thought you couldn't instantiate a FootballListener object.

A: True, you can't. But you can write a class that implements FootballListener, and instances of this class will be of type FootballListener.

Q: Why?

A: Because of polymorphism. If a class named CellPhone implements FootballListener, a CellPhone object is a FootballListener object. The design of our FootballGame class is such that the only way to be a member of the audience Vector is to write a class that implements FootballListener.

Q: What did we gain from this design?

A: We gained a benefit that might seem subtle but is an important aspect of the Java language—one that demonstrates the robustness and structure of the Java programming language. When it comes time to inform the objects in the audience Vector of a change in the score, we know that every object in that Vector is of type FootballListener. This means we can invoke any method in the FootballListener interface on every object in audience, and we are guaranteed that each object has implemented the method. Through this design, I have forced members of the audience Vector to have certain behaviors, and it was all accomplished using an interface parameter of type FootballListener.

Q: Can you do this in other programming languages?

A: This type of benefit with interfaces is difficult to accomplish in languages that are not object oriented. We are using two key OOP concepts: encapsulation and polymorphism. Interfaces in Java are a powerful design tool, as long as you understand how they can be used to improve the design of your applications. Read on!

Let's write a class that wants to listen to a football game. The following ScoreBoard class implements the FootballListener interface.

```java
public class ScoreBoard implements FootballListener
{
    private String home, visitors;
    private int homePoints, visitorPoints;
    private int currentQuarter;
    public ScoreBoard()
    {
        currentQuarter = 1;
    }
    public void updateScore()
    {
        System.out.println("*************************************");
        System.out.println(home + ": " + homePoints);
        System.out.println(visitors + ": " + visitorPoints);
        displayQuarter();
        System.out.println("*************************************");
    }
    public void displayQuarter()
    {
        if(currentQuarter > 0)
        {
            System.out.println("Game is in quarter "
                            + currentQuarter);
```

```
        }
        else
        {
            System.out.println("Final score");
        }
    }
    public void homeTeamScored(int points)
    {
        System.out.println("The home team just scored " + points);
        homePoints += points;
        updateScore();
    }
    public void visitingTeamScored(int points)
    {
        System.out.println("The visiting team just scored " + points);
        visitorPoints += points;
        updateScore();
    }
    public void endOfQuarter(int quarter)
    {
        if(quarter >= 1 && quarter <= 3)
        {
            currentQuarter++;
        }
        else
        {
            currentQuarter = -1;      //game is over
        }
        System.out.println("Quarter " + quarter + " just ended.");
        updateScore();
    }
    public void setHomeTeam(String name)
    {
        home = name;
    }
    public void setVisitingTeam(String name)
    {
        visitors = name;
    }
}
```

The ScoreBoard class contains an implementation for each method in FootballListener, and therefore successfully implements the FootballListener interface. The following OaklandAtDenver program demonstrates a ScoreBoard
object adding itself to the audience Vector of a FootballGame object. Whenever
an event occurs in the DenverAtOakland game, the ScoreBoard object is
notified.

Study the OaklandAtDenver program and try to determine its output. Run
the program to verify the output.

```
public class OaklandAtDenver
{
    public static void main(String [] args)
    {
        System.out.println("Instantiating a new FootballGame");
        FootballGame game = new FootballGame("Broncos", "Raiders");
        System.out.println("Instantiating a listener");
        ScoreBoard scoreBoard = new ScoreBoard();
        System.out.println("Registering a listener to the game");
        game.addFootballListener(scoreBoard);
        System.out.println("Simulating a game...");
        game.homeTeamScored(7);
        game.quarterEnded(1);
        game.visitingTeamScored(3);
        game.visitingTeamScored(7);
        game.quarterEnded(2);
        game.quarterEnded(3);
        game.homeTeamScored(3);
        game.homeTeamScored(7);
        game.quarterEnded(4);
    }
}
```

In the OaklandAtDenver program, a ScoreBoard object was added to the audience Vector of the FootballGame object with the statement:

```
game.addFootballListener(scoreBoard);
```

This line of code is the key to the football example. If you want to watch the game, you need to invoke addFootballListener(), which requires a FootballListener object, of which ScoreBoard is one. As the OaklandAtDenver game is played, the ScoreBoard object is updated of all score changes and end of quarters, since ScoreBoard is in the audience Vector.

 The ScoreBoard object can do anything it wants with the information about the football game. It displays the score to System.out, but a Web page could convert it to HTML and generate a Web page. A cell phone company could send a text message to a Broncos or Raiders fan. A television station could display the scores on a scrolling ticker across the bottom of the screen.

The FootballGame class is not concernced with how the audience is listening or what the audience is doing with the information about score changes and so on. FootballGame simply notifies everyone who is listening to the game of any score changes because everyone in the audience has implemented the FootballListener methods.

Declaring Fields in Interfaces

Interfaces can contain fields, as long as the fields are declared both static and final. They must be static because an interface cannot be instantiated, and the requirement to be final is for program reliability.

 It does not make sense for an interface to contain a nonstatic field because the interface can never be instantiated. Recall that static fields do not require an instance of a class to exist in memory, but nonstatic fields are created only when an object is instantiated. Static fields in an interface are allocated in memory when the interface is loaded by the JVM's class loader.

The following PhoneHandler interface demonstrates an interface with three fields. As with the PhoneHandler example, most examples of fields in an interface are some type of enumeration.

```
package customer.service;
public interface PhoneHandler
{
    public static final int LOCAL = 0;
    public static final int LONG_DISTANCE = 1;
    public static final int COLLECT = 2;
    public void answer();
    public boolean forward(int extension);
    public void takeMessage(String message, String recipient);
}
```

Static members of a class are accessed using the class name. Similarly, static fields in an interface are accessed using the name of the interface. For example, the following statement accesses the LOCAL field of the PhoneHandler interface:

```
if(x == PhoneHandler.LOCAL)
```

The following FieldDemo program demonstrates using the fields of the PhoneHandler interface. Study the program and try to determine its output, which is shown in Figure 10.10.

Figure 10.10 The output of the FieldDemo program.

```
import customer.service.PhoneHandler;
public class FieldDemo
{
    public static void main(String [] args)
    {
        int call = 1;

        switch(call)
        {
            case PhoneHandler.LOCAL :
                System.out.println("Dial 9");
                break;
            case PhoneHandler.LONG_DISTANCE :
                System.out.println("Dial 8");
                break;
            case PhoneHandler.COLLECT :
                System.out.println("Dial 0");
                break;
        }
    }
}
```

Extending Interfaces

An interface can extend another interface, similarly to the way that a class can extend another class. The extends keyword is used to extend an interface, and the child interface inherits the methods of the parent interface.

The following SportsListener interface is extended by HockeyListener and FootballListener interfaces.

```
//Filename: SportsListener.java
public interface SportsListener
{
    public void setHomeTeam(String name);
    public void setVisitingTeam(String name);
}

//Filename: FootballListener.java
public interface FootballListener extends SportsListener
{
    public void homeTeamScored(int points);
    public void visitingTeamScored(int points);
    public void endOfQuarter(int quarter);
}

//Filename: HockeyListener.java
```

```
public interface HockeyListener extends SportsListener
{
    public void homeGoalScored();
    public void visitingGoalScored();
    public void endOfPeriod(int period);
    public void overtimePeriod(int ot);
}
```

The HockeyListener interface has four methods, but it inherits two from SportsListener; thus, a class that implements HockeyListener needs to implement all six methods. Similarly, a class that implements FootballListener needs to define the three methods from FootballListener and the two methods from SportsListener.

The following SportsTicker class implements the HockeyListener interface. Notice that the required six methods are defined to avoid declaring Sports-Ticker abstract.

```
public class SportsTicker implements HockeyListener
{
    private String home, visitors;
    private int homeGoals, visitorGoals;
    private int period, overtimePeriod;
    public void homeGoalScored()
    {
        homeGoals++;
    }
    public void visitingGoalScored()
    {
        visitorGoals++;
    }
    public void endOfPeriod(int period)
    {
        this.period = ++period;
    }
    public void overtimePeriod(int ot)
    {
        overtimePeriod = ot;
    }
    public void setHomeTeam(String name)
    {
        home = name;
    }
    public void setVisitingTeam(String name)
    {
        visitors = name;
    }
}
```

Extending Multiple Interfaces

In Java, a class can only extend one parent class. (Multiple inheritance is not allowed.) Interfaces are not classes, however, and an interface can extend more than one parent interface. The extends keyword is used once, and the parent interfaces are declared in a comma-separated list.

For example, if the HockeyListener interface extended both SportsListener and EventListener, it would be declared as:

```
public interface HockeyListener extends SportsListener, EventListener
```

Any class that implements this HockeyListener interface must implement all the methods in HockeyListener, SportsListener, and EventListener.

 You might be curious to know what happens if an interface has two parents and each parent declares the exact same method. For example, if SportsListener and EventListener both contain a playBall() method, how does this affect a class that implements HockeyListener? Well, because it does not make sense for a class to have two playBall() methods, only one is required of the class.

♦ Tagging Interfaces

The most common use of extending interfaces occurs when the parent interface does not contain any methods. For example, the MouseListener interface in the java.awt.event package extended java.util.EventListener, which is defined as:

```
package java.util;
public interface EventListener
{}
```

An interface with no methods in it is referred to as a *tagging interface.* Why define an interface with no methods in it? Well, there are two basic design purposes of tagging interfaces:

Creates a common parent. As with the EventListener interface, which is extended by dozens of other interfaces in the Java API, you can use a tagging interface to create a common parent among a group of interfaces. For example, when an interface extends EventListener, the JVM knows that this particular interface is going to be used in an event delegation scenario.

Adds a data type to a class. This situation is where the term tagging comes from. A class that implements a tagging interface does not need to define any methods (since the interface does not have any), but the class becomes an interface type through polymorphism.

continued

◆ Tagging Interfaces *(continued)*

java.io.Serializable is an example of a tagging interface that is not designed to be a parent interface, but instead is meant to be implemented by a class so that objects of the class become Serializable objects. The Serializable interface is defined as:

```
package java.io;
public interface Serializable
{
    public static final long serialVersionUID;
}
```

Notice Serializable has one field, but no methods. A class can implement Serializable simply by declaring *implements Serializable*, and no additional changes are required of the class. The following Employee class implements the Serializable interface.

```
public class Employee implements java.io.Serializable
{
    public String name, address;
    public double weeklyPay;
    public void computePay(int hoursWorked)
    {
        weeklyPay = hoursWorked * 6.50;
        System.out.println("Weekly pay for " + name
+ " is $" + weeklyPay);
    }
    public void mailCheck()
    {
        System.out.println("Mailing check to " + name
+ " at " + address);
    }
}
```

Why implement an interface with no methods in it? What is different about the Employee class now that it implements Serializable? Well, the answer is based on polymorphism. If a class implements an interface, objects of the class can be treated as the interface data type. For example, an Employee object can be treated as a Serializable object.

Consider the following statements that use this Employee class. What is the output?

```
Employee e = new Employee();
if(e instanceof Employee)
{
    System.out.println("e is an Employee object");
}
if(e instanceof java.io.Serializable)
{
    System.out.println("e is a Serializable object");
}
```

The output of these statements is:

```
e is an Employee object
e is a Serializable object
```

If the Employee class did not implement Serializable, the second line of the output would not be displayed; therefore, implementing a tagging interface, although requiring no extra work of the class, adds a data type to objects of that class.

By the way, the Serializable interface is an important tagging interface in the Java language. A JVM can serialize an object, saving its state to a file or other output, and deserialize the object at a later time. This can only be done with objects that are of type java.io.Serializable, meaning it can only be done with objects whose class implements the Serializable interface. This allows the designer of a class to decide whether or not the class should be tagged as Serializable.

Interfaces and Polymorphism

If a class implements an interface, objects of the class can take on the form of the interface data type. The capability of an object to take on the form of an interface is an example of polymorphism. I have used this fact several times throughout this chapter, but now I want to formally discuss the details of polymorphism and interfaces.

For example, in the OaklandAtDenver program discussed earlier, a ScoreBoard object is passed in to a method that has a FootballListener reference. The reason that this is valid is that the ScoreBoard class implements the Football-Listener interface.

 In fact, we could have instantiated a ScoreBoard object using a FootballListener reference:

```
FootballListener scoreBoard = new ScoreBoard();
```

The *is a* relationship carries over to interfaces. ScoreBoard implements FootballListener, so a ScoreBoard object *is a* FootballListener object.

Let's look at an example that demonstrates how interfaces affect polymorphism. We will look at a Dog class that both has a parent class and implements an interface. The following Mammal class is the parent class.

```
public class Mammal
{
    public void breathe()
    {
        System.out.println("Mammal is breathing");
    }
}
```

The following Play interface represents objects that can play fetch and play catch, which is implemented by our Dog class.

```
public interface Play
{
    public void playFetch();
    public void playCatch();
}
```

The following Dog class extends Mammal and implements the Play interface.

```
public class Dog extends Mammal implements Play
{
    public void playFetch()
    {
        System.out.println("Dog is fetching");
    }
    public void playCatch()
    {
        System.out.println("Dog is catching");
    }
    public void sleep()
    {
        System.out.println("Dog is sleeping");
    }
}
```

I want to point out the various forms that a Dog object can take on. Through polymorphism, a Dog can take on the following forms:

Dog.   Certainly a Dog object can take the form of a Dog.

Mammal.   A Dog object is a Mammal object because Dog extends the Mammal class.

Play.   A Dog object is a Play object because Dog implements Play.

Object.   A Dog object is an Object because Dog extends Mammal and Mammal extends Object.

Therefore, the following four statements are all valid:

```
Dog fido = new Dog();
Mammal rover = new Dog();
Play spot = new Dog();
Object pooch = new Dog();
```

Each of these four Dog objects looks the same in memory; however, each is being viewed in a different form, depending on its reference. For example, with the Dog reference fido, all the methods of Dog, Mammal, Object, and Play can be invoked without requiring any casting of the Dog reference.

```
fido.sleep();
fido.playFetch();
fido.breathe();
fido.toString();
```

Compare this to the Mammal reference rover. Without casting, which methods can be invoked? Aside from the Object methods, only the breathe() method can be invoked on rover:

```
rover.breathe();
```

Similarly, what methods (aside from the Object methods) can be invoked using the Play reference spot, without casting? Because it is a Play reference, only the two methods of Play can be invoked:

```
spot.playCatch();
spot.playFetch();
```

Using the Object reference pooch, only the methods in Object can be invoked without casting. For example, the following code is valid.

```
pooch.toString();
```

However, to invoke any of the methods in Mammal, Play, or Dog requires the pooch reference to be cast. For example, the following statement is valid:

```
((Dog) pooch).sleep();
```

The following FourDogs program demonstrates a Dog object taking on these four different forms through polymorphism. Study the program, which compiles and executes successfully, and try to determine its output, which is shown in Figure 10.11.

```
public class FourDogs
{
    public static void main(String [] args)
    {
```

```
            System.out.println("Instantiating four dogs");
            Dog fido = new Dog();
            Mammal rover = new Dog();
            Play spot = new Dog();
            Object pooch = new Dog();
            System.out.println("Invoking Dog methods");
            fido.sleep();
            fido.playFetch();
            fido.breathe();
            System.out.println("fido is " + fido.toString());
            System.out.println("\nInvoking Mammal methods");
            rover.breathe();
            System.out.println("\nInvoking Play methods");
            spot.playCatch();
            spot.playFetch();
            System.out.println("\nInvoking Object methods");
            System.out.println("pooch is " + pooch.toString());
            ((Dog) pooch).sleep();
        }
    }
```

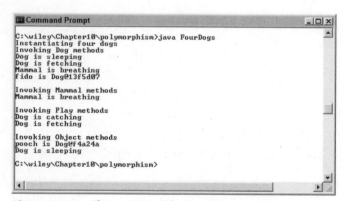

Figure 10.11   The output of the FourDogs program.

Lab 10.1: Implementing an Interface

In this lab, you will write your own version of a FootballListener and use the FootballGame class from this chapter to add your FootballListener to the audience.

1. Start by copying the FootballGame.class and FootballListener.class files into a new directory you create, named c:\football.

2. Declare a class named CellPhone that implements FootballListener.

3. Within your CellPhone class, add fields for the names of the teams, their scores, and the current quarter.

4. Add all of the methods in the FootballListener interface. The assumption here is that a CellPhone display has limited resources, so only display an output (to System.out) when the score changes or when the game is over. Try to limit the text of your output as much as possible, while still displaying the information in an informative manner.

5. Save the CellPhone class in your c:\football directory and then compile it.

6. Write a program that simulates a football game. You will need to instantiate a FootballGame object and a CellPhone object, and invoke addFootballListener(), passing in your CellPhone object.

7. Simulate a game by having the two teams score and the quarters change; then run your program to verify that your CellPhone object is listening and displaying the proper results of the game.

As the football game is played, you should be able to watch it on the CellPhone, seeing the output at the command prompt.

Lab 10.2 Interfaces and javadoc

This lab demonstrates how the javadoc tool creates documentation for interfaces.

1. In Lab 10.1, you created a directory named c:\football. Make sure that directory has the following four .class files in it: FootballGame, FootballListener, CellPhone, and your program that simulates a football game.

2. In your CellPhone class, add javadoc comments for the class and the methods, including author and version information.

3. From the command prompt, run the following javadoc command from the c:\football directory:

```
javadoc -author -version *.java
```

4. If successful, the javadoc tool should have created a file in the c:\football directory named index.html. Open this file in your Web browser, and view the documentation, specifically the FootballListener interface.

The page index.html should contain a link to each of the four classes and interfaces that you added javadoc comments to. You should be able to see your comments as you browse through the documentation.

Summary

- An interface is a collection of abstract methods that are implemented by a class. A class uses the implements keyword to implement an interface.

- A class that implements an interface must implement each method defined in the interface. If not, the class must be declared abstract.

- An interface can be used to expose certain methods of a class. An interface can also be used to force a class to contain certain methods.

- An interface can contain fields. Each field in an interface is implicitly public, static, and final.

- An interface can extend one or more interfaces.

- An interface with no methods in it is referred to as a tagging interface.

Review Questions

1. True or False: An interface is saved in a .java file that must match the name of the interface.

2. True or False: The bytecode for an interface appears in a .intf file, where the filename matches the name of the interface.

3. True or False: All methods in an interface are abstract.

4. True or False: Methods in an interface can be public, protected, or the default access, but not private.

5. If a class declares that it implements an interface but the class does not define all the methods of the interface, the class must be declared _____.

6. What is the term used to describe an interface with no methods in it?

7. Name two important uses of interfaces.

8. True or False: A class can implement more than one interface.

9. True or False: An interface can extend more than one parent interface.

10. A field in an interface must be declared as _____ and _____.

Answers to Review Questions

1. True, as with classes.

2. False. Interfaces are not classes, but their bytecode appears in .class files. The name of the .class file matches the name of the interface, and the directory structure must match the package name, as with classes.

3. True. Even if you do not use the abstract keyword, all methods in an interface are abstract.

4. False: Methods in an interface are public, even if you leave off the public keyword. Attempting to declare a method in an interface as private or protected generates a compiler error.

5. Abstract. A class that does not implement all the methods of an interface must declare itself as abstract.

6. A tagging interface is an interface with no methods in it.

7. There are many, but two that I emphasized in this chapter are exposing methods of a class, and forcing behavior on a class.

8. True. The interfaces are separated by commas after the implements keyword.

9. True. The parent interfaces are separated by commas after the extends keyword.

10. Final and static. Only final and static fields can be declared in any interface.

CHAPTER

11

Exception Handling

Exception handling is yet another fundamental aspect of Java that must be understood before the more advanced APIs of the language can be used. This chapter discusses how exception handling works in Java, including try/catch blocks, the Handle or Declare Rule, declaring exceptions, throwing exceptions, the finally keyword, and writing your own exceptions.

Overview of Exception Handling

An exception is a problem that arises during the execution of a program. An exception can occur for many different reasons, including the following: a user has entered invalid data, a file that needs to be opened cannot be found, a network connection has been lost in the middle of communications, or the JVM has run out of memory.

Some of these exceptions are caused by user error, others by programmer error, and others by physical resources that have failed in some manner. In this chapter, I will discuss the various types of exceptions, when you should throw one, and when you should catch one (and times when you do not have a choice), and how to write and throw your own exceptions.

To understand how exception handling works in Java, you need to understand the three categories of exceptions:

Checked exceptions.   A checked exception is an exception that is typically a user error or a problem that cannot be foreseen by the programmer. For example, if a file is to be opened, but the file cannot be found, an exception occurs. Because this type of exception is a checked exception, it must be dealt with in Java and cannot simply be ignored (as we will see when we discuss the Handle or Declare Rule).

Runtime exceptions.   A runtime exception is an exception that occurs that probably could have been avoided by the programmer. As opposed to checked exceptions, runtime exceptions can be ignored (and should be, in most cases). You should let a runtime exception crash your program, then find the problem and change your code so that the exception does not arise again. Examples of runtime exceptions include running off the end of an array, integer division by zero, referencing a null reference, and casting a reference to an invalid data type.

Errors.   Actually, these are not exceptions at all, but problems that arise beyond the control of the user or the programmer. Errors are typically ignored in your code because you can rarely do anything about an error, even if you wanted your program to fix the problem. For example, if a stack overflow occurs, an error will arise. However, because you are out of memory, your program will be unable to continue executing. Any code you have written that attempts to fix the problem won't get a chance to execute anyway, so errors are often ignored when designing and writing Java applications.

Even though errors are not exceptions, they behave similarly to exceptions in terms of the flow of the control when they arise. Both exceptions and errors can crash your program, as we will now discuss.

Flow of Control of Exceptions

Exceptions in Java are objects that are thrown by a method. When a method is invoked, it is pushed onto the method call stack. When a method throws an exception, the method is popped off the call stack, and the exception is thrown to the previous method on the stack.

For example, suppose that main() is at the bottom of the call stack, followed by method1() and then method2(). If method2() throws an exception, method2() is popped off the call stack, and the exception is thrown down to method1().

With an exception heading its way, method1() has three choices:

- Catch the exception so that it does not go any further down the call stack.
- Catch the exception, then throw it back down the call stack.
- Not catch the exception, thereby causing method1() to be popped off the call stack, with the exception continuing down the call stack to main().

This flow of control continues down the call stack, no matter how many methods appear on the call stack. Each method further down the call stack either catches the exception and stops this process, catches the exception and throws it again, or simply does nothing and lets the exception fall through to the next method.

What happens when we reach the bottom of the call stack? Well, if an exception is thrown to main(), then main() had better catch the exception or the program will terminate. When an exception reaches the bottom of a call stack and no method has stopped it along the way, the JVM will crash and inform you of the details of the exception.

Let's look at an example of what happens when an exception is ignored all the way down the call stack. The following CrashDemo program has three methods: main(), method1(), and method2(). Study the program and try to determine what happens when it executes. The output is shown in Figure 11.1.

```java
public class CrashDemo
{
    public static void main(String [] args)
    {
        System.out.println("Inside main...");
        int [] values = {1, 2, 3, 4};
        System.out.println("Invoking method1...");
        method1(values);
        System.out.println("*** Back in main ***");
    }
    public static void method1(int [] x)
    {
        System.out.println("\nInside method1...");
        method2(x);
        System.out.println("*** Back in method1 ***");
    }
    public static void method2(int [] y)
    {
        System.out.println("\nInside method2");
        System.out.println(y[5]);
        System.out.println("*** Leaving method2 ***");
    }
}
```

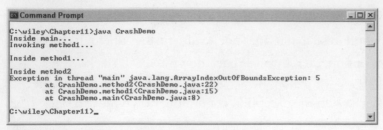

Figure 11.1   Output of the CrashDemo program.

The CrashDemo program crashes when an ArrayIndexOutOfBoundsException occurs, which is an example of a runtime exception. As I mentioned earlier, runtime exceptions are typically the result of programmer error; therefore, you want the exception to crash your program so you can find and fix the problem.

Notice from the output in Figure 11.1 of the CrashDemo program that the following statement does not execute in method2():

```
System.out.println("*** Leaving method2 ***");
```

This is because the previous statement (shown as follows) causes an ArrayIndexOutOfBoundsException:

```
System.out.println(y[5]);
```

The array referenced by y has only four elements, so three is the largest index that can be used. This exception is thrown by the JVM, which pops method2() off the call stack. Because method1() does not do anything with the exception, method1() is popped off the call stack. Because main() ignores the exception as well, main() is popped off the call stack.

The exception is then passed on to the JVM, and the JVM prints out the stack trace before terminating. Notice that the stack trace contains useful information, including the line numbers in the source code where the exception occurred.

You can print this stack trace yourself with any exception you catch by using the printStackTrace() method of the Throwable class. You will notice that I use printStackTrace() method in almost every catch block in the examples.

 Later in this chapter, I will discuss the Handle or Declare Rule, which specifies when an exception must be handled. In the earlier CrashDemo program, if method1() catches the exception and does not throw it again, the exception is considered handled (no matter what method1() actually does to fix the problem). If method1() catches the exception and then turns right around and throws it at main(), this is not considered handling the exception. Similarly, if method1() does nothing but let the exception continue on to main(), the exception has not been handled either.

An exception is considered handled by a method if the method stops the exception from continuing down the method call stack.

Throwable Classes

The three types of exceptions share a common parent: the java.lang.Throwable class. Only objects of type Throwable can be thrown by the JVM. The Throwable class has two child classes: Exception and Error.

The inheritance hierarchy of exceptions is based on the three categories. The Error class is the parent class of all Java errors; the Exception class is the parent class of all exceptions, both run time and checked.

Runtime exceptions and checked exceptions are further distinguished by where they fit in the inheritance hierarchy. If a class is a child of RuntimeException, this child class represents a runtime exception. If a class is a child of Exception but not a child of RuntimeException, this class is a checked exception.

For example, ArrayIndexOutOfBoundsException and ArithmeticException are runtime exceptions because they are both child classes of RuntimeException, whereas IOException and ClassNotFoundException are checked exceptions because they are child classes of Exception.

 Why make the distinction between runtime and checked exceptions when all the classes are children of Exception? Because the Handle or Declare Rule (discussed later in this chapter) is an essential Java feature that applies only to checked exceptions.

Methods of the Throwable Class

Exceptions are Java objects of type Throwable. When you catch an exception, you catch a reference to a Java object. Each exception class is different and has its own set of useful methods, but because all exceptions extend from Throwable, you can also invoke the methods of the Throwable class on any caught exception.

The following is a description of some of the methods in Throwable. Be sure to check the documentation for a complete description of all the methods in the Throwable class.

public String getMessage().   Returns a detailed message about the exception that has occurred. This message is initialized in the Throwable constructor.

public Throwable getCause().   Returns the cause of the exception as represented by a Throwable object. This cause is initialized using either one of the Throwable constructors or the initCause() method.

public String toString().   Returns the name of the class concatenated with the result of getMessage().

public void printStackTrace().   Prints the result of toString() along with the stack trace to System.err, the error output stream. (System.err is the command prompt for your Java programs running on Windows.) This method is overloaded for sending the stack trace to an output stream that you specify.

public StackTraceElement [] getStackTrace().   Returns an array containing each element on the stack trace. The element at index 0 represents the top of the call stack, and the last element in the array represents the method at the bottom of the call stack. This method allows your application to programmatically iterate through each line of the call stack.

public Throwable fillInStackTrace().   Fills the stack trace of this Throwable object with the current stack trace, adding to any previous information in the stack trace.

The methods in Throwable are designed to assist you in determining how and where the problem occurred. In the next section, we will discuss how an exception is caught using a try/catch block.

Catching Exceptions

A method catches an exception using a combination of the try and catch keywords. A try/catch block is placed around the code that might generate an exception. Code within a try/catch block is referred to as protected code, and the syntax for using try/catch looks like the following:

```
try
{
    //Protected code
}catch(ExceptionName e1)
{
    //Catch block
}
```

A catch statement involves declaring the type of exception you are trying to catch. If an exception occurs in protected code, the catch block (or blocks) that follows the try is checked. If the type of exception that occurred is listed in a catch block, the exception is passed to the catch block much as an argument is passed into a method parameter.

A try/catch block does not catch everything. If you say you want to catch a football and a baseball is thrown, you will not catch it. If you say you want to catch a NullPointerException and an ArithmeticException occurs, you will not catch the ArithmeticException.

 If you say you want to catch an Exception, then you will catch every exception that might arise. Remember, all exceptions are child classes of Exception, so through polymorphism, all exceptions are of type Exception.

The following try/catch block tries to catch a FileNotFoundException when attempting to open a file:

```
try
{
     System.out.println("Opening file for reading...");
     file = new FileInputStream(fileName);
}catch(FileNotFoundException f)
{
     System.out.println("** Could not find " + fileName + " **");
     f.printStackTrace();
     return -1;
}
```

If the file is found, no exception occurs, and the catch block is skipped. If the file is not found, the constructor of FileInputStream throws a new FileNot-FoundException, which is caught in the variable f of our catch block. I suppose in a real-world situation, we would give the user an opportunity to try another filename, but this catch block simply prints out the stack trace and returns a –1, causing the method to stop executing and the flow of control to return to the previous method on the call stack.

Writing try/catch Blocks

The following MyFileUtilities class has a readOneByte() method that contains two try/catch blocks. Study the method and try to determine the flow of control if an exception does or does not occur in each try/catch block.

```
import java.io.*;
public class MyFileUtilities
{
     private String fileName;
     public MyFileUtilities(String name)
     {
```

```
            fileName = name;
    }
    public byte readOneByte()
    {
        FileInputStream file = null;
        try
        {
            System.out.println("Opening file for reading...");
            file = new FileInputStream(fileName);
        }catch(FileNotFoundException f)
        {
            System.out.println("** Could not find "
                                    + fileName + " **");
            f.printStackTrace();
            return -1;
        }
        System.out.println("Just opened file: " + fileName);
        byte x = -1;
        try
        {
            System.out.println("Reading one byte from file...");
            x = (byte) file.read();
        }catch(IOException i)
        {
            System.out.println("** Error reading one byte **");
            i.printStackTrace();
            return -1;
        }
        System.out.println("Just read " + x);
        return x;
    }
}
```

The following CatchDemo program uses a filename input from the command line. The output in Figure 11.2 shows what occurs when the filename does not exist and the readOneByte() method attempts to open this nonexistent file.

```
public class CatchDemo
{
    public static void main(String [] args)
    {
        System.out.println("Instantiating a
MyFileUtilities object...");
        MyFileUtilities util = new MyFileUtilities(args[0]);
        System.out.println("Invoking readOneByte() method...");
        System.out.println(util.readOneByte());
    }
}
```

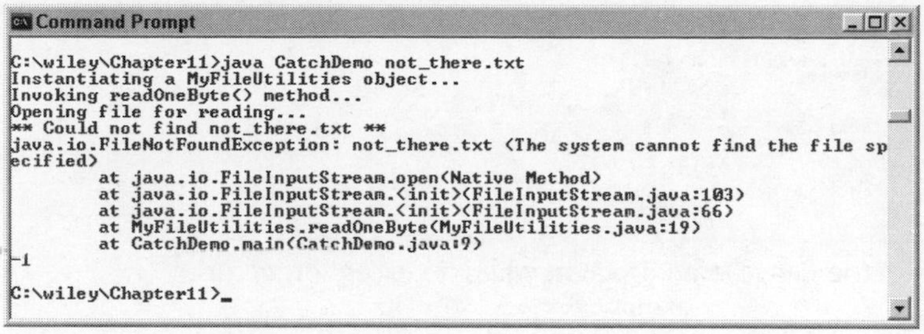

Figure 11.2 Output of the CatchDemo program when the file is not found.

In Figure 11.2, the file not_there.txt does not exist, and a FileNotFound-Exception occurs at the following statement:

```
file = new FileInputStream(fileName);
```

The FileNotFoundException catch block catches the exception in the variable f, uses f to print out the stack trace, and returns a –1. That ends the method call and flow of control returns back to main().

Now let's run the program again, this time where the file exists and the read() is also successful; hence no exceptions occur. Figure 11.3 shows an example of what the output will look like.

Multiple catch Blocks

A try block can be followed by multiple catch blocks. The syntax for multiple catch blocks looks like the following:

```
try
{
    //Protected code
}catch(ExceptionType1 e1)
{
    //Catch block
}catch(ExceptionType2 e2)
{
    //Catch block
}catch(ExceptionType3 e3)
{
    //Catch block
}
```

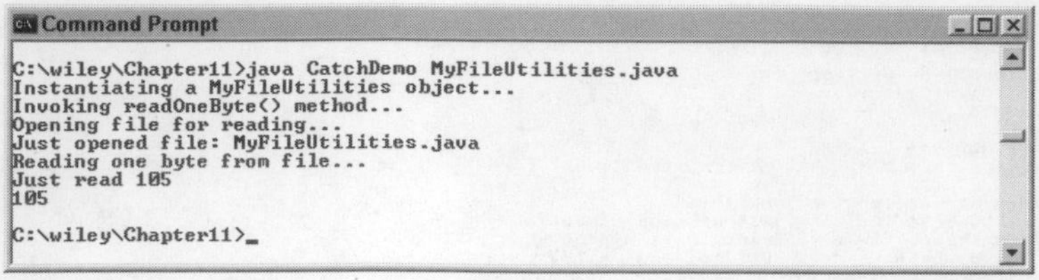

Figure 11.3 Output of the CatchDemo program when no exception occurs.

The previous statements demonstrate three catch blocks, but you can have any number of them after a single try. If an exception occurs in the protected code, the exception is thrown to the first catch block in the list. If the data type of the exception thrown matches *ExceptionType1*, it gets caught there. If not, the exception passes down to the second catch statement. This continues until the exception either is caught or falls through all catches, in which case the current method stops execution and the exception is thrown down to the previous method on the call stack.

In the readOneByte() method of the MyFileUtilities class, there are two try/catch blocks: one for the FileNotFoundException and one for the IOException. I created two try/catch blocks to demonstrate both the flow of control of exceptions and how to use try and catch. However, I would typically write a single try block that has two catch blocks, as shown in the readOneByte() method of the following MyFileUtilities2 class.

```java
import java.io.*;
public class MyFileUtilities2
{
    private String fileName;
    public MyFileUtilities2(String name)
    {
        fileName = name;
    }
    public byte readOneByte()
    {
        FileInputStream file = null;
        byte x = -1;
        try
        {
            System.out.println("Opening file for reading...");
            file = new FileInputStream(fileName);
            System.out.println("Just opened file: " + fileName);
            System.out.println("Reading one byte from file...");
            x = (byte) file.read();
        }catch(FileNotFoundException f)
        {
            System.out.println("** Could not find "
```

```
                                        + fileName + " **");
                f.printStackTrace();
                return -1;
        }catch(IOException i)
        {
                System.out.println("** Error reading one byte **");
                i.printStackTrace();
                return -1;
        }
        System.out.println("Just read " + x);
        return x;
    }
}
```

 With multiple catch blocks, the order in which the catch blocks are listed is the order they are checked when an exception occurs. This has an important side effect that I discuss in detail in the sidebar titled *Catching Exceptions and Polymorphism*.

Notice in the MyFileUtilities2 class that all the statements involved with opening and reading the file appear in the same try block. This makes the code more readable in my opinion, yet the result of the method is identical to the one in the MyFileUtilities program.

The following CatchDemo2 program invokes readOneByte() in MyFile-Utilities2 by using a file that does not exist, thereby generating a FileNot-FoundException at the following statement:

```
file = new FileInputStream(fileName);
```

Study the CatchDemo2 program and try to determine its output, which is shown in Figure 11.4. Compare this to the output of the CatchDemo program in Figure 11.2.

```
public class CatchDemo2
{
    public static void main(String [] args)
    {
        System.out.println("Instantiating a MyFileUtilities2
object...");
        MyFileUtilities2 util = new MyFileUtilities2(args[0]);
        System.out.println("Invoking readOneByte() method...");
        System.out.println(util.readOneByte());
    }
}
```

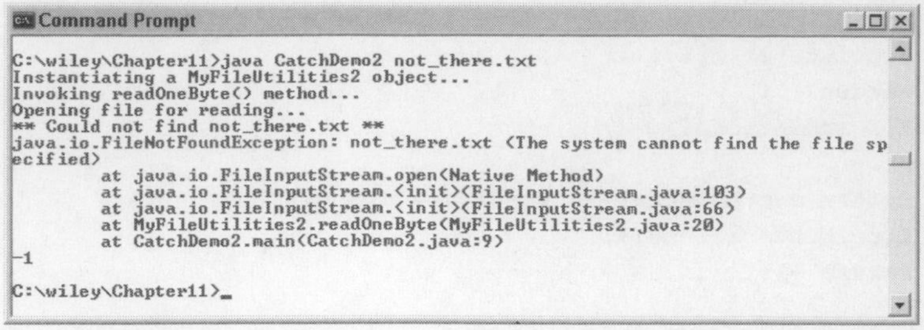

Figure 11.4 Output of the CatchDemo2 program when a nonexistent file is used.

◆ Catching Exceptions and Polymorphism

Although a try block can have multiple catch blocks, the catch blocks cannot simply appear in a random order. When an exception occurs, the catch blocks are checked in the order in which they appear. Because of polymorphism, it is possible to write a catch block that cannot be reached.

For example, the following try block has two catch blocks following it. The IOException is listed first, followed by a FileNotFoundException.

```
try
{
    file = new FileInputStream(fileName);
    x = (byte) file.read();
}catch(IOException i)
{
    i.printStackTrace();
    return -1;
}catch(FileNotFoundException f)          //Not valid!
{
    f.printStackTrace();
    return -1;
}
```

The preceding try/catch block does not compile because the FileNotFoundException block is an unreachable block of code. Why? Because FileNotFoundException is a child class of IOException. Therefore, a FileNotFoundException is an IOException (don't forget the *is a* relationship with polymorphism). If a FileNotFoundException occurs in the try block, the IOException will catch it because the IOException catch block is checked first.

Another result of exceptions and polymorphism is that you can write a "catch all" block. All exception classes are child classes of Exception, so catching an Exception catches all exceptions, both checked and run time.

For example, the following try/catch block corrects the earlier problem with IOException and FileNotFoundException by placing them in the correct order, and it also adds a third catch block to catch any other type of exception that might occur.

```
try
{
    file = new FileInputStream(fileName);
    x = (byte) file.read();
}catch(IOException i)
{
    i.printStackTrace();
    return -1;
}catch(FileNotFoundException f)          //Not valid!
{
    f.printStackTrace();
    return -1;
}catch(Exception e)
{
    e.printStackTrace();
}
```

Notice that the Exception catch block does not contain a return statement, so the current method keeps executing. The other two catch blocks cause the method to pop off the call stack because they return a value to the calling method. These are merely design decisions.

I want you to look at the next try/catch block and try to determine how it filters exceptions that may occur.

```
try
{
    //Protected code
}catch(RuntimeException r)
{
    System.out.println("Just caught a runtime exception");
    r.printStackTrace();
}catch(Exception e)
{
    System.out.println("Just caught a checked exception");
    e.printStackTrace();
}
```

You can tell by the println() statements that the first catch block catches all runtime exceptions, whereas the second catch block catches all checked exceptions. The RuntimeException catch block has to appear before the Exception catch block because RuntimeException is a child class of Exception.

Handle or Declare Rule

Java has a rule that is strictly enforced regarding checked exceptions; it is referred to as the Handle or Declare Rule. The rule states simply that a checked exception must be either handled or declared. *Handling* an exception involves catching the exception. *Declaring* an exception involves a method using the throws keyword in its signature, declaring any checked exceptions that the method is not going to handle.

> **The Handle or Declare Rule does not apply to runtime exceptions. If you do something in your program that can generate a runtime exception, you have the option of catching that exception or simply ignoring it and letting it crash your program. As I mentioned earlier, in most cases you do not try to catch runtime exceptions because they are often the result of poor code design. Let them crash your program, then find the problem and fix it.**

I want to emphasize the difference between runtime exceptions and checked exceptions, and explain why runtime exceptions do not have to adhere to the Handle or Declare Rule. For example, using the dot operator to access a field or method may generate a NullPointerException if the reference is null. The NullPointerException class is a child of RuntimeException and therefore is a runtime exception. If I had to try and catch a NullPointerException every time I used the dot operator, my code would contain more try/catch code than other code. Thankfully, you can ignore potential runtime exceptions in your code.

However, if I try to open a file and that file is not found, how does that affect the rest of my program if I simply ignore the fact that the file was not found? In Java, you cannot ignore a situation such as a file not being found. You must handle the potential checked exception, or your Java code will not compile.

> **Protected code has a higher overhead for the JVM than unprotected code. Avoid putting statements in protected code unless they need to be. That being said, often when I am in a hurry to test something, I will put my entire program in one large try/catch block that catches Exception, just so I can avoid compiler errors from the Handle or Declare Rule. Of course, I won't do that if I am writing "serious" code.**

The following Lazy class contains a readOneByte() method that does not contain any try/catch code. Because the readOneByte() method does not follow the Handle or Declare Rule, the class does not compile. Figure 11.5 shows the compiler error that is generated.

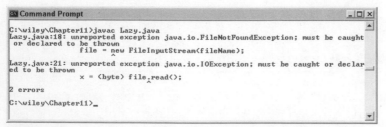

Figure 11.5   Compiler error generated by compiling the Lazy class.

```
import java.io.*;
public class Lazy
{
    private String fileName;
    public Lazy(String name)
    {
        fileName = name;
    }
    public byte readOneByte()
    {
        FileInputStream file = null;
        byte x = -1;
        System.out.println("Opening file for reading...");
        file = new FileInputStream(fileName);
        System.out.println("Just opened file: " + fileName);
        System.out.println("Reading one byte from file...");
        x = (byte) file.read();
        System.out.println("Just read " + x);
        return x;
    }
}
```

The compiler is telling us that the readOneByte() method either has to catch the FileNotFoundException that can occur from the statement new FileInput-Stream() or declare it. The compiler is saying the same about the IOException that can occur from the read() statement.

You have seen how to handle an exception using a try/catch block. Now, let's look at our other option in the Handle or Declare Rule: declaring an exception.

Declaring Exceptions

If a method does not handle a checked exception, the method must declare it using the throws keyword. The throws keyword appears at the end of a method's signature. For example, the following method declares that it throws a RemoteException:

```
public void deposit(double amount) throws RemoteException
```

A method can declare that it throws more than one exception, in which case the exceptions are declared in a list separated by commas. For example, the following method declares that it throws a RemoteException and an Insufficient-FundsException:

```
public void withdraw(double amount) throws RemoteException,
InsufficientFundsException
```

Classroom Q & A

Q: When do you handle an exception and when do you declare an exception?

A: A good question. The answer is based on design decisions. Do you want a method to deal with a problem, or do you want the problem to be passed on to the caller of the method?

Q: I would think a method should deal with its own problems.

A: I agree, if the problem is related to the method. For example, suppose that I walk into my bank and make a deposit (by invoking a deposit() method), but the teller is having problems with his computer. That should not be my problem. In this case, the deposit() method should handle this exception and fix the problem without notifying me, the caller of the method.

Q: Then why would the deposit() method throw an exception?

A: Well, if I am in the middle of a deposit and the bank's computer system fails, that might be my problem. In that case, I want to be informed that my deposit did not successfully go through. The deposit() method can tell me that the transaction was unsuccessful by throwing an exception back to me.

Q: Why not just have the method return a boolean? If the deposit worked, it returns true. Otherwise, it returns false.

A: Well, that is a common programming design. In fact, the C and C++ Windows API is filled with methods that return true or false. What I don't like about getting back an answer like false is that it doesn't tell me what went wrong. If I make a deposit and the teller simply says, "Sorry, that didn't work," I have no idea why. If the teller throws me an exception instead, I can catch the exception (which is a Java object) and determine all sorts of information about what went wrong.

Q: Throwing the exception seems like too much overhead. Is it worth it?

A: Exception handling is a part of Java, and the minimal overhead involved should not be a concern compared to the design benefits. For example, if I try to withdraw more money than I have in my checking account, just telling me that it did not work with a return value of false does not stop me from ignoring my overdraft. I can just go right on spending more money and then plead ignorance when my overdraft statement comes in the mail. I can tell the bank that I didn't check the return value of the withdraw() method.

Q: Why does an exception make that situation a better design?

A: Because I cannot ignore an exception if it is a checked exception. If the withdraw() method throws an InsufficientFundsException, I must try to handle it every time I invoke withdraw(). Sure, I can do nothing once I catch the exception, and keep spending money I don't have, but I can no longer plead ignorance to the bank and say that I had no idea I was overdrawn. Just as interfaces can be used to force behavior on a class, the Handle or Declare Rule can be used to force callers of a method to deal with potential problems and not simply ignore them.

The throws Keyword

Let's revisit the Lazy class that did not handle nor declare the two exceptions. From a design point of view, the readOneByte() method should probably not catch the exceptions anyway; otherwise, the caller of the method does not know what happened or is not given a chance to fix any problems. Therefore, the readOneByte() method should declare the exceptions, which is done using the throws keyword:

```
public byte readOneByte() throws FileNotFoundException, IOException
```

The following NotSoLazy class fixes the compiler errors of the Lazy class by declaring the exceptions.

```
import java.io.*;
public class NotSoLazy
{
    public byte readOneByte() throws FileNotFoundException, IOException
    {
        //Same as before
    }
    //Remainder of class definition
}
```

 Because FileNotFoundException is a child class of IOException, the readOneByte() method can declare just the IOException:

```
public byte readOneByte() throws IOException
```

A method that invokes readOneByte() can still try to catch the FileNotFoundException and IOException separately or try to catch just the IOException.

I want to show you an example that demonstrates how declaring a method forces it to eventually be handled. Because the readOneByte() method declares that it throws two checked exceptions, the Handle or Declare Rule applies to any method that wants to invoke readOneByte(). Look carefully at the following HandleOrDeclareWrong program. The class does not compile. See if you can determine where the problem is.

```
public class HandleOrDeclareWrong
{
    public static void main(String [] args)
    {
        System.out.println("Inside main");
        method1(args[0]);
    }
    public static void method1(String fileName)
    {
        System.out.println("Inside method1");
        method2(fileName);
        System.out.println("Leaving method1");
    }
    public static void method2(String fileName)
    {
        System.out.println("Inside method2");
        NotSoLazy util = new NotSoLazy(fileName);
        System.out.println(util.readOneByte());
        System.out.println("Leaving method2");
    }
}
```

The compiler error occurs within method2(), as shown in Figure 11.6. Within method2(), a call to readOneByte() is made, so method2() must handle or declare the exceptions declared by readOneByte().

We have two ways to fix the compiler error in Figure 11.6:

- method2() can try and catch the FileNotFoundException and IOException, thereby handling the exceptions.

- method2() can declare the two exceptions.

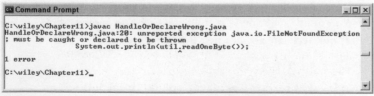

Figure 11.6   The compiler is enforcing the Handle or Declare Rule.

If method2() declares the two exceptions, method2() will compile, but method1() now has the same problem. If method1() decides to simply declare the two exceptions, the problem gets pushed all the way back to main(). However, main() is at the bottom of this calling sequence, so main() does not have anyone to declare the exceptions to. Eventually, the two exceptions need to be handled, which means that either method2(), method1(), or main() needs to contain a try/block for the FileNotFoundException and IOException.

The following HandleOrDeclare class shows the case in which method2() decided to declare the exceptions and method1()decided to handle the exceptions. That means main() does not have to worry about anything because there is no way for either exception to work its way down to main().

```java
import java.io.*;
public class HandleOrDeclare
{
    public static void main(String [] args)
    {
        System.out.println("Inside main");
        method1(args[0]);
    }
    public static void method1(String fileName)
    {
        System.out.println("Inside method1");
        try
        {
            method2(fileName);
        }catch(IOException e)
        {
            System.out.println("Something went wrong!");
            e.printStackTrace();
        }
        System.out.println("Leaving method1");
    }
    public static void method2(String fileName) throws IOException
    {
        System.out.println("Inside method2");
        NotSoLazy util = new NotSoLazy(fileName);
        System.out.println(util.readOneByte());
        System.out.println("Leaving method2");
    }
}
```

 The readOneByte() method declares FileNotFoundException and IOException. The method2() method declares only IOException, which covers both FileNotFoundException and IOException because FileNotFoundException is a child class of IOException. I would recommend in this type of situation to simply declare the parent exception, as method2() demonstrates.

```
Command Prompt                                                    _ □ ×

C:\wiley\Chapter11>java HandleOrDeclare not_there.txt
Inside main
Inside method1
Inside method2
Opening file for reading...
Something went wrong!
java.io.FileNotFoundException: not_there.txt (The system cannot find the file sp
ecified)
        at java.io.FileInputStream.open(Native Method)
        at java.io.FileInputStream.<init>(FileInputStream.java:103)
        at java.io.FileInputStream.<init>(FileInputStream.java:66)
        at NotSoLazy.readOneByte(NotSoLazy.java:18)
        at HandleOrDeclare.method2(HandleOrDeclare.java:29)
        at HandleOrDeclare.method1(HandleOrDeclare.java:16)
        at HandleOrDeclare.main(HandleOrDeclare.java:8)
Leaving method1

C:\wiley\Chapter11>_
```

Figure 11.7   Output of the HandleOrDeclare program when a FileNotFoundException occurs.

Try to determine the output of the HandleOrDeclare program, both when an exception occurs and when no exception occurs. An example of the output when an exception occurs is shown in Figure 11.7. Study the output carefully and follow the flow of control.

Throwing Exceptions

You can throw an exception, either a newly instantiated one or an exception that you just caught, by using the throw keyword. A throw statement causes the current method to immediately stop executing, much like a return statement, and the exception is thrown to the previous method on the call stack.

For example, the following statement throws a new ArrayIndexOutOf-BoundsException, with 5 being the invalid index:

```
throw new ArrayIndexOutOfBoundsException(5);
```

You can also instantiate an exception object and then throw it in a separate statement:

```
ArrayIndexOutOfBoundsException a =
    new ArrayIndexOutOfBoundsException(5);
//Some time later
throw a;
```

 note   **You can throw only objects of type java.lang.Throwable. In almost all situations, you will throw an object that is a child of java.lang.Exception. Recall that the Exception class extends the Throwable class.**

The following ThrowDemo program is similar to the HandleOrDeclare program, except that method1() catches the IOException, does something with it, and then uses the throw keyword to throw the exception after catching it using the following statement:

```
throw e;
```

Even though method1() catches the IOException, it also throws it; so, method1() must declare the IOException in order to adhere to the Handle or Declare Rule.

```java
import java.io.*;
public class ThrowDemo
{
    public static void main(String [] args)
    {
        System.out.println("Inside main");
        if(args.length == 0)
        {
            throw new ArrayIndexOutOfBoundsException(5);
        }
        try
        {
            method1(args[0]);
        }catch(IOException e)
        {
            System.out.println("Sorry, but an exception occurred.");
            return;
        }
        System.out.println("End of main");
    }
    public static void method1(String fileName) throws IOException
    {
        System.out.println("Inside method1");
        try
        {
            method2(fileName);
        }catch(IOException e)
        {
            System.out.println("Something went wrong!");
            e.printStackTrace();
            throw e;
        }
        System.out.println("Leaving method1");
    }
    public static void method2(String fileName) throws IOException
    {
```

```
        System.out.println("Inside method2");
        NotSoLazy util = new NotSoLazy(fileName);
        System.out.println(util.readOneByte());
        System.out.println("Leaving method2");
    }
}
```

So how come main() does not need to declare that it throws an ArrayIndex-OutOfBoundsException? Because it is a runtime exception, and runtime exceptions are not affected by the Handle or Declare Rule (only checked exceptions are).

By the way, I used an index of 5 just to demonstrate that the value of 5 is a part of the message that is displayed when the ArrayIndexOutOfBounds-Exception occurs. Figure 11.8 shows the output of the ThrowDemo program when no command-line argument is entered.

Figure 11.9 shows the output of the ThrowDemo program when the file cannot be found by the readOneByte() method.

 The throws keyword is used for declaring an exception, and it is used only in method signatures. The throw keyword is for throwing an exception, and it can be used anywhere you want to throw an exception.

```
Command Prompt                                                    _ □ ×
11/14/2002  01:31 PM                962 ThrowDemo.java
11/14/2002  01:31 PM              1,121 ThrowDemo.class
              2 File(s)            2,083 bytes
              0 Dir(s)  67,873,079,296 bytes free

C:\wiley\Chapter11>java ThrowDemo
Inside main
Exception in thread "main" java.lang.ArrayIndexOutOfBoundsException: Array index
 out of range: 5
        at ThrowDemo.main(ThrowDemo.java:10)

C:\wiley\Chapter11>_
```

Figure 11.8   The main() method threw a new ArrayIndexOutOfBoundsException.

```
Command Prompt                                                    _ □ ×
C:\wiley\Chapter11>java ThrowDemo not_there.txt
Inside main
Inside method1
Inside method2
Opening file for reading...
Something went wrong!
java.io.FileNotFoundException: not_there.txt (The system cannot find the file sp
ecified)
        at java.io.FileInputStream.open(Native Method)
        at java.io.FileInputStream.<init>(FileInputStream.java:103)
        at java.io.FileInputStream.<init>(FileInputStream.java:66)
        at NotSoLazy.readOneByte(NotSoLazy.java:18)
        at ThrowDemo.method2(ThrowDemo.java:43)
        at ThrowDemo.method1(ThrowDemo.java:29)
        at ThrowDemo.main(ThrowDemo.java:15)
Sorry, but an exception occurred

C:\wiley\Chapter11>_
```

Figure 11.9   The readOneByte() method threw a FileNotFoundException.

The finally Keyword

The finally keyword is used to create a block of code that follows a try block. A finally block of code always executes, whether or not an exception has occurred. Using a finally block allows you to run any cleanup-type statements that you want to execute, no matter what happens in the protected code. A finally block appears at the end of the catch blocks and has the following syntax:

```
try
{
     //Protected code
}catch(ExceptionType1 e1)
{
     //Catch block
}catch(ExceptionType2 e2)
{
     //Catch block
}catch(ExceptionType3 e3)
{
     //Catch block
}finally
{
     //The finally block always executes.
}
```

You can even write a try block that does not have any corresponding catch blocks, only a finally block:

```
try
{
     //Protected code
}finally
{
     //The finally block always executes.
}
```

Why use a finally block? Well, you may want to close a file that has been opened, even if your program could not read from the file for some reason. In other words, if a read is successful, you want to close the file, and if the read fails, you still want to close the file. A finally block can be used to simplify the way this code will look.

```
try
{
     //Try to read from a file.
}catch(IOException e)
{
```

```
        //Read failed
        return;
    }finally
    {
        //Close the file.
    }
```

If no IOException occurs in this try/catch/finally block, the catch block is skipped and the finally block executes. If an IOException does occur, the catch block executes and a return statement is reached. The method will return, but before it does, the finally block will execute.

I want you to study the readOneByte() method in the following MyFile-Utilities3 class. The try/catch block contains a finally block that closes the file opened in the try block.

```
import java.io.*;
public class MyFileUtilities3
{
    private String fileName;
    public MyFileUtilities3(String name)
    {
        fileName = name;
    }
    public byte readOneByte() throws FileNotFoundException
    {
        FileInputStream file = null;
        byte x = -1;
        try
        {
            System.out.println("Opening file for reading...");
            file = new FileInputStream(fileName);
            System.out.println("Just opened file: " + fileName);
            System.out.println("Reading one byte from file...");
            x = (byte) file.read();
        }catch(FileNotFoundException f)
        {
            System.out.println("Could not find " + fileName);
            throw f;
        }catch(IOException i)
        {
            System.out.println("Error reading one byte");
            i.printStackTrace();
            return -1;
        }finally
        {
            System.out.println("** Inside finally block **");
            try
            {
                if(file != null)
                {
```

```
                                file.close();
                    }
            }catch(IOException e)
            {}
        }
        System.out.println("Just read " + x);
        return x;
    }
}
```

The following FinallyDemo program instantiates a MyFileUtilities3 object and invokes its readOneByte() method. See if you can determine its output when no exception occurs. What happens when a FileNotFoundException occurs? What happens when an IOException occurs?

Figure 11.10 shows the output when the file is not found.

```
import java.io.FileNotFoundException;
public class FinallyDemo
{
    public static void main(String [] args)
    {
        System.out.println("Instantiating a MyFileUtilities3
object...");
        MyFileUtilities3 util = new MyFileUtilities3(args[0]);
        System.out.println("Invoking readOneByte() method...");
        try
        {
            byte b = util.readOneByte();
            System.out.println(b);
        }catch(FileNotFoundException e)
        {
            System.out.println("Could not find " + args[0]);
            e.printStackTrace();
        }
        System.out.println("End of main");
    }
}
```

```
Command Prompt                                                      _ □ X
C:\wiley\Chapter11>java FinallyDemo not_there.txt
Instantiating a MyFileUtilities3 object...
Invoking readOneByte() method...
Opening file for reading...
Could not find not_there.txt
** Inside finally block **
Could not find not_there.txt
java.io.FileNotFoundException: not_there.txt (The system cannot find the file sp
ecified)
        at java.io.FileInputStream.open(Native Method)
        at java.io.FileInputStream.<init>(FileInputStream.java:103)
        at java.io.FileInputStream.<init>(FileInputStream.java:66)
        at MyFileUtilities3.readOneByte(MyFileUtilities3.java:20)
        at FinallyDemo.main(FinallyDemo.java:14)
End of main

C:\wiley\Chapter11>_
```

Figure 11.10   Output of the FinallyDemo program when a FileNotFoundException occurs.

A finally block is like any block of code, and can perform any operations. Notice that the finally block in MyFileUtilities3 contains another try/catch block because closing a file possibly throws an IOException.

Overridden Methods and Exceptions

In Chapter 6, "Understanding Inheritance," we discussed method overriding, in which a method in a child class can override a method in the parent class. One of the rules I mentioned about method overriding is that a child method cannot throw "more" exceptions than the overridden parent method. We are now ready to discuss the details of this rule.

When I say "more" exceptions, I am not referring to the number of exceptions thrown by the child method, even though that is part of it. What I mean by "more" is that a child class cannot throw an exception that, by polymorphism, is not at least declared by the overridden method in the parent.

This is best seen by an example. Suppose that we have a class named Parent that contains a method named connect(). The connect() method declares that it throws a java.io.IOException.

```
import java.io.IOException;
public class Parent
{
    public void connect() throws IOException
    {
        System.out.println("Inside connect() in Parent");
        throw new IOException();
    }
}
```

The following Child1 class extends the Parent class and overrides the connect() method. The connect() method in Child1 declares that it throws a java .net.SocketException. Is this valid method overriding? Yes, because Socket-Exception is a child class of IOException, so SocketException is a "lesser" exception than IOException.

```
import java.net.SocketException;
public class Child1 extends Parent
{
    public void connect() throws SocketException
    {
        System.out.println("Inside connect() in Child1");
        throw new SocketException();
    }
}
```

You can override a parent method that throws an exception and not declare any exceptions in the child class method. For example, the following Child2 class extends Parent and overrides the connect() method. The child method does not declare any exceptions, which is certainly not "more" than an IOException.

```
public class Child2 extends Parent
{
    public void connect()
    {
        System.out.println("Inside connect() in Child2");
    }
}
```

Let's see an example that does not work. The following Child3 class extends Parent and attempts to override connect(). A compiler error is generated because connect() in Child3 declares that it throws Exception, which is "more" of an exception than IOException.

```
public class Child3 extends Parent
{
    public void connect() throws Exception        //Does not compile!
    {
        System.out.println("Inside connect() in Child3");
        throw new Exception();
    }
}
```

◆ Why Does This Rule Exist When Overriding a Method?

A method in a child class, overriding a method in its parent class, cannot throw more exceptions or greater exceptions than what the parent class has declared. This might seem like an odd rule in Java, but there is a specific reason for it. If you were allowed to have a child method throw a greater exception, you could create a situation in which a checked exception avoided the Handle or Declare Rule.

Let me show you with a simple example. Suppose that we have the following class named Parent:

```
public class Parent
{
    public void connect()
    {
    System.out.println("Inside connect() in Parent");
    }
}
```

continued

◆ Why Does This Rule Exist When Overriding a Method? *(continued)*

Notice that it has a connect() method that does not declare any exceptions. The following Child class extends Parent and overrides the connect() method:

```
public class Child extends Parent
{
    public void connect() throws java.io.IOException
    {
        System.out.println("Inside connect() in Child");
        throw new java.io.IOException();
    }
}
```

The Child class does not compile because its connect() method declares an IOException, and the overridden connect() method in Parent does not declare any exceptions.

Let's assume, however, that this rule involving exceptions and overriding methods did not exist and that the Child class compiled successfully. Then, through polymorphism, the following statement is valid:

```
Parent p = new Child();
```

The reference p is of type Parent, but the object is of type Child. This is valid because a Child object is a Parent object. Now, consider the following program, which invokes the connect() method using this reference p:

```
public class Test
{
    public static void main(String [] args)
    {
        Parent p = new Child();
        p.connect();
    }
}
```

This program compiles because the Parent class has a connect() method. However, because of virtual method invocation, which method executes at run time? Not the one in Parent, but the overridden method in Child. The connect() method in Child throws an IOException, but who catches it? Nobody. And we just created a situation in which a checked exception went unchecked. The compiler thought I was invoking connect() in Parent, which did not declare any exceptions. However, at run time, the connect() method in Child is what executes, and that method throws an IOException.

The compiler cannot predict the Handle or Declare Rule in this situation. This is why child class methods that override parent class methods cannot throw "more" exceptions than the parent class method; if they could, a checked exception could occur that might never be caught.

User-Defined Exceptions

You can create your own exceptions in Java. In fact, because of the way Java is designed, you are encouraged to write your own exceptions to represent problems that can arise in your classes. Keep the following points in mind when writing your own exception classes:

- All exceptions must be a child of Throwable.
- If you want to write a checked exception that is automatically enforced by the Handle or Declare Rule, you need to extend the Exception class.
- If you want to write a runtime exception, you need to extend the RuntimeException class.

 You will likely never write a class that directly extends Throwable because then it will be neither a checked nor a runtime exception. Most user-defined exception classes are designed to be checked exceptions and therefore will extend the Exception class. However, if you want to write an exception that you don't want users to have to handle or declare, make it a runtime exception by extending the RuntimeException class.

The following InsufficientFundsException class is a user-defined exception that extends the Exception class, making it a checked exception. An exception class is like any other class, containing useful fields and methods. In our case, the name of the exception class pretty much explains it all, but we have added a field to store the amount of insufficient funds and an accessor method for viewing this field.

```
public class InsufficientFundsException extends Exception
{
    private double amount;
    public InsufficientFundsException(double amount)
    {
        this.amount = amount;
    }
    public double getAmount()
    {
        return amount;
    }
}
```

To demonstrate using our user-defined exception, the following Checking-Account class contains a withdraw() method that throws an InsufficientFunds-Exception. Because this is a checked exception, it must be declared in the signature of withdraw(). Notice that the throw keyword is used to throw an InsufficientFundsException.

```
public class CheckingAccount
{
    private double balance;
    private int number;
    public CheckingAccount(int number)
    {
        this.number = number;
    }
    public void deposit(double amount)
    {
        balance += amount;
    }
    public void withdraw(double amount) throws
InsufficientFundsException
    {
        if(amount <= balance)
        {
            balance -= amount;
        }
        else
        {
            double needs = amount - balance;
            throw new InsufficientFundsException(needs);
        }
    }
    public double getBalance()
    {
        return balance;
    }
    public int getNumber()
    {
        return number;
    }
}
```

The following BankDemo program demonstrates invoking the deposit() and withdraw() methods of CheckingAccount. Notice that the deposit() method is invoked without a try/catch block around it, whereas the withdraw() method can be invoked only within a try/catch block. Study the program and try to determine its output, which is shown in Figure 11.11.

```
Command Prompt                                              _ □ ×
11/14/2002  03:26 PM                578 CheckingAccount.java
11/14/2002  03:29 PM                649 CheckingAccount.class
11/14/2002  03:29 PM                500 BankDemo.java
11/14/2002  03:29 PM              1,023 BankDemo.class
              6 File(s)            3,321 bytes
              2 Dir(s)  67,872,751,616 bytes free

C:\wiley\Chapter11\userdefined>java BankDemo
Depositing $500...

Withdrawing $100...

Withdrawing $600...
Sorry, but you are short $200.0
InsufficientFundsException
        at CheckingAccount.withdraw(CheckingAccount.java:25)
        at BankDemo.main(BankDemo.java:15)

C:\wiley\Chapter11\userdefined>_
```

Figure 11.11   Output of the BankDemo program.

```java
public class BankDemo
{
    public static void main(String [] args)
    {
        CheckingAccount c = new CheckingAccount(101);
        System.out.println("Depositing $500...");
        c.deposit(500.00);
        try
        {
            System.out.println("\nWithdrawing $100...");
            c.withdraw(100.00);
            System.out.println("\nWithdrawing $600...");
            c.withdraw(600.00);
        }catch(InsufficientFundsException e)
        {
            System.out.println("Sorry, but you are short $"
+ e.getAmount());
            e.printStackTrace();
        }
    }
}
```

Lab 11.1: Writing try/catch Blocks

The purpose of this lab is to become familiar with writing a try/catch block.

1. Write a class named Multiply and add main() within the class. The Multiply class is going to multiply two numbers together that are input by using the command-line arguments.

2. Within main(), declare a try block that parses the first two command-line arguments into ints by using the Integer.parseInt() method.

3. Your try block is going to have two catch blocks, one for an Array-IndexOutOfBoundsException and one for a NumberFormatException.

4. If an ArrayIndexOutOfBoundsException occurs, the user has not input two command-line arguments. Inform the user of this, print the stack trace, and have main() end using a return statement.

5. If a NumberFormatException occurs, the user has input invalid command-line arguments. Inform the user that the program expects two ints; then print the stack trace and have main() end.

6. If no exception occurs, print out the two ints and also their product.

7. Save, compile, and run the Mulitply program several times by using the following command lines:

```
java Multiply 10 5
java Multiply 10
java Multiply 7 hello
```

Lab 11.2: Exceptions and Polymorphism

In this lab, you will replace the two catch blocks in the Multiply program of Lab 11.1 with a single catch block.

1. Start off by making a copy of the Multiply.java file, renaming it MultiplyLazy.java. You will also need to rename the class MultiplyJava.

2. Remove the two catch blocks and replace them with a single catch block that catches RuntimeException.

3. Within the catch block, print out a message that an error has occurred and also print the stack trace.

4. The remainder of the MultiplyLazy class can remain the same. Save, compile, and run the program three times, using the following command lines:

```
java MultiplyLazy 10 5
java MultiplyLazy 10
java MultiplyLazy 7 hello
```

Lab 11.3: Checked Exceptions

In Lab 10.1, you wrote a program that instantiated a FootballGame object and simulated a football game, having the home and visiting teams score

and the quarters end. In this lab, you will modify the FootballGame so
that it uses the Thread.sleep() method to slow the program down.

1. Open the source code file for the program you wrote in Lab 10.1 that
   simulated a football game.

2. The sleep() method in the Thread class is a static method that causes
   the current thread of execution to sleep for a specified number of
   milliseconds. For example, the following statement pauses the current thread for 5 seconds:

```
Thread.sleep(5000);
```

3. Add a call the Tread.sleep() before each score change and each end
   of quarter in your football game. You can specify any sleep time you
   want. This will slow down your game so you can "watch" it being
   played.

4. Save and compile your program. It should not compile successfully.
   Why not?

5. The sleep() method throws a checked exception named Interrupted-
   Exception., so you need to add a try/catch block around each call to
   Thread.sleep(). Print out the stack trace in each catch block.

6. Save and compile your football program again. This time, it should
   compile successfully.

7. Run the program and watch your football game being played.

 **The InterruptedException will never occur in your program. The only way
to cause this exception is to have a second thread interrupt your current
thread.**

Summary

- Exception handling is an important aspect of Java programming because
  the Java language defines checked exceptions. A checked exception is
  an exception that fits under the Handle or Declare Rule, meaning that it
  must be either handled by a method using a try/catch block or declared
  using the throws keyword.

- The keywords try and catch are used to create protected code. If an
  exception occurs in a try block, the corresponding catch blocks attempt
  to catch the exception. If the data type of the exception does match the
  catch blocks, then the exception falls through to the next method on the
  call stack.

- The java.lang.Throwable class is the parent class of all exceptions. It has two child classes: java.lang.Exception and java.lang.Error.

- There are two types of exceptions: runtime exceptions and checked exceptions. Runtime exceptions are those exceptions that are child classes of java.lang.RuntimeException. All other exceptions are checked exceptions.

- A try block can have any number of corresponding catch blocks. A try block can also contain a finally block that executes whether or not an exception occurs.

- The throws keyword is used to declare that a method throws an exception.

- The throw keyword is used to throw an exception.

- A child class method that overrides a parent class method cannot declare that it throws more exceptions than the parent class method.

- A user-defined exception must extend the java.lang.Throwable class, although typically it will extend either the Exception or RuntimeException class.

Review Questions

1. What are the two types of exceptions in Java? How are they distinguished?

2. If an object is to be thrown using the throw keyword, the object must be what data type?

3. True or False: A try block must be followed by exactly one corresponding catch block.

4. What is the term used to refer to code within a try block?

5. True or False: A finally block always executes, whether or not an exception occurs in the corresponding try block.

6. The following try/catch block does not compile. Why not?

```
try
{
}catch(Exception e)
{
}catch(RuntimeException r)
{
}
```

7. Suppose that a RemoteException occurs in the following try block. What will be displayed next?

```
try
{
    //A RemoteException occurs here
}catch(RemoteException r)
{
    System.out.println("Something went wrong.");
    throw r;
}finally
{
    System.out.println("Finally!");
}
```

8. What is the output of the try/catch block in the previous question if no Remote-Exception occurs?

9. What is the output of the same try/catch block if a NullPointerException occurs in the protected code (instead of a RemoteException)?

10. The Handle or Declare Rule applies only to what type of exception?

11. What keyword is used by a method to declare an exception?

12. What keyword is used by a method to throw an exception?

13. True or False: If a parent class method declares an Exception, a child class method overriding this parent method can declare an IOException.

14. True or False: If a parent class method declares an IOException, a child class method overriding this parent method can declare an Exception.

15. All user-defined exceptions must be a child of what class?

16. If you want a user-defined exception to be a checked exception, what class should you *not* extend?

Answers to Review Questions

1. Checked exception and runtime exceptions. There is a third category—errors—but technically, an error is not an exception. A runtime exception is a child of the Runtime-Exception class, whereas checked exceptions are child classes of Exception (that do not also extend RuntimeException).

2. The object must of type java.lang.Throwable to be thrown using the throw keyword.

3. False. A try block can be followed by any number of catch blocks, including zero.

4. Protected code.

5. True. A finally block always executes, no matter what happens in the try block or any previous catch blocks.

6. RuntimeException is a child of Exception, so the RuntimeException catch block is unreachable code and should appear before the Exception catch block.

7. The string "Something went wrong." will be displayed next, followed by "Finally!", even though the catch block threw the exception again.

8. The catch block will be skipped, but the finally block always executes, and the string "Finally!" will be displayed.

9. The catch block will be skipped because it is not trying to catch a NullPointerException. The NullPointerException will therefore be thrown down the call stack, but not before the finally block executes and the string "Finally!" is displayed.

10. Checked exceptions. Runtime exceptions are not affected by the Handle or Declare Rule.

11. throws.

12. throw.

13. True, because IOException is a child of Exception, making it a lesser exception.

14. False, because Exception is the parent of IOException, making it more of an exception, which is not allowed in method overriding.

15. java.lang.Throwable (although most will extend Exception).

16. RuntimeException. If you extend RuntimeException, the class will be a runtime exception and therefore not a checked exception.

CHAPTER

12

An Introduction to GUI Programming

We are now ready to discuss one of my favorite aspects of Java: GUI programming. I started my programming career as a Windows programmer using Visual C++ and MFC, which can take months to learn how to use and longer to understand. When I learned how to write GUI programs in Java, I was relieved to find that Sun had used a logical and object-oriented design for creating a GUI and handling its events. In this chapter, I will focus on creating the window portion of the GUI by discussing containers, layout managers, and panels. (The next chapter, "GUI Components and Event Handling," discusses the details of various GUI components and how to handle their events.)

AWT versus Swing

GUI, which stands for *graphical user interface*, refers to that portion of a program that the user visually sees and interacts with. The GUI is an essential part of programs that run on windows-based operating systems such as Windows, Macintosh, and Unix. Almost every Windows program you have used is probably a GUI program: for example, Microsoft Word or Internet Explorer.

When Java was first released in 1995, it contained a GUI API referred to as the Abstract Windowing Toolkit (AWT). This API contained classes like Frame to represent a typical window, Button to represent buttons, Menu to represent a window's menu, and so on. The classes and interfaces of the AWT are in the java.awt packages.

Although it is a useful and important API, the AWT had its shortcomings, including a lack of support for many popular GUI components. It's not that the AWT is not useful, but it was a lot of work for those initial Java GUI programmers to create the look and feel that they wanted their GUI programs to have.

note   **AWT components are referred to as *heavyweight components* because their implementation relies heavily on the underlying operating system. The look and feel of AWT components depend on the platform the program is running on. For example, an AWT button will look like a Windows button when the program is run on a Windows platform. The same button will look like a Macintosh button when the program is run on a Macintosh platform.**

Aware of the need for a more robust API for creating GUI applications, Sun Microsystems teamed together with Netscape (and other industry partners) and created Swing. Swing is actually a part of the Java Foundation Classes (JFC), a collection of technologies that includes Swing, AWT, Java 2D, Java Drag and Drop, the Accessibility APIs, and others. The classes and interfaces of Swing are found in the javax.swing packages.

Swing is different from AWT in that Swing components are 100 percent Java, thereby not relying on the native operating system or platform. This allows Swing components to have a *pluggable look and feel*, meaning that you can decide what you want your GUI components to look like. For example, if you want a button to look like a Windows button, even if the program is executed on a Macintosh or Unix platform, you can denote your Swing program as having the Windows look and feel. With the Windows look and feel, the Swing program will look like a Windows program, no matter what operating system the program runs on.

note   **Swing components are referred to as *lightweight components* because their implementation does not rely on the underlying operating system. The JDK 1.1 version of Java defines how a lightweight component is implemented using the Lightweight UI Framework. Because Swing components are lightweight, their appearance is determined by you, the programmer, and not by where the program is running.**

Nowadays, most Java GUI programming is done by using Swing. We will still discuss the AWT in this chapter, though, because it is an important part of GUI programming, and many of the AWT classes are used in Swing, including the layout managers, and event-handling classes and interfaces. After you understand the way a GUI is created, you will find that using AWT and Swing is the same in terms of developing the code. For example, creating and using a Button in AWT is very similar to creating and using a JButton, Swing's version of a GUI button. And the event-handling code behind the scenes is exactly the same, no matter if you are using a Button or JButton.

 The names of the Swing classes all begin with a capital J, like JButton. For the most part, an AWT program can be converted to a Swing program by adding a capital J to the class names used in the source code and recompiling the code.

Creating Windows

The basic starting point of a GUI is the container because you need a container before you can start laying out your components. The java.awt.Frame and javax.swing.JFrame classes are containers that represent a basic window with a title bar and common windowing capabilities such as resizing, minimizing, maximizing, and closing. The Frame class is used for AWT programs and is the parent class of JFrame, which is used for Swing programs.

java.awt.Frame Class

When working with Frame objects, there are basically three steps involved to get a Frame window to appear on the screen:

1. Instantiate the Frame object in memory.
2. Give the Frame object a size using setSize(), setBounds(), or pack().
3. Make the Frame appear on the screen by invoking setVisible(true).

Let's look at instantiating a Frame object first. The java.awt.Frame class has four constructors:

public Frame(). Creates a new frame with no message in the title bar.

public Frame(String title). Creates a new frame with the given String appearing in the title bar.

public Frame(GraphicsConfiguration gc).   Creates a frame with the specified GraphicsConfiguration of a screen device.

public Frame(String title, GraphicsConfiguration gc).   Creates a frame with the specified title and GraphicsConfiguration.

Each of the preceding constructors creates a new Frame object that is initially invisible and has a size of 0 pixels wide and 0 pixels high. The String passed in to a Frame constructor appears in the title bar, and the Graphics-Configuration represents where the image is to be displayed. This is useful when working with a multiscreen environment, but in most cases you do not need to worry about a GraphicsConfiguration object. If you do not pass in a GraphicsConfiguration object, your Frame will use the default graphics destination, which in Windows is the computer screen.

The following statement demonstrates instantiating a new Frame object in memory:

```
Frame f = new Frame("My first window");
```

This Frame is not displayed on the screen, and it has an initial size of 0 by 0. You need to give your Frame a size before displaying it, which can be done by invoking one of the following five methods:

public void setSize(int width, int height).   Sets the size of the Frame to the given width and height, in pixels.

public void setSize(java.awt.Dimension d).   Sets the size of the Frame to the same width and height as the given Dimension object.

public void setBounds(int x, int y, int width, int height).   Sets both the size and initial location of the window, where *x* represents the number of pixels over from the upper-left corner of the screen, and *y* represents the number of pixels down from the upper-left corner of the screen. (See the sidebar titled *GUI Coordinates*.)

public void setBounds(java.awt.Rectangle r).   Sets the bounds of the Frame to that of the given Rectangle.

public void pack().   Sets the size of the Frame to be just big enough to display all its components with their preferred size.

 I often notice students invoking more than one of the setSize(), setBounds(), or pack() methods to set the size of a window. However, you need to invoke only one of them. For example, if you invoke setSize(200,200) and then setBounds(20,50,200,200), the first call to setSize() was overridden by the subsequent call to setBounds(), making the initial call to setSize() a waste of time. Similarly, invoking pack() and then invoking setBounds() overrides whatever the pack() method did to the size of the window.

◆ GUI Coordinates

All components and containers have a size and location, which is denoted in pixels. A pixel is a relative unit of measurement based on the settings of the user's screen. The pixels create a coordinate system, with the upper-left corner of the screen as the origin (0,0). Any point on the screen can be represented as an (x,y) value, where x is the number of pixels to the right of the origin, and y is the number of pixels down from the origin.

For example, the point (100,100) is 100 pixels over and 100 pixels down from the upper-left corner of the screen. Suppose that a Frame is instantiated and given the bounds (100,100, 300, 400):

```
Frame f = new Frame();
f.setBounds(100, 100, 300, 400);
```

The upper-left corner of the Frame is the point (100,100) relative to the computer screen. The width of this Frame is 300 and the height is 400, so the lower-right corner of the Frame is the point (400, 500) of the computer screen.

There is another coordinate system of GUI components referred to as the *relative coordinate system*. The relative coordinate system is based on the upper-left corner of the container that the component is residing in. The upper-left corner of a container is an origin (0,0), and components are placed in a container relative to the container's origin, not the screen's origin.

For example, the following statements instantiate a Button, assign it bounds (20, 200, 60, 40). The Button is then added to the Frame object instantiated earlier:

```
Button ok = new Button("OK");
ok.setBounds(20, 200, 60, 40);
f.add(ok);              //Add the Button to a Frame
```

The upper-left corner of the OK button appears 20 pixels over and 200 pixels down from the upper-left corner of the Frame. The size of the Button is 60 pixels wide and 40 pixels high.

Assuming that Frame f has not been moved, this puts the Button 120 pixels over and 300 pixels down from the upper-left corner of the screen. This point changes if the Frame is moved. However, the relative location of the Button within the Frame does not move, even if the Frame moves. This is the desired result of GUI containers and components. When we move a window, we expect all the components within the window to move along with it. Therefore, we rarely concern ourselves with the actual screen coordinates of a component. The component's relative coordinates are what are important to a programmer laying out components in a container.

After you have instantiated a Frame, given it a size, and laid out the components within it, you display the Frame on the screen by invoking the setVisible() method inherited from the Component class. The signature of setVisible() is:

```
public void setVisible(boolean show)
```

If the boolean passed in is true, the component is made visible. If the value is false, the component is hidden. The following FrameDemo program creates a Frame object, sets its bounds, and displays it on the screen. Study the program and try to determine its output, which is shown in Figure 12.1.

```java
import java.awt.*;
public class FrameDemo
{
    public static void main(String [] args)
    {
        Frame f = new Frame("My first window");
        f.setBounds(100,100, 400, 300);
        f.setVisible(true);
    }
}
```

 If you run the FrameDemo program, you will see a Frame window similar to the one in Figure 12.1. You can move, resize, minimize, and maximize the Frame window. However, you can't close the window because closing a window often implies ending the program. If the user needs to save a document or other settings before ending, your program needs a chance to do this.

Therefore, the closing of a Frame window is left to the programmer and involves handling the WindowEvent generated by a user attempting to close the window. I will show you how to do this in the next chapter, so to close the window for now you need to stop the JVM. In Windows, this can be done by pressing Ctrl+c from the command prompt.

javax.swing.JFrame Class

The javax.swing.JFrame class represents a window similar to Frame, except that JFrame adds support for the Swing component architecture. A JFrame is a heavyweight component, meaning that it has the look and feel of the native platform. From a user's point of view, a JFrame and a Frame look the same. Creating and displaying a JFrame is also similar to creating and displaying a Frame.

However, a JFrame is different in terms of how components are added to the JFrame. As opposed to a Frame, a JFrame has three panes that components can be added to: a content pane, a glass pane, and a root pane. Typically, the content pane will contain all of the components of the JFrame. We will see several examples in this chapter of adding components to the content pane of a JFrame.

Figure 12.1   Frame created in the FrameDemo program.

Let's look at the steps involved in creating a JFrame. You start by instantiating a JFrame using one of the following constructors:

public JFrame().   Creates a new JFrame with no message in the title bar.

public JFrame(String title).   Creates a new JFrame with the given String appearing in the title bar.

public JFrame(GraphicsConfiguration gc).   Creates a JFrame with the specified GraphicsConfiguration of a screen device.

public JFrame(String title, GraphicsConfiguration gc).   Creates a JFrame with the specified title and GraphicsConfiguration.

The constructors are similar to those in the Frame class, and the parameters have the same uses. The following statement instantiates a JFrame with "My first JFrame" in the title bar:

```
JFrame f = new JFrame("My first JFrame");
```

As with Frame objects, this JFrame is initially not visible and has a size of 0 pixels by 0 pixels. You invoke one of the setSize(), setBounds(), or pack() methods to give the JFrame a size and then invoke setVisible() to make it visible. The following JFrameDemo program demonstrates creating and displaying a JFrame object. Study the program and try to determine its output, which is shown in Figure 12.2.

```
import javax.swing.*;
public class JFrameDemo
{
    public static void main(String [] args)
    {
        JFrame f = new JFrame("My first JFrame");
        f.setSize(400, 300);
        f.setDefaultCloseOperation(WindowConstants.EXIT_ON_CLOSE);
        f.setVisible(true);
    }
}
```

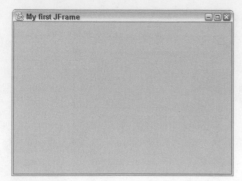

Figure 12.2   JFrame created by the JFrameDemo program.

 Clicking the X in the title bar of a JFrame causes the window to be hidden by default, but this does not cause your program to stop executing. You need to press Ctrl+c at the command prompt to stop the JVM, even though your JFrame is no longer visible on the screen.

As with Frame objects, you can handle the WindowEvent of the JFrame and use the System.exit() method to stop execution of the program. However, unlike the Frame class, the JFrame class contains a setDefault-CloseOperation() method that allows you to decide what action to take when the user closes the JFrame. The method takes in an int, which can be one of the following values:

WindowConstants.HIDE_ON_CLOSE.   Hides the JFrame. This is the default behavior.

WindowConstants.DO_NOTHING_ON_CLOSE.   Does nothing, which is similar to the behavior of Frame objects.

WindowConstants.DISPOSE_ON_CLOSE.   Hides and disposes the JFrame, but does not terminate the program.

WindowConstants.EXIT_ON_CLOSE.   Causes the program to stop executing.

Notice that the JFrameDemo program contains the statement:

```
f.setDefaultCloseOperation(WindowConstants.EXIT_ON_CLOSE);
```

The JFrameDemo program terminates when the window is closed, as opposed to the FrameDemo program, which did nothing when the window was closed.

Containers and Components

There are two basic elements of a GUI: containers and components. A container is for displaying components, and components must be displayed within a container. A Button is an example of a component, whereas a Frame is an example of a container. To display a Button, you place it within a Frame and display the Frame.

Component is an abstract class that is the parent class of the various GUI components of the AWT: Button, Checkbox, Choice, Label, List, and Text-Component. Container is an abstract class that is the parent class of the containers of the AWT: Window, Panel, and ScrollPane. Child objects of Component are placed within child objects of Container. For example, a Button can be placed within a Panel, or a List can be placed within a Frame.

 Components are placed inside containers. However, notice that Container is a child of Component. Therefore, a container is a component, which allows a Container object to be placed inside another Container object. For example, a Panel is a Container, and a Frame is a Container. Because Panel is also a Component, a Panel can be placed inside a Frame. (Using the same logic, a Frame can also be placed inside a Panel.)

The nesting of containers is an important aspect of creating the look of your GUI. The section *Panels* later in this chapter shows you how to add a Panel to a Frame and demonstrates why this is commonly done.

The JComponent class is a child of Container, and it is the parent class of all of the Swing components, such as JComboBox, JLabel, JSlider, JSpinner, and JMenuBar. One of the ways that Swing is different from AWT is that not all AWT components are containers. However, all Swing components extend JComponent, which extends Container. Therefore, all Swing components are also containers, allowing them to be nested within each other. For example, a JButton can be placed within a JFrame (a typical use of JButton). However, because JButton is a child of Container, you can place a JFrame inside a JButton (which is not a typical GUI feature, but nonetheless this can be done in Swing).

Adding Components to a Container

A Component is added to a Container using one of the following add() methods found in the java.awt.Container class:

public Component add(Component c).   Adds the Component to the Container and returns a reference to the newly added Component

public Component add(Component c, int index).   Adds the Component to the Container at the position specified by index

public Component add(Component c, Object constraints).   Adds the Component to the Container using the specified constraints

Components are added to a JFrame differently from the way they are added to a Frame. When using a Frame, you invoke the add() method directly on the Frame object, adding the components directly to the Frame. When using a JFrame, you still invoke the add() method, but not on the JFrame. Instead, you add the components to the content pane of the JFrame by invoking the add() method on the JFrame's content pane.

You use the getContentPane() method in the JFrame class to obtain a reference to the content pane of a JFrame. For example, the following statements add a JButton to the content pane of a JFrame:

```
JFrame f = new JFrame();
JButton b = new JButton();
Container contentPane = f.getContentPane();
contentPane.add(b);
```

Notice that the return value of getContentPane() is Container. The add() method is invoked on the content pane, adding b by using the layout manager of the content pane.

Which add() method you use depends on which layout manager you are using. (Layout managers are discussed in the upcoming section called *Layout Managers*.) To demonstrate using the add() method, the following AddDemo program creates a Frame object and adds a Button.

```
import java.awt.*;
public class AddDemo
{
    public static void main(String [] args)
    {
        Frame f = new Frame("A simple window");
        Button cancel = new Button("Cancel");
        f.add(cancel);       //Add the Button to the Frame
        f.setSize(100,100);
        f.setVisible(true);
    }
}
```

Notice that the cancel Button is added to the Frame f. Whenever f is displayed, the cancel button is also displayed. Figure 12.3 shows the output of the AddDemo program. Notice that the Button consumes the entire interior of the Frame, no matter what size you make the Frame.

Figure 12.3 The Button is the same size as the Frame.

The button shown in Figure 12.3 looks a little unusual. I haven't seen many GUI programs that are one large button.

Classroom Q & A

Q: OK, I'll ask the obvious question here. Why is the Button the same size as the Frame?

A: The answer involves the concept of a layout manager. A container uses a layout manager to determine how components are laid out within the container. The Frame class uses a BorderLayout manager by default, and the BorderLayout manager has placed the Button in the center of the Frame.

Q: But that is an unusual layout. What if we want the Button to have a normal size and appear in a certain location?

A: In the AddDemo example, I could have given the button a normal size by using a different layout manager such as FlowLayout. However, with layout managers, you do not specify the exact size and location of a GUI component. Instead, you simply add components to your container, and *the layout manager determines where each component will go and what its size will be.*

Q: That sounds odd. How does the layout manager know what you want the GUI to look like?

A: You determine the look of the GUI by selecting the appropriate layout manager and giving the components to the layout manager in a specific order or with specific constraints.

Q: I have done some GUI programming using Visual Basic, and all I did was visually place the components exactly where I wanted them in the window using the Visual Basic IDE. Can you do that in Java?

A: You can if you have an IDE like Visual Café or Visual Age. These IDEs have GUI editors that let you place components exactly where you want them. You can also organize components by assigning a null layout manager to your container and specifying the exact location and size of each component added. There is an example of this later in the chapter in the section *Using No Layout Manager*.

Q: So why would you ever use one of the layout managers? Why not just use the IDE or lay out the components exactly where you want them?

A: Two reasons: First, you might not have an IDE, and if you do, there is a certain complexity to figuring out how to use it. If you understand layout managers, this will help you comprehend the code that the IDE is generating for you. Second, using a layout manager to lay out your components makes your GUI more portable. You might be surprised to see that a GUI that you created using an IDE looks great on Windows, but not so great on a Unix or Macintosh platform. The same problem can occur if you try to lay out components exactly where you want them.

Q: How does the layout manager know how you want your GUI to look?

A: Good question. You need to understand the way each type of layout manager behaves. For example, you need to know that the FlowLayout manager gives components their preferred size, and that BorderLayout places components in specific regions of the container. By using the different layout managers and nesting containers, you have great control over the look of the GUI, while at the same time letting the layout managers determine the exact location and size of your GUI components. Let's look at some of these layout managers so you can get a feel for how they are used.

Layout Managers

A container uses a layout manager to determine both the location and size of the components within the container. A container can be assigned one layout manager, which is done using the setLayout() method of the java.awt .Container class:

```
public void setLayout(LayoutManager m)
```

LayoutManager is an interface that all the layout managers' classes must implement. You can create your own layout manager by writing a class that implements the methods of the LayoutManager interface (no small task), or you can use one of the many layout managers of the AWT and Swing APIs, including the following:

java.awt.FlowLayout.   Lays out components in a left-to-right flow, with each component given its preferred size. A Panel has FlowLayout by default.

java.awt.BorderLayout.   Divides a container into five regions, allowing one component to be added to each region. A Frame and the content pane of a JFrame have BorderLayout by default.

java.awt.GridLayout.   Divides a container into a grid of rows and columns, with one component added to each region of the grid and each component having the same size.

java.awt.GridBagLayout.   Divides a container into regions similar to GridLayout, except that components do not need to be the same size. Components can span more than one row or column.

java.awt.CardLayout.   Each component added to the container is treated as a card, with only one card being visible at a time (similar to a deck of cards).

javax.swing.BoxLayout.   Allows components to be laid out vertically or horizontally. BoxLayout is similar to GridBagLayout, but it is generally easier to use.

javax.swing.SpringLayout.   Lays out components with a specified distance between the edges of each component.

javax.swing.OverlayLayout.   Displays components over the top of each other, similarly to CardLayout. This is a useful layout manager for creating tabbed panes.

Any container can use any layout manager. Notice that Frame objects and the content pane of JFrame objects have BorderLayout by default. However, you can assign them any layout manager you need. Similarly, Panel objects have FlowLayout by default, but a Panel can be assigned any other layout manager.

We will not discuss all these layout managers in this book, but I will show you the more commonly used ones, including FlowLayout, BorderLayout, GridLayout, and BoxLayout. After you get a feel for using these layout managers, it will be easier for you to learn how to use the other layout managers.

FlowLayout Manager

The java.awt.FlowLayout class represents a layout manager that aligns components in a left-to-right flow, such as words in a sentence. FlowLayout has the following properties:

- Components are given their preferred size.

- The order in which the components are added determines their order in the container. The first component added appears to the left, and subsequent components flow in from the right.

- If the container is not wide enough to display all of the components, the components wrap around to a new line.

- You can control whether the components are centered, left-justified, or right-justified.

- You can control the vertical and horizontal gap between components.

I always emphasize the importance of what a layout manager does to your components in terms of resizing them. What is nice about FlowLayout is that components get their preferred size, meaning that a FlowLayout manager will not attempt to override the width or height of a component if you have previously declared a specific size for the component.

To use FlowLayout in a Frame or JFrame, you need to invoke setLayout() on the container and pass in a new FlowLayout object. The FlowLayout class has three constructors:

public FlowLayout().   Creates a new FlowLayout that centers the components with a horizontal and vertical gap of five units (where the unit is pixels in most GUI operating systems).

public FlowLayout(int align).   Creates a FlowLayout object with the specified alignment, which is one of the following values: FlowLayout .CENTER, FlowLayout.RIGHT, or FlowLayout.LEFT. The horizontal and vertical gap between components is five units.

public FlowLayout(int align, int hgap, int vgap).   Creates a FlowLayout object with the specified alignment, horizontal gap, and vertical gap.

For example, the following statement instantiates a new FlowLayout manager that justifies components to the right. The horizontal and vertical gap is not specified, so they will have the default value of 5.

```
Frame f = new Frame();
f.setLayout(new FlowLayout(FlowLayout.RIGHT));
```

What FlowLayout does to components in a container is best understood by an example. The following FlowLayoutDemo program creates a Frame and assigns it FlowLayout. Components are then added using the add() method. Study the program and see if you can determine its output, which is shown in Figure 12.4.

```java
import java.awt.*;
public class FlowLayoutDemo
{
    public static void main(String [] args)
    {
        Frame f = new Frame("FlowLayout demo");
        f.setLayout(new FlowLayout());
        f.add(new Button("Red"));
        f.add(new Button("Blue"));
        f.add(new Button("White"));
        List list = new List();
        for(int i = 0; i < args.length; i++)
        {
            list.add(args[i]);
        }
        f.add(list);
        f.add(new Checkbox("Pick me", true));
        f.add(new Label("Enter name here:"));
        f.add(new TextField(20));
        f.pack();
        f.setVisible(true);
    }
}
```

The FlowLayoutDemo demonstrates using some of the AWT components. Three Button components are added to the Frame first. Then, a List is created, filled with the command-line arguments, and added to the Frame. Next, a Checkbox, Label, and TextField are added. The pack() method sizes the Frame so all the components fit nicely, as you can see by the output shown in Figure 12.4.

Figure 12.4   Output of the FlowLayoutDemo program.

♦ Pluggable Look and Feel

Swing components have what is referred to as a *pluggable look and feel* (PLAF), allowing their appearance to be independent of the underlying platform. You can create your own look and feel—determining colors, fonts, and backgrounds for all your components. Creating your own look and feel involves a fair amount of coding and artistic skills and is beyond the scope of this book.

However, Swing comes with a built-in look and feel for Windows, Macintosh, and Motif, which is a Unix look and feel. There is also a default Swing look and feel, known as the Metal look and feel. (In its earliest stages, Swing was referred to as Metal.)

The javax.swing.UIManager class maintains the current look and feel for a Java program using Swing. In particular, the UIManager class contains methods for determining and changing the current look and feel:

public static void setLookAndFeel(LookAndFeel x). Throws Unsupported-LookAndFeelException. Changes the current look and feel for this Java program to the given LookAndFeel object.

public static void setLookAndFeel(String s). Throws UnsupportedLookAnd-FeelException. Changes the current look and feel for this Java program to the given class name, which is a class that implements LookAndFeel.

public static LookAndFeel getLookAndFeel(). Returns the current look and feel for this Java program as a LookAndFeel object.

The LookAndFeel class is in the javax.swing package and encapsulates a pluggable look and feel. The following classes represent the four built-in pluggable look-and-feel components of Swing:

com.sun.java.swing.plaf.motif.MotifLookAndFeel. Creates a Motif look and feel, which is the user interface for many Unix operating systems.

com.sun.java.swing.plaf.windows.WindowsLookAndFeel. Creates a Microsoft Windows look and feel.

com.sun.java.swing.plaf.mac.MacLookAndFeel. Creates a Macintosh look and feel. (Note that as of J2SE 1.4, this look and feel is not completed yet.)

javax.swing.plaf.metal.MetalLookAndFeel. Creates a Metal look and feel, which is the default for Swing applications.

The PLAFDemo program available on the Web site demonstrates a Swing JFrame with various Swing components added to the JFrame. The JFrame class represents a typical GUI window, and is one of the few heavyweight Swing components. You will notice in the outputs of the PLAFDemo program that the window containing the components is not affected by the selected look and feel.

Figure 12.5 shows the output of the PLAFDemo program using the Metal, Motif, and Windows look and feel. Compare the three windows and notice that the components are similar, but each has its own unique "look." The "feel" comes from the actual response of the components when the user interacts with them.

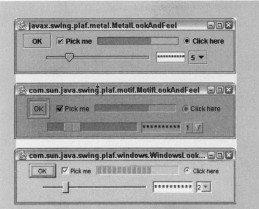

Figure 12.5 This figure provides the Metal look and feel of the PLAFDemo program (top), Motif look and feel of the PLAFDemo program (center), and Windows look and feel of the PLAFDemo program (bottom).

You can resize the Frame from FlowLayoutDemo, and the components will adjust their location so they remain centered in the window. If the Frame is not wide enough to display all the components, the components will wrap around to a new line.

BorderLayout Manager

The java.awt.BorderLayout class represents a BorderLayout manager, which divides a container into five different regions: north, south, east, west, and center. Only one component can be added to a given region, and the size of the component is determined by the region it appears in. BorderLayout has the following properties:

- When a component is added, you pass in an int to the add() method that denotes the region of the container in which the component is to be added. The possible values are NORTH, SOUTH, EAST, WEST, and CENTER, which are all static fields in the BorderLayout class.

- You do not need to add a component to each region. If a region is left empty, the area is filled with the other components in the neighboring regions.

- A component added to the north or south gets its preferred height, but its width will be the width of the container.

- A component added to the east or west will get its preferred width, but its height will be the height of the container minus any components in the north or south.

- A component added to the center gets neither its preferred height nor width, but instead will be the size of the remaining space not filled by components in the other four regions.

If you want a Frame or JFrame to use BorderLayout, you do not need to invoke setLayout() because they use BorderLayout by default. If your container does not have BorderLayout, you need to instantiate a new BorderLayout object using one of its two constructors:

public BorderLayout().   Creates a new BorderLayout with a horizontal and vertical gap of five units between components.

public BorderLayout(int hgap, int vgap).   Creates a BorderLayout object with the specified horizontal and vertical gap.

The following BorderLayoutDemo program demonstrates both how to add components to a container with BorderLayout and how the five regions look. In the program, a Button object is added to each of the five regions. The output is shown in Figure 12.6.

```java
import java.awt.*;
public class BorderLayoutDemo extends Frame
{
    private Button north, south, east, west, center;
    public BorderLayoutDemo(String title)
    {
        super(title);
        north = new Button("North");
        south = new Button("South");
        east = new Button("East");
        west = new Button("West");
        center = new Button("Center");
        this.add(north, BorderLayout.NORTH);
        this.add(south, BorderLayout.SOUTH);
        this.add(east, BorderLayout.EAST);
        this.add(west, BorderLayout.WEST);
        this.add(center, BorderLayout.CENTER);
    }
    public static void main(String [] args)
    {
        Frame f = new BorderLayoutDemo("BorderLayout demo");
        f.pack();
        f.setVisible(true);
    }
}
```

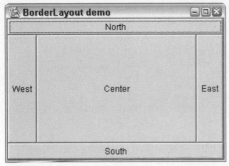

Figure 12.6 Output of the BorderLayoutDemo program.

 Notice that the BorderLayoutDemo takes a more object-oriented approach to creating a Frame. The BorderLayoutDemo class extends Frame and uses fields for each of the components in the Frame. I will try to use this object-oriented design with the examples from here on.

The north and south buttons have their preferred height, but are as wide as the window. The east and west buttons have their preferred width, but run the height of the window. The center button fills in the remaining space, getting neither its preferred width nor height.

Your initial reaction to BorderLayout might be the following: Why would you use it? First, it can contain only five components, which seems like a serious drawback. And the way it resizes your components can make their appearance seem irregular, as with the buttons shown in Figure 12.6. Well, it has been my experience that BorderLayout can be quite useful, especially with top-level containers such as Frame and JFrame (which have BorderLayout by default). You will probably never add a Button to one of the five regions in BorderLayout because of the way BorderLayout resizes buttons. Instead, you will probably add either a component that looks appropriate in the region in which it is placed, or you will nest a panel inside one of the regions, which is demonstrated in the next section, *Panels*. I will show you how BorderLayout can be used along with FlowLayout to create just about any GUI layout you need to create.

Panels

A *panel* is a simple container used for holding components. A panel is like an invisible container, and it must be placed in a top-level container, such as a Frame or JFrame before it can be viewed. The java.awt.Panel class represents panels in AWT, and the javax.swing.JPanel class represents panels in Swing. Panels have the following properties:

- The default layout manager of both Panel and JPanel is FlowLayout, but since they are containers, they can have any layout manager assigned to them.

- A panel can be nested within another panel, a common occurrence when working with complex GUIs.

- A JPanel can take advantage of the double-buffering features in Swing, allowing them to be updated quickly and avoid flickering.

The Panel class has two constructors:

public Panel().   Creates a new Panel with FlowLayout.

public Panel(LayoutManager m).   Creates a new Panel with the specified layout manager.

The JPanel class has four constructors:

public JPanel().   Creates a new JPanel with FlowLayout and double-buffering turned on.

public JPanel(boolean isDoubleBuffered).   Creates a new JPanel with FlowLayout. It will use a double buffer if the boolean parameter is true.

public JPanel(LayoutManager m).   Creates a new JPanel with the specified layout manager and double-buffering turned on.

public JPanel(LayoutManager m, boolean isDoubleBuffered).   Creates a new JPanel with the specified layout manager, with double-buffering used when the boolean parameter is true.

You might be wondering what the purpose of panels is, so let's look at an example that illustrates when a panel is useful. Suppose that you are using a Frame with BorderLayout and you want three buttons displayed in the south. However, you cannot add three components to the south of a BorderLayout, so how can this be done? Well, the trick is to put a panel in the south. We can do this because a panel is a container, and containers are also components. If the one component we add in the south is a panel, we can add three buttons to the panel.

The following PanelDemo program does just this. Study the program and see if you can determine what the output will look like. Notice that the layout manager of the Frame was not changed, so it is BorderLayout. Similarly, the layout manager of the Panel was not changed, so it is FlowLayout by default. The output of the PanelDemo program is shown in Figure 12.7.

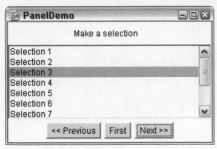

Figure 12.7   Output of the PanelDemo program.

```java
import java.awt.*;
public class PanelDemo extends Frame
{
    private Button next, prev, first;
    private List list;
    public PanelDemo(String title)
    {
        super(title);
        next = new Button("Next >>");
        prev = new Button("<< Previous");
        first = new Button("First");
        Panel southPanel = new Panel();
        southPanel.add(prev);
        southPanel.add(first);
        southPanel.add(next);
        this.add(southPanel, BorderLayout.SOUTH);
        Panel northPanel = new Panel();
        northPanel.add(new Label("Make a selection"));
        this.add(northPanel, BorderLayout.NORTH);
        list = new List();
        for(int i = 1; i <= 10; i++)
        {
            list.add("Selection " + i);
        }
        this.add(list, BorderLayout.CENTER);
    }
    public static void main(String [] args)
    {
        Container f = new PanelDemo("PanelDemo");
        f.setSize(300,200);
        f.setVisible(true);
    }
}
```

The PanelDemo class extends Frame and has four fields: three Button references and a List reference. Notice in the PanelDemo constructor that the three Button objects are placed in a Panel named southPanel, and southPanel is added to the south of the Frame. Because the Buttons are in a Panel with FlowLayout, they will get their preferred size. A Label is put on a Panel named northPanel, and the northPanel is placed in the north of the Frame. Putting the Label on a Panel allows it to be centered along the top of the window because the FlowLayout manager of the northPanel centers its components.

A List is added to the center of the Frame to demonstrate that the remaining space in the Frame is filled with whatever component is placed there. The List is not placed on a Panel, but is simply added directly to the Frame. If the window in Figure 12.7 is resized, the Buttons and Label will be recentered, and the List will be resized to fill the center region of the Frame.

After I discuss the GridLayout and BoxLayout managers, I will show you an example using JPanel that nests panels within each other.

GridLayout Manager

The java.awt.GridLayout class represents a layout manager that divides a container into a grid of rows and columns. The GridLayout manager has the following properties:

- Only one component can be added to each region of the grid. (Of course, that one component can be a panel containing any number of components.)

- Each region of the grid will have the same size. When the container is resized, each region of the grid will be resized accordingly.

- No components get their preferred height or width. Each component in the container is the same size, which is the current size of the regions of the grid.

- The order in which components are added determines their locations in the grid. The first component added appears in the first row and column, and subsequent components fill in the columns across the first row until that row is filled. Then, the second row is filled, and then the third, and so on.

To instantiate a GridLayout object, you use one of its three constructors:

public GridLayout(int rows, int cols).   Creates a new GridLayout with the specified number of rows and columns. The horizontal and vertical gap between components is five units.

public GridLayout(int rows, int cols, int hgap, int vgap). Creates a new GridLayout with the specified number of rows and columns and also with the specified horizontal and vertical gap.

public GridLayout(). Creates a GridLayout object with one row and any number of columns.

One (but not both) of the values for rows and columns can be zero. If the value of columns is 0, the grid will have the specified number of rows, but any number of columns. Similarly, if the value of rows is 0, the grid will have the specified number of columns, but any number of rows.

For example, suppose that we instantiate a GridLayout manager with three columns and 0 rows:

```
GridLayout grid = new GridLayout(0, 3);
```

If 10 components are added to a container with grid as its layout manager, the components will be displayed in four rows and three columns, with the last row containing only one component.

 The no-argument constructor of GridLayout creates a GridLayout with one row and an indeterminate number of columns. This is equivalent to the following statement:

```
new GridLayout(1,0);
```

The following GridLayoutDemo program creates a JPanel, assigns its content pane to have GridLayout, and six JButton components are added to the content pane. Study the program and see whether you can determine what the JFrame will look like. In particular, try to determine the layout of the six buttons relative to the order they are added to the JFrame. The output is shown in Figure 12.8.

```
import java.awt.*;
import javax.swing.*;
public class GridLayoutDemo extends JFrame
{
    private JButton [] buttons;
    public GridLayoutDemo(String title)
    {
        super(title);
        Container contentPane = this.getContentPane();
        contentPane.setLayout(new GridLayout(2,3,10,15));
        buttons = new JButton[6];
        for(int i = 0; i < buttons.length; i++)
        {
```

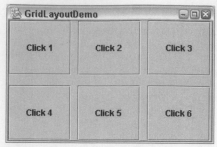

Figure 12.8   Output of the GridLayoutDemo program.

```
                buttons[i] = new JButton("Click " + (i + 1));
                contentPane.add(buttons[i]);
            }
        }
        public static void main(String [] args)
        {
            JFrame f = new GridLayoutDemo("GridLayoutDemo");
            f.setSize(300,200);
            f.setVisible(true);
        }
    }
```

 In the GridLayoutDemo program, notice that the components are added to the JFrame's content pane, not to the JFrame directly. If you invoke add() on the JFrame instead of its content pane, your code will still compile. However, you will get an exception at run time, stating that components cannot be added to a JFrame directly.

BoxLayout Manager

The javax.swing.BoxLayout class represents a box layout, which is used for displaying components either vertically or horizontally. The BoxLayout manager has the following properties:

- Components are displayed either vertically or horizontally, depending on the value of its axis, which is set in the constructor of BoxLayout.

- The components do not wrap as they do with FlowLayout.

- If the components are aligned horizontally, the BoxLayout manager attempts to give them all the same height, based on the component with the largest height. Components in this axis get their preferred width.

- If the components are aligned vertically, the BoxLayout manager attempts to give them all the same width, based on the component with the largest width. Components in this axis get their preferred height.

- In most situations, the Box class is used when working with BoxLayout, as opposed to creating a BoxLayout manager directly. You can think of a Box as a Panel with BoxLayout.

The BoxLayout class has one constructor:

public BoxLayout(Container target, int axis).   Creates a new BoxLayout manager for the specified target and given axis.

The possible values of axis are as follows:

BoxLayout.X_AXIS.   The components are displayed horizontally from left to right.

BoxLayout.Y_AXIS.   The components are displayed vertically from top to bottom.

BoxLayout.LINE_AXIS.   Similar to X_AXIS, the components are laid out horizontally. The order they are displayed is different, depending on the container's ComponentOrientation property, which allows components to be displayed from right to left or from left to right.

BoxLayout.PAGE_AXIS.   Components are laid out like words on a page based on the container's ComponentOrientation property, which allows the components to be laid out from right to left, from left to right, from top to bottom, or from bottom to top.

You can assign BoxLayout to a Panel, JFrame, or any other container, but the simplest way to use BoxLayout is to instantiate a Box object, place your components in the Box, and place the Box into your container. The constructor of the Box class takes in one of these axis values as well:

```
public Box(int axis)
```

The following BoxLayoutDemo program demonstrates how to use the Box class to align a collection of components vertically within a JFrame. Study the program and try to determine its output, which is shown in Figure 12.9.

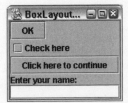

Figure 12.9   Output of the BoxLayoutDemo program.

```java
import java.awt.*;
import javax.swing.*;
public class BoxLayoutDemo extends JFrame
{
     public BoxLayoutDemo(String title)
     {
          super(title);
          //Create a Box with a vertical axis.
          Box box = new Box(BoxLayout.Y_AXIS);
          //Add some components to the Box.
          box.add(new JButton("OK"));
          box.add(new JCheckBox("Check here."));
          box.add(new JButton("Click here to continue."));
          box.add(new JLabel("Enter your name:"));
          box.add(new JTextField());
          //Add the Box to the content pane of this JFrame.
          Container contentPane = this.getContentPane();
          contentPane.add(box, BorderLayout.CENTER);
     }
     public static void main(String [] args)
     {
          JFrame f = new BoxLayoutDemo("BoxLayoutDemo");
          f.pack();
          f.setVisible(true);
     }
}
```

 In the output of the BoxLayoutDemo program shown in Figure 12.9, notice that the width of the components was determined by the widest component in the Box, which in this example is the JButton with the label "Click here to continue."

Nesting Panels

Now that we have discussed a variety of different layout managers, I want to show you a fairly complex GUI that contains a variety of components. Figure 12.10 shows a GUI similar to a program I worked on about 5 years ago when Swing first started becoming popular.

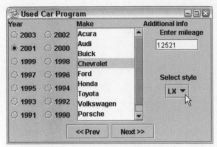

Figure 12.10 The UsedCarFrame program is used to compute the book value of used cars.

I want you to study the GUI in Figure 12.10 and try to determine how you might create it by using various layout managers and containers. Of course, there is no single correct answer, but I have provided a solution in the Used-CarFrame class available on the Web site. As you study the code, you will notice that panels were nested within panels to create parts of the GUI.

I want to point out a few of the details of the UsedCarFrame:

- The UsedCarFrame class extends JFrame, and its content pane uses BorderLayout (because it was not changed from its default).

- A JPanel is added to the south, north, and center of the content pane.

- The JPanel in the south has FlowLayout and contains two JButton components.

- The JPanel in the north has GridLayout with one row and three columns and contains three JLabel components.

- The JPanel in the center of the content pane has GridLayout with one row and three columns. The component in the first column is a JPanel named left, the component in the second column is a JScrollPane named scrollPane, and the component in the third column is a Box named right.

- The left JPanel has GridLayout with seven rows and two columns. The 14 components are radio buttons.

- The scrollPane houses a JList containing various strings.

- The right Box contains a JLabel, a JTextField, another JLabel, and a JComboBox.

I realize that throughout this chapter I have used the various AWT and Swing components without properly describing them or how they are created and used. In Chapter 13, "GUI Components and Event Handling," I will discuss these components in detail, including how to handle the various events that each component generates.

◆ Dialog Windows

A *dialog window* is used to interact with the user, either to share information with the user or obtain information from the user. The java.awt.Dialog class represents an AWT dialog window, and the javax.swing.JDialog class represents a Swing dialog window. Note that the JDialog class extends the Dialog class.

A dialog window is either modal or modeless. A *modal* dialog window must be closed before the program can continue. A *modeless* dialog window is one that does not need to be closed, and you still can interact with the program or programs behind the modeless dialog.

A dialog window often has an owner window that is either another dialog window or a frame window. The owner of a dialog window is assigned by using one of the constructors of the Dialog or JDialog classes:

public Dialog(Frame owner, String title, boolean modal).   Creates a Dialog with the given Frame as its owner. The String appears in the title bar, and if the boolean is true, the Dialog will be modal.

public Dialog(Dialog owner, String title, boolean modal).   Creates a Dialog with the given Dialog as its owner.

public JDialog(Frame owner, String title, boolean modal).   Creates a JDialog with the given Frame as its owner.

public JDialog(Dialog owner, String title, boolean modal).   Creates a JDialog with the given Dialog as its owner.

public JDialog().   Creates a JDialog with no owner or title. It will be modeless by default.

There are other constructors in the Dialog and JDialog classes that contain a variation of the parameters listed above.

After you have instantiated a dialog window, you invoke the show() method to activate the dialog window and the hide() method to hide the dialog window. These methods are defined as follows:

public void show().   This method makes the Dialog visible. If the Dialog is modal, this method will not return until the hide() or dispose() method is invoked on this Dialog object. If the Dialog is modeless, this method returns immediately.

public void hide().   This method hides the Dialog and causes the show() method to return if the Dialog is modal.

Notice that the dispose() method can also be used to hide a Dialog window. (The difference between hide() and dispose() is that the dispose() method frees up any resources involving the screen and other native devices. A disposed window can still be redisplayed using the show() method.)

The following ModalDemo program creates a Dialog window with a Frame as its owner. The dialog is modal, so when the dialog is displayed, it must be closed before the user can interact with the Frame.

```
import java.awt.*;
import java.awt.event.*;
import javax.swing.*;
```

```
public class ModalDemo extends Frame implements ActionListener
{
    private Dialog modal;
    private JButton go, ok;
    public ModalDemo(String title)
    {
        super(title);
        //Prepare the buttons.
        go = new JButton("Go");
        go.addActionListener(this);
        ok = new JButton("OK");
        ok.addActionListener(this);
        //prepare the Dialog window
        modal = new Dialog(this, "A modal dialog", true);
        modal.setLayout(new FlowLayout());
        modal.add(ok);
        modal.setBounds(60,100,180,60);
        //Add the "Go" button to the Frame.
        JPanel center = new JPanel();
        center.add(go);
        this.add(center, BorderLayout.CENTER);
    }
    //Clicking either button causes this method to be invoked
    public void actionPerformed(ActionEvent e)
    {
        String label = e.getActionCommand();
        if(label.equals("Go"))
        {
            modal.show();
        }
        else if(label.equals("OK"))
        {
            modal.hide();
        }
    }
    public static void main(String [] args)
    {
        Frame f = new ModalDemo("Modal Demo");
        f.setSize(300, 300);
        f.setVisible(true);
    }
}
```

Figure 12.11 shows the output of the ModalDemo program. Notice that true was passed in to the Dialog constructor, making the Dialog modal. The ActionListener interface and actionPerformed() method are discussed in detail in Chapter 13.

continued

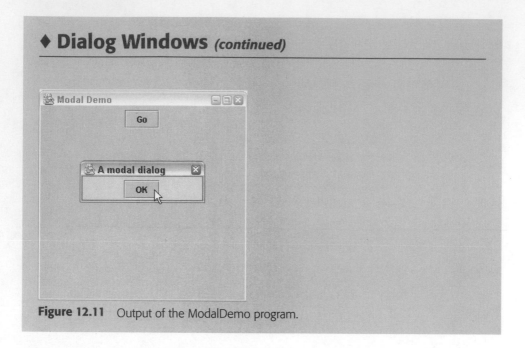

Figure 12.11 Output of the ModalDemo program.

Using No Layout Manager

You can create a GUI with components in the exact location and size that you want. To do this, you set the layout manager of the container to null and then set the bounds for each component within the container.

The following JDialogDemo program creates a JDialog and sets its layout manager to null. Three components are added: a JLabel and two JButtons. The bounds of each component are set using the setBounds() method. Because there is no layout manager, the bounds of the component are not overridden (as they often are when you are using a layout manager), causing the components to appear exactly where you specify with setBounds(). Study the JDialogDemo program and try to determine what the GUI will look like. The output is shown in Figure 12.12.

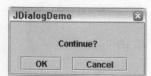

Figure 12.12 Output of the JDialogDemo program.

```
import java.awt.*;
import javax.swing.*;
public class JDialogDemo extends JDialog
{
    private JButton ok, cancel;
    public JDialogDemo(String title)
    {
        this.setTitle(title);
        Container contentPane = this.getContentPane();
        contentPane.setLayout(null);
        JLabel message = new JLabel("Continue?");
        message.setBounds(70, 20, 125, 20);
        ok = new JButton("OK");
        ok.setBounds(15,50, 60, 20);
        cancel = new JButton("Cancel");
        cancel.setBounds(90, 50, 80, 20);
        contentPane.add(message);
        contentPane.add(ok);
        contentPane.add(cancel);
    }
    public static void main(String [] args)
    {
        JDialog f = new JDialogDemo("JDialogDemo");
        f.setSize(200,100);
        f.setResizable(false);
        f.setVisible(true);
    }
}
```

Lab 12.1: Using JFrame

The purpose of this lab is to become familiar with creating a JFrame.

1. Write a class named Calculator that extends JFrame.

2. Within the constructor of the Calculator class, use panels and layout managers to create a GUI similar to the one shown in Figure 12.13. Note that the class uses JButton for the buttons and JTextField for the display above the buttons.

3. Add a main() method to your Calculator class that instantiates and displays your Calculator GUI.

4. Save, compile, and run the Calculator class.

Your Calculator should be similar to the one in Figure 12.13. Do not worry if it is not exactly the same, especially because we have not discussed the details of the various components yet.

Figure 12.13 Create a GUI that looks similar to this Calculator window.

Lab 12.2: The Instant Message Window

This lab is the beginning of a project that you will work on throughout the remainder of this book: You will write an instant messaging program. Instant messaging has become a very popular Internet application because it enables you to "talk" to someone by sending messages back and forth that are instantly read by the receiver. This project will use Swing, and you will create the GUI portion of the program first.

Write a class named InstantMessageFrame. Have it extend the JFrame class.

1. Add a constructor that contains a single parameter of type String to represent the title bar of the JFrame. Within the constructor, pass the String parameter up to the parent JFrame constructor that takes in a String.

2. Within the constructor, use the setDefaultCloseOperation() method so that your JFrame will cause the program to exit when the user closes the JFrame.

3. Add a main() method within your InstantMessageFrame class. Within main(), instantiate a new InstantMessageFrame object, passing in "My IM Program" for the title bar.

4. Within main(), set the size of your window to be 220 pixels wide by 450 pixels high.

5. Within main(), invoke setVisible() to make your window visible on the screen.

6. Save, compile, and run your InstantMessageFrame program.

You should see a JFrame that is 220 pixels wide by 450 pixels high. Your program should exit when you close the JFrame.

Lab 12.3: The Instant Message GUI

The purpose of this lab is to become familiar with using layout managers and panels to lay out components in a window. This lab, which is a continuation of Lab 12.2, uses an object-oriented approach to creating the GUI. I will have you write separate methods for each nested container.

1. Open the source code file of your InstantMessageFrame class from Lab 12.2.

2. Add the following three fields to the InstantMessageFrame class: a JTextField named message, a JList named friends, and a JButton named send.

3. Add a method to your InstantMessageFrame class named getMessagePanel() that returns a JPanel and has no parameters. (This method will create a JPanel that will appear in the south border of your JFrame. It will contain a text field in which a message can be entered and a button that sends an instant message to all the friends in the list.)

4. Within getMessagePanel(), instantiate a new JPanel and give it BorderLayout. Assign a message equal to a new JTextField by using the no-argument constructor of JTextField. Assign send to a new JButton, passing in "Send" to the constructor. (This will be the label on the button.)

5. Within getMessagePanel(), add the message text field to the center of the JPanel and add the send button to the east border of the JPanel. The panel is now ready, so return the JPanel reference.

6. Add a method to your InstantMessageFrame class named getFriendsPane() that returns a JScrollPane and has no parameters. (This method will create a scrollable list that will contain the names of others that you can chat with.)

7. Within getFriendsPane(), assign friends to a new JList by using the no-argument constructor of JList.

8. Within getFriendsPane(), instantiate a new JScrollPane using the following statement:

   ```
   JScrollPane pane = new JScrollPane(friends);
   ```

9. The scroll pane is ready, so return the reference pane at the end of getFriendsPane().

10. Within the constructor of InstantMessageFrame, invoke getMessagePanel(), placing the returned panel in the south border of the content pane of InstantMessageFrame.

11. Within the constructor of InstantMessageFrame, invoke get-FriendsPane(), placing the returned scroll pane in the center of the content pane of InstantMessageFrame.

12. Save, compile, and run the InstantMessageFrame class.

Your InstantMessageFrame now has three visible components: a JList, a JTextField, and a JButton.

Lab 12.4: Creating a Dialog Window

Sending an instant message is typically done using a dialog window in which you enter the message in a text field. In this lab, you will write a class to represent the GUI for this dialog window that will look similar to that shown in Figure 12.14.

1. Write a class named InstantMessageDialog that extends JDialog.

2. Add three fields to the InstantMessageDialog class: a JButton named send, a JButton named cancel, and a JTextField named message.

3. Add a constructor that has two parameters: a Frame to represent the owner of the dialog and a String to represent the recipient of the instant message. Pass the Frame parameter up to the parent constructor, as well as a String for the title of the window and true to make it a modal dialog.

4. Within the constructor, initialize the two JButton fields to be a "Send" and "Cancel" button. Initialize the message field to a new JTextField by using the no-argument constructor of JTextField.

5. Add the two buttons to the south border of the dialog's content pane, as shown in Figure 12.14.

6. Add the JTextField to a new JScrollPane using the statement:

```
JScrollPane center = new JScrollPane(message);
```

7. Add the center pane to the center of the dialog's content pane.

8. Add a JLabel to the north border of the dialog's content pane that displays a message containing the name of the recipient, similar to the label in Figure 12.14.

9. Set the size of the dialog window to be 400 pixels wide by 200 pixels high.

10. Add a main() method to the InstantMessageDialog class that instantiates a new InstantMessageDialog object. Pass in null for the owner

and any name you want for the recipient. Invoke the show() method on your dialog window.

11. Save, compile, and run the InstantMessageDemo program.

The main() method you added to InstantMessageDialog is strictly for testing purposes. When you run the program, you should see a dialog window similar to the one shown in Figure 12.14. To close this dialog window, you will need to terminate the JVM (press Ctrl+c at the command prompt).

Figure 12.14   Your InstantMessageDialog should look similar to this one.

Summary

- There are two APIs for creating GUI applications in Java: Swing and AWT. The Swing API uses many of the AWT classes and interfaces.

- Components reside in containers. The java.awt.Component class is the parent class of all AWT components. The java.awt.Container class is the parent class of all AWT containers and also of all Swing components.

- The java.awt.Frame and javax.swing.JFrame classes are used to create a top-level window.

- A container uses a layout manager to determine how the components are laid out in the container. A container can use any of the available layout managers.

- The common layout managers are FlowLayout, BorderLayout, GridLayout, GridBagLayout, CardLayout, BoxLayout, SpringLayout, and OverlayLayout.

- Swing components are displayed using a Pluggable Look and Feel (PLAF) that can be changed dynamically.

- A panel can be nested within a container. Panels can be nested within other panels as well to allow greater control of where components are laid out within a container.

Review Questions

1. What does GUI stand for?

2. What does AWT stand for?

3. What does Swing stand for?

4. Which of the following statements is (are) true about lightweight and heavyweight components? (Select all that apply.)

   a. The look and feel of a heavyweight component relies heavily on the native platform.

   b. The look and feel of a lightweight component relies heavily on the native platform.

   c. Lightweight components are written entirely in Java, allowing them to control their appearance.

   d. All the AWT components are heavyweight components.

   e. All the class names that represent Swing components begin with a capital J.

   f. All the Swing components are lightweight components.

5. What is the initial size of a java.awt.Frame object immediately after one is instantiated?

6. How big is a JFrame if setBounds(120, 200, 340, 280) is invoked on the JFrame?

7. Which one of the following statements is *not* true?

   a. The java.awt.Container class is a child of java.awt.Component.

   b. The javax.swing.JComponent class is the parent class of all Swing components.

   c. All Swing components can act as containers.

   d. All AWT components can act as containers.

   e. The javax.swing.JComponent class is a child of java.awt.Container.

8. Which method in the java.awt.Container class is used to add a component to the container?

9. What is the default layout manager of a java.awt.Frame?

10. What is the default layout manager of the content pane of a javax.swing.JFrame?

11. What is the default layout manager of a java.awt.Panel? Of a javax.swing.JPanel?

12. Which of the following statements is (are) true about layout managers? (Select all that apply.)

   a. Components with FlowLayout receive their preferred size.

   b. Components with BorderLayout receive only their preferred width.

   c. Components with GridLayout do not receive their preferred width or height.

   d. Components with BoxLayout receive their preferred height or width, depending on the axis.

   e. The order in which components are added to a container with GridLayout does not affect where they appear in the grid.

   f. You can add at most only five components to a container with BorderLayout.

13. True or False: A java.awt.Panel can be assigned BorderLayout.

14. True or False: A java.awt.Panel can be nested within another java.awt.Panel.

15. Suppose that a new GridLayout manager is instantiated using the statement new Grid-Layout(0,1). If five components are added to a container using this layout manager, how will the components be arranged?

16. If a dialog window is instantiated using the statement new JDialog(), is it modal or modeless?

Answers to Review Questions

1. GUI stands for graphical user interface, and it refers to the visual portion of your application that a user sees and interacts with.

2. AWT stands for Abstract Windowing Toolkit, and it refers to a collection of classes and interfaces for developing GUI programs.

3. Sorry to say, Swing is not an acronym, nor does it refer to anything. Swing is a collection of GUI components and APIs that are more robust and versatile than the AWT. The story I heard from Sun was that someone used the comment "That really swings" when first seeing Metal, the initial name given to the Swing project.

4. Answer a is true because that is the definition of a heavyweight component. Answer b is not true; the look and feel of a lightweight component is determined by the component, which is why answer c is true. Answer d is also true, but answer f is not entirely true. (Swing has several heavyweight components, including the windows such as JFrame and JDialog.) Answer e is true.

5. The initial size of Frame, JFrame, Dialog, and JDialog objects is 0 pixels high by 0 pixels wide.

6. It will be 340 pixels wide by 280 pixels high. The 120 and 200 denote its location on the screen, but do not affect the size of the JFrame.

7. Not all AWT components are containers, only those that are child classes of java.awt.Container, so the correct answer is d.

8. You use one of the overloaded add() methods.

9. FlowLayout.

10. BorderLayout.

11. Both have FlowLayout by default.

12. Answer a is true; FlowLayout gives all components their preferred size. Answer b is false; the east and west components get their preferred width, but the north and south components do not. Instead, they get their preferred height, and the center component does not get its preferred width or height. Answer c is true; components in GridLayout are all the size of the regions in the grid, which are all the same size. Answer d is true; horizontal components get their preferred width and vertical components get their preferred height. Answer e is false; in fact, the exact opposite is true. The order components are added in exactly the way they appear in the grid. Answer f is true; only five components can be added to a container with BorderLayout. However, any one of those components can be a container (like a Panel) that contains any number of components.

13. True. A Panel can be assigned to any layout manager.

14. True. Panels are often nested within other panels.

15. The number of rows is defined as 0, which means that any arbitrary number of rows can appear. Because the number of columns is one, the five components will appear vertically in one column spanning five rows.

16. The no-argument constructor of JDialog creates a modeless dialog window.

CHAPTER

13

GUI Components and Event Handling

Now that you can create a nice-looking GUI for your programs, you are probably anxious to get started on this chapter, especially because your GUI programs from the last chapter do not have any functionality beyond looking good. In this chapter, I will discuss the delegation model, the architecture behind event handling in Java. We will then look at the various components of the AWT and Swing APIs, discussing how to create them and how to handle their events.

The Delegation Model

Events in Java are fired and handled using a design known as the delegation model. With the delegation model, a source generates an event and a listener handles it, creating an object-oriented approach to handling events. (A class is written to handle the events of a component.) There are three major players in the delegation model:

The source of the event.   In GUI programming, the component is the source of the event. Events are Java objects that are instantiated by the component and passed as an argument to any listeners.

An event listener.   A listener of an event registers itself with the source of the event. When an event occurs, the source of the event invokes a method on the listener.

An interface.   The interface contains the methods that the listener must implement and that the source of the event invokes when the event occurs.

For example, when a user clicks a java.awt.Button, the Button generates a java.awt.event.ActionEvent. The Button invokes the actionPerformed() method on each registered listener of the Button, passing in the ActionEvent object. The actionPerformed() method is defined in the java.awt.event.ActionListener interface, which each listener must implement. In this scenario, the Button is the source of the event, the interface is ActionListener, and the listener is any class that implements ActionListener and registers itself with the Button.

Classroom Q & A

Q: How do you register a listener with a Button?

A: Two steps are involved. You first need to write a class that implements ActionListener. You then invoke the addActionListener() method on the Button, passing in an instance of your class.

Q: So do all components generate an ActionEvent?

A: No. There are many types of events, and each event has a corresponding listener interface. For example, windows generate WindowEvent objects and invoke a method from the WindowListener interface. A check box generates an ItemEvent and invokes a method in the ItemListener interface.

Q: How do you know what events a component generates?

A: Well, one of my main goals in this chapter is to show you how to determine the events that a component generates. The simplest way to tell is to look for methods in the component's class of the form add<event_name>Listener(). For example, if a component has an addMouseListener() method, the component generates a MouseEvent.

Q: So what interface do you implement to listen to a MouseEvent?

A: Java components use a standard naming convention for events. If the name of the event is MouseEvent, the name of the corresponding interface is MouseListener, and the name of the method you invoke to register a listener is addMouseListener().

Q: Can a component have more than one listener?

A: Sure. Any number of listeners can register themselves with a GUI component. When an event occurs, each listener is notified one at a time (in no particular order).

Q: Can a component generate more than one type of event?

A: Yes. In fact, all components generate multiple types of events because all components can generate a FocusEvent, KeyEvent, MouseEvent, MouseMotionEvent, and others.

Q: That must mean that all components have methods named addFocusListener() method, addKeyListener(), addMouseListener(), addMouseMotionListener(), and so on.

A: You're catching on. The add<event_name>Listener() methods for these events are found in the java.awt.Component class (the parent class of all components). What I want to do now is discuss the event interfaces, which provide the communication between the source of the event and the listener. After that, I will show you how to write a listener and register it with the event source.

The Event Listener Interfaces

The *event listener interface* contains the methods that the event source invokes on the listener, and it provides the means of communication between the source of the event and the listener of the event. Each type of event has a corresponding listener interface.

 Java uses a standard naming convention for event classes and listener interfaces: The name of the event class uses the convention *<Name>*Event, and the corresponding listener interface uses the convention *<Name>*Listener. For example, the ActionEvent class is associated with the one method of the ActionListener interface, and the WindowEvent class is associated with the seven methods of the WindowListener interface.

An event listener interface extends the java.util.EventListener interface. The EventListener interface does not contain any methods, but is used for tagging an event listener interface for use with the delegation model of event handling. For example, the ActionListener interface is defined as:

```
package java.awt.event;
public interface ActionListener extends java.util.EventListener
{
    public void actionPerformed(ActionEvent e);
}
```

Notice that ActionListener extends EventListener and is in the java.awt.event package, which is where all the AWT event classes and listener interfaces are defined. The javax.swing.event package contains the event classes and listener interfaces unique to Swing. The AWT components only generate AWT events, while Swing components generate both AWT and Swing events. For example, a Swing JButton is the source of java.awt.event.ActionEvent (an AWT event class) and a javax.swing.event.ChangeEvent (a Swing event class).

Notice also that the ActionListener interface contains one method, and the parameter is an ActionEvent. When an action event occurs, the source of the event instantiates an ActionEvent object and invokes actionPerformed() on all listeners, passing in the ActionEvent object.

An event listener interface can contain any number of methods. The methods are used to determine what caused the event. With ActionEvent, there is only one method, actionPerformed(), which simply means that the action has occurred. For example, with buttons it means the button was clicked.

The WindowListener interface has seven methods, and the method that the event source invokes depends on what caused the WindowEvent. WindowListener is defined as:

```
package java.awt.event;
public interface WindowListener extends java.util.EventListener
{
    public void windowOpened(WindowEvent e);
    public void windowClosing(WindowEvent e);
    public void windowClosed(WindowEvent e);
    public void windowIconified(WindowEvent e);
    public void windowDeiconified(WindowEvent e);
    public void windowActivated(WindowEvent e);
    public void windowDeactivated(WindowEvent e);
}
```

For example, when a user clicks the X to close a window, the window instantiates a new WindowEvent and invokes the windowClosing() method on all registered listeners. Similarly, minimizing a window causes windowIconified() to be invoked, restoring a window causes windowDeiconified() to be invoked, and so on. The window invokes the appropriate method on the listener, depending on what caused the WindowEvent.

Each type of event has an event class and an event listener interface. They share a common name, such as **ActionEvent** and **ActionListener**, **ItemEvent** and **ItemListener**, and so on. A listener of an event must implement the corresponding event listener interface. For example, if you want to listen to an **ItemEvent**, you write a class that implements the **ItemListener** interface.

Now that we've discussed the interfaces, let's look at how to create a listener and register it with an event source.

Creating an Event Listener

If a listener wants to listen to a particular type of event, then the listener must implement the corresponding event listener interface. From a programming point of view, this means you need to write a class that implements the listener interface. If you want to listen for an ActionEvent, you write a class that implements ActionListener. If you want to listen for a WindowEvent, you write a class that implements WindowListener.

I want to show you an example that demonstrates a common design issue of event handling. I want to write a simple program that contains a Frame with a Button in it. When the user clicks the Button, I want the color of the Frame to change to a random color. We have not discussed Button components in detail yet, but I can tell you that clicking a Button generates an ActionEvent.

Therefore, I need to write a class that implements ActionListener. When the actionPerformed() method is invoked, I know that the Button has been clicked, but I want to change the background color of the window. I need to design my ActionListener class so that it has a reference to the window.

The following RandomColor class is an ActionListener that, in its constructor, initializes a field to point to a Container whose color is to be changed. By using a reference of type Container, this allows the RandomColor class to change the color of not just a window, but any Container.

 Storing the data and other components that a listener needs as fields in the listener class is a common technique when designing a listener class. Typically, these fields are initialized in the constructor or by adding mutator (set) methods.

```
import java.awt.*;
import java.awt.event.*;
public class RandomColor implements ActionListener
{
```

```
      private Container container;

      public RandomColor(Container c)
      {
          container = c;
      }
      public void actionPerformed(ActionEvent e)
      {
          System.out.println(e + " just occurred.");
          int red, green, blue;
          red = (int) (Math.random() * 256);
          green = (int) (Math.random() * 256);
          blue = (int) (Math.random() * 256);
          Color color = new Color(red, green, blue);
          container.setBackground(color);
      }
  }
```

Registering a Listener with an Event Source

After writing a listener class, you register it with the component from which you want to handle events. If a component generates an event, the component has a method of the form add<*Event_Name*>Listener(). For example, a Button generates an ActionEvent, and the Button class contains the following method:

```
public void addActionListener(ActionListener a)
```

Similarly, a Frame generates a WindowEvent and contains the following method:

```
public void addWindowListener(WindowListener w)
```

Notice that the data types of the parameters of these two methods are interface types. These methods are designed to force the listener class to implement a specific interface. If you want to listen for the ActionEvent of a Button, you need to write a class that implements ActionListener so you can pass an instance to the addActionListener() method. If you want to listen for the WindowEvent of a Frame, you need to write a class that implements WindowListener so you can pass an instance to the addWindowListener() method.

The following EventDemo class creates a button and registers an instance of the RandomColor class discussed earlier as a listener of the button. Study the program and try to determine what the GUI looks like and what the program does.

```
import java.awt.*;public class EventDemo extends Frame
{
    private Button go;
    public EventDemo(String title)
    {
        super(title);
        go = new Button("Go");
        //Instantiate a listener object.
        RandomColor changer = new RandomColor(this);
        //Register the listener with the button.
        go.addActionListener(changer);
        //Add the button to the frame.
        this.setLayout(new FlowLayout());
        this.add(go);
    }
    public static void main(String [] args)
    {
        Frame f = new EventDemo("Click the button...");
        f.setSize(300,300);
        f.setVisible(true);
    }
}
```

I want to make a few observations about the EventDemo program:

- When the RandomColor object is instantiated, a reference to the Frame is passed in to the constructor. This reference is stored as a field in the RandomColor object.

- The RandomColor object is registered as a listener of the *go* button.

- Each time the *go* button is clicked, the button generates an ActionEvent and invokes actionPerformed() on the RandomColor object.

- Within actionPerformed(), the RandomColor object generates a random color and sets it as the background color of the Frame.

The output of the EventDemo program is shown in Figure 13.1. Notice that the program does not terminate because it is a Frame and we have not handled the WindowEvent yet. I will show you how to do that next when I discuss the event adapter classes.

Figure 13.1   Output of the EventDemo program.

The Event Adapter Classes

A listener class must implement a listener interface, meaning that all of the methods of the interface must be defined in the class. For the listener interfaces with one method, this is not too much work; however, for the listener interfaces with multiple methods, it can be fairly tedious—especially when you have to define methods in which you are not interested.

For example, suppose that you want to handle the windowClosing() cause of a WindowEvent so that the program terminates. Then the listener class needs to implement WindowListener and define all seven of its methods. The class might look similar to the following:

```java
import java.awt.event.*;
public class TediousWindowCloser implements WindowListener
{
    public void windowClosing(WindowEvent e)
    {
        System.exit(0);
    }
    public void windowOpened(WindowEvent e)
    {}
    public void windowClosed(WindowEvent e)
    {}
    public void windowIconified(WindowEvent e)
    {}
    public void windowDeiconified(WindowEvent e)
    {}
    public void windowActivated(WindowEvent e)
    {}
```

```
    public void windowDeactivated(WindowEvent e)
    {}
}
```

The TediousWindowCloser class must define all seven methods of WindowListener, even though six of them do not have any implementation. There is nothing wrong with this class except that it was a lot of typing for really only defining one method.

This is where the adapter classes come in. The event listener interfaces that contain more than one method have a corresponding *event adapter class* that implements the interface and defines each method in the interface with an empty method body. Instead of implementing an event listener interface, you can extend the corresponding event adapter class and define only those methods in which you are interested.

The WindowAdapter class is an example of an event adapter class. It implements WindowListener, and defines its seven methods with empty method bodies. Other event adapter classes in the AWT and Swing include:

ComponentAdapter.   Defines the four methods of ComponentListener.

ContainerAdapter.   Defines the two methods of ContainerListener.

FocusAdapter.   Defines the two methods of FocusListener.

KeyAdapter.   Defines the three methods of KeyListener.

MouseAdapter.   Defines the five methods of MouseListener.

MouseMotionAdapter.   Defines the two methods of MouseMotionListener.

InternalFrameAdapter.   Defines the seven methods of InternalFrameListener.

MouseInputAdapter.   Defines the seven methods of MouseInputListener.

To demonstrate using an adapter class, the following SimpleWindowCloser class extends WindowAdapter instead of implementing WindowListener. The class fulfills the same purpose as the TediousWindowCloser class, but notice that it is simpler to write:

```
import java.awt.event.*;
public class SimpleWindowCloser extends WindowAdapter
{
    public void windowClosing(WindowEvent e)
    {
        System.exit(0);
    }
}
```

Because the SimpleWindowCloser class extends WindowAdapter and WindowAdapter implements WindowListener, that makes SimpleWindowCloser a

WindowListener that can listen for a WindowEvent. The EventDemo2 program that follows demonstrates using SimpleWindowCloser to end a program when a user closes the Frame. It is similar to the EventDemo program earlier. Study the program, and try to determine how the event handling ends the program.

```java
import java.awt.*;
public class EventDemo2 extends Frame
{
    private Button go;
    public EventDemo2(String title)
    {
        super(title);
        go = new Button("Go");
        RandomColor changer = new RandomColor(this);
        go.addActionListener(changer);
        this.setLayout(new FlowLayout());
        this.add(go);
        //Register a listener to this Frame.
        SimpleWindowCloser closer = new SimpleWindowCloser();
        this.addWindowListener(closer);
    }
    public static void main(String [] args)
    {
        Frame f = new EventDemo2("SimpleWindowCloser");
        f.setSize(300,300);
        f.setVisible(true);
    }
}
```

The output of the EventDemo2 program looks the same as the window shown in Figure 13.1. When the "X" is clicked, the Frame generates a WindowEvent and invokes the windowClosing() method on the SimpleWindowCloser object. The following statement causes the JVM to terminate (which closes the Frame as well):

```java
System.exit(0);
```

note   A Frame can be closed by invoking either the setVisible() method and passing in false, or invoking the dispose() method. Both of these methods are defined in the java.awt.Window class, which is the parent class of Frame. Both methods hide the window, but the dispose() method also frees up any screen resources that the window may be consuming.

We have discussed the delegation model and how listeners must implement the event listener interfaces. I want to spend the remainder of this chapter focusing on the various GUI components. Specifically, I want to discuss how each component is instantiated and the types of events each generates.

♦ The Event Objects

When an event occurs, the source of the event instantiates an object that represents the event. The java.awt.event and javax.swing.event packages contain the various classes that represent these events. Each event class contains different attributes and behaviors, depending on the type of event. For example, the MouseEvent class contains the x and y coordinates of the location of the mouse pointer when the event occurred. The ActionEvent class contains an action command denoting what action took place.

The java.util.EventObject class is the parent class of all event classes. There are two methods in the EventObject class:

public Object getSource(). Returns a reference to the component that generated the event.

public String toString(). Returns the event as a String.

Every event object contains a reference to the component that was the source of the event, and a listener can obtain this reference using the getSource() method.

Suppose that you wanted to write a GUI that highlighted components as the mouse hovered over them. To accomplish this, a listener would need to handle the MouseEvent generated by a component when the user moves the mouse over the component. To highlight the component, the listener would need a reference to the component, which can be obtained using the getSource() method.

The following HighlightComponent class demonstrates how this might be done. Notice that the class extends MouseAdapter and implements the mouseEntered() and mouseExited() methods, which are invoked when the mouse enters and leaves a component, respectively.

```
import java.awt.event.*;
import java.awt.*;
public class HighlightComponent extends MouseAdapter
{
    private Color previousColor;
    public void mouseEntered(MouseEvent e)
    {
        Component component = (Component) e.getSource();
        previousColor = component.getBackground();
        component.setBackground(Color.WHITE);
    }
    public void mouseExited(MouseEvent e)
    {
        Component component = (Component) e.getSource();
        component.setBackground(previousColor);
    }
}
```

continued

◆ The Event Objects (continued)

The java.awt.Component class, which is the parent of all components, contains an addMouseListener() method. This implies that all components are the source of MouseEvent, which is true because all components can interact with the mouse in some manner. The following code from the HighlightDemo program (see the Web site for this book for a complete listing) creates six JButton components and registers a HighlightComponent listener with each component, as well as the JFrame's content pane. What do you think happens when this program executes and the user moves the mouse over the various components in the window?

```
buttons = new JButton[6];
HighlightComponent listener =new HighlightComponent();
contentPane.addMouseListener(listener);
for(int i = 0; i < buttons.length; i++)
{
buttons[i] = new JButton("Click " + (i + 1));
contentPane.add(buttons[i]);buttons[i].addMouseListener(listener);
}
```

Figure 13.2 shows the output of the HighlightDemo program when the mouse is hovering over the button labeled Click 2.

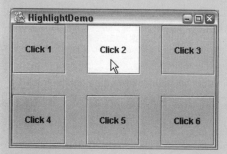

Figure 13.2   The Click 2 button is highlighted when the mouse is over it.

When the mouse leaves the Click 2 button, the button changes back to its regular color and the background of the window becomes white. When the mouse moves back over a button, the window goes back to its regular color and the corresponding mouse becomes white. Note that the HighlightComponent listener class was simplified by the listener's being able to get the source of the event invoking getSource(), which can be invoked on any event object.

As I discuss the various components in this chapter, I will discuss many of the event classes and how to use them to obtain useful information about the event that is being listened for.

Buttons

We have seen the Button and JButton class used in many of the GUI examples of Chapter 12, "An Introduction to GUI Programming," and also the examples earlier in this chapter. Now, let's look at buttons in detail. The java.awt.Button class represents an AWT button, and the javax.swing.JButton class represents a Swing button.

AWT Buttons

The java.awt.Button class has two constructors:

public Button().   Creates a Button with no label.

public Button(String label).   Creates a Button with the specified label.

The methods in the Button class related to events include:

public void addActionListener(ActionListener a).   Registers the given listener with the button to receive the ActionEvent generated when the button is clicked.

public void setActionCommand(String c).   Sets the action command for the button. A component that generates an ActionEvent can assign a command to the event, which by default is the label on the button. This method is used to assign the action command to something other than the button's label.

 The java.awt.event.ActionEvent class represents an action event. Action events are typically generated by a user making a selection, such as clicking a button or selecting a menu item. The methods in the ActionEvent class include:

> **public String getActionCommand().**   Returns the action command of the source of the component.
>
> **public int getModifiers().**   Returns an int containing information about modifier keys that were pressed when the event occurs. Modifier keys include the Shift, Ctrl, and Alt keys. Sometimes an event is handled slightly differently when a modifier key is pressed.

In addition, because ActionEvent extends java.util.EventObject, you can also obtain a reference to the source of the event using the getSource() method.

Swing Buttons

The javax.swing.JButton class has several constructors, including:

public JButton(String label).   Creates a JButton with the given label.

public JButton(Icon icon).   Creates a JButton with the specified icon. Swing buttons can have an icon displayed on the button.

public JButton(String label, Icon icon).   Creates a JButton with both text and an icon.

The methods in the JButton class related to events include:

public void addActionListener(ActionListener a).   Registers the given listener with the button to receive the ActionEvent generated when the button is clicked.

public void addChangeListener(ChangeListener c).   Registers the given listener to receive the ChangeEvent generated when the state of the button changes.

public void setActionCommand(String c).   Sets the action command for the button.

public void doClick().   Programmatically clicks the button, just as if the user had done it.

public void setMnemonic(int mnemonic).   Assigns a virtual key to the button so that it can be clicked using the keyboard. The argument passed in is one of the static fields in the KeyEvent class. For example, if the mnemonic is set to be VK_B, pressing Alt+B when the button has focus will cause the button to be clicked.

public void setPressedIcon(Icon icon).   Assigns an icon that is displayed when the button is clicked.

The JButton class has dozens more methods, so check the documentation to find out other features of JButton. You will notice with buttons (and all the other components) that the Swing version of the component has many more methods and features than its AWT counterpart. For example, the doClick() and setMnemonic() methods are not in the java.awt.Button class.

The following ButtonDemo program instantiates three JButton components and adds them to a JFrame. The ColorChanger class (defined immediately after the ButtonDemo class) provides the event handling for the three buttons. Study the two classes and try to determine what the program does.

```java
import java.awt.*;
import javax.swing.*;
public class ButtonDemo extends JFrame
{
    private JButton red, blue, white;
    public ButtonDemo(String title)
    {
        super(title);
        this.setDefaultCloseOperation(WindowConstants.EXIT_ON_CLOSE);
        red = new JButton("Red");
        blue = new JButton("Blue");
        white = new JButton("White");
        //add the buttons to the frame
        JPanel south = new JPanel();
        south.add(red);
        south.add(blue);
        south.add(white);
        Container contentPane = this.getContentPane();
        contentPane.add(south, BorderLayout.SOUTH);
        //register the event listener
        ColorChanger changer = new ColorChanger(this);
        red.addActionListener(changer);
        blue.addActionListener(changer);
        white.addActionListener(changer);
    }
    public static void main(String [] args)
    {
        JFrame f = new ButtonDemo("ButtonDemo");
        f.setSize(300,300);
        f.setVisible(true);
    }
}
import java.awt.*;
import java.awt.event.*;
import javax.swing.JFrame;
public class ColorChanger implements ActionListener
{
    private Container container;

    public ColorChanger(JFrame c)
    {
        container = c.getContentPane();
    }

    public void actionPerformed(ActionEvent a)
    {
```

```
            String label = a.getActionCommand();
            if(label.equals("Red"))
            {
                container.setBackground(Color.RED);
            }
            else if(label.equals("Blue"))
            {
                container.setBackground(Color.BLUE);
            }
            else if(label.equals("White"))
            {
                container.setBackground(Color.WHITE);
            }
        }
    }
```

Within the actionPerformed() method of the ColorChanger class, the label on the button is obtained by invoking the getActionCommand() on the ActionEvent object:

```
String label = a.getActionCommand();
```

The action command of a button by default is the label. The if/else block sets the background of a Container to the color represented by the button's label. The Container in this example is the JFrame window ButtonDemo. Figure 13.3 shows the output of the ButtonDemo program.

Figure 13.3   Clicking a button changes the background color of the window.

Check Boxes

A check box is a component that is either selected or deselected. When selected, a check mark (or an x) appears in the box. A check box has a label associated with it that typically appears to the right of the check box. The java.awt.Checkbox class represents an AWT check box, and the javax.swing.JCheckBox class represents a Swing check box.

AWT Check Boxes

The java.awt.Checkbox class has five constructors, but two of them are for creating radio buttons (discussed in the next section). The three constructors for creating a check box are:

public Checkbox(String label). Creates a check box with the given label. The initial state of the check box is deselected.

public Checkbox(String label, boolean selected). Creates a check box with the given label that is initially selected if the boolean argument is true.

public Checkbox(). Creates a check box with no label that is initially deselected.

The methods in Checkbox related to event handling include:

public void addItemListener(ItemListener i). Generates an ItemEvent when they are clicked by the user.

public void setState(boolean state) and public boolean getState(). For changing or determining the state of the check box. The state is true when the check box is selected and false when it is deselected.

 The java.awt.event.ItemEvent class represents an item event. When a check box is clicked, an ItemEvent is instantiated and passed in to the itemStateChanged() method from the ItemListener interface (the only method in ItemListener).

The method in the ItemEvent class that is typically of interest to the event handler returns the type of state change. The possible return values are ItemEvent.SELECTED or ItemEvent.DESELECTED.

```
public int getStateChange().
```

For example, when a user clicks a check box so that a check mark appears in the box, the getStateChange() method returns ItemEvent.SELECTED. The getItem() method of ItemEvent is also useful. For an AWT check box, it returns the label of the Checkbox. For a Swing check box, it returns a reference to the JCheckBox that was clicked.

The following CheckboxDemo program creates a GUI with four check boxes. The item events are handled by the MixColors class, which can be found on the Web site. Study the CheckboxDemo program carefully, then try to determine how the GUI looks, and what the event handler is doing to the window.

```
import java.awt.*;
public class CheckboxDemo extends Frame
{
    private Checkbox red, yellow, blue;
    public CheckboxDemo(String title)
    {
        super(title);
        red = new Checkbox("Red");
        blue = new Checkbox("Blue");
        yellow = new Checkbox("Yellow");
        //add the checkboxes to the frame
        Panel north = new Panel();
        north.add(red);
        north.add(blue);
        north.add(yellow);
        this.add(north, BorderLayout.NORTH);
        //register the event listener
        MixColors listener = new MixColors(this);
        red.addItemListener(listener);
        blue.addItemListener(listener);
        yellow.addItemListener(listener);
    }
    public static void main(String [] args)
    {
        Frame f = new CheckboxDemo("CheckboxDemo");
        f.setSize(300,300);
        f.setVisible(true);
    }
}
```

The MixColors listener uses the getItem() method of ItemEvent to determine which check box generated the event. It then uses getStateChange() to determine if the check box was selected or deselected. The three booleans in MixColors represent the three check boxes in the GUI, and the color of the window is determined by which check boxes are selected.

For example, selecting red causes the window to be red. Selecting red and yellow causes the window to be orange. Selecting blue and yellow makes it green, blue and red makes it purple, and so on. A sample output is shown in Figure 13.4.

Figure 13.4   Selecting red and blue creates a purple window.

Swing Check Boxes

Now, let's look at Swing check boxes. The javax.swing.JCheckBox class has several constructors, each of which takes in a combination of the following three parameters:

String label.   For the label of the check box.

Icon icon.   For an icon associated with the check box.

boolean selected.   For denoting the initial state of the check box.

A JCheckBox is a source of both an ItemEvent and also a ChangeEvent, both of which are generated when the check box is clicked on by the user. The ItemEvent can be used to determine the current state of the check box, while the ChangeEvent only denotes that the state has changed.

 Creating and laying out Swing check boxes is essentially identical to doing so for AWT check boxes; however, some minor modifications are needed for our ItemListener. For an AWT check box, invoking getItem() on the ItemEvent returns the label of the check box. With Swing check boxes, invoking getItem() returns a reference to the check box.

The MixSwingColors class found on the Web site is similar to the MixColors listener, except that it works for JCheckBox components instead of Checkbox components. The MixSwingColors listener is used in the JCheckBoxDemo program.

The following JCheckboxDemo program looks quite similar to the earlier CheckboxDemo program. Compare the two and notice what changes were needed since Swing is being used instead of AWT. For example, a JFrame is used instead of a Frame, and the components are added to the content pane. Sample output from the JCheckBoxDemo program is shown in Figure 13.5. Compare the output to that in Figure 13.4.

```java
import javax.swing.*;
import java.awt.*;
public class JCheckBoxDemo extends JFrame
{
    private JCheckBox red, yellow, blue;

    public JCheckBoxDemo(String title)
    {
        super(title);
        this.setDefaultCloseOperation(WindowConstants.EXIT_ON_CLOSE);
        Container contentPane = this.getContentPane();
        red = new JCheckBox("Red");
        blue = new JCheckBox("Blue");
        yellow = new JCheckBox("Yellow");
        //add the checkboxes to the frame
        Panel north = new Panel();
        north.add(red);
        north.add(blue);
        north.add(yellow);
        contentPane.add(north, BorderLayout.NORTH);
        //register the event listener
        MixSwingColors listener = new MixSwingColors(contentPane);
        red.addItemListener(listener);
        blue.addItemListener(listener);
        yellow.addItemListener(listener);
    }
    public static void main(String [] args)
    {
        JFrame f = new JCheckBoxDemo("JCheckBoxDemo");
        f.setSize(300,300);
        f.setVisible(true);
    }
}
```

Figure 13.5   Swing check boxes have a different look and feel from AWT check boxes, but their functionality is the same.

Radio Buttons

A radio button is a component that is either selected or deselected, similar to a check box. The difference with radio buttons is that they are associated with a group, and only one radio button in the group can be selected. When a radio button in the group is selected, any other previously selected one in the group is deselected.

It takes two classes to create a group of radio buttons: one for the radio button component, and one for the group. Let's discuss how to create them for both AWT and Swing.

AWT Radio Buttons

When using AWT, the java.awt.Checkbox and java.awt.CheckboxGroup classes are used to create a group of radio buttons. You start by creating a CheckboxGroup object using its only constructor:

public CheckboxGroup().   Creates a new CheckboxGroup object.

The following methods in the CheckboxGroup class are used to set or determine which radio button in the group is selected:

public void setSelectedCheckbox(Checkbox c).   Sets the given check box as the currently selected radio button in the group. Passing in null deselects all check boxes.

public Checkbox getSelectedCheckbox(). Returns a reference to the currently selected radio button in the group, or null if none is selected.

After you have instantiated a CheckboxGroup object, you use it in the constructors of Checkbox to denote which radio buttons are in the group. You use one of the following two constructors of Checkbox:

public Checkbox(String label, boolean state, CheckboxGroup group). Creates a radio button with the given label and initial state, belonging to the given group.

public Checkbox(String label, CheckboxGroup group, boolean state). Same as the previous constructor, except the order of the parameters is different. (Don't ask me why Sun did this.)

The RadioButtonDemo program found on the Web site for this book demonstrates using AWT radio buttons. The event handling is done by the following ItemListener class named ChangeSize.

```java
import java.awt.*;
import java.awt.event.*;
public class ChangeSize implements ItemListener
{
    private Component component;

    public ChangeSize(Component c)
    {
        component = c;
    }
    public void itemStateChanged(ItemEvent e)
    {
        String size = (String) e.getItem();
        if(size.equals("small"))
        {
            component.setSize(75,20);
        }
        else if(size.equals("medium"))
        {
            component.setSize(100,50);
        }
        else if(size.equals("large"))
        {
            component.setSize(150, 75);
        }
    }
}
```

The getItem() method of the ItemEvent class returns the label for AWT radio buttons. The itemStateChange() method changes the size of the component passed in to the constructor, which in this example is a button. A sample output of the RadioButtonDemo program is shown in Figure 13.6.

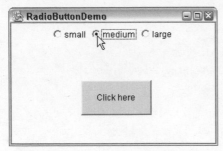

Figure 13.6 The button changes size as the radio buttons are selected.

Swing Radio Buttons

Swing radio buttons are created using the javax.swing.JRadioButton and javax.swing.ButtonGroup classes. The JRadioButton class has several constructors that take in a variation of the following parameters:

String label. For the label of the radio button.

Icon icon. For an icon associated with the radio button.

boolean selected. For denoting the initial state of the radio button.

The ButtonGroup class only has one constructor:

public ButtonGroup(). Creates a new ButtonGroup object.

To create a Swing group of radio buttons, you instantiate a ButtonGroup object, instantiate the JRadioButton objects, and pass each JRadioButton in to the following ButtonGroup method:

public void add(AbstractButton button). Adds the given button to the ButtonGroup object.

 The AbstractButton class in the javax.swing package is the common parent class for JButton, JCheckBox, and JRadioButton. This means that in Swing you can create a ButtonGroup of buttons, check boxes, and radio buttons, although radio buttons are the most common use of the ButtonGroup class.

The following JRadioButtonDemo program is similar to the RadioButton-Demo program, except that it uses Swing components. The event handling needed some slight modifications also, which are shown in the SwingChange-Size class that is available on the Web site.

```
import javax.swing.*;
import java.awt.*;
public class JRadioButtonDemo extends JFrame
{
    private JRadioButton small, medium, large;
    private JButton button;
    public JRadioButtonDemo(String title)
    {
        super(title);
        this.setDefaultCloseOperation(WindowConstants.EXIT_ON_CLOSE);
        Container contentPane = this.getContentPane();
        ButtonGroup group = new ButtonGroup();
        small = new JRadioButton("small");
        medium = new JRadioButton("medium");
        large = new JRadioButton("large");
        //add the radio buttons to the same group
        group.add(small);
        group.add(medium);
        group.add(large);
        button = new JButton("Click here.");
        button.setBounds(100,50,100, 50);
        JPanel center = new JPanel();
        center.setLayout(null);
        center.add(button);
        contentPane.add(center, BorderLayout.CENTER);
        //add the radio buttons to the frame
        JPanel north = new JPanel();
        north.add(small);
        north.add(medium);
        north.add(large);
        contentPane.add(north, BorderLayout.NORTH);
        //register the event listener
        SwingChangeSize listener = new SwingChangeSize(button);
        small.addItemListener(listener);
        medium.addItemListener(listener);
        large.addItemListener(listener);
    }
    public static void main(String [] args)
    {
        JFrame f = new JRadioButtonDemo("JRadioButtonDemo");
        f.setSize(300,200);
        f.setVisible(true);
    }
}
```

In the SwingChangeSize class, the getItem() method of the ItemEvent object returns a reference to the radio button that was clicked. The getText() method is used to obtain the label of the radio button, and the component is resized accordingly, as demonstrated in Figure 13.7.

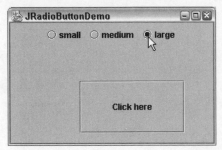

Figure 13.7 A sample output of the JRadioButtonDemo program.

Labels

A label is a string or icon that is displayed within a container. Labels generate the events that all components generate, like focus and mouse events, but they do not generate any other events such as action or item events. In most cases, you will not be interested in the events that a label generates because the purpose of the label is to simply display the text or icon.

The java.awt.Label class represents an AWT label and has three constructors:

public Label().   Constructs an empty label.

public Label(String text).   Constructs a label with the given text.

public Label(String text, int alignment).   Creates a label with the specified alignment; possible alignment values are Label.RIGHT, Label.LEFT, and Label.CENTER.

 An AWT label can only represent text, while a Swing label can represent either text or an icon.

For example, the following statement creates a Label that will be centered in the region that it is laid out in by the layout manager:

```
Label hi = new Label("Hello", Label.CENTER);
```

The ListDemo program in the upcoming *Lists* section demonstrates using an AWT label.

The javax.swing.JLabel class represents a Swing label and has six constructors that take in a variation of the following parameters:

String text.   Represents the text of the label.

Icon icon.   Represents the icon of the label. A JLabel can have both text and an icon.

int horizontalAlignment.   Represents where the text and/or icon appear within the bounds of the label when it is laid out in the container. The possible values are LEFT, RIGHT, CENTER, LEADING, and TRAILING, which are static variables in the javax.swing.SwingConstants interface.

For example, the following statement creates a JLabel that will be centered:

```
JLabel bye = new JLabel("Goodbye", SwingConstants.CENTER);
```

The JTextComponentDemo program in the next section demonstrates using the JLabel class.

Text Components

There are two types of GUI text components: text fields and text areas. A text field is a single line of text, while a text area can be any number of lines of text and often has vertical and horizontal scroll bars for navigating through the text area. Let's look at both the AWT and Swing versions of the text components.

AWT Text Components

The java.awt.TextField class represents a text field, and the java.awt.TextArea class represents a text area. They share a common parent class, java.awt.Text-Component, which contains many useful methods, including:

public void addTextListener(TextListener t).   Both the TextField and TextArea components generate a TextEvent, which occurs when the text changes.

public String getText().   This returns the current text in the text component.

public void setText(String s).   This sets the text of the text component.

public void setEditable(boolean b).   When the argument is false, the user cannot edit the text in the text component. Text components are editable by default.

public String getSelectedText().   This returns the text that is currently selected in the text component.

public void setCaretPosition(int position).   This sets the position of the caret in the text component.

Be sure to browse the documentation and check the other methods of the class if you need to work with a TextComponent.

The TextField class contains four constructors that take in a variation of the following two parameters:

String text.   Represents the initial text that appears in the TextField.

int columns.   The initial size of the TextField, based on the platform-dependent average width of the current character font.

In addition to generating a TextEvent when the text changes, a TextField also generates an ActionEvent when the user hits the Enter key while typing in the text field. Therefore, the TextField class contains the addActionListener() method for registering an ActionListener. Handling the action event is commonly done because users often expect some behavior to happen when they press Enter while in a text field. The TextComponentDemo program that I will discuss shortly demonstrates doing this.

The TextArea class has five constructors that take in a variation of the following parameters:

String text.   Represents the initial text displayed in the text area.

int rows.   The number of rows of text to display.

int columns.   The number of columns to display, based on the platform-dependent average width of the current character font.

int scrollbars.   Denotes the scrollbar property of the text area. The possible values are static fields in the TextArea class: SCROLLBARS_NONE, SCROLLBARS_VERTICAL_ONLY, SCROLLBARS_HORIZONTAL_ONLY, and SCROLLBARS_BOTH.

 Both the TextField and TextArea constructors allow you to assign an initial number of columns and rows. The actual size of these values depends on the character font being displayed in the text component.

Keep in mind that the values you pass in to these constructors for rows and columns become the preferred size of the text component. As with all components in both Swing and AWT, most layout managers override a component's preferred size. The TextComponentDemo program in this chapter creates a TextField and TextArea whose rows and columns are zero because both are laid out with a BorderLayout manager that overrides any preferred size anyway.

A TextArea does not generate an ActionEvent as a TextField does. In most situations, you will not listen to the events generated from a text area. Instead, another component such as a button or menu item often signals when a user is done entering text in a text area.

The following code from the TextComponentDemo, available on the Web site for this book, demonstrates using the TextField and TextArea components. Study the program, determining how the GUI looks and what the program does.

```
textField = new TextField();
textArea = new TextArea("", 0, 0,
                            TextArea.SCROLLBARS_VERTICAL_ONLY);
textArea.setEditable(false);
//setup the event handling
CreateList listener = new CreateList(textField, textArea);
textField.addActionListener(listener);
```

The event handling is done using the following CreateList class, and I want you to pay special attention to its actionPerformed() method.

```
import java.awt.*;
import java.awt.event.*;
public class CreateList implements ActionListener
{
    private int counter;
    private TextField source;
    private TextArea destination;
    public CreateList(TextField s, TextArea d)
    {
        source = s;
        destination = d;
    }
    public void actionPerformed(ActionEvent e)
    {
        Object component = e.getSource();
        String action = e.getActionCommand();
        if(component instanceof TextField || action.equals("Enter"))
        {
            String text = source.getText();
            counter++;
            destination.append(counter + ". " + text + "\n");
            source.setText("");
        }
        else if(action.equals("Clear"))
        {
            destination.setText("");
            counter = 0;
        }
    }
}
```

The component with focus is the component that receives keyboard input. When I first wrote the TextComponentDemo program, the text area was given focus by default; however, I wanted the text field to have the initial focus because that is where the user is going to type right away.

To accomplish this, I used the requestFocus() method of the Component class. I needed to invoke this method after the Frame was displayed, so I added a getTextField() method to the TextComponentDemo class that allows me to invoke requestFocus() on the TextField object within main() after invoking setVisible() on the Frame. Now, when the program is executed, the cursor is blinking in the text field and is ready for the user to begin typing!

The CreateList class listens to events from both buttons and the text field. There are two ways that the following statement is true:

```
if(component instanceof TextField || action.equals("Enter"))
```

- When the source of the event is a TextField object, which will occur when the user types in the TextField and hits the Enter key.
- When the action command of the component is Enter, which will occur when the user clicks the Enter button.

If the expression is true, the text from the TextField is appended to the TextArea, and the TextField is cleared using the statement:

```
source.setText("");
```

Figure 13.8 shows a sample output of the TextComponentDemo program, which displays a numbered list in the TextArea created from the text entered in the TextField.

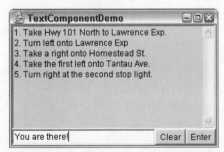

Figure 13.8   Output of the TextComponentDemo program.

Swing Text Components

The JTextField, JTextArea, and JPasswordField represent Swing text components. The JTextField and JTextArea classes are child classes of JTextComponent, while JPasswordField is a child class of JTextField.

The methods of JTextComponent are similar to those in TextComponent, with a notable exception: JTextComponent objects do not generate a TextEvent, so the addTextListener() is not in JTextComponent. Notice, however, some interesting methods in JTextComponent, including:

public void addCaretListener(CaretListener c). This is for listening to a CaretEvent, which occurs when changes are made to the caret.

public void setKeymap(Keymap map). A Keymap binds keystrokes to actions. A keymap takes the place of a TextListener in AWT.

public void setCaretColor(Color c). This changes the color of the caret.

public void setSelectionColor(Color c). This sets the color used when text is selected.

public void write(Writer w). This writes the text to the specified output writer.

The constructors of JTextField are identical to those of TextField, with the addition of:

public JTextField(Document doc). This creates a JTextField with the given Document. A Document object contains the content of the text field and allows the content to be separated from its view in the text component.

Similarly, the JTextArea constructors look similar to those of TextArea, with the inclusion of a constructor that takes in a Document. The JTextArea class, however, does not contain a constructor that involves the policies of the scroll bars. This is because the JTextArea does not handle its own scroll bars as TextArea does. See the sidebar *Working with Scroll Panes* to see how to add scroll bars to a JTextArea.

♦ Working with Scroll Panes

When using text areas with AWT, scroll bars are managed by the TextArea object. In Swing, scroll bars in a JTextArea are managed by a separate object. You can use the JScrollPane class to add scroll bars to a JTextArea using the constructor:

```
public JScrollPane(Component view, int vsbPolicy, int hsbPolicy)
```

The Component parameter represents the component that needs scroll bars. The vsbPolicy and hsbPolicy parameters represent the scroll bar policies for the JScrollPane. The possible values are found in the javax.swing.ScrollPaneConstants interface. Examples include HORIZONTAL_SCROLLBAR_ALWAYS and VERTICAL_SCROLLBAR_AS_NEEDED.

For example, the following ScrollPaneDemo program demonstrates adding scroll bars to a JTextArea. Study the program and try to determine how the GUI looks.

```
import javax.swing.*;
import java.awt.*;
public class ScrollPaneDemo extends JFrame
{
     JTextArea textArea;

     public ScrollPaneDemo(String title)
     {
          super(title);
this.setDefaultCloseOperation(WindowConstants.EXIT_ON_CLOSE);
          Container contentPane = this.getContentPane();
          textArea = new JTextArea();
          JScrollPane pane = new JScrollPane(textArea,

ScrollPaneConstants.VERTICAL_SCROLLBAR_ALWAYS,

ScrollPaneConstants.HORIZONTAL_SCROLLBAR_AS_NEEDED);
          contentPane.add(pane, BorderLayout.CENTER);
     }
     public static void main(String [] args)
     {
          JFrame f = new ScrollPaneDemo("ScrollPaneDemo");
          f.setSize(300,200);
          f.setVisible(true);
     }
}
```

Figure 13.9 shows what happens when enough text is entered to display the horizontal scroll bar, which does not appear initially.

continued

◆ **Working with Scroll Panes** *(continued)*

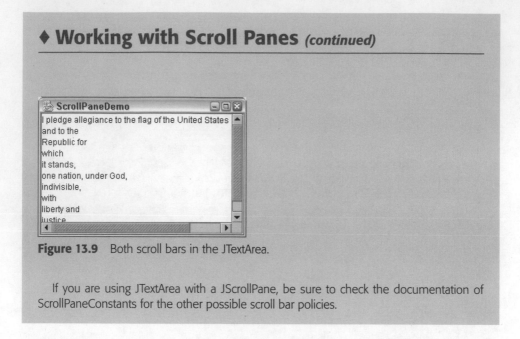

Figure 13.9　Both scroll bars in the JTextArea.

If you are using JTextArea with a JScrollPane, be sure to check the documentation of ScrollPaneConstants for the other possible scroll bar policies.

The JPasswordField class is used for the common occurrence of a user needing to enter a password. A JPasswordField is similar to a JTextField except the characters typed in by the user are not echoed back to the user. Instead, an alternate character such as an asterisk is displayed for each character typed in the field. You can set the echo character using the method:

```
public void setEchoChar(char c)
```

The JTextComponentDemo program available on the Web site demonstrates using the Swing text components JTextField, JPasswordField, and JLabel. Study the program and try to determine how the GUI will look. The output is shown in Figure 13.10. Notice that this program does not contain any event handling. It demonstrates, however, the power of using panels and layout managers to obtain the specific GUI you want.

Figure 13.10　GUI created from the JTextComponentDemo program.

Lists

A list component represents a list of items from which a user can select one or more of the items. The java.awt.List class represents an AWT list, which can only contain text entries. The javax.swing.JList class represents a Swing list, which can contain text, images, and any other Object type. Let's look at both classes.

AWT Lists

The java.awt.List class has three constructors:

public List().   Creates a new, empty single-selection list.

public List(int rows).   Creates an empty single-selection list with the specified numbered of rows visible.

public List(int rows, boolean multipleMode).   If the boolean value is true, multiple items can be selected.

Some of the methods in the List class include:

public void add(String item).   Adds the specified item to the end of the list.

public void add(String item, int index).   Adds the item to the list at the specified position, where 0 is the first position in the list.

public void addActionListener(ActionListener a).   Adds the ActionListener to the list. An ActionEvent occurs when the use double-clicks on an item in the list.

public void addItemListener(ItemListener i).   Adds the ItemListener to the list. An ItemEvent occurs when the user clicks on an item in the list.

public void setMultipleMode(boolean multiple).   Passes in true to allow multiple selection in the list.

public String getSelectedItem().   Returns the currently selected item of the list.

public String [] getSelectedItems().   Returns the currently selected items. Use this method when the list allows multiple selection.

public void remove(int position).   Removes the item at the specified position.

public void remove(String item).   Removes the first occurrence of the given item.

public void select(int index).   Selects the specified item in the list.

There are other methods, so check the documentation when working with List components. The following code from the ListDemo program, available on the Web site for this book, demonstrates filling a List with the days of the week.

```
items = new List();
items.add("Sunday");
items.add("Monday");
items.add("Tuesday");
items.add("Wednesday");
items.add("Thursday");
items.add("Friday");
items.add("Saturday");
```

The ListDemo program displays the selected list item as a Label in the window. You need to double-click the item in the list so that an ActionEvent occurs, and the following ShowSelection listener class handles this event. Study the ListDemo program and the ShowSelection class, and try to determine how the output of the program looks. The output is shown in Figure 13.11.

```java
import java.awt.event.*;
public class ShowSelection implements ActionListener
{
    private Label display;

    public ShowSelection(Label d)
    {
        display = d;
    }
    public void actionPerformed(ActionEvent a)
    {
        Object source = a.getSource();
        if(!(source instanceof List))
        {
            return;
        }
        List list = (List) source;
        String selected = list.getSelectedItem();
        display.setText(selected);
    }
}
```

Figure 13.11 Double-clicking an item in the list displays it in the label.

 An AWT list manages its own scroll bars; however, when using the Swing list component JList, you need to use the JScrollPane class to create scroll bars. The process is similar to using JScrollPane for the JTextArea component. See the earlier sidebar *Working with Scroll Panes* for an example of how to use the JScrollPane class.

Swing Lists

The javax.swing.JList class represents a Swing list. The JList class has four constructors:

public JList(). Creates a new, empty single-selection list.

public List(Object [] listData). Creates a list with the given array of objects as its initial data.

public JList(Vector listData). Creates a list with the elements of the Vector as its initial data.

public JList(ListModel listData). Creates a list with the given ListModel. A ListModel object uses a Vector to maintain the elements of the list.

I want to make a couple of comparisons between List and JList:

- When using a List, items are added to the list one at a time using the add() methods. With a JList, items are added from a data structure such as a Vector or an array using either a constructor or one of the setListData() methods. (There are no add() methods in JList.)

- A List generates an ItemEvent, while a JList generates a ListSelection-Event when the selected item or items change.

- A List generates an ActionEvent when an item is double-clicked, while a JList does not generate any action events.

Some of the methods in JList include:

public void addListSelectionListener(ListSelectionListener s).   Generates a ListSelectionEvent each time the selected list of items changes.

public void setListData(Object [] listData).   Changes the items in the list to the elements in the array.

public void setListData(Vector listData).   Changes the items in the list to the elements in the Vector.

public Object getSelectedValue().   Returns the currently selected item of the list.

public Object [] getSelectedValues().   Returns the currently selected items. Use this method when the list allows multiple selection.

public void setSelectionMode(int mode).   Sets the selection mode of this list. The possible values are SINGLE_SELECTION, SINGLE_INTERVAL_SELECTION, MULTIPLE_INTERVAL_SELECTION, fields in the ListSelectionModel interface.

I want to demonstrate how to use JList because lists are a common component. Let's take a look at combo boxes first, then I will show you an example (the upcoming SelectionDialog program) that demonstrates using both lists and combo boxes.

Combo Boxes

A combo box is a drop-down list that only displays the currently selected item. The java.awt.Choice class represents an AWT combo box, and the javax.swing.JComboBox class represents a Swing combo box. Let's take a look at both classes.

AWT Choice

The Choice class is similar to the List class. (A combo box is basically a single-selection list that only displays one item.) The Choice class has one constructor:

public Choice().   Creates a new, empty combo box.

Items are added to a Choice using the add() method, which takes in a String. The getSelectedItem() method returns the currently selected item. When a selection is made, the Choice generates an ItemEvent containing the currently selected item.

The ChoiceDemo program (see the Web site for this book for a complete listing) is similar to the ListDemo program, except that the items appear in a Choice, created using the following code.

```
items = new Choice();
items.add("");
items.add("Sunday");
items.add("Monday");
items.add("Tuesday");
items.add("Wednesday");
items.add("Thursday");
items.add("Friday");
items.add("Saturday");
```

The following event handler ShowChoice is an ItemListener that displays the currently selected item in a Label. Study the program and try to determine how it works. Figure 13.12 shows the output.

```java
import java.awt.*;
import java.awt.event.*;
public class ShowChoice implements ItemListener
{
    private Label display;

    public ShowChoice(Label d)
    {
        display = d;
    }
    public void itemStateChanged(ItemEvent a)
    {
        Object source = a.getSource();
        if(!(source instanceof Choice))
        {
            return;
        }
        Choice list = (Choice) source;
        String selected = list.getSelectedItem();
        display.setText(selected);
    }
}
```

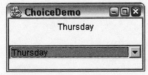

Figure 13.12   Output of the ChoiceDemo program.

I want to make a comment about the ItemEvent generated from a combo box, and how it applies to both Choice and JComboBox components. When an item is selected, it has been my experience that two item events occur. (The documentation states that one or two item events may occur, but it is not clear when you get one and when you get two.) You often need to make sure you aren't handling the same event twice when working with a Choice. When using a JComboBox, you can take advantage of the ActionEvent that occurs when a user selects an item in the combo box, and not handle the ItemEvent. (See the SelectionDialog program in this chapter for an example of handling the ActionEvent of a JComboBox.)

Swing Combo Boxes

A Swing combo box is different from an AWT one in that a JComboBox can be made editable, allowing the user to add items to the combo box. Also, a JComboBox generates both an ItemEvent and an ActionEvent when the user makes a selection. A JComboBox also generates a PopupMenuEvent when the user clicks the arrow to display the contents of the combo box.

The JComboBox class has four constructors:

public JComboBox().   Creates a new, empty combo box.

public JComboBox (Object [] items).   Creates a combo box with the given array of objects as its initial data.

public JComboBox (Vector items).   Creates a combo box with the elements of the Vector as its initial data.

public JComboBox (ComboBoxModel items).   Creates a combo box with the given ComboBoxModel. A ComboBoxModel object uses a Vector to maintain the elements of the combo box.

The following code from the SelectionDialog program available on the Web site for this book demonstrates using JComboBox, as well as a JList. Study the program and try to determine how the GUI looks.

```
String [] comboBoxItems = {"Right", "Left"};
direction = new JComboBox(comboBoxItems);
String [] listItems = {"Sunday", "Monday", "Tuesday", "Wednesday",
"Thursday", "Friday", "Saturday"};
left = new JList(listItems);
right = new JList();
left.setSelectionMode(ListSelectionModel.SINGLE_SELECTION);
right.setSelectionMode(ListSelectionModel.SINGLE_SELECTION);
```

The following SelectionHandler class provides the event handling for the two JList components. Study this class carefully and try to determine what is happening with this GUI. The GUI is shown in Figure 13.13.

```java
import javax.swing.*;
import java.awt.event.*;
import javax.swing.event.*;
import java.util.Vector;
public class SelectionHandler implements ActionListener,
ListSelectionListener
{
    private JLabel direction;
    private JList source, destination;

    public SelectionHandler(JLabel d, JList left, JList right)
    {
        direction = d;
        source = left;
        destination = right;
    }
    public void actionPerformed(ActionEvent a)
    {
        JComboBox cb = (JComboBox) a.getSource();
        String selected = (String) cb.getSelectedItem();
        String current = direction.getText();
        if(!selected.equals(current))
        {
            direction.setText(selected);
            JList temp = source;
            source = destination;
            destination = temp;
            source.clearSelection();
            destination.clearSelection();
        }
        //Else do nothing
    }
    public void valueChanged(ListSelectionEvent e)
    {
        JList list = (JList) e.getSource();
        String item = (String) source.getSelectedValue();
        System.out.println(item);
        if(item != null && !item.equals(""))
        {
            removeFromSource(item);
            addToDestination(item);
        }
    }
    private void removeFromSource(String item)
    {
        ListModel model = source.getModel();
```

```
                    Vector listData = new Vector();
                    for(int i = 0; i < model.getSize(); i++)
                    {
                         listData.addElement(model.getElementAt(i));
                    }
                    listData.removeElement(item);
                    source.setListData(listData);
           }
           private void addToDestination(String item)
           {
                    ListModel model = destination.getModel();
                    Vector listData = new Vector();
                    for(int i = 0; i < model.getSize(); i++)
                    {
                         listData.addElement(model.getElementAt(i));
                    }
                    listData.addElement(item);
                    destination.setListData(listData);
           }
      }
```

 In the SelectionHandler class, items are added to and removed from the two JList components. There are no add() or remove() methods in the JList class. To change the items in each JList, I used the getModel() method to retrieve the elements as a ListModel object. Then, I iterated through the ListModel, adding each element to a Vector. (See the removeFromSource() and addToDestination() methods.) I made changes to the Vector and then set the Vector as the new elements in the JList. It seems kind of tedious, but I haven't seen a better way to do it.

Figure 13.13   Output of the SelectionDialog program.

Progress Bars

A progress bar is a component that visually displays a value within an interval, and typically represents the progress of a certain task being performed. If you have ever downloaded a file off the Internet, you have seen a progress bar in action. The AWT does not have a class for progress bars, so if you want to use a progress bar in AWT you are going to have write one from scratch.

Swing contains the javax.swing.JProgressBar class to represent a progress bar, and has five constructors that take in a variation of the following parameters:

int min.   The lower bound of the progress bar, which is 0 by default.

int max.   The upper bound of the progress bar, which is 100 by default.

int orient.   Can be one of two values: JProgressBar.VERTICAL or JProgressBar.HORIZONTAL, and determines which way the progress bar appears in its container. The default orientation is a horizontal progress fire.

BoundedRangeModel model.   Represents a data model that consists of a range with a minimum, maximum, extent, and current value.

A JProgressBar generates a ChangeEvent when the current value changes, and a listener is added using the addChangeListener() method. The current value is accessed using the setValue() and getValue() methods, and there are similar methods for accessing the orientation and minimum and maximum values.

The MenuDemo program in the next section demonstrates using the JProgressBar class to create and manage a progress bar.

Menus

A menu is a common feature of Frame and JFrame windows. There are three components to a menu:

- A menu bar, which is attached to the window. The menu bar is typically shown at the top of a window.

- A menu, which is attached to the menu bar or another menu. The menus have a label, and clicking on the label causes the menu to drop down and display its menu items.

- A menu item, which is attached to a menu. Selecting a menu item generates an ActionEvent.

The AWT classes MenuBar, Menu, and MenuItem are used to create a menu for a Frame. The Swing classes JMenuBar, JMenu, and JMenuItem are used to create a menu for a JFrame. The process is similar for both AWT and Swing, so I will only discuss how it works for Swing.

To add a menu to a JFrame, you perform the following steps:

1. Instatiate a new JMenuBar object, and attach it to the JFrame using the setJMenuBar() method of the JFrame class.

2. Instantiate one or more JMenu objects, and add them to the JMenuBar using the add(JMenu menu) method of the JMenuBar class.

3. Instantiate one or more JMenuItem objects, and add them to a JMenu object using the add(JMenuItem) method of the JMenu class.

4. Add an ActionListener to each menu item to handle the ActionEvent that is generated when a user selects the menu item.

To demonstrate menus, the following MenuDemo program adds a menu to a JFrame. (The MenuColorChanger class that handles the events is available on the Web site for this book.) Study the createMenu() method and try to determine how the menu will look. (I sneaked in a cascading menu and a check box menu item just to demonstrate their use, as shown in the output in Figure 13.14.) Notice that the event handling for the buttons and menu items is identical, which is possible because they both generate an ActionEvent with the same action command. For example, clicking the Red button and selecting Red from the menu both generate an ActionEvent with a Red action command.

```java
import java.awt.*;
import javax.swing.*;

public class MenuDemo extends JFrame
{
    private JButton red, blue, white;
    private JProgressBar progress;

    public MenuDemo(String title)
    {
        super(title);
        Container contentPane = this.getContentPane();
        this.setDefaultCloseOperation(WindowConstants.EXIT_ON_CLOSE);

        red = new JButton("Red");
        blue = new JButton("Blue");
        white = new JButton("White");
```

```
            //Add the buttons to the frame.
            JPanel south = new JPanel();
            south.add(red);
            south.add(blue);
            south.add(white);
            contentPane.add(south, BorderLayout.SOUTH);

            //Add the progress bar.
            progress = new JProgressBar(0,3);
            contentPane.add(progress, BorderLayout.NORTH);


            //Register the event listener.
            MenuColorChanger changer = new MenuColorChanger(contentPane,
progress);
            red.addActionListener(changer);
            blue.addActionListener(changer);
            white.addActionListener(changer);

            createMenu(changer);
        }


    public void createMenu(MenuColorChanger changer)
        {
            //Create a menu bar and attach it to this JFrame.
            JMenuBar menuBar = new JMenuBar();
            this.setJMenuBar(menuBar);

            //Create three menus, and add them to the menu bar.
            JMenu fileMenu = new JMenu("File");
            JMenu colorMenu = new JMenu("Color");
            JMenu helpMenu = new JMenu("Help");

            menuBar.add(fileMenu);
            menuBar.add(colorMenu);
            menuBar.add(helpMenu);

            //Add three menu items to the "Color" menu.
            JMenuItem redMenuItem = new JMenuItem("Red");
            JMenuItem blueMenuItem = new JMenuItem("Blue");
            JMenuItem whiteMenuItem = new JMenuItem("White");
            colorMenu.add(redMenuItem);
            colorMenu.add(blueMenuItem);
            colorMenu.add(whiteMenuItem);
            redMenuItem.addActionListener(changer);
```

```
        blueMenuItem.addActionListener(changer);
        whiteMenuItem.addActionListener(changer);

        //Add one menu item to the "File" menu.
        JMenuItem exit = new JMenuItem("Exit");
        fileMenu.add(exit);
        exit.addActionListener(changer);

        //Add one menu item and one menu to the "Help" menu.
        JMenuItem about = new JMenuItem("About MenuDemo...");
        helpMenu.add(about);
        JMenu cascade = new JMenu("Tip of the day");
        helpMenu.add(cascade);
        JCheckBoxMenuItem show = new JCheckBoxMenuItem("Show");
        cascade.add(show);
    }

    public static void main(String [] args)
    {
        MenuDemo f = new MenuDemo("MenuDemo");
        f.setSize(300,300);
        f.setVisible(true);
    }

}
```

Figure 13.14 Output of the MenuDemo program.

Lab 13.1: Event Handling

The purpose of this lab is to become familiar with handling the events of GUI components. You are going to add the necessary event handlers so that your Calculator from Lab 12.1 works.

1. Write a class named CalculatorListener that implements ActionListener. This class is going to handle the ActionEvent from all 16 JButtons in your calculator.

2. Add a field of type JTextField and a constructor that has a JTextField parameter. Assign the field to the parameter within this constructor.

3. Your actionPerformed() method is going to perform the arithmetic of the calculator. Use if/else statements to determine which button was clicked, and include all the necessary logic for your CalculatorListener class so that the calculator functions properly.

You should see a fully functional calculator. Be sure to perform some quality assurance on your calculator, testing to make sure everything is working properly.

Lab 13.2: Handling the Instant Message Events

In this lab, you will start working on the event handling for the instant message program started in Chapter 12. This lab is a continuation of Lab 12.3, and you will add some event handling to your InstantMessageFrame.

1. Write a class named IMHandler that implements ActionListener. This class will handle the events from the Send button and text field of your InstantMessageFrame.

2. Add a field of type JTextField and JList, and initialize each field using a constructor.

3. The actionPerformed() method will be invoked when the user either clicks the Send button or presses the Enter key in the text field. In either case, get the text from the text field and print it out at the command prompt using System.out.println() for each friend in the JList. For example, if the text is "Hello" and there are four friends in the list, the output should say "Hello" four times, with each friend's name being displayed next to "Hello."

4. Save and compile your IMHandler class.

5. Within your InstantMessageFrame constructor, instantiate a new IMHandler, passing in the JList and JTextField of the InstantMessageFrame.

6. Register your IMHandler object with the text field and the Send button.

7. Write a class named DisplayMessageDialog that extends the Mouse-Adapter class. This class does not need any fields or constructors.

8. Add the mouseClicked() method to DisplayMessageDialog. Use the getClickCount() method of MouseEvent to determine if the user double-clicked the mouse. If yes, print out the item double-clicked, which will be the name of the person that the instant message is intended for.

9. Within your InstantMessageFrame constructor, instantiate a new DisplayMessageDialog object, and register it as a listener to the JList.

10. Add a collection of Strings to the JList. These will represent the screen names of your friends who are currently online and awaiting an instant message.

11. Save, compile, and run your InstantMessageFrame program.

When you type something in the text field and click the Send button, the message should appear at the command prompt of the window along with the names of each friend. If you click on a friend in the list, the name of the friend should be displayed at the command prompt.

Lab 13.3: The InstantMessageDialog Events

This lab is a continuation of Lab 12.4. You will add some event handling to your InstantMessageDialog.

1. Write a class named SendMessage that implements ActionListener. This class will handle the events from the Send and Cancel buttons of your InstantMessageDialog.

2. Add a field of type JTextArea which will contain the message to send, a String to represent the recipient of the message, and JDialog to represent dialog window. Add a constructor that initializes these three fields.

3. Within the actionPerformed() method, determine which button was clicked. If the Send button is clicked, get the text from the text area and display it using a call to System.out.println(), printing out the recipient and the message. Then hide the dialog window referred to by your JDialog field.

4. If the Cancel button is clicked, hide the dialog window.

5. Within the constructor of InstantMessageDialog, instantiate a new SendMessage object, passing in the JTextArea of InstantMessageDialog, the recipient's name, and the this reference as the JDialog argument.

6. Register your SendMessage object as an ActionListener of the Send and Cancel buttons.

7. Save, compile, and run the InstantMessageDemo program.

When you click the Send button, the message should appear at the command prompt of the window, along with the recipient's name, and the dialog window should disappear. Clicking the Cancel button should simply hide the dialog window.

 ## Lab 13.4 Displaying the InstantMessageDialog

In this lab, you will tie together the two classes InstantMessageFrame and InstantMessageDialog.

1. Modify your DisplayMessageDialog event handler so that when the user selects a friend from the list in InstantMessageFrame, the InstantMessageDialog is displayed. Within the mouseClicked() method, you will need to instantiate an InstantMessageDialog and display it using the show() method.

2. Save and compile your DisplayMessageDialog class.

3. Run the InstantMessageFrame program.

The appearance of your InstantMessageFrame has not changed; however, clicking on a friend in the list should cause the InstantMessageDialog window to appear. Entering a message and clicking the Send button should display the message at the command prompt and also hide the dialog window. Clicking the Cancel button should hide the dialog window.

Summary

- Java GUI programming uses the Delegation Model for handling the events of components and containers. The source of an event invokes a method on a registered listener of the event, with the two objects communicating via a common interface.

- An event consists of an event class that extends java.util.EventObject and an interface that extends the java.util.EventListener interface.

- You can determine which events a component generates by viewing the add<event_name>Listener() methods of the component's class.

- This chapter discussed the commonly used Swing and AWT components, focusing on how to construct them and what types of events they generate.

Review Questions

1. What three entities are involved in the event delegation model?

2. When a Button is clicked, which event occurs:

   a. ItemEvent

   b. ActionEvent

   c. MouseClickedEvent

   d. Both a and b

   e. Both b and c

3. How many methods are in the ActionListener interface? Name them.

4. True or False: All components generate an ActionEvent.

5. True or False: All components generate a MouseEvent.

6. True or False: A component can have either 0 or 1 listener for an event.

7. If a component generates a KeyEvent, name the interface that a listener must implement. What method in the component's class is invoked to register this listener?

8. When the user clicks the X on a Frame or JFrame, a WindowEvent is generated. Which method in WindowListener is invoked?

   a. public void windowClosed(WindowEvent w)

   b. public void windowIconified(WindowEvent w)

   c. public void windowClosing(WindowEvent w)

   d. First a, then c

   e. none of the above

9. The MouseListener has five methods in it. Does it have a corresponding event adapter class? If yes, what is the name of the adapter class?

10. Clicking a java.awt.Checkbox generates what type of event? What about clicking a javax.swing.JCheckBox?

11. What two classes are used to create a group of AWT radio buttons?

12. What two classes are used to create a group of Swing radio buttons?

13. Pressing the Enter key while typing in a TextArea generates which event?

    a. ActionEvent

    b. TextEvent

    c. KeyEvent

    d. All of the above

    e. Both a and b

    f. Both b and c

    g. None of the above

14. True or False: The JScrollPane class can be used to add scroll bars to any Swing component.

15. What does it mean for a component to have focus?

16. Clicking once on an item in a List generates what event? What about clicking once on an item in a JList?

17. Double-clicking on an item in a List generates what event? What about double-clicking on an item in a JList?

18. Selecting an item in a Choice generates what event?

    a. ActionEvent

    b. TextEvent

    c. KeyEvent

    d. ItemEvent

    e. Both a and d

19. Selecting an item in a JComboBox generates which event?

    a. ActionEvent

    b. TextEvent

    c. KeyEvent

    d. ItemEvent

    e. Both a and d

20. List the three components that compose a menu of a top-level window (such as Frame or JFrame).

21. True or False: A menu can be added to a menu bar.

22. True or False: A menu can be added to another menu.

Answers to Review Questions

1. The source of the event, the listener of the event, and interface that provides the mechanism for the source and listener to communicate.

2. Clicking a button generates an ActionEvent, so the answer is b. There is no such event as MouseClickedEvent, although clicking a button does generate a MouseEvent.

3. One method named public void actionPerformed(ActionEvent a).

4. False. There are many components that do not generate an ActionEvent.

5. True. All components are the source of mouse events, as can be determined by the addMouseListener() method of the java.awt.Component class.

6. False. A component can have any number of listeners (zero or more).

7. To listen to a KeyEvent, you need to write a class that implements the KeyListener interface. Register your listener by invoking the addKeyListener() method on the component you want to listen to.

8. The windowClosing() method is invoked when a user attempts to close a window by clicking the X, so the answer is c.

9. Yes, the MouseListener interface has a corresponding event adapter class named MouseAdapter.

10. Clicking a Checkbox generates an ItemEvent. Clicking a JCheckBox generates an ItemEvent and also a ChangeEvent.

11. The Checkbox and CheckboxGroup classes.

12. The JCheckBox and ButtonGroup classes.

13. Typing anything in a text area generates both a key event and a text event. Note that a text area does not generate action events, so the answer is f.

14. True. The constructor of JScrollPane has a parameter of type java.awt.Component, so it can actually be used as a scroll pane for AWT components as well.

15. The component that has focus is the component that receives the key events generated from the user's typing on the keyboard.

16. Clicking once on a List item generates an ItemEvent. Doing the same on a JList item generates a ListSelectionEvent. Note that JList components never generate an ItemEvent.

17. Double-clicking on a List item generates an ActionEvent. Again, doing the same on a JList item generates a ListSelectionEvent. Note that JList components never generate an ActionEvent either.

18. A Choice generates an ItemEvent, so the answer is d.

19. A JComboBox generates both an ItemEvent and an ActionEvent when the user selects an item in the combo box, so the answer is e.

20. A top-level menu typically consists of a menu bar consisting of menus, and each menu consists of menu items. So the three components are menu bar, menu, and menu item.

21. True. In fact, menus are the only thing that can be attached to a menu bar.

22. True. Adding a menu to another menu creates a cascading menu.

Applets

In this chapter, I will discuss the details of writing and viewing applets. You will find that writing an applet is similar to creating a graphical user interface (GUI) program, especially because an applet is a container object. Containers, components, layout managers, and event handling are a big part of developing applets. I will also cover some basic HTML concepts because applets are embedded inside HTML documents.

An Overview of Applets

An *applet* is a Java program that runs in a Web browser. The term applet is derived from application, as if to imply that an applet is a small application. This does not need to be the case, however. An applet can be a fully functional Java application because it has the entire Java API at its disposal.

There are some important differences between an applet and a standalone Java application, including the following:

- An applet is a Java class that extends the java.applet.Applet class.
- A main() method is not invoked on an applet, and an applet class will (typically) not define main().

- Applets are designed to be embedded within an HTML page.

- When a user views an HTML page that contains an applet, the code for the applet is downloaded to the user's machine.

- A user must have a JVM on his or her machine. The JVM can be either a plug-in of the Web browser or a separate runtime environment.

- The JVM on the user's machine creates an instance of the applet class and invokes various methods during the applet's lifetime.

- Applets have strict security rules that are enforced by the Web browser. The security of an applet is often referred to as *sandbox security*, comparing the applet to a child playing in a sandbox with various rules that must be followed.

- Other classes that the applet needs can be downloaded in a single Java Archive (JAR) file.

What is impressive about applets is that they are truly platform-independent programs. I have seen many Java applications that are, of course, portable, but there is no need for them to run on different devices. Because applets are a part of a Web page, however, they can be accessed by any Web browser using any operating system on any device, and therefore can be executed on many different platforms and devices. I can run an applet using Windows XP and Internet Explorer, and you can run the same applet on a Macintosh running Netscape Navigator.

 If you are going to be developing applets, you should keep in mind that they may be executed on many different machines. My experience with applets is that they are great for developing Web applications, but that you must be willing to accept the fact that some potential users of your applet will not be able to run them. For example, if you write an applet using J2SE 1.4, the user needs an up-to-date JVM. If my grandmother needs to download and install the latest JVM plug-in to run your applet, I can assure you she won't be visiting your Web site!

When the Internet was first popular in the mid-to-late 1990s, so were applets. Nowadays, I see applets used for some amazing Web applications, but I do not see them used for everyday Web pages. Don't be discouraged, though. Applets play a key role in Java Web development. Keep in mind that most Java code is written for the business world. It's a lot easier to make sure everyone in your company has the right JVM for their Web browser than to make sure that everyone else on the planet does. Knowledge of applets is a must in real-world, distributed Java applications, so do not downplay the importance of applets in Java. You need to have realistic expectations about when and how they are used.

In this chapter, I will show you how to write an applet and embed it in an HTML page. This will involve writing some HTML, but don't worry if you are not familiar with it. Only a little HTML is needed, and I promise to keep to the basics. JAR files will also be discussed in detail because they are important aspects of applets. I will begin with a discussion on the Applet class, the starting point for writing an applet.

The java.applet.Applet Class

An applet is a Java class; if the applet is to be viewed in a Web browser, the class must extend the java.applet.Applet class. The Applet class provides a common interface so that a Web browser can communicate with the applet.

An interesting note about the Applet class is that it extends java.awt.Panel. This means that an applet is a panel, which is a java.awt.Container; therefore, an applet can have components added to it just like any container, as well as have a layout manager assigned to it, and you can even nest panels within an applet to create the GUI you want.

 An applet has FlowLayout by default, but any layout manager can be assigned to an applet using the setLayout() method.

Let's take a look at a simple Applet class. The following HelloWorldApplet extends applet and adds a button to the applet. The event handling is done in the ensuing PrintHello class. Study the following code, and try to determine what this applet does.

```
import java.applet.*;
import java.awt.*;

public class HelloWorldApplet extends Applet
{
    private Button go;
    private TextField name;
    private Label hello;

    public void init()
    {
        go = new Button("Go");
        name = new TextField();
        hello = new Label("", Label.CENTER);

        this.setLayout(new BorderLayout());

        this.add(name, BorderLayout.NORTH);

        Panel center = new Panel();
```

```
            center.add(go);
            this.add(center, BorderLayout.CENTER);

            this.add(hello, BorderLayout.SOUTH);

            //Set up the event handling.
            PrintHello listener = new PrintHello(hello, name);
            go.addActionListener(listener);
        }
    }


import java.awt.*;
import java.awt.event.*;

public class PrintHello implements ActionListener
{
    private Label label;
    private TextField textField;

    public PrintHello(Label s, TextField t)
    {
        label = s;
        textField = t;
    }

    public void actionPerformed(ActionEvent a)
    {
        String name = textField.getText();
        if(name != null && !(name.equals("")))
        {
            label.setText("Hello, " + name);
        }
    }
}
```

I want to make a few comments about this applet:

- Most of the code of the HelloWorldApplet appears in the init() method, which is overriding the init() method from the parent class Applet. The Web browser invokes init() immediately after it creates an instance of HelloWorldApplet. I could have used a constructor, but I wanted to demonstrate the init() method.

- Within init(), the layout of the applet is changed to BorderLayout. (It had FlowLayout by default.)

- A PrintHello object is listening for an ActionEvent from the Go button.

- At no point in the code is the size of the applet specified, even though it is a container. The size of an applet is determined by the HTML that contains the applet. Any attempt to set the size of the applet is overridden by the HTML.

This applet is displayed in a Web page named hello.html using the <applet> tag. The HTML looks similar to:

```
<html>
    <body>
        <h2>Enter your name and click the button.</h2>

        <applet code="HelloWorldApplet"
                width="200"
                height="75">
        </applet>
    </body>
</html>
```

 An applet is embedded in an HTML page by using the <applet> tag. There are several attributes of the <applet> tag, which are discussed in detail in the upcoming section *The <applet> Tag*. For now, I need to discuss the three attributes of the <applet> tag that are required:

code.   The name of the applet class for this applet.

width.   The width in pixels of the applet.

height.   The height in pixels of the applet.

For example, if the name of your applet class is com.wiley.MyApplet, the following HTML embeds an instance of MyApplet in a Web page:

```
<applet code="com.wiley.MyApplet"  width="400" height="500">
</applet>
```

The size of the applet will be 400 pixels wide and 500 pixels high.

Figure 14.1 shows the hello.html file opened in Internet Explorer, displaying the HelloWorldApplet.

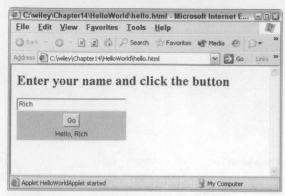

Figure 14.1 HelloWorldApplet displayed in a Web browser.

 An applet can actually be embedded within any other application, not just a Web browser. If your applet is going to be embedded in a Web page, it must extend the Applet class. If your applet is going to be embedded in some other application, extending Applet is not required. That being said, I have never seen an applet whose class did not extend either Applet or JApplet, so I assume that not extending Applet is rarely done.

Swing Applets

The javax.swing.JApplet class is for creating an applet that uses Swing components. The JApplet class is a child of Applet, so JApplet inherits all the methods of Applet. Web browsers do not distinguish between a regular applet and a Swing applet. The purpose of the JApplet class is to provide support for Swing.

 Probably the biggest difference between an applet and a JApplet is how components are added to them. A JApplet has three panes, much like a JFrame, and components are added to the content pane of the JApplet (as opposed to an applet where components are added directly to the Applet). The content pane of a JApplet has BorderLayout by default.

The following HelloSwingApplet extends JApplet. The event handling is done by using a class named FourColors. Study these two classes and try to determine what the applet does.

```java
import java.applet.*;
import java.awt.*;
import javax.swing.*;

public class HelloSwingApplet extends JApplet
{
    public void init()
    {
        Container contentPane = this.getContentPane();

        contentPane.setLayout(new GridLayout(2,2));
        JPanel [] quadrants = new JPanel[4];

        for(int i = 0; i < quadrants.length; i++)
        {
            quadrants[i] = new JPanel();
            contentPane.add(quadrants[i]);
        }

        FourColors listener = new FourColors(quadrants,
 this.getWidth(), this.getHeight());
        this.addMouseMotionListener(listener);
    }
}

import java.awt.*;
import java.awt.event.*;

public class FourColors extends MouseMotionAdapter
{
    private Container [] quadrants;
    private int width, height;

    public FourColors(Container [] q, int w, int h)
    {
        quadrants = q;;
        width = w;
        height = h;
    }

    public void mouseMoved(MouseEvent m)
    {
        int x = m.getX();
        int y = m.getY();

        int current = 0;
        if(x < width/2 && y < height/2)
        {
```

```
            //First quadrant
            quadrants[0].setBackground(Color.RED);
            current = 0;
        }
        else if(x > width/2 && y < height/2)
        {
            //Second quadrant
            quadrants[1].setBackground(Color.GREEN);
            current = 1;
        }
        else if(x < width/2 && y > height/2)
        {
            //Third quadrant
            quadrants[2].setBackground(Color.BLUE);
            current = 2;
        }
        else if(x > width/2 && y > height/2)
        {
            //Fourth quadrant
            quadrants[3].setBackground(Color.YELLOW);
            current = 3;
        }

        for(int i = 0; i < quadrants.length; i++)
        {
            if(i != current)
            {
                quadrants[i].setBackground(Color.WHITE);
            }
        }
    }
}
```

Figure 14.2 shows the output of the HelloSwingApplet in a Web page named colors.html, which is defined as:

```
<html>
    <body>
        <p>Move the mouse around the applet.</p>

        <applet code="HelloSwingApplet"
                width="300"
                height="300">
        </applet>
    </body>
</html>
```

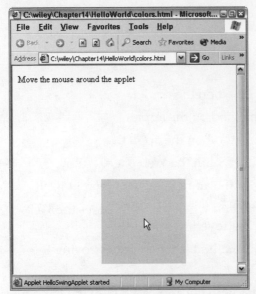

Figure 14.2   HelloSwingApplet displayed in a Web page.

I want to make a few comments about the HelloSwingApplet:

- The size of the applet in the colors.html page is 300 pixels wide by 300 pixels high. The content pane of the JApplet is divided into a grid of two rows and two columns, so each will be of size 150 x 150 pixels.

- A JPanel is placed into each grid.

- The four JPanel containers are passed into the FourColors listener object. When the mouse moves over the JApplet, this listener handles the MouseEvent.

- Within the mouseMoved() method of FourColors, some math is done to calculate which JPanel the mouse is moving over. The color of that JPanel is changed, while the other JPanel quadrants are made white to match the background.

Life Cycle of an Applet

When a user views a Web page that contains an applet, the following sequence of events occurs regarding the life cycle of the applet:

1. The Web browser downloads the necessary bytecode and JAR file from the Web server where the code is located. (This Web server is referred to as the code base.)

2. The browser creates an instance of the Applet class, invoking the default constructor.

3. The applet is displayed in the Web page, with the location and size of the applet determined by the HTML.

4. The browser invokes the init() method on the applet.

5. The browser invokes the start() method on the applet.

6. The browser invokes the paint() method on the applet.

7. The applet is now live and running within the Web page.

8. The browser calls paint() whenever the applet needs to repaint itself.

9. The browser invokes the stop() method when the user leaves the Web page or the applet is about to be destroyed.

10. The browser invokes the destroy() method just before destroying the applet.

Notice that the browser communicates with the applet by invoking methods on the applet. The methods invoked by the browser are defined in the Applet class, and your Applet class can override any of these methods to perform whatever tasks it wants to.

Let's look at the five methods that the browser invokes on your applet.

public void init(). The first method invoked on the applet when it is initially instantiated. This is your chance to perform any initialization, such as locating resources or preparing event handlers.

public void start(). Invoked by the browser to inform the applet that it should start executing. The start() method is called right after the init() method, and is also called when the page is revisited. This is a good time to start any threads or other tasks like displaying animation or playing sound.

public void stop(). Invoked by the Web browser to inform the applet that it should stop executing. The stop() method is called right before the destroy() method is invoked, and also when a user leaves the Web page. Typically, anything you started in the start() method is stopped in the stop() method.

public void destroy(). Invoked by the Web browser to inform the applet that it is about to be destroyed (in other words, garbage collected). Typically, any resources allocated in the init() method are freed in the destroy() method.

public void paint(Graphics g). Invoked immediately after the start() method, and also any time the applet needs to repaint itself in the browser. The paint() method is actually inherited from the java.awt. Container class (the grandparent class of Applet), and is a feature of all containers. The java.awt.Graphics parameter is the graphics context, representing the portion of the screen on which your applet is allowed to paint.

Each time I teach students about applets, I have them write an applet similar to the LifecycleDemo class that follows. The LifecycleDemo applet uses calls to System.out.println() to demonstrate when the browser invokes these methods on the applet. This applet not only demonstrates the life cycle of an applet, but also demonstrates how to view an applet that you created in a Web browser. I also need to show you where the output is of System.out.printn(). Let's do this example together, so perform the following steps:

Step 1: Write the Applet Class

Begin by opening your text editor and then typing in the LifecycleDemo class shown in Figure 14.3. Notice the LifecycleDemo class overrides the five methods that the browser invokes, and prints out a message within each method. The paint() method uses the Graphics object to display a value in the applet.

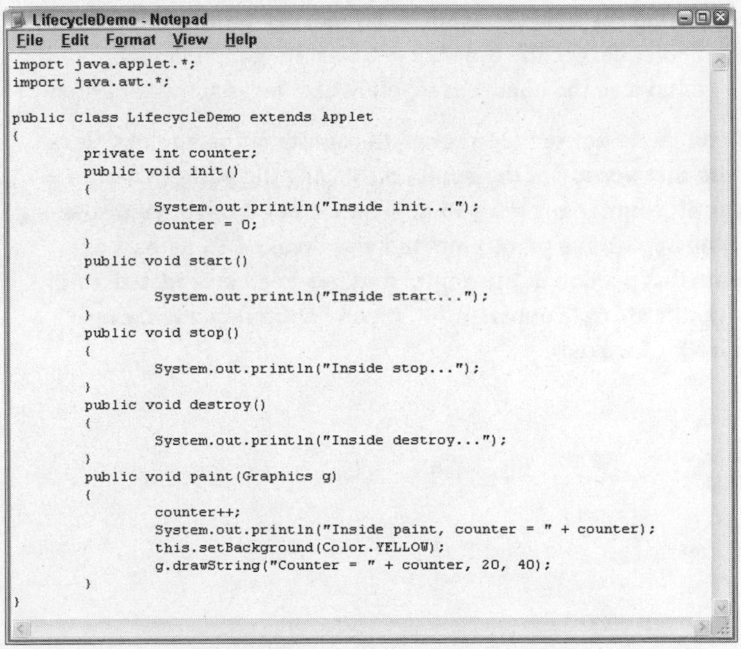

```
LifecycleDemo - Notepad
File  Edit  Format  View  Help
import java.applet.*;
import java.awt.*;

public class LifecycleDemo extends Applet
{
        private int counter;
        public void init()
        {
                System.out.println("Inside init...");
                counter = 0;
        }
        public void start()
        {
                System.out.println("Inside start...");
        }
        public void stop()
        {
                System.out.println("Inside stop...");
        }
        public void destroy()
        {
                System.out.println("Inside destroy...");
        }
        public void paint(Graphics g)
        {
                counter++;
                System.out.println("Inside paint, counter = " + counter);
                this.setBackground(Color.YELLOW);
                g.drawString("Counter = " + counter, 20, 40);
        }
}
```

Figure 14.3 Type in the LifecycleDemo class, which overrides five methods inherited from Applet.

Save the file LifecycleDemo.java in a new folder named c:\applets. After you have it typed in and saved, compile it using javac. Note that LifecycleDemo is not a program. You can try to run it using the java VM, but this will only result in an exception.

Step 2: Write the HTML Page

We do not need anything fancy here; just a Web page with the <applet> tag. Create a new document in your text editor, and type in the HTML shown in Figure 14.4.

Save the document in a file named lifecycle.html. Be sure to save it in the directory c:\applets (or wherever you compiled LifecycleDemo.java).

Step 3: View the HTML Page

Open the file lifecycle.html in your Web browser. Assuming that your first two steps were accomplished successfully, you should see the applet shown in Figure 14.5.

 One of the purposes of the LifecycleDemo applet is to demonstrate when the paint() method is invoked. Initially, the counter is 1. Try minimizing and then restoring the browser window. Try moving another window in front of the applet. Resize the browser window. (It won't take long for the counter to get up into the hundreds if you resize the window continually.)

Note that you might not see the change to counter in the applet unless you cover up that portion of the applet displaying the string "Counter = x". In other words, counter might be 35 in memory, but it might be displaying only 10 in the applet. The paint() method was invoked 35 times, but it only repaints that portion of the applet that has been invalidated. Until you cover up the string "Counter = 10", it will not be repainted, even though paint() is invoked.

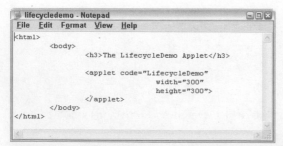

Figure 14.4 The lifecycle.html page contains the LifecycleDemo applet.

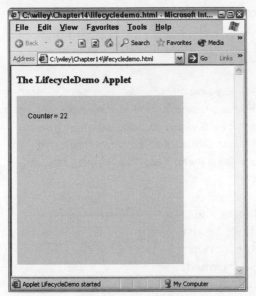

Figure 14.5 LifecycleDemo applet displays the number of times the paint() method is invoked.

Step 4: View the Java Console

A good question to ask now is: Where did the output of the System.out.println() calls go? There is no command prompt because this is an applet, and the output did not appear anywhere on the Web page.

Invoking the System.out.println() method in an applet sends the output to the *Java console*. How you view the Java console depends on which browser you are using.

If you are using a JVM that is a part of Internet Explorer, follow these steps to display the Java console. (If you see the Java logo down on your taskbar when you view an applet, your browser is using the Java plug-in and you can skip the following steps):

1. Select the Internet Options menu item, which is found on either the View menu or the Tools menu, to open the Internet Options dialog box.

2. Click the Advanced tab, and page down about halfway to the section titled Java.

3. Check the Show Java console (requires restart) box.

4. Press the OK button to close the Internet Options dialog box.

5. Close Internet Explorer and then open it again.

6. On the View menu, you should now see a menu item titled Java Console. Select it, and the Java Console will be displayed. You should see output similar to that in Figure 14.6.

 Netscape Navigator does not hide the Java console like Internet Explorer does. When using Netscape, the Java console is viewed from a menu item on the Tools menu. The exact menu item varies slightly, depending on your version of Netscape, but it is not difficult to find. If you are using Netscape, look on the Tools menu for a menu item that looks similar to Display Java Console.

If the JVM being used is the Java plug-in, the console is displayed by clicking the Java Plug-in icon in your Windows taskbar. If you are using Windows XP, you are probably using the Java plug-in. When you installed the J2SDK on your machine, the Java plug-in was also installed.

When you view a Web page that contains an applet, the Java Plug-in icon appears on the taskbar by the clock. The icon looks like a steaming cup of coffee (the Java logo). Right-click the icon, and then select Show Console. Figure 14.6 shows the console for the Java plug-in.

Notice in Figure 14.6 that the init() method is invoked first, followed by the start() method, then numerous calls to paint(). To get the output in Figure 14.6, I left the lifecycle.html page, which caused stop() and destroy() to be invoked.

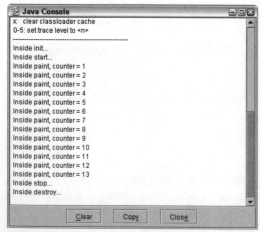

Figure 14.6 Java console displays the System.out.println() output of the LifecycleDemo applet.

♦ Introduction to HTML

HTML stands for HyperText Markup Language and is the language of the Internet. A Web page is an HTML document, and HTML looks nothing like the page you actually view. Your Web browser takes the HTML and marks it up (thus the term "markup" language).

This is not an HTML book, but I want to cover a few of the basics so you can create the necessary Web pages to view your applets. HTML consists of tags, which appear in angle brackets <>. Most tags come in pairs, with an opening and closing tag. For example, the following <strong> tag makes the string "Hello, HTML" appear in bold.

```
<strong>Hello, World</strong>
```

Notice that a forward slash is used to denote the closing tag. Not all tags require a closing tag, most noticeably the line break tag <br>; however, most tags come in pairs with an opening and closing tag.

An HTML document is a text file saved with either a .htm or .html extension. The root tag of an HTML document is <html>, and the <html> tag can nest the optional <head> and <body> tags:

```
<html>
      <head>
      </head>
      <body>
      </body>
</html>
```

The <head> tag can contain the <title> tag, which denotes the text to appear in the title bar of the browser's window. Other tags that typically appear within <head> include:

<meta>.   Used to define variables like the search keywords, content type, description of the page, and so on.

<style>.   Used for defining styles on the page (fonts, colors, cursors, and so on).

<script>.   Used for defining programming functions in languages like javascript.

For example, the following Web page displays Welcome in the title bar of the browser and defines keywords that are used by search engines to determine the content of the page:

```
<header>
      <title>Welcome</title>
      <meta name="keywords" content="java, training, courseware,
books">
</header>
```

Search engines rank their search results on the <meta> keywords. If someone searches for "java training," ideally this Web page will appear early on in the search results.

continued

♦ Introduction to HTML *(continued)*

The <body> tag contains the content of the Web page. Common tags in the body of a page include:

<p>.   The paragraph tag.

<hx>.   The heading tag. Possible values of x and 1–6. For example, <h1> is the heading 1 tag, which creates a large heading. <h6> is the smallest heading.

<center>.   For centering items.

<img src="*url*">.   Displays the image at the specified URL.

<font face="*font_name*" size="*size*" color="*#color*">.   Displays the nested text with the given font, size, and color.

<a href="*url*">.   The anchor tag; it creates a hyperlink to some other URL.

<applet>.   Embeds an applet in the HTML document.

<table>.   For creating a table. Nest <tr> within <table> to create a table row, and nest <td> within <tr> to create columns for the table data.

The following HTML displays the HelloSwingApplet and demonstrates the use of some of the other HTML tags. Study the HTML, and see if you can determine how the page will look.

```
<html>
    <head>
        <title>An Introduction to HTML</title>
    </head>
    <body>
    <h2>The HelloSwingApplet</h2>
    <p>This applet demonstrates using the JApplet class.</p>
    <center>
        <table border="1">
        <tr><td>
        <applet code="HelloSwingApplet"
                width="250"
                height="250">
        </applet>
        </tr></td>
        <tr><td>
        <p><font size="-1" color="#B21445">
         Move the mouse around the area above
        </font></p>
        </td></tr>
        </table>
    </center>
    <br>
    <p><a href="HelloSwingApplet.java">Click here</a>
      to view the source code.</p>
    </body>
</html>
```

The previous HTML was saved in a file named sidebar.html. Figure 14.7 shows this page viewed in Internet Explorer.

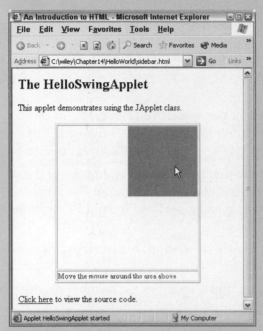

Figure 14.7   HTML page viewed marked up in a Web browser.

If you are viewing a Web page and are curious to see what the HTML looks like, you can view the source by selecting the Source menu item of the View menu (on Internet Explorer). The HTML for that page will be shown as a text document, displaying all the HTML tags used to create that page.

The <applet> Tag

The <applet> tag is used to embed an applet within an HTML page. I discussed earlier how the applet tag has three required attributes: code, width, and height. The following is a list of the other applet tags attributes, each of which is optional:

codebase.   The location where the browser can find the bytecode for the applet. It is not uncommon for the HTML file to be in a different directory or even on a different Web server than the bytecode. The code base represents a URL (relative to where the HTML document is located) where the necessary applet bytecode is located. The next section, *Document and Code Base*, discusses the code base in detail.

archive.   The name of a JAR file (or files) that contains any additional files required by the applet. Use a comma to separate multiple filenames. All .class files in the archives are loaded by the JVM's class loader, making the classes available to the applet. Note that the applet class itself can be located in one of the archives as well. Examples of files in an archive include .class files, images (such as .gif or .jpg files), audio files, and data files. The upcoming section *JAR File and Applets* discusses how to create and use an archive.

name.   The name of this instance of the applet. You can create multiple applets on a Web page, and they can locate each other by using this name attribute and the AppletContext class. You will do this in Lab 14.4.

align.   A standard HTML attribute that specifies the alignment of the applet relative to other items around it on the Web page. The possible values are left, right, top, bottom, middle, texttop, absmiddle, absbottom, and baseline.

vspace.   A standard HTML attribute that specifies the number of pixels to appear above and below the applet.

hspace.   A standard HTML attribute that specifies the number of pixels to appear to the left and right of the applet.

alt.   A standard HTML attribute that allows you to specify text that appears if the browser understands the <applet> tag but cannot run the applet.

 If a Web browser does not understand the <applet> tag, it will ignore the tag and display any HTML that appears within the opening and closing <applet> tags. For example, the following HTML displays a message that the user is unable to see the applet that was intended to appear:

```
<applet      code="com.wiley.MyApplet"
             width="200"
             height="348"
             alt="MyApplet failed">
    <h2>Your browser does not support applets!</h2>
    <p>To view this page correctly, you will need to find a Web
    browser that provides support for applets, or install the
    Java Plug-in.</p>
</applet>
```

Visitors to this page who have a Web browser that supports applets will not see the message about their browser not supporting applets. Note that if their browser supports applets but, for some reason, cannot run applets, the visitor will see the alt message "MyApplet failed."

In addition to these attributes, an <applet> tag can also contain any number of parameters, which are defined using the <param> tag. The <param> tag is nested within the <applet> tag, and has two attributes: name and value. The syntax for using <param> is:

```
<applet>
     <param name="parameter name" value="value">
     <param name="parameter name" value="value">
     ...
</applet>
```

An applet can obtain the parameters using the following Applet method:

public String getParameter(String name).   Returns the value of the given parameter. The return value is null if the parameter is not defined.

Parameters allow the writer of an applet to customize the applet based on input from the writer of the HTML page. Proper use of parameters can make your applets flexible and capable of being used in many different situations. For example, the following HTML document, paramdemo.html, displays an applet named HelloWorldApplet2, which is similar to the HelloWorldApplet discussed earlier, except that it uses two parameters to determine the label on the button and the greeting.

```
<html>
     <body>
          <h2>Enter your name and click the button.</h2>

          <applet code="HelloWorldApplet2"
                    width="200"
                    height="75"
                    name="HelloWorld"
                    align="center"
                    vspace="15"
                    alt="The HelloWorld2 applet">
               <param name="greeting" value="Merry Christmas">
               <param name="buttonLabel" value="Click here">
          </applet>
     </body>
</html>
```

Notice that this applet will be centered and have a vertical space of 15 pixels above and below it in the browser. The HelloWorldApplet2 class is defined next, and demonstrates how to use the getParameter() method to obtain the values of the <param> tags. The event handling is done by the DisplayGreeting class, which is also defined here.

```java
import java.applet.*;
import java.awt.*;
public class HelloWorldApplet2 extends Applet
{
    private Button go;
    private TextField name;
    private Label hello;
    public void init()
    {
        String buttonLabel = this.getParameter("buttonLabel");
        if(buttonLabel == null)
        {
            //No buttonLabel parameter was defined.
            buttonLabel = "Go";
        }
        go = new Button(buttonLabel);
        String greeting = this.getParameter("greeting");
        if(greeting == null)
        {
            greeting = "Hello";
        }
        hello = new Label(greeting, Label.CENTER);
        this.setLayout(new BorderLayout());
        name = new TextField();
        this.add(name, BorderLayout.NORTH);
        Panel center = new Panel();
        center.add(go);
        this.add(center, BorderLayout.CENTER);
        this.add(hello, BorderLayout.SOUTH);
        //setup the event handling
        DisplayGreeting listener = new DisplayGreeting(hello, name);
        go.addActionListener(listener);
    }
}

import java.awt.*;
import java.awt.event.*;
public class DisplayGreeting implements ActionListener
{
    private Label label;
    private TextField textField;
    private String greeting;
    public DisplayGreeting(Label s, TextField t)
    {
```

```
        label = s;
        textField = t;
        greeting = s.getText();
    }
    public void actionPerformed(ActionEvent a)
    {
        String name = textField.getText();
        if(name != null && !(name.equals("")))
        {
            label.setText(greeting + ", " + name);
        }
    }
}
```

The buttonLabel parameter of HelloWorldApplet2 becomes the label on the button. The greeting parameter becomes the greeting displayed in the applet. Figure 14.8 shows HelloWorldApplet2 displayed in a Web browser using the paramdemo.html page, where the buttonLabel parameter is "Click here" and the greeting parameter is "Merry Christmas."

 In the HelloWorldApplet2 class, if the buttonLabel parameter is not defined, the button label will be Go. Similarly, the greeting defaults to Hello if no greeting parameter is provided. When writing an applet, you should always have meaningful default values for parameters to allow for situations where the parameters are not provided by the HTML author.

Figure 14.8   Greeting and button label are determined by parameters.

Document and Code Base

The document and code bases are important topics in applets because of how they relate to sandbox security. The document base is the base URL of the HTML document, and the code base is the base URL of the applet's bytecode. These do not need to be in the same location; however, security restrictions force an applet to only use classes that are located at the applet's code base.

For example, suppose a Web page is located at the following URL:

```
http://www.javalicense.com/jeopardy/index.htm
```

The document base for the index.htm page is:

```
http://www.javalicense.com/jeopardy
```

Suppose that an applet named com.javalicense.JeopardyApplet is embedded in the index.htm page, and the URL of the .class file is

```
http://www.wiley.com/applets/com/javalicense/JeopardyApplet.class
```

The code base for this applet is:

```
http://www.wiley.com/applets
```

Notice that the /com/javalicense/ portion of the URL is required as part of the package name and is not a part of the code base. The codebase attribute of the <applet> tag is used to denote in the HTML file where the applet code can be found. For example, the index.htm page that embeds the JeopardyApplet might look similar to the following.

```html
<html>
    <head>
        <title>Java Jeopardy</title>
    </head>
    <body>
        <h2>Java Jeopardy</h2>
        <applet code="com.javalicense.JeopardyApplet"
                width="400"
                        height="450"
                codebase=" http://www.wiley.com/applets"
                align="center"
                archive="jeopardy.jar">
```

```
                    <param name="questions" value="introquestions.txt">
                    <p>You must have a browser that supports applets
                    to play Java Jeopardy.</p>
                </applet>
            </body>
        </html>
```

No matter where this HTML document is located, the JeopardyApplet can be found because the codebase attribute is defined. Notice that the JeopardyApplet uses an archive named jeopardy.jar, which contains several other .class files as well as a file named introquestions.txt that contains the questions for the game. This example also uses a parameter to denote this filename, which allows the questions to be easily changed.

 An applet can determine its document base and code base by using the following methods, which are found in the Applet class.

public URL getDocumentBase().   Returns a java.net.URL object, which represents the document base of the page that embeds this applet

public URL getCodeBase().   Returns a java.net.URL object, which represents the location where this applet is located

These are useful methods when developing applets, especially when you need an applet to locate another file or document. At development time, the applet author does not need to know the URL of the location where the applet is to be deployed, nor does the applet author need to know the location of the Web page that will be embedding the applet. Both of their URLs can be obtained by using the getCodeBase() and getDocumentBase() methods, respectively. The upcoming *Displaying Images* and *Playing Audio* sections contain typical uses of these methods.

The appletviewer Tool

The J2SDK comes with a tool known as appletviewer that is used for testing applets during their development stage. The appletviewer tool opens an HTML file, but it ignores all <html> tags except for those pertaining to applets. Figure 14.9 shows the options of the appletviewer tool.

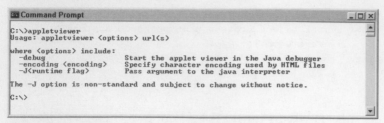

Figure 14.9 Options for running the appletviewer tool.

To view an applet using appletviewer, you enter the name of any .html file that embeds the applet. For example, the HelloSwingApplet is embedded in the colors.html page. Figure 14.10 shows the command line to view this applet in appletviewer. Note that the first time you run appletviewer a message appears about using a default properties file. This is perfectly fine.

Figure 14.11 shows the HelloSwingApplet being displayed by the appletviewer tool.

 When you are developing applets, it is common to view them in a Web browser, change a few things, recompile the applet, and go back and view your changes in the browser. You will soon find out that refreshing the Web page in the browser may or may not reload the applet class. I have noticed this with Internet Explorer using the Java plug-in while I was writing the applets for this chapter.

The only remedy I found was to close the browser window and start it back up again so that the applet class was reloaded by the JVM. One nice benefit of appletviewer is that you can view an applet, make a change to the code, recompile it, and simply reload the applet by selecting Reload from the appletviewer menu. After you know that the applet is working properly, you can try it out in a Web browser such as Internet Explorer or Netscape Navigator.

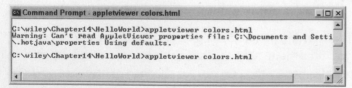

Figure 14.10 appletviewer will display any applets embedded in the colors.html file.

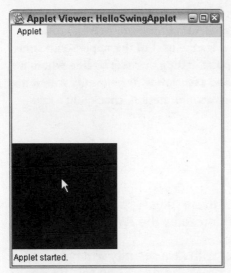

Figure 14.11   appletviewer displaying the HelloSwingApplet.

Sandbox Security

Applets run in a Web browser restricted to a set of security policies referred to as *sandbox security*. The purpose of the sandbox security model is to ensure that the applet you are downloading and executing is not going to do terrible things to your computer. This is especially important in today's Internet world of viruses and other undesirable side effects of software applications.

Applets that are downloaded and executed in a Web browser must adhere to the following rules:

- An applet cannot access any files on a user's operating system.
- An applet can only create network connections to the applet's code base, and cannot connect to other network addresses.
- An applet cannot execute a program on the user's machine.
- An applet cannot access system information or use system dialog boxes such the Open File or Print dialog boxes.

 An applet can be granted permission to leave the sandbox and perform an otherwise restricted operation. For example, you can grant an applet permission to access files on your local hard drive. Of course, you will want to make sure you trust the source of the applet before granting such permission.

An applet can also be signed, which involves creating a security certificate. This is the typical way to create an applet that needs to perform tasks outside the sandbox because it provides the user of the applet with some assurance as to the source of the applet, letting the user decide whom he or she trusts. Creating a certificate and associating permissions with it are beyond the scope of this book. For more information, check Sun's Java Web site at http://java.sun.com/.

Classroom Q & A

Q: How does the sandbox enforce these rules?
A: The security permissions are enforced by the JVM.

Q: Suppose a programmer familiar with Java security writes an applet that grants itself permission to break the rules. Can this be done?
A: I should say no, but there always seem to be holes in any security mechanism. I will say this: It would be extremely difficult to write an applet that steps outside its sandbox without the user granting it permission. It is probably easier for someone to write an applet that tricks a user into agreeing to a signed certificate so that the applet could do anything it wanted on the person's machine than it is to write Java code that bypasses the built-in security features of applets and the JVM.

Q: So applets really are not that secure, are they?
A: No, I didn't say that. Applets by their nature are much safer than other Web applications that do not have a sandbox-type security. If a user has security turned on, an applet cannot leave its sandbox without the express permission of the user. An applet has much tighter security restrictions than HTML, JavaScript, and other widely used Web development technologies.

Q: Can I turn off the security permissions so my own applets can run on my machine and perform actions such as accessing the local file system?
A: Certainly. Let me show you how to do this using Microsoft Internet Explorer. You will find that Microsoft has hidden this feature deep in the browser settings, so you will need to follow along closely.

To view and/or change the sandbox security settings for applets running in your Web browser, perform the following steps:

1. Open the Internet Options dialog box found on the Tools menu of Internet Explorer. (Older versions of Internet Explorer have the Internet Options on the View menu.)

2. Select the Security tab. You should see a dialog box similar to the one shown in Figure 14.12.

3. Click the Custom Level button. The Security Settings dialog box is displayed.

4. Scroll down the list of security settings until you see either a Java heading or a Java Permissions heading. Select the Custom radio button under this heading, and you should see a Java Custom Settings button appear at the bottom of the Security Settings dialog box, similar to Figure 14.13.

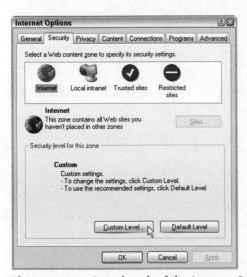

Figure 14.12   Security tab of the Internet Options dialog box.

Figure 14.13   Select the Custom radio button to display the Java Custom Settings button.

5. Click the Java Custom Settings button to display the Internet dialog box. Select the Edit Permissions tab. You will see a dialog box similar to the one in Figure 14.14.

You probably do not want to change any of the settings at this time, but I recommend that you browse through the list of permissions. They show you exactly what an applet can and cannot do. You can cancel your way out of the dialog boxes when you are finished browsing through the permissions.

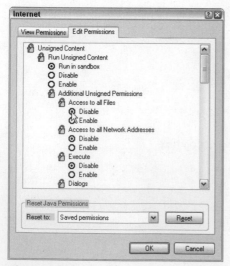

Figure 14.14   Use this dialog box to change the sandbox security settings for applets.

The Applet Context

The *applet context* refers to the environment that the applet is running in, which for most applets is a Web page. The java.applet.AppletContext interface contains methods that an applet can use to communicate with the environment, allowing the applet to perform tasks like finding another applet on the page or loading a different Web page into the user's browser.

An applet obtains a reference to the AppletContext object using the getAppletContext() method, found in the Applet class:

public AppletContext getAppletContext().   Returns a reference to this applet's context, which is typically a Web document.

Here are some of the methods in the AppletContext interface.

public Applet getApplet(String name).   Returns a reference to the applet on this page that has the given name, which is determined by the name attribute of the <applet> tag.

public void showDocument(URL url).   Replaces the current Web page with the document at the specified java.net.URL.

public void showDocument(URL url, String target).   Shows the document at the specified java.net.URL. The target parameter is an HTML attribute that determines where the document is displayed. The possible values are:

_self.   Show the document in the same window and frame as the applet.

_parent.   Show the document in the applet's parent frame.

_top.   Show the document in the top-level frame of the applet's window.

_blank.   Show the document in a new window.

"name".   Show the document in a currently opened browser window with the given name. If a window does not match *name*, then the document is shown in a new window.

public AudioClip getAudioClip(URL url).   Creates a new AudioClip object from the audio file at the specified URL. Audio clips are discussed in the upcoming section *Playing Audio*.

public Image getImage(URL url).   Returns an Image object associated with the image file at the specified URL. Images are discussed in the upcoming section *Displaying Images*.

public void showStatus(String status).   Displays the status String in the status bar of the browser's window.

The following ContextDemo applet demonstrates using some of the methods in the AppletContext. The events of the two buttons are handled by the ShowDocument class, which also follows. Study the classes, and try to determine how the applet looks and what it does.

```java
import java.applet.*;
import java.awt.*;
import javax.swing.*;
public class ContextDemo extends JApplet
{
      private JButton show1, show2;
      private JTextField url;
      private AppletContext context;
      public void init()
      {
            context = this.getAppletContext();

            Container contentPane = this.getContentPane();

            url = new JTextField(30);
            show1 = new JButton("Show");
            show2 = new JButton("Open in new window");
            contentPane.add(new JLabel("Enter a URL:",
                  SwingConstants.CENTER), BorderLayout.NORTH);
            JPanel center = new JPanel();
            center.add(url);
            contentPane.add(center, BorderLayout.CENTER);
            JPanel south = new JPanel();
            south.add(show1);
            south.add(show2);
            contentPane.add(south, BorderLayout.SOUTH);
            //Register event handlers.
            ShowDocument listener = new ShowDocument(context, url);
            show1.addActionListener(listener);
            show2.addActionListener(listener);
      }
      public void start()
      {
            context.showStatus("ContextDemo has started!");
      }
}


import java.awt.event.*;
import java.applet.AppletContext;
import java.net.*;
import javax.swing.JTextField;
public class ShowDocument implements ActionListener
{
      private AppletContext context;
      private JTextField textField;
```

```
public ShowDocument(AppletContext c, JTextField t)
{
    context = c;
    textField = t;
}
public void actionPerformed(ActionEvent a)
{
    context.showStatus("Showing document");
    URL url = null;
    try
    {
        url = new URL(textField.getText());
    }catch(MalformedURLException e)
    {
        e.printStackTrace();
        context.showStatus("Unable to display URL");
        return;
    }
    String label = a.getActionCommand();
    if(label.equals("Show"))
    {
        context.showDocument(url);
    }
    else if(label.equals("Open in new window"))
    {
        context.showDocument(url, "_blank");
    }
}
}
```

Figure 14.15 shows the ContextDemo displayed in a Web browser. Let me make a few comments about this applet:

- The AppletContext for this applet is saved as a field in the class and initialized in the init() method. This is standard procedure with applets.

- The start() method attempts to display a message on the status bar of the browser's window. I noticed that each time I ran the applet, the browser would override the status bar after this, so I never saw the message.

- When either button is clicked, the actionPerformed() method in the ShowDocument class is invoked. Setting the status bar to Showing document worked every time.

- The java.net.URL constructor throws a MalformedURLException if the String passed in is not in the proper URL format.

- Clicking the button labeled Show replaces the current page (contextdemo.html) with the URL entered in the text field.

- Clicking the other button shows the entered URL in a new browser window.

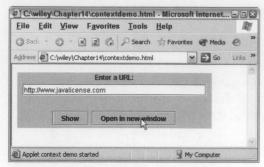

Figure 14.15 ContextDemo applet displays the document entered in the text field.

Displaying Images

An applet can display images of the format GIF, JPEG, BMP, and others. To display an image within the applet, you use the drawImage() method found in the java.awt.Graphics class. This is done using the Graphics object passed in to the applet's paint() method. The Graphics class has six overloaded versions, which take in a variation of the following parameters:

Image image. The java.awt.Image object to be displayed. This is obtained using the getImage() method of the applet's context.

int x and int y. The (x,y) coordinate of the upper-left corner of the image.

int width and int height. The width and height of the rectangular region that the image is to be displayed in.

Color color. The background color of the image. This only shows through if the image does not fill the rectangular region or is opaque in places.

ImageObserver observer. An optional parameter that allows a separate object to be notified of changes to the Image object.

The image passed in to the drawImage() method must be of type java.awt.Image. You do not instantiate the Image object, though. Instead, you obtain the Image instance by invoking the getImage() method of the Applet-Context interface:

```
public Image getImage(URL url)
```

The getImage() method associates an Image object with the given URL. The following ImageDemo applet demonstrates displaying a JPEG image within an applet. Notice that the Image is a field in the class, initialized in the init() method from an applet parameter named image. It is then drawn onscreen in the paint() method. Figure 14.16 shows how the applet looks when displayed in a browser.

 The getImage() method returns immediately and does not actually look for the image file at the given URL until the browser attempts to draw the image on the screen. At that time, the URL is resolved, and the image is downloaded. Any problems with the URL will not be realized until you attempt to display the image.

```java
import java.applet.*;
import java.awt.*;
import java.net.*;
public class ImageDemo extends Applet
{
    private Image image;
    private AppletContext context;

    public void init()
    {
        context = this.getAppletContext();
        String imageURL = this.getParameter("image");
        if(imageURL == null)
        {
            imageURL = "default.jpg";
        }
        try
        {
            URL url = new URL(this.getDocumentBase(), imageURL);
            image = context.getImage(url);
        }catch(MalformedURLException e)
        {
            e.printStackTrace();
            context.showStatus("Could not load image!");
        }
    }
    public void paint(Graphics g)
    {
        context.showStatus("Displaying image");
        g.drawImage(image, 0, 0, 200, 84, null);
        g.drawString("www.javalicense.com", 35, 100);
    }}
```

The following imagedemo.html file embeds the ImageDemo applet, and assigns the image parameter to a JPEF file named LogoD.jpg. Note that the way the URL is initialized in the init() method, the image file needs to be in the same root directory as the imagedemo.html document. This page is shown in Figure 14.16.

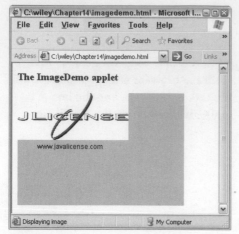

Figure 14.16   ImageDemo applet paints a JPEG image in the applet.

```
<html>
    <body>
        <h3>The ImageDemo applet</h3>
        <applet code="ImageDemo"
                    width="300"
                    height="200"
                    align="center">
            <param name="image" value="LogoD.jpg">
        </applet>
    </body>
</html>
```

Playing Audio

An applet can play an audio file represented by the AudioClip interface in the java.applet package. The AudioClip interface has three methods, including:

public void play().   Plays the audio clip one time, from the beginning.

public void loop().   Causes the audio clip to replay continually.

public void stop().   Stops playing the audio clip.

To obtain an AudioClip object, you must invoke the getAudioClip() method of the Applet class:

```
public AudioClip getAudioClip(URL url)
```

The getAudioClip() method returns immediately, whether or not the URL resolves to an actual audio file. The audio file is not downloaded until an attempt is made to play the audio clip.

The following AudioDemo applet demonstrates playing an audio clip that is specified as an applet parameter. Study the class, and try to determine how it looks and what it does.

```java
import java.applet.*;
import java.awt.*;
import java.net.*;
public class AudioDemo extends Applet
{
    private AudioClip clip;
    private AppletContext context;
    public void init()
    {
        context = this.getAppletContext();
        String audioURL = this.getParameter("audio");
        if(audioURL == null)
        {
            audioURL = "default.au";
        }
        try
        {
            URL url = new URL(this.getDocumentBase(), audioURL);
            clip = context.getAudioClip(url);
        }catch(MalformedURLException e)
        {
            e.printStackTrace();
            context.showStatus("Could not load audio file!");
        }
    }
    public void start()
    {
        if(clip != null)
        {
            clip.loop();
        }
    }
    public void stop()
    {
        if(clip != null)
        {
            clip.stop();
        }
    }
}
```

The audio clip begins playing in the start() method of the AudioDemo applet, and does not stop playing until the stop() method is invoked, which occurs when the user leaves the page. Notice that the applet does not have any visual elements to it, and the following audiodemo.html Web page embeds the applet with a size of 0 by 0 pixels. When the audiodemo.html page is viewed in a browser, the clip plays continually.

```
<html>
    <body>
        <h3>The AudioDemo applet</h3>
        <applet code="AudioDemo"
                width="0"
                height="0">
            <param name="audio" value="jeopardy.wav">
        </applet>
    </body>
</html>
```

 The audio file "jeopardy.wav" is specified as the audio parameter of the AudioDemo applet. The URL passed in to the getAudioClip() uses the document base as the location of this file; therefore, the file jeopardy.wav needs to appear in the same directory as the audiodemo.html file.

♦ Working with JAR files

The J2SDK comes with a tool called jar for creating JAR (Java ARchive) files. JAR files are used in all aspects of Java, and the further you progress in your Java programming, the more you will realize that JAR files are everywhere. The reason they are so widely used is because both Java compilers and JVMs can read files from a JAR without requiring the JAR file to be uncompressed. You can take the largest of Java applications, consisting of any number of .class files, and compress all these files into a single JAR file. Your application can then be deployed by simply giving someone the JAR file, and they do not even have to uncompress it to execute it.

It is no surprise, therefore, that JAR files are a common aspect of applets. When a user views a Web page that embeds an applet, the necessary files can be downloaded to the user's machine in one or more JAR files. The JVM of the Web browser handles the task of uncompressing and extracting the archives to access the various files within.

The jar tool is run from the command prompt, and is used for creating or extracting a JAR file. Figure 14.17 shows the options of the jar tool. This should be in your PATH on your computer, so open a command prompt, type in jar, and press Enter.

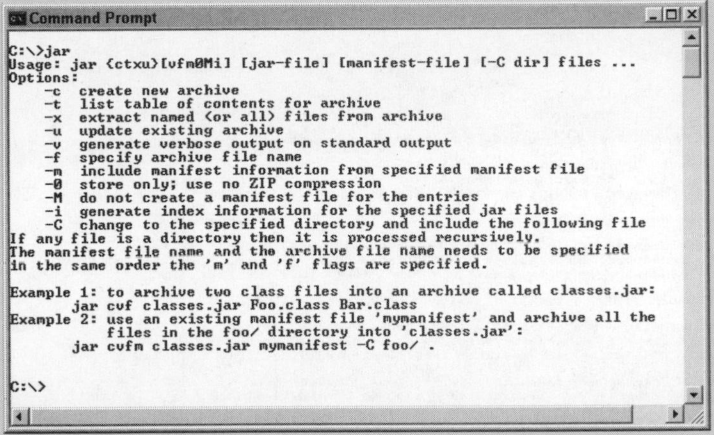

Figure 14.17   Various options of the jar tool.

The c option is used for creating a new JAR file, and the x option is used for extracting an existing JAR. I like to use the v option for verbose so I can see what the tool is doing. The f option is used to specify the name of the new file. Another common option is m, which is used to add a manifest file to the JAR. Manifest files are required for all JAR files, and the jar tool will create one for you if you do not specify an existing manifest file using the m option. For example, the following manifest file is used for a JAR file that contains an application:

```
Manifest-Version: 1.0
Main-Class: com.javalicense.JeopardyGame
```

To demonstrate the jar tool, the following command line creates a new JAR file named jeopardy.jar that contains the directory \com and all of its subdirectories, plus the text file questions.txt:

```
jar -cvmf my_manifest.mf jeopardy.jar .\com questions.txt
```

Notice the order of the options m and f relative to the subsequent filenames: The m appears before the f, and the name of the manifest file appears before the name of the new file to create. The order in which the options appear is the order in which the respective filenames need to appear. For example, the following command creates the same JAR file:

```
jar -cvfm jeopardy.jar my_manifest.mf .\com questions.txt
```

Figure 14.18 shows the verbose output of creating this JAR.

continued

◆ Working with JAR files *(continued)*

```
Command Prompt                                                    _ □ ×

C:\jeopardy>jar -cvmf my_manifest.mf jeopardy.jar .\com questions.txt
added manifest
adding: com/(in = 0) (out= 0)(stored 0%)
adding: com/javalicense/(in = 0) (out= 0)(stored 0%)
adding: com/javalicense/JeopardyWindow.class(in = 3019) (out= 1679)(deflated
)
adding: com/javalicense/JeopardyWindow$1.class(in = 526) (out= 336)(deflated
)
adding: com/javalicense/JeopardyMenu.class(in = 2088) (out= 1090)(deflated 4
adding: com/javalicense/JeopardyGame.class(in = 3307) (out= 1811)(deflated 4
adding: com/javalicense/JeopardyQuestion.class(in = 2104) (out= 1099)(deflat
7%)
adding: com/javalicense/JeopardyQuestion$1.class(in = 546) (out= 344)(deflat
6%)
adding: com/javalicense/DailyDouble.class(in = 1302) (out= 750)(deflated 42%
adding: com/javalicense/JeopardyTeam.class(in = 538) (out= 334)(deflated 37%
adding: com/javalicense/AddTeamDialog.class(in = 1862) (out= 1021)(deflated

adding: com/javalicense/ScoreKeeper.class(in = 1574) (out= 918)(deflated 41%
adding: com/javalicense/JeopardyWindow$2.class(in = 634) (out= 410)(deflated
)
adding: questions.txt(in = 49) (out= 48)(deflated 2%)

C:\jeopardy>
```

Figure 14.18   All files in the .\com directory are added to jeopardy.jar.

The jeopardy.jar now contains all the files necessary to run the Jeopardy application. The program can be executed with the following command:

```
java -jar jeopardy.jar
```

There are 11 .class files in the archive jeopardy.jar, but the JVM knows which one contains the main() method by checking the Main-Class entry of the manifest file.

JAR Files and Applets

An applet can place the files it needs in an *archive*, a single, compressed file containing bytecode, images, sound files, and any other files that the applet needs. Archive files simplify the task of an applet trying to locate other files, and also improves performance of downloading, since the files are compressed using the same compression format as ZIP files.

 You can open JAR files to view their contents by using the standard ZIP utility programs such as WinZip or PKUnzip.

The archive is typically a JAR file, or Java Archive, although ZIP files can also be used. The jar tool that comes with the J2SDK is used to create JAR files. With applets, you can place all the necessary bytecode and other files needed by the applet in the JAR file.

Figure 14.19 imagedemo.jar file contains all the necessary files for the ImageDemo applet.

To demonstrate using JAR files and applets, the following example creates a JAR file for the ImageDemo applet, adding the bytecode ImageDemo.class, and the image file LogoD.jpg. Figure 14.19 shows the jar command that is used to create the new JAR file named imagedemo.jar.

The following jardemo.html page demonstrates embedding the ImageDemo applet using the archive attribute of the <applet> tag.

```
<html>
    <body>
        <h3>The ImageDemo applet</h3>
        <applet code="ImageDemo"
                width="300"
                height="200"
                align="center"
                archive="imagedemo.jar">
            <param name="image" value="LogoD.jpg">
        </applet>
    </body>
</html>
```

When the <applet> tag is reached, the imagedemo.jar file is downloaded and uncompressed by the JVM of the browser. The jardemo.html file creates the same output as the one in Figure 14.16.

Lab 14.1: Writing an Applet

This lab will help you become familiar with writing applets.

1. Write a class named MyFirstApplet that extends Applet.

2. Within the paint() method, use the drawString() method of the Graphics class to display your name in the applet.

3. Save and compile the MyFirstApplet class.

4. Write an HTML document named myfirst.html that embeds the MyFirstApplet applet. Add a <h1> heading displaying "My First Applet", and any other HTML code you want.

5. Save the HTML document in the same directory as the bytecode file MyFirstApplet.class.

6. Open the HTML document in appletviewer.

7. Open the HTML document in a Web browser.

In appletviewer, you should see just the apple; in the Web browser, you should see the applet plus any HTML code that appears in myfirst.html.

Lab 14.2: Using Applet Parameters

This lab will help you become familiar with using applet parameters. This lab makes some modifications to the MyFirstApplet class from Lab 14.1.

1. Add the init() method to your MyFirstApplet class, and also a field of type String called name.

2. Within the init() method, initialize the name field to be the value of a parameter called username. If no username parameter is defined, have the name field default to be your name.

3. Modify the paint() method so that it displays the name field instead of your name.

4. Save and compile the MyFirstApplet class.

5. View the myfirst.html page in a browser or appletviewer. You should see your name because you have not defined a username applet parameter yet.

6. Modify your myfirst.html file so that it defines a username parameter. Assign the value of this parameter to be something other than your name.

7. View the myfirst.html page again in a browser or appletviewer.

The output is similar to that of Lab 14.1, except that the name displayed should be the value of the username parameter defined in myfirst.html.

Lab 14.3: The Calculator Applet

The purpose of this lab is to demonstrate the similarities and differences between applets and GUI applications. You will modify your Calculator program from Chapter 13, "GUI Components and Event Handling," so that it can be used as an applet.

1. Copy all of the code from your solutions to Lab 13.1 in a new directory. You are going to modify your Calculator program, but I do not want you to lose the work you did already. Make all of the following changes to the copied version of your Calculator program.

2. Modify your Calculator class so that it extends JApplet instead of JFrame.

3. Perform all the initialization and setup of your GUI and event handling in the init() method. This might be as simple as renaming your constructor to be the init() method, depending on how you wrote your Calculator class.

4. Make any other necessary changes so that your Calculator class compiles. (You might get some compiler errors because you changed the parent class from JFrame to JApplet.)

5. Write a Web page that embeds your Calculator applet.

6. View your Web page, and test the Calculator to ensure that it works properly.

Your Calculator applet should work similarly to your Calculator program, except that now it can be viewed as an applet.

Lab 14.4: Applet Communication

The purpose of this lab is to demonstrate how two applets on the same Web page can communicate with each other using the applet context. You will write two applets: one that plays an audio clip, and a second applet that controls which audio clip is played.

1. Write a class named PlayClipApplet that extends Applet. Add a field of type AudioClip called clip, and a field of type String called clipName.

2. Add a method called setAudioClip() that has a java.net.URL parameter. This URL represents the location of an audio clip. Within the setAudioClip() method, use the getAudioClip() method of the AppletContext to initialize the field clip. Use the getFile() method of the URL class to initialize the clipName field.

3. Add the start() and stop() methods to the PlayClipApplet class, having them play and stop the audio clip, respectively.

4. Within the start() method, use the showStatus() method of the AppletContext interface to display the text "Playing *clip_name*", where *clip_name* is the value of the field clipName.

5. Save and compile the PlayClipApplet class.

6. Write a class named EnterASongApplet that extends JApplet. Add two JButton fields—play and stop—and a JTextField field called songName. Also add a field of type AppletContext.

7. Within the init() method, initialize the three component fields. Use the labels Play and Stop for the buttons. Add the two buttons and text field to the content pane of this JApplet, laying them out in a nice fashion.

8. Also within the init() method, initialize the AppletContext field, then instantiate a new PlayListener object, passing a reference to the songName text field and the AppletContext field. (You will write the PlayListener class next.) Register the PlayListener object with both buttons.

9. Save your EnterASongApplet class, and write a new class named PlayListener that implements ActionListener.

10. Add a field of type JTextField and a field of type PlayClipApplet.

11. Add a constructor that has a JTextField parameter and an AppletContext parameter. Initialize the JTextField field with the corresponding parameter. Use the getApplet() method, passing in "playclip", of the given AppletContext to initialize the PlayClipApplet field. You will need to cast the return value to the appropriate data type.

12. Within actionPerformed(), determine which button was clicked. If the Play button is clicked, get the text from the JTextField, which will be the name of an audio file, and use it to create a new URL object. Pass in this URL object to the setAudioClip() method of the PlayClipApplet field, then invoke the start() method on the PlayClipApplet field.

13. If the Stop button is pressed, invoke the stop() method on the PlayClipApplet field.

14. Save and compile both your PlayListener class and EnterASongApplet class.

15. Write an HTML page named playclip.html. Add the PlayClipApplet and EnterASongApplet applets to the page, using two separate <applet> tags. Assign the name attribute of the PlayClipApplet as playclip.

16. View the playclip.html page in your Web browser.

You should be able to enter a filename representing an audio clip, play the clip by clicking the Play button, and stop it by clicking the Stop button.

Lab 14.5: Using JAR Files

The purpose of this lab is to become familiar with creating a JAR file using the jar tool, and also how to use JAR files with applets. This lab uses the classes you created in Lab 14.4.

1. Using the jar tool, create a new file called songapplet.jar that contains all the .class files from Lab 14.4. Also include in the JAR any audio files that the applets will use.

2. Modify the playclip.html file, adding the archive attribute to both <applet> tags. The value of the archive attributes should be songapplet.jar.

3. Move the files songapplet.jar and playclip.html into a new directory by themselves.

4. Open the playclip.html file in a browser to ensure that everything is still working properly.

The output is the same as your output in Lab 14.4. The difference is that now all of the necessary files are compressed into a single JAR file, allowing your applets to be easily deployed and downloaded by clients. I had you move the files into a new directory to ensure that the JAR file was working and that the Web page wasn't finding the unarchived class files from the previous lab.

Summary

- An applet is a Java program that runs in a Web browser. An applet is written by extending the java.awt.Applet class.

- When an applet is instantiated in a browser, the browser communicates with the applet by invoking the init(), start(), stop(), paint(), and destroy() methods.

- A Swing applet extends the javax.swing.JApplet class.

- Applets run in a security context referred to as a sandbox. This limits what an applet can do on a person's PC. For example, applets cannot access the local file system or start other applications.

- The appletviewer tool that comes with the SDK is useful for the development of applets.

- An applet uses the AppletContext to communicate with the browser, allowing the applet to communicate with other applets on the same page or to display a URL.

- An applet can display images and play audio files.

- The applet class and all the corresponding files that it uses can be placed in a JAR file for faster downloading and simplifying deployment.

Review Questions

1. List the three required attributes of the <applet> tag.

2. For an applet class to be viewed in a browser, the class must extend:

    a. java.applet.Applet

    b. java.awt.Panel

    c. javax.swing.JApplet

    d. Any of the above

    e. a or b

3. True or False: If an applet class defines main(),the browser will invoke main() when the applet is instantiated.

4. Of the following applet methods, which ones are invoked by the browser when the applet is first initialized, and in what order are they invoked?

    a. start()

    b. init()

    c. stop()

    d. paint()

    e. destroy()

5. True or False: For security reasons, the bytecode for an applet must appear on the same Web server as the HTML source code.

6. True or False: The size of an applet is determined by the HTML page that embeds the applet.

7. True or False: The stop() method is invoked on an applet when the user clicks the Stop button or selects the Stop menu item of the Web browser.

8. What method does an applet use to obtain the value of an applet parameter?

9. How is an applet parameter defined?

10. True or False: The getCodeBase() method returns the URL of the server where the applet's bytecode is located.

11. True or False: The getDocumentBase() method returns the URL of the server where the HTML page is located that embeds the applet.

12. True or False: An applet can never access files on the local file system.

13. How does an applet obtain a reference to its corresponding AppletContext object?

14. True or False: The bytecode for an applet can be placed in a JAR file.

15. True or False: All necessary files for an applet must be placed in a JAR file that is specified using the archive attribute of the <applet> tag.

Answers to Review Questions

1. code, width, and height.

2. An applet must extend applet. An Applet class can also extend JApplet because JApplet is a child of Applet; therefore, the answer is e.

3. False. An Applet class can define main(), but it will not be invoked by the browser.

4. The methods invoked when an applet is initialized are init(), start(), and paint(), in that order.

5. False. The bytecode can reside anywhere, and the HTML can denote the location of the applet's bytecode using the codebase attribute of the <applet> tag.

6. True. The size of an applet is based on the width and height attributes of the <applet> tag.

7. False. Selecting Stop in a browser stops the page from downloading further, but has no effect on an applet that is already running on the page.

8. The getParameter() method of the Applet class.

9. By nesting the <param> tag within the <applet> tag of the corresponding HTML page.

10. True. That is the purpose of the getCodeBase() method.

11. True. That is the purpose of the getDocumentBase() method.

12. False. By default, an applet cannot access local files; however, the security permissions can be changed for an applet so that it can step outside of the sandbox and perform tasks such as accessing local files.

13. By invoking the getAppletContext() method in the Applet class.

14. True. In fact, this is commonly done.

15. False. You do not need to use JAR files with applets; however, using JAR files greatly reduces the risk of files not being found or classes not being loaded properly on the client's machine.

CHAPTER

15

Threads

Threads allow you to perform multiple tasks at the same time. In this chapter, I will discuss how threads are created in Java and how they behave after they start running. Creating threads has advantages, but using multiple threads creates data integrity issues, so I will need to discuss the various synchronization issues that arise. Topics discussed include the Runnable interface; the Thread, Timer, and TimerTask classes; the synchronization keyword; and avoiding deadlock.

Overview of Threads

A *thread* is defined as a path of execution, a collection of statements that execute in a specific order. The programs we have written up until now in the course have had a single path of execution: the main() method. When a Java application is executed, the main() method runs in its own thread. Within the path of execution of main(), you can start new threads to perform different tasks.

From a programming point of view, creating multiple threads is equivalent to being able to invoke multiple methods at the same time. You can have a thread that is displaying a GUI on the screen, a second thread in the background that is downloading a file from the Internet, and a third thread that is waiting for the user to interact with the GUI.

I need to define another term related to threads: *process*. A process consists of the memory space allocated by the operating system that can contain one or more threads. A thread cannot exist on its own; it must be a part of a process. A process remains running until all of the non-daemon threads are done executing.

You are familiar with processes, because each time you run a program on your computer, you start a process. Today's operating systems are multiprocessing (often called multitasking). You can run multiple processes at the same time. For example, you can play Solitaire while checking your email with Outlook and surfing the Internet with Netscape Navigator. Just to clarify, we will not discuss multiple processes in this chapter. What we will discuss is multiple threads in a single process.

A *daemon thread*, by definition, is a thread that does not keep the process executing. Use a daemon thread for a task that you want to run in the background only while the program is still running. The garbage collector of the JVM process is a good example of a daemon thread. The JVM wants the garbage collector to always be running in the background, freeing memory of unused objects. However, if the garbage collector is the only thread running, there is no need for the JVM process to continue executing.

Classroom Q & A

Q: How many threads can a process have?

A: As many threads as it can handle in its memory space. I have seen applications with thousands of threads. Of course, these applications were running on large servers with lots of memory and multiple CPUs.

Q: And all of these threads are running at the same time?

A: Well, yes and no. To be more precise, a process can have multiple threads that are *runnable* at the same time. However, the number of threads actually *running* at any given time is dependent on the number of CPUs (processors) available.

Q: So how many threads can run on a CPU at one time?

A: Just one! That means your typical desktop computer with its one CPU can execute only one thread at a time.

Q: Then what are the other threads doing?

A: They are still runnable, but they are waiting in a queue for the *thread scheduler* (which is really the JVM) to schedule CPU time for them. For example, suppose that you have two processes and each process has two threads. If one CPU is available, then only one of those threads can be executing at a time, and the other three are waiting.

Q: How long do they wait?

A: Well, to be precise, it depends. The amount of time a thread gets on the CPU depends on an indeterminate number of factors. Some platforms (such as Windows 95/NT/XP) use *time-slicing*, meaning that a thread gets a certain amount of CPU time, and that's it. Other platforms do not time-slice, but instead schedule threads based on their priority. The thread scheduler for the JVM uses *fixed priority scheduling*. This term means that threads are scheduled based on their priority, with higher-priority threads running before lower-priority threads. The JVM thread scheduler is also *preemptive*, which means that if a higher-priority thread comes along, it preempts any currently running lower-priority thread.

Q: So I can create a Java thread, give it a high priority, and it will hog the CPU until it is finished?

A: Perhaps, but doubtful. Many operating systems take certain measures to ensure that threads do not hog the CPU, like intentionally scheduling a lower-priority thread over a higher one. Therefore, *you should never rely on thread priority as part of your algorithm logic*. If you need one thread to finish before another, do not assume that this can be accomplished by using priorities. The purpose of thread priorities is only to allow you to denote one task as more important than another.

Q: Why use threads at all if you do not have control over which one is running?

A: Well, that's a good question. A good rule of thumb is to not use multithreading if you can solve the problem at hand without it. However, in many real-world programming situations, they can't be avoided. In fact, threads can often make a problem easier to solve, while improving the performance of the application at the same time. Therefore, it is important to understand not just how to write a thread, but how the thread behaves after it starts running.

Life Cycle of a Thread

A thread goes through various stages in its life cycle. For example, a thread is born, started, runs, and then dies. What I want to do now is discuss these various stages of a thread's life:

Born. When a thread is first created, it is referred to as a *born* thread. Every thread has a priority, with a new thread inheriting the priority of the thread that created it. This priority can be changed at any time in the thread's life cycle. Thread priority is an int value, and your Java threads can have any priority between 1 and 10. A born thread does not run until it is started.

Runnable. After a newly born thread is started, the thread becomes *runnable*. For each of the 10 priorities, there is a corresponding priority queue (the first thread in is the first thread out). When a thread becomes runnable, it enters the queue of its respective priority. For example, the main() thread has the normal thread priority, which is 5. If main() starts a thread Y, then Y enters the priority 5 queue. If Y starts a thread Z and assigns Z a priority of 8, Z will enter the priority 8 queue. If Z is the highest-priority thread, it will preempt the current thread and start running immediately.

note Keep in mind that the Java thread scheduler is *preemptive*. If the priority 5 queue has two runnable threads in it, say X and Y, and these threads are the highest priority of all other threads, X and Y will dominate the CPU. If a priority 8 thread comes along, say Z, it will immediately preempt the currently running priority 5 thread and start running. The X and Y threads must now wait until the Z thread is no longer runnable.

Running. The thread scheduler determines when a runnable thread gets to actually run. In fact, the only way a thread is running is if the thread scheduler grants it permission. If for any reason a thread has to give up the CPU, it must eventually work its way through the runnable priority queues before it can run again.

Blocked. A thread can become blocked, which occurs when multiple threads are synchronizing on the same data and need to take turns. A blocked thread is not running, nor is it runnable. It waits until the synchronization monitor allows it to continue, at which point it becomes runnable again and enters its appropriate priority queue.

Other blocked states. A thread can become blocked for other reasons besides synchronization. For example, a thread can invoke the wait() method on an object, which blocks the thread until notify() is invoked on the same object. A thread can sleep for a certain number of milliseconds, or a thread can call the join() method and wait for another thread to finish. As is always the case, when a thread is no longer blocked and becomes runnable again, the thread is placed in its corresponding priority queue and gets to run again when the thread scheduler schedules it.

Dead. A thread that runs to completion is referred to as a dead thread. The term *dead* is used because it cannot be started again. If you need to repeat the task of the thread, you need to instantiate a new thread object.

Now that you have seen how threads behave, I will show you the various ways to write a thread in Java.

Creating a Thread

There are three common ways to write a thread in Java:

- You can write a class that implements the Runnable interface, then associate an instance of your class with a java.lang.Thread object.
- You can write a class that extends the Thread class.
- You can write a class that extends the java.util.TimerTask class, and then schedule an instance of your class with a java.util.Timer object.

I want to point out that although each of these techniques is different, all three involve implementing the Runnable interface. Either you write a class that implements Runnable, or you extend a class that already implements Runnable. (Both the Thread and TimerTask classes implement Runnable.) In either case, you define the one method in Runnable:

```
public void run()
```

The body of the run() method is the path of execution for your thread. When the thread starts running, the run() method is invoked, and the thread becomes dead when the run() method runs to completion.

Each of these various ways to create a thread has its advantages and disadvantages, but they are mostly design issues. Therefore, whichever technique you choose will likely be based on your own design and personal preferences. I will now discuss each of these three techniques, throwing in some important information about threads along the way.

Implementing Runnable

After all this discussion about threads, we are now ready to finally write one. I will start by creating a thread using a class that implements the Runnable interface. The following DisplayMessage class implements Runnable and uses a while loop to continually display a greeting:

```
public class DisplayMessage implements Runnable
{
    private String message;

    public DisplayMessage(String message)
    {
        this.message = message;
    }

    public void run()
    {
        while(true)
        {
            System.out.println(message);
        }
    }
}
```

Objects of type DisplayMessage are also of type Runnable because the DisplayMessage class implements the Runnable interface. However, DisplayMessage objects are not threads. For example, the following two statements are valid, but be careful about what their result is:

```
DisplayMessage r = new DisplayMessage ("Hello, World");
r.run();
```

The run() method is invoked, but not in a new thread. The infinite while loop will print "Hello, World" in the current thread that these two statements appear in. To run DisplayMessage in a separate thread, you need to instantiate and start a new object of type java.lang.Thread.

 The purpose of the Runnable class is to separate the Thread object from the task it is performing. When you write a class that implements Runnable, there are two objects involved in the thread: the Runnable object and the Thread object. The Runnable object contains the code that executes when the thread finally gets to run. It is the Thread object that is born, has a priority, starts, is scheduled, runs, blocks, and eventually dies. When the Thread object is actually running, the run() method of the Runnable object is the code that executes.

The Thread class has eight constructors, which take in a variation of the following parameters:

String name.   Every Thread object has a name associated with it. You can assign a thread any name you like because the purpose of the name is to allow you to distinguish the various threads you create. If you do not assign your threads a name, the Thread class names them Thread0, Thread1, Thread2, and so on.

Runnable target.   Associates a Runnable object as the target of the Thread. If you write a separate class that implements Runnable, use one of the Thread constructors that has a Runnable parameter.

ThreadGroup.   The group that the thread belongs to. All threads belong to a group. If you create your own ThreadGroup object, use one of the Thread constructors that has a ThreadGroup parameter to associate the new thread with your group. If you do not explicitly put a thread into a group, the thread is placed in the default thread group.

long stackSize.   The number of bytes you want allocated for the size of the stack used by this thread. The documentation warns that this value is highly platform dependent and may be ignored on some JVMs.

 Every thread belongs to a *thread group*. The java.lang.ThreadGroup class represents a thread group, and Thread objects are associated with a group using one of the Thread constructors with a ThreadGroup parameter. If a thread is not specifically added to a thread group, it belongs to the default thread group created by the JVM called main. Creating a ThreadGroup is useful when managing a large number of threads.

After you instantiate the Thread object and associate it with the Runnable target, this new thread is started by invoking the start() method of the Thread object. The following RunnableDemo program demonstrates instantiating both a Runnable object (the DisplayMessage object) and a corresponding Thread object. Then, the start() method is invoked on the Thread object, which causes the run() method of DisplayMessage to execute in a separate thread. Study the program and see if you can determine what the output is.

```
public class RunnableDemo
{
    public static void main(String [] args)
    {
        System.out.println("Creating the hello thread...");
        DisplayMessage hello = new DisplayMessage("Hello");
        Thread thread1 = new Thread(hello);
```

```
                System.out.println("Starting the hello thread...");
                thread1.start();

                System.out.println("Creating the goodbye thread...");
                DisplayMessage bye = new DisplayMessage("Goodbye");
                Thread thread2 = new Thread(bye);
                System.out.println("Starting the goodbye thread...");
                thread2.start();
        }
}
```

I want to make a few comments about the RunnableDemo program:

- Two Runnable objects are instantiated: hello and bye.

- Each of the two Runnable objects is associated with a Thread object: thread1 and thread2.

- Invoking start() on the Thread objects causes the thread to become runnable.

- When the thread gets scheduled, the run() method on the corresponding Runnable object is invoked.

- Just after thread2 is started, there are three threads in this process: the main() thread, thread1, and thread2.

- The program does not terminate, even though main() runs to completion. Once main() is done executing, the process still has two non-daemon threads: thread1 and thread2. The process does not terminate until both of these threads finish executing.

- That being said, this process never terminates because the two threads do not stop (their corresponding run() methods contain infinite loops). To stop this process, you need to stop the JVM process. (In Windows, press Ctrl+c at the command prompt.)

Figure 15.1 shows a sample output of running the RunnableDemo program. The output was created by running the program on Windows XP, which uses time-slicing. Notice that Hello is printed for a while; Goodbye is then printed for a while; then the program goes back to Hello again, and so on. Running this program probably produces a different output each time, depending on the platform and how many other threads are running.

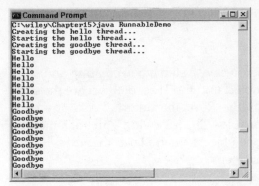

Figure 15.1   Sample output of the RunnableDemo program.

Extending the Thread Class

You can create a thread by writing a class that extends the java.lang.Thread class and overrides the run() method in Thread. To demonstrate, the following GuessANumber class extends Thread and randomly picks a number between 1 and 100 until it guesses the int stored in the field number.

```java
public class GuessANumber extends Thread
{
    private int number;

    public GuessANumber(int number)
    {
        this.number = number;
    }

    public void run()
    {
        int counter = 0;
        int guess = 0;
        do
        {
            guess = (int) (Math.random() * 100 + 1);
            System.out.println(this.getName()
                                        + " guesses " + guess);
            counter++;
        }while(guess != number);

        System.out.println("** Correct! " + this.getName()
```

```
                                        + " in " + counter + " guesses.**");
        }
    }
```

When you extend the Thread class, you save a step when creating and starting the thread because the Runnable object and the Thread object are the same object. (The Thread class implements the Runnable interface, so any child classes of Thread are also of type Runnable.) The following ThreadDemo program instantiates two GuessANumber objects, then starts them. Study the program and try to determine what happens.

```java
public class ThreadDemo
{
    public static void main(String [] args)
    {
        System.out.println("Pick a number between 1 and 100...");

        GuessANumber player1 = new GuessANumber(20);
        GuessANumber player2 = new GuessANumber(20);

        player1.start();
        player2.start();
    }
}
```

Each thread runs until it guesses the number 20, which takes an arbitrary number of guesses. Figure 15.2 shows a sample output of the ThreadDemo program.

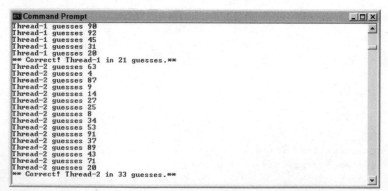

Figure 15.2 Sample output of the ThreadDemo program.

Although it is easier to extend Thread, there are certain times when you may not have that option. Keep in mind that you get only one parent class in Java. If you write a class that already extends a class, extending Thread is not an option. For example, suppose that you write an applet named MyApplet. Because the MyApplet class must extend java.applet.Applet, extending Thread is not an option. To make MyApplet a thread, it must implement Runnable:

```
public class MyApplet extends Applet implements Runnable
```

It is my opinion that implementing Runnable is a better choice in regard to object-oriented design. The purpose of extending a class is to add functionality to it. The GuessANumber example extends Thread, but adds no functionality to the Thread class. From an object-oriented point of view, GuessANumber is not a Thread (even though it runs *in* a thread) and therefore does not satisfy the *is a* relationship.

That being said, I see developers extend Thread all the time. In fact, in many of the examples in this chapter, I will extend Thread instead of implementing Runnable just because it saves me a step. However, when I do "real" Java development, my threads will be classes that implement Runnable.

◆ Yielding Threads

Notice in the output of the ThreadDemo in Figure 15.2 (created on Windows XP) that each thread gets about 5–10 guesses before its time slice runs out. If this program were to run on a non-time-slicing platform, one thread would likely get a lot of guesses, while the other thread waited to get scheduled. Of course, there are many indeterminate factors involved in scheduling the threads, so the output of the program is different each time it runs. Because the program runs differently each time, the design of the program should not depend on whether the platform time-slices or not.

If we want this game to be fairer, with each thread getting a chance to guess a number without waiting too long for the other threads playing, we can design the threads to *yield* to one another. A thread yields by invoking the yield() method in the Thread class, which looks like this:

```
public static void yield()
```

This method causes the currently running thread to pause so that other threads can have a chance to execute. Yielding is a good programming design with threads, but note that it is only a moderately polite thing for a thread to do because it will yield only to other threads of the same priority.

continued

◆ Yielding Threads *(continued)*

For example, suppose that you have two threads currently runnable: A of priority 5 and B of priority 10. If B calls yield(), the A thread does not get a chance to run. In fact, the B thread does not even leave the CPU. It just keeps on running. However, if A and B are of the same priority and B calls yield(), B will go to the back of the priority queue and A will get a chance to run.

The following GuessANumber2 class modifies the GuessANumber class by adding a call to yield in the run() method:

```java
public class GuessANumber2 extends Thread
{
    private int number;

    public GuessANumber2(int number)
    {
        this.number = number;
    }

    public void run()
    {
        int counter = 0;
        int guess = 0;
        do
        {
            Thread.yield();

            guess = (int) (Math.random() * 100 + 1);
            System.out.println(this.getName()
+ " guesses " + guess);
            counter++;
        }while(guess != number);

        System.out.println("** Correct! " + this.getName()
+ " in " + counter + " guesses.**");
    }
}
```

Study the following YieldDemo program and try to determine what happens when the three threads are started:

```java
public class YieldDemo
{
    public static void main(String [] args)
    {
        System.out.println("Pick a number between 1 and 100...");

        Thread player1 = new GuessANumber2(85);
```

```
        Thread player2 = new GuessANumber2(85);
        Thread player3 = new GuessANumber2(85);


        player3.setPriority(Thread.MAX_PRIORITY);


        player1.start();
        player2.start();
        player3.start();
    }
}
```

Notice in the YieldDemo program that player3 has the maximum priority of a Thread, which is 10. After each guess, each thread invokes the yield() method. However, because player3 has a higher priority, it does not yield to player1 or player2. Figure 15.3 shows a sample output of running the YieldDemo program.

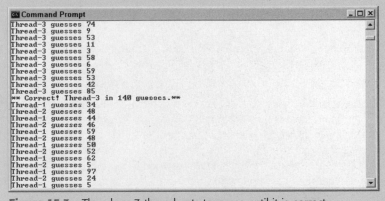

Figure 15.3   The player3 thread gets to guess until it is correct.

The player3 thread hogs the CPU until it is finished executing. After the player3 thread is done, player1 and player2 politely take turns guessing numbers because each one calls yield() after each guess. The output of YieldDemo will be similar on any platform, whether or not time slicing is used.

If you want player3 to actually give up the CPU for lower-priority threads, player3 can sleep for a short amount of time. You use the sleep() method in the Thread class to cause the currently running thread to sleep:

```
public static void sleep(int millisec) throws InterruptedException
```

I was curious to see what effect sleep() would have on the GuessANumber2 class, so I took out the call to Thread.yield() and replaced it with the following:

```
try
{
    Thread.sleep(1);
}catch(InterruptedException e)
{}
```

continued

◆ Yielding Threads *(continued)*

Notice that calls to sleep() require the exception to be handled or declared. Figure 15.4 shows the difference that occurred between using yield() and using sleep().

Figure 15.4   The player3 thread gave up the CPU to the lower-priority threads player1 and player2.

Notice that each thread took turns guessing, even though player3 has a higher priority. Sleeping allowed the three threads to share the CPU more consistently, but it also took away from the fact that thread3 has a higher priority. If I give player3 a high priority, it makes sense that player3 should get more CPU time than player1 or player2. In that case, because sleep() negated the higher priority that was assigned to player3, I would say it is a better design to use the yield() method, which allowed the higher-priority thread to run and threads of the same priority to share the CPU among themselves.

Methods of the Thread Class

Now, let's look at the Thread class in more detail. The Thread class has many useful methods for determining and changing information about a thread, including:

public void start().   Starts the thread in a separate path of execution, then invokes the run() method on this Thread object.

public void run().   If this Thread object was instantiated using a separate Runnable target, the run() method is invoked on that Runnable object. If you write a class that extends Thread, the overridden run() method in the child class is invoked.

public final void setName(String name).   Changes the name of the Thread object. There is also a getName() method for retrieving the name.

public final void setPriority(int priority). Sets the priority of this Thread object. The possible values are between 1 and 10. However, developers are encouraged to use the following three values: Thread.NORM_PRIORITY, Thread.MIN_PRIORITY, and Thread.MAX_PRIORITY (whose values are 5, 1, and 10, respectively).

public final void setDaemon(boolean on). A parameter of true denotes this Thread as a daemon thread. For the thread to be a daemon thread, this method must be invoked before the thread is started.

public final void join(long millisec). The current thread invokes this method on a second thread, causing the current thread to block until the second thread terminates or the specified number of milliseconds passes. If the long passed in is 0, the first thread waits indefinitely.

public void interrupt(). Interrupts this thread, causing it to continue execution if it was blocked for any reason.

public final boolean isAlive(). Returns true if the thread is alive, which is any time after the thread has been started but before it runs to completion.

The previous methods are invoked on a particular Thread object. The following methods in the Thread class are static. Invoking one of the static methods performs the operation on the currently running thread:

public static void yield(). Causes the currently running thread to yield to any other threads of the same priority that are waiting to be scheduled.

public static void sleep(long millisec). Causes the currently running thread to block for at least the specified number of milliseconds.

public static boolean holdsLock(Object x). Returns true if the current thread holds the lock on the given Object. Locks are discussed later in this chapter in the section *synchronized Keyword*.

public static Thread currentThread(). Returns a reference to the currently running thread, which is the thread that invokes this method.

public static void dumpStack(). Prints the stack trace for the currently running thread, which is useful when debugging a multithreaded application.

The following ThreadClassDemo program demonstrates some of these methods of the Thread class. It uses the DisplayMessage and GuessANumber classes discussed previously in this chapter. Study the program and try to determine what it does:

```
public class ThreadClassDemo
{
    public static void main(String [] args)
    {
        Runnable hello = new DisplayMessage("Hello");
```

```
              Thread thread1 = new Thread(hello);
              thread1.setDaemon(true);
              thread1.setName("hello");
              System.out.println("Starting hello thread...");
              thread1.start();

              Runnable bye = new DisplayMessage("Goodbye");
              Thread thread2 = new Thread(hello);
              thread2.setPriority(Thread.MIN_PRIORITY);
              thread2.setDaemon(true);
              System.out.println("Starting goodbye thread...");
              thread2.start();
              System.out.println("Starting thread3...");
              Thread thread3 = new GuessANumber(27);
              thread3.start();
              try
              {
                  thread3.join();
              }catch(InterruptedException e)
              {}
              System.out.println("Starting thread4...");
              Thread thread4 = new GuessANumber(75);
              thread4.start();

              System.out.println("main() is ending...");
      }
}
```

Let me make a few comments about the ThreadClassDemo program:

- There are a total of five threads involved. (Don't forget the thread that main() executes in.)

- thread1 and thread2 are daemon threads, so they will not keep the process alive, which is relevant in this example because thread1 and thread2 contain infinite loops.

- thread2 is assigned the minimum priority.

- The main() thread invokes join() on thread3. This causes main() to block until thread3 finishes, which is an indefinite amount of time because thread3 runs until it guesses the number 27.

- While main() is waiting for thread3, there are three runnable threads: thread1, thread2, and thread3.

- When thread3 terminates, main() becomes runnable again and starts thread4. Then main() ends and its thread dies, leaving thread1, thread2, and thread4 as the remaining runnable threads of the process.

- thread4 runs until it guesses the number 75, at which point there are only two daemon threads left. This causes the process to terminate.

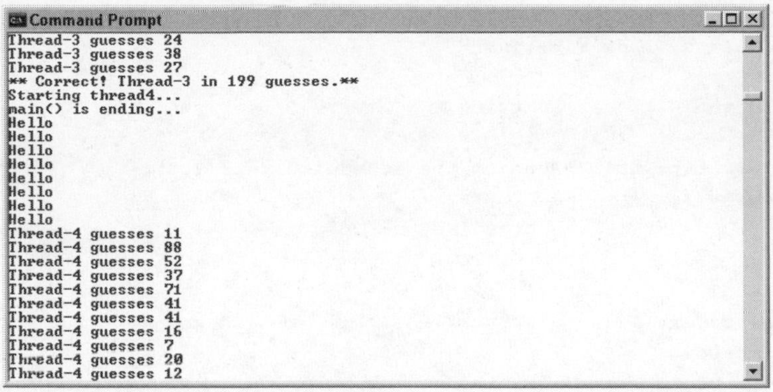

Figure 15.5 The main() thread blocks until thread3 guesses the correct number and dies.

Figure 15.5 shows the output of the ThreadClassDemo program right after thread3 runs to completion. I should point out that I ran this program a dozen times on Windows XP, and at no point did thread2 get a chance to run and print out Goodbye.

Timer and TimerTask Classes

The java.util.Timer class is used to create a thread that executes based on a schedule. The task can be scheduled for a single running at a specified time or to run after a certain amount of time has elapsed, or the task can be scheduled to run on an ongoing basis. A single Timer object can manage any number of scheduled tasks.

Each task is created by writing a class that extends the java.util.TimerTask class. The TimerTask class implements Runnable, but does not implement the run() method. Your child class of TimerTask defines the run() method, and when the task is scheduled to run, your run() method is invoked.

Let me show you a simple example to demonstrate how these two classes are used together to create a scheduled thread. In this example, suppose that you have a memory-intensive program that frequently allocates and frees memory. Garbage collection is constantly running in the background, but you can invoke the System.gc() method to attempt to force immediate garbage collection. Instead of trying to conveniently place calls to System.gc() throughout your program, you want to create a scheduled task that invokes this method every 5 seconds. The following GCTask runs the garbage collector, and the ensuing TimerDemo program creates a Timer and schedules the task to repeat every 5 seconds.

```
import java.util.TimerTask;
public class GCTask extends TimerTask
{
    public void run()
    {
        System.out.println("Running the scheduled task...");
        System.gc();
    }
}


import java.util.Timer;
public class TimerDemo
{
    public static void main(String [] args)
    {
        Timer timer = new Timer();
        GCTask task = new GCTask();
        timer.schedule(task, 5000, 5000);

        int counter = 1;
        while(true)
        {
            new SimpleObject("Object" + counter++);
            try
            {
                Thread.sleep(500);
            }catch(InterruptedException e)
            {}
        }
    }
}
```

Notice the following about this example:

- The GCTask class extends the TimerTask class and implements the run() method.

- Within the TimerDemo program, a Timer object and a GCTask object are instantiated.

- Using the Timer object, the task object is scheduled using the schedule() method of the Timer class to execute after a 5-second delay and then continue to execute every 5 seconds.

- The infinite while loop within main() instantiates objects of type Sim-pleObject (whose definition follows) that are immediately available for garbage collection.

```
public class SimpleObject
{
    private String name;

    public SimpleObject(String n)
    {
        System.out.println("Instantiating " + n);
        name = n;
    }
    public void finalize()
    {
        System.out.println("*** " + name + " is getting garbage
collected ***");
    }
}
```

The SimpleObject class overrides the finalize() method and prints out a message. (Recall that the finalize() method is invoked by the garbage collector just before an object's memory is freed.) Figure 15.6 shows a sample output of the TimerDemo program. Notice that even when the main() thread is sleeping, the objects are not garbage collected until the GCTask is scheduled by the timer, which invokes the System.gc() method. This behavior will vary, depending on the JVM.

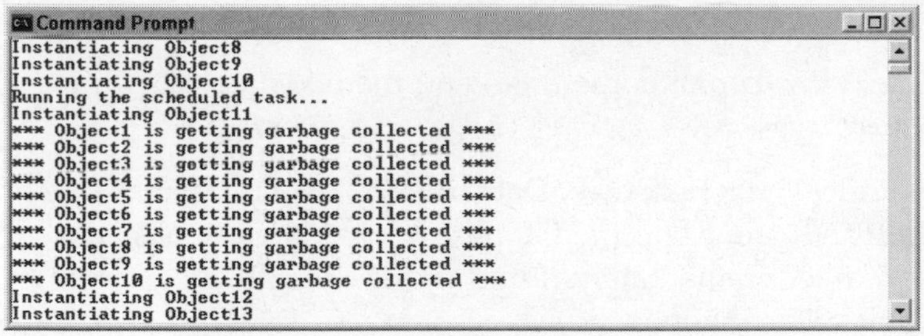

Figure 15.6 Sample output of the TimerDemo program.

Scheduling Tasks

The TimerDemo program demonstrates scheduling a repeated task. The run() method of the GCTask object is invoked every 5 seconds. You can also schedule a task for a single execution, which is scheduled at a specific time or after a specified delay.

Repeating tasks are assigned a period that denotes the time between executions, and they fit into two categories:

Fixed-delay execution.   The period is the amount of time between the *ending* of the previous execution and the beginning of the next execution.

Fixed-rate execution.   The period is the amount of time between the *starting* of the previous execution and the beginning of the next execution.

For example, the GCTask task in the TimerDemo program is a fixed-delay task with a period of 5 seconds, which means that the 5-second period starts after the current task ends. Compare this to a fixed-rate execution with a period of 5 seconds. The fixed-rate task is scheduled every 5 seconds, no matter how long the previous task takes to execute. If the previously scheduled task has not finished yet, subsequent tasks will execute in rapid succession. Fixed-rate scheduling is ideal when you have a task that is time-sensitive, such as a reminder application or clock.

 Each schedule() method can throw an IllegalStateException if the task has already been scheduled. A TaskTimer object can be scheduled only once. If you need to repeat a task, you need to schedule a new instance of your TimerTask class.

The java.util.Timer class contains the following methods for scheduling a TimerTask:

public void schedule(TimerTask task, Date time).   Schedules a task for a single execution at the time specified. If the time has already past, the task will be scheduled immediately. If the task has already been scheduled, an IllegalStateException is thrown.

public void schedule(TimerTask task, long delay).   Schedules a task for a single execution after the specified delay has elapsed.

public void schedule(TimerTask task, long delay, long period).   Schedules a task for fixed-delay execution. The delay parameter represents the amount of time to wait until the first execution, which can be different from the period it is scheduled to run.

public void schedule(TimerTask task, Date firstTime, long period).
Schedules a task for fixed-delay execution. The Date parameter represents the time of the first execution.

public void scheduleAtFixedRate(TimerTask task, long delay, long period). Schedules a task for fixed-rate execution. The delay parameter represents the amount of time to wait until the first execution, which can be different from the period during which it runs.

public void scheduleAtFixedRate(TimerTask task, Date firstTime, long period). Schedules a task for fixed-rate execution. The Date parameter represents the time of the first execution.

Notice that each schedule() method takes in either a start time or a delay time (the amount of the time before the first scheduled execution). Also, each method has a TimerTask parameter to represent the code that runs when the task is scheduled. The TimerTask class has three methods in it:

public abstract void run(). The method invoked by the Timer. Notice that this method is abstract and therefore must be overridden in the child class.

public boolean cancel(). Cancels the task so that it will never run again. If the task is currently running, its current execution will finish. The method returns true if an upcoming scheduled task was canceled.

public long scheduledExecutionTime(). Returns the time at which the most recent execution of the task was scheduled to occur. This method is useful for fixed-delay tasks, whose scheduled times vary.

For example, the following *if* statement checks to see whether an execution of the previous task took longer than three seconds. If it did, this execution will voluntarily skip its turn to run by simply returning from the run() method.

```
if(System.currentTimeMillis() - this.scheduledExecutionTime() >= 3000)
{
     System.out.println("Previous execution took too long");
     return;
}
```

To demonstrate a fixed-rate execution, the following Phone class uses a PhoneRinger task to simulate the ringing of a telephone, with a 3-second period. Study the code of these two classes and try to determine what the output of main() is, which is shown in Figure 15.7.

```java
import java.util.TimerTask;
public class PhoneRinger extends TimerTask
{
     int counter;
     public PhoneRinger()
     {
          counter = 0;
     }
     public void run()
     {
          counter++;
          System.out.println("Ring " + counter);
     }
     public int getRingCount()
     {
          return counter;
     }
}

import java.util.Timer;
public class Phone
{
     private boolean ringing;
     private PhoneRinger task;
     private Timer timer;

     public Phone()
     {
          timer = new Timer(true);
     }
     public boolean isRinging()
     {
          return ringing;
     }
     public void startRinging()
     {
          ringing = true;
          task = new PhoneRinger();
          timer.scheduleAtFixedRate(task, 0, 3000);
     }
     public void answer()
     {
          ringing = false;
          System.out.println("Phone rang " + task.getRingCount()
                              + " times");
          task.cancel();
     }
```

```
    public static void main(String [] args)
    {
        Phone phone = new Phone();
        phone.startRinging();
        try
        {
            System.out.println("Phone started ringing...");
            Thread.sleep(20000);
        }catch(InterruptedException e)
        {}
        System.out.println("Answering the phone...");
        phone.answer();
    }
}
```

Let me make a few comments about the PhoneRinger and Phone classes:

- The PhoneRinger class is a TimerTask that keeps track of the number of rings and displays a simple message in the run() method.

- The Phone class instantiates a daemon Timer, so that the Timer will not keep the application running.

- Each time the startRinging() method is invoked to simulate a new incoming phone call, a new PhoneRinger object is instantiated. You cannot reuse a previous PhoneRinger object because a task cannot be rescheduled.

- The task is scheduled at a fixed rate, with 0 delay (it starts immediately) and a 3-second period.

- When the Phone is answered, the task is canceled (but not the timer). This means that the task will not execute again, which in our example means that the phone will not ring again.

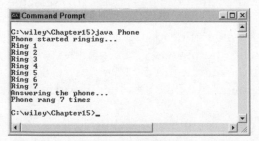

Figure 15.7 Output of the Phone program.

A Timer object is used to create threads that execute on a schedule. Note that the Timer object itself runs in a background thread that executes all the tasks of the timer. This Timer thread sequentially invokes the scheduled tasks at their appropriate time, so a task should not take too long to execute. If it does, other scheduled tasks may be bunching up waiting for their turn to be scheduled. Therefore, if you have a task that could possibly take a long time to execute, this task should use its own Timer object.

The thread for a Timer is non-daemon by default. To make a Timer thread a daemon thread, you must use the following Timer constructor:

```
public Timer(boolean isDaemon)
```

A Timer thread marked as daemon will not keep the application alive, which is useful for timers that schedule maintenance tasks such as garbage collection.

A Timer thread can be stopped by invoking the cancel() method of the Timer class. The cancel() method cancels any scheduled tasks. The currently running task will complete, but no other tasks can be scheduled on the timer.

Multithreading Issues

I have discussed three ways to create a thread, and at this point in the book, I need to point out that I have shown you just enough about threads to be dangerous! Creating and starting a thread is the easy part. The hard part is making sure that your threads behave in a manner that maintains the integrity of your program and the data involved. Keep in mind that the threads in a program are in the same process memory, and therefore have access to the same memory.

Because you do not have control over when a thread is scheduled, you never know when the thread will stop running and have to go back in the priority queues. The thread might have been in the middle of a data-sensitive task, and the currently running thread can mess things up while the other thread is waiting to run.

It is not difficult to come up with an example to demonstrate how two threads can make the data in a program invalid. Take the following BankAccount class, which represents a simple bank account with a number, balance, and methods for making deposits and withdrawals:

```
public class BankAccount
{
     private double balance;
     private int number;
     public BankAccount(double initialBalance)
     {
          balance = initialBalance;
     }
     public int getNumber()
     {
          return number;
     }
     public double getBalance()
     {
          return balance;
     }
     public void deposit(double amount)
     {
          double prevBalance = balance;
          balance = prevBalance + amount;
     }
     public void withdraw(double amount)
     {
          double prevBalance = balance;
          balance = prevBalance - amount;
     }
}
```

The BankAccount class seems simple enough, but I am obviously setting you up here. Check out the following BankTeller class that makes a $100 deposit on a BankAccount object:

```
public class BankTeller extends Thread
{
     private BankAccount account;
     public BankTeller(BankAccount a)
     {
          account = a;
     }
     public void run()
     {
          System.out.println(this.getName() + " depositing $100...");
          account.deposit(100.00);
     }
}
```

Again, the BankTeller class seems simple enough. To test out the BankTeller and BankAccount classes, I wrote the following program named Some-thingsWrong that creates a single BankAccount object and two BankTeller threads. Study the program and try to determine the output, which is shown in Figure 15.8.

```java
public class SomethingsWrong
{
    public static void main(String [] args)
    {
        BankAccount account = new BankAccount(101, 1000.00);
        System.out.println("Initial balance: $"
                        + account.getBalance());
        Thread teller1 = new BankTeller(account);
        Thread teller2 = new BankTeller(account);
        teller1.start();
        teller2.start();
        Thread.yield();
        System.out.println("Withdrawing $200...");
        account.withdraw(200);
        System.out.println("\nFinal balance: $"
                        + account.getBalance());
    }
}
```

 I added the call to yield() so that the main() thread would give the two BankTeller threads a chance to execute first, thereby increasing the likelihood that the two deposits occur before the withdrawal. This does not guarantee that the deposits will occur first, and the final balance is still $1000.00 with or without the call to yield() in main().

The output of the SomethingsWrong program seems to be consistent with the logic of the program: The initial balance is $1000, two deposits of $100 are made and a withdrawal of $200 is made, so the final balance should be $1000, which it is.

```
Command Prompt                                              _ □ x
C:\wiley\Chapter15\BankAccount>java SomethingsWrong
Initial balance: $1000.0
Thread-1 depositing $100...
Thread-2 depositing $100...
Withdrawing $200...

Final balance: $1000.0

C:\wiley\Chapter15\BankAccount>_
```

Figure 15.8 The SomethingsWrong program appears to be working fine.

I didn't name the program SomethingsWrong without a reason, though. I claim that this program worked because of sheer luck. The two BankTeller threads have a reference to the same BankAccount object. In other words, these two threads share the same memory. The threads ran quickly enough that they did not ever block in the middle of running. However, if they had blocked for any reason, a different result might have occurred. To test out my theory, I added a call to sleep() in both the deposit() and withdraw() methods of BankAccount, forcing the BankTeller threads to become blocked in the middle of a transaction:

```
public void deposit(double amount)
{
    double prevBalance = balance;
    try
    {
        Thread.sleep(4000);
    }catch(InterruptedException e)
    {}

    balance = prevBalance + amount;
}
public void withdraw(double amount)
{
    double prevBalance = balance;
    try
    {
        Thread.sleep(4000);
    }catch(InterruptedException e)
    {}
    balance = prevBalance - amount;
}
```

Adding the calls to sleep() forces the threads to take turns executing. Running the SomethingsWrong program again generates a different result, as shown in Figure 15.9. Notice that after two $100 deposits, followed by a $200 withdrawal, the balance should be $1000, but for some reason is only $800.

Figure 15.9 The SomethingsWrong program demonstrates a problem with our BankAccount class.

In a real-world environment in which actual money is involved, this result would not be acceptable, especially for the customer who appears to have lost $200. The problem arises because three threads (main() and the two bank tellers) are accessing the same data in memory at the same time. When working with data-sensitive information such as a bank account balance, multiple threads accessing the data should take turns. For example, if a deposit is being made, no other transactions that affect the balance should be allowed until the deposit is finished. You can do this by synchronizing your threads, which I will now discuss.

synchronized Keyword

The BankAccount class from the previous section is clearly not thread-safe. Multiple threads can make deposits and withdrawals that are not successfully implemented. To make the class thread-safe, you can take advantage of the synchronization features built into the Java language.

The synchronized keyword in Java creates a block of code referred to as a *critical section*. Every Java object with a critical section of code gets a lock associated with the object. To enter a critical section, a thread needs to obtain the corresponding object's lock.

To fix the problem with the BankAccount class, we need to create a critical section around the data-sensitive code of the deposit and withdraw methods. When using the synchronized keyword to create this critical section, you specify which lock is being requested by passing in a reference to the object that owns the lock. For example, the following deposit() method synchronizes on this BankAccount object:

```
public void deposit(double amount)
{
    synchronized(this)
    {
        double prevBalance = balance;
        try
        {
            Thread.sleep(4000);
        }catch(InterruptedException e)
        {}
        balance = prevBalance + amount;
    }
}
```

 The synchronized keyword is commonly used within a class to make a class thread-safe. In this situation, the critical section is synchronized on the *this* reference. An alternate way to synchronize on the *this* reference is to declare the entire method as synchronized. For example:

```
public synchronized void withdraw(double amount)
{
     //Method definition
}
```

When the synchronized withdraw() method is invoked, the current thread will attempt to obtain the lock on this object and will release this object when the method is done executing. Synchronizing the entire method is preferred over synchronizing on the *this* reference within the method because it allows the JVM to handle the method call and synchronization more efficiently. Also, it allows users of the class to see from the method signature that this method is synchronized.

That being said, do not arbitrarily synchronize methods unless it is necessary for thread safety, and do not create unnecessary critical sections. If a method is 50 lines of code, and you need to synchronize only three lines of it, do not synchronize the entire method. Hanging on to a lock when it is not needed can have considerable performance side effects, especially if other threads are waiting for the lock.

I created a new class named ThreadSafeBankAccount that contains this deposit() method. In addition, I added the synchronized keyword to the withdraw() method. I also modified the BankTeller class, naming it BankTeller2, so that it makes a $100 deposit on a ThreadSafeBankAccount object. The following SomethingsFixed program is identical to the SomethingsWrong program, except that it uses the ThreadSafeBankAccount and BankTeller2 classes.

```
public class SomethingsFixed
{
     public static void main(String [] args)
     {
          ThreadSafeBankAccount account =
                    new ThreadSafeBankAccount(101, 1000.00);
          System.out.println("Initial balance: $"
                              + account.getBalance());
          Thread teller1 = new BankTeller2(account);
          Thread teller2 = new BankTeller2(account);
          teller1.start();
          teller2.start();
          Thread.yield();
          System.out.println("Withdrawing $200...");
          account.withdraw(200);
          System.out.println("\nFinal balance: $"
                              + account.getBalance());
     }
}
```

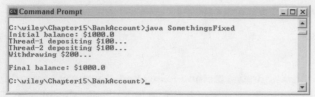

Figure 15.10 The bank account is now thread-safe, and deposits and withdrawals are successful, even in a multithreaded application.

There are two things you will notice about running the SomethingsFixed program: It takes longer to run and it works this time. This is because the deposits and withdrawals are not occurring at the same time as they were in the SomethingsWrong program, but rather they are executing sequentially (one at a time). Figure 15.10 shows the output of the SomethingsFixed program.

Deadlock Issues

Well, if you were dangerous after learning how to create a thread, you are probably just as dangerous now that I have shown you the synchronized keyword. Before synchronizing, our program's data was being corrupted. After synchronizing, our program now becomes susceptible to *deadlock*, which occurs when a thread is waiting for a lock that never becomes available.

There are ways to avoid deadlock, including ordering locks and using the wait() and notify() methods, both of which I will discuss. However, let me show you a simple but realistic example of how deadlock can occur. The following LazyTeller class contains a transfer() method that transfers money from one bank account to another. In order to transfer money, the teller needs the lock on both accounts to ensure that the transaction is successful. Study the transfer() method and see if you can predict where a problem might arise:

```java
public class LazyTeller extends Thread
{
     private ThreadSafeBankAccount source, dest;
     public LazyTeller(ThreadSafeBankAccount a, ThreadSafeBankAccount b)
     {
          source = a;
          dest = b;
     }
     public void run()
     {
          transfer(250.00);
     }
     public void transfer(double amount)
```

```
    {
        System.out.println("Transferring from "
                + source.getNumber() + " to " + dest.getNumber());
        synchronized(source)
        {
            Thread.yield();
            synchronized(dest)
            {
                System.out.println("Withdrawing from "
                                        + source.getNumber());
                source.withdraw(amount);
                System.out.println("Depositing into "
                                        + dest.getNumber());
                dest.deposit(amount);
            }
        }
    }
}
```

It wasn't hard to create deadlock with this class, especially because I had the
LazyTeller thread yield after obtaining its first of two locks. The following
DeadlockDemo program creates two bank accounts, checking and savings.
Then, two LazyTeller objects transfer money between them. Notice that teller1
transfers $250 from checking to savings, whereas teller2 transfers $250 from
savings to checking. Figure 15.11 shows the output of the DeadlockDemo program. Study the output to try to determine how far the program ran before it
locked up.

```
public class DeadlockDemo
{
    public static void main(String [] args)
    {
        System.out.println("Creating two bank accounts...");
        ThreadSafeBankAccount checking =
                new ThreadSafeBankAccount(101, 1000.00);
        ThreadSafeBankAccount savings =
                new ThreadSafeBankAccount(102, 5000.00);
        System.out.println("Creating two teller threads...");
        Thread teller1 = new LazyTeller(checking, savings);
        Thread teller2 = new LazyTeller(savings, checking);

        System.out.println("Starting both threads...");
        teller1.start();
        teller2.start();
    }
}
```

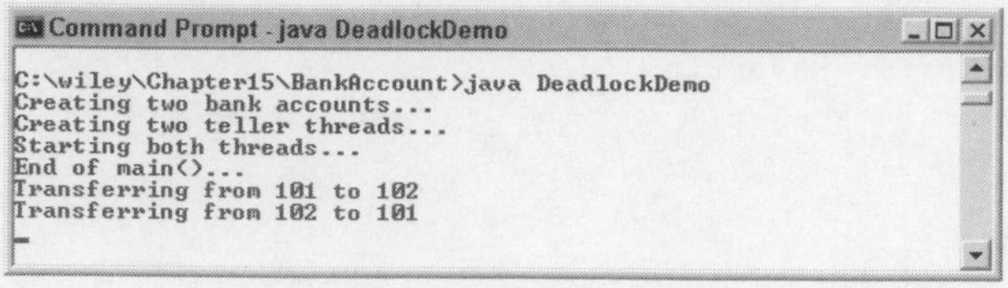

Figure 15.11 The DeadlockDemo program locks up and does not generate any further output than what is shown here.

The problem with the LazyTeller class is that it does not consider the possibility of a race condition, a common occurrence in multithreaded programming. After the two threads are started, teller1 grabs the checking lock and teller2 grabs the savings lock. When teller1 tries to obtain the savings lock, it is not available. Therefore, teller1 blocks until the savings lock becomes available. When the teller1 thread blocks, *teller1 still has the checking lock and does not let it go*. Similarly, teller2 is waiting for the checking lock, so *teller2 blocks but does not let go of the savings lock*. This leads to one result: deadlock! The two threads are now blocked forever, and the only way to end this application is to terminate the JVM.

There is a solution to this problem with the race condition. Whenever a thread needs more than one lock, the thread should be careful not to simply randomly grab the locks. Instead, all threads involved need to agree on a specified order in which to to obtain the locks so that deadlock can be avoided. Let me show how this is done.

Ordering Locks

A common threading trick to avoid the deadlock of the LazyTeller threads is to order the locks. By ordering the locks, it gives threads a specific order to obtain multiple locks. For example, when transferring money, instead of a bank teller obtaining the lock of the source account first, the teller could grab the account with the smaller number first (assuming that each bank account has a unique number). This ensures that whoever wins the race condition (whichever teller obtains the lower account number first), that thread can continue and obtain further locks, whereas other threads block without taking locks with them.

The following transfer() method, in a class named OrderedTeller, is a modification of the LazyTeller class. Instead of arbitrarily synchronizing on locks, this transfer() method obtains locks in a specified order based on the number of the bank account.

```
public class OrderedTeller extends Thread
{
    private ThreadSafeBankAccount source, dest;
    public OrderedTeller(ThreadSafeBankAccount a,
```

```
                              ThreadSafeBankAccount b)
        {
            source = a;
            dest = b;
        }

        public void run()
        {
            transfer(250.00);
        }

        public void transfer(double amount)
        {
            System.out.println("Transferring from " + source.getNumber()
                            + " to " + dest.getNumber());

            ThreadSafeBankAccount first, second;
            if(source.getNumber() < dest.getNumber())
            {
                first = source;
                second = dest;
            }
            else
            {
                first = dest;
                second = source;
            }

            synchronized(first)
            {
                Thread.yield();
                synchronized(second)
                {
                    System.out.println("Withdrawing from "
                                            + source.getNumber());
                    source.withdraw(amount);
                    System.out.println("Depositing into "
                                            + dest.getNumber());
                    dest.deposit(amount);
                }
            }
        }
    }
```

Notice in this transfer() method that the code within the critical section did not change from the LazyTeller class. The difference is in the order the locks are synchronized. I modified the DeadlockDemo program (in a class named DeadlockFixedDemo) to use the OrderedTeller instead of the LazyTeller. Figure 15.12 shows the output. The program runs successfully, does not deadlock, and the data in the account is correct.

Figure 15.12   After ordering the locks, deadlock does not occur.

wait() and notify() Methods

The java.lang.Object class (the parent of every Java object) contains wait() and notify() methods that allow threads to communicate with each other. These methods are typically used in a producer/consumer model, in which one thread is producing and another thread is consuming. If the producer is producing faster than the consumer is consuming, the producer can wait for the consumer. The consumer can notify the producer to inform the producer to stop waiting.

Similarly, the consumer may be consuming faster than the producer is producing, in which case the consumer can wait until the producer notifies it to continue consuming.

The producer/consumer model is a common occurrence in thread programming, and in this section I will show you how to implement this in Java using the following methods in the Object class:

public final void wait(long timeout).   Causes the current thread to wait on this Object. The thread continues when another thread invokes notify() or notifyAll() on this same Object, or when the specified timeout number of milliseconds elapses. The current thread must own the Object's lock, and it will release the lock when this method is invoked.

public final void wait(long timeout, int nanos).   Similar to the previous wait() method, except that the timeout is denoted in milliseconds and nanoseconds.

public final void wait().   Causes the current thread to wait indefinitely on this Object for a notify() or notifyAll().

public final void notify().   Wakes up one thread that is waiting on this Object. The current thread must own the object's lock to invoke this method.

public final void notifyAll(). Similar to notify(), except that all waiting threads are awoken instead of just one.

 An object's lock is often referred to as its *monitor*. The term monitor refers to that portion of the object responsible for monitoring the behavior of the wait() and notify() methods of the object. To invoke any of the wait() or notify() methods, the current thread must own the monitor (lock) of the Object, meaning that calls to wait() and notify() always appear in a critical section, synchronized on the Object.

The following example demonstrates a producer/consumer model that uses wait() and notify(). The producer is a pizza chef, and the consumer is a lunch crowd at a buffet. The following Buffet class represents the object that will be used as the monitor:

```
public class Buffet
{
    boolean empty;
    public synchronized boolean isEmpty()
    {
        return empty;
    }
    public synchronized void setEmpty(boolean b)
    {
        empty = b;
    }
}
```

The following PizzaChef class is a thread that contains a reference to a Buffet object. If the buffet is not empty, the chef waits for a notify() to occur on the Buffet object. If the buffet is empty, the chef cooks pizza for a random amount of time. If the cooking time is long enough, the buffet is no longer empty and the thread invokes notify() on the Buffet object.

```
public class PizzaChef extends Thread
{
    private Buffet buffet;

    public PizzaChef(Buffet b)
    {
        buffet = b;
    }

    public void run()
    {
```

```
        int cookingTime = 0;
        while(true)
        {
            synchronized(buffet)
            {
                while(!buffet.isEmpty())
                {
                    try
                    {
                        System.out.println("Chef is waiting...");
                        buffet.wait();
                    }catch(InterruptedException e)
                    {}
                }
            }

            //Bake some pizzas
            try
            {
                System.out.println("Chef is cooking...");
                cookingTime = (int) (Math.random()*3000);
                Thread.sleep(cookingTime);
            }catch(InterruptedException e)
            {}

            if(cookingTime < 1500)
            {
                buffet.setEmpty(true);
            }
            else
            {
                buffet.setEmpty(false);
                synchronized(buffet)
                {
                    buffet.notify();
                }
            }
        }
    }
}
```

The following LunchCrowd class is the consumer of the Buffet object. If the buffet is empty, the lunch crowd waits for the chef to cook some pizzas and invoke notify(). If the buffet is not empty, the lunch crowd eats for a random amount of time. If enough pizza is eaten to empty the buffet, the chef is notified.

```java
public class LunchCrowd extends Thread
{
    private Buffet buffet;

    public LunchCrowd(Buffet b)
    {
        buffet = b;
    }

    public void run()
    {
        int eatingTime = 0;
        while(true)
        {
            synchronized(buffet)
            {
                while(buffet.isEmpty())
                {
                    try
                    {
                        System.out.println("Lunch crowd is
                        waiting...");
                        buffet.wait();
                    }catch(InterruptedException e)
                    {}
                }
            }

            //Eat some pizzas.
            try
            {
                System.out.println("Lunch crowd is eating...");
                eatingTime = (int) (Math.random()*3000);
                Thread.sleep(eatingTime);
            }catch(InterruptedException e)
            {}

            if(eatingTime < 1500)
            {
                buffet.setEmpty(false);
            }
            else
            {
                buffet.setEmpty(true);
                synchronized(buffet)
                {
```

```
                                   buffet.notify();
                    }
                }
            }
        }
    }
```

The following ProduceConsumeDemo program instantiates a producer and consumer thread and starts them. Figure 15.13 shows a sample output.

```java
public class ProduceConsumeDemo
{
    public static void main(String [] args)
    {
        Buffet buffet = new Buffet();

        PizzaChef producer = new PizzaChef(buffet);
        LunchCrowd consumer = new LunchCrowd(buffet);

        producer.start();
        consumer.start();
    }
}
```

Figure 15.13 Producer and consumer threads communicate with each other using the wait() and notify() methods.

♦ Waiting for a Notify

When a thread invokes wait() on an object, the following sequence of events occurs before the thread runs again. Suppose that there are two threads, A and B:

1. Thread A invokes wait() on an object and gives up the lock on the object. Thread A is now blocked.

2. Thread B grabs the lock and invokes notify() on the object.

3. Thread A wakes up, but the lock is not available because Thread B has it. Therefore, Thread A is now waiting for the lock. In other words, Thread A just went from one blocked state to another. Before, Thread A was waiting for a notify(). Now, it is waiting for a lock to become available.

4. Thread B releases the lock (hopefully), and Thread A becomes runnable.

5. Before running again, Thread A must obtain the lock on the object.

Because multiple threads may be waiting and awoken at the same time, it is important for a waiting thread to make sure that they should have been woken up. The PizzaChef does this using a while loop:

```
synchronized(buffet)
{
    while(!buffet.isEmpty())
    {
        try
        {
            System.out.println("Chef is waiting...");
            buffet.wait();
        }catch(InterruptedException e)
        {}
    }
}
```

When the PizzaChef thread receives a notify, it checks to make sure that the buffet is actually empty. Why bother if it just received a notify? Well, suppose that by the time this thread has a chance to run again, a second PizzaChef thread has already filled the buffet with pizzas. If our first thread did not check that the buffet was empty, it would have filled the buffet as well, causing overproduction, which is what we are trying to avoid in the first place.

Placing a call to wait() in a while loop is a standard design when working with producer and consumer threads.

Lab 15.1: Creating a Thread

To become familiar with creating a thread by implementing the Runnable interface.

1. Write a class named PrintNumbers that implements the Runnable interface. Add a field of type boolean called keepGoing and a constructor that initializes keepGoing to true.

2. Add a method to the PrintNumbers class called stopPrinting() that assigns the keepGoing field to false.

3. Within the run() method, write a while loop using System.out.printl(), which prints out the numbers 1, 2, 3, 4, and so on for as long as the keepGoing field is true. In between printing each number, the thread should sleep for 1 second.

4. Save and compile the PrintNumbers class.

5. Write a class named Print that contains main(). Within main(), instantiate a PrintNumbers object. Instantiate a Thead object that will be used to run the PrintNumbers object in a separate thread and then start the thread.

6. The Print program will take in a single command-line argument to represent the number of milliseconds that the main() thread will sleep. Parse this argument into an int and then have the main() thread sleep for that amount of milliseconds.

7. When the main() thread wakes up, have it invoke the stopPrinting() method on the PrintNumbers object.

8. Save, compile, and run the Print program. Don't forget to pass in an int to represent how long the program will run in milliseconds.

The numbers 1, 2, 3, and so on will be printed for approximately the number of seconds you specified with the command-line argument. For example, if the command-line argument is 10,000, you should see about 10 numbers printed. This lab demonstrates a common need in thread programming: creating a mechanism for a thread to stop executing. The stopPrinting() method can be invoked from any other thread to inform PrintNumbers that it should stop running.

Lab 15.2: Simulating a Car Race

To become familiar with writing a thread by extending the Thread class.

1. Write a class named RaceCar that extends the Thread class and contains the run() method.

2. Add an int field named finish and a String field called name. Add a constructor that initializes both fields.

3. Within run(), add a *for* loop that executes *finish* number of times. Within the *for* loop, use System.out.println() to print out the *name* field and also the current iteration through the loop. For example, the third time through the loop should output "Mario: 3" for a car named Mario. Then, have the thread sleep for a random amount of time between 0 and 5 seconds.

4. At the end of the *for* loop, print out a message stating that the race car has finished the race, and print out the *name* field as well. For example, "Mario finished!"

5. Save and compile the RaceCar class.

6. Write a class named Race that contains main().

7. Within main(), declare and create an array large enough to hold five Thread references.

8. Write a *for* loop that fills the array with five RaceCar objects. The names should be retrieved from five command-line arguments, and the int should be the same for each RaceCar. This value will represent how long the race will last, and it should also be input from the command line.

9. Write a second *for* loop that invokes start() on each Thread in the array.

10. Save, compile, and run the Race program.

The Race program will look like a car race that slowly progresses as you watch it. The winner will be whichever RaceCar thread reaches the finish line first.

Lab 15.3: Using Timer and TimerTask

To become familiar with using the Timer and TimerTask class.

1. Write a class named Reminder that extends TimerTask. Add a field of type String named message, and a constructor that initializes this field.

2. Within the run() method, simply print out the message field using System.out.println().

3. Write a class named TestReminder that contains main().

4. Within main(), instantiate a new Timer object.

5. Within main(), instantiate three Reminder objects, each with a different message.

6. Using the schedule() method of the Timer class that creates a single execution task, schedule your three Reminder objects with the Timer. Have the first Reminder scheduled immediately, the second reminder after 30 seconds, and the third reminder after 2 minutes.

7. Save, compile, and run the TestReminder program.

   The three reminders should be displayed at the command prompt. You should have to wait 2 minutes before seeing the final reminder.

Lab 15.4: An Applet Game

This lab ties together many of the aspects of Java that you have learned up until now. I won't give you much help here, except to explain the applet that I want you to write, which is a game that tests a user's skill and quickness with the mouse. I want you to write a game that displays a small image moving across the screen. The player of the game scores points by clicking on the image. Here are some of the expectations for the game.

1. The game should be an applet so that it can be embedded in a Web page.

2. Use JApplet for your applet and Swing components for any GUI components you use.

3. To create the image that moves across the screen, you can create a bitmap image using a program such as Microsoft Paint. Alternately, an easier way is to use one of the drawing methods of the java.awt.Graphics class. Check the documentation for the Graphics class and browse through the methods. For example, the fillOval() method can be used to draw a circle, or the fillRect() method draws a rectangle. (Hint: A rectangle can simplify your math considerably when you try to determine whether the user clicked on the image or not.)

4. Write a thread that contains a reference to the content pane of the JApplet. The thread should draw the image on the screen, sleep for a specified amount of time, and then redraw the image somewhere else on the screen. You can also display the image in different sizes to make the game more challenging.

5. Provide a JTextField that displays the sleep time of the thread. The users should be able to change this value, depending on how fast they think they are. Add the corresponding event handling that changes the sleep time in the thread class.

6. Add a JLabel that displays the score. You can score the game however you like. A simple scoring might be 10 points for hitting the object, or perhaps you can offer more points for hitting the object quickly or for hitting the object when it is smaller.

7. You will need a MouseListener to handle the mouseClicked() event. This class will need to determine whether the object was hit, and if so, how many points to award.

8. Write an HTML page that embeds your JApplet. This program will probably require lots of testing, so the appletviewer might come in handy.

You should be able to embed your applet in a Web page and play the game.

Summary

- A thread is a path of execution that executes within a process. When you run a Java program, the main() method runs in a thread. The main() method can start other threads.

- A process terminates when all its non-daemon threads run to completion.

- A thread is created by writing a class that implements java.lang.Runnable and associating an instance of this class with a new java.lang.Thread object. The new Thread is initially in the born state.

- Invoking the start() method on a Thread object starts the thread and places it in its appropriate runnable queue, based on its priority.

- Java uses a preemptive scheduling mechanism where threads of higher priority preempt running threads of a lower priority. However, the actual behavior of threads also relies on the underlying platform.

- A thread can also be written by writing a class that extends java.util.TimerTask and associating an instance of this class with a java.util.Timer object. This type of thread is useful when performing scheduled tasks.

- The synchronized keyword is used to synchronize a thread on a particular object. When a thread is synchronized on an object, the thread owns the lock of the object. Any other thread attempting to synchronize on this object will become blocked until the object's lock becomes available again.

- Care needs to be taken when synchronizing threads, since deadlock may occur. Ordering locks is a common technique for avoiding deadlock.

- The wait() and notify() methods from the Object class are useful when multiple threads need to access the same data in any type of producer/consumer scenario.

Review Questions

1. Name the one method in the java.lang.Runnable interface.

2. True or False: A process that has no threads running in it will terminate.

3. True or False: If the only threads left in a process are daemon threads, the process will terminate.

4. Which one of the following statements is not true?

   a. The maximum priority of a Java thread is the value Thread.MAX_PRIORITY.

   b. If a thread of priority 5 is running and a priority 8 thread becomes runnable, it will preempt the priority 5 thread.

   c. Because Java programs run on a JVM, the behavior of the underlying platform does not affect your Java threads.

   d. By default, a new thread inherits the priority of the thread that started it.

5. True or False: A born thread does not run until the start() method is invoked.

6. True or False: The number of threads currently running depends on how many threads are waiting in the runnable priority queues.

7. List three different ways to create a thread in Java.

8. Suppose that threads A and B are the only two threads in a process, and A has priority 5 and B priority 10. Which of the following statements is (are) guaranteed to be true? Select all that apply.

   a. Thread B will run to completion before A gets a chance to execute.

   b. If thread B invokes yield(), thread A will be scheduled to run.

   c. If thread B invokes sleep(), thread A will be scheduled to run.

   d. If the underlying platform uses time slicing, threads A and B will receive equal time on the CPU.

   e. Deadlock cannot occur because B has a higher priority.

   f. If B calls join() on A, B will block until A runs to completion.

9. Suppose that a task is scheduled using the following statement:

   ```
   someTimer.schedule(someTask, 0, 10000);
   ```

   Which of the following statements is (are) true? Select all that apply.

   a. The task will be scheduled immediately.

   b. The task will be scheduled in exactly 10 seconds.

   c. The task will be scheduled 10 seconds after its first completion.

   d. The task will execute once, in 10 seconds.

   e. The task will execute exactly 10,000 times.

10. Suppose that a task is scheduled using the following statement:

    ```
    someTimer.scheduleAtFixedRate(someTask, 0, 60000);
    ```

    Which of the following statements is true? Select all that apply.

    a. The task will be scheduled immediately.

    b. The task will be scheduled 60 seconds after its first completion.

    c. The task will be scheduled every 60 seconds, no matter how long the task takes to execute.

    d. If the timer is canceled, the task will not be scheduled again.

    e. If the task is canceled, the task will not be scheduled again.

11. True or False: Declaring a method as synchronized causes the method to run in its own thread.

12. True or False: A synchronized method synchronizes on the this reference of the object.

13. True or False: When a thread that invoked wait() receives a notify(), it still is blocked waiting for the lock to become available.

14. True or False: The notify() method wakes up only one waiting thread.

15. True or False: When a thread invokes the wait() method, the thread releases the corresponding object's lock.

Answers to Review Questions

1. public void run()

2. True. A process cannot exist without at least one non-daemon thread.

3. True. That is the definition of a daemon thread, that it does not keep the process alive.

4. c is not correct. The underlying platform plays a large role in the way your threads will actually behave at run time. Running a multithreaded application on different platforms can have quite different results.

5. True. Threads do not run until the start() method of the Thread class is invoked.

6. False. The number of threads running depends on the number of CPUs available.

7. You can do the following: (1) write a class that implements Runnable and wrap it in a Thread object, (2) write a class that extends Thread, or (3) extend TimerTask and schedule it with a Timer object.

8. a is not true because many platforms give lower-priority threads a chance to run to avoid higher-priority threads hogging the CPU. b is not true because B will yield only to threads of priority 10. c is true because calling sleep() causes B to block, which makes A the only runnable thread, meaning that A will get scheduled. d is false because time slicing does not affect priority. e is false because deadlock has nothing to do with priorities. f is true because that is how the join() method works.

9. a is true because the delay is 0. b is false because this is fixed-delay scheduling. Instead, c is true. d is false because this task has a period of 10 seconds. e is false.

10. a is true because the delay is 0. b is false because this is fixed-rate scheduling. Instead, c is true. Both d and e are true.

11. False. The statement basically makes no sense.

12. True. That is the effect of the synchronized keyword on methods.

13. True.

14. True. To wake up all waiting threads, use notifyAll() instead of notify().

15. True. Otherwise, another thread would be unable to invoke notify(). Recall that a thread must own the object's lock to invoke wait() or notify() on the object.

CHAPTER 16

Input and Output

The java.io package contains nearly every class you might ever need to perform input and output (I/O) in Java. In this chapter, I will discuss how the java.io classes are used, including an overview of the java.io package, streams versus readers and writers, low-level and high-level streams, chaining streams, serialization, and logging.

An Overview of the java.io Package

The java.io package contains dozens of classes and interfaces for performing input and output. At first, the java.io package might seem intimidating, but after you understand the various categories of streams, you will be able to quickly find the classes you need to perform any I/O.

Almost all of the classes in the java.io package fit into one of the following two categories:

Streams. The stream classes are for performing I/O on bytes of data.

Readers and Writers. The reader and writer classes are for performing I/O on characters.

The stream classes are child classes of java.io.OutputStream and java.io.InputStream. The reader classes are child classes of java.io.Reader, and the writer classes are child classes of java.io.Writer. These four classes are abstract and represent the common functionality among their child classes.

The Output Streams

The OutputStream class is the parent class of all the output streams. It contains five methods:

public void close().   Closes the output stream.

public void flush().   Flushes any buffers.

public void write(int b).   Writes a single byte.

public void write(byte [] b).   Writes an array of bytes.

public void write(byte [] b, int offset, int length).   Writes length number of elements in the array starting at the index specified by offset.

The methods of the java.io.OutputStream class are not very exciting. They only write a byte or an array of bytes. Writing bytes to an output stream is important functionality, but what if the data you are sending comprises more complex data such as ints, doubles, booleans, Strings, and objects? It would be a lot of work to write the code behind the scenes that parses the bytes into their appropriate data types. Thankfully, there are many child classes of OutputStream that will do this type of work for you.

In fact, you will probably never need to write a class that performs low-level I/O because there is likely a class in the java.io package that already provides what you need. The trick is learning what each class does and how to combine them to create the perfect stream for your needs (my main objective in this chapter).

Each child class of OutputStream implements the write() methods inherited from OutputStream in their own unique way. For example, the FileOutput-Stream class writes the bytes to a file, and the BufferedOutputStream writes the bytes to a buffer. The filtered output stream classes (those that subclass FilterOutputStream) contain additional write() methods for writing different data types or objects. For example, the DataOutputStream class contains methods for writing ints, shorts, doubles, Strings, and so on.

The Input Stream Classes

For each output stream class, there is a corresponding input stream class for reading in the data. The abstract InputStream class is the parent class of all the input streams, and it contains read() methods that correspond to the write() methods of the OutputStream class. It also contains several other methods, including:

public int read().   Reads a single byte from the stream.

public int read(byte [] b).   Reads in a collection of bytes and places them in the given array. The return value is the actual number of bytes read.

public int read(byte [] b, int offset, int length).   Reads a collection of bytes into the specified location of the array.

public void close().   Closes the stream.

public long skip(long n).   Skips the next *n* bytes in the stream.

public void mark(int readLimit).   Marks the current location of the stream. This method is used in conjunction with the reset() method on streams that allow support for pushback. After readLimit number of bytes are read, the marked location becomes invalid.

public void reset().   Resets the position of the stream to the location of the most recent mark() call, assuming that the marked location is still valid.

public int available().   Returns the number of bytes that can be read from the input stream without blocking.

 A stream (or reader/writer) is opened automatically when the object is instantiated. You can close a stream by using the close() method. This is a good programming design, but not mandatory. The garbage collector implicitly closes a stream before the corresponding stream object is garbage collected.

The Writer Class

The Writer class is the parent of all the writer classes in the java.io package. A writer is used for outputting data that is represented as characters. The Writer class contains the flush() and close() methods, which are similar to the ones in OutputStream. It also contains five write() methods:

public void write(int c).   Writes a single character to the stream.

public void write(char [] c).   Writes the array of characters to the stream.

public void write(char [] c,int offset, int length).   Writes length number of characters in the array starting at the index specified by offset.

public void write(String s).   Writes the given String to the stream.

public void write(String s, int offset, int length).   Writes the specified subset of the given String to the stream.

The child classes of Writer implement the write() methods in their own unique ways. For example, the PipedWriter class writes the characters to a pipe (a stream between two threads), and the OutputStreamWriter class converts the writer into an output stream, converting the characters into bytes.

The Reader Class

The Reader class is the parent of all the reader classes in the java.io package. The Reader class has a close() and skip() method similar to the ones in InputStream. It also contains read() methods that correspond to the write() methods in Writer:

public int read().   Reads a single character from the stream.

public int read(char [] c).   Reads in a collection of characters and places them in the given array. The return value is the actual number of characters read.

public int read(char [] c, int offset, int length).   Reads in a collection of characters and places them into the specified portion of the array.

For each Writer class, there is a corresponding Reader class.

♦ The java.io.File class

The java.io.File class is a utility class for working with files and directories. It is not a stream class and cannot be used for performing any I/O. However, it is widely used by the other classes in the java.io package.

Think of a File object as a String representing the name and location of a file or directory. The File class has four constructors:

public File(String pathname).   Creates a File object associated with the file or directory specified by pathname.

public File(String parent, String child).   Creates a File object using the given parameters. The parent parameter represents a directory, and the child parameter represents a subdirectory or file located within parent.

public File(File parent, String child).   Similar to the previous constructor, except that the directory is denoted by a File object instead of a String.

public File(URI uri).   Creates a File object using the given java.net.URI object. A URI is a uniform resource identifier. A file URI is of the format file:///*directory/filename*.

Keep in mind that a File object is similar to a String and only represents the path name of a file or directory. The constructors are successful even if the given file or directory does not exist. For example, the following statement is successful, whether or not somefile.txt is an actual file:

```
File f = new File("somefile.txt");
```

However, you now have a File object associated with a file named somefile.txt, and the File class contains many useful methods for determining information about this file. For example, you can check to see if it exists using the exists() method:

```
if(f.exists())
{
    //Use the file now that we know it exists
}
```

Other methods in the File class include:

public String getName(). Returns the name of the file or directory.

public String getParent(). Returns the pathname of the parent directory of this file or directory.

public String getPath(). Returns the File object as its String representation.

public boolean canRead(). Returns true if the File object is a file that can be read from. There is also a corresponding canWrite() method.

public boolean isDirectory(). Returns true if the File object is a directory.

public boolean isFile(). Returns true if the File object is a file.

public boolean delete(). Deletes the file or directory, and returns true if successful.

public String [] list(). Returns a list of all the filenames in the directory.

To demonstrate the File class, the following FileDemo program creates a File object and uses the methods of the File class to determine information about the file or directory. Study the program and see if you can determine what it does.

```
import java.io.File;
public class FileDemo
{
    public static void main(String [] args)
    {
        File file = new File(args[0]);

        if(!file.exists())
        {
            System.out.println(args[0]
                    + " does not exist.");
            return;
        }

        if(file.isFile() && file.canRead())
```

continued

◆ The java.io.File class *(continued)*

```
            {
                    System.out.println(file.getName()
    + " can be read from.");
            }


            if(file.isDirectory())
            {
                    System.out.println(file.getPath()
    + " is a directory containing...");
                    String [] files = file.list();
                    for(int i = 0; i < files.length; i++)
                    {
                            System.out.println(files[i]);
                    }
            }
        }
    }
}
```

Figure 16.1 shows a sample output of running the FileDemo program when an actual file is used as the command-line argument. Figure 16.2 shows the output when the command-line argument is a valid directory.

Figure 16.1   The command-line argument is a file that exists.

Figure 16.2   The FileDemo program lists the contents of the given directory.

Notice the File class used throughout the java.io package, typically as a parameter or return value type. It is a good programming design to use File objects instead of Strings to represent files. This allows you to perform certain checks on the files, similar to those done in the FileDemo program, before using the File for I/O operations. Be sure to check the documentation of the File class for a complete list of the methods in the class.

Low-Level and High-Level Streams

In the previous section, I discussed the difference between streams and readers and writers. I will now discuss the details of using the various stream and reader/writer classes. I am going to begin with input and output streams, which can be separated into two categories:

Low-level streams.   An input or output stream that connects directly to a data source, such as a file or socket.

High-level streams.   An input or output stream that reads or writes to another input or output stream.

You can tell which streams are low-level and which streams are high-level by looking at their constructors. The low-level streams take in actual data sources in their constructors, while the high-level streams take in other streams. For example, FileOutputStream is a low-level stream, and each of its constructors takes in a variation of a filename. The DataOutputStream is a high-level stream, and it only has one constructor, which takes in an existing output stream:

```
public DataOutputStream(OutputStream out)
```

In other words, the only way to create a FileOutputStream is to provide a filename, while the only way to create a DataOutputStream is to have an existing OutputStream already.

Low-Level Streams

The following is a list of the low-level input and output streams in the java.io package and their corresponding data source:

FileInputStream and FileOutputStream.   For writing and reading binary data from a file.

ByteArrayInputStream and ByteArrayOutputStream.   For writing and reading data from an array of bytes.

PipedInputStream and PipedOutputStream.   For writing and reading data between two threads.

InputStream and OutputStream.   The abstract parent classes are often used for physical connections to data sources (other than files, which use the FileInputStream and FileOutputStream classes). For example, a socket connection uses these classes to represent the input and output streams of the socket.

Let's look at an example. The following EchoFile program uses the FileInputStream class to read the elements from a file and print them out to the console output. Study the program and try to determine its output, which is shown in Figure 16.3.

```java
import java.io.*;
public class EchoFile
{
    public static void main(String [] args)
    {
        File file = new File(args[0]);

        if(!file.exists())
        {
            System.out.println(args[0] + " does not exist.");
            return;
        }

        if(!(file.isFile() && file.canRead()))
        {
            System.out.println(file.getName()
                                    + " cannot be read from.");
            return;
        }

        try
        {
            FileInputStream fis = new FileInputStream(file);
            char current;
            while(fis.available() > 0)
            {
                current = (char) fis.read();
                System.out.print(current);
            }
        }catch(IOException e)
        {
            e.printStackTrace();
        }
    }
}
```

```
Command Prompt                                    _ □ ×
C:\wiley\Chapter16>java EchoFile scores.html
<html>
        <body>
        <table border="1">
                <tr>
                        <td>Home:</td>
                        <td>Denver Broncos</td>
                        <td>34</td>
                </tr>
                <tr>
                        <td>Visitor:</td>
                        <td>Oakland Raiders</td>
                        <td>27</td>
                </tr>
        </table>
        </body>
</html>

C:\wiley\Chapter16>
```

Figure 16.3   A sample output of the EchoFile program.

 The purpose of a low-level stream is to communicate with a specific data source. The low-level streams only read in data at the byte level. In other words, the low-level streams do not provide extra functionality for performing advanced reading or writing of primitive data types or object types. This is done using a high-level stream, chaining the low-level stream to one or more high-level streams.

High-Level Streams

The following is a list of the high-level input and output streams in the java.io package, as well as a few others in the J2SE:

BufferedInputStream and BufferedOutputStream.   This is used for buffering input and output.

DataInputStream and DataOutputStream.   This is a filter for writing and reading primitive data types and Strings.

ObjectInputStream and ObjectOutputStream.   This is used for serialization and deserialization of Java objects.

PushbackInputStream.   This represents a stream that allows data to be read from the stream, then pushed back into the stream if necessary.

AudioInputStream.   This is used for reading audio from an input stream. This class is in the javax.sound.sampled package.

CheckedInputStream and CheckedOutputStream.   This is used for filtering data using a checksum that can be used to verify the data. These classes are found in the java.util.zip package.

CypherInputStream and CypherOutputStream.   This is used for working with encrypted data. These classes are found in the javax.crypto package.

ZipInputStream and ZipOutputStream.   This is used for working with ZIP files. These classes are found in the java.util.zip package.

JarInputStream and JarOutputStream.   This is used for reading and writing to JAR files. These classes are found in the java.util.jar package.

ProgressMonitorInputStream.   This monitors the progress of an input stream, and displays a dialog window to the user if the input is taking too long, allowing the user to cancel the input stream. This class is in the javax.swing package.

 The J2SE contains an API known as the Image I/O API for reading and writing images. The classes and interfaces of the Image I/O API are found in the javax.imageio packages. If you are working with images, be sure to check the documentation for a description of the various streams available in this API.

Classroom Q & A

Q: Why make the distinction between low-level and high-level streams? Why not just use the stream you want?

A: Because you often need to use both a low-level stream and one or more high-level streams. The high-level streams perform the type of I/O that you typically need done in an application, similarly to reading and writing primitive data types or objects, while the low-level stream communicates the actual source of the data, similarly to the file or network socket.

Q: But if I want to read from a file, don't I need to use the low-level FileInputStream class?

A: Yes, if the data in the file is to be read in as bytes. (If it contains character data, you would likely use the FileReader class.)

Q: But the FileInputStream class only reads in data as bytes, so can I only read in bytes at a time?

A: No, you can take the FileInputStream and chain it to a high-level filter like the DataInputStream, which converts the bytes into primitive data types.

Q: Why not just start with a DataInputStream?

A: You can't. A DataInputStream cannot attach to a file or any other physical resource. The high-level streams are not instantiated on their own. They require the existence of either a low-level stream or some other existing high-level stream.

Q: You mentioned the BufferedInputStream class that buffers the data. What if I want to buffer the data read from the file?

A: That's a good idea. Reading one byte at a time from a file is terribly inefficient, so I recommend buffering any time you can. You can attach the high-level BufferedInputStream class to the FileInputStream object, and the data will be buffered automatically.

Q: OK, but I want to read the data from the file using the buffer *and* filter it using the DataInputStream class.

A: Then you use all three classes—one low-level stream and two high-level streams. You start with a FileInputStream object that reads from the file. Chain to that a BufferedInputStream object that buffers the file input, and then chain to the buffer a DataInputStream object that filters the data into primitive data types. That's how the java.io classes are chained together to create the exact type of input you want. Let me show you an example of chaining streams.

Chaining Streams Together

The following ChainDemo example demonstrates the DataOutputStream class, which contains methods such as:

- public void writeDouble(double d)
- public void writeFloat(float f)
- public void writeInt(int x)
- public void writeLong(long x)
- public void writeShort(short s)
- public void writeUTF(String s)

There are similar methods for writing bytes, chars, and booleans. Similarly, the DataInputStream contains corresponding read() methods for reading in these data types. In addition, the ChainDemo program buffers the output to improve efficiency using the BufferedOutputStream class. The BufferedOutputStream class has two constructors:

public BufferedOutputStream(OutputStream source).   Buffers the output to the specified stream using a 512-byte buffer.

public BufferedOutputStream(OutputStream source, int size).   Buffers the output to the specified stream using a buffer of the specified size.

The constructors in the high-level stream classes take in other streams. I can tell that BufferedOutputStream is a high-level stream because both of its constructors take in an object of type OutputStream. Checking the constructor's parameters is the simplest way to determine if a stream is high level or low level. I can tell that FileOutputStream is a low-level stream because the parameters of its constructors are types like String and File.

Study the following ChainDemo program and try to determine what the program is doing.

```java
import java.io.*;

public class ChainDemo
{
    public static void main(String [] args)
    {
        try
        {
            FileOutputStream fileOut =
                    new FileOutputStream("data.txt");
            BufferedOutputStream buffer =
                    new BufferedOutputStream(fileOut);
            DataOutputStream dataOut =
                    new DataOutputStream(buffer);

            dataOut.writeUTF("Hello!");
            dataOut.writeInt(4);
            dataOut.writeDouble(100.0);
            dataOut.writeDouble(72.0);
            dataOut.writeDouble(89.0);
            dataOut.writeDouble(91.0);

            dataOut.close();
            buffer.close();
            fileOut.close();
        }catch(IOException e)
        {
            e.printStackTrace();
        }
    }
}
```

The ChainDemo program does not display any output, but it does create a new file named data.txt. Because the data is created using a DataOutputStream, you need to use a DataInputStream to read the data. And because the data is in a file, you need to also use a FileInputStream. If you want to buffer the data, a BufferedInputStream can also be used. In the following ReadData program, I decided to just use a DataInputStream and FileInputStream. Study the ChainDemo and ReadData programs and try to determine the output of ReadData, which is shown in Figure 16.4.

```java
import java.io.*;

public class ReadData
{
    public static void main(String [] args)
    {
        try
        {
            FileInputStream fileIn =
                            new FileInputStream("data.txt");
            DataInputStream dataIn = new DataInputStream(fileIn);

            System.out.println(dataIn.readUTF());

            int counter = dataIn.readInt();
            double sum = 0.0;

            for(int i = 0; i < counter; i++)
            {
                double current = dataIn.readDouble();
                System.out.println("Just read " + current);
                sum += current;
            }

            System.out.println("\nAverage = " + sum/counter);

            dataIn.close();
            fileIn.close();
        }catch(IOException e)
        {
            e.printStackTrace();
        }
    }
}
```

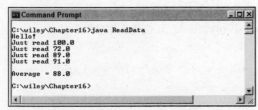

Figure 16.4   Output of the ReadData program.

Low-Level Readers and Writers

A reader is used for performing character I/O, and the java.io.Reader class is the parent class of all readers. Similarly, the java.io.Writer class is the parent class of all writers. Readers and writers, similarly to streams, can be broken down into two categories: low level and high level. The low-level readers and writers connect directly to a data source, similarly to memory or a file, while the high-level readers and writers connect to existing readers and writers.

The low-level readers in the java.io package are:

CharArrayReader and CharArrayWriter.   For reading from and writing to arrays of characters.

FileReader and FileWriter.   For reading from and writing to files containing character data.

PipedReader and PipedWriter.   For creating character streams between two threads. An example of pipes is discussed in the upcoming *Using Pipes* section.

StringReader and StringWriter.   For reading from and writing to String objects.

The upcoming section, *File I/O*, demonstrates using the FileWriter class. Using the other low-level readers and writers is similar.

High-Level Readers and Writers

The high-level readers and writers in the java.io package are:

BufferedReader and BufferedWriter.   For buffering the characters in the character stream. Using these classes is similar to using the BufferedInputStream and BufferedOutputStream classes.

InputStreamReader and OutputStreamWriter.   For converting between byte streams and character streams. The sidebar *Reading Input from the Keyboard* in this chapter demonstrates converting a stream to a reader.

PrintWriter.   For printing text to either an output stream or a Writer. You have seen a PrintWriter used extensively: System.out is a PrintWriter object.

PushbackReader.   For readers that allow characters to be read and then pushed back into the stream.

Now that we have seen how the classes in the java.io package break down into streams, readers and writers, and low-level and high-level streams, let's look at some of the more commonly used classes in detail. I will start with a discussion on file I/O.

File I/O

When performing file I/O, you have three options:

FileInputStream and FileOutputStream.   Use these classes when working with bytes.

FileReader and FileWriter.   Use these classes when working with characters.

RandomAccessFile.   Use this to both read and write to a file, allowing you to access any location in the file.

The ChainDemo and ReadData classes discussed earlier in this chapter demonstrated the FileInputStream and FileOutputStream classes. The constructors in FileInputStream, FileOutputStream, FileReader, and FileWriter are similar, taking in a variation of the following parameters:

File file.   A File object representing the file to be read from or written to.

String file.   The string name of the file to be read from or written to.

boolean append.   Used in the FileOutputStream and FileWriter constructors, a value of true specifies that the data written to the file should be appended to the end of the file. By default, writing to these streams does not append, but instead overwrites the data in the file.

To demonstrate using these classes, the following CreateFileDemo program creates a text file using the FileWriter class as the low-level writer. Study the CreateFileDemo program, which creates a new file named scores.html, and try to determine what the file will look like. Figure 16.5 shows the generated file.

```
scores_original - WordPad
File  Edit  View  Insert  Format  Help

<html>
      <body>
      <table border="1">
            <tr>
            <td>Home:</td>
            <td>Denver Broncos</td>
            <td>27</td>
            </tr>
            <tr>
            <td>Visitor:</td>
            <td>Oakland Raiders</td>
            <td>24</td>
            </tr>
      </table>
      </body>
</html>

For Help, press F1                                        NUM
```

Figure 16.5   HTML file generated from the CreateFileDemo program.

```java
import java.io.*;
public class CreateFileDemo
{
    public static void main(String [] args)
    {
        try
        {
            FileWriter file = new FileWriter("scores.html");
            BufferedWriter buffer = new BufferedWriter(file);
            PrintWriter out = new PrintWriter(buffer);

            out.println("<html>\n\t<body>");
            out.println("\t<table border=\"1\">\n\t\t<tr>");
            out.println("\t\t<td>Home:</td>\n\t\t<td>
                    Denver Broncos</td>\n\t\t<td>27</td>");
            out.println("\t\t</tr>\n\t\t<tr>");
            out.println("\t\t<td>Visitor:</td>\n\t\t<td>
                    Oakland Raiders</td>\n\t\t<td>24</td>");
            out.println("\t\t</tr>\n\t</table>");
            out.println("\t</body>\n</html>");

            out.close();
            buffer.close();
            file.close();
        }catch(IOException e)
        {
            e.printStackTrace();
        }
    }
}
```

The RandomAccessFile Class

The upcoming RandomAccessDemo program uses a RandomAccessFile object to view and modify the scores.html file created from the Create-FileDemo program. The RandomAccessFile class has two constructors:

public RandomAccessFile(File file, String mode).   The File parameter represents the file to be accessed.

public RandomAccessFile(String name, String mode).   The name parameter represents the name of the file to be accessed.

Both RandomAccessFile constructors contain a String parameter called mode to represent how the file is to be used. The possible values of the mode parameter are:

r.   For reading only.

rw.   For reading and writing.

rwd.   For reading and writing, and in addition, causes all changes to the file in memory to be written out to the file on the physical storage device at the same time.

rws.   Similar to rws, except the metadata is updated on the file as well. This typically involves one more I/O operation than rwd mode.

A RandomAccessFile object contains an index referred to as the *file pointer* that represents its current location in the file. The RandomAccessFile class contains both read and write methods, with each operation occurring relative to the current location of the file pointer. Some of the methods in the RandomAccessFile class include:

public long getFilePointer().   Returns the current location of the file pointer in bytes. This is often referred to as the offset since it represents the distance in bytes from the beginning of the file.

public void seek(long offset).   Moves the file pointer to the specified offset, measured in bytes relative to the beginning of the file.

public long length().   Returns the length of the file.

public final String readLine().   Reads the next line of text in the file.

The read and write methods of the RandomAccessFile class come in pairs, such as:

readInt() and writeInt().   For reading and writing ints.

readLong() and writeLong().   For reading and writing longs.

readDouble() and writeDouble().   For reading and writing doubles.

readUTF() and writeUTF().   For reading and writing String objects.

There are similar read and write methods for the other Java primitive data types. Study the following RandomAccessDemo program and try to determine what it does. You will have to follow along carefully, referring often to the scores.html file in Figure 16.5. Figure 16.6 shows the generated file.

```java
import java.io.*;

public class RandomAccessDemo
{
    public static void main(String [] args)
    {
        try
        {
            RandomAccessFile file =
```

```
                           new RandomAccessFile("scores.html", "rw");
            for(int i = 1; i <= 6; i++)
            {
                System.out.println(file.readLine());
            }
            long current = file.getFilePointer();
            file.seek(current + 6);

            file.write("34".getBytes());

            for(int i = 1; i <= 5; i++)
            {
                System.out.println(file.readLine());
            }
            current = file.getFilePointer();
            file.seek(current + 6);
            file.write("27".getBytes());
            file.close();
        }catch(IOException e)
        {
            e.printStackTrace();
        }
    }
}
```

Figure 16.6 Scores.html file after running the RandomAccessDemo program.

♦ Reading Input from the Keyboard

You have seen and used System.out extensively throughout this book and its labs for displaying output to the console, but we have not read any input from the console yet. There is a corresponding System.in object that represents the keyboard input from the console. The reason I have not discussed System.in yet is because it is an InputStream, meaning that it reads in bytes at a time. However, keyboard input is typically characters.

Therefore, to read in characters from the command prompt, you need to convert the System.in stream from a byte stream to a reader using the InputStreamReader class. Since keyboard input typically involves a user's entering a line of text, the BufferedReader class can also be used to simplify processing lines of text entered by the user.

The following KeyboardInput program demonstrates how to chain together System.in, InputStreamReader, and BufferedReader to read in lines of text from the standard console input. Study the program and try to determine its output, which is shown in Figure 16.7.

```java
import java.io.*;
public class KeyboardInput
{
    public static void main(String [] args)
    {
        try
        {
            System.out.print("Enter your name: ");
            InputStreamReader reader =
new InputStreamReader(System.in);
            BufferedReader in =
new BufferedReader(reader);

            String name = in.readLine();
            System.out.println("Hello, " + name
+ ". Enter three ints...");
            int [] values = new int[3];
            double sum = 0.0;
            for(int i = 0; i < values.length; i++)
            {
                System.out.print("Number " + (i+1)
+ ": " );
                String temp = in.readLine();
                values[i] = Integer.parseInt(temp);
                sum += values[i];
            }
            System.out.println("The average equals "
+ sum/values.length);

        }catch(IOException e)
        {
```

continued

◆ Reading Input from the Keyboard *(continued)*

```
                e.printStackTrace();
        }
    }
}
```

```
Command Prompt                                     _ □ ×
C:\wiley\Chapter16>java KeyboardInput
Enter your name: Rich
Hello, Rich. Enter three ints...
Number 1: 14
Number 2: 10
Number 3: 8
The average equals 10.666666666666666

C:\wiley\Chapter16>
```

Figure 16.7 Sample output of the KeyboardInput program.

Notice the use of the Integer.parseInt() method to parse the String input into ints. Also note that the readLine() method blocks until the user presses the Enter key on the keyboard.

Using Pipes

A pipe refers to a stream between threads, which allows for interthread communication. The PipedInputStream and PipedOutputStream classes are used when the data is bytes, and the PipedReader and PipedWriter classes are used when working with character data. The constructors for the pipe stream classes look similar to:

public PipedInputStream().   Creates a new, unconnected pipe input stream.

public PipedInputStream(PipedOutputStream).   Creates a new pipe input stream that is connected to the given pipe output stream.

public PipedOutputStream().   Creates a new, unconnected pipe output stream.

public PipedOutputStream(PipedInputStream).   Creates a new pipe output stream that is connected to the given pipe input stream.

Creating a pipe is a two-step process. One thread creates a new unconnected pipe, then a second thread comes along and connects to this existing pipe. Alternatively, two unconnected pipes can be connected using the connect() method of the corresponding class:

public void connect(PipedInputStream dest). Connects the given pipe input stream to the pipe output stream that this method is invoked on.

public void connect(PipedOutputStream dest). Connects the given pipe output stream to the pipe input stream that this method is invoked on.

The PipedReader and PipedWriter classes work in a similar fashion. Their constructors look similar to:

public PipedReader(). Creates a new, unconnected pipe reader.

public PipedReader(PipedWriter). Creates a new pipe reader that is connected to the given pipe writer.

public PipedWriter(). Creates a new, unconnected pipe writer.

public PipedWriter(PipedReader). Creates a new pipe writer that is connected to the given pipe reader.

As with the pipe streams, if the PipedReader and PipedWriter are not connected using the constructors, they can be connected using the connect() method.

The following PipeDemo program demonstrates two threads communicating with each other, using the PipedInputStream and PipedOutputStream classes. The data being sent back and forth is an int and a String object, so the pipes are chained with a DataInputStream and DataOutputStream, respectively.

The data being sent is generated from the following RandomWeather class:

```java
import java.io.*;
import java.util.*;

public class RandomWeather extends TimerTask
{
    private DataOutputStream out;

    public RandomWeather(OutputStream dest)
    {
        out = new DataOutputStream(dest);
    }

    public void run()
    {
        try
        {
            int temp = (int) (Math.random() * 110);
            out.writeInt(temp);

            int random = (int) (Math.random() * 4);
            String conditions;
            switch(random)
            {
                case 0:
```

```
                              conditions = "sunny";
                              break;
                    case 1:
                              conditions = "rainy";
                              break;
                    case 2:
                              conditions = "windy";
                              break;
                    default:
                              conditions = "snowy";
              }
         out.writeUTF(conditions);

    }catch(IOException e)
    {
         e.printStackTrace();
    }
  }
}
```

 You are probably wondering why the RandomWeather class does not use the PipedOutputStream class, especially because this section is on pipes. Well, pipes are going to be used, but I made a design decision when writing the RandomWeather class. Because the RandomWeather class chains the output stream with a DataOutputStream, it does not really care if the low-level stream is a pipe, file, or other stream; therefore, I have designed the RandomWeather class to work with any OutputStream. In the following PipeDemo program, the actual OutputStream is going to be a PipedOutputStream.

Similarly, the WeatherViewer class uses a DataInputStream to read the data, and it is designed to read data from any InputStream. Since PipedInputStream is a child of InputStream, the WeatherViewer can read from pipes, which is the case in the PipeDemo program.

The RandomWeather thread is going to send the output to the following WeatherViewer thread:

```
import java.io.*;
public class WeatherViewer extends Thread
{
     private DataInputStream in;

     public WeatherViewer(InputStream src)
     {
          in = new DataInputStream(src);
     }
```

```
        public void run()
        {
            while(true)
            {
                try
                {
                    int currentTemp = in.readInt();
                    System.out.println("\nThe current temp is "
                                        + currentTemp);

                    String conditions = in.readUTF();
                    System.out.println("Conditions are "
                                        + conditions);
                }catch(IOException e)
                {
                    e.printStackTrace();
                    break;
                }
            }
        }
    }
}
```

The PipeDemo program creates two threads and a pipe between them. Study the PipeDemo program along with the RandomWeather and WeatherViewer classes and try to determine its output, which is shown in Figure 16.8.

```
import java.io.*;
import java.util.*;
public class PipeDemo
{
    public static void main(String [] args)
    {
        try
        {
            PipedInputStream pipeIn = new PipedInputStream();
            PipedOutputStream pipeOut =
                            new PipedOutputStream(pipeIn);

            TimerTask task = new RandomWeather(pipeOut);
            Thread viewer = new WeatherViewer(pipeIn);

            Timer timer = new Timer();
            timer.schedule(task, 0, 4000);
            viewer.start();
        }catch(IOException e)
        {
            e.printStackTrace();
        }
    }
}
```

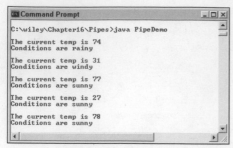

Figure 16.8 Sample output of the PipeDemo program.

An Overview of Serialization

One of the most impressive features of the Java language is its built-in use of serialization. *Serialization* refers to the process of saving the state of an object by sending it to an output stream, and deserialization is the process of retrieving the object back into memory. Most impressive is that the entire process is JVM independent, meaning an object can be serialized on one platform and deserialized on an entirely different platform.

Java practically trivializes the process of serialization because the JVM does most of the work for you. The ObjectOutputStream and ObjectInputStream classes are high-level streams that contain the methods for serializing and deserializing an object. The ObjectOutputStream class contains many write methods for writing various data types, but one method in particular stands out:

```
public final void writeObject(Object x) throws IOException
```

This method serializes an Object and sends it to the output stream. Similarly, the ObjectInputStream class contains the following method for deserializing an object:

```
public final Object readObject() throws IOException, ClassNotFoundException
```

This method retrieves the next Object out of the stream and deserializes it. The return value is Object, so you will need to cast it to its appropriate data type.

Classroom Q & A

Q: What exactly does the writeObject() method send to the output stream?

A: The purpose of serialization is to save the state of an Object. If you think about it, the state of an Object that makes it unique is the value of its fields. The writeObject() method, among other information, sends the values of the object's fields to the output stream.

Q: Does it send them in a specific order?

A: To be honest, the order doesn't matter. The JVM handles all the details of serialization and deserialization. The implementation details are discussed in the Java Language Specification, if you are interested in the seeing exactly how the process works behind the scenes.

Q: Can I serialize any Object in Java?

A: No. You can only serialize objects that are *serializable*. An Object is serializable if its class implements the java.io.Serializable interface. This interface does not contain any methods. It simply tags the class so instances of the class can be serialized.

Q: If you don't have to write any extra methods to make a class serializable, why didn't Sun just make all classes serializable by default?

A: Two reasons: It does not make sense to serialize some classes because their state is not something that can be saved and recreated. The Thread class is a good example of a class that is not serializable. It really does not make sense to serialize a thread and then deserialize it later. For the same reason, none of the stream classes in the java.io package are serializable. Also, implementing Serializable allows you to decide, from a design point of view, if you want instances of your classes to be serialized or not.

Q: Why would you not want a class to be serializable, assuming that it makes sense to serialize its fields?

A: Well, you probably *do* want most of your classes to be serializable. In most situations, if you write a class whose state can be maintained, you will make it serializable for the benefit of others using the class. You might have a class, however, that contains sensitive data that you do not want anyone to ever serialize.

Q: What if you want some of the fields of a class to be serializable, but not all them?

A: You can mark a particular field as transient, a keyword in Java, so that it will be ignored during serialization. There are also situations in which the transient keyword must be used for fields that are not serializable. For example, if a serializable class has a Thread field, the field must be marked as transient or a java.io.NotSerializable-Exception will occur if an attempt is made to serialize the object.

Q: What will the value be of a transient field when the object is deserialized?

A: Transient fields have a zero value when they are deserialized. For example, numeric types will be 0 and references will be null.

To demonstrate how serialization works in Java, I am going to use the Employee class that we discussed early on in the book. Suppose that we have the following Employee class, which implements the Serializable interface:

```
public class Employee implements java.io.Serializable
{
    public String name;
    public String address;
    public int transient SSN;
    public int number;
    public void mailCheck()
    {
        System.out.println("Mailing a check to " + name
+ " " + address);
    }
}
```

 The fields in the Employee class are public just to simplify this example; however, if they were private, they would be serialized in the same manner. The access specifier of a field has no effect on serialization.

The SSN field of Employee is transient to demonstrate what happens to transient fields during serialization. Notice that for a class to be serialized successfully, two conditions must be met:

- The class must implement the java.io.Serializable interface.
- All of the fields in the class must be serializable. If a field is not serializable, it must be marked transient.

Employee objects will be successfully serialized because its nontransient fields (one int and two String references) are serializable. Note that the String class is serializable, as are all eight primitive data types. The Employee class is ready to be serialized, so let's look at how to do this.

 If you are curious to know if a class is serializable or not, check the documentation for the class. The test is simple: If the class implements java.io.Serializable, then it is serializable; otherwise, it's not. In the documentation for String, the class is declared as:

```
public final class String extends Object
                implements Serializable, Comparable, CharSequence
```

Therefore, the String class is serializable. You will find that many of the classes in the J2SE API are serializable.

Serializing an Object

The ObjectOutputStream class is used to serialize an Object. The following SerializeDemo program instantiates an Employee object and serializes it to a file. When the program is done executing, a file named employee.ser is created. The program does not generate any output, but study the code and try to determine what the program is doing.

 When serializing an object to a file, the standard convention in Java is to give the file a .ser extension.

```java
import java.io.*;
public class SerializeDemo
{
     public static void main(String [] args)
     {
          Employee e = new Employee();
          e.name = "Neil Young";
          e.address = "Mobile, AL";
          e.SSN = 11122333;
          e.number = 101;

          try
          {
               FileOutputStream fileOut =
                         new FileOutputStream("employee.ser");
               ObjectOutputStream out =
                         new ObjectOutputStream(fileOut);

               out.writeObject(e);

               out.close();
               fileOut.close();
          }catch(IOException i)
          {
               i.printStackTrace();
          }
     }
}
```

Deserializing an Object

The following DeserializeDemo program deserializes the Employee object created in the SerializeDemo program. Study the program and try to determine its output, which is shown in Figure 16.9.

```java
import java.io.*;
public class DeserializeDemo
{
    public static void main(String [] args)
    {
        Employee e = null;
        try
        {
            FileInputStream fileIn =
                        new FileInputStream("employee.ser");
            ObjectInputStream in = new ObjectInputStream(fileIn);

            e = (Employee) in.readObject();
            in.close();
            fileIn.close();
        }catch(IOException i)
        {
            i.printStackTrace();
            return;
        }catch(ClassNotFoundException c)
        {
            System.out.println("Employee class not found");
            c.printStackTrace();
            return;
        }
        System.out.println("Just deserialized Employee...");
        System.out.println("Name: " + e.name);
        System.out.println("Address: " + e.address);
        System.out.println("SSN: " + e.SSN);
        System.out.println("Number: " + e.number);

    }
}
```

Figure 16.9   Output of the DeserializeDemo program.

I want to make a few comments about the DeserializeDemo program:

- The try/catch block tries to catch a ClassNotFoundException, which is declared by the readObject() method. For a JVM to be able to deserialize an object, it must be able to find the bytecode for the class. If the JVM can't find a class during the deserialization of an object, it throws a ClassNotFoundException.

- Notice that the return value of readObject() is cast to an Employee reference.

- The value of the SSN field was 11122333 when the object was serialized, but because the field is transient, this value was not sent to the output stream. The SSN field of the deserialized Employee object is 0.

The Logging APIs

Version 1.4 of the J2SE introduced a new package called java.util.logging that provides classes and interfaces for logging information about an application, such as errors, problems, security breaches, performance bottlenecks, and so on. The classes are referred to as the Logging APIs, and the process of logging an event involves the following classes:

Logger.   The Logger class creates the LogRecord objects and passes them to a Handler.

LogRecord.   This class contains the information to be logged.

Handler.   This class formats the LogRecord into a specific format, such as plaintext or XML, using a Formatter, and publishes the record to an output stream.

Formatter.   This class is responsible for formatting a LogRecord into a specific format.

You can write your own Formatter class, or you can use one of the two provided in the java.util.logging package:

SimpleFormatter.   Formats the LogRecord into simple text.

XMLFormatter.   Formats the LogRecord into an XML document of type <log>, using a standard XML set of tags.

The Formatter gets associated with a Handler, which publishes the LogRecord. There are several types of built-in Handler classes, including:

ConsoleHandler.   Sends the formatted log record to System.err, which in Windows is the console.

FileHandler.   Sends the formatted log record to a file.

StreamHandler. Sends the formatted log record to any OutputStream.

MemoryHandler. Writes the formatted log record to memory.

SocketHandler. Sends the formatted log record to a socket.

The process of logging starts with the Logger class, which contains the methods that an application uses to log a LogRecord. Messages are logged for different reasons and at different levels, as the following methods in the Logger class illustrate:

public static Logger getLogger(String name). A static method an application uses to obtain a Logger object. The name parameter represents the name of the Logger object to obtain. If a Logger with the given name already exists, the method returns this Logger; otherwise, this method creates a new Logger with the given name. This allows Logger objects to be shared among threads and applications.

public void addHandler(Handler h). Adds the given Handler to the Logger so that the Handler will now receive any logged messages.

public void log(Level level, String message). Logs the given message at the specified level. The possible values of level are static fields in the Level class and include, in descending order of severity, SEVERE, WARNING, INFO, CONFIG, FINE, FINER, and FINEST. This method is identical to invoking one of the following methods.

public void fine(String message). Logs a FINE message, which indicates the level of tracing information to provide. A FINE message contains the least amount of tracing information.

public void finer(String message). Logs a FINER message, which contains a fairly detailed tracing message.

public void finest(String message). Logs a FINEST message, which contains a highly detailed tracing message.

public void config(String message). Logs a CONFIG message for static configuration messages, such as the current Swing look and feel or monitor resolution.

public void severe(String message). Logs a SEVERE message for indicating a serious problem with the application.

public void warning(String message). Logs a WARNING message for indicating a warning of a potential problem.

public void info(String message). Logs an INFO message for general information messages.

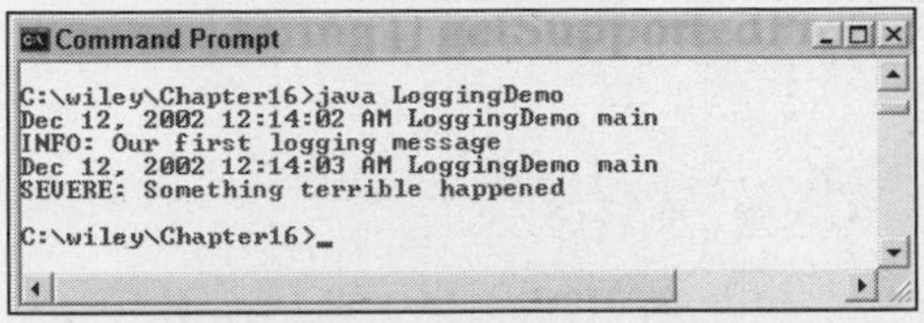

Figure 16.10 Output of the LoggingDemo program.

An Example of Logging

Let's look at an example that puts together these various logging classes so you can see how they are used. The following LoggingDemo program logs messages to a file named messages.log. The XMLFormatter is used to demonstrate how messages look in XML.

```java
import java.util.logging.*;
import java.io.IOException;
public class LoggingDemo
{
    public static void main(String [] args)
    {
        Logger logger = Logger.getLogger("my.log");

        Handler handler = null;

        try
        {
            handler = new FileHandler("messages.log");
        }catch(IOException e)
        {
            System.out.println("Using the console handler");
            handler = new ConsoleHandler();
        }

        logger.addHandler(handler);
        handler.setFormatter(new XMLFormatter());
        logger.info("Our first logging message");
        logger.severe("Something terrible happened");
    }
}
```

Figure 16.10 shows the console output from running the LoggingDemo. Notice that even though the output was sent to a file, the INFO and SEVERE logs also display a message at the console output.

The file messages.log contains the output of the two logged messages in XML format. The XML tags used are the standard for log messages, and using XML allows you to write applications that display the logged messages in many different ways. Here is what the messages.log file looks like:

```
<?xml version="1.0" encoding="windows-1252" standalone="no"?>
<!DOCTYPE log SYSTEM "logger.dtd">
<log>
<record>
  <date>2002-12-12T00:14:02</date>
  <millis>1039677242522</millis>
  <sequence>0</sequence>
  <logger>my.log</logger>
  <level>INFO</level>
  <class>LoggingDemo</class>
  <method>main</method>
  <thread>10</thread>
  <message>Our first logging message</message>
</record>
<record>
  <date>2002-12-12T00:14:03</date>
  <millis>1039677243083</millis>
  <sequence>1</sequence>
  <logger>my.log</logger>
  <level>SEVERE</level>
  <class>LoggingDemo</class>
  <method>main</method>
  <thread>10</thread>
  <message>Something terrible happened.</message>
</record>
</log>
```

In the release of version 1.4, a new API referred to as the new I/O (NIO) APIs was added to the J2SE. The API has various packages, including:

java.nio. This consists of classes designed to improve the performance of buffering in I/O operations.

java.nio.channels. This package contains classes and interfaces for defining channels, connections to physical devices such as files or network sockets.

java.nio.charset. This defines classes for working with charsets, encoders, and decoders, all of which define mappings between bytes and Unicode characters.

javax.util.regex. This defines two classes, Matcher and Pattern, for matching character sequences against patterns, where the pattern represents a regular expression.

Using the new I/O APIs is beyond the scope of an introductory Java course, but if you are interested in using them, a good place to start is the J2SE documentation.

Lab 16.1: Using Streams

The purpose of this lab is for you to become familiar with reading from a file and chaining streams.

1. Suppose that you are given a file in the following format that represents final scores of football games:

```
Dallas Cowboys
21
San Francisco 49ers
30
Denver Broncos
34
Oakland Raiders
0
```

For example, the Cowboys lost to the 49ers 30 to 21, and the Broncos beat the Raiders 34 to 0. The home team is listed first, followed by their score, and then the visiting team and their score are listed. Locate the file scores.txt in the lab solutions and copy it to the directory in which you are working.

2. Write a program that reads in all of the scores in the file and displays them in the following format at the console output:

```
Home: Dallas Cowboys  21
Visitor: San Francisco 49ers  30*
```

Place an asterisk next to the winning score.

Run the program reading the file scores.txt, and you should see the output of seven football games.

Lab 16.2: Using Logging

In this lab, you modify your game from Lab 15.2 so that it keeps track of the winners of the race in a file and uses logging.

1. Within the main() method of the Race class from Lab 15.2, output the winner of the race in a file named winners.dat. Be sure to append the winner at the end of the file. Use whichever output streams or writer classes that you feel are appropriate.

2. In addition to saving the winner to a file, generate a logging message of level INFO that states that the race has been won and also

gives the name of the winning car. Have the logging message use the SimpleFormatter and the ConsoleHandler.

3. Write a program named ShowWinners that displays all of the winners in the winners.dat file, using the corresponding input streams or reader classes.

Each time you run the Race program, the winner is added to the end of the winners.dat file and an INFO log message should appear at the console output. Running the ShowWinner program should display all the entries in the file.

Lab 16.3: Using Serialization

In this lab, you will write a class that is serializable. The class will represent an instant message and will be used as part of the Instant Messaging project you started in Chapter 12.

1. Write a class named InstantMessage, making it serializable.

2. Add three private String fields: recipient, sender, and message.

3. Add a constructor that takes in three String parameters that are used to initialize the three fields.

4. Add three accessor methods, one for each of the three fields.

5. Save and compile your InstantMessage class.

You shouldn't see anything yet. You will use this class in the next lab.

Lab 16.4: Using Pipes

In this lab, you will become familiar with using pipes to perform I/O between two threads You will modify the SendMessage listener class from Lab 13.3.

1. Open your SendMessage.java file from Lab 13.3. Add a field of type ObjectOutputStream and a String to represent the sender.

2. Add an OutputStream parameter and String parameter (for the sender field) to the constructor of SendMessage. Initialize the ObjectOutputStream field by chaining the OutputStream parameter to a new ObjectOutputStream.

3. Within the actionPerformed() method, if the Send button is clicked, instantiate a new InstantMessage object (using your InstantMessage class from Lab 16.3) and serialize it to the Object OutputStream field of the SendMessage class.

4. Save and compile the SendMessage class.

5. Write a class named Participant that extends Thread. Add a field of type ObjectInputStream and a field of type String to represent a user's name.

6. Add a constructor that takes in an InputStream and a String. Initialize the ObjectInputStream field by chaining the InputStream parameter to a new ObjectInputStream object. Store the String in your String field.

7. Within the run() method, add an infinite while loop. Within the while loop, invoke readObject() on the ObjectInputStream field. This will cause the thread to block until an object becomes available in the stream.

8. Cast the return value of readObject() to an InstantMessage reference. The InstantMessage read from the stream represents an incoming message from a friend.

9. Display a modeless dialog window that displays the name of the sender and the message. This may require writing additional classes for laying out the dialog and performing any necessary event handling to close the dialog. A handy feature is a Reply button, which allows the user to quickly reply to the sender.

10. You will now modify your InstantMessageDialog.java class from Lab 13.4 because it will no longer compile with all the changes you made to SendMessage. Within the constructor of InstantMessage Dialog, instantiate a PipedOutputStream and PipedInputStream and connect them.

11. Pass in the PipedOutputStream to the SendMessage constructor.

12. Instantiate a new Participant object, passing in the PipedInput-Stream to the constructor. Start the Participant thread.

13. Save, compile, and run the InstantMessageDialog class.

When you click a friend in the JList of the InstantMessageFrame window, a dialog window should appear (as before). Typing in a message and clicking the Send button should close this dialog and display a new modeless dialog window with the message you just sent to somebody else. (In the next chapter, "Network Programming," you will finish this project by sending the message to an actual recipient on a different computer instead of sending it to yourself, which is what your program does now.)

Lab 16.5: A Reminder Application

You will write a Reminder Application that ties together many of the Java topics we have discussed so far in this book. I won't give you much help because I want you to design the application, but I will give you a list of requirements.

1. The GUI for the program needs to provide an interface for users to enter a message to represent a reminder, such as a meeting, conference call, birthday, anniversary, doctor's appointment, and so on. The message can be any String.

2. The GUI needs to provide a way for the user to specify when he or she wants the reminder to be scheduled. The simplest way (from the point of view of the programmer) is to have the user enter the number of seconds or minutes to wait; however, a more user-friendly GUI would allow the user to enter a date and time.

3. When it's time to display the reminder, a modeless dialog window should appear on screen. Provide an OK button or something similar so the user can close the reminder dialog box. An optional feature might be to let the user choose to have the reminder appear in 5 minutes (or a time they specify), similar to an extra reminder.

4. Use the Timer and TimerTask classes to implement the actual schedule.

5. Another optional feature would be to allow the user to schedule a recurring reminder, similar to "Pay phone bill" at the 10th of each month, or "Take out trash" every Friday.

6. Check out the java.awt.Toolkit class, and see if you can figure out how to make your computer beep when a reminder is displayed.

The GUI that allows users to enter a new task will be displayed when the program is executed, and it will remain open until the Reminder Application terminates. Because it is a Java program, there will also be a command prompt window open at all times as well. You should be able to enter a reminder and a scheduled time, and the reminder should appear in a separate dialog window at the appropriate scheduled time.

Summary

- The java.io package contains useful classes for performing most any type of input and output.

- Most of the classes in the java.io package fit into one of two categories: streams, and readers or writers. The stream classes are for performing IO with different data types, and readers and writers are used for performing IO at the character level.

- The java.io.OutputStream and java.io.InputStream classes are the parent classes of all the streams. The java.io.Reader and java.io.Writer classes are the parent classes of all the reader and writer classes.

- The classes in the java.io package can be chained together. A low-level stream is used to communicate with the source of the IO, and high-level streams can be chained to the low-level stream to perform buffering and filtering of the data.

- Object serialization is a built-in feature of the Java language. It allows the state of objects to be saved and transmitted to other streams. The java.io.ObjectOutputStream and java.io.ObjectInputStream classes are used for performing serialization, and a class must implement the java.io.Serializable interface for instances of the class to be serialized.

- The new Logging APIs provide a mechanism for Java applications to log certain events and errors.

Review Questions

1. What is the difference between a stream and a reader or writer?

2. Name the parent class of all input streams.

3. Which of the following methods is (are) in java.io.OutputStream class? Select all that apply.

    a. public void writeUTF(String string)

    b. public void write(int b)

    c. public void write(byte [] b)

    d. public void write(byte [] b, int offset, int length)

    e. public void close()

4. Which of the following classes is (are) low-level input streams? Select all that apply.

    a. FileInputStream

    b. DataInputStream

    c. FilterInputStream

    d. PushbackInputStream

    e. PipedInputStream

5. True or False: A PipedInputStream can be chained to a FileInputStream.

6. True or False: A BufferedReader can be chained to a PipedReader.

7. True or False: A DataInputStream can be chained to a BufferedInputStream.

8. If you were going to perform I/O that involved working with the eight primitive data types and String objects, which I/O classes would you likely use?

9. Suppose that in the previous question the I/O took place between two threads. Which classes would you use?

10. If you were going to perform I/O that involved working with characters and String objects in a file, which I/O classes would you likely use?

11. If you were going to perform I/O that involved working with Java objects, which I/O classes would you likely use?

12. The read() method in the java.io.InputStream class declares that it returns an int. What data type does it actually return?

    a. int

    b. byte

    c. short

    d. char

    e. none of the above

13. True or False: The read methods of the various input streams block and wait for input when none is available.

14. True or False: A field marked as transient throws a NotSerializableException when the corresponding object is serialized.

15. True or False: A value of a transient field is ignored by the JVM during serialization.

16. How many methods are in the java.io.Serializable interface?

17. Which two exceptions does the readObject() method in the ObjectInputStream class possibly throw?

18. True or False: An object must be of type java.io.Serializable to be successfully serialized.

19. True or False: An object serialized on Windows XP can only be deserialized by a Windows JVM.

20. Which one of the following logging levels is the most severe (compared to the others)?

    a. FINE

    b. FINEST

    c. INFO

    d. WARNING

21. Name the two Formatter classes in the Logging API.

22. Where does the ConsoleHandler publish a logged message?

Answers to Review Questions

1. A stream treats data as bytes, while a reader and writer treats data as characters.

2. java.io.InputStream is the abstract parent class of all the input stream classes.

3. They all are, except a writeUTF(String), which is the kind of method you will find in the high-level streams.

4. a and e. The other three are high-level streams that only attach to existing streams.

5. False. PipedInputStream and FileInputStream are both low-level streams, and two low-level streams cannot be chained together.

6. True. BufferedReader is a high-level reader and PipedReader is a low-level reader.

7. True. They are both high-level streams, and any two high-level streams can be chained together.

8. You would likely use DataInputStream and DataOutputStream because they contain methods for reading and writing primitive data types and Strings.

9. You would likely use the PipedInputStream and PipedOutputStream classes for the two threads, *and* the DataInputStream and DataOutputStream classes for filtering the I/O.

10. I would suggest the FileReader and FileWriter because they are used specifically for that purpose. In addition, I would recommend the BufferedReader and BufferedWriter classes to improve performance.

11. You would likely use the ObjectInputStream and ObjectOutputStream classes, which perform serialization and deserialization of Java objects.

12. The read() method returns a single byte, so the answer is b.

13. True.

14. False. Marking a field as transient avoids the NotSerializableException.

15. True. That is the purpose of the transient keyword.

16. Serializable is a tagging interface and contains no methods.

17. An IOException if an I/O problem arises, and a ClassNotFoundException if the deserialized object contains a class that the JVM cannot find.

18. True.

19. False. Serialized objects are JVM, and are platform independent.

20. The WARNING level is just below SEVERE (the highest level) in terms of severity, so the answer is d.

21. SimpleFormatter, which formats the messages into text, and XMLFormatter, which formats the messages into XML documents.

22. System.err, the standard error output, which is typically the console.

CHAPTER

17

Network Programming

In this chapter, I will discuss the various built-in features of the J2SE that provide support for network programming. Computer networks have become so common that you may even have one in your own home, and almost certainly at your place of work. Then there's the Internet, which can be pictured as one global network of computers. For this reason, network programming is a fundamental and essential part of any programming language. Java, being a newer language, has plenty of built-in classes and interfaces for network programming. I will begin with an overview of networks and the two common protocols: TCP and UDP. Then, I will show you how to connect two computers using sockets, allowing them to perform TCP/IP communication. Then, I will discuss the Java Secure Sockets Extension (JSSE), which allows for secure socket connections. I will then discuss how to send and receive UDP datagram packets, and how to use the URLConnection class to communicate with a URL.

An Overview of Network Programming

The term *network programming* refers to writing programs that execute across multiple devices (computers), in which the devices are all connected to each other using a network. The java.net package of the J2SE APIs contains a collection of classes and interfaces that provide the low-level communication details, allowing you to write programs that focus on solving the problem at hand. The java.net package provides support for the two common network protocols:

TCP. TCP stands for Transmission Control Protocol, which allows for reliable communication between two applications. TCP is typically used over the Internet Protocol, which is referred to as TCP/IP.

UDP. UDP stands for User Datagram Protocol, a connection-less protocol that allows for packets of data to be transmitted between applications.

In the following sections, we take a look at the way these two protocols compare.

Transmission Control Protocol

Transmission Control Protocol (TCP) is often compared to making a telephone call. If you want to telephone someone, the person needs to have a phone, needs a phone number, and needs to be waiting for an incoming call. After the person you are calling answers the telephone, you now have a reliable, two-way communication stream, allowing either person to talk to the other (even at the same time). If one person hangs up the phone, the communication is over.

With a TCP network connection, the client computer is similar to the person placing the telephone call, and the server computer is similar to the person waiting for a call. When the client attempts to connect to the server, the server needs to be running, needs to have an address on the network, and needs to be waiting for an incoming connection on a port. When a TCP connection is established, the client and server have a reliable, two-way communication stream that allows data to be transmitted in either direction. The two computers can communicate until the connection is closed or lost.

The java.net.ServerSocket and java.net.Socket classes are the only two classes you will probably ever need to create a TCP/IP connection between two computers unless you require a secure connection, in which case you would use the SSLServerSocket and SSLSocket classes in the javax.net.ssl package. I will discuss both of these techniques later in this chapter.

User Datagram Protocol

User Datagram Protocol (UDP) provides a protocol for sending packets of data called *datagrams* between applications. If TCP is similar to placing a telephone call, UDP can be compared to mailing someone a letter. The datagram packet is like a letter, where a client sends a datagram to a server without actually connecting to the server. This makes UDP an unreliable communication protocol when compared to TCP, where the client and server are directly connected.

If I mail you two letters on the same day, they might be delivered on the same day, but this is hardly guaranteed. In fact, there is no guarantee that both letters will even get delivered at all. It's possible that one will be delivered the next day, whereas the other doesn't arrive for two weeks. The same is true for datagram packets. UDP does not guarantee that packets will be received in the order they were sent or that they will even be delivered at all.

If this type of unreliability is unacceptable for the program you are developing, you should use TCP instead. However, if you're developing a network application in which reliable communication is not essential to the application, UDP is probably a better option because it does not carry the overhead of TCP.

The java.net.DatagramPacket and java.net.DatagramSocket classes are used to send and receive datagram packets; I will show you how this is done in the upcoming section *Overview of Datagram Packets*.

Classroom Q & A

Q: How does a computer find another computer on the network?

A: Every computer on the network has a unique numeric value, which is referred to as its *IP address*. Each computer also probably has a name, which makes it easier for other computers to locate it, especially if its IP address changes on the network but its name doesn't.

Q: Can two computers have multiple TCP connections between them?

A: Certainly. In fact, it is often the case that two computers have multiple applications running and communicating between each other. Servers will have HTTP applications, FTP applications, and so on, all running at the same time.

Q: So if two computers have multiple connections, how do you distinguish which application you want to communicate with?

A: Well, when data is sent from one application to another, the data has two values associated with it: the computer's IP address and a *port number*. The IP address denotes which computer the data is intended for, and the port number denotes which application the data is intended for.

Q: Do you need to associate a port number with all your network programs?

A: Yes. You will find that port numbers are used throughout the Java networking APIs, especially in constructors when applications are starting up.

Q: Do I just make up a port number?

A: Sure. A port number can be any 16-bit integer (between 0 and 65,535). However, you should use only port numbers larger than 1,024 because the lower ports are reserved for common protocols such as HTTP, FTP, Telnet, and others. Often, a port number needs to be assigned to you by a network administrator. However, if I am just testing applications or writing program for a small network, I just pick large numbers. Ports greater than 10,000 seem to be pretty safe because many common applications such as Web servers use ports up into the 9,000 range.

Q: What if I pick a port number that is already being used?

A: You will get an exception in your Java program. In that case, I would handle the exception and try another port until you are successful. In most methods that require a port number, you can pass in 0 and let the JVM find a port for you.

I am now ready to show you how to do some network programming, so let's start with creating a TCP connection using sockets.

Using Sockets

If TCP is similar to placing a telephone call, a *socket* is the telephone. Sockets provide the communication mechanism between two computers using TCP. A client program creates a socket on its end of the communication and attempts to connect that socket to a server. When the connection is made, the server creates a socket object on its end of the communication. The client and server can now communicate by writing to and reading from the socket.

The java.net package contains classes that provide all of the low-level communication for you. For example, the java.net.Socket class represents a socket, and the java.net.ServerSocket class provides a mechanism for the server program to listen for clients and establish connections with them.

The following steps occur when establishing a TCP connection between two computers using sockets:

1. The server instantiates a ServerSocket object, denoting which port number communication is to occur on.

2. The server invokes the accept() method of the ServerSocket class. This method waits until a client connects to the server on the given port.

3. After the server is waiting, a client instantiates a Socket object, specifying the server name and port number to connect to.

4. The constructor of the Socket class attempts to connect the client to the specified server and port number. If communication is established, the client now has a Socket object capable of communicating with the server.

5. On the server side, the accept() method returns a reference to a new socket on the server that is connected to the client's socket.

 When a client establishes a socket connection to a server, the client needs to specify a port number. This port number denotes the port that the server is listening on. However, after a client and server are connected using sockets, their connection is actually taking place on a different port. This allows the server, in a separate thread, to continue listening on the original port for other clients. This all takes place behind the scenes and should not affect your code, but it is an important tidbit to understand.

After the connections are established, communication can occur using I/O streams. Each socket has both an OutputStream and an InputStream. The client's OutputStream is connected to the server's InputStream, and the client's InputStream is connected to the server's OutputStream. TCP is a two-way communication protocol, so data can be sent across both streams at the same time.

 The socket streams are low-level I/O streams: InputStream and OutputStream. Therefore, they can be chained together with buffers, filters, and other high-level streams to allow for any type of advanced I/O you need to perform. This is why I discussed the java.io package before network programming. You are about to find out that creating the connection is the easy part, and most of your work in network programming involves the actual transmitting of data back and forth. Of course, this is how network programming should be, allowing you to focus on the problem being solved and not worrying about the low-level communication and protocol details. This is one of the reasons why Java is so popular among network programmers.

Let's look at an example using sockets. I will start with a program that runs on the server, listening on a port for client requests. Then I will show you how to write the client code that connects to the server application.

The ServerSocket Class

The java.net.ServerSocket class is used by server applications to obtain a port and listen for client requests. The ServerSocket class has four constructors:

public ServerSocket(int port) throws IOException. Attempts to create a server socket bound to the specified port. An exception occurs if the port is already bound by another application. The port parameter can be 0, which creates the socket on any free port.

public ServerSocket(int port, int backlog) throws IOException. Similar to the previous constructor, the backlog parameter specifies how many incoming clients to store in a wait queue. If the queue is full, clients attempting to connect to this port will receive an exception. If the value is 0, the default queue size of the native platform is used.

public ServerSocket(int port, int backlog, InetAddress address) throws IOException. Similar to the previous constructor, the InetAddress parameter specifies the local IP address to bind to. The InetAddress is used for servers that may have multiple IP addresses, allowing the server to specify which of its IP addresses to accept client requests on.

public ServerSocket() throws IOException. Creates an unbound server socket. When using this constructor, use the bind() method when you are ready to bind the server socket.

Notice that each of the constructors throws an IOException when something goes wrong. However, if the ServerSocket constructor does not throw an exception, it means that your application has successfully bound to the specified port and is ready for client requests. Here are some of the common methods of the ServerSocket class:

public int getLocalPort(). Returns the port that the server socket is listening on. This method is useful if you passed in 0 as the port number in a constructor and let the server find a port for you.

public Socket accept() throws IOException. Waits for an incoming client. This method blocks until either a client connects to the server on the specified port or the socket times out, assuming that the time-out value has been set using the setSoTimeout() method. Otherwise, this method blocks indefinitely.

public void setSoTimeout(int timeout). Sets the time-out value for how long the server socket waits for a client during the accept().

public void bind(SocketAddress host, int backlog). Binds the socket to
the specified server and port in the SocketAddress object. Use this method
if you instantiated the ServerSocket using the no-argument constructor.

The accept() method is the one I want you to focus on because this is how
the server listens for incoming requests. When the ServerSocket invokes
accept(), the method does not return until a client connects (assuming that no
time-out value has been set). After a client does connect, the ServerSocket
creates a new Socket on an unspecified port (different from the port it was listening on) and returns a reference to this new Socket. A TCP connection now
exists between the client and server, and communication can begin.

 **If you are writing a server application that allows for multiple clients, you
want your server socket to always be invoking accept(), waiting for clients.
When a client does connect, the standard trick is to start a new thread for
communication with the new client, allowing the current thread to
immediately invoke accept() again. For example, if you have 50 clients
connected to a server, the server program will have 51 threads: 50 for
communicating with the clients and one additional thread waiting for a
new client via the accept() method.**

The following SimpleServer program is an example of a server application
that uses the ServerSocket class to listen for clients on a port number specified
by a command-line argument. Notice that the server doesn't do much with the
client, but the program demonstrates how a connection is made with a client.
The return value of accept() is a Socket, so I need to discuss the Socket class
before we can do anything exciting with the connection. Study the Simple-
Server program and try to determine what its output will be.

```
import java.net.*;
import java.io.*;
public class SimpleServer extends Thread
{
    private ServerSocket serverSocket;
    public SimpleServer(int port) throws IOException
    {
        serverSocket = new ServerSocket(port);
        serverSocket.setSoTimeout(10000);
    }
    public void run()
    {
        while(true)
```

```
        {
            try
            {
                System.out.println("Waiting for client on port "
                            + serverSocket.getLocalPort() + "...");
                Socket client = serverSocket.accept();
                System.out.println("Just connected to "
                            + client.getRemoteSocketAddress());
                client.close();
            }catch(SocketTimeoutException s)
            {
                System.out.println("Socket timed out!");
                break;
            }catch(IOException e)
            {
                e.printStackTrace();
                break;
            }
        }
    }
    public static void main(String [] args)
    {
        int port = Integer.parseInt(args[0]);
        try
        {
            Thread t = new SimpleServer(port);
            t.start();
        }catch(IOException e)
        {
            e.printStackTrace();
        }
    }
}
```

Figure 17.1 shows the output of the SimpleServer program when 5001 is the command-line argument. The server program is waiting for a client, which I will show you how to create next. Because no client comes along and connects, this accept() method blocks for 10 seconds (why?) and the SocketTimeoutException occurs, causing the thread to run to completion and the program to terminate.

Figure 17.1 Output of the SimpleServer program.

Socket Class

The java.net.Socket class represents the socket that both the client and server use to communicate with each other. The client obtains a Socket object by instantiating one, whereas the server obtains a Socket object from the return value of the accept() method. The Socket class has five constructors that a client uses to connect to a server:

public Socket(String host, int port) throws UnknownHostException, IOException. Attempts to connect to the specified server at the specified port. If this constructor does not throw an exception, the connection is successful and the client is connected to the server. This is the simplest constructor to use when connecting to a server.

public Socket(InetAddress host, int port) throws IOException. Identical to the previous constructor, except that the host is denoted by an InetAddress object.

public Socket(String host, int port, InetAddress localAddress, int localPort) throws IOException. Connects to the specified host and port, creating a socket on the local host at the specified address and port. This is useful for clients who have multiple IP addresses or who want the socket to bind on a specific local port.

public Socket(InetAddress host, int port, InetAddress localAddress, int localPort) throws IOException. Identical to the previous constructor, except that the host is denoted by an InetAddress object instead of a String.

public Socket(). Creates an unconnected socket. Use the connect() method to connect this socket to a server.

When the Socket constructor returns, it does not simply instantiate a Socket object. Within the constructor, it actually attempts to connect to the specified server and port. If the constructor returns successfully, the client has a TCP connection to the server!

Some methods of interest in the Socket class are listed here. Notice that both the client and server have a Socket object, so these methods can be invoked by both the client and server.

public void connect(SocketAddress host, int timeout) throws IOException. Connects the socket to the specified host. This method is needed only when you instantiated the Socket using the no-argument constructor.

public InetAddress getInetAddress(). Returns the address of the other computer that this socket is connected to.

public int getPort(). Returns the port the socket is bound to on the remote machine.

public int getLocalPort(). Returns the port the socket is bound to on the local machine.

public SocketAddress getRemoteSocketAddress(). Returns the address of the remote socket.

public InputStream getInputStream() throws IOException. Returns the input stream of the socket. The input stream is connected to the output stream of the remote socket.

public OutputStream getOutputStream() throws IOException. Returns the output stream of the socket. The output stream is connected to the input stream of the remote socket.

public void close() throws IOException. Closes the socket, which makes this Socket object no longer capable of connecting again to any server.

The Socket class contains many more methods, so check the documentation for a complete list. You will notice that many of the methods in the Socket class involve accessing and changing the various TCP properties of a connection, such as a time-out value or keep-alive setting. Of all the methods in Socket, probably the two most important ones are getInputStream() and getOutput-Stream(), which I will now discuss in detail.

Communicating between Sockets

The InputStream and OutputStream attributes of a Socket are the ways the two computers communicate with each other. For example, if the server wants to send data to the client, the server needs to write to the OutputStream of its socket, which is then read by the InputStream of the client's socket. Similarly, data can be sent from the client to the server using the client's OutputStream and the server's InputStream.

The following GreetingClient is a client program that connects to a server by using a socket and sends a greeting, and then waits for a response. Study the program and try to determine exactly how the client accomplishes this.

```java
import java.net.*;
import java.io.*;
public class GreetingClient
{
    public static void main(String [] args)
    {
        String serverName = args[0];
        int port = Integer.parseInt(args[1]);
        try
        {
```

```
            System.out.println("Connecting to " + serverName
                        + " on port " + port);
            Socket client = new Socket(serverName, port);
            System.out.println("Just connected to "
                        + client.getRemoteSocketAddress());
            OutputStream outToServer = client.getOutputStream();
            DataOutputStream out =
                        new DataOutputStream(outToServer);
            out.writeUTF("Hello from "
                        + client.getLocalSocketAddress());
            InputStream inFromServer = client.getInputStream();
            DataInputStream in =
                        new DataInputStream(inFromServer);
            System.out.println("Server says " + in.readUTF());
            client.close();
        }catch(IOException e)
        {
            e.printStackTrace();
        }
    }
}
```

The following code from the GreetingServer class (available on the Web site for this book) is identical to the SimpleServer class discussed earlier, except that it reads in a string from a client and sends a message back to the client. The server then closes the socket and invokes accept() again for the next client that comes along. Study the program carefully to see how this is accomplished:

```
System.out.println("Waiting for client on port " +
serverSocket.getLocalPort() + "...");
Socket server = serverSocket.accept();
System.out.println("Just connected to "
                                    + server.getRemoteSocketAddress());
DataInputStream in =
                new DataInputStream(server.getInputStream());
System.out.println(in.readUTF());
DataOutputStream out =
                new DataOutputStream(server.getOutputStream());
out.writeUTF("Thank you for connecting to "
                + server.getLocalSocketAddress() + "\nGoodbye!");
server.close();
```

 The GreetingServer and GreetingClient programs can be executed on two different computers that are on the same network, or you can run them both on the same computer. When the client and server are on the same computer, the client can use localhost as the name of the server to connect to. Note that running the two programs on the same computer requires two command prompts.

Figure 17.2   Output of the GreetingServer program.

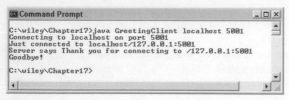

Figure 17.3   Output of the GreetingClient program.

Figure 17.2 shows the output of the GreetingServer program, which needs to be executed first.

Figure 17.3 shows the output of the GreetingClient program. Notice that the GreetingServer program does not terminate because it invokes accept() in an infinite *while* loop. You can run the client again and again without having to restart the server program.

Java Secure Socket Extension (JSSE)

A socket connection can be made using the Secure Sockets Layer (SSL) protocol, which provides a secure connection between the client and server. Using SSL ensures a high level of security in regard to the data being sent between the two computers. When you purchase an item online and send your credit card number over the Internet, SSL is likely the security method used to protect your credit card number from being seen and used maliciously.

Version 1.4 of the J2SE introduced new support for using SSL and sockets with the Java Secure Socket Extension (JSSE). The classes involved in creating a secure socket connection with JSSE are found in the javax.net and javax.net.ssl packages and include the following:

javax.net.ssl.SSLServerSocket.   Used by the server application to accept client connections and create an SSLSocket. Compare this class to the java.net.ServerSocket class.

javax.net.ssl.SSLSocket.   Represents the secure socket on both the client and the server. Compare this class to the java.net.Socket class.

javax.net.ssl.SSLServerSocketFactory.   The server program uses this class to obtain an SSLServerSocket object.

javax.net.ssl.SSLSocketFactory.   The client program uses this class to obtain an SSLSocket object.

The steps involved in creating a secure socket connection are slightly different from those in a non-secure-socket connection (using the Socket and SocketServer classes in the java.net package), so let's go through the details.

Secure Server Socket

The server application performs the following steps to create a secure server socket:

1. The server program starts with an SSLServerSocketFactory object, which is not instantiated using the new keyword, but instead is obtained using the following static method found in the SSLServerSocketFactory class:

```
public static ServerSocketFactory getDefault()
```

 The getDefault() method returns the default SSL server socket factory. If you have written your own factory, you can override the default factory by denoting its class name using the ssl.ServerSocketFactory.provider property.

2. Use the server socket factory to create an SSLServerSocket object, which listens on a specified port for client requests.

3. Initialize the server socket with any necessary security settings.

4. The SSLServerSocket invokes the accept() method to block and wait for client connections.

The first step is to locate a server socket factory using the getDefault() method. Notice that the return type of getDefault() is javax.net.ServerSocketFactory, the parent class of SSLServerSocketFactory. The ServerSocketFactory class has four methods for creating a ServerSocket:

public ServerSocket createServerSocket(int port) throws IOException.   Creates a ServerSocket on the given port.

public ServerSocket createServerSocket(int port, int backlog) throws IOException.   Creates a ServerSocket on the given port with the specified backlog, which determines the size of the queue containing clients waiting to connect.

public ServerSocket createServerSocket(int port, int backlog, InetAd-dress address) throws IOException.   Creates a ServerSocket on the given port using the specified local address, which is useful when the server has multiple IP addresses.

public ServerSocket createServerSocket() throws IOException.   Creates an unbound ServerSocket that can be bound using the bind() method of the ServerSocket class.

The createServerSocket() methods of the ServerSocketFactory class have identical parameters to the constructors in the java.net.ServerSocket class discussed earlier in this chapter. When you are not using SSL, you can either instantiate a ServerSocket object using one of its constructors (the technique I showed you earlier in the SimpleServer program) or you can use the ServerSocketFactory class and one of the createServerSocket() methods. When you are using SSL, you must use a socket factory to obtain a server socket.

Which technique you use for nonsecure sockets is a matter of choice, but it is apparent from my experiences with other Java APIs that using a factory class has its advantages, especially in making your code easier to deploy on different platforms and in setting various properties of the factory. For example, using a SocketFactory allows you to determine the properties of a ServerSocket, such as its time-out value, without hard-coding the values in your program.

After you have obtained an SSLServerSocket object using the factory, you are now ready to initialize the server socket with any specific security settings. The SSLServerSocket class extends java.net.ServerSocket, so you can invoke those methods discussed earlier, such as accept() and close(), plus the methods in SSLServerSocket, which include the following:

public void setEnabledCipherSuites(String [] suites).   Sets the cipher suites available for this connection. A *cipher suite* defines the security algorithms for authentication, encryption, and key agreements, a process referred to *handshaking*. The upcoming SSLServerDemo program shows the common cipher suite values.

public String [] getSupportedCipherSuites().   Returns an array containing the cipher suites that can be enabled for this particular socket connection.

public String [] getSupportedProtocols().   Returns an array containing the security protocols that can be enabled for this particular socket connection. You can expect SSL as well as TLS, the Transport Layer Security, to be supported.

public void setNeedClientAuth(boolean flag).   Denotes that clients connecting to this server socket *must* be authenticated. By default, clients' connections do not require authentication. If turned on, clients must be authenticated, or else the connection will close immediately after the server accepts the client connection.

public void setWantClientAuth(boolean flag).   Denotes that clients connecting to this server socket *should* be authenticated. Clients should provide authentication information, but the connection is still maintained if they do not.

A server program for SSL sockets uses a factory to create a secure server socket. The following SSLServerDemo program demonstrates the steps a server takes to accept secure client connections. Study the program and its output carefully, which is shown in Figure 17.4.

```java
import java.net.*;
import javax.net.ssl.*;
import java.io.*;
public class SSLServerDemo
{
    public static void main(String [] args)
    {
        int port = Integer.parseInt(args[0]);
        try
        {
            System.out.println("Locating server socket factory for
            SSL...");
            SSLServerSocketFactory factory =
(SSLServerSocketFactory) SSLServerSocketFactory.getDefault();
             System.out.println("Creating a server socket on port " +
             port);
            SSLServerSocket serverSocket =
           (SSLServerSocket) factory.createServerSocket(port);
            String [] suites =
                    serverSocket.getSupportedCipherSuites();
            System.out.println("Support cipher suites are:");
            for(int i = 0; i < suites.length; i++)
            {
                System.out.println(suites[i]);
            }
            serverSocket.setEnabledCipherSuites(suites);
            System.out.println("Support protocols are:");
            String [] protocols =
                    serverSocket.getSupportedProtocols();
            for(int i = 0; i < protocols.length; i++)
```

```
          {
              System.out.println(protocols[i]);
          }
          System.out.println("Waiting for client...");
          SSLSocket socket = (SSLSocket) serverSocket.accept();
          System.out.println("Starting handshake...");
          socket.startHandshake();
          System.out.println("Just connected to "
                      + socket.getRemoteSocketAddress());
       }catch(IOException e)
       {
          e.printStackTrace();
       }
    }
}
```

I want to make a few comments about the SSLServerDemo program:

- The getDefault() method declares that it returns a ServerSocketFactory, but its actual data type is SSLServerSocketFactory, so I cast it to this type.

- Similarly, the createServerSocket() method declares that it returns a ServerSocket reference. However, because we are using the SSLServerSocketFactory, the actual return type is SSLServerSocket, so I had to cast this return value as well.

- This program displays the supported cipher suites and protocols for the environment it is executed in. The output in Figure 17.4 was generated by using the JSSE implementation of the J2SE 1.4.

- I enabled all the cipher suites that are supported on this platform with the following statement:

```
serverSocket.setEnabledCipherSuites(suites);
```

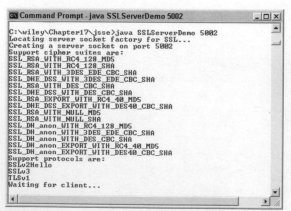

Figure 17.4   Output of the SSLServerDemo program.

- When I didn't enable the supported cipher suites, I got an exception that looked like the following:

```
javax.net.ssl.SSLException: No available certificate corresponds
  to the SSL cipher suites which are enabled.
        at
com.sun.net.ssl.internal.ssl.SSLServerSocketImpl.a(DashoA6275)
        at
com.sun.net.ssl.internal.ssl.SSLServerSocketImpl.accept(DashoA6275)
        at SSLServerDemo.main(SSLServerDemo.java:35)
```

- If you get this exception, try enabling at least one supported cipher suite. In a real-world environment, you probably will not enable all cipher suites as I did in the SSLServerDemo program, but instead you will only enable those that are being used by the security mechanisms of your platform.

- The program displays the supported protocols of this JSSE implementation, which are SSL version 3 and version 2Hello, and also TLS version 1.

- The program hangs because the server socket is waiting for a client connection, which I will show you how to create next.

Secure Client Socket

A client that wants to connect to an SSLServerSocket must use an SSLSocket object, which is accomplished by performing the following steps:

1. The client starts with an SSLSocketFactory object, which is not instantiated using the new keyword, but instead is obtained by using the following static method found in the SSLSocketFactory class:

```
public static SocketFactory getDefault()
```

2. Use the socket factory to create an SSLSocket object, which listens on a specified port for client requests.

After a secure connection is made, the client and server have an SSLSocket object to handle communication. The SSLSocket class extends java.net.Socket, so the client and server can invoke the methods discussed earlier from the Socket class, such as getOutputStream() and getInputStream(). There are also methods in SSLSocket unique to secure socket connections, including the following:

public void startHandshake() throws IOException. Starts an SSL handshake for this connection, which establishes the security and protection of the connection. Handshaking is successful only if both the client and server have a common cipher suite. A handshake is started automatically when an attempt is made to read or write from the socket, but you can start the handshake explicitly with this method.

public void setEnabledCipherSuites(String [] suites). Sets the cipher suites available for this connection. The client and server need to share at least one common cipher suite before handshaking can occur.

public void addHandshakeCompletedListener(HandshakeComplet-edListener h). Adds the specified listener to the connection. Whenever a handshake is completed successfully, the listener is notified via the handshakeCompleted() method in the HandshakeCompletedListener interface.

public SSLSession getSession(). Gets the session of this SSL connection, which is created after handshaking occurs. The SSLSession object contains information about the connection, for example, which cipher suite and protocol is being used, as well as the identity of the client and server.

Notice that the SSLSocket class is a source of a HandshakeCompletedEvent. This allows you to determine information about the security parameters used to establish the connection, such as the cipher suite used or any security certificates used. The following MyHandshakeListener class demonstrates writing a listener for this event.

```
import javax.net.ssl.*;
public class MyHandshakeListener
                    implements HandshakeCompletedListener
{
    public void handshakeCompleted(HandshakeCompletedEvent e)
    {
        System.out.println("Handshake succesful!");
        System.out.println("Using cipher suite: "
                        + e.getCipherSuite());
    }
}
```

The following SSLClientDemo program demonstrates a client creating an SSL connection to the SSLServerDemo application by using the SSLSocket class. Study the program and try to determine what is happening and what the output will be, which is shown in Figure 17.5.

Figure 17.5 Output of the SSLClientDemo program, which starts a handshake with the server to ensure that secure communication can occur successfully.

```java
import java.net.*;
import javax.net.ssl.*;
import java.io.*;
public class SSLClientDemo
{
    public static void main(String [] args)
    {
        String host = args[0];
        int port = Integer.parseInt(args[1]);
        try
        {
            System.out.println("Locating socket factory for SSL...");
            SSLSocketFactory factory =
                    (SSLSocketFactory) SSLSocketFactory.getDefault();
            System.out.println("Creating secure socket to "
                        + host + ":" + port);
            SSLSocket socket =
                    (SSLSocket) factory.createSocket(host, port);
            System.out.println("Enabling all available cipher
                        suites...");
            String [] suites = socket.getSupportedCipherSuites();
            socket.setEnabledCipherSuites(suites);
            System.out.println("Registering a handshake
                                listener...");
            socket.addHandshakeCompletedListener(
                    new MyHandshakeListener());
            System.out.println("Starting handshaking...");
            socket.startHandshake();
            System.out.println("Just connected to "
                        + socket.getRemoteSocketAddress());
        }
        catch(IOException e)
        {
            e.printStackTrace();
        }
    }
}
```

Let me make a few comments about the SSLClientDemo program:

- The getDefault() static method of SSLSocketFactory is used to obtain a reference to the default secure socket factory.

- The socket factory is used to create an SSLSocket on the localhost at port 5002. In this example, the server program is the SSLServerDemo program discussed earlier.

- The client and server need a common cipher suite, so the client needs to enable at least one cipher suite that the server understands. I just enabled all of them in this example and let the underlying implementation choose a cipher suite.

- A MyHandshakeListener object is registered to receive notification of when the handshake completes.

- The client specifically starts a handshake with the server, which is successful because the listener is notified. The listener displays the cipher suite that was used to establish this secure connection.

Communicating over a Secure Socket

The JSSE is used to establish a secure socket connection between two computers, as demonstrated by the SSLServerDemo and SSLClientDemo programs discussed in this chapter. After you have made a secure connection, communication can occur similar to that with nonsecure sockets. (A nonsecure socket is one created with the java.net.SocketServer and java.net.Socket classes.)

For example, suppose that you need an application to process credit card orders from customers. You want a secure connection so that the data passed between computers cannot be intercepted by malicious applications. I want to show you a simple but useful example of how this can be accomplished by tying together secure sockets and serialization (as discussed in Chapter 16, "Input and Output").

Suppose that the order is represented by a serializable class named CustomerOrder that contains fields for a customer's name, credit card number, and amount of order. (See the Web site for a listing of the CustomerOrder class.)

The following code from the OrderHandler class (available on the Web site) runs in a thread that waits for a secure client to connect, reads in a single CustomerOrder object, processes the order, and then closes the socket connection and waits for a new order to be sent:

```
System.out.println("Waiting for order...");
SSLSocket socket =
    (SSLSocket) serverSocket.accept();
socket.startHandshake();
ObjectInputStream in = new ObjectInputStream(socket.getInputStream());
CustomerOrder order = (CustomerOrder) in.readObject();
System.out.println("** Processing order **");
System.out.println("Amount: " + order.amountOfOrder);
System.out.println("Card info: " +
    order.creditCardNumber + " " +
    order.expMonth + "/" + order.expYear);
socket.close();
```

Figure 17.6 Output of the PurchaseDemo program, which sends a single CustomerOrder object to the OrderHandler program over a secure socket.

The following code from the PurchaseDemo program (available on the Web site) simulates an order being sent to the OrderHandler application. Study the code and try to determine the output of both the PurchaseDemo program and the OrderHandler program, shown in Figure 17.6 and Figure 17.7, respectively.

```
SSLSocketFactory factory =
    (SSLSocketFactory) SSLSocketFactory.getDefault();
System.out.println("Creating secure socket to " + host + ":" + port);
SSLSocket socket = (SSLSocket) factory.createSocket(host, port);
System.out.println("Enabling all available cipher suites...");
String [] suites = socket.getSupportedCipherSuites();
socket.setEnabledCipherSuites(suites);
ObjectOutputStream out =
    new ObjectOutputStream(socket.getOutputStream());
System.out.println("Sending order...");
CustomerOrder order =
    new CustomerOrder(1111222233334444L, 1, 2010, 853.79);
out.writeObject(order);
```

Notice in Figure 17.7 that the OrderHandler waits for an order, processes the order, and then immediately waits for another one.

Also notice that the client did not start a handshake explicitly using the startHandshake() method. However, a handshake occurs automatically when the client attempts to write a CustomerOrder object to the output stream of the socket.

Figure 17.7 Output of the OrderHandler program, which deserializes the CustomerOrder object and displays its information.

Overview of Datagram Packets

The User Datagram Protocol (UDP) is a connectionless protocol used for sending binary data from one computer to another. The data is referred to as a datagram packet, which also contains the destination server and port number that the data is to be delivered to. The sender of a message uses a datagram socket to send a packet, and a recipient uses a datagram socket to receive a message. When a message is sent, the recipient does not need to be available. Similarly, when a message is received, the sender does not need to be still available.

DatagramSocket Class

The java.net.DatagramSocket class is used by both the sender and the recipient of a datagram packet to send and receive a packet, respectively. The DatagramSocket class has four public constructors:

public DatagramSocket(int port) throws SocketException.   Creates a datagram socket on the localhost computer at the specified port.

public DatagramSocket(int port, InetAddress address) throws Socket-Exception.   Creates a datagram socket using the specified port and local address, which is useful if the computer has multiple addresses.

public DatagramSocket(SocketAddress address) throws SocketException. Creates a datagram socket at the specified SocketAddress, which encapsulates a server name and port number.

public DatagramSocket() throws SocketException.   Creates an unbound datagram socket. Use the bind() method of the DatagramSocket class to bind the socket to a port.

Here are some of the methods of interest in the DatagramSocket class:

public void send(DatagramPacket packet) throws IOException.   Sends the specified datagram packet. The DatagramPacket object contains the destination information of the packet.

public void receive(DatagramPacket packet) throws IOException. Receives a datagram packet, storing it in the specified argument. This method blocks and does not return until a datagram packet is received or the socket times out. If the socket times out, a SocketTimeoutException occurs.

public void setSoTimeout(int timeout) throws SocketTimeoutException. Sets the time-out value of the socket, which determines the number of milliseconds that the receive() method will block.

public void connect(InetAddress address, int port).   Although UDP is a connectionless protocol, this method has been added to the DatagramSocket class, as of J2SE 1.4. Packets are still sent and received using the send() and receive() methods, but connecting two datagram sockets improves delivery performance since security checks only need to be performed once.

public void disconnect().   Disconnects any current connection.

DatagramPacket Class

Notice that the send() and receive() methods of the DatagramSocket class have a DatagramPacket parameter. The DatagramPacket class represents a datagram packet, and (like DatagramSocket) it is used by both the sender and receiver of a packet. The DatagramPacket class has six constructors: two for receivers and four for senders.

The following two DatagramPacket constructors are used for receiving a datagram packet:

public DatagramPacket(byte [] buffer, int length).   Creates a datagram packet for receiving a packet of the specified size. The buffer will contain the incoming packet.

public DatagramPacket(byte [] buffer, int offset, int length).   Same as the previous constructor, except that the data of the incoming packet is stored in the position of the byte array specified by the offset parameter.

The array of bytes passed in to these constructors is used to contain the data of the incoming packet, and typically are empty arrays. If they are not empty, then the incoming datagram packet overwrites the data in the array.

The following four constructors are used for sending a datagram packet:

public DatagramPacket(byte [] buffer, int length, InetAddress address, int port).   Creates a datagram packet for sending a packet of the specified size. The buffer contains the data of the packet, and the address and port denote the recipient.

public DatagramPacket(byte [] buffer, int length, SocketAddress address).   Similar to the previous constructor, except that the name and port number of the recipient are contained in a SocketAddress argument.

public DatagramPacket(byte [] buffer, int offset, int length, InetAddress address, int port).   Allows you to denote an offset into the array, which (along with the length argument) determines a subset of the byte array that represents the data.

public DatagramPacket(byte [] buffer, int offset, int length, SocketAddress address).   Similar to the previous constructor, except that the name and port number of the recipient are contained in a SocketAddress argument.

Notice that each of the six constructors takes in an array of bytes. When receiving a packet, the array starts out empty and is filled with the incoming datagram packet. When sending a packet, the array of bytes contains the data of the packet to be sent.

The DatagramPacket class contains accessor and mutator methods for the various attributes of the datagram packet:

public byte [] getData(). Returns the data buffer.

public void setData(byte [] buffer). Sets the data of the packet.

public int getLength(). Returns the length of the data to be sent or received.

public void setLength(int length). Sets the length of the data to be sent or received.

public SocketAddress getSocketAddress(). Returns the address of the remote host where the message is being sent to or received from.

public void setSocketAddress(SocketAddress address). Sets the address of the remote host where the message is being sent to or received from.

Now, let's look at an example of how to use these classes to send and receive datagram packets using UDP.

Receiving a Datagram Packet

To receive a datagram packet, the following steps are performed:

1. Create an array of bytes large enough to hold the data of the incoming packet.
2. A DatagramPacket object is instantiated using the array of bytes.
3. A DatagramSocket is instantiated, and it is specified which port (and specific localhost address, if necessary) on the localhost the socket will bind to.
4. The receive() method of the DatagramSocket class is invoked, passing in the DatagramPacket object. This causes the thread to block until a datagram packet is received or a time out occurs.

After the receive() method returns, a new packet has just been delivered successfully. (Note that if a time out occurs, the receive() method does not return, but instead throws an exception.) The getData() method of the DatagramPacket class can be used to retrieve the array of bytes containing the data of this packet.

The following PacketReceiver program demonstrates the steps involved in receiving a datagram packet.

```
import java.net.*;
import java.io.*;

public class PacketReceiver
{
    public static void main(String [] args)
    {
        try
        {
            byte [] buffer = new byte[1024];
            DatagramPacket packet =
                    new DatagramPacket(buffer, buffer.length);
            DatagramSocket socket = new DatagramSocket(5002);
            System.out.println("Waiting for a packet...");
            socket.receive(packet);
            System.out.println("Just received packet from "
                    + packet.getSocketAddress());
            buffer = packet.getData();
            System.out.println(new String(buffer));
        }catch(IOException e)
        {
            e.printStackTrace();
        }
    }
}
```

Sending a Datagram Packet

To receive a datagram packet, the following steps are performed:

1. Create an array of bytes large enough to hold the data of the packet to be sent, and fill the array with the data.

2. Create a new DatagramPacket object that contains the array of bytes, as well as the server name and port number of the recipient.

3. A DatagramSocket is instantiated, and it is specified which port (and specific localhost address, if necessary) on the localhost the socket will bind to.

4. The send() method of the DatagramSocket class is invoked, passing in the DatagramPacket object.

The following PacketSender class sends a packet containing a string. Notice that the String object is converted to an array of bytes using the getBytes() method of the String class.

```
import java.net.*;
import java.io.*;
public class PacketSender
{
```

```
public static void main(String [] args)
{
    try
    {
        String data =
        "You have just received a packet of data sent using UDP";
        byte [] buffer = data.getBytes();
        DatagramPacket packet = new DatagramPacket(buffer,
                        buffer.length,
                        new InetSocketAddress("localhost", 5002));
        DatagramSocket socket = new DatagramSocket(5003);
        System.out.println("Sending a packet...");
        socket.send(packet);
    }catch(IOException e)
    {
        e.printStackTrace();
    }
}
}
```

The PacketSender program sends a datagram packet to the PacketReceiver program discussed earlier. Figure 17.8 shows the output of the PacketSender program.

Figure 17.9 shows the output generated by PacketReceiver when the packet is delivered. Note that the blank space in Figure 17.9 is caused by the array of bytes not being entirely filled with the incoming datagram.

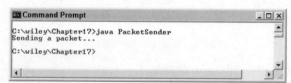

Figure 17.8 The PacketSender sends a datagram packet containing a string.

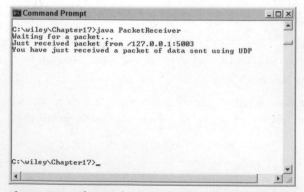

Figure 17.9 The receive() method invoked within PacketReceiver returns after the datagram packet is delivered.

Working with URLs

So far in this chapter, I have discussed sockets and datagram packets as options for creating network applications in Java. In this section, I will show you how to write Java programs that communicate with a URL. URL, which stands for Uniform Resource Locator, represents a resource on the World Wide Web, such as a Web page or FTP directory.

 A URL is actually a type of URI, Uniform Resource Identifier. A URI identifies a resource, but doesn't contain information about how to access the resource. A URL identifies a resource and a protocol for accessing the resource. A URI is represented in Java using the java.net.URI class.

A URL can be broken down into parts, as follows:

```
protocol://host:port/path?query#ref
```

The path is also referred to as the filename, and the host is also called the authority. Examples of protocols include HTTP, HTTPS, FTP, and File. For example, the following is a URL to a Web page whose protocol is HTTP:

```
http://www.javalicense.com/training/index.html?language=en#j2se
```

Notice that this URL does not specify a port, in which case the default port for the protocol is used. With HTTP, the default port is 80.

The java.net.URL class represents a URL. The URL class has several constructors for creating URLs, including the following:

public URL(String protocol, String host, int port, String file) throws MalformedURLException. Creates a URL by putting together the given parts.

public URL(String protocol, String host, String file) throws MalformedURLException. Identical to the previous constructor, except that the default port for the given protocol is used.

public URL(String url) throws MalformedURLException. Creates a URL from the given String.

public URL(URL context, String url) throws MalformedURLException. Creates a URL by parsing the together the URL and String arguments.

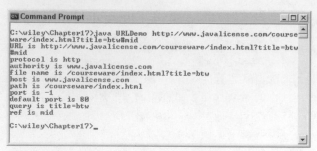

Figure 17.10 The URLDemo class displays each part of a URL.

The URL class contains many methods for accessing the various parts of the URL being represented. Some of the methods in the URL class include the following:

public String getPath().   Returns the path of the URL.

public String getQuery().   Returns the query part of the URL.

public String getAuthority().   Returns the authority of the URL.

public int getPort().   Returns the port of the URL.

public int getDefaultPort().   Returns the default port for the protocol of the URL.

public String getProtocol().   Returns the protocol of the URL.

public String getHost().   Returns the host of the URL.

public String getFile().   Returns the filename of the URL.

public String getRef().   Returns the reference part of the URL.

public URLConnection openConnection() throws IOException.   Opens a connection to the URL, allowing a client to communicate with the resource.

The following URLDemo program demonstrates what these methods do and also demonstrates the various parts of a URL. A URL is entered on the command line, and the URLDemo program outputs each part of the given URL. Study the program and try to determine what the output is when the command-line argument is:

```
http://www.javalicense.com/courseware/index.html?title=btw#mid
```

The output of the URLDemo program with this URL is shown in Figure 17.10.

```
import java.net.*;
import java.io.*;
public class URLDemo
{
    public static void main(String [] args)
    {
```

```
        try
        {
            URL url = new URL(args[0]);
            System.out.println("URL is " + url.toString());
            System.out.println("protocol is "
                                    + url.getProtocol());
            System.out.println("authority is "
                                    + url.getAuthority());
            System.out.println("file name is " + url.getFile());
            System.out.println("host is " + url.getHost());
            System.out.println("path is " + url.getPath());
            System.out.println("port is " + url.getPort());
            System.out.println("default port is "
                                    + url.getDefaultPort());
            System.out.println("query is " + url.getQuery());
            System.out.println("ref is " + url.getRef());
        }catch(IOException e)
        {
            e.printStackTrace();
        }
    }
}
```

URL Connections

Using the openConnection() method of the URL class, you can connect to a
URL and communicate with the resource. The openConnection() method
returns a java.net.URLConnection, an abstract class whose subclasses represent the various types of URL connections. For example, if you connect to a
URL whose protocol is HTTP, the openConnection() method returns an
HttpURLConnection object. If you connect to a URL that represents a JAR file,
the openConnection() method returns a JarURLConnection object.

The URLConnection class has many methods for setting or determining
information about the connection, including the following:

public void setDoInput(boolean input). Passes in true to denote that the
connection will be used for input. The default value is true because
clients typically read from a URLConnection.

public void setDoOutput(boolean output). Passes in true to denote that
the connection will be used for output. The default value is false because
many types of URLs do not support being written to.

public InputStream getInputStream() throws IOException. Returns the
input stream of the URL connection for reading from the resource.

public OutputStream getOutputStream() throws IOException. Returns the output stream of the URL connection for writing to the resource.

public URL getURL(). Returns the URL that this URLConnection object is connected to.

The URLConnection class also contains methods for accessing the header information of the connection, allowing you to determine the type and length of the URL's content, the date it was last modified, the content encoding, and so forth. Be sure to check the documentation for a listing of all the methods in the URLConnection class.

The following URLConnectionDemo program connects to a URL entered from the command line. If the URL represents an HTTP resource, the connection is cast to HttpURLConnection, and the data in the resource is read one line at a time. Figure 17.11 shows the output of the program for the URL www.javalicense.com.

```java
import java.net.*;
import java.io.*;
public class URLConnectionDemo
{
    public static void main(String [] args)
    {
        try
        {
            URL url = new URL(args[0]);
            URLConnection urlConnection = url.openConnection();
            HttpURLConnection connection = null;
            if(urlConnection instanceof HttpURLConnection)
            {
                connection = (HttpURLConnection) urlConnection;
            }
            else
            {
                System.out.println("Please enter an HTTP URL.");
                return;
            }
            BufferedReader in = new BufferedReader(
                            new InputStreamReader(
                            connection.getInputStream()));
            String urlString = "";
            String current;
            while((current = in.readLine()) != null)
            {
                urlString += current;
            }
            System.out.println(urlString);
        }catch(IOException e)
        {
            e.printStackTrace();
        }
    }
}
```

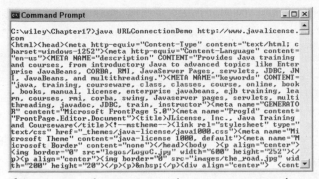

Figure 17.11   The URLConnectionDemo program shows the contents of an HTML page. This figure shows part of the output of the URL http://www.javalicense.com.

Lab 17.1: Using Sockets

The purpose of this lab is to become familiar with working with sockets. You will write a client/server network program that allows a simple conversation to take place between two computers.

1. Write a program named TalkServer that uses a ServerSocket object to listen for clients on port 5050.

2. When a client connects, have the TalkServer program read in a String from the client using the readUTF() method of the DataInputStream class. You will need to create a new DataInputStream by using the input stream of the socket. Print out the String that is read.

3. The TalkServer program should then send a String to the client using the writeUTF() method of the DataOutputStream class, sending the String to the client's socket. The string sent to the client should be input from the console input using the keyboard.

4. This process should continue until the connection is lost somehow. In other words, the TalkServer reads in a String, displays it, and then inputs a String from the keyboard and sends it to the client.

5. Write a program named TalkClient that uses the Socket class to connect to the server socket of the TalkServer program.

6. The client should send a String input from the keyboard to the server using the writeUTF() method. Then, the TalkClient should read in a String from the Server using the readUTF() method, displaying the String.

7. This process should continue until the connection is lost. The client and server are now communicating with each other in a simple conversation.

The initial output of the server should be a String read from the client. The initial output on the client should be a prompt to enter a message to be sent to the server. When the client enters a message and presses Enter, the message should be displayed on the server. Similarly, when a message is entered on the server and the user presses Enter, the message should be displayed on the client.

Lab 17.2: Using Datagram Packets

The purpose of this lab is to become familiar with sending and receiving datagram packets. You will write a program that simulates a weather-updating process, in which weather updates are sent to a listener every 15 seconds using datagram packets.

1. Write a class named WeatherUpdater that extends TimerTask. Add a field of type DatagramSocket, a String field named recipientName, and an int field named recipientPort. Add a constructor that takes in a String and an int for these two fields, and also initialize the DatagramSocket object in the constructor using any available port.

2. Within the run() method of the WeatherUpdater class, create a String that looks like "Current temp: 40", where 40 is a randomly generated number between 0 and 100 that changes each time the method is invoked.

3. Within run(), instantiate a DatagramPacket appropriate for sending a packet. The array of bytes should be the String in the previous step converted to bytes. Send it to the recipient denoted by the recipientName and recipientPort fields of the class.

4. Add main() to your WeatherUpdater class. Within main(), instantiate a new WeatherUpdater object, using the first two command-line arguments for the recipient's name and port number.

5. Within main(), instantiate a Timer object and use it to schedule the WeatherUpdater with a fixed-rate schedule of every 15 seconds.

6. Save and compile the WeatherUpdater class.

7. Write a class named WeatherWatcher that contains main().

8. Within main(), instantiate a DatagramSocket on port 4444. Also, instantiate a DatagramPacket suitable for receipt, by using an array of bytes of size 128.

9. Invoke the receive() method within main() so that the thread blocks until a datagram packet is delivered.

10. After a packet is delivered, print out its contents. Create a loop so that the WeatherWatcher then invokes receive() again, to be ready for the next packet to be delivered.

11. Save, compile, and run the WeatherWatcher program.

12. Run the WeatherUpdater program, passing in the appropriate host name (localhost if both are on the same computer) and port number 4444.

The WeatherUpdater probably will not display any output. However, in the WeatherWatcher program, you should see the statement "Current temp: N" every 15 seconds or so, with the temperature changing randomly.

Lab 17.3: The InstantMessage Server

This lab is a continuation of the Instant Messaging project from previous chapters. In this lab, you will write the server application that receives an InstantMessage object from a sender and sends the message to its intended recipient.

1. Write a class named IMServer that implements Runnable. Add a field of type Vector to contain all Participant objects currently logged on.

2. Within the run() method, create a ServerSocket on port 5555. Invoke the accept() method and wait for a client to connect.

3. When a client connects, they will send you a String using the writeUTF() method of DataOutputStream. Read in this String using the readUTF() method of DataInputStream, which will be their username. Then, instantiate a new Participant, passing in the socket and their username into the constructor.

4. Because Participant is a Thread, start it. Perform these steps in a loop so that accept() is invoked on the ServerSocket after the new Participant thread is started.

5. Save, compile, and run the IMServer program.

There will not be any output until we write the client program in the next lab. For now, your IMServer program should be blocked, waiting for a client to connect.

Lab 17.4: Finishing the InstantMessage Program

In this lab, you will finish the InstantMessage program.

1. To make your Instant Message application communicate with the server, the only modifications need to appear in the constructor of the InstantMessageDialog class. Open this class in your text editor.

2. Comment out or remove any code involving pipes.

3. Within the constructor of InstantMessageDialog, create a Socket connection to the IMServer program. Use the input and output streams of this socket to instantiate the SendMessage and Participant objects.

4. Save, compile, and run the InstantMessageDialog class.

Your Instant Message program can now be executed on two different computers on a network, or you can simply run it twice on your computer. When a message is sent, it should appear in the appropriate friend's instant message window.

Lab 17.5: Connecting to URLs

The purpose of this lab is to become familiar with connecting to URLs. In this lab, you will create a Swing GUI that can be used to view the source code of HTML documents. I will give you the guidelines for the application and let you decide how to design and write it.

1. Create a JFrame that contains a text area in the center for viewing an HTML page and a text field in the south for entering a URL.

2. When the user enters a URL in the text field, your program should connect to the URL, read its contents, and display them in the text area.

3. Use the HttpURLConnection class to read the contents of the URL.

4. Check out the javax.swing.text.html package for classes that might be of interest, notably the HTMLEditorKit class.

5. To make your class more functional, consider adding a menu with menu items that allow the user to save the contents of the text area in an HTML file on his or her hard drive. The javax.swing.JFile-Chooser class might come in handy here.

When the program is executed, the user should be able to type in a URL in the text field, and then see the source code of that HTML in the text area.

Summary

- Java contains APIs for developing network applications that use TCP/IP and UDP protocols.

- The java.net.ServerSocket and java.net.Socket classes are used for creating a TCP/IP connection between two Java applications. Communication is performed using the java.io classes.

- The Java Secure Socket Extension (JSSE) allows for a secure connection between two machines, using the Secure Sockets Layer (SSL) protocol. This is performed using the javax.net.ssl.SSLServerSocket and javax.net.ssl.SSLSocket classes.

- The java.net.DatagramSocket class is used to send and receive datagram packets. The java.net.DatagramPacket class is used to represent the data in the packet.

- The java.net.URL class is used for connecting to and reading data from a URL.

Review Questions

1. Name the two common networking protocols discussed in this chapter.

2. True or False: To create a TCP connection, both the client and server applications need to be running and available at the same time.

3. True or False: When a sender sends a datagram packet, the recipient is guaranteed to receive it, even though this may not happen instantly.

4. Name the two classes in the Java API used to create a nonsecure socket connection using TCP.

5. Name the two classes in the Java API used to send and receive datagram packets.

6. True or False: Multiple applications on a server can bind the same port and share it.

7. True or False: I can write a server application that binds to port 80.

8. List the two ways that the accept() method in the ServerSocket class will stop blocking.

9. What is the data type of the return value of the accept() method in the ServerSocket class?

10. True or False: If a ServerSocket is listening on port 3000 and a client connection is accepted, the server and client are now communicating by using port 3000.

11. True or False: The following statement creates a Socket object in memory that is not yet connected to the server, but can be connected by using the bind() method in the Socket class:

    ```
    Socket s = new Socket("server_name", 1090);
    ```

12. What does SSL stand for?

13. Which two classes are used to obtain a secure server socket using the JSSE?

14. Which two classes are used to obtain a secure socket using the JSSE?

15. What does URL stand for?

16. What does URI stand for?

17. What is the query part of the following URL?

    ```
    http://www.wiley.com/index.html?language=en#Java
    ```

18. What is the default port of the previous URL? The authority?

19. What is the actual data type returned from the openConnection() method of the URL class when invoked on a URL object representing an HTTP resource?

Answers to Review Questions

1. Transmission Control Protocol (TCP) and User Datagram Protocol (UDP).

2. True. TCP is a "live" connection between two computers.

3. False. UDP does not guarantee delivery of packets.

4. java.net.ServerSocket and java.net.Socket.

5. java.net.DatagramSocket and java.net.DatagramPacket.

6. False. A port can be bound by only one application at a time.

7. True. However, port 80 is the port used by most Web servers, so it isn't a good idea to use port 80 unless you are developing a Web server application.

8. When a client connects, or when the server socket times out.

9. java.net.Socket.

10. False. The ServerSocket is using port 3000; the socket for the client uses an arbitrary port for communicating with that client.

11. False. If that statement is successful, then a connection is made with the server and no further steps need to be taken. The two computers are ready to begin communication.

12. Secure Sockets Layer.

13. javax.net.ssl.SSLServerSocketFactory and javax.net.ssl.SSLServerSocket.

14. javax.net.ssl.SSLSocketFactory and javax.net.ssl.SSLSocket.

15. Uniform Resource Locator.

16. Uniform Resource Identifier, which is similar to URL except it does not contain any information about how to locate the resource.

17. language=en.

18. 80 because the protocol is HTTP.

19. HttpURLConnection.

CHAPTER

18

Database Programming

Almost every real-world programming application I have ever been a part of has involved a database. Accessing data in a database is an essential aspect of any language, and it's no surprise that Java contains extensive support for database programming. The JDBC API contains the classes and interfaces a Java program uses to connect to a database and access its contents. In this chapter, I will discuss an overview of JDBC, how to connect to a database, how to execute an SQL statement on a database, and how to work with result sets.

An Overview of JDBC

The JDBC API is an API for accessing data in a tabular format, which includes every popular database as well as spreadsheet applications such as Microsoft Excel and files that contain tabular data. The latest version of JDBC is 3.0 and is a part of the J2SE 1.4. JDBC 3.0 is broken down into two packages:

java.sql. Referred to as the JDBC Core API.

javax.sql. Referred to as the JDBC Optional Package API. (In JDBC 2.0, this package was formerly known as the JDBC Standard Extension API.)

JDBC is not an acronym, but rather a trademarked name, although you will commonly hear it referred to as Java Database Connectivity. The term JDBC evolved from the acronym ODBC, which stands for Open Database Connectivity, a technology designed to simplify database programming by making the code to access a database independent of the actual database used.

JDBC provides the same capabilities as ODBC, allowing Java programs to contain database-independent code. This means that a Java program that accesses a database is not only portable across JVMs (since it's a Java program), but portable across databases, since it uses JDBC.

The JDBC API provides a mechanism for Java code to be portable across databases. JDBC simplifies the creation and execution of Structured Query Language (SQL) statements. SQL is a language used to communicate with a database and access its contents. Be sure to read the upcoming section *An SQL Primer* later in this chapter if you are new to SQL.

Classroom Q & A

Q: It seems impressive that a Java program can move from one database to another without changing any of the code that involves accessing the database. Does this really happen in the real world?

A: Well, yes and no. If you write a Java application that uses JDBC, and you stick to the standard SQL statements, yes. If you write a program that takes advantage of the unique features of a particular database, no. Keep in mind that this lack of portability is not a Java or JDBC issue, but a database issue. In the competitive database market, unique features or behaviors of a database are common. Any code in any language that takes advantage of a specific feature of a database will not be portable across databases.

Q: Suppose my program uses everyday SQL, nothing fancy. How is it possible that my program can communicate with different databases?

A: The answer is based on having a JDBC driver. Before you can access a database using JDBC, you need a JDBC driver for that particular database. For example, in this chapter I will show you how to access a Microsoft Access database. This means that we will need a JDBC driver for Access. We will just happen to use a driver that comes with the J2SE.

Q: Where do I get these drivers?

A: Typically, the manufacturer of your database provides you with one. As Java has become more and more popular, more and more database vendors provide efficient, robust JDBC drivers so Java applications can take advantage of the features of the database.

Q: What if I use a database that does not provide a JDBC driver?

A: Not to worry. There are plenty of third-party drivers available for all types of databases. JDBC drivers exist for virtually every possible type of database access you will ever need, and virtually every database. In the next section, *JDBC Drivers*, I discuss the various types of drivers and where you can find them.

Q: Is the driver a separate program that I need to download?

A: It depends on the type of driver. A database driver is a class, and to use a driver you need to make sure the class for the driver is loaded by your JVM and registered with the DriverManager class, which I discuss in detail in the upcoming section *Connecting to a Database*. Some drivers require a separate application to be running.

Q: You mentioned JDBC works on databases that use a tabular format. What does that mean?

A: Tabular format means the data is stored in tables. Most databases store their contents by using tables. In fact, a database can be thought of as a collection of tables, where a table is a collection of rows, and a row is a collection of columns. The items in the columns represent the actual contents of the database. You will soon find out that the JDBC API contains many methods for accessing the rows and columns of database tables.

Q: You mentioned SQL is used to communicate with a database. Do I need to learn SQL to use JDBC?

A: Yes! Although JDBC may eventually eliminate the need to learn SQL, right now SQL is the de facto means for accessing the contents of a database. If you are new to database programming, I might as well let you in on what database programmers have known for years: You need to know SQL. JDBC provides you with a mechanism for connecting to a database, but the actual access to the data in the database is done using SQL.

Q: What if I don't know any SQL?

A: That's no problem. If you have made it this far in the book, you are clearly someone who understands languages. I can show you enough SQL to have you writing database programs within the hour. Just check out the section *An SQL Primer* in this chapter and carefully study the sample programs throughout this chapter.

Now that we have discussed how JDBC works, let's look at the important topic of JDBC drivers. I will then show you how to select a driver in your Java program, and connect to a database.

JDBC Drivers

To connect to a database and access its contents, you need a JDBC driver that works with that particular database. There are many different JDBC drivers available, and Sun keeps an updated, searchable list of them on their Web site at:

```
http://industry.java.sun.com/products/jdbc/drivers
```

JDBC drivers fit into four categories referred to as *types*, denoted simply by the numbers 1 through 4. The four types of drivers are:

type 1 driver.   A *bridge driver*, which allows JDBC to communicate with any database that uses ODBC. When Java first came out, this was a useful driver because most databases only supported ODBC access. Nowadays, however, the bridge driver is not recommended beyond testing purposes. The J2SE comes with a bridge driver that we will use in the examples in this chapter.

type 2 driver.   A *native API driver*, meaning that the driver converts JDBC calls into native API calls unique to the database. Type 2 drivers are typically provided by the database vendor and require native code to be deployed to any client using a type 2 driver.

type 3 driver.   A *JDBC-Net driver*, which converts JDBC calls into a database-independent net protocol, which is then translated into the database-specific calls. A type 3 driver has advantages because it does not require anything of the client, and the same driver can be used for multiple databases. The conversions are made by using a middleware application. Third-party vendors typically provide type 3 drivers.

type 4 driver.   A *native protocol driver*, meaning that JDBC calls are converted directly into native calls to the database. They are pure-Java drivers that do not require native code on the client side. The JDBC drivers provided by the database vendor are typically type 4 drivers.

If you are accessing one type of database, such as Oracle, Sybase, or IBM, the preferred driver type is 4. If your Java application is accessing multiple types of databases at the same time, type 3 is the preferred driver. Type 2 drivers are useful in situations where a type 3 or type 4 driver is not available yet for your database. The type 1 driver is not considered a deployment-level driver and is typically used for development and testing purposes only.

The J2SE comes with the following type 1 bridge driver:

```
sun.jdbc.odbc.JdbcOdbcDriver
```

This is the driver we will use for the examples in the course because it comes with the J2SE API, which means that you have it on your computer.

 If you are using a version of the Windows operating system, you can find detailed instructions on this book's Web site showing how to create a database using Microsoft Access. More importantly, you will find step-by-step instructions on how to create a Data Source Name for your database so that your Java programs can connect to your Access database. See the Introduction for the site's URL.

Connecting to a Database

After you have a data source name created, there are two ways to establish a connection to the database using JDBC. (See the Web site's URL provided in the Introduction for instructions on how to do this for Windows and Microsoft Access.)

- Use the static method getConnection() in the java.sql.DriverManager class, which takes in a URL representing the data source name.
- Use JNDI (Java Naming and Directory Interface) to look up the data source name, which is returned as a javax.sql.DataSource object, and then use the getConnection() method of the DataSource class.

The Java documentation states that the technique using the DataSource class is preferred over the DriverManager class; however, DataSource is a newer class (J2SE 1.4), so there is lots of existing database code out there that still uses DriverManager, not to mention that using the DataSource class typically involves using a third-party application such as an application server and a naming service. If you are writing a standalone Java application, such as all of the examples in this book, the DriverManager class is the technique most often used.

No matter which technique you choose, they are similar in terms of coding, so I will show both of them to you.

♦ Connecting to a JDBC Data Source

To connect to a JDBC data source, its name must be represented as a URL of the following format:

```
jdbc:<subprotocol>:<dsn>
```

All JDBC URLs start with jdbc. The subprotocol is actually determined by the driver you are using. For example, the bridge driver we will use has a subprotocol ODBC. The DSN is whatever the name is of the data source.

For example, the following URL represents a data source named moviesDSN, which is being accessed using the bridge driver:

```
jdbc:odbc:moviesDSN
```

The following URL represents the same data source being accessed from a type 3 driver from a company called JDataConnect:

```
jdbc:JDataConnect://localhost/musicDSN
```

JDBC URLs are driver dependent, so be sure to check any documentation that comes with your driver for determining the proper URL syntax.

Using the DriverManager Class

There are two steps involved in connecting to a database using the Driver-Manager class: Load the appropriate JDBC driver, and then invoke the getConnection() method of the DriverManager class.

The driver is loaded when the corresponding bytecode class is loaded by the JVM, so you need to make sure the driver class is loaded. One way to do this is to use the Class.forName() method. For example, the following statement loads the sun.jdbc.odbc.JdbcOdbcDriver type 1 driver that comes with the J2SE:

```
Class.forName("sun.jdbc.odbc.JdbcOdbcDriver");
```

After the driver is loaded, the connection is made using one of the following methods in the DriverManager class:

public static Connection getConnection(String url) throws SQLException. Establishes a connection to the given database. The DriverManager will select an appropriate JDBC driver if more than one has been loaded.

public static Connection getConnection(String url, String user, String password) throws SQLException.   Same as the previous version, except that a username and password are passed in if the database requires authentication.

public static Connection getConnection(String url, Properties info)
throws SQLException. The Properties object contains information
about the connection to be made and typically includes user and
password entries.

Notice that the return value of each of these methods is a java.sql.Connection object, which represents the connection to the database. I will discuss the
Connection class in the upcoming section *Creating Statements*. The following
DriverManagerDemo program demonstrates using the DriverManager class
to connect to the moviesDSN data source. After the connection is made, the
getCatalog() method is invoked on the Connection object, which displays the
name of the database file. Study the program and try to determine its output,
which is shown in Figure 18.1.

```java
import java.sql.*;
public class DriverManagerDemo
{
    public static void main(String [] args)
    {
        String url = "jdbc:odbc:" + args[0];
        System.out.println("Attempting to connect to " + url);
        try
        {
            System.out.println("Loading the driver...");
            Class.forName("sun.jdbc.odbc.JdbcOdbcDriver");

            System.out.println("Establishing a connection...");
            Connection connection =
                    DriverManager.getConnection(url);

            System.out.println("Connect to "
                    + connection.getCatalog() + " a success!");
        }
        catch (Exception e)
        {
            e.printStackTrace();
        }
    }
}
```

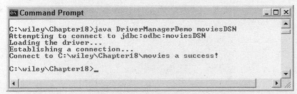

Figure 18.1 Output of the DriverManagerDemo program.

Using the DataSource Class

The javax.sql.DataSource class can also be used to establish a connection to a database. A naming service is used to locate the database, meaning that the database needs to bind its data source name with the naming service. This step is typically not done by the programmer, but instead is accomplished using a tool provided by the naming service, application server, or database vendor.

When using drivers and the DriverManager class, the URL for a data source looks similar to:

```
jdbc:<protocol>:<data_source_name>
```

When using a naming service and the DataSource class, the URL for a data source looks similar to:

```
jdbc/<context>/<data_source_name>
```

For example, the following URL might be used to represent our movies database:

```
jdbc/moviesDSN
```

◆ Binding the Data Source Name

The DataSourceDemo program will not run on your computer unless you bind the data source name in a naming service and then specify the naming service as a property when running the program using the java.naming.factory.initial property.

For example, the following command line runs the DataSourceDemo program using the rmiregistry as its naming service. (The rmiregistry comes with the J2SE SDK):

```
java -Djava.naming.factory.initial=
com.sun.jndi.rmi.registry.RegistryContextFactory
DataSourceDemo jdbc/moviesDSN
```

This still does not fix the problem of running this program on your computer, however, because jdbc/moviesDSN is not a bound data source name in the rmiregistry. This is the problem you will run into when using DataSource in a standalone application: You need a naming service as well as a way to bind your database's data source name into the naming service. The J2SE API does not provide the classes for you to do this on your own. You need to use third-party software.

So, why did I show you the DataSource technique for connecting to a database? Because it is the preferred way to connect to a database, even though in standalone Java applications such as the ones in this book, you will probably use the DriverManager class. You will most often see the DataSource class used in J2EE applications. That being said, I wouldn't feel too bad about choosing DriverManager instead of the preferred DataSource class for establishing database connections, especially because DriverManager has been the only way to connect to a database for the first 5 years of Java database programming!

The javax.naming.InitialContext class is used to communicate with the naming service, and its lookup() method is used to look up a name in the naming service. The following DataSourceDemo program demonstrates the steps involved in connecting to a database using the DataSource class.

```java
import java.sql.*;
import javax.sql.DataSource;
import javax.naming.InitialContext;
public class DataSourceDemo
{
    public static void main(String [] args)
    {
        String dsn = args[0];
        System.out.println("Attempting to connect to " + dsn);
        try
        {
            System.out.println("Initializing the naming context...");
            InitialContext init = new InitialContext();

            System.out.println("Looking up " + dsn);
            DataSource source = (DataSource) init.lookup(dsn);
            System.out.println("Establishing a connection...");
            Connection connection = source.getConnection();
            System.out.println("Connect to "
                + connection.getCatalog() + " a success!");
        }
        catch (Exception e)
        {
            e.printStackTrace();
        }
    }
}
```

When using the DataSource class to connect to a database, you do not typically load a JDBC driver; however, if you need to, you can. The drivers are typically specified either from a command-line property or a properties file managed by the application server or naming service tool you are using.

An SQL Primer

Structured Query Language (SQL) is a standardized language that allows you to perform operations on a database, such as creating entries, reading content, updating content, and deleting entries. SQL is supported by most any database you will likely use, and it allows you to write database code independently of the underlying database.

SQL is a standard, but most database vendors provide an extension to SQL unique to their database. In this book, I am going to show you the basics of SQL, but keep in mind there is more to it than what is discussed here. I will show you enough SQL to be able to create, read, update, and delete (often referred to as CRUD operations) data from a database, which are far and away the most common types of SQL operations.

Creating Data

The CREATE TABLE statement is used for creating a new table in a database. The syntax is:

```
CREATE TABLE table_name
(
    column_name column_data_type,
    column_name column_data_type,
    column_name column_data_type
    ...
)
```

For example, the following SQL statement creates a table named Employees with four columns: number, which is an int; payRate, which is a double; and first and last, which are strings of up to 255 characters.

```
CREATE TABLE Employees
(
    number INT NOT NULL,
    payRate DOUBLE PRECISION NOT NULL,
    first VARCHAR(255) ,
    last VARCHAR(255)
)
```

After you have a table created, you can insert rows into the table using the INSERT statement. The syntax for INSERT looks similar to the following, where column1, column2, and so on represent the new data to appear in the respective columns:

```
INSERT INTO table_name VALUES (column1, column2, column3, ...)
```

For example, the following INSERT statement inserts a new row in the Employees database created earlier:

```
INSERT INTO Employees VALUES (101, 20.00, 'Rich', 'Raposa')
```

You can also specify into which columns to insert the data; this is useful if you are not inserting data into each column of the new row. The following INSERT statement does not insert a payRate for the new row:

```
INSERT INTO Employees (number, first, last) VALUES (102, 'Rich', 'Little')
```

In this case, the payRate column will assume a default value or be empty, depending on the database.

Reading Data

The SELECT statement is used to retrieve data from a database. The syntax for SELECT is:

```
SELECT column_name, column_name, ...
    FROM table_name
    WHERE conditions
```

The WHERE clause can use the comparison operators such as =, !=, <, >, <=, and >=, as well as the BETWEEN and LIKE operators.

For example, the following statement selects the payRate, first and last columns from the Employees table where the number column is 101:

```
SELECT first, last, payRate FROM Employees WHERE number = 101
```

To select all columns from a row, you can use the asterisk *:

```
SELECT * FROM Employees WHERE number = 101
```

The LIKE operator allows you to select entries containing a particular substring. The following SELECT statement selects employee numbers whose last name starts with an R:

```
SELECT number FROM Employees WHERE last LIKE 'R%'
```

Notice the percent symbol (%) is used to denote a wildcard in a LIKE operation. The following SELECT statement selects all employees whose last name contains the pattern 'er' anywhere in their last name:

```
SELECT * FROM Employees WHERE last LIKE '%er%'
```

The AND and OR operators are used to combine WHERE expressions. The following SELECT statement selects all employees whose pay is greater than 10.0 and less than or equal to 20.0:

```
SELECT * FROM Employees WHERE payRate > 10.0 AND payRate <= 20.0
```

The BETWEEN statement also uses AND. The following statement selects all employees whose last name is between Saunders and Smith:

```
SELECT * FROM Employees WHERE last BETWEEN 'Saunders' AND 'Smith'
```

The NOT operator can be used in a WHERE clause to negate a Boolean expression. The following SELECT statement selects employees whose first name does not start with an R:

```
SELECT * FROM Employees WHERE first NOT LIKE 'R%'
```

By default, the SELECT statement returns all elements that match the WHERE condition, even if the result set is not unique. For example, searching the Employees table for all first names that start with an R will return Rich twice if the database contains a Rich Raposa and a Rich Little. If the DISTINCT keyword is used, the result set will only contain Rich once:

```
SELECT DISTINCT first FROM Employees WHERE first LIKE 'R%'
```

The SELECT statement can contain an optional ORDER BY clause that sorts the elements in the result set. For example, the following SELECT statement returns all employees in the database, sorting the result set by last name:

```
SELECT * FROM Employees ORDER BY last
```

When using ORDER BY, you can use the ASC to denote ascending order, which is the default, and DESC to denote descending order. The following statement returns all employees whose last name starts with R, sorting them in descending order of their pay rate, but ascending order by their last name:

```
SELECT * FROM Employees WHERE last LIKE 'R%' ORDER BY payRate DESC, last ASC
```

Updating Data

The UPDATE statement is used to update data. The syntax for UPDATE is:

```
UPDATE table_name
    SET column_name = value, column_name = value, ...
    WHERE conditions
```

The following UPDATE statement changes the payRate column of the employee whose number is 101:

```
UPDATE Employees SET payRate=40.00 WHERE number=101
```

The following UPDATE statement changes two columns in the row of employee 102:

```
UPDATE Employees SET payRate=10.00, first='Richard' WHERE number=102
```

Deleting Data

The DELETE statement is used to delete rows from a database. The DELETE has the syntax:

```
DELETE FROM table_name
    WHERE conditions
```

The following statement deletes the row from the Employees database whose number column is 101:

```
DELETE FROM Employees WHERE number=101
```

The following DELETE statement deletes all employees whose first name starts with Rich:

```
DELETE FROM Employees WHERE first LIKE 'Rich%'
```

You can delete a table from a database using the DROP TABLE statement, which looks similar to:

```
DROP TABLE table_name
```

For example, the following statement removes the Employees table from the database:

```
DROP TABLE Employees
```

Creating Statements

After you connect to a database using either the DriverManager class or the DataSource class, you get a java.sql.Connection object. The Connection class contains the methods you need for creating SQL statements. The java.sql.Statement interface represents a SQL statement, and there are three types of Statement objects:

java.sql.Statement.   Represents a simple SQL statement with no parameters.

java.sql.PreparedStatement.   A child interface of Statement, a Prepared-Statement object represents a precompiled SQL statement that contains parameters that need to be set before the statement is executed.

java.sql.CallableStatement.   A child interface of PreparedStatement, a CallableStatement object is used to call a stored procedure in the database.

 A Statement is useful for executing a SQL statement that will likely only occur once and has no parameters. If you have a SQL statement that executes a number of times, you should use a PreparedStatement, whether or not parameters are needed. A prepared SQL statement executes more efficiently because the statement is precompiled by the database. In addition, the in parameters of a prepared statement allow you to reuse a common SQL statement repeatedly with different values. If you are invoking a stored procedure in a database, you need to use a CallableStatement.

Stored procedures represent multiple SQL statements, and invoking a stored procedure is similar to invoking a method. Not all databases support stored procedures, but enterprise-level databases definitely will and are commonly used in large-scale database applications. The CallableStatement interface is used to invoke a stored procedure, which can have both in and out parameters.

No matter which type of statement you need, each is obtained using the Connection object. I will now discuss how to create and use each of the three types of SQL statements, starting with simple statements.

Simple Statements

The java.sql.Statement interface represents a simple SQL statement. The Connection interface contains the following methods for creating Statement objects:

public Statement createStatement() throws SQLException.   Creates a simple SQL statement. The result set of this statement will be read-only and forward scrolling only.

public Statement createStatement(int resultSetType, int concurrency) throws SQLException.   Creates a simple SQL statement whose result set will have the given properties. The resultSetType is either TYPE_FORWARD_ONLY, TYPE_SCROLL_INSENSITIVE, or TYPE_SCROLL_SENSITIVE, which are static fields in the java.sql.ResultSet interface. These values are discussed in the next section, *Working with Result Sets*. The concurrency type is CONCUR_READ_ONLY or CONCUR_UPDATABLE, for denoting whether the result set is updatable or not.

public Statement createStatement(int resultSetType, int concurrency, int holdability) throws SQLException.   Similar to the previous method, except a result set holdability property is denoted. The possible values for holdability are HOLD_CURSORS_OVER_COMMIT or CLOSE_CURSORS_AT_COMMIT, static fields in the ResultSet interface. These are also discussed in the next section. For example, the following statements create a Statement object using the default result set properties:

```
Class.forName("sun.jdbc.odbc.JdbcOdbcDriver");
Connection connection =
    DriverManager.getConnection("jdbc:odbc:someDSN");
Statement statement = connection.createStatement();
```

A Statement object can represent any SQL statement, and the Statement interface contains methods for defining and executing the SQL statement. Some of the methods in the Statement interface include:

public ResultSet executeQuery(String sql) throws SQLException.   Executes a SQL statement that returns a single result set. Use this method for SELECT statements.

public int executeUpdate(String sql) throws SQLException.   Executes the given SQL statement. Use this method for executing UPDATE, INSERT, or DELETE statements or other statements that do not return a result set. The return value is a row count of the number of rows affected by the SQL statement.

public boolean execute(String sql) throws SQLException.   Executes the given SQL statement. This method is useful if you do not know what type of SQL statement is being executed. If the statement generates a result set, it can be obtained using the getResultSet() method.

For example, the following code executes an INSERT statement:

```
statement.executeUpdate("INSERT INTO Employees VALUES (101, 20.00,
'Rich', 'Raposa')");
```

 You can also use a Statement object to create a batch of SQL statements and then execute the entire batch at once. This is accomplished using the following methods of the Statement interface:

public void addBatch(String sql) throws SQLException.   Add the given SQL statement to the current batch.

public int [ ] executeBatch() throws SQLException.   Executes all of the SQL statements in the batch. The array of return values corresponds to the statements in the batch and typically represents a row count for each batch statement executed successfully.

Let's look at an example that uses a Statement object to add data to our movies database. I wanted to make this example object oriented, so the first step I took was to write a class named Movie that represented a movie. This class is available on the Web site. The Movie class has fields to represent the title of the movie, the category (drama, comedy, kids, and so on), the format available, and a unique number for inventory purposes.

 Be sure to view the Movie class from the book's Web site. You will notice that the Movie class does not contain any database programming. This was a design decision. I wanted the Movie class to be able to be used in many different situations, not just representing data in a database. I wrote a separate class, MovieDatabase, that contains the database code for performing operations on the Movies table of the movies.mdb database using the Movie class.

The following MovieDatabase class contains an addMovie() method that adds an entry in the Movies table of a database. Study the class carefully and then try to determine what the code is doing:

```java
import java.sql.*;
public class MovieDatabase
{
    private Connection connection;
    public MovieDatabase(Connection connection)
    {
        this.connection = connection;
    }
    public void addMovie(Movie movie)
    {
        System.out.println("Adding movie: " + movie.toString());
        try
        {
            Statement addMovie = connection.createStatement();
            String sql = "INSERT INTO Movies VALUES("
                    + movie.getNumber() + ", "
                    + "'" + movie.getMovieTitle() + "', "
                    + "'" + movie.getCategory() + "', "
                    + "'" + movie.getFormat() + "')";
            System.out.println("Executing statement: " + sql);
            addMovie.executeUpdate(sql);
            addMovie.close();
            System.out.println("Movie added successfully!");
        }
        catch(SQLException e)
        {
            e.printStackTrace();
        }
    }
}
```

The following AddMovies program adds six movies to the database. Study the program carefully and try to determine what it does and what its output will be, which is shown in Figure 18.2.

```java
import java.sql.*;
public class AddMovies
{
     public static void main(String [] args)
     {
          String url = "jdbc:odbc:" + args[0];
          System.out.println("Attempting to connect to " + url);
          try
          {
               System.out.println("Loading the driver...");
               Class.forName("sun.jdbc.odbc.JdbcOdbcDriver");

               System.out.println("Establishing a connection...");
               Connection connection =
                         DriverManager.getConnection(url);
               System.out.println("Connect to "
                         + connection.getCatalog() + " a success!");
               MovieDatabase db = new MovieDatabase(connection);
               Movie [] movies = new Movie[6];
               movies[0] = new Movie(1, "Star Wars: A New Hope",
                                   "Science Fiction", "DVD");
               movies[1] = new Movie(2, "Citizen Kane", "Drama",
                                     "VHS");
               movies[2] = new Movie(3, "The Jungle Book",
                                   "Children", "VHS");
               movies[3] = new Movie(4, "Dumb and Dumber",
                                   "Comedy", "DVD");
               movies[4] = new Movie(5, "Star Wars: Attack of the
                                   Clones", "Science Fiction", "DVD");
               movies[5] = new Movie(6, "Toy Story", "Children",
                                   "DVD");
               for(int i = 0; i < movies.length; i++)
               {
                    db.addMovie(movies[i]);
               }
               System.out.println("Closing the connection...");
               connection.close();
          }
          catch(Exception e)
          {
             e.printStackTrace();
          }
     }
}
```

Figure 18.2   Part of the output of the AddMovies program.

 warning The first few times I ran the AddMovies program, the last movie wasn't showing up in the database. What was the problem? I forgot to close the database connection when I was done with it. The SQL statement that inserted the movie executed, but it did not commit to the database because I left the connection open. After adding the statement

```
connection.close();
```

at the end of the AddMovies program, I saw all six movies added to the database successfully. Keep in mind I had this problem using Microsoft Access. Other databases may behave differently, but closing the connection when you are finished with it is still an important step.

After running the AddMovies program, the six entries appear in the movies database, as shown in Figure 18.3.

number	title	category	format
1	Star Wars: A New Hope	Science Fiction	DVD
2	Citizen Kane	Drama	VHS
3	The Jungle Book	Children	VHS
4	Dumb and Dumber	Comedy	DVD
5	Star Wars: Attack of the Clones	Science Fiction	DVD
6	Toy Story	Children	DVD
0			

Record: |◄ ◄ [1] ► ►| ►* of 6

Figure 18.3   Six movies now appear in the Movies table of the movies.mdb database.

Working with Result Sets

The SQL statements that read data from a database query return the data in a *result set*. The SELECT statement is the standard way to select rows from a database and view them in a result set. The java.sql.ResultSet interface represents the result set of a database query.

A ResultSet object maintains a *cursor* that points to the current row in the result set. The methods of the ResultSet interface can be broken down into three categories:

- Navigational methods used to move the cursor around.
- Get methods that are used to view the data in the columns of the current row being pointed to by the cursor.
- Update methods that update the data in the columns of the current row. The updates can then be updated in the underlying database as well.

Let's look at some of these methods in the ResultSet interface because working with result sets is an essential task of any database application. We'll start with the methods that let you move the cursor around.

Navigating a Result Set

The cursor is movable based on the properties of the ResultSet. These properties are designated when the corresponding Statement that generated the ResultSet is created. (See the createStatement() methods in the section *Simple Statements*.) The possible properties of a result set cursor are:

ResultSet.TYPE_FORWARD_ONLY.   The cursor can only move forward in the result set.

ResultSet.TYPE_SCROLL_INSENSITIVE.   The cursor can scroll forwards and backwards, and the result set *is not* sensitive to changes made by others to the database that occur after the result set was created.

ResultSet.TYPE_SCROLL_SENSITIVE.   The cursor can scroll forwards and backwards, and the result set *is* sensitive to changes made by others to the database that occur after the result set was created.

If the type is forward only, you can only navigate through the result set once, and only moving the cursor forward. Scrollable cursors can be moved forward and backward in the result set. If a result set is marked as insensitive, the result set is a snapshot of the corresponding data in the database at the time the result set was created, and subsequent changes to the database do not affect the result set. If the result is marked as sensitive, changes to the database should appear in the result set as well.

There are several methods in the ResultSet interface that involve moving the cursor, including:

public void beforeFirst() throws SQLException.   Moves the cursor to just before the first row.

public void afterLast() throws SQLException.   Moves the cursor to just after the last row.

public boolean first() throws SQLException.   Moves the cursor to the first row.

public void last() throws SQLException.   Moves the cursor to the last row.

public boolean absolute(int row) throws SQLException.   Moves the cursor to the specified row.

public boolean relative(int row) throws SQLException.   Moves the cursor the given number of rows forward or backwards from where it currently is pointing.

public boolean previous() throws SQLException.   Moves the cursor to the previous row. This method returns false if the previous row is off the result set.

public boolean next() throws SQLException.   Moves the cursor to the next row. This method returns false if there are no more rows in the result set.

public int getRow() throws SQLException.   Returns the row number that the cursor is pointing to.

public void moveToInsertRow() throws SQLException.   Moves the cursor to a special row in the result set that can be used to insert a new row into the database. The current cursor location is remembered.

public void moveToCurrentRow() throws SQLException.   Moves the cursor back to the current row if the cursor is currently at the insert row; otherwise, this method does nothing.

Viewing a Result Set

The ResultSet interface contains dozens of methods for getting the data of the current row. There is a get method for each of the possible data types, and each get method has two versions: one that takes in a column name, and one that takes in a column index.

For example, if the column you are interested in viewing contains an int, you need to use one of the getInt() methods of ResultSet:

public int getInt(String columnName) throws SQLException. Returns the int in the current row in the column named columnName.

public int getInt(int columnIndex) throws SQLException. Returns the int in the current row in the specified column index. The column index starts at 1, meaning the first column of a row is 1, the second column of a row is 2, and so on.

 Using the column index is more efficient in terms of performance as opposed to using the column name. The get methods that use the column name have to determine which index to use. They then actually invoke the get method that takes in an index. Knowing the column index saves you at least two method calls behind the scenes. That being said, I like to use the column name whenever feasible because it makes the code easier to use, and I do not have to worry about the order of the columns in the result set.

As you may expect, there are get methods in the ResultSet interface for each of the eight Java primitive types, as well as common types such as java.lang.String, java.lang.Object, and java.net.URL. There are also methods for getting SQL data types java.sql.Date, java.sql.Time, java.sql.TimeStamp, java.sql.Clob (Character Large Object), and java.sql.Blob (Binary Large Object). (Check the documentation for more information about using these SQL data types.)

I added the following showAllMovies() method to the MovieDatabase class from earlier to demonstrate how a ResultSet object is navigated from start to finish, and also to demonstrate how to access the data in each row of a Result-Set. Study the method carefully and try to determine what it does.

```
public void showAllMovies()
{
    try
    {
        Statement selectAll = connection.createStatement();
        String sql = "SELECT * FROM Movies";
        ResultSet results =      selectAll.executeQuery(sql);
        while(results.next())
        {
            int number = results.getInt(1);
            String title = results.getString("title");
            String category = results.getString(3);
            String format = results.getString(4);

            Movie movie = new Movie(number, title,
                                    category, format);
```

```
                        System.out.println(movie.toString());
                }
                results.close();
                selectAll.close();
        }
        catch(SQLException e)
        {
            e.printStackTrace();
        }
    }
```

The following ShowMovies program calls the showAllMovies() method to test the program and make sure that it is successful. Study the ShowMovies and MovieDatabase classes to determine the output of running the Show-Movies program, which is shown in Figure 18.4.

```
import java.sql.*;
public class ShowMovies
{
    public static void main(String [] args)
    {
        String url = "jdbc:odbc:" + args[0];
        try
        {
            Class.forName("sun.jdbc.odbc.JdbcOdbcDriver");
            Connection connection =
                        DriverManager.getConnection(url);
            MovieDatabase db = new MovieDatabase(connection);
            db.showAllMovies();
            connection.close();
        }
        catch(Exception e)
        {
            e.printStackTrace();
        }
    }
}
```

Figure 18.4 Output of the ShowMovies program.

Updating a Result Set

The ResultSet interface contains a collection of update methods for updating the data of a result set. As with the get methods, there are two update methods for each data type: one that uses the column name and one that uses the column index.

For example, to update a String column of the current row of a result set, you would use one of the following updateString() methods:

public void updateString(int columnIndex, String s) throws SQLException. Changes the String in the specified column to the value of s.

public void updateString(String columnName, String s) throws SQLException. Similar to the previous method, except that the column is specified by its name instead of its index.

There are update methods for the eight primitive data types, as well as String, Object, URL, and the SQL data types in the java.sql package.

Updating a row in the result set changes the columns of the current row in the ResultSet object, but not in the underlying database. To update your changes to the row in the database, you need to invoke the following method:

public void updateRow(). Updates the current row by updating the corresponding row in the database.

In the next section, *Prepared Statements*, I will demonstrate how to use the update methods to update the data in the database.

 The updateRow() method updates any changes to the current row in the result set to the underlying database. Here are some other methods in the ResultInterface that deal with the current result set row and the corresponding database row:

> **public void deleteRow().** Deletes the current row from the database.
>
> **public void refreshRow().** Refreshes the data in the result set to reflect any recent changes in the database.
>
> **public void cancelRowUpdates().** Cancels any updates made on the current row.
>
> **public void insertRow().** Inserts a row into the database. This method can only be invoked when the cursor is pointing to the insert row.

Prepared Statements

A *prepared statement* is an SQL statement that contains parameters, and the java.sql.PreparedStatement interface is used to represent a prepared SQL statement. Before a prepared statement can be executed, each parameter needs to be assigned using one of the set methods in the PreparedStatement interface. A question mark is used to denote a parameter.

For example, the following prepared statement inserts a new row in a table called Employees:

```
INSERT INTO Employees VALUES (?, ?, ?, ?)
```

This prepared statement contains four parameters. When the Prepared-Statement object is created using the Connection object, this statement is sent to the database and precompiled, allowing the database to execute the statement at a faster rate.

 Prepared statements are preferred over simple statements for two good reasons:

- **Prepared statements execute faster because they are precompiled.**

- **As you soon may discover, prepared statements are easier to code because you do not have to worry about things like single quotes around text or missing commas.**

My second point is demonstrated in the addMovie() method of the MovieDatabase class, which contains a simple but still tedious SQL statement.

Using a prepared statement involves the following steps:

1. Create a PreparedStatement object using one of the prepareStatement() methods of the connection.

2. Use the appropriate set methods of the PreparedStatement interface to set each of the parameters of the prepared statement.

3. Invoke one of the execute() methods of the PreparedStatement interface to execute the statement.

Step 1: Preparing the Statement

Let's start with the Connection interface, which contains the following six methods for creating a PreparedStatement:

public PreparedStatement prepareStatement(String sql) throws SQLException. Creates a prepared SQL statement. The SQL is sent to the database for precompilation.

public PreparedStatement prepareStatement(String sql, int resultSetType, int concurrency, int holdability) throws SQLException. Creates a prepared statement using the specified properties for result sets. The resultSetType is either TYPE_FORWARD_ONLY, TYPE_SCROLL_INSENSITIVE, or TYPE_SCROLL_SENSITIVE. The concurrency type is either CONCUR_READ_ONLY or CONCUR_UPDATABLE, and holdability is either HOLD_CURSORS_OVER_COMMIT or CLOSE_CURSORS_AT_COMMIT.

public PreparedStatement prepareStatement(String sql, int resultSetType, int concurrency) throws SQLException. Similar to the previous method, except that only the scroll type and concurrency type are specified.

public PreparedStatement prepareStatement(String sql, int pk) throws SQLException. Creates a prepared SQL statement used for INSERT statements in a database that generates the primary key for you. The possible values of pk are RETURN_GENERATED_KEYS or NO_GENERATED_KEYS, and only applies to INSERT statements.

public PreparedStatement prepareStatement(String sql, String [ ] keys) throws SQLException. Creates a prepared SQL statement used for INSERT statements in a database that generates the primary key for you. The array of Strings represents the column name or names that compose the primary key.

public PreparedStatement prepareStatement(String sql, int [ ] keys) throws SQLException. Similar to the previous method, except that the array of columns is denoted by the column index instead of the column name.

Notice that these last three prepareStatement() methods contain information about autogenerated primary keys, which only applies to INSERT statements.

 Creating a Statement did not involve the actual SQL, since it is done using the Statement interface; however, when creating a prepared statement, SQL is needed so the statement can be precompiled and the PreparedStatement object can be created.

The following code demonstrates preparing a statement using a connection:

```
PreparedStatement insert = connection.prepareStatement(
        "INSERT INTO Employees VALUES (?, ?, ?, ?)");
```

Each question mark in a prepared statement denotes a parameter. The order in which the parameters appear determines their index, with the first parameter being index 1, the second parameter index 2, and so on. This is important when you go to set the values using the various set methods in the PreparedStatement interface.

Step 2: Setting the Parameters

Before a prepared statement can be executed, each of its parameters must be assigned a value. The PreparedStatement interface contains a set method for each of the possible data types of a parameter. Each set method takes in an index to denote which parameter to set. For example, if the data type of the parameter is a double, then you use the method:

public void setDouble(int index, double value).   Sets the specified index to the double value argument.

The following statements prepare a statement and assign each of its four parameters a value using the appropriate set method:

```
PreparedStatement insert = connection.prepareStatement(
"INSERT INTO Employees VALUES (?, ?, ?, ?)");
insert.setDouble(2, 2.50);
insert.setInt(1, 103);
insert.setString(3, "George");
insert.setString(4, "Washington");
```

Notice that the order in which you set the parameters does not matter, as long as you set a value for each parameter of the prepared statement.

Step 3: Executing a Prepared Statement

After the values of all the parameters are set, the prepared statement is executed using one of the following methods in the PreparedStatement interface:

public ResultSet executeQuery() throws SQLException.   Use this method if the SQL statement returns a result set, like a SELECT statement.

public int executeUpdate() throws SQLException.   Use this method for statements like INSERT, UPDATE, or DELETE. The return value is the number of rows affected.

public boolean execute() throws SQLException.   This method executes any type of SQL statement. Use the getResultSet() method to obtain the result set if one is created.

To demonstrate prepared statements, I added a changeCategory() method to the MovieDatabase class that changes the category of a movie in the database.

Because the class uses prepared statements, the PreparedStatement objects only need to be created once, so I did this in the constructor. Study the class carefully to see how the statements are prepared and executed.

```java
import java.sql.*;
public class MovieDatabase
{
    private Connection connection;
    private PreparedStatement findByNumber, updateCategory;
    public MovieDatabase(Connection connection) throws SQLException
    {
        this.connection = connection;
        findByNumber = connection.prepareStatement(
                "SELECT * FROM Movies WHERE number = ?");
        updateCategory = connection.prepareStatement(
                "UPDATE Movies SET category = ? WHERE number = ?");
    }
    public void changeCategory(int number, String newCategory)
    {
        try
        {
            updateCategory.setString(1, newCategory);
            updateCategory.setInt(2, number);
            updateCategory.executeUpdate();

            System.out.println("Verifying change...");
            findByNumber.setInt(1, number);
            ResultSet results = findByNumber.executeQuery();
            if(results.next())
            {
                System.out.println("Category of "
                            + results.getString("title") + " is "
                            + results.getString("category"));
            }
            else
            {
                System.out.println("No movie found matching number "
                            + number);
            }
        }
        catch(SQLException e)
        {
            e.printStackTrace();
        }
    }
}
```

The following UpdateCategory program inputs a movie number and category, then changes the category of the given movie. Study the program along with the MovieDatabase class and try to determine what the output is and what changes occur in the database.

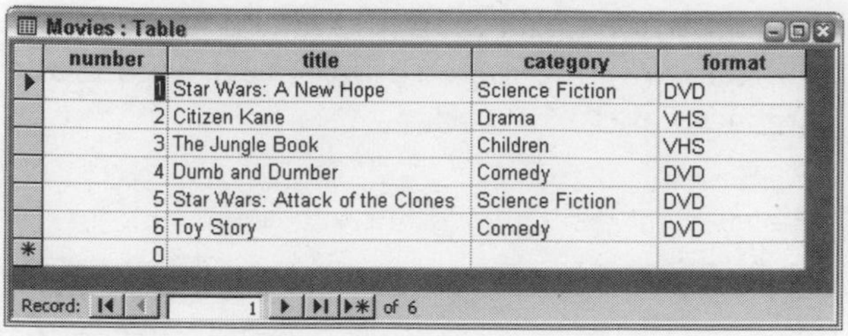

number	title	category	format
1	Star Wars: A New Hope	Science Fiction	DVD
2	Citizen Kane	Drama	VHS
3	The Jungle Book	Children	VHS
4	Dumb and Dumber	Comedy	DVD
5	Star Wars: Attack of the Clones	Science Fiction	DVD
6	Toy Story	Comedy	DVD
0			

Figure 18.5 Movies table after the UpdateCategory program executes.

```
import java.sql.*;
public class UpdateCategory
{
     public static void main(String [] args)
     {
          String url = "jdbc:odbc:" + args[0];
          int number = Integer.parseInt(args[1]);
          String category = args[2];
          try
          {
               Class.forName("sun.jdbc.odbc.JdbcOdbcDriver");
               Connection connection =
                             DriverManager.getConnection(url);
               MovieDatabase db = new MovieDatabase(connection);
               System.out.println("Changing category of movie number "
                                    + number + " ...");
               db.changeCategory(number, category);
               connection.close();
          }
          catch(Exception e)
          {
             e.printStackTrace();
          }
     }
}
```

Figure 18.5 shows the Movies table of the movies.mdb database after the program executes. The category of Toy Story was Children, but now it is Comedy.

Callable Statements

A CallableStatement object is used to invoke a stored procedure in a database. A stored procedure allows you to repeat a sequence of tasks repeatedly in an efficient manner, much like writing a method in Java. There are several ways to create a stored procedure, which is database dependent. In the sidebar *Stored Procedures in Microsoft Access*, I show you how to create a stored procedure in Access.

 The **CREATE PROCEDURE** statement can be used to create a procedure using SQL. The syntax looks similar to:

```
CREATE PROCEDURE ShowMovies (IN category varchar(32))
LANGUAGE SQL
BEGIN
    SELECT * FROM Movies
    WHERE Movies.category = category;
END;
```

Keep in mind that the syntax is database dependent, so you will need to check the documentation of your database for using the correct CREATE PROCEDURE statement.

◆ Stored Procedures in Microsoft Access

The CallableDemo program at the end of this chapter demonstrates how to invoke a stored procedure in a database. The program invokes a procedure named SelectByCategory, which I wrote in Microsoft Access using Visual Basic. I'll be honest with you: I don't know Visual Basic at all, so it is fitting when I say that this is not a lesson in Visual Basic. However, I will show you the steps involved in creating this stored procedure in Access, and those of you familiar with Visual Basic will quickly find some useful and interesting uses of stored procedures.

Start by opening the movies.mdb database in Access. Click the Modules tab, and then click the New button. Figure 18.6 shows the Module dialog that appears.

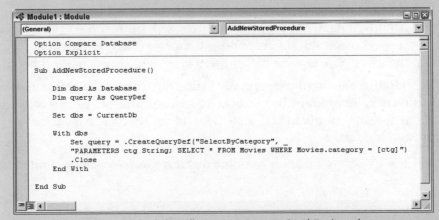

Figure 18.6 The Module dialog allows you to enter Visual Basic code.

continued

♦ Stored Procedures in Microsoft Access *(continued)*

Enter the procedure defined in Figure 18.6. After you have entered it, click File and then Save. Save the module as "StoredProcedures".

The Visual Basic statements of interest in this procedure are:

```
Set query = .CreateQueryDef("SelectByCategory", _
        "PARAMETERS category String; SELECT * FROM Movies WHERE
Movies.category = [category]")
```

The CreateQueryDef function creates a stored procedure. The first argument is the name of the stored procedure, which in this example is SelectByCategory. The second argument is the SQL of the procedure, which in this example selects the rows in the Movies table that match the given category parameter.

After you have entered the AddNewStoredProcedure() subroutine from Figure 18.6, you need to run it so that the stored procedure gets created. Run the subroutine by Go/Continue from the Run menu (or by selecting F5).

After you have successfully run the subroutine, the stored procedure SelectByCategory is now ready to be invoked from your Java applications using the SQL statement:

```
{call SelectByCategory(?)}
```

of a CallableStatement object, as demonstrated by the showByCategory() method of the MovieDatabase class. Be sure to close the Module window and the movies.mdb database before running the CallableDemo program.

Use one of the prepareCall() methods of the Connection interface to create a CallableStatement object:

public CallableStatement prepareCall(String sql) throws SQLException. Creates a callable statement using the given SQL statement.

public CallableStatement prepareCall(String sql, int resultSetType, int concurrency) throws SQLException. Creates a callable statement using the given SQL statement, result set type, and concurrency type.

public CallableStatement prepareCall(String sql, int resultSetType, int concurrency, int holdability) throws SQLException. Creates a callable statement using the given SQL statement, result set type, concurrency type, and holdability type.

The SQL for invoking a callable procedure that has parameters looks similar to:

```
{call procedure_name(?, ?, ...)}
```

As with prepared statements, the parameters need to be set before the callable procedure can be invoked. If the procedure does not have any parameters, it is invoked using the statement:

```
{call procedure_name}
```

For example, the following statements create a CallableStatement object for a procedure named UpdateScores that has one parameter:

```
CallableStatement c = connection.prepareCall("{call UpdateScores(?)}")
```

Before the statement can be executed, the parameter is set using one of the set methods in the CallableStatement interface, which are similar to the set methods of the PreparedStatement interface. For example, the following statement sets the first parameter of a CallableStatement to an int value of 27:

```
c.setInt(1, 27);
```

To execute a CallableStatement, invoke one of the execute methods inherited from PreparedStatement, which is the parent interface of CallableStatement. For example:

```
c.execute();
```

To demonstrate invoking a stored procedure, I added a showByCategory() method to the MovieDatabase class that uses a CallableStatement to invoke a stored procedure named SelectByCategory. (Read the sidebar *Stored Procedures in Microsoft Access* to see how this stored procedure was created.) Study the showByCategory() method to determine what it does.

```java
import java.sql.*;
public class MovieDatabase
{
    private Connection connection;
    private PreparedStatement findByNumber, updateCategory;
    private CallableStatement findByCategory;
    public MovieDatabase(Connection connection) throws SQLException
    {
        this.connection = connection;
        findByNumber = connection.prepareStatement(
            "SELECT * FROM Movies WHERE number = ?");
```

```
                    updateCategory = connection.prepareStatement(
                            "UPDATE Movies SET category = ? WHERE number = ?");
                    findByCategory = connection.prepareCall(
                            "{call SelectByCategory(?)}");
            }
            public void showByCategory(String category)
            {
                try
                {
                    findByCategory.setString(1, category);
                    System.out.println("Calling stored procedure
                                    SelectByCategory");
                    ResultSet result = findByCategory.executeQuery();

                    System.out.println("Found the following movies in "
                                    + category);
                    while(result.next())
                    {
                        System.out.println(result.getString("title"));
                    }
                }
                catch(SQLException e)
                {
                    e.printStackTrace();
                }
            }
        }
```

The following CallableDemo program shows what happens when the showByCategory() method is invoked. Study the program and MovieDatabase class and try to determine the output of the CallableDemo program, which is shown in Figure 18.7.

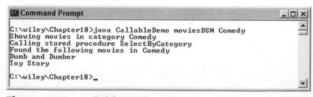

Figure 18.7 CallableDemo program prints out the movies that match the given category on the command line.

Lab 18.1: Using JDBC

This lab is designed to help you become familiar with using JDBC.

1. Start by creating a database to store music CDs. Add a table named CDs and columns for the artist and title.

2. Write a class to represent a music CD that does not contain any database code, similar to the Movie class in this chapter.

3. Write a class named CDDatabase. Add a method to CDDatabase called insertCD() that takes in a CD object and inserts it in the database.

4. Add a method named removeCD() to CDDatabase that takes in a CD object and removes it from the database.

5. Add a method named findByTitle() that takes in a String and returns an array of CD objects. The array represents CDs in the database whose title matches any part of the given string.

6. Add a method named findByArtist() that takes in an artist's name and returns an array containing all CDs in the database that match the given artist.

7. Save and compile the CDDatabase class.

8. Write a program named FillDatabase that fills the database with a collection of CDs, or simply add CDs to the database manually using your database program.

9. Write a program that tests all the methods of the CDDatabase, making sure they work correctly.

   When you invoke a method on the CDDatabase object, the results should be consistent with the data in the database. For example, invoking insertCD() should insert a row in the table, and invoking removeCD() should remove a row from the table.

Lab 18.2: Using Result Sets

In this lab, you will create a GUI for the results in Lab 18.1 and then add a feature that allows you to scroll through the CDs in the database.

1. Write a class named CDFrame that extends javax.swing.JFrame. Add a JTextArea in the center, two JTextField components in the north (one for entering an artist and one for entering a title), and add four buttons to the south: First, Previous, Next, and Last.

2. Write a class named CDListener that implements ActionListener. Add two JTextField and one JTextArea fields and initialize them in a constructor. They will be references to the GUI components of the CDFrame.

3. Within the actionPerformed() method of CDListener, determine the source of the action event. If it is a button, determine which of the four navigation buttons was clicked and then perform the appropriate action, displaying the CD in the text area. For example, if the First button was clicked, so the first CD in the database. If the Next button is clicked, show the next CD in the database and so on. Use your CDDatabase class from Lab 18.1.

4. If the source of the ActionEvent is a JTextField, the user has typed something in one of the text fields and has pressed Enter. This means that the user wants to search the database for a given artist, a given title, or both. Perform the desired search using the appropriate methods of your CDDatabase class, then display the results in the text area.

5. Save and compile your CDListener class.

6. In the constructor or your CDFrame class, instantiate a new CDListener and register it as an action listener to the four buttons and the two text fields.

7. Add main() to your CDFrame class. Within main() instantiate a CDFrame object, resize it, and make it visible.

8. Save, compile, and run your CDFrame class.

You should see your CDFrame GUI appear, and clicking the navigational buttons should display the corresponding CD in the text area. Entering an artist's name and pressing Enter should display in the text area all of the CDs in the database from that artist. Entering a title should display all CDs in the database that contain the given text in part of the title's name. For example, entering The in the title text field should display all CDs in the database with *The* in their title.

Lab 18.3: The Reminder Application

This lab is a continuation of Lab 16.5, *A Reminder Application*. The Reminder application you wrote in Lab 16.5 is useful to the extent that your reminders are remembered and successful as long as the program is running. After you shut down the program, all of your reminders are lost. In this lab, you will use a database to keep track of the reminders.

1. Start by creating a new database. Add a table called Reminders that contains columns for keeping track of the time and message of each reminder. You might want to add a number column to the table to represent a primary key.

2. When a user creates a reminder, add the information to the database. (Your program should still do whatever it performed previously.)

3. When a reminder goes off, delete it from the database.

4. Now, when the program is exited, all upcoming reminders are maintained in the database. When the program starts up, it should retrieve the reminders from the database and schedule them.

5. If a reminder should have occurred while the program was not running, have the reminder displayed immediately when the program starts up.

6. Test your program and make sure it works successfully.

Your Reminder application is now useful. Reminders are not lost, although they might be missed if the program isn't running when a reminder is scheduled. (However, that's true with any reminder-type application.)

Summary

- The JDBC API contains classes and interfaces for connecting to a database and performing SQL statements.
- You need a JDBC driver for a Java application to connect to a database. There are four types of drivers referred to as Type 1, 2, 3, and 4. Each type of driver has its benefits.

- The java.sql.DriverManager class can be used to obtain a connection to a database. The java.sql.Connection interface represents the database connection.

- The javax.sql.DataSource class can also be used to obtain a connection to a database. This is the preferred technique when connecting to a database from within a J2EE application or environment that provides JNDI.

- SQL stands for Structured Query Language and is the language used by most databases for accessing and updating data.

- There are three types of statements: simple statements, prepared statements, and callable statements, which are used for stored procedures.

- The java.sql.Statement interface represents simple statements, the java.sql.PreparedStatement interface represents prepared statements, and the java.sql.CallableStatement interface represents callable statements. Each of these is obtained using the Connection object.

- The java.sql.ResultSet interface represents a result set, the data returned from an SQL query.

Review Questions

1. What does JDBC stand for?

2. If you have a JDBC driver that was provided by your database vendor, written entirely in Java, what type of driver do you probably have?

   a. type 1

   b. type 2

   c. type 3

   d. type 4

3. If you have a JDBC driver that works on multiple databases from different vendors, what type of driver do you probably have?

   a. type 1

   b. type 2

   c. type 3

   d. type 4

4. If you have a JDBC driver that requires a middleware application to convert the JDBC calls into native calls using an intermediate protocol, which type of driver do you have?

   a. type 1

   b. type 2

   c. type 3

   d. type 4

5. How do you load a JDBC driver so that it is available in your Java application?

6. If I am using the JDBC-ODBC bridge driver that comes with the J2SE and my database has a data source name of "contactsDSN", what is the URL used to connect to this database using the getConnection() method?

7. Describe the result set of the SQL statement:

   ```
   SELECT * FROM SomeTable WHERE someColumn LIKE '%java%'
   ```

8. List the three types of statements you can create from a java.sql.Connection object.

9. Suppose that you want to execute an SQL statement once. Which of the three types of statements would best fit this situation?

10. Suppose you want to execute an SQL statement repeatedly. Which of the three types of statements would best fit this situation?

11. What is the parent interface of PreparedStatement?

12. What is the parent interface of CallableStatement?

13. Which properties would you use to create a statement whose result set is scrollable and updatable? Select all that apply.

    a. TYPE_FORWARD_ONLY

    b. TYPE_SCROLL_INSENSITIVE

    c. CONCUR_READ_ONLY

    d. CONCUR_UPDATABLE

    e. CLOSE_CURSORS_AT_COMMIT

14. Suppose that you have a java.sql.Statement object and you want to use it to execute a DELETE statement. Which of the following methods in Statement can be used to execute the DELETE statement? (Select all that apply.)

    a. execute(String sql)

    b. executeUpdate(String sql)

    c. executeQuery(String sql)

    d. executeBatch()

    e. runSQL(String sql)

15. True or False: The cursor of a ResultSet initially points to just before the first row.

16. True or False: Invoking next() causes an SQLException to occur if the ResultSet is empty.

17. What is the effect of invoking relative(5) on a ResultSet object?

18. True or False: A result set must be scrollable for the previous() method to execute successfully.

19. True or False: Invoking updateString(1, "Hello") on a ResultSet object changes the first column of the current row of the ResultSet to "Hello".

20. True or False: Invoking updateString(1, "Hello") on a ResultSet object changes the data in the database that corresponds to the current row.

21. True or False: The first parameter of a PreparedStatement has the index value 0.

22. Which method in the Connection interface is used to create a CallableStatement?

    a. createStatement()

    b. prepareCall()

    c. prepareStatement()

    d. createCall()

Answers to Review Questions

1. Okay, that's a trick question. It is commonly referred to as Java Database Connectivity, but it officially does not stand for anything.

2. Type 4 drivers are pure-Java drivers typically provided by the database vendor, so the answer is d.

3. Type 3 drivers work on different databases, so the answer is c.

4. The question describes exactly how type 3 drivers work, so the answer is c again.

5. A driver is loaded by having the JVM load its corresponding class. This is typically done using the Class.forName() method.

6. jdbc:odbc:contactsDSN.

7. The result will be all columns from the rows in SomeTable whose someColumn data contains the substring 'java' in any part of it.

8. Simple statements of type Statement, prepared statements of type PreparedStatement, and callable statements of type CallableStatement.

9. A simple statement would probably work best when only executing the statement once.

10. A prepared statement is more efficient when used repeatedly because its SQL is pre-compiled by the database. A stored procedure might also work well too.

11. java.sql.Statement.

12. java.sql.PreparedStatement.

13. b makes the result set scrollable, and d makes it updatable.

14. b is the likely choice, although a works for any SQL statement, and d actually works if you add the statement to a batch. The only two that don't work are c, which is for SQL statements that return a ResultSet, and the runSQL() method is one I made up.

15. True. You must invoke next() on a ResultSet, even if it only contains one row.

16. False. The next() method returns false if there is no next row.

17. The cursor moves five rows ahead of its current position.

18. True. Nonscrollable result sets can only be navigated forward.

19. True. The data of the ResultSet object changes.

20. False. The data in the database does not change. You need to invoke updateRow() before any updates appear in the database.

21. False. The first parameter has an index 1.

22. b. createCall() is not a method in Connection, prepareStatement() is for prepared statements, and createStatement() is for simple statements.

CHAPTER

19

JavaBeans

JavaBeans are software components for the Java programming language. In this chapter, I will discuss what JavaBeans are, how they are written, and how they are used. Topics discussed include an overview of JavaBeans, simple, bound, and constrained properties, events, the Bean Builder tool, and long-term persistence of beans.

Overview of JavaBeans

The JavaBeans components API defines a mechanism for writing software components in Java. A *software component* is a reusable piece of software that is hooked together with other components, creating an application or new component.

The concept of software components is not unique to Java. You may have heard of ActiveX components, which are software components for developing Windows applications. The goal of software components is to simplify and accelerate application development. Instead of writing a program by developing all new code from scratch, you develop a program by hooking together existing components in your own unique way.

669

For example, suppose that you need to develop a program that allows customers to purchase items online. You could use an existing bean that searches the database for inventory, a bean that handles credit card payments, and a collection of beans to create the GUI. You could write new beans for creating a shopping cart and enabling users to log in. Using existing beans accelerates development time, and writing new beans allows them to easily be used in other applications.

A JavaBean has three basic components:

Properties. The properties of a bean describe characteristics of the bean that can be viewed and can be changed by other beans.

Methods. The methods of a bean are the behaviors of the bean that can be invoked by other beans.

Events. A bean can be the source of an event. Events provide the mechanism that enables beans to communicate with each other.

Each of these components of a JavaBean is determined by the public methods that are defined within a bean's class. The JavaBeans specification defines how methods are named and which methods need to appear in a class to denote the bean's properties and events.

Classroom Q & A

Q: How do you create a JavaBean?

A: A JavaBean is simply a class. What makes the class a JavaBean are the methods you add to the class. The JavaBeans specification defines how methods are named to denote properties and events of a bean. In this chapter, I will discuss the JavaBeans specification for naming the methods of a bean class.

Q: So to write a bean, all I need to do is follow a certain naming convention for methods in a class?

A: Well, there is more to it than that. A JavaBean is not just a class describing an object. It is a software component that can be plugged into an application and used by other components, and it has properties that other beans can view and change. It fires events to communicate with other components.

Q: What if I have an existing class that I want to make into a JavaBean, but I didn't follow the specification for naming methods?

A: No problem. A JavaBean can have a separate class, called a Bean-Info class, which specifies the properties, methods, and events of a bean. Most beans have a BeanInfo class, whether or not they started out as a JavaBean.

Q: Suppose that I have a collection of JavaBeans. How do I hook them together?

A: Beans are hooked together using a GUI builder tool, typically one of the popular IDEs such as Visual Café or JBuilder. These builder tools generate the code that hooks the beans together in the manner that you need. In this book, I will show you how to use Sun's Bean Builder tool, which is freely downloadable from its Web site.

Q: What if the bean is not a GUI component, such as a bean that searches a database?

A: You still hook it together with other beans using a GUI builder tool. A bean does not need to be a GUI component, and in fact, most beans do not have any GUI aspect to them.

Q: Why not just write the code yourself, instead of relying on the tool?

A: I suppose you could, but why not let a tool do the work for you? An interesting aspect of JavaBeans is that you do not need to be a Java programmer to hook them together. As long as you understand properties, events, and methods, you can create a Java application by hooking together a collection of JavaBeans.

Q: Do these builder tools need the source code of my beans so they can determine the method names in my bean class?

A: No. The bean builder tools use a process called *introspection* to determine the properties, methods, and events of a bean, which are determined by public methods in the bean class. As a part of introspection, the builder tools use the Java Reflection API to determine the signatures of the methods in a bean class. The Reflection API is not exclusive to JavaBeans; you can perform reflection on any bytecode file.

Now that I have introduced you briefly to JavaBeans, let's look at the details of how they are written and used. I will start with a discussion on simple properties, which will help demonstrate the simpler aspects of beans. Then, I will show you how to view and change the simple properties of a bean using Sun's Bean Builder.

Think of software components as being similar to hardware components. Suppose, for example, that you want to build a computer. You could start by trying to build a computer chip (no small task) or you could go down to your local electronics store and purchase a chip. While you're there, you might as well purchase the other various hardware components that make up a computer, such as a motherboard, video card, sound card, keyboard, monitor, mouse, and so on. Note that you don't have to understand how the components work to hook them together. You just need to understand how to hook them together using your tools. I have no idea how a video card works, but I do know how one plugs into a PC's motherboard.

Similarly, you don't have to understand how a software component works to use it, as long as you understand what the purpose is of the component and how it is hooked to other components. For example, you do not need to know how to program in Java to use JavaBeans. (Of course, to write them, you do.) When hooking beans together, the builder tool generates all the necessary code.

Simple Properties

A *simple property* of a JavaBean is an attribute of the bean that can be viewed and can be changed by other beans. A simple property can be a read-only, a write-only, or a read-write property, and the simple properties of a bean are determined by the set and get methods in a bean's class, which have the following syntax:

```
public void set<Property>(data_type x)
public data_type get<Property>()
```

If both a set and get method appear that have the same property name and data type, the bean will have a read-write property of the specified name. If only a get method appears, the property is read-only; similarly, if only a set method appears, the property is write-only.

For example, suppose that a bean has the following methods:

```
public void setTitle(String t)
public String getTitle()
```

Then, the bean has a read-write property named title, and the data type of this property is a String. When the data type is a Boolean, an *is* method can be used in place of a get method. For example, the following two method signatures create a Boolean property named atHome:

```
public void setAtHome(boolean b)
public boolean isAtHome()
```

 The name of a property is determined by the method signatures for the property. The set or get portion of the method name is removed, and the next letter is decapitalized. For example, the following two methods create a property named length of type int:

```
public void setLength(int x)
public int getLength()
```

The exception to the decapitalization rule occurs when the property name is all capitals, such as the following:

```
public String getURL()
public void setURL(String s)
```

These two methods create a read-write property of type String whose name is URL.

Study the following Movie class and see if you can determine its bean properties, including their name, their data type, and whether they are read-only, write-only, or read-write:

```
package video.store;

public class Movie implements java.io.Serializable
{
    private String title;
    private int length;
    private boolean rented;
    private String customer;

    public Movie()
    {
        System.out.println("Constructing a movie...");
        customer = "";
    }

    public void setTitle(String t)
    {
        System.out.println("Setting the title to " + t);
        title = t;
    }

    public String getTitle()
    {
```

```
            System.out.println("Getting the title: " + title);
            return title;
        }

    public void setLength(int seconds)
    {
            System.out.println("Setting the length to " + seconds);
            length = seconds;
    }

    public int getLength()
    {
            System.out.println("Getting the length: " + length);
            return length;
    }

    public void setCustomerName(String s)
    {
            System.out.println("Setting customer name to " + s);
            customer = s;
    }

    public boolean isRented()
    {
            return rented;
    }

    public void rentMovie()
    {
            if(customer.equals(""))
            {
                System.out.println("Customer name needs to be set");
            }
            else if(rented)
            {
                System.out.println(title + " is rented");
            }
            else
            {
                System.out.println("Renting " + title + " to "
                                    + customer);
                rented = true;
            }
    }

    public void returnMovie()
    {
            System.out.println("Returning " + title);
            rented = false;
            customer = "";
    }
}
```

Let me make a few comments about the Movie class:

- First, the rentMovie() and returnMovie() methods are simply methods in the class and do not define any properties of this bean.
- The class implements java.io.Serializable and contains a no-argument constructor, both features of all JavaBeans.
- The bean has two read-write properties: title, which is a String, and length, which is an int.
- The bean has a write-only property named customerName of type String.
- The bean has a read-only property named rented of type boolean.
- The Movie class has four fields, but they have nothing to do with bean property names or data types. In fact, bean builder tools are not aware of these fields because they are private.

Now that you have seen a bean (the Movie class) and how to create simple properties for a bean, I will show you how to package the bean in a JAR file and use the bean in a builder tool.

Packaging a Bean

JavaBeans are accessed by builder tools in the following formats:

JAR files.   The bean class and any other utility classes that the bean needs are packaged in a JAR file. I will show you this technique first.

Serialized files.   The bean to be accessed is a serialized object in a file whose extension is .ser. The file was created using the java.io.ObjectOutputStream class.

XML archive.   The bean was serialized using the java.beans.XMLEncoder class. This is the preferred technique to serialize a bean, and it is also a new technique as of J2SE 1.4.

 Serializing beans is a common aspect of JavaBeans, and this was done using the standard Java serialization up until J2SE 1.4. However, with XML becoming widely used in all aspects of Java programming, the new XMLEncoder and XMLDecoder classes offer an alternate way to persist beans. See the upcoming sidebar *Bean Persistence*.

Figure 19.1 Compile the Movie class using the –d flag.

When writing a class to represent a JavaBean, the class must be placed in a JAR file along with a manifest file listing the contents of the JAR. There are several steps involved in creating this JAR file, so let's work through them together. Start by opening your text editor and following along with the ensuing steps:

Step 1: Write the Bean Class

For this example, you will write and package the Movie bean class discussed in the previous section. Type this Movie class into your text editor. Be sure to compile it using the -d flag, as shown in Figure 19.1, because the Movie class is in a package.

Step 2: Write the Manifest File

A *manifest file* is a text file that lists the files in a JAR. In many situations, the manifest file is created for you automatically by the jar tool. However, when using JavaBeans, you must write your own manifest file for the bean's JAR. This manifest file needs to list which class files in the JAR are JavaBeans.

In our example, the JAR file will contain only one class: Movie.class. Because this is a bean, we will denote the Java-Bean property of the file as True in the manifest file, as shown in Figure 19.2. Type the file shown in Figure 19.2 in your text editor, and save it as movie.mf. Be sure to save it in the same directory as your file Movie.java.

Figure 19.2 Manifest file for the Movie bean (save it in a file named movie.mf).

A common problem I always see with the jar tool is that it does not seem to read the last line in a manifest file. Therefore, after you type the following in your movie.mf file, hit Enter a couple of times so that the last line of the manifest file is a blank line:

```
Java-Bean: True
```

This is important because if the Java-Bean line is not read by the jar tool, the builder tool will think that Movie.class is not a JavaBean. If you don't see the Movie bean in the list of available beans in the tool, check the manifest file first.

Step 3: Create the JAR File

After you have written the manifest file, you are ready to create a JAR file for your bean. We will use the jar tool that comes with the J2SE SDK. Open a command prompt and change directories to the directory containing the Movie.java and movie.mf files. Then, enter the following jar command:

```
jar -cvfm movie_bean.jar movie.mf .\video
```

Figure 19.3 shows the output of this command.

I want to make a couple of comments about the jar command in Figure 19.3:

- The f and m flags are for filename and manifest filename, respectively. Placing the f before the m denotes that you specify the new filename before the name of the manifest file, which was done in Figure 19.3.

- The file Movie.class is in a directory named \video\store because it is in a package named video.store. Therefore, the \video\store directory must appear in the JAR file. Adding the directory .\video adds all its subdirectories, so notice in Figure 19.3 that this included the Movie.class file in the appropriate directory structure.

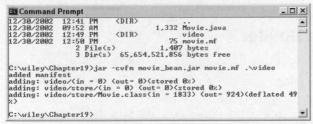

Figure 19.3 A JAR file named movie_bean.jar is created using the movie.mf manifest file.

After you run the jar command, you should see a new file named movie_bean.jar in the current working directory. This JAR file is now ready for use by a JavaBean builder tool, so the next step is to download Sun's Bean Builder tool and install it on your PC.

Step 4: Download the Bean Builder

Sun provides a JavaBean builder tool called the Bean Builder for working with and hooking together JavaBeans. The Bean Builder is free to download and use, so let's do that now. Open your Web browser and go to the following URL: http://java.sun.com/products/javabeans/beanbuilder/index.html.

Toward the bottom of this Web page is a button to click to download the latest version of the Bean Builder. Click this button and follow the directions to download the installation file.

 You do not need to download the Bean Builder. Instead, you can start the program using Java Web Start, a program that allows applications to be loaded and executed over the Internet. You can do this if you like, and you may already have Java Web Start installed in your PC. However, if you do not have a continuous connection to the Internet, you will probably be better off downloading the Bean Builder application and installing it on your local hard drive.

You don't really install the Bean Builder; you just unzip the file that you downloaded. I suggest unzipping to your root directory, such as c:\, because all necessary subdirectories already exist in the compressed file. Unzip the file you downloaded now, and you should see a new directory named c:\ beanbuilder-1_0 or something similar.

Figure 19.4 shows the contents of this directory. The run.bat executable is used for running the Bean Builder on Windows, and the run.sh executable is used for running the Bean Builder on Unix platforms. Before running the Bean Builder, you need to define the JAVA_HOME environment variable, which we will now do.

Step 5: Run the Bean Builder

To run the Bean Builder, you must first set the JAVA_HOME environment variable. Setting environment variables is done differently, depending on your version of Windows. If you have Windows 95/98/ME, you define the JAVA_HOME environment variable in the autoexec.bat file. Add the following line to your autoexec.bat file:

```
set JAVA_HOME=c:\j2sdk1.4.1_01
```

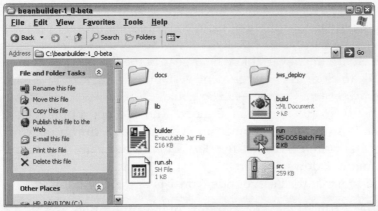

Figure 19.4 The c:\beanbuilder-1_0-beta directory contains the files used to run the Bean Builder application (this directory name may be different, depending on the version you downloaded).

Be sure to enter the home directory of whatever version of Java you have installed on your PC, which may be slightly different from this example. You will have to restart your computer for this addition to take effect.

If you are using Windows NT/2000/XP or later, the JAVA_HOME environment variable is defined in the System properties found in the Control Panel. (On XP, the System icon is found in the Performance and Maintenance option of the Control Panel.) On the Advanced tab of the System Properties dialog box is a button named Environment Variable. Click it to display the Environment Variables dialog box, shown in Figure 19.5.

Figure 19.5 Add the JAVA_HOME environment variable in the Environment Variables dialog box.

Click the New button (either as a system variable or a user variable) to add the JAVA_HOME environment variable, assigning it to the directory on your PC in which you installed the J2SE SDK. Click OK when you are finished, and the JAVA_HOME environment variable will appear in the list of environment variables. Click OK to close the Environment Variables dialog box, and click OK again to close the System Properties dialog box.

You are now ready to run the Bean Builder. Run the appropriate Bean Builder executable now, which is run.bat on Windows and run.sh on Unix (refer to Figure 19.4). Figure 19.6 shows the Bean Builder program, which consists of three different windows.

Notice in Figure 19.6 that the Bean Builder consists of three windows:

The Bean Builder.   This is the main window of the application, and it contains a tabbed pane displaying all the JavaBeans currently loaded into the Bean Builder. The Swing components, which all happen to be JavaBeans, are automatically loaded by default.

Property Inspector.   This window on the lower left of the screen displays the properties of the currently selected bean.

The Bean window.   By default, the Bean Builder starts with an empty JFrame for you to lay out your beans in. It is within this window that you will lay out your beans and hook them together.

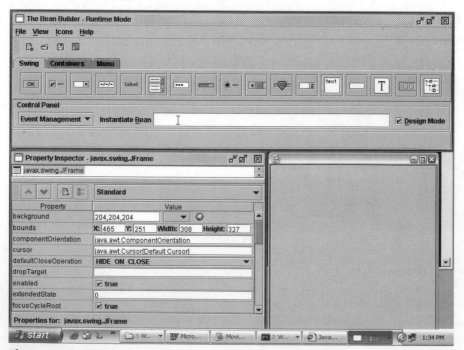

Figure 19.6   Bean Builder program runs after the JAVA_HOME environment variable is set.

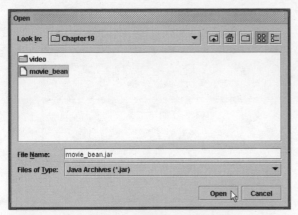

Figure 19.7   Load the movie_bean.jar file.

We are now ready to load our Movie bean into the Bean Builder and view its properties, which we will do in the next step.

Step 6: Load the Movie Bean into the Bean Builder

To load a bean into the Bean Builder from a JAR file, click File and then Load Jar File from the menu of the Bean Builder window. Figure 19.7 shows the dialog box that appears.

Browse to the directory in which you created the movie_bean.jar file, select it, and click the Open button. If it works successfully, you will see a new tab named User on the Bean Builder's main window. Click the User tab, and you will see the Movie bean as the only item on the list, as shown in Figure 19.8.

 The icon for the Movie bean is empty because we did not associate an icon with the Movie bean. However, the BeanInfo class can be used to denote an icon for a bean, and the builder tools can use the icons in whatever fashion they want. A JavaBean can have up to four icons associated with it: a 32x32 bit color icon, a 16x16 bit color icon, a 32x32 bit monochrome icon, and a 16x16 bit monochrome icon.

Step 7: Using the Movie Bean in the Builder Tool

Now that the Movie bean is loaded in the Bean Builder, it is ready to be used. Click on the Movie bean in the User tab (refer to Figure 19.8), and the mouse pointer becomes a cross. Move the mouse down to the empty JFrame in the lower-right window, and click the mouse again anywhere inside the window. A Movie bean object is instantiated by the builder tool, and a small rectangle is created to view the bean, as shown in Figure 19.9.

Figure 19.8 User tab of the Bean Builder window displays the beans you load from JAR files.

 note **If a JavaBean is a GUI component, what you see in the builder tool is the actual component. Because the Movie bean is not a GUI component, the Bean Builder displays it in a small rectangular region so that you can still visually hook the Movie bean to other beans in the builder tool. This is strictly for convenience and other Bean Builder tools may handle non-GUI beans differently.**

The small boxes around the corners and in the center of the Movie bean in Figure 19.9 are for resizing and moving the bean. The small boxes that are off-center of the edges of the Movie bean are for hooking this bean to other beans in the builder tool, which I will discuss in the next step. When the Movie bean is selected, its properties appear in the Property Inspector window of the Bean Builder, as shown in Figure 19.10.

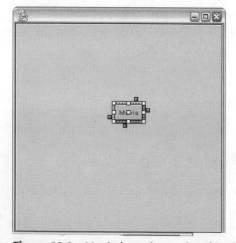

Figure 19.9 Movie bean instantiated in the Bean Builder.

Figure 19.10   Property Inspector window shows the properties of the Movie bean.

You can change the title and length properties of the Movie bean, and they will appear in the Property Inspector window. You can also enter a customer-Name property, but it will disappear after you enter it because it is not a readable property. This does not mean the customerName property wasn't changed, because it was. This only means that you can't view the value of customerName because the Movie bean class does not have a get method for that property.

Notice in Figure 19.10 that the Bean Builder only displays the read-write and write-only properties of the Movie bean by default. To view all of the properties, click the drop-down list that says Standard and select All. You will see all of the properties of the Movie bean, as shown in Figure 19.11.

 The rented property shown in Figure 19.11 is read-only; therefore, the Property Inspector will not allow you to change its value. It is currently not rented, so the check box is not selected. Note that the various bean builder tools handle read-only and write-only properties differently. The JavaBeans specification does not define how bean builder tools are implemented, and I have noticed that they all have their own unique way of displaying and editing properties.

Figure 19.11   All the properties of the Movie bean.

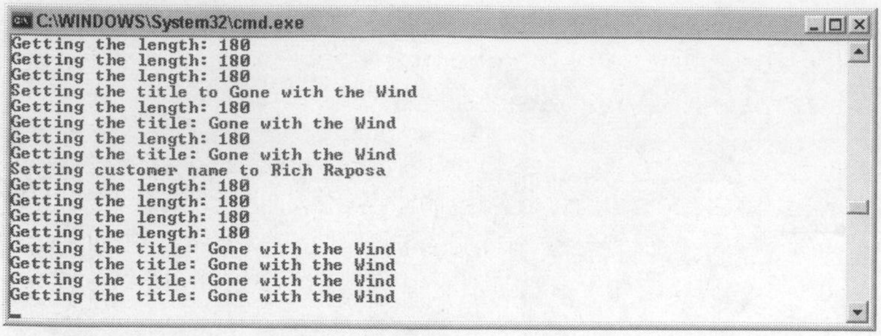

Figure 19.12 Bean Builder invokes the set and get methods of the beans behind the scenes.

If you have changed the properties of the Movie bean (and even if you haven't), you will notice that the bean builder tool is invoking the appropriate set and get methods on the bean object behind the scenes. If you typed in the Movie bean class just as it appears earlier in this chapter, you will notice that I added System.out.println() statements inside the set and get methods. The output of these calls appears in the command prompt window that is running the Bean Builder application. Figure 19.12 shows this window after some of the properties of the Movie bean have been changed in the Property Inspector window.

Now that you have seen how to write a bean, package it in a JAR file, and load it into the Bean Builder tool, I want to show you how the other types of properties work in JavaBeans, which are bound properties and constrained properties.

Bound Properties

A *bound property* of a JavaBean allows a bean property to be bound to the property of another bean. When the property changes in the first bean, its changes are automatically reflected in the second bean. This is a common aspect of Java-Beans development, and the JavaBeans API contains the java.beans.Property-ChangeSupport class to simplify the process of creating bound properties.

To give a bean bound properties, you perform the following steps:

1. Add a field of type PropertyChangeSupport.

2. Add the method addPropertyChangeListener() to the bean class, which takes in a PropertyChangeListener object. Within this method, you add the given listener object to the PropertyChangeSupport object.

3. Add the method removePropertyChangeListener() to the bean class, which also takes in a PropertyChangeListener object. Using the PropetyChangeSupport object, remove the given listener.

4. Add the method getPropertyChangeListeners(), which returns an array containing all listeners currently bound to properties of this bean.

5. Whenever a bound property changes, have the PropertyChangeSupport object notify all listeners by invoking one of the firePropertyChange() methods of the PropertyChangeSupport class.

The last step is the critical step. The first four steps are essentially maintenance steps to register and keep track of listeners. When a property actually changes, the set method of the property is invoked. Within the set method, you need to notify all listeners bound to that property by invoking one of the following methods:

public void firePropertyChange(String propertyName, Object oldValue, Object newValue).   Use this method for properties of any data type because the old and new values are of type Object.

public void firePropertyChange(String propertyName, int oldValue, int newValue).   Use this method for properties of type int.

public void firePropertyChange(String propertyName, boolean oldValue, boolean newValue).   Use this method for properties of type boolean.

To demonstrate bound properties, examine the following bean class named Customer, which has two properties, both of them bindable to other bean properties. Study the class and notice how it follows the previously discussed steps for creating bound properties.

```
package video.store;

import java.beans.*;

public class Customer implements java.io.Serializable
{
    private String name;
    private int number;
    private PropertyChangeSupport pcs;

    public Customer()
    {
        name = "";
        pcs = new PropertyChangeSupport(this);
    }

    public void addPropertyChangeListener(PropertyChangeListener p)
    {
        pcs.addPropertyChangeListener(p);
    }

    public void removePropertyChangeListener(PropertyChangeListener p)
    {
        pcs.removePropertyChangeListener(p);
    }
```

```
public PropertyChangeListener [] getPropertyChangeListeners()
{
    return pcs.getPropertyChangeListeners();
}

public void setName(String s)
{
    String oldName = name;
    name = s;
    pcs.firePropertyChange("name", oldName, name);
}

public String getName()
{
    return name;
}

public void setAccountNumber(int n)
{
    int oldNumber = number;
    number = n;
    pcs.firePropertyChange("accountNumber", oldNumber, number);
}

public int getAccountNumber()
{
    return number;
}
}
```

I want to point out a few items about the Customer bean class:

- As with all JavaBeans, the Customer class implements Serializable and contains a no-argument constructor.

- The Customer bean has two properties: name, which is a String, and accountNumber, which is an int.

- The Customer bean class has the three methods for adding, removing, and getting PropertyChangeListener objects. These are required for a bean to have bound properties.

- Within the setName() method, the firePropertyChange() method is invoked for the name property, passing in the old and new value of name.

- Within the setAccountNumber() method, the firePropertyChange() method is invoked for the accountNumber property, passing in the old and new value of accountNumber.

Step 8: Binding Properties in the Bean Builder

I want you see how bound properties work first-hand, so begin by using the Customer bean discussed previously. Start by creating a new bean object in the Bean Builder by clicking File the New on the main menu. If your Movie bean was previously shown in the JFrame window, it will be deleted and a new empty window will appear.

I already created a JAR file for you, so all you have to do is load it into the Bean Builder using the Load Jar File menu item on the File menu. To download this file, go to the book's Web site at the URL provided in this book's Introduction.

After you have loaded the Customer bean, place one in the JFrame window, as shown in Figure 19.13. I also want you to add a JSlider component (see Figure 19.13), which is found on the Swing tab of the Bean Builder window.

We will now bind the account number property of the Customer bean to the value property of the slider. (The value property is an int between 1 and 100 that denotes where the slider appears.) To bind this property, start by clicking one of the event boxes on the end of the Customer bean in the JFrame. An arrow appears. Drag the arrow over to one of the event boxes on the slider, as shown in Figure 19.14.

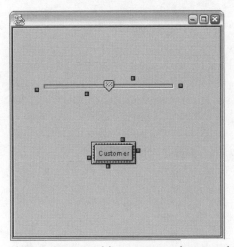

Figure 19.13   Add a Customer bean and a JSlider component to the design window.

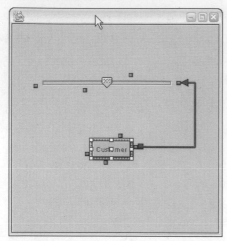

Figure 19.14 Drag the event arrow from the Customer bean to the JSlider bean.

The Interaction Wizard dialog box shown in Figure 19.15 appears. The wizard steps through the process of hooking these two beans together. To bind two properties together, the Create Interaction option should be Event Adapter, which it is by default. The only event that the Customer bean generates is a propertyChange event, which again is already selected.

Click the Next button of the wizard, and you will see a list of target methods found in the JSlider class, as shown in Figure 19.16. This is where you determine which method is invoked on the JSlider bean when the accountNumber property changes in the Customer bean. We will bind accountNumber to the value property of the JSlider, so select the setValue() method, as shown in Figure 19.16, and click the Next button.

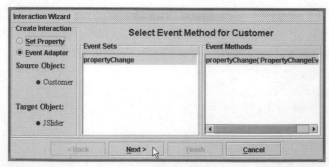

Figure 19.15 Interaction Wizard dialog box assists in hooking two beans together.

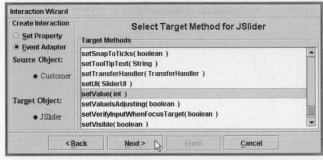

Figure 19.16   Select a target method to be invoked on the JSlider bean.

Figure 19.17 shows the list of get methods from the Customer bean that are compatible with the setValue() method of the JSlider class. (These are the methods of Customer that return an int.) Select getAccountNumber() because it is the property we want to bind to value, and click the Finish button to end the wizard. A bluish line now appears between the Customer bean and the JSlider bean to denote that a relationship exists between the two beans.

To verify that your properties are bound successfully, click the Customer bean and enter a value for the accountNumber property (between 1 and 100). Figure 19.18 shows the accountNumber set to 75.

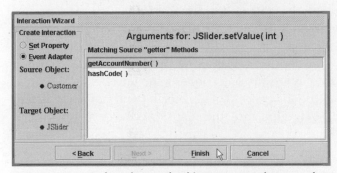

Figure 19.17   Select the method in Customer that sets the value property of the JSlider.

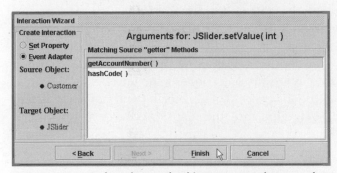

Figure 19.18   Change the value of the accountNumber property of the Customer bean.

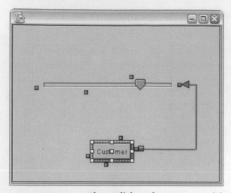

Figure 19.19   The JSlider changes position depending on the value of the Customer bean's accountNumber property.

Figure 19.19 shows what happens to the JSlider bean when the account-Number property is changed.

Constrained Properties

A *constrained property* is a bean property whose changes are monitored by one or more other beans. These other beans validate any changes to the constrained property and can veto a change if they do not find it appropriate. If a change is vetoed, the bean should not make the change and should notify all listeners of this decision.

As with bound properties, because constrained properties are a common occurrence in JavaBeans, the JavaBeans API contains the java.beans.Vetoable-ChangeSupport class to handle the process of registering and notifying listeners of a constrained property. Here are the steps involved in creating a constrained property:

1. Add a field of type VetoableChangeSupport.

2. Add the method addVetoableChangeListener() to the bean class, which takes in a VetoableChangeListener object. Within this method, you add the given listener object to the VetoableChangeSupport object.

3. Add the method removeVetoableChangeListener() to the bean class, which also takes in a VetoableChangeListener object. Using the VetoableChangeSupport object, remove the given listener.

4. Add the method getVetoableChangeListeners(), which returns an array containing all listeners currently constrained to properties of this bean.

5. Before a constrained property is changed, have the VetoableChange-Support object notify all listeners by invoking one of the fireVetoable-Change() methods of the VetoableChangeSupport class. If no one vetoes the change, then the bean can go ahead and make the requested change. If one listener vetoes the change, the change should not be made to the property and the bean should notify all listeners of this.

To veto a change, a listener throws a PropertyVetoException. If this exception occurs, the VetoableChangeSupport handles it for the bean and also notifies all listeners that the new value is not being used; instead, the bean is reverting to the old value. As a bean developer, your set method can simply declare the PropertyVetoException.

When a constrained property is changed (within a set method of the bean class), the bean needs to invoke one of the following fireVetoableChange() methods found in the VetoableChangeSupport class:

public void fireVetoableChange(String propertyName, Object oldValue, Object newValue). Use this method for properties of any data type because the old and new values are of type Object.

public void fireVetoableChange(String propertyName, int oldValue, int newValue). Use this method for properties of type int.

public void fireVetoableChange(String propertyName, boolean oldValue, boolean newValue). Use this method for properties of type boolean.

The following Customer class is a modification of the earlier Customer class, except that the accountNumber is now both a bound property and a constrained property. Study this Customer class and notice that it follows the steps for creating a constrained property.

```
package video.store;

import java.beans.*;

public class Customer implements java.io.Serializable
{
    private String name;
    private int number;
    private PropertyChangeSupport pcs;
    private VetoableChangeSupport vcs;

    public Customer()
    {
        name = "";
```

```
            pcs = new PropertyChangeSupport(this);
            vcs = new VetoableChangeSupport(this);
    }

    public void addVetoableChangeListener(VetoableChangeListener p)
    {
            vcs.addVetoableChangeListener(p);
    }

    public void removeVetoableChangeListener(VetoableChangeListener p)
    {
            vcs.removeVetoableChangeListener(p);
    }

    public VetoableChangeListener [] getVetoableChangeListeners()
    {
            return vcs.getVetoableChangeListeners();
    }


    public void setAccountNumber(int newNumber) throws
PropertyVetoException
    {
            int oldNumber = number;
            vcs.fireVetoableChange("accountNumber", oldNumber, newNumber);
            number = newNumber;
            pcs.firePropertyChange("accountNumber", oldNumber, number);
    }

    //Remainder of Customer stays the same as before
}
```

Let me make a few comments about this Customer class and its constrained accountNumber property:

- The only property that is constrainable is accountNumber.

- Within setAccountNumber(), notice carefully the sequence of events. The vetoable listeners are notified first, then the change is made, then bound property listeners are notified.

- If a constrained listener vetoes the change, this is done by throwing a PropertyVetoException. Since the setAccountNumber() method does not catch this exception when fireVetoableChange() is invoked, the remainder of setAccountNumber() does not execute. More specifically, the property is not changed and bound property listeners are not notified of any change.

- If a PropertyVetoException occurs, the VetoableChangeSupport object catches the exception and notifies all listeners that the bean is reverting to the old account number.

Vetoing an Event

To veto a constrained property, a listener must implement the java.beans. VetoableChangeListener interface. This interface contains one method:

```
public void vetoableChange(PropertyChangeEvent e)
    throws PropertyVetoException
```

This method is invoked on registered listeners before the property is changed. The PropertyChangeEvent parameter contains the name of the property, its old value, and the new value being requested. To demonstrate a listener of constrained properties, the following StoreOwner bean is a listener of changes made to the accountNumber property of Customer beans. Study the class and try to determine when changes are vetoed.

```
package video.store;

import java.beans.*;

public class StoreOwner implements VetoableChangeListener,
                        java.io.Serializable
{
    public void vetoableChange(PropertyChangeEvent e) throws
    PropertyVetoException
    {
        if(e.getPropertyName().equals("accountNumber"))
        {
            Integer temp = (Integer) e.getNewValue();
            int newValue = temp.intValue();
            if(newValue <= 0 || newValue > 100)
            {
                System.out.println("Vetoing change!");
                throw new PropertyVetoException("Out of range", e);
            }
            else
            {
                System.out.println(newValue + " is OK with me!");
            }
        }
    }
}
```

Note the following about the StoreOwner bean:

- I will point this out one last time: The bean class implements Serializable and contains a no-argument constructor (which in this case is the default constructor).

- The getPropertyName() method of the PropertyChangeEvent object is used to make sure that the listener is validating the correct property.

- The getNewValue() method is used to determine what the new value of the accountNumber property is being requested.

- If the newValue is not between 1 and 100, the property change is vetoed. Otherwise, the listener does nothing.

Hooking up a constrained property is similar to hooking up a bound property in the Bean Builder, except that the target method for the listener is vetoableChange(). If you are interested in seeing constrained properties in action, load the customer_bean2.jar file. (To download this file, go to this book's Web site.) Hook up the Customer bean to the StoreOwner bean, registering the StoreOwner as a listener to the accountNumber property.

Overview of Events

JavaBeans communicate with each other through events. You have seen events already with the bound and constrained properties, except that you used utility classes such as PropertyChangeSupport to register and notify listeners. In this section, I will show you how to write a bean that generates an event and how to register another bean to listen to that event.

During the introspection process, a builder tool looks for methods of the following format:

```
public void add<event_name>Listener(<event_name>Listener x)
public void remove<event_name>Listener(<event_name>Listener x)
public <event_name>Listener [] get<event_name>Listeners()
```

These three methods are used to denote that a bean is the source of an event named <event_name>. The <event_name>Listener interface contains the methods that the source of the event invokes and must match the name used in the add and remove methods.

For example, if you want a bean to be the source of a java.awt.ActionEvent, the following three methods need to appear in the bean class:

```
public void addActionListener(ActionListener x)
public void removeActionListener(ActionListener x)
public ActionListener [] getActionListeners()
```

A bean can be the source of any event object that extends java.util.EventObject and whose listener interface extends java.util.EventListener. Thus, all the Swing and AWT events can be used in JavaBeans, as well as any events that you define.

As of J2SE 1.4, the JavaBeans specification recommends that a bean class should contain the get<event_name>Listeners method, which returns an array containing all registered listeners for the event. Adding this method is not a requirement, but I would recommend adding its implementation, especially if you are developing new JavaBeans.

Let's take a look at event handling in action. We will hook together the Movie bean with a couple of JButton components, which are the source of ActionEvents. Open the Bean Builder and follow along.

Step 9: Hooking up Buttons to the Movie Bean

Start with a new design window in the Bean Builder by clicking File, New from the main menu. Load the movie_bean.jar file, and add a Movie bean to the design window. Then add two JButton objects, as shown in Figure 19.20. Change the label on one button to say Rent and the other button to say Return.

Click an event hookup button on the Rent button and drag it over to an event hookup button on the Movie bean. The Interaction Wizard appears, as shown in Figure 19.21. Click on action for the event and actionPerformed() for the method, and then click the Next button.

Figure 19.22 shows the next step of the wizard, which prompts for the target method in the Movie bean. I want the Rent button to cause the movie to be rented, so select the rentMovie() method, as shown in Figure 19.22, and click the Next button.

The next step of the wizard is prompting for a get method in the JButton bean, but this does not apply in our situation, so you can simply click the Finish button to finish the wizard.

Perform similar steps for the Return button, except choose the method returnMovie() as the target method for the action event.

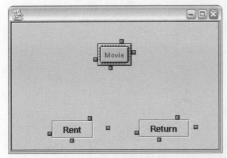

Figure 19.20   Add a Movie bean and two JButton objects, changing the labels on the two buttons.

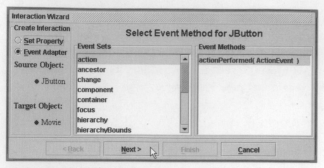

Figure 19.21   Select action event, and click the Next button.

Step 10: Viewing Beans in Preview Mode

After you get the two JButton beans hooked up to the Movie bean, you can test them out by viewing the beans in preview mode. Before you do that, you need to enter a customerName property for the Movie bean and assign the title property as well. Keep in mind that the customerName is a write-only property, so after you set it, you won't see it in the property window anymore.

After you have entered a title and customerName property for the Movie bean, click View, Design Mode on the main menu to turn off design mode and view the bean in preview mode. You should see a window similar to the one shown in Figure 19.23.

 The Movie bean shown in Figure 19.23 is not displayed because the Movie bean is not a GUI component. It is still a part of the application, however; you just can't see it.

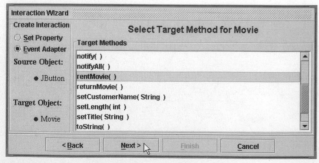

Figure 19.22   Select the rentMovie() method as the target method.

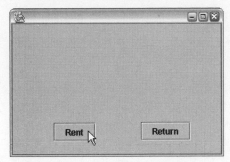

Figure 19.23   Viewing the Movie bean and two JButton beans in preview mode.

Click the Rent button while in preview mode, then change back to design view by selecting View, Design View on the main menu again. Click the Movie bean and view all of its properties. The read-only property rented should be checked, as shown in Figure 19.24. You should also be able to see the output in the command prompt window that the Bean Builder is running in because the Movie bean contained several calls to System.out.println() to show when the various methods of the bean are invoked.

Similarly, clicking the Return button in the preview mode causes the movie to no longer be rented and resets the customerName property to an empty String.

Now that I have shown you how to hook two beans together, let's go through an example of writing your own events, which is an important aspect of JavaBean programming.

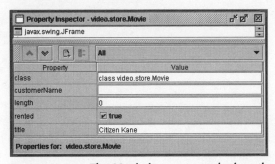

Figure 19.24   The Movie is now rented when the Rent button is clicked.

Generating User-Defined Events

You can write your own events by performing the following steps:

1. Write an event class that extends java.util.EventObject.

2. Write an event listener interface that extends java.util.EventListener.

3. Add the appropriate add, remove, and get listener methods to your bean class.

4. Whenever the event occurs, instantiate an event object and notify all listeners by invoking one of the methods in the event listener interface on each listener.

Let's look at an example that performs each of these steps. Suppose that we have a bean named Radio, and we want it to be the source of an event named volume that is generated each time the volume changes on the radio. Then, we need to begin by writing a class named VolumeEvent that extends EventObject:

```
public class VolumeEvent extends java.util.EventObject
{
    private int volume;

    public VolumeEvent(Object source, int volume)
    {
        super(source);
        this.volume = volume;
    }

    public int getVolume()
    {
        return volume;
    }
}
```

The corresponding listener interface for VolumeEvent must be named VolumeListener and extend EventListener, as the following interface demonstrates. Notice that each method has a single parameter of type VolumeEvent.

```
public interface VolumeListener extends java.util.EventListener
{
    public void volumeIncreased(VolumeEvent e);
    public void volumeDecreased(VolumeEvent e);
    public void muted(VolumeEvent e);
}
```

The bean class that is the source of a VolumeEvent must contain an addVolumeListener() and removeVolumeListener() method. Within these methods, the listeners need to be maintained by the bean in some type of data structure, such as an array or Vector. The following Radio bean class keeps track of VolumeListener objects in a Vector. Study the Radio class, and try to determine the situations in which the various events occur.

```java
import java.util.*;

public class Radio implements java.io.Serializable
{
    private int volume;
    private float station;
    private Vector listeners;

    public Radio()
    {
        listeners = new Vector();
    }

    public void addVolumeListener(VolumeListener v)
    {
        listeners.add(v);
    }

    public void removeVolumeListener(VolumeListener v)
    {
        listeners.remove(v);
    }

    public VolumeListener [] getVolumeListeners()
    {
        return (VolumeListener []) listeners.toArray();
    }

    public void setVolume(int v)
    {
        int difference = volume - v;
        if(difference == 0)
        {
            return;
        }
        volume = v;

        //Notify listeners.
        VolumeEvent event = new VolumeEvent(this, volume);
        Vector clone = (Vector) listeners.clone();
        for(int i = 0; i < clone.size(); i++)
        {
            VolumeListener current = (VolumeListener)
```

```
                    clone.elementAt(i);
                    if(volume == 0)
                    {
                        current.muted(event);
                    }else if(difference > 0)
                    {
                        current.volumeDecreased(event);
                    }else if(difference < 0)
                    {
                        current.volumeIncreased(event);
                    }
                }
            }

            public int getVolume()
            {
                return volume;
            }

            public void setStation(float s)
            {
                station = s;
            }

            public float getStation()
            {
                return station;
            }
        }
```

Let me make a few comments about the Radio bean class:

- The Radio bean is a source of volume events because of the add, remove, and get volume listener methods.

- The listeners are stored in a Vector, and the add() and remove() methods of the Vector class simplify adding and removing listeners.

- The volume events occur when the volume changes, which is within the setVolume() method.

- Within setVolume(), the Vector of listeners is traversed, and each object in the Vector is notified of the event by having a VolumeListener method invoked on it.

- I cloned the Vector before notifying listeners to demonstrate a standard trick in JavaBeans programming. Cloning the Vector is done for thread safety. Notifying the listeners might take a while, and a listener might remove itself from the Vector right before it is to be notified of a VolumeEvent. Because the Vector is cloned, the listener removes itself from the original Vector, but it still gets notification of the event because the listener is still in the cloned Vector.

Because you are developing the bean, you get to decide how to keep track of listeners of an event. In addition, you get to decide how many listeners a bean can have for a particular event. For example, you might have a situation in which only one listener makes sense for an event. In this situation, you would not need a data structure, but would need only a field to keep track of the listener.

The java.util package contains a class named TooManyListenersException that can be thrown by the add<event_name>Listener method when the bean does not want any more listeners registering for the event.

Now that the Radio bean is a source of a VolumeEvent, it can be hooked up to other beans that listen for this event. To deploy this bean, it needs to appear in a JAR file along with the VolumeEvent and VolumeListener classes. The manifest file should look like the following:

```
Manifest-Version: 1.0

Name: Radio.class
Java-Bean: True

Name: VolumeEvent.class
Java-Bean: False

Name: VolumeListener.class
Java-Bean: False
```

After the bean is deployed, the Bean Builder tool will recognize the Radio as a source of a VolumeEvent and let other beans register for it. Figure 19.25 shows the first step of the Interaction Wizard that appears when the Radio bean is hooked up to another bean. Notice that the methods of the VolumeListener interface appear in the list of available event sources.

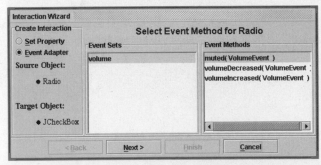

Figure 19.25 Methods of the VolumeListener interface appear as events for the Radio bean.

♦ Bean Persistence

A common activity with beans is to hook them together in a builder tool, then serialize this new bean to a file or other persistent location. Bean persistence is an important capability in JavaBeans development, and up until J2SE 1.4 the persistence was achieved by using object serialization and the ObjectOutputStream and ObjectInputStream classes of the java.io package.

As of J2SE 1.4, XML is used to create a textual way to persist beans. Two new classes have been added to the java.beans package: XMLEncoder and XMLDecoder. The XMLEncoder class takes the properties of one or more beans and archives them into a file using XML tags. Bean Builder tools can then use the XMLDecoder class to extract the properties of the beans from the XML file.

For example, the following EncodeDemo program instantiates a Radio bean and archives it to a file named my_radio.xml:

```java
import java.beans.*;
import java.io.*;

public class EncodeDemo
{
    public static void main(String [] args)
    {
        Radio radio = new Radio();
        radio.setVolume(10);
        radio.setStation(100.3F);

        try
        {
            FileOutputStream file =
                new FileOutputStream("my_radio.xml");
            XMLEncoder out = new XMLEncoder(file);
            out.writeObject(radio);

            out.close();
            file.close();
        }catch(IOException e)
        {
            e.printStackTrace();
        }
    }
}
```

The volume is set to 10 and the station is set to 100.3. The resulting file my_radio.xml looks like this:

```xml
<?xml version="1.0" encoding="UTF-8"?>
<java version="1.4.1_01" class="java.beans.XMLDecoder">
    <object class="Radio">
```

```
            <void property="station">
                    <float>100.3</float>
            </void>
            <void property="volume">
                    <int>10</int>
            </void>
        </object>
    </java>
```

Similarly, you could use the readObject() method of the XMLDecoder class to read in the Radio object into an application. Typically, you do not need to write the code to encode an XML object because the bean builder tools do this for you.

For example, in the Bean Builder program, if you hook together a collection of Java-Beans, you can save the design in an XML file by selecting File, Save on the main menu of the Bean Builder. You could then extract the information in a Java program using the XMLDecoder class.

BeanInfo Class

Every bean can have a BeanInfo class that denotes the properties, methods, and events of a bean. The BeanInfo class is useful for many situations, including the following:

- If you have an existing class that you want to make into a bean, but the class did not follow the naming conventions of the JavaBeans specification, you can use the BeanInfo class to denote the set and get methods of properties and the add and remove methods of events.

- You might have some properties that are simple, some that are bound, and others that are constrained. The BeanInfo class lets you denote this.

- You can use the BeanInfo class to denote default properties, those that will most often be used by other beans.

- Similarly, you can denote a default event that most beans will likely use. Smart builder tools will use these default values to make themselves more user-friendly.

- You can create a *customizer* for a bean, which allows you to write your own GUI for changing and viewing the properties of a bean in a builder tool.

- You can specify icons for a bean for use in various situations by the bean builder tools.

A BeanInfo class for a bean must satisfy the following requirements:

- The name of the BeanInfo class must be the name of the bean class appended with BeanInfo. For example, if the bean class is named Movie, its BeanInfo class must be named MovieBeanInfo.

- The BeanInfo class of a bean must implement the java.beans.BeanInfo interface. Alternatively, the BeanInfo class can extend the SimpleBeanInfo class in the java.beans package, which is a utility class that implements the methods of the BeanInfo class for you with empty method bodies.

Some of the methods in the BeanInfo interface include the following:

public int getDefaultEventIndex().   Returns the index of the event that is most likely used by other beans.

public int getDefaultPropertyIndex().   Returns the index of the property that is most likely used by other beans.

public Image getIcon(int kind).   Returns the icon for the bean specified by the kind argument, which is either ICON_COLOR_32x32, ICON_COLOR_16x16, ICON_MONO_32x32, or ICON_MONO_16x16.

public EventSetDescriptor [ ] getEventSetDescriptors().   Returns an array containing the types of events that this bean generates and their corresponding add and remove methods.

public PropertyDescriptor [ ] getPropertyDescriptors().   Returns an array containing the properties of this bean.

public MethodDescriptor [ ] getMethodDescriptors().   Returns an array containing the methods of this bean.

 A bean can have a BeanInfo class that does not implement all the methods of the BeanInfo interface. For those methods in a BeanInfo class that are not implemented, the builder tools will use introspection instead. This allows you to use a BeanInfo class for some aspects of a bean and have the builder tool determine other aspects of your bean.

The following MovieBeanInfo class demonstrates writing a BeanInfo class for a bean. Study this class and try to determine what type of information it is providing to the builder tool, versus the information about the Movie bean that the builder tool will have to figure out by itself using introspection.

```
package video.store;

import java.beans.*;
```

```
public class MovieBeanInfo extends SimpleBeanInfo
{
    public PropertyDescriptor [] getPropertyDescriptors()
    {
        try
        {
            PropertyDescriptor [] pds = {
new PropertyDescriptor("title", video.store.Movie.class),
        new PropertyDescriptor("length", video.store.Movie.class),
        new PropertyDescriptor("customerName",
video.store.Movie.class,
    null, "setCustomerName"),
        new PropertyDescriptor("rented",
    video.store.Movie.class, "isRented", null)};

            return pds;
        }catch(IntrospectionException e)
        {
            e.printStackTrace();
            return null;
        }
    }

    public int getDefaultPropertyIndex()
    {
        return 0;
    }
}
```

The MovieBeanInfo class needs to appear in the JAR file with the Movie bean, and builder tools automatically look for and invoke the methods on MovieBeanInfo to determine this additional information about the bean.

Lab 19.1: A Stock Bean

To become familiar with writing a JavaBean. In this lab, you will write a bean to represent a stock traded on the stock exchange.

1. Write a bean class named Stock that implements Serializable and contains a no-argument constructor. Have the class extend JPanel so that it will be a visual bean.

2. Add the necessary set and get methods so that the Stock bean has a property named symbol of type String, price of type int, and sharesTraded of type double.

3. Override the paint() method inherited from JPanel, and use the drawString() method of the Graphics class to display the symbol, price, and sharesTraded properties within the JPanel.

4. Save and compile the Stock class.

5. Create a manifest file for the Stock bean, and use it to package the Stock bean in a JAR file.

6. Open the Stock bean in the builder tool, and change some of its properties.

Because this Stock bean is a GUI component, you should be able to see its properties displayed on the bean itself. You may need to force a repaint by covering up the design window and then restoring it.

Lab 19.2: Using Bound Properties

In this lab, you will modify the Stock bean so that its properties are bindable.

1. Open your Stock.java file from Lab 19.1. Add a field of type PropertyChangeSupport, and initialize this field in the constructor.

2. Add the necessary add and remove methods so that other beans can register themselves as PropertyChangeEvent listeners.

3. Within the set methods of the Stock bean, invoke the firePropertyChange() method of the PropertyChangeSupport object, passing in the appropriate arguments.

4. Save and compile the Stock class.

5. Re-create the JAR file, and reload it in the Bean Builder.

6. Add a Stock bean to the design window and a JSlider component. Bind the Stock's price property to the value property of the JSlider.

Change the price property of the Stock bean, and you should see the JSlider move accordingly.

Lab 19.3: Using Constrained Properties

To become familiar with constrained properties. In this lab, you will modify the Stock bean so that its sharesTraded property is constrained.

1. Add the necessary fields and methods to make the Stock class able to handle VetoableChange listeners.

2. Within the setSharesTraded() method, notify all listeners that the property is about to be changed before changing the property. If any listener vetoes, be sure that the property does not change.

3. Save and compile the Stock class.

4. Write a bean called StockVetoer that implements the VetoableChangeListener interface.

5. Within the vetoableChange() method, determine how many shares are being traded. If the value is greater than 5000, veto the change.

6. Save and compile the StockVetoer class.

7. Modify your manifest file so that StockVetoer is denoted as a Java-Bean. Create a new JAR file that contains both the Stock and StockVetoer beans.

8. Load this JAR file in the Bean Builder, and hook these two beans together to verify that they are working.

You should not be able to change the sharesTraded property of the Stock bean to a value greater than 5000.

Lab 19.4: User-Defined Events

To become familiar with writing beans that fire events. In this lab, you will modify your Stock bean so that it fires a StockPriceChange event.

1. Write a class named StockPriceChangeEvent that extends EventObject. Add a field named price and a constructor that initializes the field.

2. Save and compile the StockPriceChangeEvent class.

3. Write an interface named StockPriceChangeListener that contains two methods: priceIncreased() and priceDecreased().

4. Save and compile the StockPriceChangeListener interface.

5. Modify your Stock bean class so that it is the source of stock-PriceChange events.

6. Within the setPrice() method, notify all listeners that the price of the stock is changing.

7. Save and compile the Stock bean class.

8. Create a manifest file and JAR file for these classes.

9. Load this JAR file into the Bean Builder. Place a Stock object in the design window along with two JList components.

10. Set up the event handling so that when the price of the stock goes up, the prices appears in one list, and when the price goes down, it appears in the other list. Thus, one list will grow only when the price goes up, and the other list will grow only when the price goes down.

11. Change the price of the Stock bean to verify that the events are working properly.

When you change the price of the stock so that it goes up, you should see the new price in the list you denoted for price increases. When the price goes down, you should see the new price in the other list.

Summary

- A JavaBean is a reusable software component designed to be used either in a GUI bean builder tool or in other Java technologies such as JavaServer Pages.

- A JavaBean is a class that adheres to the JavaBeans specification. For example, the class must implement the java.io.Serializable interface and contain a public no-argument constructor.

- JavaBeans have three basic components: properties, events, and methods. Each of these features of a JavaBean is determined by the public methods declared within the class.

- A bean's properties are determined by the public set and get methods in the class.

- A bean's events are determined by the public add<event_name>Listener() and remove<event_name>Listener() methods in the class.

- Beans are deployed by placing them in a JAR file with a corresponding manifest file that lists the beans in the JAR file.

- The Bean Builder is a free tool available from Sun that allows you to test and work with JavaBeans.

- Bound properties allow a bean to have its properties bound to the properties of another bean. Constrained properties allow a bean to have a property verified before any changes are made to the property. Constrained listeners have the option of vetoing any changes to a property.

- A user-defined event is created by writing an event class that extends java.util.EventObject and a corresponding interface that extends java.util.EventListener.

- The java.beans.XMLEncoder and java.beans.XMLDecoder classes are used to persist the state of a JavaBean.

- A JavaBean can have an optional BeanInfo class that contains detailed information about the properties, events, and methods of a bean.

Review Questions

1. Which of the following statements is (are) true about JavaBeans? Select all that apply:

   a. JavaBeans are software components.

   b. JavaBeans are hooked together in a GUI builder tool.

   c. You do not need to know how to write Java code to hook JavaBeans together.

   d. JavaBeans are used widely in JavaServer Pages.

   e. A JavaBean can be converted into an ActiveX component.

2. If a bean has a read-write property named color of type String, what two methods appear in the bean class?

3. Suppose that a bean class declares the following two methods. Which of the following statements is (are) true? Select all that apply.

   ```
   public void setCompleted(boolean complete)
   public boolean isCompleted()
   ```

   a. The bean has a read-write property named completed.

   b. The bean has a read-write property named Completed.

   c. The bean has a write-only property named complete.

   d. The property name for this bean depends on the name of the corresponding field.

   e. No property is determined from these two methods.

4. True or False: A bean class should implement the java.io.Serializable interface.

5. True or False: A bean class must contain a no-argument constructor.

6. True or False: A bean in a JAR file must be denoted as a JavaBean in the manifest file of the JAR.

7. Suppose that you want a bean to be the source of an event named football. What methods must appear in the bean class?

8. True or False: A listener vetoes a constrained property change by returning false from the vetoableChange() method.

9. True or False: Adding a field of type PropertyChangeSupport to a bean class makes all of the properties of the bean bound properties.

10. True or False: If a constrained property is vetoed, a bean should go back and notify all listeners that the bean is reverting back to the old value of the property.

11. True or False: A bean can limit the number of registered listeners it has for a particular event by throwing a TooManyListenersException when too many listeners register for the event.

12. An event class must extend what class?

13. An event listener interface must extend what interface?

14. If you have bean class named Television, what must the name of its corresponding BeanInfo class be?

15. What two classes are used for archiving and extracting JavaBeans in XML format?

Answers to Review Questions

1. They are all true.

2. public void setColor(String c) and public String getColor().

3. Only a is true.

4. True. Beans are often serialized, either on their own or after being hooked to other beans.

5. True. According to the JavaBeans specification, bean classes must have a no-argument constructor.

6. True. This is done using the Java-Bean parameter in a manifest file. If you forget to do this in the manifest file, your bean will not appear in the builder tool as an available bean.

7. Two methods must appear: public void addFootballListener() and removeFootballListener(), both with FootballListener parameters. The other recommended but optional method is getFootballListeners(), which returns all registered FootballListener objects as an array.

8. False. A listener vetoes a change by throwing a PropertyVetoException.

9. False. The step that makes a property a bound property is when the firePropertyChange() method is invoked in the corresponding set method.

10. True. This is the recommended behavior of a vetoed change. Keep in mind that if you use the VetoableChangeSupport class to handle constrained properties, it does this for you.

11. True. A bean gets to determine exactly how many listeners it wants to register for an event.

12. java.util.EventObject.

13. java.util.EventListener.

14. TelevisionBeanInfo.

15. java.beans.XMLEncoder and java.beans.XMLDecoder.

APPENDIX

A

About the 60 Minutes Web Site

This appendix provides you with information on the contents of the Web site that accompanies this book. On this site, you will find information that will help you with each of the book's chapters.

This Web site contains:

- Streaming video presentations that introduce you to each chapter of the book. These presentations are intended to provide late-breaking information that can help you understand the content of the chapter.

- Sample code that is used throughout the book. The sample code is presented as files with a .java and .class extensions.

To access the site, visit www.wiley.com/compbooks/60minutesaday.

System Requirements

Make sure that your computer meets the minimum system requirements listed in this section. If your computer doesn't match up to most of these requirements, you may have a problem using the contents of the Knowledge Publisher Studio.

- PC with a Pentium processor running at 266 MHZ or faster with Windows NT4, Windows 2000, or Windows XP.

- At least 256MB of total RAM installed on your computer; for best performance, we recommend at least 512MB.

- A high-speed Internet connection of at least 100K is recommended for viewing online video.

- Internet Explorer 6.0 or higher.

- Browser settings need to have Cookies enabled; Java must be enabled (including JRE 1.2.2 or higher installed) for chat functionality and live Webcast.

- Screen Resolution of 1024x768 pixels.

60 Minutes a Day Presentations

To enhance the learning experience and further replicate the classroom environment, *Java in 60 Minutes a Day* is complemented by a multimedia Web site which aggregates a streaming video and audio presentation. The multimedia Web site includes an online presentation and introduction to each chapter. The presentation, hosted by Rich Raposa, includes a 10- to 15- minute video segment for each chapter that helps to deliver the training experience to your desktop and to convey advanced topics in a user-friendly manner.

Each video/audio segment introduces a chapter and details the important concepts and details of that chapter. After viewing the online presentation, you are prepped to read the chapter.

Upon reaching the companion site that contains the video content for this book you will be asked to register using a valid email address and self-generated password. This will allow you to bookmark video progress and manage notes, email, and collaborative content as you progress through the chapters. All video content is delivered "on demand," meaning that you can initiate the viewing of a video at any time of the day or night at your convenience.

Any video can be paused and replayed as many times as you wish. The necessary controls and widgets used to control the delivery of the videos use strict industry standard symbols and behaviors, thus eliminating the necessity to learn new techniques. If you would like to participate in a complete five-minute online tutorial on how to use all features available inside the presentation panel, visit http://www.propoint.com/solutions/ and click on the DEMO NOW link on the left side of the Web page.

This video delivery system may be customized somewhat to enhance and accommodate the subject matter within a particular book. A special effort has been made to ensure that all information is readily available and easy to understand. In the unlikely event that you should encounter a problem with the content on the site please do not hesitate to contact us at Wiley Product Technical Support.

Code and Bonus Content

In addition to the presentations, you can download the sample code files and view additional resources.

Troubleshooting

If you have trouble with the Web site, please call the Wiley Product Technical Support phone number: (800) 762-2974. Outside the United States, call 1 (317) 572-3994. You can also visit our Web site at www.wiley.com/techsupport. Wiley Publishing, Inc., will provide technical support only for installation and other general quality control items; for technical support on the applications themselves, consult the program's vendor or author.

Index

SYMBOLS

&& (and operator), 43, 55
& (and operator), 43, 55
{} (curly brackets)
  for array elements, 259
  in class declaration, 89
  if statement, 59
— (decrement operator), 39
== (equal to operator), 43, 156
^ (exclusive or operator), 43, 56, 57
> (greater than operator), 42
>= (greater than or equal to operator), 42
++ (increment operator), 39
< (less than operator), 42
<= (less than or equal to operator), 42
! (not operator), 56
!= (not equal to operator), 43
| (or operator), 43, 56
|| (or operator), 43, 56
<< (shift operator), 40–41
> (shift operator), 41
>> (shift operator), 41
[] (square brackets), 254

A

abstract classes. *See also* abstraction;
    classes
  changes of, 238
  declaring, 239
  defined, 238
  example, 240–241
  hierarchy of, 242
  subclassing, 238
  use benefits, 244
abstract keyword, 239
abstract methods. *See also* abstraction;
    methods
  benefits, 242
  collection of, 295
  declarating, 242
  declaration results, 242
  defined, 242
  implementation, 242
  in parent class, 242
  use benefits, 244
  uses, 242
Abstract Windowing Toolkit. *See* AWT
AbstractButton class, 427
AbstractDemo program, 240–241

abstraction
   benefits, 244
   defined, 238
   overview, 238–239
   summary, 248
accept() method, 597
access specifiers
   class, 194
   default access, 111, 190
   defined, 90, 190
   example, 191–194
   in method overriding, 154
   private access, 111, 190
   program design and, 190
   protected access, 111, 190
   public access, 111, 190
   values, 111
AccessDemo program, 192–193
accessor methods
   defined, 194
   naming, 195
ActionEvent class, 417
ActionListener interface
   actionPerformed() method, 408, 409
   class implementation of, 409
   defined, 408
actionPerformed() method, 408, 409
add() method, 275, 375–376
addActionListener() method, 417, 418
addAll() method, 275
addBatch() method, 643
addChangeListener() method, 418
AddDemo program
   defined, 376
   output, 377
   source code, 376
addElement() method, 275
addHandler() method, 580
addItemListener() method, 421
addListSelectionListener() method, 440
addMouseListener() method, 416
AddMovies program
   defined, 645
   MovieDatabase class, 644
   output, 646

   running, 646
   source code, 645
addTextListener() method, 430
addWindowListener() method, 410
Alphabet program, 78
and operator, 52–53
<applet> tag. *See also* HTML
   attributes, 473–474
   browser not understanding, 474
   defined, 473
   parameters, 475
Applet class
   defined, 459
   example, 459–462
   extending, 462
applet context
   defined, 485
   example, 486–488
AppletContext interface, 485
applets
   class, writing, 467–468
   code base, 478–479
   defined, 457
   developing, 479
   document base, 478–479
   embedding, 461, 462
   image display, 488–490
   JAR files and, 494–495
   life cycle, 465–470
   overview, 457–459
   parameters, 475
   platform independence, 458
   playing audio, 490–492
   security rules, 458
   size, 461
   standalone Java applications
      versus, 457–458
   Swing, 462–465
   uses, 458
   viewing, in Web browser, 480
   viewing, with appletviewer, 480
appletviewer
   defined, 479
   display, 480, 481
   options, 480

sandbox security, 481–484
viewing applets with, 480
arguments
defined, 113
passing, 116–119
promoting, 125
this method as, 101
ArithmeticDemo program, 38–39
ArithmeticException, 333, 335
array elements
accessing, 255
data types, 253
deleting, 281
first, 253
index, 253, 256
initial values, 255
listing, 259
printing, 256
in two-dimensional arrays, 263
Vector class, 273–274
array initializers
benefits, 259
defined, 259
example, 259–261
new keyword and, 259
use of, 260
array references
creating, by polymorphism, 266
declaring, 253, 254, 256
example, 257–259
passing, 261
sums, 254
three-dimensional, 263
arraycopy() method
defined, 261
signature, 261
use example, 261–262
ArrayCopyDemo program, 261–262
ArrayDemo program
defined, 257
observations, 258
output, 259
source code, 258
ArrayIndexOutOfBoundsException,
256, 332, 333, 348, 350

ArrayInitDemo program
defined, 259
output, 261
source code, 259–260
arrays. *See also* collections
accessing, 254, 255
assigning sums to, 254
in contiguous memory, 254
copying, 261–262
creation steps, 253
defined, 253
of doubles, 255
instantiating, 253
Java versus other, 256
multidimensional, 263–265
as objects, 256
of primitive data types, 256
resizeable, 281
size, specifying, 253, 254
three-dimensional, 263
two-dimensional, 263
types of, 256
using, 288
assignment operators, 40
attributes. *See also* objects
defined, 85
denoting, 86
length, 255–256
AudioClip interface, 490–491
AudioDemo applet
defined, 491
source code, 491
start() method, 492
available() method, 553
AWT (Abstract Windowing Toolkit).
See also Swing
Buttons, 369, 417
check boxes, 375, 421–423
Choice, 375, 440–442
classes, 369
combo boxes, 440–442
components, 358, 375
defined, 368
labels, 375, 429
lists, 375, 437–439

AWT *(continued)*
  program conversion, 369
  radio buttons, 425–427
  shortcomings, 368
  Swing versus, 368
  text components, 375, 430–433

B

BankDemo program, 359
base classes. *See* parent classes
Bean Builder. *See also* JavaBeans
  bean instantiated in, 682
  Bean window, 680
  binding properties in, 687–690
  defined, 678
  downloading, 678
  JAVA_HOME environment
      variable and, 680
  loading beans into, 681
  main window, 680
  Property Inspector, 680, 683
  running, 678–681
  set/get method invocation, 684
  User tab, 682
BeanInfo class
  defined, 671, 703
  methods, 704
  requirements, 704
  uses, 703
behaviors. *See also* objects
  becoming methods, 86, 90
  defined, 85
  forcing, on classes, 304, 310–315
bind() method, 597
blocked threads. *See also* threads
  defined, 506
  states, 507
boolean data type
  defined, 30
  min/max values, 23
  size, 23
  true/false values, 30, 31
  variable, 30
Boolean logic
  defined, 52
  exclusive or operator, 52, 54

not operator, 52, 54
and operator, 52–53
or operator, 52, 53–54
types of, 52
Boolean operators
  && (and), 55
  & (and), 55
  ^ (exclusive or), 56, 57
  ! (not), 56
  | (or), 56
  || (or), 56
  combining, 57
  defined, 43
  list of, 56
  logic, 52–54
  types of, 43
BooleanDemo program, 30–31
BorderLayout class, 383–384
BorderLayout manager. *See also*
    layout managers
  defined, 379, 383
  properties, 383–384
  use example, 384–385
BorderLayoutDemo program, 384–385
born threads, 506
bound properties. *See also* JavaBeans
  addition steps, 684–685
  creating, 687–690
  defined, 684
  example, 685–686
  using, 706
BoxLayout class
  assigning, 391
  constructor, 391
  defined, 390
BoxLayout manager. *See also* layout
    managers
  defined, 379
  example, 391–392
  properties, 390–391
BoxLayoutDemo program, 391–392
break keyword
  common use of, 75
  defined, 74
  excessive use of, 77

in while loops, 75
BreakDemo program, 75–76
breaks
example, 75–76
flow of control and, 74
bridge drivers. *See also* JDBC drivers
defined, 632
J2SE, 633
BufferedOutputStream class, 561
Button class, 417
ButtonDemo program
defined, 418
output, 420
source code, 419–420
Buttons
creating, 369
displaying, 375
listener registration, 406
size, 377
buttons
AWT, 417
Swing, 418–420
byte data type, 23
bytecode
in arbitrary directories, 186
files, 187
of interfaces, 295
in JAR files, 187

C

C++, virtual methods, 233
call stacks. *See also* methods
current method execution in, 107
defined, 107
exceptions and, 330, 331
method removal from, 107
multiple, 108
callable statements, 656–660
CallableDemo program, 659–660
CallableStatement object
creating, 658, 659
defined, 656
call-by-pointer, 116
call-by-reference, 116

call-by-value
argument specification and, 116
changing argument contents and, 120
defined, 116
example, 116–119
cancel() method, 523
canRead() method, 555
capacity() method, 276
CardLayout manager, 379
case. *See also* switch statement
default, 62
defined, 61
value after, 64
case sensitivity, 184
cast operator, 26, 27
CastDemo program, 220–221
casting
defined, 26
down hierarchy tree, avoiding, 234
float to double, 218
floating-point numbers, 26
inheritance hierarchy and, 219
casting references
casting of primitive data
types and, 219
example, 220–221
inheritance hierarchy and, 219
catch blocks
defined, 334–335
multiple, 337–340
syntax, 337
catch keyword, 334
CatchDemo2 program, 339–340
CatchDemo program
defined, 336
output when file not found, 337
output when no exception occurs, 338
source code, 336
catching exceptions. *See also* exceptions
defined, 334
multiple catch blocks, 337–340
polymorphism and, 340–341
process, 334–335
try/catch block, 334, 335–337
ChainDemo program, 561–562

char data type
  defined, 31
  as integer value, 31
  min/max values, 23
  size, 23
character literals, 31
characters
  escape sequence, 31
  Unicode value, 32
CharDemo program, 32
check boxes
  AWT, 421–423
  defined, 421
  Swing, 423–425
Checkbox class, 421
CheckboxDemo program, 422–423
CheckboxGroup class
  constructor, 425
  methods, 425–426
checked exceptions. *See also* exceptions
  avoiding Handle or Declare Rule, 355
  declaring, 342
  defined, 330
  runtime exceptions versus, 333, 342
child classes. *See also* classes;
   inheritance
  access, 146
  defined, 139
  method overriding, 154–157, 158
  methods, 154
  nonabstracted, 242
child objects
  instantiating, 146–148
  parent class references to, 214–218
  as parent class type, 214
  reference to inherited fields, 160
  reference to parent object, 157–160
Choice class, 440–441
ChoiceDemo program, 441
.class extension, 14
class keyword, 89
class members, 198
ClassCastException, 224, 225

classes
  abstract, 238, 239–241
  AbstractButton, 427
  access specifiers, 194
  ActionEvent, 417
  adding, to packages, 176–178
  adding fields to, 89–90
  adding methods to, 90–91
  Applet, 459–465
  AWT, 369
  BeanInfo, 671, 703–705
  BorderLayout, 383–385
  BoxLayout, 390–391
  BufferedOutputStream, 561
  bytecode file, 186
  Checkbox, 421
  child, 139
  Choice, 440–442
  common elements, 143
  compiling, 98–99, 182
  Component, 371–372, 375
  Container, 375
  CreateList, 433
  curly brackets ({}), 89
  data types and, 24
  DatagramPacket, 613–614
  DatagramSocket, 612–613
  DataOutputStream, 561
  DataSource, 633, 636–637
  declaring, 89
  defined, 12, 85
  Dialog, 394
  DisplayMessage, 508
  DriverManager, 633, 634–635
  Error, 333
  event adapter, 412–414
  EventObject, 415–416
  Exception, 333
  extending, 145–146
  field content control, 197
  fields, 89
  final, 160–161
  FlowLayout, 379–383
  forcing behaviors on, 304, 310–315

Formatter, 579
Frame, 369
fully qualified name, 181, 182, 184
Graphics, 488
GridLayout, 388–389
Handler, 579
HashSet, 273
Hashtable, 281–287
importing, 181, 182–183
inheritance, 145
InputStream, 553
interface implementation, 300
interfaces versus, 296
introduction to, 12
JApplet, 462
JCheckbox, 423
JComboBox, 442
JComponent, 375
JDialog, 394
JFrame, 369, 372–374
JLabel, 429–430
JPanel, 386
JPasswordField, 436
JProgressBar, 445
JRadioButton, 427
JScrollPane, 435–436
JTextArea, 434
JTextComponent, 434
Label, 429–430
LinkedList, 290
List, 437
Logger, 579, 580
LogRecord, 579
methods, 89
Object, 150–154
ObjectInputStream, 574
ObjectOutputStream, 574, 577
OutputStream, 552
overview, 85–86
packages, 175–180
Panel, 385–386
parent, 139
PipedInputStream, 570
PipedOutputStream, 570

PipedReader, 570
PipedWriter, 570
public, 89
RandomAccessFile, 566–568
Reader, 554
in same package, 180
saving, 185
SelectionHandler, 443–444
ServerSocket, 592, 595, 596–598
ServerSocketFactory, 603–604
Socket, 592, 595, 599–600
SSLServerSocket, 604–605
SSLSocket, 607–608
StringBuffer, 35
Swing, 369
System, 261
this reference usage, 157
Thread, 507, 509
ThreadGroup, 509
Throwable, 332, 333–334
Timer, 519–521
TimerTask, 507, 519–521
TreeSet, 273
URLConnection, 619–620
Vector, 273–281, 287, 289
VetoableChangeSupport, 690–691
WindowAdapter, 413
without main() method, 121
wrapper, 229
Writer, 553–554
writing, 24, 89–91, 97–99, 102–103, 185
XMLDecoder, 702–703
XMLEncoder, 702
ClassNotFoundException, 333
CLASSPATH environment variable
bytecode and, 186
contents, 187
current definition of, 187
defining, 188
package directory structure and, 189
setting, 187–188
setting, in Control Panel, 188
CLDC (Connected Limited Device
    Configuration), 5

clear() method, 278, 285
clone() method, 152
close() method, 552, 553, 600
code base, 478–479
collections
  arrays, 253–265
  defined, 253
  heterogeneous, 229–230, 265–267
  implementing, 273
  interfaces, 295–328
  performance and, 273
  types of, 253
collections framework
  classes, 287
  data structures, 230, 272–273
  defined, 229, 253, 272
  Hashtable class, 281–287
  overview, 272–273
  purpose, 273
  Vector class, 273–281
  wrapper classes, 229
combo boxes
  AWT, 440–442
  defined, 440
  Swing, 442–444
command-line arguments, 16–17
comments
  constructor, 269
  field, 269
  javadoc, 269–271
  method, 269
  techniques, 44
  use example, 44
comparison (<, <=, >, >=, ==, !=,
  instanceof) operators, 42–43
compiler errors, 14
compiling
  classes, 98–99
  Hello, World program, 13–14
  user-defined interfaces, 299
Component class
  add() methods, 375–376
  addMouseListener() method, 416
  Child objects, 375

  defined, 375
  setVisible() method, 371–372
components. *See also* GUI (graphical
  user interface)
  added to JFrames, 372
  adding, 375–377
  AWT, 358
  containers and, 375–378
  heavyweight, 368
  lightweight, 368
  pluggable look and feel, 382–383
  Swing, 368
config() method, 580
CongratulateStudent program, 62–63
connect() method, 570–571, 599
Connected Limited Device Configuration (CLDC), 5
Connection interface, 642–643
connectors, 6
constants, 37
constrained properties. *See also*
  JavaBeans
  creation steps, 690–691
  defined, 690
  using, 706–707
ConstructorDemo program
  defined, 130
  main(), 164, 198, 199
  output, 131
  source code, 130
constructors. *See also* methods
  adding, 127
  benefits of, 126
  BoxLayout class, 391
  BufferedOutputStream class, 561
  Button class, 417
  Checkbox class, 421
  CheckboxGroup class, 425
  Choice class, 440
  comments, 269
  DatagramPacket class, 613
  DatagramSocket class, 612–613
  default, 127, 128–129, 167
  defined, 125

Dialog class, 394
File class, 554
FlowLayout class, 380
Frame class, 369–370
GridLayout class, 388–389
Hashtable class, 283
instance initializers versus, 205
invoking, 127
invoking, within same class, 132
JButton class, 418
JCheckbox class, 423
JFrame class, 373
JList class, 439
JTextArea, 434
Label class, 429
List class, 437
method overloading with, 121
multiple, 130–131
multiple, adding, 126
names, 126
no-argument, 130, 164, 167
Object class, 163
Panel class, 386
parameter lists, 126
parent class, 165–168
properties satisfied by, 126
purpose, 125
RandomAccessFile class, 566
ServerSocket class, 596
signatures, 129, 130
Sockets class, 599
TextArea class, 431
TextField class, 431
this keyword in, 131–134
Threads class, 509
URL class, 617
using, 129–131, 135
Vector class, 274
Container class
  defined, 375
  setLayout() method, 378
containers. *See also* GUI (graphical
    user interface)
  components and, 375–378

layout manager use, 378
need for, 369
nesting, 375
panels, 385–388
containsKey() method, 285
containsValue() method, 285
ContextDemo applet
  defined, 486
  display, 488
  source code, 486–487
continue keyword
  defined, 76
  in do/while loop, 76
  example, 76–77
  excessive use of, 77
  in for loop, 76, 77
  in while loop, 76, 77
ContinueDemo program, 76–77
control structures
  Boolean, 52–57
  break keyword, 74–76
  continue keyword, 76–77
  decision-making statement, 52
  defined, 52
  do/while loop, 67–70
  flow, 51–52
  if statement, 57–59
  if/else, 59–61
  for loop, 70–74
  looping, comparison, 72
  nested loops, 78
  repetition statement, 52
  switch statement, 61–64
  while loop, 64–67
copying, arrays, 261–262
CrashDemo program
  crash, 332
  defined, 331
  methods, 331
  output, 332
  source code, 331
CreateFileDemo program, 565–566
CreateList class, 433
createServerSocket() method, 603–604

critical sections, 530
curly brackets ({})
  for array elements, 259
  in class declaration, 89
  if statement, 59
currentThread() method, 517
cursors
  defined, 647
  moving, 648
  properties, 647
  scrollable, 647

D
daemon threads, 504
data
  creating, 638–639
  deleting, 641
  reading, 639–640
  updating, 640–641
data structures. *See also* Java Collections Framework
  categories, 272–273
  Hashtable, 230, 281–287
  lists, 273
  maps, 273
  sets, 273
  Vector, 230, 273–281
data types
  array element, 253
  boolean, 23, 30–31
  byte, 23, 28
  char, 23, 31–32
  classes and, 24
  creating, 24
  defined, 23
  double, 23, 29–30
  float, 23, 29–30
  floating-point, 29–30
  int, 23, 28
  integer, 27–28
  list of, 23
  long, 23, 28
  short, 23, 28
  size definition, 23
  strictness, 26

  variables and, 25
  wrapper classes, 229
databases
  connecting to, 633–637
  programming, support for, 629
  stored procedures in, 656
datagram packets. *See also* UDP
  (User Datagram Protocol)
  attributes, 614
  defined, 592, 612
  overview, 612–614
  receiving, 614–615
  sending, 615–616
  using, 622–623
datagram sockets, 612
DatagramPacket class, 613–614
DatagramSocket class
  constructors, 612–613
  defined, 612
DataOutputStream class, 561
DataSource class
  defined, 633
  naming service, 636
  using, 636–637
DataSourceDemo program, 636–637
DateProgram program
  defined, 109
  flow of control, 110
  output, 111
  source code, 109
dead threads, 507
deadlock. *See also* threads
  avoiding, 532
  defined, 532
  example, 533–534
  issues, 532–534
  ordering locks and, 534–536
DeadlockDemo program, 533–534
decapitalization rule, 673
decision-making techniques, 52
decrement (—) operator, 39
default access. *See also* access specifiers
  for classes, 194
  defined, 111, 190

default constructor. *See also* constructors
  adding constructors and, 129
  compiler generation of, 128, 167
  defined, 128
  empty parameter list, 127
  example, 128
  no, 128
  super() and, 167
default package, 176
delegation model
  defined, 405
  elements, 405–406
delete() method, 555
deleting
  array elements, 281
  data, 641
  objects, 94–96
derived classes. *See* child classes
deserialization. *See also* serialization
  defined, 574
  process, 578–579
DeserializeDemo program
  defined, 578
  output, 578
  source code, 578
  try/catch block, 579
destroy() method, 466
Dialog class, 394
dialog windows
  defined, 394
  example, 394–396
  modal, 394
  modeless, 394
directories
  bytecode, 186
  com, 184
  current, 188
  manually creating, 184
  output, 184
  structure of packages, 183–190
DisplayMessage class, 508
dispose() method, 394
doClick() method, 418
document base, 478

documentation
  for interfaces, 325–326
  J2SE, 268
  online, 269
dot operator
  defined, 97
  using, 97–100
double data type
  concatenation, 34
  float passed to, 125
  min/max values, 23
  size, 23
DoubleArray program
  defined, 264
  nested for loops, 264
  output, 265
  source code, 264
do/while loops. *See also* control
  structures
  continue keyword, 76
  defined, 67
  example, 69–70
  loop counter, 68
  number of repetitions, 72
  semicolon, 68
  statement execution, 67
  using, 79
  while loop versus, 68–69
drawImage() method, 488
DriverManager class
  defined, 633
  getConnection() method, 634–635
  using, 634–635
DriverManagerDemo program, 635
dumpStack() method, 517

E
EchoFile program
  defined, 558
  sample output, 559
  source code, 558
EJB (Enterprise JavaBeans), 5
EmployeeDemo program, 99–100

encapsulation
  benefits, 196–198
  defined, 194
  as fundamental concept, 194
  public methods and, 194
Enterprise JavaBeans (EJB), 5
environment variables
  CLASSPATH, 186–187
  current definition of, 187
  defining, 188
  JAVA_HOME, 678–680
Environment Variables dialog box, 188
equals() method. *See also* Object class
  == comparison operator, 156
  defined, 152
  example, 155–156
  not equal objects by, 281
  overriding, 155
Error class, 333
errors
  behavior, 330
  compiler, 14
  defined, 330
escape sequence characters, 31
event listener interfaces. *See also*
    listeners
  ActionListener, 408
  defined, 407
  events and, 409
  naming conventions, 407
  WindowListener, 408
event objects, 415–416
EventDemo2 program, 414
EventDemo program
  defined, 410
  output, 412
  source code, 411
EventListener interface, 298
EventObject class, 415
events
  determination, 406
  listener interface, 406, 407–410
  multiple, 407
  overview, 694–697

source, 405
user-defined, 698–701
vetoing, 693–694
Exception class, 333
exception handling
  overhead, 344
  overview, 329–330
exceptions
  ArithmeticException, 333, 335
  ArrayIndexOutOfBoundsException,
    256, 332, 333, 348
  catching, 334–335
  categories, 330
  causes, 329
  checked, 330
  ClassCastException, 224, 225
  ClassNotFoundException, 333
  declaring, 113, 341, 343–345
  defined, 329
  errors and, 330
  FileNotFoundException, 335, 337,
    340, 345
  flow of control, 330–333
  handled, 332–333
  handling, 341–342
  InsufficientFundsException, 343
  IOException, 75, 333, 340, 343, 345
  list of, 113
  NullPointerException, 335, 342
  as objects thrown by methods, 330
  overridden methods and, 354–355
  overriding, 154
  passed to JVM, 332
  PropertyVetoException, 691
  RemoteException, 343
  runtime, 330
  RuntimeException, 333
  throwing, 108, 330, 348–350
  TooManyListenersException, 701
  user-defined, 357–359
exclusive or operator (^), 53–54
execute() method, 654
executeBatch() method, 643
executeQuery() method, 654

executeUpdate() method, 655
exit() method, 374
extends keyword
  adding, 151
  defined, 145
  in extending interfaces, 317
  in extending multiple interfaces, 319
  use example, 145
Extensible Markup Language. *See* XML

F
false literal, 22
FieldDemo program, 316–317
fields. *See also* classes
  accessing, 97
  adding, 89–90
  in class declaration, 89
  comments, 269
  contents, 89–90
  declaring, in interfaces, 316–317
  example, 90
  initial values, 126
  memory allocation, 97
  methods access of, 91
  nonstatic, 203
  object, 92
  for object type determination, 141
  private, 194, 196
  static, 198–202
  transient, 575
File class
  constructors, 554
  defined, 554
  example, 555–556
  methods, 555
file I/O
  example, 565–566
  options, 565
file structure, 184
FileDemo program, 555–556
FileNotFoundException, 335, 337, 340, 345
fillInStackTrace() method, 334

final classes
  defined, 160
  examples, 161
  use situations, 161
final keyword, 160
final methods
  child classes and, 161
  declaring, 161, 233
  defined, 160
  virtual methods and, 233
final variables, 160
finalize() method, 152
finally blocks
  appearance, 351
  characteristics, 354
  creating, 351
  example, 353
  uses, 351
finally keyword, 351
FinallyDemo program, 353
fine() method, 580
finer() method, 580
finest() method, 580
firePropertyChange() method, 685
firstElement() method, 278
fixed priority scheduling, 505
fixed-delay execution, 522
fixed-rate execution, 522
float data type
  floating-point literal, 29
  min/max values, 23
  passed to double data type, 125
  size, 23
FloatDemo program, 29–30
floating-point types, 29–30
flow of control
  breaks and, 74
  exceptions, 330–333
  ListenToRadio program, 117–119
  for loop, 70, 71
  methods and, 107, 108–109
  techniques, 52
  while loop, 64

FlowLayout class
  constructors, 380
  defined, 379
FlowLayout manager. *See also* layout
    managers
  defined, 379
  properties, 379–380
  use example, 381–383
  using, 380
FlowLayoutDemo program
  defined, 381
  Frame resize, 383
  output, 381
  source code, 381
flush() method, 552
for loops. *See also* control structures
  Boolean expression evaluation, 70
  continue keyword, 76, 77
  defined, 70
  example, 72–74
  execution, 71, 74
  flow of control, 70, 71
  infinite, 71
  initialization step, 70, 73, 74
  nested, 264
  number of repetitions, 72, 73
  scope outside of, 73
  syntax, 70
  update statement, 70, 71
ForDemo program
  defined, 72
  first for loop, 73
  second for loop, 73–74
  source code, 72–73
  third for loop, 74
Formatter class, 579
FourDogs program
  defined, 323
  output, 324
  source code, 323–324
Frame class
  BorderLayout manager, 377
  constructors, 369–370
  defined, 369

pack() method, 370
  setBounds() method, 370
  setSize() method, 370
  usage, 369
FrameDemo program, 372–373
Frames
  height, 371
  instantiating, 371
  size, 370
  width, 371
  window appearance and, 369
fully qualified name classes,
    181, 182, 184

G
garbage collection
  benefits, 94
  defined, 94
  example, 95–96
  references and, 94–95
  streams and, 553
gc() method, 95
GCDemo program, 95–96
get() method, 278, 285
get methods. *See also* specific get
    methods
  defined, 194
  naming convention, 195
getActionCommand() method, 417
getAppleContext() method, 485
getApplet() method, 485
getAudioClip() method, 485, 490–491
getBytes() method, 616
getCause() method, 334
getClass() method
  defined, 151
  implementation, 161
getConnection() method, 634–635
getData() method, 614
getDefaultEventIndex() method, 704
getDefaultPropertyIndex() method, 704
getEventSetDescription() method, 704
getFilePointer() method, 567
getIcon() method, 704

getImage() method, 485, 488, 489
getInetAddress() method, 599
getInputStream() method, 600
getInt() method, 649
getItem() method, 426, 428
getLocalPort() method, 596, 600
getLogger() method, 580
getMessage() method, 334
getMethodDescriptors() method, 704
getModifiers() method, 417
getName() method, 555
getNewValue() method, 694
getOutputStream() method, 600
getParameter() method, 475
getParent() method, 555
getPath() method, 555
getPort() method, 600
getPropertyDescriptors() method, 704
getRemoteSocket() method, 600
getSelectedChcckbox() method, 426
getSelectedText() method, 430
getSelectedValue() method, 440
getSource() method, 415
getStackTrace() method, 334
getSupportedCipherSuites()
    method, 604
getSupportedProtocols() method, 605
getText() method, 428, 430
getURL() method, 620
graphical user interface. *See* GUI
Graphics class, 488
GreetingClient program
  defined, 600
  output, 602
  source code, 600–601
GreetingServer program, 601
GridBagLayout manager, 379
GridLayout class
  constructors, 388–389
  defined, 388
GridLayout manager. *See also* layout
    managers
  defined, 379, 388
  example, 389–390

instantiating, 388, 389
  properties, 388
GridLayoutDemo program, 389–390
GUI (graphical user interface)
  API, 368
  coordinates, 371
  defined, 367
  instant message, 399–400
  pixels, 371
  programming, 367–404
GUI builder tool, 671

H
Handle or Declare Rule
  checked exceptions avoiding, 355
  compiler enforcing, 346
  defined, 341
  runtime exceptions and, 342
HandleOrDeclareWrong program
  defined, 346
  output, 348
  source code, 346
Handler class, 579
hash codes, 281, 283
hash tables
  accessing elements in, 285–286
  adding elements to, 273, 283–285
  adding objects to, 281
  creating, 283
  defined, 281
  growth in memory, 282
  implementing, 282
  load factor, 282, 283
  resize, 282–283
hashcode() method, 151, 281
HashSet class, 273
Hashtable class
  clear() method, 285
  constructors, 283
  containsKey() method, 285
  containsValue() method, 285
  defined, 282, 287
  get() method, 285
  hash table process, 283

Hashtable class *(continued)*
  isEmpty() method, 285
  put() method, 283
  remove() method, 285
  size() method, 284
HashtableDemo2 program, 285–286
HashtableDemo program
  defined, 283
  output, 285
  source code, 284
heavyweight components, 368
Hello, World program. *See also* Java
    programs
  compiling, 13–14
  defined, 11
  running, 14–15
  source code, 11
  writing, 11–13
HelloSwingApplet
  defined, 462
  display, 465
  source code, 463–464
HelloWorld.class file, 14
HelloWorldApplet2
  buttonLabel parameter, 477
  code, 476–477
  defined, 475
  display, 477
HelloWorldApplet
  defined, 459
  display, 462
  source code, 459–460
heterogeneous collections. *See also*
    collections
  creating, 265–267
  defined, 229
  example, 230, 265–267
  of listeners, 310
  polymorphism for, 229–230
hide() method, 394
high-level readers, 564
high-level streams. *See also* low-level
    streams; streams
  class constructors, 562
  defined, 557

  identifying, 557
  list of, 559–560
high-level writers, 564
HighlightDemo program, 416
holdsLock() method, 517
HRDemo program, 309
HTML
  <applet> tag, 468, 473–477
  <body> tag, 472
  defined, 471
  documents, 471, 475
  example, 472
  <head> tag, 471
  <html> tag, 471
  introduction, 471–473
  page, viewing, 468–469, 473
  page, writing, 468

I

identifiers
  defined, 22
  example, 23
  rules, 22
if statement. *See also* control structures
  curly brackets ({}), 59
  defined, 57
  example, 57–58
  syntax, 57
IfDemo program, 457–458
if/else statement. *See also* control
    structures
  as decision-making technique, 52
  defined, 59
  else block, 59
  example, 60–61
  execution, 59
  final else block, 60
  series, 59–60
  syntax, 59
  truth logic, 61
  using, 79
ImageDemo applet
  defined, 489
  display, 490

JAR file for, 495
source code, 490
import keyword
compiler removal of, 182
with wildcard (*), 181, 183
importing
classes, 181, 182–183
packages, 183
increment (—) operator, 39
indexOf() method, 278
info() method, 580
inheritance
benefits, 142, 143
child class, 139
defined, 139
example, 140–144
as fundamental concept, 194
implementing, 145–146
importance, 140
is a relationship, 144
multiple, 149
overview, 139–144
parent class, 139
program maintenance and, 143
repeating code and, 143
single, 149–150
testing, 144
when to use, 141–142
InheritDemo program
defined, 146
mailCheck() method and, 148
output, 148
source code, 146–147
init() method, 466
initializers
array, 259–261
instance, 205–206
static, 203–204
InputStream class, 553
insertElementAt() method, 275
Install Wizard, 7
instance initializers
constructors versus, 205
defined, 205
examples, 206

statement execution, 205–206
use of, 206
instance members
defined, 198
static methods and, 202–203
InstanceInitDemo program, 206
instanceof keyword
defined, 223
demonstration of, 233
syntax, 223
instanceof operator
false, 223
syntax, 43
true, 223
InstanceOfDemo program, 224–225
instant message windows, 398
instantiating objects
child, 146–148
defined, 12
example, 92–94
process, 92–94, 162–165
InstantMessageDialog display, 451
InsufficientFundsException, 343
int data type
integer arithmetic and, 28
min/max values, 23
size, 23
integer types. *See also* data types
example, 27–28
signed, 27
IntegerDemo program, 27–28
Interaction Wizard dialog box, 688, 701
interface keyword, 296
interface parameters
examples, 310
using, 310–312
interfaces
ActionListener, 408
AppletContext, 485
AudioClip, 490–491
benefits, 296
bytecode, 295
characteristics, 295
classes versus, 296

interfaces *(continued)*
  Connection, 642–643
  declaring, 296–298
  defined, 295
  in delegation model, 406
  EventListener, 298
  exposing methods via, 304–310
  extending, 317–319
  field declarations in, 316–317
  file extension, 295
  FootballListener, 310, 312, 313–314
  HockeyListener, 317, 318, 319
  implementing, 300–303
  javadoc documentation for, 325–326
  LayoutManager, 378
  listener, 298
  as method parameters, 310
  methods, 295, 297
  MouseListener, 297–298, 304
  multiple, extending, 319
  overview, 295–296
  in packages, 295
  Paintable, 299, 300–301
  PhoneHandler, 316
  Play, 322
  polymorphism and, 321–324
  PreparedStatement, 652
  properties, 296–297
  ResultSet, 647
  Runnable, 297, 508–511
  Serializable, 320–321, 576
  source code file format, 296
  SportsListener, 317
  Statement, 641–642
  tagging, 298, 319–321
  user-defined, 298–299
  uses, 296, 303
  using, 303–304
  VetoableChangeListener, 693
  WindowListener, 408
  writing, 296
Internet Options dialog box, 483
interrupt() method, 517

introspection, 671
invoking methods. *See also* methods
  for changing flow of control, 52, 107
  on class instances, 111
  defined, 107
  method signatures and, 113
  process, 108–111
  static, 111
I/O API, 560
IOException, 75, 333, 340, 343, 345
is a relationship. *See also* inheritance
  defined, 144
  failure, 144
  maintaining, 150
  polymorphism and, 213
isAlive() method, 517
isDirectory() method, 555
isEmpty() method, 285
isFile() method, 555
ItemEvent class, 426

J

J2EE
  defined, 5
  packages, 180
  technologies, 5–6
J2ME, 5
J2SE
  defined, 4
  documentation, 268
  packages, 175
JApplet class, 462
JAR (Java Archive) files
  applets and, 494–495
  bytecode in, 187
  in CLASSPATH, 188
  creating, 493, 677–678
  defined, 187
  example, 495
  JavaBeans, 675
  opening, 494
  uses, 492
  viewing, 494
  working with, 492–494

jar tool
  defined, 492
  options, 493
  running, 492
Java
  C++ versus, 1–2
  case sensitivity, 184
  documentation, 268–272
  editions, 4–6
  J2EE, 5–6
  J2ME, 5
  J2SE, 4–5
  learning, 2
Java Archive files. *See* JAR files
java.awt package, 175
Java Collections Framework
  classes, 287
  data structures, 230, 272–273
  defined, 229, 253, 272
  overview, 272–273
  purpose, 273
  wrapper classes, 229
Java Community Process (JCP), 5
Java Database Connectivity. *See* JDBC
Java Foundation Classes (JFC), 368
Java IDL, 6
java.io package
  class categories, 551
  contents, 175
  File class, 554–557
  overview, 551–554
  reader classes, 551, 552
  stream classes, 551, 552
java.lang package. *See also* packages
  as fundamental class, 175
  implicit importation, 183
  wrapper classes, 229
Java Messaging Service (JMS), 6
Java Naming and Directory Interface
  (JNDI), 6, 633
Java Native Interface (JNI), 204
java.net package, 175, 591–592
java.nio.channels package, 582
java.nio.charset package, 582

java.nio package, 175, 582
Java programs
  AbstractDemo, 240–241
  AccessDemo, 192–193
  AddDemo, 376–377
  AddMovies, 644–646
  Alphabet, 78
  ArithmeticDemo, 38–39
  ArrayCopyDemo, 261–262
  ArrayDemo, 257–259
  ArrayInitDemo, 259–261
  BankDemo, 358–359
  BooleanDemo, 30–31
  BorderLayoutDemo, 384–385
  BoxLayoutDemo, 391–392
  BreakDemo, 75–76
  ButtonDemo, 418–420
  CallableDemo, 659–660
  CastDemo, 220–221
  CatchDemo2, 339–340
  CatchDemo, 336–337
  ChainDemo, 561–563
  CharDemo, 32
  CheckboxDemo, 422–423
  ChoiceDemo, 441
  compiling, 13–14
  CongratulateStudent, 62–63
  ConstructorDemo, 130–131, 164, 198
  ContinueDemo, 76–77
  CrashDemo, 331–332
  CreateFileDemo, 565–566
  DataSourceDemo, 636–637
  DateProgram, 109–111
  DeadlockDemo, 533–534
  DeserializeDemo, 578–579
  DoubleArray, 264–265
  DriverManagerDemo, 635
  EchoFile, 558–559
  EmployeeDemo, 99–100
  EventDemo2, 414
  EventDemo, 410–412
  FieldDemo, 316–317
  FileDemo, 555–556
  FinallyDemo, 353

Java programs *(continued)*
  FloatDemo, 29–30
  FlowLayoutDemo, 381–382
  ForDemo, 72–74
  FourDogs, 323–324
  FrameDemo, 372
  GCDemo, 95–96
  GreetingClient, 600–602
  GreetingServer, 601
  GridLayoutDemo, 389–390
  HandleOrDeclareWrong, 346–348
  HashtableDemo2, 285–286
  HashtableDemo, 283–285
  HighlightDemo, 416
  HRDemo, 309
  IfDemo, 57–58
  InheritDemo, 146–148
  InstanceInitDemo, 206
  InstanceOfDemo, 224–225
  IntegerDemo, 27–28
  JCheckBoxDemo, 423–425
  JDialogDemo, 396–397
  JFrameDemo, 374
  JRadioButtonDemo, 427–429
  JTextComponentDemo, 436
  KeyboardInput, 569–570
  ListDemo, 429, 438–439
  ListenToRadio, 116–119, 121
  LoggingDemo, 581–582
  MenuDemo, 446–448
  ModalDemo, 394–396
  MyCompany, 266–267
  OrderHandler, 611
  OverloadDemo, 124–125
  PacketReceiver, 614–615
  PacketSender, 615–616
  PanelDemo, 386–388
  ParentDemo, 166–168
  PayableDemo, 307
  PayDemo2, 236–237
  PayDemo, 227–228
  PayEmployees, 244–245
  Phone, 523–525
  PipeDemo, 571–574
  PLAFDemo, 382–383
  ProduceConsumeDemo, 537–540
  PurchaseDemo, 611
  RadioButtonDemo, 426–427
  RandomAccessDemo, 567–568
  RandomLoop, 69–70
  ReadData, 562–563
  RunnableDemo, 509–511
  running, 14–15
  SelectionDialog, 443–444
  ShiftDemo, 41–42
  ShowMovies, 650
  SimpleServer, 597–598
  SomethingsFixed, 531–532
  SomethingsWrong, 528–529
  source code, writing, 11–13
  speed, 3
  SSLClientDemo, 608–610
  SSLServerDemo, 605–607
  StaticDemo, 200–202
  StaticInitDemo, 204
  StringDemo, 34
  StudentGrade, 60–61
  SuperDemo, 158–159
  TextComponentDemo, 431–433
  ThisDemo, 132–134
  ThreadClassDemo, 517–519
  ThreadDemo, 512
  ThrowDemo, 349–350
  TimerDemo, 519–521
  ToStringDemo, 152–153
  UpdateCategory, 655–656
  URLConnectionDemo, 620–621
  URLDemo, 618–619
  UsedCarFrame, 393
  VectorDemo2, 278–280
  VectorDemo, 275–277
  VirtualDemo, 231–233
  WhileDemo, 66–67
  YieldDemo, 514–515
Java Secure Socket Extension. *See* JSSE
Java servlets, 5
Java Standard Developer's Kit (SDK).
  See also JVM (Java Virtual Machine)
component selection, 8
contents, 7

downloading, 6–7
installing, 7–8
javac compiler, 9
releases, 6–7
tools, running, 8–10
using, 1
java.swing package, 175
Java Transaction API (JTA), 6
Java Transaction Service (JTS), 6
java.util package, 579
Java Virtual Machine. *See* JVM
Java Web Services, 6
JavaBeans
  bound properties, 684–690
  builder tool, 671, 678
  button hookup, 695–696
  components, 670
  constrained properties, 690–692
  creating, 670
  defined, 669
  formats, 675
  JAR files, creating, 677–678
  overview, 669–672
  packaging, 675–684
  persistence, 702–703
  properties, 683
  serializing, 675
  simple properties, 672–675
  specification, 670, 695
  using, 681–684
  viewing, in preview mode, 696–697
javac compiler
  -d flag, 184, 185
  defined, 9
  running, 9–10
javadoc
  command example, 271
  comments, 269–271
  comments, practicing, 272
  defined, 268
  format, 269
  interfaces and, 325–326
  options, 271
  page example, 268

running, 268, 269
  successful functioning of, 272
  using, 288–289
JAVA_HOME environment variable
  Bean Builder program and, 680
  defining, 678–681
JavaMail, 6
JavaServer Pages (JSP), 6
javax.util.regex package, 582
JButton class, 418
JButtons
  adding, 695
  components, instantiating, 418–420
  creating, 369
  viewing, in preview mode, 697
JCheckbox class, 423
JCheckBoxDemo program
  defined, 424
  MixSwingColors listener, 423
  output, 425
  source code, 424
JComboBox class, 442
JComponent class, 375
JCP (Java Community Process), 5
JDBC (Java Database Connectivity)
  API, 629
  data source, connecting to, 634
  defined, 6, 630
  overview, 629–632
  SQL and, 631–632
  tabular format and, 631
  URLs, 634
  using, 661
JDBC drivers
  bridge, 632
  JDBC-NET, 632
  native API, 632
  native protocol, 632
  need for, 630
  obtaining, 631
  specifying, 637
  types, 632
JDBC-Net drivers, 632
JDialog class, 394

JDialogDemo program
  defined, 396
  output, 396
  source code, 397
JeopardyApplet, 478–479
JFC (Java Foundation Classes), 368
JFrame class
  constructors, 373
  defined, 369
  Frame class versus, 372
  methods, 373
  setDefaultCloseOperation()
    method, 374
  Swing architecture support, 372
JFrameDemo program, 374
JFrames
  adding menus to, 446
  components added to, 372
  content pane, 372
  creating, 373
  glass pane, 372
  illustrated, 374
  root pane, 372
  title bar, 374
  using, 397–398
  WindowEvent, 374
JIT (Just-In-Time) compilers
  defined, 3
  work in RAM, 4
JLabel class, 429–430
JList class
  constructors, 439
  defined, 439
  List versus, 439
  methods, 440
JMS (Java Messaging Service), 6
JNDI (Java Naming and Directory
    Interface), 6, 633
JNI (Java Native Interface), 204
join() method, 517
JPanel class, 386
JPasswordField class, 436
JProgressBar class, 445
JRadioButton class, 427

JRadioButtonDemo program
  defined, 427
  sample output, 429
  source code, 428
JScrollPane class, 435–436
JSlider
  dragging event arrow to, 688
  illustrated, 690
  value property, 688
JSP (JavaServer Pages), 6
JSSE (Java Secure Socket Extension)
  classes, 662–663
  defined, 662
  uses, 610
JTA (Java Transaction API), 6
JTextArea class, 434
JTextComponent class, 434
JTextComponentDemo program, 436
JTS (Java Transaction Service), 6
Just-In-Time compilers. See JIT
    compilers
JVM (Java Virtual Machine)
  JIT compilers, 3, 4
  language, 3
  need for, 2–3
  running, 10
  stack trace printing, 332
  as target, 3
  thread scheduler, 505

K

KeyboardInput program
  defined, 569
  sample output, 570
  source code, 569–570
keywords
  abstract, 239
  break, 74–76
  catch, 334
  class, 89
  const, 22
  continue, 76–77
  defined, 21
  extends, 145, 317, 319

false, 21
final, 160–162
finally, 351–354
goto, 22
import, 180–183
instance of, 221–225, 233
interface, 296
list of, 21–22
new, 92, 97, 126, 255
null, 21
package, 176
private, 190
protected, 190
public, 190
static, 198, 203
super, 157–160
synchronized, 530–532
this, 100, 131–134
throw, 348, 349, 358
throws, 343, 345–348
transient, 575
true, 21
try, 334

L

Label class, 429
labels
    AWT, 429
    defined, 429
    Swing, 429–430
labs
    abstract classes, 247
    applet communication, 497–499
    applet game, 544–545
    applet parameters, 496
    arrays, 288
    bound properties, 706
    Calculator applet, 497
    car race simulation, 543
    cell phone bill, 78–79
    checked exceptions, 360–361
    command-line arguments, 16–17
    constrained properties, 706–707
    constructors, 135

datagram packets, 622–623
dialog window creation, 400–401
do/while loop, 79
encapsulation, 207–208
event handling, 449
exceptions and polymorphism, 360
first Java program, 15
handling instant message events,
    449–450
if/else statement, 79
implementing inheritance, 168–169
instant message GUI, 399–400
instant message window, 398
InstantMessage finish, 624
InstantMessage server, 623–624
InstantMessageDialog events,
    450–451
interface implementation, 325
interfaces and javadoc, 325–326
JAR files, 499
javadoc, 288–289
JDBC, 661
JFrame, 397–398
LinkedList class, 290
logging, 583–584
mortgage calculator, 45–46
overriding methods, 169
pipes, 584–585
polymorphism, 245–247
Powerball lottery, 80
Powerball lottery, redesigning, 135
Reminder application, 586, 663
result sets, 661–662
serialization, 584
simulating an elevator, 134
sockets, 621–622
static methods, 208–209
Stock bean, 705–706
streams, 583
summation problem, 79
temperature converter, 45
thread creation, 542
Timer class, 544

labs *(continued)*
   TimerTask class, 544
   URL connections, 624–625
   user-defined events, 707–708
   Vector class, 289
   video rental store, 102
   working with packages, 207
   writing applets, 495–496
   writing classes, 102–103
   writing try/catch blocks, 359–360
lastElement() method, 278
layout managers
   BorderLayout, 377, 379, 383–385
   BoxLayout, 379, 390–392
   CardLayout, 379
   FlowLayout, 379–383
   GridBagLayout, 379
   GridLayout, 379, 388–390
   list of, 379
   no, using, 396–397
   OverlayLayout, 379
   SpringLayout, 379
   use of, 378
LayoutManager interface, 378
length() method, 567
length attribute, 255–256
LifecyleDemo applet, 470
lightweight components, 368
linked lists, 290
LinkedList class, 290
list() method, 555
List class, 437, 439
ListDemo program, 438–439
listeners. *See also* event listener
   interfaces
   creating, 409–410
   defined, 406
   multiple, 407
   registering, 406, 410–412
ListenToRadio program
   defined, 116
   flow of control, 117
   initial volume, 118

   sample output, 119
   source code, 116–117
lists
   adding elements to, 273
   AWT, 437–439
   component, 437
   defined, 273
   linked, 290
   Swing, 439–440
log() method, 580
Logger class
   defined, 579
   methods, 580
logging
   APIs, 579–582
   example, 581–582
   using, 583–584
LoggingDemo program, 581–582
LogRecord class, 579
long data type
   min/max values, 23
   size, 23
   variable declaration as, 28
loop() method, 490
loop counters
   breaks and, 74
   defined, 65
   do/while loop, 68
   while loop, 65
loops
   comparison, 72
   do/while, 67–70
   for, 70–74
   nested, 78
   while, 64–67
low-level readers, 564
low-level streams. *See also* high-level
   streams; streams
   defined, 557
   example, 558–559
   identifying, 557
   list of, 557–558
   purpose, 559
low-level writers, 564

M

main() method
  classes without, 121
  ConstructorDemo program, 164
  Hello, World program, 13
  invocation, 108
  signature, 13, 111
  static, 199
  StaticDemo program, 201
manifest files, 676
maps, 273
mark() method, 553
Math.random() function, 80
memory leaks, 94
MenuDemo program
  defined, 446
  output, 448
  source code, 446–448
menus
  AWT classes, 446
  components, 445
  Swing classes, 446
method overloading
  child method invocation and, 159
  with constructors, 121
  defined, 121
  example, 124–125
  parameter lists and, 123
  parent method, 355
  printIn() method, 121–122
  return values and, 123
  simplification, 122
  usage, 121
  valid, 123, 124
method overriding
  defined, 154
  equals() method, 155
  exception, 154, 354–355
  parent class, 237
  rules, 154
  virtual method invocation and, 237
method signatures
  access specifier, 111
  arraycopy(), 261

components, 111–113
defined, 111
information, 111
invoking methods and, 113
main(), 111
method name, 112
optional specifier, 112
parameter list, 112–113
return value, 112
thrown exceptions list, 113
methods. *See also* constructors
  abstract, 241–245, 295
  accept(), 597
  accessing, 97
  accessor, 194
  actionPerformed(), 408, 409
  add(), 275, 375–376
  addActionListener(), 417, 418
  addAll(), 275
  addBatch(), 643
  addChangeListener(), 418
  addElement(), 275
  addHandler(), 580
  adding, to classes, 90–91
  addItemListener(), 421
  addition example, 91
  addListSelectionListener(), 440
  addMouseListener(), 416
  addTextListener(), 430
  addWindowListener(), 410
  appearance, 87, 111
  arraycopy(), 261–262
  AudioClip interface, 490
  available(), 553
  bind(), 597
  body, 91
  Button class, 417
  call stack, 107–108, 330
  call-by-value, 116–120
  cancel(), 523
  canRead(), 555
  capacity(), 276
  child class, 154, 355
  clear(), 278, 285

methods *(continued)*
  clone(), 152
  close(), 552, 553, 600
  comments, 269
  config(), 580
  connect(), 570–571, 599
  containsKey(), 285
  containsValue(), 285
  contents, 90–91
  createServerSocket(), 603–604
  currentThread(), 517
  DataOutputStream class, 561
  definition of, 91
  delete(), 555
  destroy(), 466
  dispose(), 394
  doClick(), 418
  drawImage(), 488
  dumpStack(), 517
  equals(), 152, 155–156, 281
  execute(), 654
  executeBatch(), 643
  executeQuery(), 654
  executeUpdate(), 655
  execution results, 108
  exit(), 374
  exposing, via interfaces, 304–309
  fields access, 91
  File class, 555
  fillInStackTrace(), 334
  final, 160–161
  finalize(), 152
  fine(), 580
  finer(), 580
  finest(), 580
  firePropertyChange(), 685
  firstElement(), 278
  flow of control and, 107, 108–109
  flush(), 552
  gc(), 95
  get(), 278, 285
  get, 194, 195
  getActionCommand(), 417
  getAppleContext(), 485

getApplet(), 485
getAudioClip(), 485, 490–491
getBytes(), 616
getCause(), 334
getClass(), 151, 161
getConnection(), 634–635
getData(), 614
getDefaultEventIndex(), 704
getDefaultPropertyIndex(), 704
getEventSetDescription(), 704
getFilePointer(), 567
getIcon(), 704
getImage(), 485, 488, 489
getInetAddress(), 599
getInputStream(), 600
getInt(), 649
getItem(), 426, 428
getLocalPort(), 596, 600
getLogger(), 580
getMessage(), 334
getMethodDescriptors(), 704
getModifiers(), 417
getName(), 555
getNewValue(), 694
getOutputStream(), 600
getParameter(), 475
getParent(), 555
getPath(), 555
getPort(), 600
getPropertyDescriptors(), 704
getRemoteSocket(), 600
getSelectedCheckbox(), 426
getSelectedText(), 430
getSelectedValue(), 440
getSource(), 415
getStackTrace(), 334
getSupportedCipherSuites(), 604
getSupportedProtocols(), 605
getText(), 428, 430
getURL(), 620
hashcode(), 151, 281
hide(), 394
holdsLock(), 517
indexOf(), 278

info(), 580
init(), 466
InputStream class, 553
insertElementAt(), 275
interface, 295, 297
interrupt(), 517
invoking, 52, 107, 108–111
isAlive(), 517
isDirectory(), 555
isEmpty(), 285
isFile(), 555
JButton class, 418
JFrame class, 373
JList class, 440
join(), 517
lastElement(), 278
length(), 567
list(), 555
log(), 580
Logger class, 580
loop(), 490
main(), 13, 108
mark(), 553
memory allocation, 97
mouseClicked(), 304
mutator, 194
name of, 112
notify(), 152, 161, 536–541
Object class, 151–154
objects and, 96
openConnection(), 619
OutputStream class, 552
overloading, 121–125
pack(), 370
paint(), 466–467
parent, 355
play(), 490
prepareCall(), 658
prepareStatement(), 653
print(), 66
printIn(), 33, 121–122
printStackTrace(), 332, 334
put(), 283
RandomAccessFile class, 567

read(), 553
readDouble(), 567
readInt(), 567
readLine(), 567, 570
readLong(), 567
readOneByte(), 338, 339, 342, 343, 345
readUTF(), 567
receive(), 614
remove(), 278, 281, 285
removeAll(), 278
reset(), 553
ResultSet interface, 648
retainAll(), 278
return value, 108
run(), 297, 507, 508, 516, 523
schedule(), 522, 522–523
scheduleAtFixedRate(), 523
scheduledExecutionTime(), 523
seek(), 567
send(), 615
ServerSocket class, 596–597
set, 194, 195
setActionCommand(), 417, 418
setBounds(), 370, 396
setCaretPosition(), 430
setDaemon(), 517
setDefaultCloseOperation(), 374
setDoInput(), 619
setDoOutput(), 619
setDouble(), 654
setEditable(), 430
setElementAt(), 278
setEnabledCipherSuites(), 604
setLayout(), 378
setListData(), 440
setListDataObject(), 440
setMnemonic(), 418
setName(), 516
setNeedClientAuth(), 605
setPressedIcon(), 418
setPriority(), 517
setSelectedCheckbox(), 425
setSelectionMode(), 440
setSize(), 370

methods *(continued)*
  setSoTimeout(), 596
  setState(), 421
  setText(), 430
  setValue(), 689
  setVisible(), 371–372
  setWantClientAuth(), 605
  severe(), 580
  show(), 394
  showDocument(), 485
  showStatus(), 485
  size(), 276, 284
  skip(), 553
  sleep(), 516, 517
  Socket class, 599–600
  start(), 466, 470, 492, 516
  static, 111, 198–203
  stop(), 466, 490
  synchronizing, 531
  TextComponent class, 430–431
  Throwable class, 333–334
  Timer class, 522–523
  toArray(), 278
  toString(), 33, 152, 334, 415
  updateString(), 651
  URL class, 618
  virtual, 230–237
  wait(), 152, 161, 536–541
  warning(), 580
  windowClosing(), 412, 414
  write(), 552, 553–554
  writeDouble(), 567
  writeInt(), 567
  writeLong(), 567
  writeObject(), 574
  writeUTF(), 567
  yield(), 513, 514, 515, 517
ModalDemo program
  defined, 394
  output, 396
  source code, 394–395
modeless dialog windows, 394
monitor, 537

mouseClicked() method, 304
MouseListener interface, 297–298, 304
multidimensional arrays
  defined, 263
  elements, 263
  example, 264–265
  instantiating, 263
  as objects, 263
  three-dimensional, 263
  two-dimensional, 263
multiple inheritance, 149
multithreading issues, 526–530
mutator methods
  defined, 194
  naming, 195
MyCompany program
  defined, 266
  sample output, 267
  source code, 266–267

N
namespaces
  benefits, 178
  created by packages, 178–179
  examples, 179–180
  purpose of, 179
native API drivers, 632
native protocol drivers, 632
nested loops, 78
nesting, panels, 392–393
network programming
  defined, 591
  overview, 591–594
network protocols, 592
new keyword, 92, 97, 126, 255
not operator, 54
notify() method
  defined, 152, 536–537
  implementation, 161
  monitoring behavior of, 537
  use example, 537–540
null literal, 22
NullPointerException, 335, 342

O

Object class
clone() method, 152
constructor, 163
defined, 150
equals() method, 152, 155–156
example, 150–151
finalize() method, 152
getClass() method, 151, 161
hashcode() method, 151
location, 150
methods, 151–154
notify() method, 152, 161, 536–537
as parent class, 150, 228
toString() method, 152
wait() method, 152, 161, 536
ObjectInputStream class, 574
object-oriented analysis and design
(OOAD), 89
object-oriented programming
core, 89
data passed in, 88
defined, 87
example, 87–88
procedural programming versus,
87, 88
ObjectOutputStream class, 574, 577
objects
adding, to hash tables, 281
arrays as, 256
attributes, 85–86
behaviors, 85–86
child, 146–148, 214
defined, 12, 85
deleting, 94–96
deserializing, 578
event, 415–416
fields, initial value, 92
instantiating, 12, 92–93
introduction to, 12
lock, 537
memory allocation and, 126
methods and, 96
monitor, 537

multidimensional arrays as, 263
overview, 85–86
polymorphism, 213–237
references versus, 94
serializing, 577
unreachable, 95
OOAD (object-oriented analysis and
design), 89
openConnection() method, 619
operators
assignment, 40
Boolean (||, &&, &, |, ^, !), 43, 55–57
comparison (<, <=, >, >=, ==, !=,
instanceof), 42–43
decrement (—), 39
dot, 97–100
increment (++), 39
instanceof, 43, 223
list of, 37–38
precedence, 37
shift (<<, >, >>), 40–42
syntax, 37–38
ternary, 43–44
optional specifiers, 112
or operator
defined, 53
truth table, 54
OrderHandler program, 611
ordering locks, 534–536
OutputStream class, 552
OverlayLayout manager, 379
OverloadDemo program
defined, 124
multiply(), 125
output, 124
source code, 124
overridden methods. *See* method
overriding

P

pack() method, 370
package access. *See* default access
package declaration, 177
package keyword, 176

package statement, 176
packages. *See also* classes
  adding classes to, 176–178
  bytecode storage and, 184
  classes placed in, 183
  default, 176
  defined, 175
  directory structure, 183–190
  importing, 183
  interfaces in, 295
  J2EE, 180
  J2SE, 175
  java.awt, 175
  java.io, 175, 551–554
  java.lang, 175, 183
  java.net, 157, 591–592
  java.nio, 175, 582
  java.nio.channels, 582
  java.nio.charset, 582
  java.swing, 175
  java.util, 579
  javax.ejb, 180
  javax.servlet, 180
  javax.util.regex, 582
  namespace, 176, 178–179
  naming, 179–180
  naming convention, 178
  purposes, 175
PacketReceiver program, 614–615
PacketSender program, 615–616
paint() method, 466–467
Paintable interface
  in·display package, 299
  as method parameter, 303
  writing class implementing, 300–301
Panel class
  constructors, 386
  defined, 385–386
PanelDemo program
  defined, 386
  output, 387
  source code, 387
panels
  defined, 385
  example, 386–388

nesting, 392–393
  properties, 386
parameter lists
  constructors, 126
  defined, 112
  empty, 127
  example, 113
  method overloading and, 123
  parentheses, 112
parameters
  <applet> tag, 475
  applets, 475
  changing name of, 123
  declaring, 113
  defined, 112–113, 113
  interface, 310
  method overloading and, 123
  passing arguments to, 116–117
  polymorphic, 225–228
parent class constructors
  example, 166–168
  invoking, 165–168
parent classes. *See also* classes;
    inheritance
  abstract methods in, 242
  creating, 143
  defined, 139
  methods, 154
  methods, invoking, 237
  methods, overriding, 237
  Object class, 150, 228
  overridden methods hidden in, 230
  references to child objects, 214–218
ParentDemo program
  defined, 166
  output, 168
  source code, 166–167
parentheses
  empty, 127
  parameter list, 112
PATH environment variable
  editing, 9
  setting, in Windows 2000/NT/XP, 8
  setting with SET command, 9
PayableDemo program, 307

PayDemo 2 program
  defined, 236
  output, 237
  source code, 236–237
PayDemo program
  defined, 227
  output, 228
  source code, 227
PayEmployees program
  defined, 244
  output, 245
  source code, 245
Phone program
  defined, 523
  output, 525
  source code, 524–525
PipeDemo program
  defined, 571
  RandomWeather thread, 572
  sample output, 574
  source code, 571–572
PipedInputStream class, 570
PipedOutputStream class, 570
PipedReader class, 570
PipedWriter class, 570
pipes
  creation process, 570
  defined, 570
  using, 584–585
pixels, 371
PLAF (pluggable look and feel),
  382–383
PLAFDemo program, 382–383
play() method, 490
pluggable look and feel (PLAF),
  382–383
pointers, 36
polymorphic parameters
  defined, 225
  example, 226
  Object, 261
polymorphism
  arrays of references creation by, 266
  benefits, 214

catching exceptions and, 340–341
defined, 213
for heterogeneous collections,
  229–230
interfaces and, 321–324
is a relationship and, 213
overview, 213–214
parent class references to child
  objects, 214–218
summary, 247–248
prepareCall() method, 658
prepared statements
  defined, 652
  executing, 654–656
  parameters, setting, 654
  question mark, 654
  simple statements versus, 652
  steps, 652
PreparedStatement interface, 652
prepareStatement() method, 653
primitive types. *See* data types
print() method, 66
printIn() method, 33, 121–122
printStackTrace() method, 332, 334
private access, 111, 190
private keyword, 190
procedural programming
  defined, 86
  example, 86–87
  object-oriented programming versus,
    87, 88
  procedures, 86, 87, 88
procedures. *See* methods
processes. *See also* threads
  defined, 504
  multiple threads in, 504
ProduceConsumeDemo program
  Buffet class, 537
  defined, 537
  LunchCrowd class, 538–540
  PizzaChef class, 537–538
  sample output, 540
  source code, 540

programming
database, 629–667
network, 591–627
object-oriented, 87–88
procedural, 86–87
progress bars, 445
PropertyVetoException, 691
protected access, 111, 190
protected keyword, 190
public access. *See also* access specifiers
for classes, 194
defined, 111, 190
public classes
class usage of, 194
in source code file, 89
public keyword, 190
PurchaseDemo program, 611

R
radio buttons
AWT, 425–427
defined, 425
Swing, 427–429
RadioButtonDemo program
defined, 426
output, 427
source code, 426
RandomAccessDemo program
defined, 567
output, 568
source code, 567–568
RandomAccessFile class
constructors, 566
defined, 566
methods, 567
mode parameter values, 566–567
RandomLoop program
defined, 69
Math.random() function, 69
sample outputs, 70
source code, 69
read() method, 553
ReadData program, 562–563
readDouble() method, 567

Reader class, 554
readers
classes, 551, 552
high-level, 564
low-level, 564
readInt() method, 567
readLine() method, 567, 570
readLong() method, 567
readOneByte() method, 338, 339, 342, 343, 345
readUTF() method, 567
receive() method, 614
references
array, 253, 254, 256–259
casting, 218–221
declaring, 93
defined, 35, 93
objects versus, 94
parent class, 214–218
pointers versus, 36
primitive data versus, 35–37
this, 100–101, 118, 157
understanding, 93
relationships, is a, 144
relative coordinate system, 371
RemoteException, 343
remove() method, 278, 281, 285
removeAll() method, 278
repetition, 52
reset() method, 553
result sets
cursors, 647
defined, 647
navigating, 647–648
updating, 651
using, 661–662
viewing, 648–650
working with, 647
ResultSet interface
defined, 647
getInt() method, 649
methods, 648
update methods, 651
retainAll() method, 278

return values
    method overloading and, 123
    in method overriding, 154
    possible, 112
RMI-IIOP, 6
run() method
    body, 507
    invoking, 297, 508
    overriding, 511
    Runnable interface, 297
    Thread class, 516
    Timer class, 523
Runnable interface
    implementing, 507, 508–511, 513
    run() method, 297
    uses, 297
    while loop, 508
runnable threads, 506
RunnableDemo program
    defined, 509, 509–510
    sample output, 511
running programs
    from command prompt, 16
    Hello, World, 14–15
runtime exceptions
    checked exceptions vs., 333, 342
    defined, 330
    Handle or Declare Rule and, 342
RuntimeException, 333

S

sandbox security
    changing, 483
    defined, 481
    permissions, 482
    permissions, changing, 484
    purpose, 481
    rules, 481
    viewing, 483
saving
    classes, 185
    source files, 12
schedule() method, 522–523
scheduleAtFixedRate() method, 523

scheduledExecutionTime() method, 523
scroll panes, 435–436
secure sever sockets, creating, 603
Secure Sockets Layer. *See* SSL
seek() method, 567
SelectionDialog program, 443–444
SelectionHandler class, 443–444
send() method, 615
Serializable interface, 320–321, 576
serialization. *See also* deserialization
    defined, 574
    example, 576
    JavaBeans, 675
    limitations, 575
    overview, 574–576
    process, 577
    using, 584
serialized files, 675
ServerSocket class
    constructors, 596
    defined, 596
    example, 597–598
    methods, 596–597
    use of, 592
ServerSocketFactory class, 603–604
set methods
    defined, 194
    invoking, 196
    naming convention, 195
setActionCommand() method, 417, 418
setBounds() method, 370, 396
setCaretPosition() method, 430
setDaemon() method, 517
setDefaultCloseOperation()
    method, 374
setDoInput() method, 619
setDoOutput() method, 619
setDouble() method, 654
setEditable() method, 430
setElementAt() method, 278
setEnabledCipherSuites() method, 604
setLayout() method, 378
setListData() method, 440
setListDataObject() method, 440

setMnemonic() method, 418
setName() method, 516
setNeedClientAuth() method, 605
setPressedIcon() method, 418
setPriority() method, 517
sets, 273
setSelectedCheckbox() method, 425
setSelectionMode() method, 440
setSize() method, 370
setSoTimeout() method, 596
setState() method, 421
setText() method, 430
setValue() method, 689
setVisible() method, 371
setWantClientAuth() method, 605
severe() method, 580
shift operators (<<, >, >>), 40–42
ShiftDemo program
  defined, 41
  output, 42
  source code, 42
short data type, 23
show() method, 394
showDocument() method, 485
ShowMovies program, 650
showStatus() method, 485
simple properties. *See also* JavaBeans
  defined, 672
  names of, 673
  read-only, 672
  read-write, 672
  write-only, 672
SimpleServer program, 597–598
size() method, 276, 284
skip() method, 553
sleep() method, 516, 517
Socket class
  constructors, 599
  defined, 599
  methods, 599–600
  use of, 592
sockets. *See also* TCP (Transmission
  Control Protocol)
  communicating between, 600–602

  connection establishment using,
    594–595
  datagram, 612
  defined, 594
  secure, communicating over, 610–611
  secure client, 607–610
  secure server, 603–607
  SSL, 605
  streams, 595
  using, 621–622
software components, 669, 672
SomethingsFixed program, 531–532
SomethingsWrong program, 528–529
source files, saving, 12
SpringLayout manager, 379
SQL (Structured Query Language)
  CREATE PROCEDURE statement,
    657
  CREATE TABLE statement, 638
  creating data, 638–639
  defined, 637
  DELETE statement, 641
  deleting data, 641
  DROP TABLE statement, 641
  extensions, 638
  INSERT statement, 638–639
  JDBC and, 631–632
  prepared statements, 652–656
  primer, 637–641
  reading data, 639–640
  result sets, 647–651
  SELECT statement, 639–640
  statements, 641–646
  support, 637
  UPDATE statement, 640–641
  updating data, 640–641
square brackets ([]), in array
  declarations, 254
SSL (Secure Sockets Layer), 602
SSLClientDemo program, 608–609
SSLServerDemo program, 605–606
SSLServerSocket class, 604–605
SSLSocket class, 607–608

start() method
  AudioDemo applet, 492
  browser-invoked, 466
  Thread class, 516
Statement interface
  defined, 641–642
  methods, 643
Statement objects
  for batch creation, 643
  creation method, 642–643
  example, 644–646
  types of, 641–642
statements. *See also* SQL (Structured
    Query Language)
  batch creation, 643
  callable, 656–660
  creating, 641–642
  prepared, 652–656
  simple, 642–646
static fields
  accessing, 199–202
  defined, 198
  understanding, 198–199
static initializers
  declaring, 203
  defined, 203
  example, 203–204
  purpose, 204
static keyword, 198, 203
static methods
  accessing, 199–203
  defined, 198
  instance members and, 202–203
  main(), 199
  nonstatic fields and, 203
  understanding, 198–199
StaticDemo program, 200–201
StaticInitDemo program, 204
stop() method, 466, 490
stored procedures
  creation methods, 657
  defined, 656
  invoking, 656, 659
  in Microsoft Access, 657–658

streams
  chaining, together, 561–563
  closing, 553
  high-level, 559–561
  input, 553
  low-level, 557–559
  opening, 553
  output, 552
  pipes, 570–574
  socket, 595
  using, 583
StringBuffer class, 35
StringDemo program, 34
strings
  class representation, 33
  defined, 33
  handling of, 2
Structured Query Language. *See* SQL
StudentGrade program
  defined, 60
  if/else blocks, 61
  sample outputs, 61
  source code, 60
subclasses. *See* child classes
super classes. *See* parent classes
super keyword
  call to, 166
  in child class, 158
  compiler generation of, 165
  default constructor and, 167
  defined, 157
  example, 158–159
  in parent method invocation, 237
  requirement, 159
  within overriding method, 230
SuperDemo program, 158–159
Swing. *See also* AWT (Abstract
    Windowing Toolkit)
  applets, 462–465
  AWT versus, 368
  check boxes, 423–425
  classes, 369
  combo boxes, 442–444
  component appearance, 368

Swing *(continued)*
  components, 368, 375, 382
  defined, 368
  GUI programming with, 369
  JButton, 369, 418
  JComboBox, 375
  JLabel, 375
  JMenuBar, 375
  JSlider, 375
  JSpinner, 375
  JTextField, 434
  labels, 429–430
  lists, 439–440
  radio buttons, 427–429
  text components, 434–436
SwingChangeSize class, 428
switch statement. *See also* control
    structures
  benefits, 64
  breaks and, 62
  case, 61
  as decision-making technique, 52
  default case, 62
  defined, 61
  equality checking, 64
  example, 62–63
  output determination, 62
  rules, 62
  syntax, 61–62
  usefulness, 64
synchronized keyword, 530
System class
  arraycopy() method, 261–262
  exit() method, 374

T

tagging interfaces. *See also* interfaces
  defined, 319
  EventListener interface, 298
  purposes, 319
  Serializable, 320–321
target platforms, 3
tasks
  creating, 519
  fixed-delay execution, 522

fixed-rate execution, 522
  repeating, 522
  scheduling, 522–526
TCP (Transmission Control Protocol)
  choosing, 593
  defined, 592
  multiple connections, 593
  network connection, 592
  sockets, 594–595
ternary operator, 43
text components
  AWT, 430–433
  Swing, 434–436
  types of, 430
TextArea class, 431
TextComponent class, 430–431
TextComponentDemo program
  defined, 431, 432
  output, 433
  source code, 432
TextField class
  constructors, 431
  defined, 430
  parameters, 431
this keyword
  in constructors, 131–134
  defined, 100
  uses, 132
this reference
  adding, 101
  as argument to method, 101
  class usage of, 157
  compiler addition of, 101
  defined, 157
  example, 101
  need for, 101
  synchronizing, 531
  usage, 100, 118
ThisDemo program
  defined, 132
  output, 134
  source code, 132–133
  Television objects, 133

Thread class
  constructors, 509
  currentThread() method, 517
  dumpStack() method, 517
  extending, 507, 511–513
  holdsLock() method, 517
  interrupt() method, 517
  isAlive() method, 517
  join() method, 517
  methods, 516–519
  run() method, 516
  setDaemon() method, 517
  setName() method, 516
  setPriority() method, 517
  sleep() method, 517
  start() method, 516
  yield() method, 513, 514, 515, 517
thread groups, 509
thread schedulers, 505, 506
ThreadClassDemo program
  defined, 517
  output, 519
  source code, 517–518
ThreadDemo program, 512
ThreadGroup class, 509
threads. *See also* processes
  blocked, 506
  blocked states, 507
  born, 506
  creating, 503–504, 507
  dead, 507
  deadlock issues, 532–534
  defined, 503
  life cycle, 506–507
  multiple, 504
  multithreading, 526–530
  number running, 504
  overview, 503–505
  pipes, 570–574
  priority, 505
  runnable, 506
  running, 506
  scheduling and, 526
  Timer, 526

wait() method use, 540
  yielding, 513–516
three-dimensional arrays, 263
throw keyword, 348, 349, 358
Throwable class
  child classes, 333
  fillInStackTrace() method, 334
  getCause() method, 334
  getMessage() method, 334
  getStackTrace() method, 334
  methods, 333–334
  printStackTrace() method, 332, 334
  toString() method, 334
throwable classes, 333
ThrowDemo program
  defined, 349
  main(), 350
  output, 350
  output when file cannot be found, 350
  source code, 349–350
throwing exceptions. *See also* exceptions
  exception types for, 348
  limitations, 348
  methods, 330
throws keyword, 343
Timer class
  cancel() method, 523
  defined, 519
  methods, 522–523
  run() method, 523
  schedule() method, 522–523
  scheduleAtFixedRate() method, 523
  scheduledExecutionTime()
    method, 523
Timer threads, 526
TimerDemo program
  defined, 519
  sample output, 521
  SimpleObject class, 521
  source code, 520
TimerTask class
  defined, 519
  extending, 507
time-slicing, 505

toArray() method, 278
TooManyListenersException, 701
toString() method
  adding, 154
  declaring, 156
  default, 154
  defined, 152
  EventObject class, 415
  example, 152–153
  invoking, 152, 157, 158
  objects having, 33
  overridden, 157
  Throwable class, 334
ToStringDemo program, 152–153
  defined, 152
  output, 153
  source code, 153
transient keyword, 575
Transmission Control Protocol. *See* TCP
trees, 273
TreeSet class, 273
true literal, 22
try keyword, 334
try/catch blocks. *See also* catching
    exceptions
  code within, 334
  writing, 335–337, 359–360
two-dimensional arrays, 263

U

UDP (User Datagram Protocol)
  choosing, 593
  datagram packets, 592, 612–617
  defined, 592, 612
Uniform Resource Locators. *See* URLs
UpdateCategory program
  defined, 655
  Movies table, 656
  source code, 656
updateString() method, 651
URL class
  constructors, 617
  defined, 617
  methods, 618
  openConnection() method, 619

URLConnection class, 619–620
URLConnectionDemo program,
    620–621
URLDemo program
  defined, 618
  output, 618
  source code, 618–619
URLs (Uniform Resource Locators)
  connections, 619–621
  defined, 617
  JDBC, 634
  parts, 617
  working with, 617–619
UsedCarFrame program, 393
User Datagram Protocol. *See* UDP
user-defined events, 698–701
user-defined exceptions
  example, 357–359
  rules, 357
  writing, 357
user-defined interfaces
  compiling, 299
  example, 298
  writing, 299

V

variables
  assigning, 25–26
  declaring, 24
  defined, 24
  final, 160
  primitive data type, 25, 36
  reference, 36
Vector class
  add() method, 275
  addAll() method, 275
  addElement() method, 275
  capacity() method, 276
  clear() method, 278
  constructors, 274
  defined, 273, 287
  firstElement() method, 278
  get() method, 278
  indexOf() method, 278
  insertElementAt(), 275

lastElement() method, 278
remove() method, 278, 281
removeAll() method, 278
resizeable arrays and, 281
retainAll() method, 278
setElementAt() method, 278
size() method, 276
toArray() method, 278
using, 289
VectorDemo2 program
  defined, 278
  output, 280
  source code, 279–280
VectorDemo program
  defined, 275
  output, 277
  source code, 275–276
Vectors
  accessing elements in, 277–281
  adding elements to, 275–277
  adding primitive data type to, 274
  as array, 273
  attributes, 274, 275
  capacity attribute, 274, 275
  capacity increment attribute, 274
  element access, 274
  elements, 273
  empty, instantiating, 274
  removing elements in, 277–281
  size, 275
VetoableChangeListener interface, 693
VetoableChangeSupport class, 690–691
virtual methods. *See also* methods
  avoiding, 233
  behavior, 237
  C++, 233
  default, 233
  defined, 232
  examples, 231–233, 236–237
  inheritance hierarchy and, 232
  invocation, 232, 233, 241
  taking advantage of, 233–237
VirtualDemo programs
  defined, 231
  execution, 233

output, 232, 233
source code, 231–232

W

wait() method
  defined, 152, 536
  implementation, 161
  monitoring behavior of, 537
  threads use of, 541
  use example, 537–540
warning() method, 580
while loops. *See also* control structures
  break keyword, 75
  continue keyword, 76, 77
  defined, 64
  do/while loop versus, 68–69
  examples, 65, 66–67
  execution, 65
  flow of control, 64
  infinite, 65–66
  number of repetitions, 72
  in Runnable interface implementa-
    tion, 508
  syntax, 64
WhileDemo program
  defined, 66
  first while loop, 66–67
  output, 67
  second while loop, 67
  source code, 66
  third while loop, 67
WindowAdapter class, 413
windowClosing() method, 412, 414
WindowListener interface
  class implementation of, 409
  defined, 408
  methods, 408
windows
  containers, 369
  creating, 369–372
  dialog, 394–396
  instant message, 398
  size, setting, 370
wrapper classes, 229
write() method, 552, 553–554

writeDouble() method, 567
writeInt() method, 567
writeLong() method, 567
writeObject() method, 574
Writer class
  defined, 553
  methods, 553–554
writers
  classes, 553–554
  high-level, 564
  low-level, 564
writeUTF() method, 567

X
XML (Extensible Markup Language)
  archives, 675
  defined, 6
XMLDecoder class, 702–703
XMLEncoder class, 702

Y
yield() method, 513, 514, 515, 517
YieldDemo program, 514–515

If you don't take
your skills to
new boundaries,

www.propoint.com

you could
find yourself
deserted.

IF you need to take your programming skills to new boundaries THEN

Let Productivity Point be your Guide.
Learn the new, emerging technologies to work smarter and faster.
Strengthen your career.

ELSE

You could find yourself deserted.

ENDIF

Productivity Point provides programmers with the latest coding
innovations to keep our students competitive. Join the legions of satisfied
programmers who have benefited from training with our expert instructors.

Call 1.800.774.2727 or visit www.propoint.com to learn the
emerging technologies that will be tomorrow's essential skillset.